JEAN HÉLION

for Jacqueline Hélion

This book accompanies the exhibition of the
same title at the Centre Georges Pompidou,
Paris, 8 December 2004–6 March 2005,
which has been realised with exceptional help
from the Bibliothèque nationale de France.

The exhibition is also shown
at the Museu Picasso, Barcelona,
17 March–19 June 2005 and, in reduced form,
at the National Academy Museum, New York,
14 July–9 October 2005.

Première edition en langue française
© Éditions du Centre Pompidou, Paris 2004

This English edition © 2004 Paul Holberton publishing
37 Snowsfields, London SE1 3SU
www.paul-holberton.net

Translations by Trista Selous (essays, chronology),
Judith Hayward and Simon Knight (chronology)

ISBN 1 903470 27 7
British Library Cataloguing in Publication Data
A catalogue record for this book is available from the
British Library

Cover:
Jean Hélion, *Big pumpkin event*, 1948 (detail; see p. 146)

Page 9:
Jean Hélion's studio, 1 rue Marcel-Sembat, Paris, 1929

Pages 14–15:
Carnet, 1970
Bibliothèque nationale de France,
département des Estampes et de la Photographie

JEAN HÉLION

THANKS

This exhibition could not have taken place without the active support and engagement of Jean Hélion's family, and, in particular, without the full participation of Mme Jacqueline Hélion and MM. David and Nicolas Hélion.

We offer our thanks to the museums, galleries, institutions and private collectors who have very generously lent to the exhibition, as follows:

France
Galerie Art Attitude Hervé Bize, Nancy
BNP/PARIBAS
Bibliothèque nationale de France, Paris
Galerie Louis Carré, Paris
Fonds national d'Art contemporain – Ministère de la culture et de la communication, Paris
Fonds régional d'Art contemporain d'Auvergne
Fonds régional d'Art contemporain de Bretagne
Fonds régional d'Art contemporain de Picardie
Collection of David Hélion
Collection of Jacqueline Hélion
Collection of Nicolas Hélion
Collection of Raphaël and Emmanuel Hélion
Collection of Daniel Malingue, Paris
Musée de Grenoble
Musée Malraux, Le Havre
Musée d'Art moderne, St-Étienne
Musée d'Art moderne de la Ville de Paris, Paris
Galerie Piltzer
Renou et Poyet, Tableaux Modernes, Paris
Musée Zervos, Vézelay

Germany
Hamburger Kunsthalle, Hambourg
Städtische Galerie im Lenbachhaus, Munich

Italy
Peggy Guggenheim Collection, Venice (Solomon R. Guggenheim Foundation, New York)
Collection of Paolo Zanasi, Modena

Luxembourg
Collection Cour Grand-Ducale, Luxembourg
Musée national d'Histoire et d'Art du Grand Duché de Luxembourg

Spain
IVAM, Instituto Valenciano de Arte moderno, Generalitat Valenciana, Valence

United Kingdom
Tate, London

United States
Collection of Herta and Paul Amir
Rachel Adler Fine Art, New York
Albright-Knox Art Gallery, Buffalo (New York)
The Art Institute of Chicago, Chicago
Collection of Louis Hélion Blair
The Metropolitan Museum of Art, New York
The Robert Miller Gallery, New York
San Diego Museum of Art, San Diego
Solomon R. Guggenheim Museum, New York

Venezuela
Collection Jean-Jacques Bichier

and those lenders who have preferred to remain anonymous.

Liberal thanks are also due to

Les galeries Pierre Brullé (Paris), Marwan Hoss (Paris), Daniel Malingue (Paris), Gérard Piltzer, Patrice Trigano (Paris), Mme Marie-Laure Amrouche, Mme Constance Boscher (Étude Francis Briest), Mme Laetitia Catoir (Christie's London), M. Maurice Covo (Renou et Poyet), Mme Catherine Gary, M. Jean-Jacques Goron (BNP/PARIBAS), Mme Gisèle Lambert (conservateur en chef du département des Estampes et de la Photographie, Bibliothèque nationale de France), M. Pascal Lansberg (Galerie Darga et Lansberg)

for their aid in the arrangement of particular loans.

Our thanks are directed also to the **Musée des Beaux-Arts de Nantes** and **Musée des Beaux-Arts d'Orléans** for releasing works in the ownership of the Centre Pompidou that have been on deposit with them.

We further express our appreciation to the following for their help and support in different capacities: **Mme Laure Bouvot** and **Mme Valérie Gaydier** (Galerie Piltzer), **M. Philippe Bruguière**, **M. Cyril Chazal** (Bibliothèque nationale de France), **M. Jacques Faujour**, **Mme Catherine Goeres** (Bibliothèque nationale de France), **Mrs Mary Anne Goley** (The Board of Governors of The Federal Reserve System, Washington, D.C.), **M. Koutsomallis** (Fondation Basil et Elise Goulandris), **M. Mark Vail**.

Within the **Musée national d'art moderne**, we have benefitted from the assistance of **Mmes Brigitte Léal, Nathalie Leleu, Necha Mamod, Nathalie Roussel.**

In pursuance of the documentary research necessary to the realisation of the exhibition, the **Institut Mémoire de l'Édition Contemporaine (IMEC)** generously granted acces to the fonds Jean Hélion. We would like to thank **MM. Olivier Corpet** (directeur) and **Yves Chèvrefils-Desbiolles** and **Mmes Hélène Favard** and **Martine Ollion**.

CONTENTS

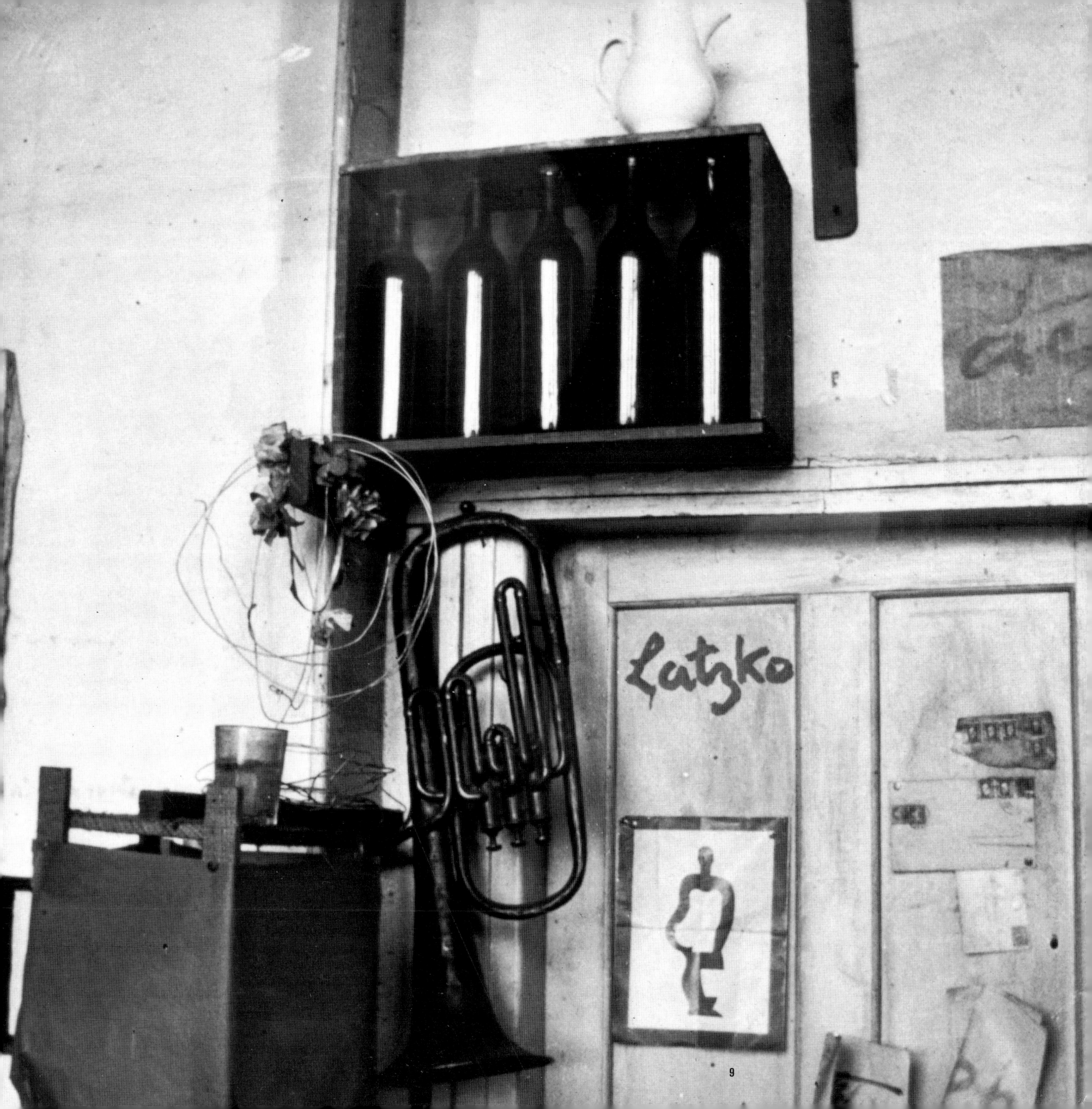
Łatzko

The Freedom of Jean Hélion

Jean Hélion can be seen as a perpetual escapee. In both his life and his art, he seems to have been gifted with a higher instinct, a prescience that allowed him to sense the slightest movement of the doors that threatened to close in on him. It might be the very real doors of the German prison from which he succeeded in escaping in 1942. More insidiously, they could take the shape of the aesthetic or political certainties which threatened to restrict the field of his creative activity.

Hélion paid a high price for his freedom, risking being misunderstood or rejected. Early on a cosmopolitan activist in the cause of abstraction, he renewed his links with figurative art at the very moment he had attained social and commercial recognition as a practitioner of abstraction. Abstract art carried hopes of reform that extended well beyond the aesthetic field. It had become the vehicle for political projects, the standard for modern values – an ideal that, for Hélion, fell apart almost as soon as he made it his own.

In 1931, his journey to the Soviet Union had made him aware of the divorce between innovatory art and a revolutionary society. Back in France, he found the avant-garde too eager to transform itself into a clique, too impatient to elevate its values into dogmas. At the end of a slow period of ripening – the metaphor seems right, as the development of his painting at that time was much inspired by the biological model – in the mid 1940s, in the United States where he had just spent almost a decade, Hélion caused his American admirers consternation by exhibiting his recent figurative experiments. Abstraction, partly thanks to his activities, had finally taken root in New York. From 1936 abstract artists had set up as a group, the Association of American Abstract Artists. Abstract painting was soon going to be the spearhead of the 'triumph of the New York School'.

In 1946, back in France, expressing its regained faith in the future and in modernity by adherence to abstract art, symbol of that modernity, Hélion's recent nudes were greeted with an oppressive silence. Hélion was consigned to the 'apostates', between Alberto Giacometti, who went back to model-based studies in 1935, and Philip Guston, who reverted to figurative work at the end of the 1960s.

Over the decades, from his 'wrong moves' in relation to the straight line of what was being called the mainstream of modern art, Hélion elaborated a body of work governed solely by the laws of his inner necessities. He invented a unique art, not influenced by rhetoric or slogans, an art governed by scruple and vigilance, a form of aesthetic Cartesianism permanently testing out each of its gestures and assumptions.

Hélion could have applied to himself the words of Willem de Kooning to Philip Guston, dejected by the reception of his new paintings: "You know what your real subject is? It's freedom!"

Bruno Racine

Président du Centre Pompidou

This year Jean Hélion would have been a hundred years old. This retrospective, his first at the Musée national d'art moderne, gives us an opportunity to trace through the century the successive evolutions of an extraordinary artist. For Hélion's was indeed a singular path. An active supporter of constructivist abstraction in the early 1930s, he later adopted curved, intertwined forms hanging in space, but remained faithful to abstract art until a certain *Fallen figure* in 1939, which marks the end of this first phase and his definitive break with abstraction. From this point on, Hélion worked with his eyes turned towards the world, reintroducing human figures linked to elements from everyday life – objects, shop-window mannequins, newspapers and even historical events – in an aesthetic evolution that departed from modernist assumptions and for a long time was met with incomprehension. This journey in the opposite direction from that of the modern classics of the twentieth century has given rise to a great many questions, although comparable examples of such a trend are provided by other modernist artists, such as Alberto Giacometti and Philip Guston, who with the passage of time have become widely celebrated.

Hélion certainly participated in the historic currents of abstract art, which he actively promoted in the 1930s. He was one of the founders of the magazine *Art Concret* alongside Théo van Doesburg, and became its editor-in-chief, countering surrealism with rigorous precepts aimed at the creation of a universal art. Shortly afterwards Hélion was involved in setting up the Abstraction-Création group, a broad international association bringing together the best in abstract art between the wars. He co-ordinated its publications, demonstrating both pedagogical abilities and a considerable theoretical reach. While his painting went through clearly differentiated stages during this period, it remained faithful to the aesthetic norms common to the period's avant-gardes and fell within the parameters set by major artists from Mondrian to Arp. This did not prevent Hélion from gradually distancing himself from Art Concret dogma and from setting forms free to move on his picture surface.

In these pre-war years Hélion made an important contribution to the international, and particularly American, recognition of modern art. His studios in Paris, and subsequently in the United States, where he mostly lived after the mid 1930s, were centres for the exchange for ideas and information. Hélion was an essential relay in the process by which the theories of abstraction penetrated Britain and the United States (exemplified by his role in the creation of the British magazine *Axis* and in the formation of the American Abstract Artists organization).

An active supporter of contemporary artists, Hélion gained the confidence of the great art collector and patron Albert E. Gallatin, who at New York Universityset up the first public collection of modern art (The Gallery of Living Art) in the United States. It was thanks to Hélion that the first picture by Mondrian to enter an American public collection was acquired and also that the Gallery of Living Art was enriched by works such as Fernand Léger's *The city* and Pablo Picasso's *Three musicians*. Only Marcel Duchamp played a comparable role in the development of the great American collections of modern art and the foundation of magazines there.

Hélion is not forgotten in America, and many museums have major works by him in their collections, but he does not occupy his rightful place in the United States. Above and beyond more general historical conditions, this is almost certainly due to a failure to understand the later phases of his painting. Initially influenced by Fernand Léger's modernist figuration, creating monumental, sculptural figures, Hélion then moved towards a realism that was increasingly out of step with the canons of the avant-garde. In a fine letter of 1939, cited by Didier Ottinger in his essay for this catalogue, Hélion announced his artistic programme: "I shall give painting back its moral and didactic power". He looked at the modern city in its most everyday aspects, extracting archetypes such as the seated man, the shop-window mannequin or the newspaper-reader, who later occupy strange, dreamlike scenes and participate in all kinds of variations on still lifes and street scenes. Today, it is almost certainly in these later decades of free, independent painting that Hélion's work is most interesting to us. At any rate it is this aspect that has caught the attention of many artists of later generations, as Gilles Aillaud and Eduardo Arroyo demonstrate in the Musée national d'art moderne itself. It is time, we feel, to return to Hélion's lesson in realism, in painting that reintroduces the great myths, constantly surprising and sometimes disturbing us. It is time to enable both the general public and the members of today's art world to view or review this work for themselves, not least among them many foreign museums who have good reason to take an interest in Hélion's work.

In this light I am very glad that, after its time in Paris, our exhibition will be moving to the Museu Picasso in Barcelona, and would like to thank that museum's director, Maria Teresa Ocaña. A reduced version of the exhibition will also be on show in New York, thanks to the energy of Isabelle Dervaux, who will host it at the National Academy Museum in New York, enabling the American public to rediscover Hélion's work.

Lastly, I should like to express my enormous gratitude for the support of Jacqueline Hélion and the other members of the painter's family and to thank all the public and private lenders. Together they have enabled us to mount an exhibition which is both a much-needed homage and an expression of our admiration for the art of Jean Hélion.

Alfred Pacquement
Directeur du Musée national d'art moderne–Centre de création industrielle

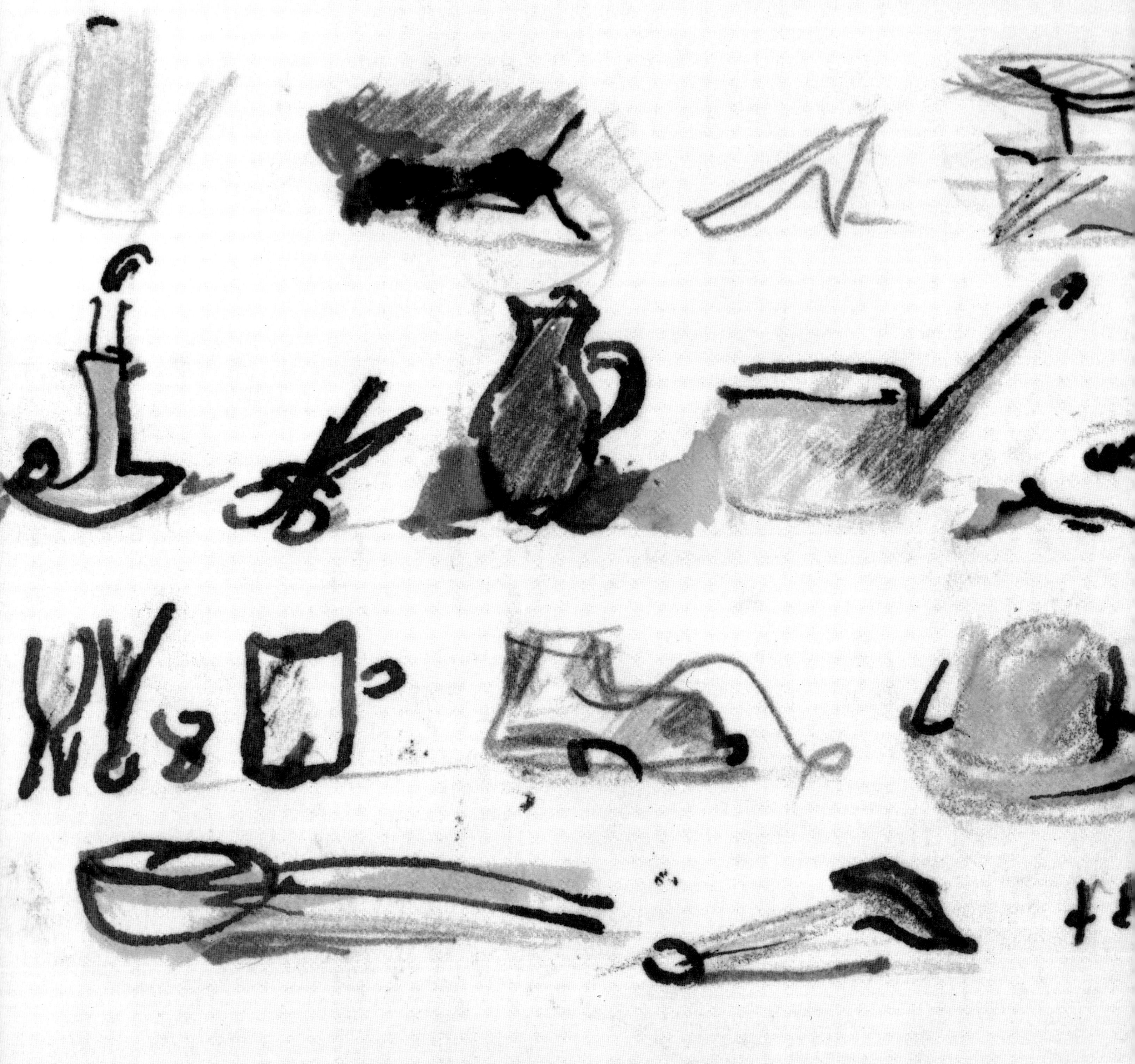

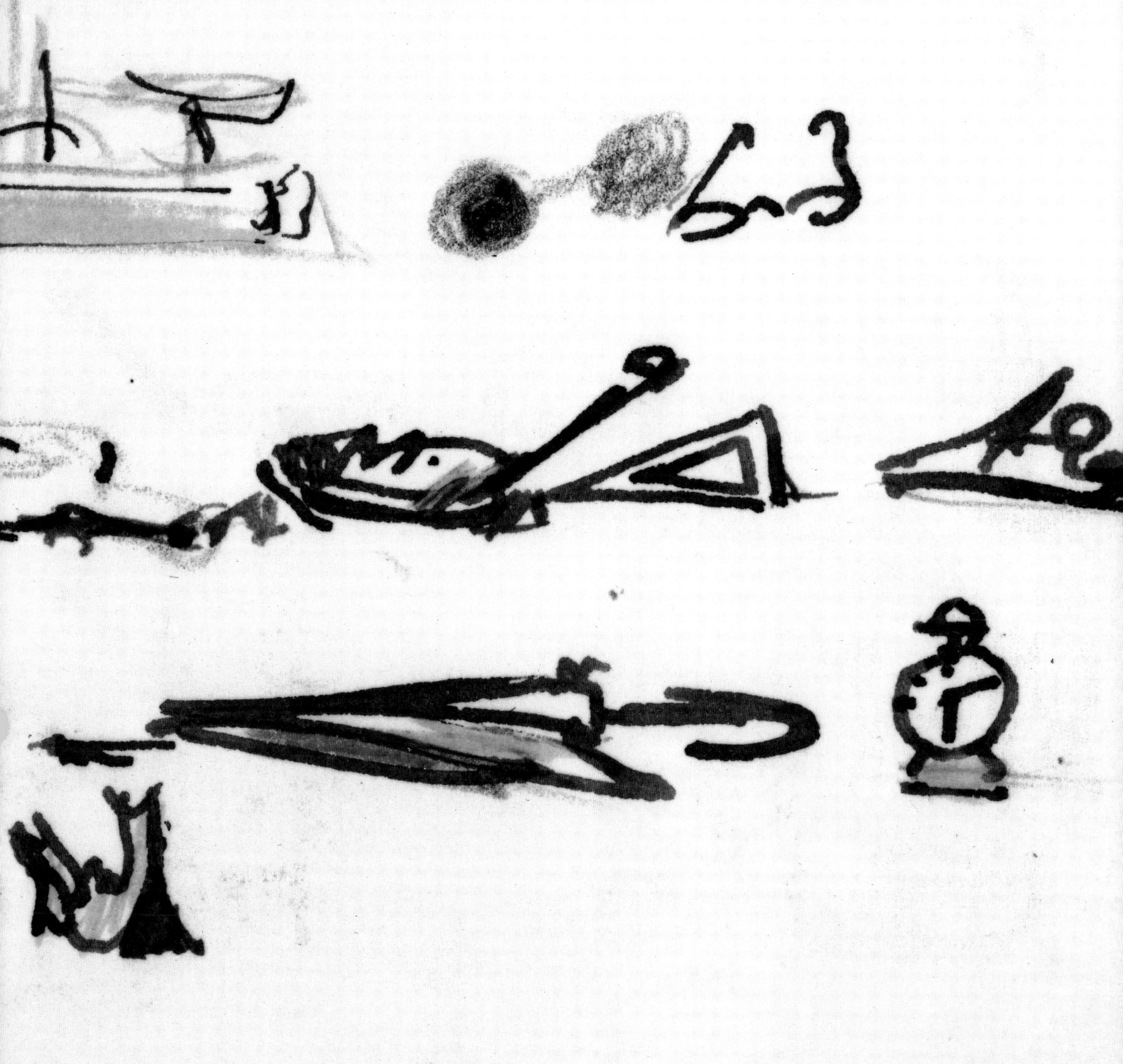

HÉLION: THE ART OF DECLARING

Jean Hélion's work, and lifelong approach, is epitomized in a memory from his youth. He remembered being amazed, while working in a pharmacy at the age of fourteen, by the chemistry that was still carried out in such places at that time. "When a beautiful lady came in with a flask of urine, [the pharmacist] obliged me to perform an experiment the name of which I have forgotten but which involves injecting crystallizable acetic acid into the bottom of a test-tube full of urine. Its vapours cause the urine above it to separate into layers of colour. 'There, in red', he said, 'is the uric acid, reduced to a line. Above that are the biliary pigments, greenish, just as you would imagine. Then the flocculent phosphates and even albumens …. I was amazed by the appearance of these signs in a conical glass. Before the acids were introduced they had been dissolved in the liquid, now they were revealed. Was it this that gave me the idea of extracting from each thing the sign it might have concealed within it?"[1]

Thus Hélion's art might perhaps be summed up by the principle of 'separating out', in an approach that seeks to abstract intelligible 'signs' from the chaos of appearances. The consistency behind his artistic changes of direction is certainly underpinned by the issue of signifying, by a concern for simple, clear communication, with the painter as its vehicle. This interest transcends the division of his work into abstract and figurative phases, a division, or opposition, that is easily exaggerated and over-simplified.

In adopting the principles of neo-plasticist abstraction in the early 1930s, in taking on its codified grammar and its vocabulary, evolved in the history and incorporating the myths of abstraction, Hélion took over a language that sought to be universal. After the Second World War, he strove in his art to come up with 'signs' of a quite different nature. Behind every gesture, every figure, he sought the archetype, the allegory each potentially expressed, in a quest that led him back to the timeless figures of myth-making.

In tracing the *iter* of Jean Hélion's artistic career we are forced to reconsider many categorical oppositions hitherto regarded as irreconcilable. Hélion's abstraction and figuration cannot be fitted into the bitter dialectic in which these terms have been fixed by their interpreters and hagiographers. Hélion was not of his time in his effort to steer clear of dogmatic schisms; he chose the worst possible historical moment, when aesthetic choices signalled ideological positions and divergent schools of thought amounted to political divisions. The 'acid' that Hélion kept throwing on to the world to precipitate its meanings also ate into a number of cast-iron certainties.

1 From Montmartre to social utopia

Jean Hélion produced his first paintings in the early 1920s, when he was still an apprentice draughtsman in an architect's office. In 1924 he showed them at the Foire aux Croûtes in Montmartre. They were typical of amateur painting: their expressionism reflected the 'rage for expression' felt by a young talent, while their bold impasto conveys Hélion's pleasure in working the substance of which pictures were made. They took their motifs from the simple objects which which art students might decorate their apartments.

In September 1926, while waiting for a studio to become available, the Uruguayan painter Joaquín Torres-García and his family moved in temporarily with Hélion. Torres was fifty-two at the time, with a rich store of varied, cosmopolitan experience. His arrival put an end to Hélion's rather conventional bohemianism. From 1892 to 1920 in Barcelona Torres had come into contact with modern painting through the pioneering exhibitions at the Dalmau gallery and had participated in the discussions of the avant-garde at the *Quatre Gats*. In Paris he had known Joan Miró and Jean Arp and sought advice from Picasso. In 1920 he left for the United States, where he joined forces with Joseph Stella, who promoted an American brand of futurism, and met Duchamp, the "well-known cubist".[2] Some of his canvases were bought by Katherine S. Dreier for the modern-art collection of her Société Anonyme. From the classicism of his earliest works, linking him to the 'neo-Greek' current of the Catalan Noucento, to the 'futurism' of his exhibition at the Dalmau gallery in 1917, the art of Torres-García is marked by a quest for order and by constructive rigour. In the year of his meeting with Hélion he summed up his aesthetic ambitions as follows: "I have tried all the genres and I think the only one that really suits me is architectural art. And I'm proud to possess that quality rare in modern painters, architectural form – and another that is rarer still, serenity."[3] In 1926 Torres's painting was that of a 'cubist Puvis': he took the hieraticism and the monumentality of his figures from Puvis de Chavanne, while from cubism deriving a strong sense of geometry.

Hélion explained exactly what it was that Torres brought him: "After the precious, academic example of Lafnet came that of Torres-García, constructive and magnificent. He also talked of cubism and surrealism, things about which Lafnet knew absolutely nothing and which did not become clear to me immediately. However, the idea of them sent cracks through all my mass of knowledge …. With Torres-García I learned to talk about facts, about rebellions of the

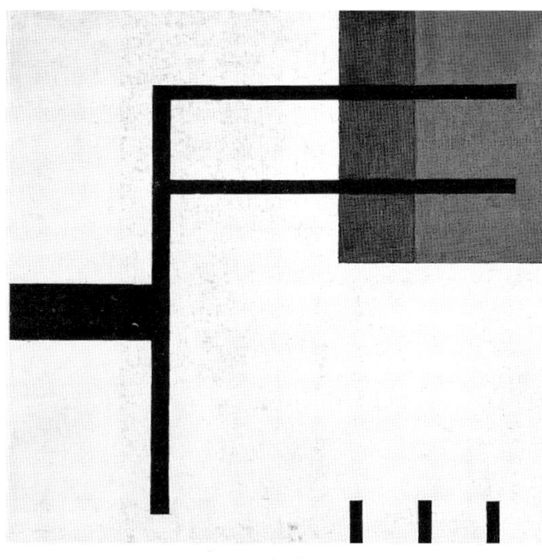

Jean Hélion
Open composition, 1930
Oil on canvas, 50 x 50 cm
Private collection

hand and the eye, about outrageous simplifications and magnificent passions."[4] Such "simplifications" can be seen in the paintings Hélion produced 1926–29, in which he applied the lessons of synthetic cubism. The objects in his still lifes, such as soup-dishes and pitchers, are geometrically separated out and reduced to their graphic outlines, which are powerfully emphasized. In addition to this constructive principle, Hélion also borrowed Torres's palette, characterized by a predilection for harmonies in black and red. His most recent canvases were shown alongside those of his new mentor at the exhibition *5 réfusés* (five rejects – from the Salon d'Automne) at the Marck gallery, 3–5 November 1928.[5] Theo van Doesburg, who visited the exhibition, appreciated the 'constructed' aspect of Torres-García's painting. He wrote to the Uruguayan artist and sent him a few issues of the magazine *De Stijl*, which he had founded with Mondrian in 1917. The discovery of neo-plasticism was a revelation to Torres and soon also to Hélion. Its echoes are immediately visible in the paintings of both, which become resolutely abstract. But then, after this time during which their works were so similar that it can be hard to tell them apart, the paths of Hélion and Torres were suddenly to diverge.

In Paris Van Doesburg was seeking to create an alternative, based on neo-plasticism, to what he regarded as the surrealist hegemony. He armed himself for the battle ahead with a dogmatic intransigence that led him to break with Torres-García, setting himself up as the apostle of art that took modern technology as its model and that should be impersonal in its execution and rigorous in its abstraction. Torres could not follow Van Doesburg either in his radical rejection of figuration or in his advocacy of impersonality. As his art remained indebted to the manual values of craftsmanship, he was more at home with the less sharply defined approach of Michel Seuphor's Cercle et Carré, pursuing an abstraction of theoretical parameters sufficiently elastic to encompass both the figuration of Fernand Léger and the surrealism of Jean Arp.

Hélion, whom Torres described as "very intelligent" and "very ambitious",[6] took over the Uruguayan's now vacant place alongside Van Doesburg, whose movement drew together its ranks under the banner of Art Concret in 1930. Hélion's paintings of the time show that he had abandoned the palette of broken colours, the sort of pictorial *cuisine* he was still practising in 1929, under the influence of Torres-García. *Composition* (1929) and *Complex tensions* (1930) use flat, pure colours set in a network of geometrical lines. His *Open composition* (1930) shows the completion of his conversion to the orthogonalistic order of neo-plasticism. Shaped by Van Doesburg's intended assault against surrealism, the founding manifesto of Art Concret asserted values that radically opposed to all forms of romanticism and expressionism. "The work of art must be entirely conceived and formed by the mind before its execution. It must take nothing from the formal elements of nature, from sensuality or sentiment. We want to exclude lyricism, drama and symbolism."[7]

'Mathematical' abstraction (purged of the spiritualist and theosophical notions that had provided the context from which De Stijl emerged) now appeared as the most effective weapon in Art Concret's planned battle against surrealism. In the year the movement was founded Van Doesburg wrote a piece in which he advocated the opposite of the principles advanced by André Breton: "Speculative and risky approaches in art have been exhausted. Intuition has led us to adventure and dreams.

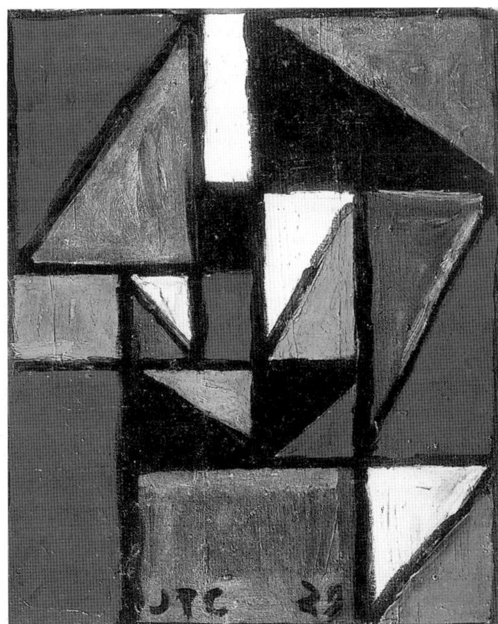

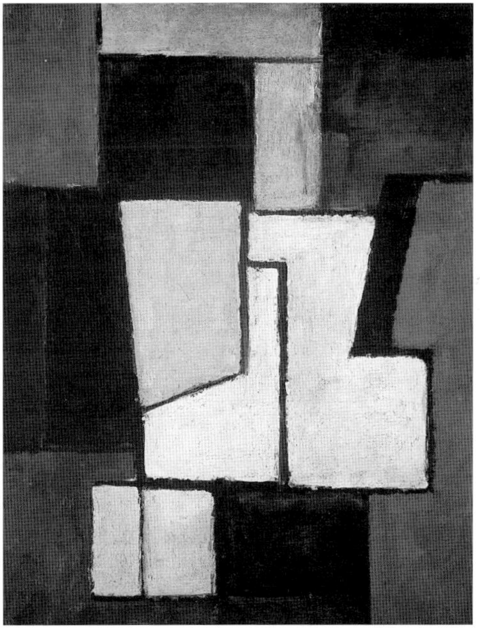

Painting cannot be carried out by means of a conjuring trick or whilst sleepwalking. It is to this decadence that we have been brought by that magnificent conductor, intuition."[8] The clarion call was all the more needed as surrealism was ceaselessly expanding its empire in the late 1920s. "At that time the surrealists, who had established a gallery in the rue Jacques-Callot and were seeking to spread the movement into general society by influencing

1. Jean Hélion, *À perte de vue* followed by *Choses revues*, ed. Claire Paulhan and Patrick Fréchet, Paris, IMEC, 1996, p. 17.
2. Joaquín Torres-García, *Histoire de ma vie*, Neuchâtel, Ides et Calendes, 1998, p. 182.
3. Id., (conversation with Régine Clary), "Les lettres et les arts – Torres-García", in *Le Phare de Villefranche*, 16 January 1926; cited in *Joaquín Torres-García, Un monde construit*, exh. cat. Strasbourg, Musée d'Art Moderne et Contemporain, 24 May-8 September 2002, p. 233.
4. J. Hélion, *À perte de vue, op. cit.*, p. 32.
5. Daura, Engel-Rozier and Aberdam were the other artists rejected by the Salon d'Automne.
6. J. Torres-García, *Histoire de ma vie, op. cit.*, p. 221.
7. *Art Concret*, Paris, n° 1, April 1930, p. 1.
8. Theo Van Doesburg, "De l'intuition à la certitude" (Paris, 1930), reprinted in the catalogue of the exhibition *Van Doesburg 1883–1931*, The Hague, 1983, p. 171.

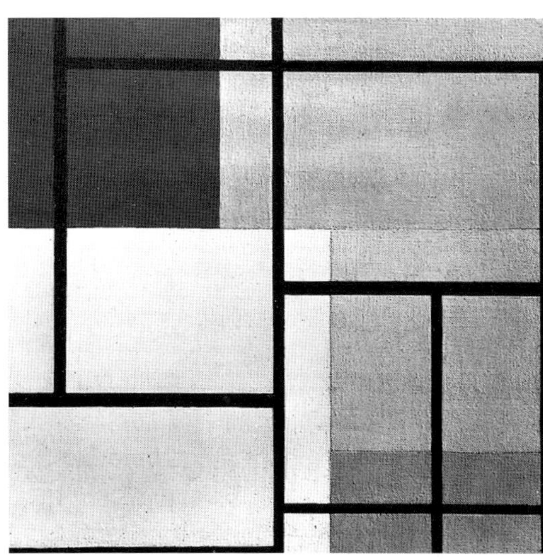

Theo van Doesburg
Simultaneous composition XXIV, 1929
Oil on canvas, 79.7 x 69.8 cm
Yale University Art Gallery, New Haven

the way people behaved (refusing to accept that their movement was only literary or artistic), were gaining more and more ground and countering the cubist and neo-plasticist movements".[9]

The struggle between surrealism and neo-plasticism was particularly fierce because, over and above any questions of form, both movements had a similar ideal. The dogmatic intransigence of the Art Concret manifestos is explained by this modern 'quarrel of the universals'. Confronted with surrealism's discovery of the invariables of human behaviour in psychoanalytic research (narcissism, the Oedipus complex, archetypes and Jungian mythology), Van Doesburg stated that the only universal values were those of an abstract, mathematical order. In opposition to the trends of surrealism, which it regarded as retrograde, Art Concret advocated the rational, progressive values that lay at the core of the 'modern spirit'. To the universality of the figures of dreams and of the mind, it opposed another, based on reason. Asked in 1929 about the future and meaning of modern art, Van Doesburg anticipated the programme of Art Concret in stating: "In each country [there are] a few humble, disinterested creators who are the faithful bearers of the future. They don't work for toffs or the market, but for the future, for a new, serious-minded world. I'm talking here about a new generation of real artists who are not trying to lash out at a blasé bourgeoisie with pictorial conjuring tricks and illusions, but who, in their studio-laboratories, backed up by modern science, are seeking the elements and laws of a universal art."[10] In asserting the "universality" of 'constructed' art, Van Doesburg was situating himself within a tradition that had sought to link the emergence of abstract art with that of a new *lingua franca*. Frantisek Kupka, a pioneer of abstraction, summed up this project for a universal language as follows: "'The art of the future' will be carried by the direct communication of emotion, the Esperanto of complete communion, raised to the level of a collectivity united in art."[11]

The articles published in the magazine *Art Concret* (of which Jean Hélion was the editor) in turn describe an art endowed with 'universal' powers. "The dominance of individualism and localism was always the great obstacle to the birth of a universal art. Only if the means of expression are free of any particularisms are they in accord with the aim of art itself, which is to bring a universal language into being."[12] This universalist demand did not escape the notice of the critic Camille Mauclair, for whom the paintings of Hélion and Van Doesburg were expressions of a "pictorial Esperanto".[13] The "universal" (or at

least international) dimension of Art Concret was illustrated first of all by the cosmopolitanism of its members. The artists who signed the founding manifesto were Dutch (Van Doesburg), Armenian (Tutundjian), Swedish (Carlsund) and French (Marcel Wantz and Hélion).

Armed with his "pictorial Esperanto", Hélion became the international spokesman for the values of constructivist art. From 1932 he showed his works in the United States, advised the collector Albert E. Gallatin and kept American artists informed about recent developments in European art. Ad Reinhardt acknowledged Hélion's crucial role for the abstract artists of New York: "You can't deal with the AAA [American Abstract Artists] in the late thirties or early forties without the presence of Hélion."[14] In Britain Hélion contributed to *Axis*, the first British magazine devoted to the promotion of abstraction.

2. Disenchantment with the (abstract) world

In the year that Art Concret was founded Otto Carlsund left Paris for Sweden. His departure compromised the future of both group and magazine, which he had funded. Van Doesburg's death in 1931 was also the death of Art Concret. A new group was formed to – as Hélion put it – "expand the bases". The "bases" of Abstraction-Création were in fact considerably enlarged. In its early days the ranks of the new movement included Arp, Kupka, Gleizes, Herbin, Valmier and, a little later, Mondrian, Vantongerloo, Calder and Nicholson. By 1935 it had 416 members from fourteen different countries. Like Art Concret, Abstraction-Création had utopian ambition, and dreamed of a "universal" language.[15] However "pictorial Esperanto" had considerably expanded its vocabulary.

Hélion's contacts with Arp and his graceful, curvilinear compositions, and also with the lightness and humour of Calder's constructions, led him to reconsider the dogmatic rigour of Art Concret. At first his paintings became enlivened by curves (*Circular tensions*, 1931–32) and then by complex, dancing colours, hanging in space (*Equilibrium,* 1933), following the example of Calder's 'mobiles'. The centre of *Abstract composition* (1933) contains an irregularly shaped form, a 'spud', an escapee from Arp's biomorphic repertoire. In a few months Hélion covered so much ground in his embrace of artistic complexity that he rebelled against the stubborn intransigence showed by Auguste Herbin in his defence of abstraction. "He thought it was faith; I could already see that it was bigotry. I remember a meeting of Abstraction-Création, where the committee was examining photos submitted for an issue of the magazine. Valmier had brought one in showing a very fine painting, on which Arp and I complemented him, when Vantongerloo burst out, 'It's a fish'. Surprised, Valmier peered at it. In fact, from some distance, you could see it as a fish, but really there was almost nothing left of it. I was in favour, but the rule prevailed and this picture, which made only the most passing reference to nature, was thrown out."[16]

Hélion's irritation at the bigotry of the abstract clique was merely a symptom of a far deeper disillusionment, resulting from what he saw as the gradual separation of abstract art from the social and political ideals that gave it its ethos, its supposed *raison d'être*. In the spring of 1931, in the company of the American William Einstein (who provided the finance), he took a trip to the Soviet Union. To his great disappointment Hélion observed that for the Societs art existed only in so far as it served the imperatives of propaganda. He saw nothing beyond the most conventional, academic, official realism. There was no trace of 'universal' abstract art, that catalyst of change and promoter of social progress, to be found in the U.S.S.R.

As was the case for most artists in the first half of the twentieth century, Hélion's involvement with abstraction could not be dissociated from the path taken by his political activism. In 1925 he joined Tristan Rémy and his circle of proletarian writers.[17] The following year he was involved in the project for an Association of Revolutionary Writers and Artists, which Rémy wanted to set up and whose members "came from the people and believed they had something to say to them", as Hélion put it.[18] The AEAR eventually came into being in 1932, under the leadership of Paul Vaillant-Couturier. Hélion was one of its founding members. His membership of Art Concret may even seem an extension of this activism to promote "social progress".[19] However, some years later, Hélion described rather different political positions to Pierre-Georges Bruguière: "Some years ago I was a very fervent communist and Marx and Lenin have left many precious traces within me. But I have gradually distanced myself from activist circles, first because painting was taking up more and more of my time and strength and also because politics, with all its tactics, its positioning, its violence, its deceits – even for the best of ends – runs counter to the attitude of perpetual truth which an artist must seek to retain in order to understand anything of the edifice of nature and himself within it .... Simple friends and workers ... have taught me a great deal, and yet have distanced me from them, because their watchword was 'comrade, help the necessary revolution ... by every means'. Whereas I was split between a desire to take refuge in Giotto's convent, where I would do nothing but adore forms and paint, and the desire to enter the fray, being very poor and suffering hardship at that time, and to become a humble everyday hero in action .... It is much easier to be a hero in the street, struggling and singing, with opinions that are black and white – for or against – than to be a quiet man ... to be sure of oneself."[20]

The movement's 'scientific' principles, its 'mathematical objectivity', its adherence to the values of modern technology and even its name, which rejected any kind of metaphysics, met the requirements of the most rigorous forms of 'dialectical materialism'. While Hélion may temporarily have believed in the political efficacy of art, his tour of the U.S.S.R. in 1931 dispelled his illusions. Looking back he described the thoughts the trip inspired in him: "I became convinced that a worker was truthful when he said that I did not believe in the 'rôle directeur du prolétariat', since I did not fulfill his daily needs and was not willing to do whatever it needed for its fight against capitalism .... What happens is that anybody who is not doing something popular, successful, regarding public opinion, is progressively led to meeting the opposition in politique, and especially the opposition that pretends to be progressive .... I have positively no more hopes in what the proletariat would do for artists of my kind if it came into power."[21]

In 1934 Jean Hélion left the AEAR and Abstraction-Création.[22] These resignations set the seal on his questioning of abstraction. The theoretical basis of Art Concret was a 'mathematics' which Hélion radically reconsidered in the mid 1930s. ('Art and mathematics' was the subtitle of a piece he had written for the first and only issue of the magazine *Art Concret*). In 1933 he abandoned the mathematical principle and the formal register of geometry in favour of its aesthetic and philosophical antithesis, the naturalist paradigm. He replaced the stability of crystalline forms with the principle of the organic growth of nature. In the second issue of *Abstraction-Création art non figuratif* he published an article reflecting the "epistemological break" that had changed his art. This development brought him suddenly closer to Arp than to Mondrian. (Mondrian's rejection of forms taken from the biological world had become proverbial.)

Since the mid-1920s the surrealists had been passionate admirers of the scientific films of Jean Painlevé, who fixed a film camera to a microscope to reveal the life of micro-organisms and the feverish world of cells. On the macroscopic scale Salvador Dalí celebrated in *Minotaure* the proliferating energy of the plant world as

9. J. Torres-García, *Histoire de ma vie, op. cit.*, p. 238.
10. T. Van Doesburg, "Réponse à l'enquête de la revue *Europa*" (June 1929), reprinted in *Van Doesburg 1883–1931, op. cit.*, p. 159.
11. F. Kupka, cited by Pascal Rousseau in "Un langage universel. L'esthétique scientifique aux origines de l'abstraction", in *Aux origines de l'abstraction 1800–1914*, exh. cat. Musée d'Orsay, Paris, 2003–04, p. 30. In his article Rousseau analyses a great many sources from the intersection of science and art which led the early abstract artists to believe that their painting might have a power of immediate communication. With Humbert de Superville and his *Essai sur les signes inconditionnels dans l'art* (Leyden, Hoek, 1827), P.M. Demainieux, in his *Lettre sur la pasigraphie* (Paris, Gillé, 1806) stated that the new vocabulary enabled "inhabitants of any land on Earth to paint their thoughts in a way that could be read and understood everywhere" (cited by Rousseau, p. 21). In relation to the science of colours, Albert de Rochas in "La notation des couleurs" (*La Nature*, 21 February 1891, p. 187) observes "the creation of a language more universal than any Volapük, which colorists can wield" (cited by P. Rousseau, p. 23).
12. J. Hélion, "Commentaires sur la base de la peinture construite", *Art Concret*, n° 1, April 1930, p. 2.
13. In his column in *L'Ami du peuple* ("Vers un espéranto pictural", cited by Merle S. Schipper, *Hélion, the Abstract Years: 1929–1939*, Los Angeles, UCLA, 1974 (unpublished thesis), p. 77, note 6.
14. Interview with Ad Reinhardt by Ruth Gurin [Bowman] (10 May 1964), cited by Merle S. Shipper, *Hélion, op. cit.*, p. 193.
15. "Any attempt to limit artistic effort on grounds of race, ideology or nationality is odious", Editorial committee, *Abstraction-Création*, n° 2, 1933, p. 1.
16. J. Hélion, *À perte de vue, op. cit.*, p. 55.
17. *Id.*, *Mémoire de la chambre jaune*, Paris, École Nationale Supérieure des Beaux-Arts, "Écrits d'artistes", 1994, p. 18.
18. *Ibid.*, p. 19.
19. Can we speak of Jean Hélion's "communism"? In 1984, looking back over the 1920s, he said, "[Tristan Rémy] wasn't a communist. Nor was I. But we did feel nostalgia for a time when we had believed it would be possible to organize a world favourable to all that would be sensitive to art and poetry", *ibid.*, pp. 19–20.
20. Unpublished letter from J. Hélion to P.-G. Bruguière, Rockbridge Baths, Virginia, 18 October 1936.
21. Jean Hélion, letter to Meyer Schapiro, 22 November 1938, cited by Merle S. Shipper, *Hélion, op. cit.*, p. 138.
22. The AEAR became an organ for promoting the realism that had become the 'official' movement of Soviet aesthetics. The French Communist Party joined some right-wing parties in voting for rearmament.

23. Salvador Dalí, "De la beauté terrifiante et comestible de l'architecture Modern'style", *Minotaure*, nos. 3–4, December 1933, pp. 69–77.

24. Exhibition at the Pierre [Loeb] gallery. In this context he and Pevsner were the only artists whose work reflected "constructive" art. On 15 April 1933 he wrote to Miró: "Do you remember my asking you last winter if you would agree to exhibit with four or five of our friends? The thing is ready to happen": letter from Hélion to Joan Miró (Successió Miró, Palma de Majorca). My thanks to Rémi Labrusse for informing me about this letter.

25. Henri Focillon, *Vie des formes* followed by *Éloge de la main*, Paris, PUF (Quadrige), 1996, p. 8.

26. J. Hélion, "From Reduction to Growth", *Axis*, London, no. 2, April 1935, p. 24.

27. *Id., Abstraction-Création*, no. 2, 1933, p. 20.

28. *Id.,* "Poussin, Seurat and Double Rythm", *Axis*, no. 6, summer 1936, p. 9.

29. *Ibid.,* p. 13.

30. *Ibid.,* p. 14.

31. *Ibid.,* p. 16.

32. J. Hélion to Raymond Queneau, Rockbridge Baths, 18 August 1939, in J. Hélion, *Lettres d'Amérique. Correspondance avec Raymond Queneau 1934–1967*, ed. Claude Rameil, Paris, IMEC, 1996, p. 146.

33. Unpublished letter from J. Hélion to P.-G. Bruguière, Rockbridge Baths, 18 October 1936.

34. Unpublished letter from J. Hélion to P.-G. Bruguière, Rockbridge Baths, 9 October 1937.

35. Unpublished letter from J. Hélion à P.-G. Bruguière, Rockbridge Baths, 7 April 1939.

36. J. Hélion, *À perte de vue, op. cit.*, p. 69.

37. Unpublished letter from J. Hélion to P.-G. Bruguière, 18 November 1939.

38. Unpublished letter from J. Hélion to P.-G. Bruguière, 18 October 1936.

39. J. Hélion, *Journal d'un peintre, Carnets 1963–1984*, ed. Anne Moeglin-Delcroix, Paris, Maeght, 1992, April or May 1965, p. 27.

represented in Gaudí.[23] In June 1933 Hélion's new sympathy for surrealist poetics led him to exhibit his paintings alongside those of Arp, Calder, Miró, Pevsner and Seligmann.[24] During the 1930s the influence of the biological model on art and its theory extended beyond surrealism. Henri Focillon took it as a model for his *Vie des formes*: "We believe that they [three-dimensional forms] constitute an order and that this order is animated by the movement of life. They are subject to the principle of metamorphosis, which endlessly renews them."[25] Hélion met this 'biologism' almost term for term in the essay 'From Reduction to Growth', which he published in the British magazine *Axis*: ""The work considered as an organism in growth. As much as possible got out of the canvas, as well as out of the artist. More, instead of less."[26] He consciously espoused the change in his artistic objectives brought about by his abandonment of the perfect forms of *eidos* in favour of the vitalism of *physis*. "Should we compare pictures to trees? It would be high time. We have too readily laid claim to the justification of grand words – universality, generality, permanence and so on."[27]

The conception of the work of art as an "organism" led Hélion to interpret modern painting in an original way and to rehabilitate traditions incompatible with his adherence to Art Concret. In 1934 he wrote a homage to the classicism of Nicolas Poussin, whose "figures appear among trees as if they were born there for that purpose. They are brothers to the trees …. The order of their elements, the internal rhythm of each, the external rhythm of all, are such that the trees function."[28] The "classicism" to which Hélion referred overturned the hierarchies set in place by modernism. He praised Cézanne for his "solidity", but characterized him as a painter of no more than "fragments", and the world he bequeathed to the cubists as a chequered Harlequin costume, a juxtaposition of parts that could not reconstitute a whole, full form. "Cézanne … had saved one part of the tradition and killed the rest",[29] concluded Hélion. In his eyes only Seurat in the modern period had given a new form to the "organic" plenitude of Poussin, to the classicism in which forms are put together so every part, like the whole, must be "both compact, closed, and opened, like a tree".[30]

After having gone along briefly with radical solutions, Hélion planned to react to "the exterior anarchy of the 'fauvisme' and the interior anarchy of the 'surréalisme'".[31] He implemented this programme to the letter in the monumental paintings he produced in the late 1930s, in his American studio at Rockbridge Baths. For from 1936 Jean Hélion lived in the United States, in New York and then in Virginia. Far away from the aesthetic and political quarrels of the Parisian avant-garde (around realism in 1936, and in disputes stemming from activism within the Communist Party, as advocated by the surrealists), he developed the figurative strengths of his painting. His correspondence reveals the precautions he took and the guilt he felt as he fostered the figurative metamorphosis of his art. He forged a theory for his own use to explain the process by which his formal means became more complex. He knew that, for many of his former fellow-travellers of Art Concret and Abstraction-Création, his recent evolution was liable to be interpreted as a denial of his 'universal' political ideals, which were consubstantial with the project of abstraction. His movement "*à rebours* [against the grain]" would probably be judged 'reactionary'. The abstract avant-garde was not alone in condemning the apostasy of a 'return to the real'. In 1935 André Breton thundered against Alberto Giacometti for having abandoned the "interior model" of his works of the 1920s for the study of models from nature. Beyond the formal categories that pitted them against each other, all the avant-gardes condemned the temptation of realism.

In the letters he wrote from America to Raymond Queneau and Pierre-Georges Bruguière, Hélion described his first figurative explorations, but asked his correspondents to keep them secret. To Queneau he said, "I'm asking you to keep these confidences about my studies to yourself because I am still too far from success to describe and discuss them publicly".[32] To Bruguière, "The drawing I have here would make a lot of people swear, with its three figures depicted in an obvious space and its volumes drawn in light".[33] "I have begun (this is strictly between ourselves, please) study drawings of my wife, drawings that are still clumsy as I'm out of practice in the genre."[34] Hélion's reluctance to hasten the movement leading him towards figuration is partly related to his 'tempo', to the principle of evolution that he had defined for his work. On 7 April 1939 he described to Bruguière the schedule he had set himself: "Ten years ago I was producing my first graphic works free from the natural image; exactly ten years. I shall soon be thirty-five, I still have time to accomplish great work. For ten years I think I shall look, admire and love the life around us – passers-by, houses, gardens, shops, trades and everyday movement. Then, when I have mastered the means and acquired the baggage of characters and attitudes to give me the ease I now have in non-figurative art, I shall begin on a new period, which I have glimpsed in the last few days: I shall give painting back its moral and didactic power. I shall attack great scenes that will no longer be simply descriptive, administrative, but also 'significant', like the great works of Poussin."[35]

Hélion was determined to close the abstract chapter of his œuvre with a significant picture. This was to be the 1939 work *Fallen figure*. The cylinders and cones he had assembled to make a monument to the social and political values of abstraction are dismembered, thrown to the ground, as were his dreams and hopes at the time. "Other manoeuvres, other revolutions, other troubles were agitating and demolishing the world just as I myself had destroyed my abstraction. On the pretext of maturing, it was crumbling by itself. The sound of boots could be heard. Hitler was thundering; the radio reported his incoherent speeches like boiling words. Everyone could sense the coming disaster."[36] *Fallen figure* closed a cycle. Its form and meaning are programmatic, in harmony with the 'meta-discourse' that Hélion the theorist was building up around his work. The painter, meanwhile, curious and henceforwards fascinated by the ticklish complexity of reality, ignored such speculations and strategies.

In 1939 he was developing the new figuration he was exploring in three directions. The first consisted of tightly framed heads. *Émile*, shown from the front, demonstrates in a clearly didactic way the overturning of perspective that led Hélion to complicate instead of purifying, to restore to an interplay of cylinders and spheres the form of a face. *Still life with umbrella* indicates the second possible path. It was intended as a rigorous, descriptive study, the realism of which prefigures the paintings of the early 1950s. The third path was that of monumentality and schematization. The figures of *With cyclist* express the essential characteristics of the art to which Hélion would henceforth become attached. This approach was a literal response to Baudelaire's conception of modernity. Hélion's *carnets* and correspondence document his assiduous reading of Baudelaire in the late 1930s. He adopted the poet's characterization of modernity as born of a reconciliation between feelings arising from the most ephemeral manifestations of one's time (Baudelaire's fashion, morality and passion) and an "eternal immutable" inherent in the structure, in the geometrical, architectural foundation of great works. This balance was embodied in Poussin and Seurat, abundantly cited during the 1930s. Among contemporary artists, *With cyclist* is a clear statement that, for Hélion, the renewal of this Baudelairian modernism was to be found in the painting of Fernand Léger. To Pierre-Georges Bruguière he wrote, "... to prolong and add muscle to the impulse of Seurat, the last great master, and

Léger, the greatest after him ...".[37] Léger (and Balthus perhaps, in some of his paintings) was implementing a plan to render modern life heroic. He also knew how to find 'popular' values in the vocabulary of forms. Léger alone was able to give his works a monumental scale, a dimension that was also fundamental to Hélion's artistic ambitions. In 1936 Hélion dreamed of receiving a commission to paint a mural, like the American artists enrolled by the Hoover government on the Work Progress Administration programme, designed to aid artists in the context of the 1930s recession. "I also hope – and it's important, very important – to find a big wall to paint [in America]."[38] As if to prove the permanence of this aspiration, as late as 1965 Hélion wrote in his *carnets*, "Very kindly, the Minister of State (André Malraux) offered me ... a decoration for my buttonhole. I had the honour to refuse him, also very kindly .... The only decoration I want is the one I would be asked to paint on the walls of, for example, an official building."[39] Whatever its actual scale or subject, Hélion's painting continually aspired to reach the monumental, edifying form natural to mural painting.

In 1939 Hélion took part in the 'phoney war'. He was taken prisoner on the Ardennes front and interned in a German camp in Stettin, from which he eventually managed to escape. After an odyssey across Europe, which he described in his book *They Shall Not Have Me*, he returned to America, went back to his studio and began working once more on his paintings, which he found where he had left them. In 1943 he painted *Man with umbrella*, which reworked the central figure of *With cyclist*. Like its prototype, the figure is built from simple, geometric forms. It is the offspring of the abstract constructions of the mid 1930s. A year later, the same figure (in *Man with umbrella and woman at window*, 1944) is testament to a style reinvented. Hélion has abandoned the metallic tones and stylized forms that had turned the figures of *With cyclist* into stove-pipe dummies. His palette has become richer and experiments with a new intensity. His lines are no longer improbable thresholds generated by chiaroscuro, but gain their independence, enlivened with upstrokes and downstrokes. The form is no longer created by a gradation of light and shade, but by a tapestry of flat, pure colours. Thus, after the war Hélion took his art in a new direction, in an even more decisive break than the Damascene conversion that severs his abstract from his figurative works. *Charles*, *Édouard*, *Émile* and the pictures of 1939 had not challenged the constructive, 'mathematical' principles of the paintings produced at the time

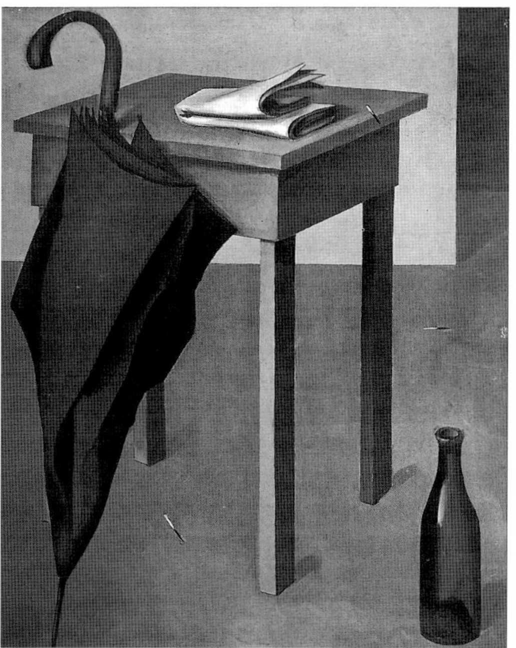

40. J. Hélion to R. Queneau, Rockbridge Baths, 18 August 1939, in *Lettres d'Amérique…, op. cit.*, pp. 146–48.
41. J. Hélion, interview, in Bernard Dahan, *Jean Hélion, peintre au confluent de la peinture, de la sémiologie et de la littérature*, Paris, Université Paris III, December 1983 (unpublished thesis), p. 138.
42. J. Hélion, *Journal d'un peintre, Carnets 1929–1962, op. cit.*, p. 103.
43. Cf. Didier Ottinger, *Surréalisme et mythologie moderne, les voies du labyrinthe d'Ariane à Fantômas*, Paris, Gallimard, 2002.
44. J. Hélion, *Journal d'un peintre. Carnets 1929–1962, op. cit.*, Paris, 28 September 1947, p. 101.
45. *Volontés*, monthly magazine founded by Georges Pelorson and Raymond Queneau. The first issue appeared in December 1937.
46. Henry Miller, "Lettre aux surréalistes en tous lieux", *Volontés*, no. 3, 20 February 1938, p. 13.
47. J. Hélion, *Journal d'un peintre. Carnets 1929–1962, op. cit.*, 20 January 1952, p. 232.
48. *Ibid.*, 19 November 1948, p. 164.
49. *Ibid.*, p. 259.

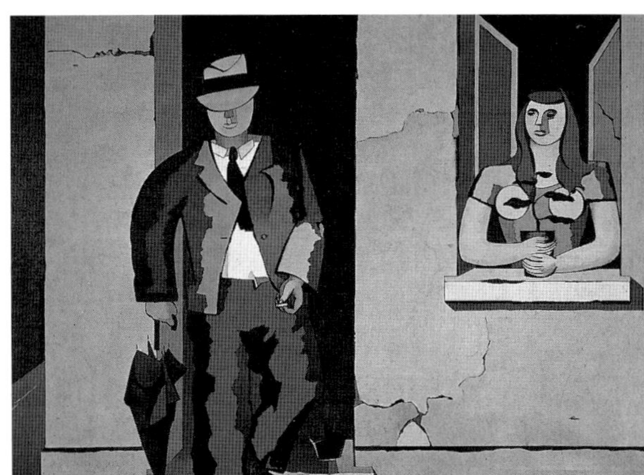

Jean Hélion
Man with umbrella and woman at window, 1944
Oil on canvas, 131 x 172 cm
Private collection

Jean Hélion
With cyclist, 1939 (detail)
Oil on canvas, 132 x 180.5 cm
Centre Georges Pompidou, Musée national d'art moderne, Paris

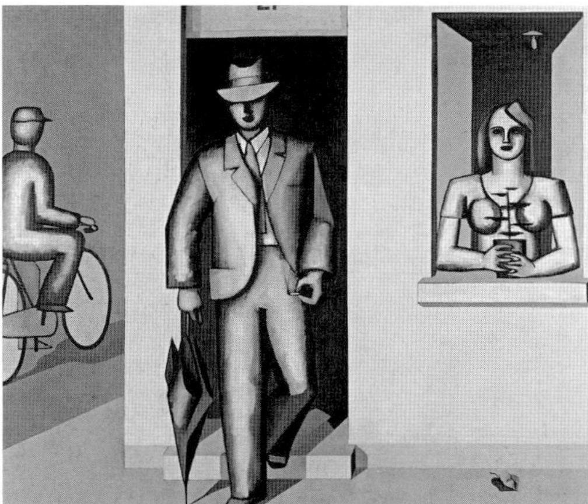

of Art Concret. Everything, however, changed with *Greeters* (*Saluers*; also known as *Saluters*) of 1944, which opened a new stylistic chapter. From then on Hélion took his pure colours and expressive lines from Arp, Miró and Kandinsky.

In the right-hand part of *Girl with yellow hair* (1944) hangs a twisted thread. In the background of *Man with red underpants* (1944) we see the lines of a calligraphy that looks 'automatic'. Such entirely new forms in Hélion's painting could be emblems, symbols, of the non-regulation that prevailed in his new pictures. *Défense d'* sums up this development. In its lower part it shows *Émile*, that child of abstraction; above, separated by a rigid line, are the free forms and erratic graphics of the post-war style.

In a letter he wrote to Raymond Queneau in 1939, Hélion explained how the question of meaning essential to his work had developed from his abstract period to the figurative work he was then creating. "Poetry should be capable of reading and writing the newspaper and all the rest of the everyday world, as well as a secret one …. It matters little that the symbol of an unknown quantity is a letter from the French or Greek alphabet; the main thing is to know the letter, to recognize the symbol. A bearded fellow represents God and all the power expressed by things and by life much better than a big X, a formula or a silence …. Why not stay with the prettiest, the most traditional and the one that is most enriched by popular usage?"[40]

Thus, around 1939, meaning had been no more than redefined, in a shift from a transcendant conception to a search for immanence. Hélion's 'betrayal' of abstraction was motivated ultimately by a desire to give its utopian aspects a human dimension.

In 1946 Hélion left America and settled in France for good. Together with this new chapter in his life he began a new phase in his art: just as *Fallen figure* had dramatically, symbolically, put an end to his abstract period, so *Wrong way up* [*À rebours*] (1947) was also intended as a turning point or manifesto. Hélion presented it as proof "that abstraction and the figure could live together, and that each was the key to the other".[41] Despite this proclaimed ecumenicalism, the painting depicts two very contrasting worlds. Hélion's own painting *Equilibrium*, which it reproduces, is sealed into the space of a gallery, while the female nude expands in a 'real' space. Above and beyond the dialectics of abstraction and figuration, which it proffers for analysis, *Wrong way up* recapitulates the three stylistic phases that Hélion's painting had passed through. To the left is abstraction, counter-balanced on the right by a nude, of which the stylized forms and immobility echo the 'architectural' aspect of abstract construction. The figure's three-dimensionality, using chiaroscuro, gives it a direct kinship with the 'transitional' figures of *With cyclist*. In the centre of the picture, all flat colour and curving lines, Hélion announced his new approach. But this 'contour' style was short-lived. On 1 October 1947 he wrote in his *carnets*, "I miss powerful three-dimensional forms".[42] *Wrong way up*, read from left to right this time, describes the 'forward' march – in the direction of its history – of Hélion's painting, the reconquest of three-dimensionality.

Once again it is tempting to compare the painter's work with his own reading of it, to try to identify a rhythm different from the one almost too perfectly punctuated by his 'pivotal' works (such as *Fallen figure* or *Wrong way up*). We have already seen that, despite the anti-surrealist stance of Art Concret, from 1934 onwards Hélion's painting was not indifferent to the siren call of *physis*. His susceptibility to the works of Arp and Miró led him to devise an 'organic' evolutionary model for his art. Later, in the mid 1940s, his figures resemble in their line and colour those of some surrealists. After the War Hélion was once again in phase with surrealism in his exploration of meaning. From the mid 1930s mythology had been a central issue for André Breton.[43] As long as it was reinvented and 'modern', myth was one modality of the 'universal' vocabulary that provided the twentieth-century avant-gardes with a common horizon.

In 1947, when the surrealist exhibition proclaiming the

emergence of a "new mythology" opened at the Maeght gallery, Hélion wrote in his *carnets*, "*The readers*. Saga of the readers. Myth of everyday actions. *Myth* of the familiar."[44] Resolutely modern, he turned to big cities for the figures of his 'mythology'.

Surrealism inspired Hélion with many of his post-war subjects. This is true of his sleepers (such as *Sleeper and nude* of 1947), which become recurrent motifs in his pictures. Through surrealist 'contamination' these sleepers tend to transform his painted images into dreams of reality. In the early 1950s the shop-window pictures introduce the new, utterly surrealist figure of the mannequin. From the metaphysical painting of Giorgio De Chirico to Hans Bellmer's *Doll* and from Man Ray's wooden figurines to the dummies of the International Exhibition of Surrealism, mannequins had become properly a symbol of the movement. Hélion returned to them again and again, even in his flea-market pictures of the 1970s.

However, no matter how far Hélion's flirtation with surrealism may have gone, it could never lead to marriage. The painter remained fiercely loyal to the positions he had taken up in the magazine *Volontés*, to which he contributed in the late 1930s.[45] This publication provided a focus for a number of dissidents from surrealism, a movement they felt tended to set its positions in stone. Their approach was summed up by Henry Miller in his '*Lettre aux surréalistes en tous lieux*'. "In my opinion the Surrealists are guilty of a very simple mistake: they are striving to establish an Absolute. They are mobilizing all the forces of consciousness in order pompously to introduce the Unconscious in all its glory. They believe in the Demon but not in God. Adore the night and refuse to recognise the day."[46] Hélion remained faithful to this declaration, which gave only relative importance to surrealist poetics.

3. Forgetting Léger

In the early 1950s Jean Hélion's painting moved into its most hermetic phase. He adopted a realism in which the wealth of detail tends to absorb and dissimulate the formal and symbolic issues. For some years his work in the studio became an experiment in which the eye and the mind were brought into intense confrontation. The painting that emerged during that time evokes a kind of asceticism, a deliberate oblivion of the self. For a while Hélion replaced the subjective, Promethean heroism synonymous with modernist art with, apparently, the contemplative's freedom from desire.

He was accompanied and encouraged on this austere path by three 'witnesses', three assiduous visitors, the poet Francis Ponge, the sculptor Alberto Giacometti and the painter Balthus. In his post-war work Giacometti sought a visibility that was immediate, yet never definitively conquered. His pictures and sculptures renounce the spells either of delirious dreams or of the mastery of geometry. His only goal now was to identify and get as close as possible to beings and things, which are lost when they are represented in absolute, as permanent.

Francis Ponge, author of *Le Parti pris des choses* [The bias of things], invited Hélion to adopt the scrupulous discipline of observing reality with no prior assumptions. "Ponge, with whom I agree in relation to the object, observed last Sunday that one must give oneself up to it, let it speak, make it the manager of the works."[47]

Balthus and Ponge discussed Hélion's pictures; Balthus regretted that Hélion was taking to long to "forget Léger".[48] On 5 March 1953, in Hélion's studio, Balthus revised this judgement. "Unexpected visit, yesterday, from Balthus .... Very understanding of my *Still life with scattered objects* .... 'For the first time in one of your paintings,' he said, 'one can feel happiness and wonder.'"[49] In *The pumpkin event* [*La Citrouillerie*] (1952) and *The snack* (1953), Hélion attained such a high degree of realism that critics spoke of "*trompe-l'oeil*".[50]

While the 'triumph' of the New York school was being acclaimed internationally and French avant-garde painters were looking only towards abstraction, Hélion, Balthus, Giacometti and a few others (such as Kossoff, Auerbach and Bacon in London) remained attached to the human figure and the depiction of solitude. Giacometti observed to Balthus that his *Passage du commerce St-André* had

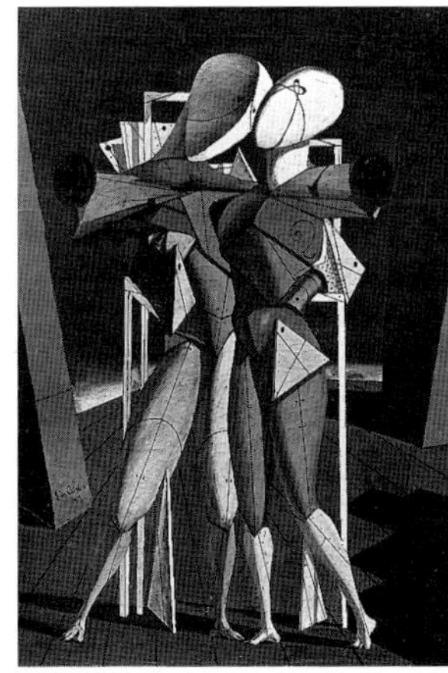

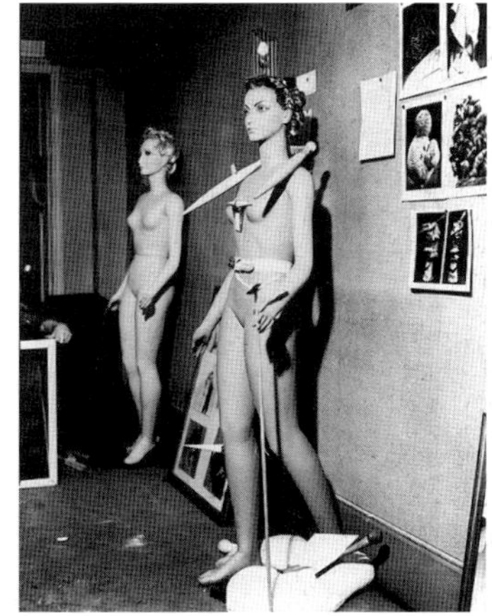

50. When these paintings were shown at the premises of the painter Mayo, *ibid.*, 30 November 1953, p. 266.
51. Recorded by Nicholas Fox Weber, in *Balthus. A Biography*, New York, Alfred A. Knopf, 1999, p. 449.
52. Jean Starobinski, "D'où venait l'enchantement", in *Balthus*, exh. cat., Paris, Centre Georges Pompidou, 1984, p. 331.
53. J. Hélion, *Journal d'un peintre. Carnets 1929–1962*, op. cit., p. 284.
54. Id., *À perte de vue, op. cit.*, p. 89.
55. G. Bataille, *Manet*, in *Œuvres complètes*, vol. IX, Paris, Gallimard, 1979, p. 145.
56. *Ibid.*, p. 132.
57. Cited by G. Bataille, *ibid.*, p. 128.
58. G. Bataille, *ibid.*, p. 127.
59. J. Hélion, *Journal d'un peintre 1929–1962, op. cit.* 29 March 1945, p. 81.
60. *Ibid.*, 14 October 1947, p. 105.
61. *Journal d'un peintre 1963–1984, op. cit.*, 28 April 1963, p. 8.
62. *Ibid.*, 3 September 1974, p. 169.

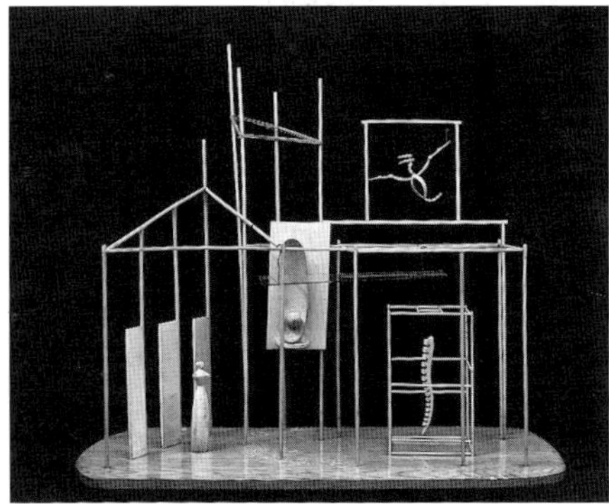

Alberto Giacometti
The palace at four o'clock 1932–33
Construction in wood, glass, wire and string
63.5 x 71.8 x 40 cm
The Museum of Modern Art, New York

the same subject as his own *Palace at four o'clock*.[51] Hélion devoted several paintings to such images of alienation, conveying the strange sense of being a stranger in the modern city.

4. *Le Grand Luxembourg*

Photographs of Hélion's studio and his studio paintings of 1953 show a monumental canvas turned to one of the walls. The picture is Balthus's *Passage du commerce St-André*. Its imagery reflects some of the issues that Hélion was exploring at the time. It shows a Parisian street full of figures frozen in quite ordinary poses. Their movements are depicted in an order and a construction reminiscent of Seurat. Like *Street* [*La Rue*; 1933], *The Passage du commerce St-André* (1952–54) transforms the everyday into myth. It "solemnizes an important moment, a moment that acquires sacred value in the way Balthus composes and fixes it".[52]

This large picture, turned to the wall in his studio, was surely the perfect answer to the questions Jean Hélion was considering. He himself thought so for a while. As though in response to Balthus's work, he started *Le Grand Luxembourg* (1953–57). He, too, composed his picture with the precision of a geometer. In explicit homage to Balthus, he gave the gardener gathering leaves a stiff figure reminiscent of the head cook of *Street*. *Le Grand Luxembourg*, larger than *The Passage du commerce St-André* (300 x 400 cm as opposed to 294 x 330 cm), was Hélion's first monument to everyday life. However, he was not to be satisfied for long by such realism which, in 'forgetting Léger', also sacrificed a formalism he had long seen as the guarantee of modernism.

The 'realism' of Ponge, Balthus or Giacometti was not an expression of objective observation. It was the mask of a subjectivism which, in Hélion's eyes, could not in itself justify a work. He still dreamed of monuments as the ultimate form of his utopian universal language. On 20 May 1954 he wrote in his *carnets*, "All in all, after a journey through nature and working only from nature for two years, I'm returning to my own domain, the world of concepts."[53]

The "concepts" had left the heaven of perfect geometrical forms in order to take on flesh. Their "universality" was that of human archetypes, their perceptible form that of allegories. "Behind ordinary gestures" Hélion sought "the sacred gesture that was the symbol of them".[54] He drew up an inventory of these gestures in a work that resembles an alphabet. *Daily allegory* (1951–52) contains the figures, the elementary 'signs', he would use to compose all his subsequent works. These include the mannequin, the newspaper-reader, the sewerage worker, the nude in the window and the seated man. Hélion now set about giving these figures a 'mythic' significance. They formed the thesaurus of 'concepts' he would use to help him decipher the world.

Almost surreptitiously, the studies of roofs Hélion undertook in the late 1950s reintroduced formalist enquiry into his painting. In this respect *Monument to a butcher* (1963), which transmutes the overall of a market porter and the carcass of an animal into an interplay of complex, synthetic three-dimensional forms, appears as a pivotal work. Four years later the *Dragon Street triptych* set the seal on this formalist reconquest of realism. Hélion returned to the metallic tones and synthetic, three-dimensional forms that had grown out of his abstract works (such as *With cyclist*). After a realism through which he had 'forgotten Léger' and an objectivity that had led him to abandon all experimentation with form, Hélion was now definitively asserting that modern subjects could not be expressed in traditional forms.

His ambition remained to paint edifying, monumental works. The events of May 68 were his inspiration for the triptych *Things seen in May*, with which he intended to give new form to history painting. Picasso, too, had sought to transpose the tumult of history into painting, with *Guernica*. However, he had opted for the timelessness of myth, to the detriment of historical record. Later, with his *Massacre in Korea,* he adorned a contemporary event in finery from the history of painting (Manet's *Execution of Maximilian*). Without recourse to quotation or scholarly distancing, Hélion covered a canvas almost nine metres long with the demonstrators and their banners, the movement of the red and black flags, and the CRS riot police in their greatcoats.

The bold anachronism of such a project sums up Hélion's eccentric relationship to modernism, which has too long been confined to the single issue of his 'betrayal' of abstraction. In the none-too-distant past, when art still had meaning and direction, Hélion's personal journey in the opposite direction from modern art's obligatory paths was enough to render him suspect. His apostasy came, however, to seem venal compared to the heresy of his desire to perpetuate a form of history painting.

When *Things seen in May* is hung in the galleries of a modern art museum it becomes possible to gauge just how singularly out of tune it is. The unease generated by a work of this kind can be encapsulated in the single word 'declaration'. Hélion's pictures are talkative; they force their figures to speak in a place where silence supposedly reigns. Hélion acknowledged this tendency in his work. He cricitized Francis Ponge for isolating the objects he chose to study, while he himself assembled them into phrases, making them "spit out" meaning. The modernity that batters through Hélion's pictures is not formalism. It is the more definitive and profound modernity of the kind identified by Georges Bataille in his book on Manet.

Manet's oeuvre reflects a modernity running counter to the lyrical, commemorative project of *Things seen in May*. "Like modern poetry, *Olympia* is the negation of the world: it is the negation of Olympia, of the poem and the mythological monument, of the monument in general and monumental conventions", claimed Bataille.[55] Faced with an event, Manet purged it of its meaning and its lyricism, its aspiration to be edifying. "Other pictures by the painter of *The balcony* tell no story, but of all of them *The execution of Maximilian* says the least .... This picture is the negation of eloquence, it is the negation of painting which, like language, expresses a feeling."[56] In the twentieth century anyone proposing to build a monument was condemned to be ridiculed and misunderstood. Max Beckmann, who wanted his art to be politically and morally edifying, found he had to drape his allegories in a veil of dreams and deliberately abstruse mythology. Philip Guston was only able to paint *Monuments* (the title of several of his works) if their ardour and spirituality were countered by grotesque forms and the darkest kind of humour. 'Monuments' such as these, which undermine their own foundations and deflate their own lyricism and eloquence, lend weight to Bataille's thesis that modern monuments can be erected only in honour of absence, and that they are condemned to be mute.

Thus Hélion, in seeking to give a new voice to painting using the forms, the symbols of modernism, was committing a two-fold act of heresy. At the dawn of modernism Baudelaire had noted the crumbling of collective values that could justify an art of eloquence: "Schools still existed under Louis XV; under the Empire there was one – one school, in other words the impossibility of doubt .... Doubt, or an absence of faith and naivety, is a vice peculiar to this century, since no one obeys."[57] Bataille draws all possible consequences from this observation: "In the old days painting had no autonomy, was merely a part of a majestic edifice, offering the crowd an intelligible *totality*. I must emphasize this fundamental point: there came to the great didactic monuments (châteaux, churches and palaces, which the past built and rebuilt in countless numbers), the monuments that spoke and proclaimed author-

ity, making the entire crowd bow down – there came a time when they lost the meaning on which their existence was based; they broke up: their language became the end of pretentious eloquence, from which the once submissive crowd turned away."[58]

Aware of this new situation, yet unable to abandon the 'monumental' motivation of his work, Hélion looked to reality as a source of "signs" that would go on reflecting meaning and offer a hope of coherence in the order of the world. Between the lines his *carnets* suggest he found fulfilment of his ambition in the last years of his work.

1945: "*My iconography*: actions, events in everyday life, in which I find, or to which I grant, an extraordinary nature or appearance. *E.g.* smoking: the rite of fire. Picking things up: humiliating oneself, etc. (The extraordinary in the ordinary).[59]

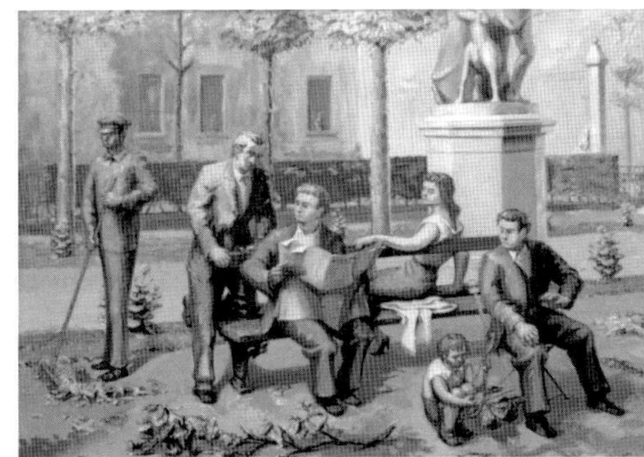

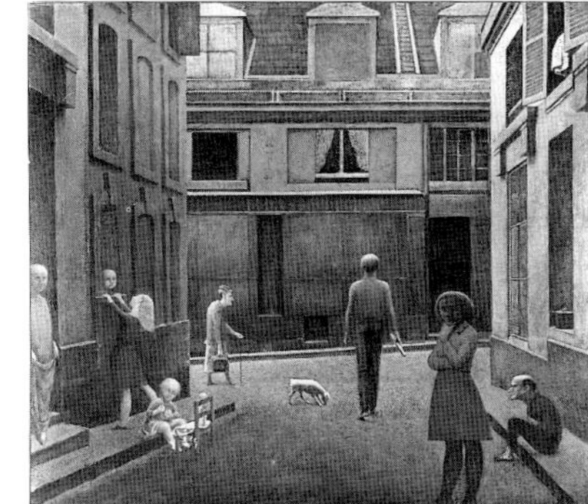

1947: "These figures having grown up, having undertaken to take something away from the gods and to assemble the important movements of the flesh and thought according to a new mythology."[60]

1963: "The newspaper-reader, the meat-porter, the woman with the shopping bag, the seated man and the flute or guitar player are the priests of a cult that I can formulate only by painting them. The meat is going to the sacrifice. The Venus with open or closed legs: temple-girl, striped girl, star-girl. Flowers and objects at the feet of all these people. This is my mythology. This is my high mass."[61]

1974: "This cycle I'm developing around people and motorcycles could be called: *Devotion to the wheel*."[62]

Jean Hélion
Le Grand Luxembourg, **1954–57**
Oil on canvas, 300 x 400 cm
Southern Illinois University at Edwardsville

Balthus
Le Passage du commerce St-André, **1952–54**
Oil on canvas, 294 x 330 cm
Private collection

63. *Ibid.*, 25 September1975, p. 214.
64. *Ibid.*, 23 February 1977, pp. 265–66.
65. *Ibid.*, 13 April 1979, p. 326.
66. *Ibid.*, 29 February 1978, p. 300.

1975: "What I have just done on a sheet of *grand aigle* paper [75 x 106 cm] is Christ as a lobster fisherman, one cooked and red in his right hand; the other alive and blue in his left hand …. The theme of the crucifixion, or the anticrucifixion, haunts this lobster saga."[63]

1977: "The gas-man (?) springing from the trap door on the left in *The city is a dream* is gesturing like an archangel. On leaving the night, the belly of the earth, perhaps every man is a prophet …. He has sprung from this tomb like a new Lazarus, like the blind man from the urinal."[64]

1979: "Myths are inscribed so deeply within us that beneath every movement we make, familiar or extraordinary, there is one expressing itself."[65]

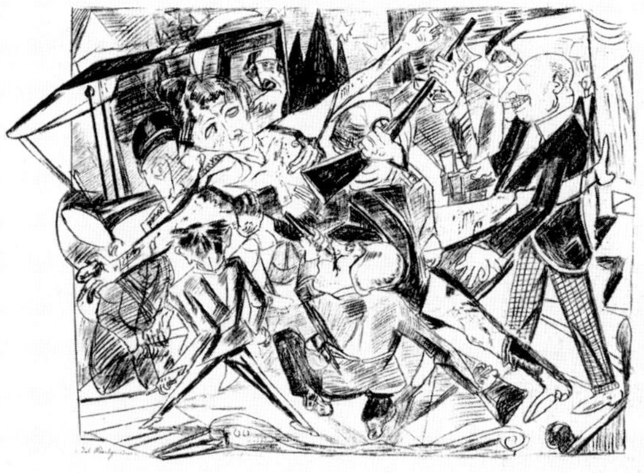

Max Beckmann
Martyrdom
Plate 4 of the portfolio *Die Holle* [Hell], 1918–19
Lithograph, 54,5 x 75 cm
Sprengel Museum, Hanover

Philippe Guston
Monument, 1976
Oil on canvas, 203 x 279.5 cm
Courtesy McKee Gallery, New York

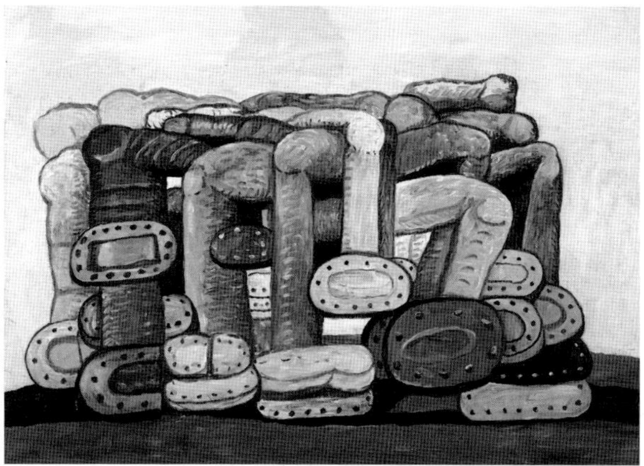

In 1983, when nearly blind, Hélion assembled on his canvases figures whose latent 'mythology' had been revealed to him by a life of observation. He had become the pharmacist whose experiments had fascinated him as a boy. Now he himself was causing the visual and symbolic chaos of the world to separate, making its signs precipitate out in figures rendered simple and abstract by a stylization of form and colour.

"It's by painting objects that I best express abstraction, seen here as the soul of the world."[66]

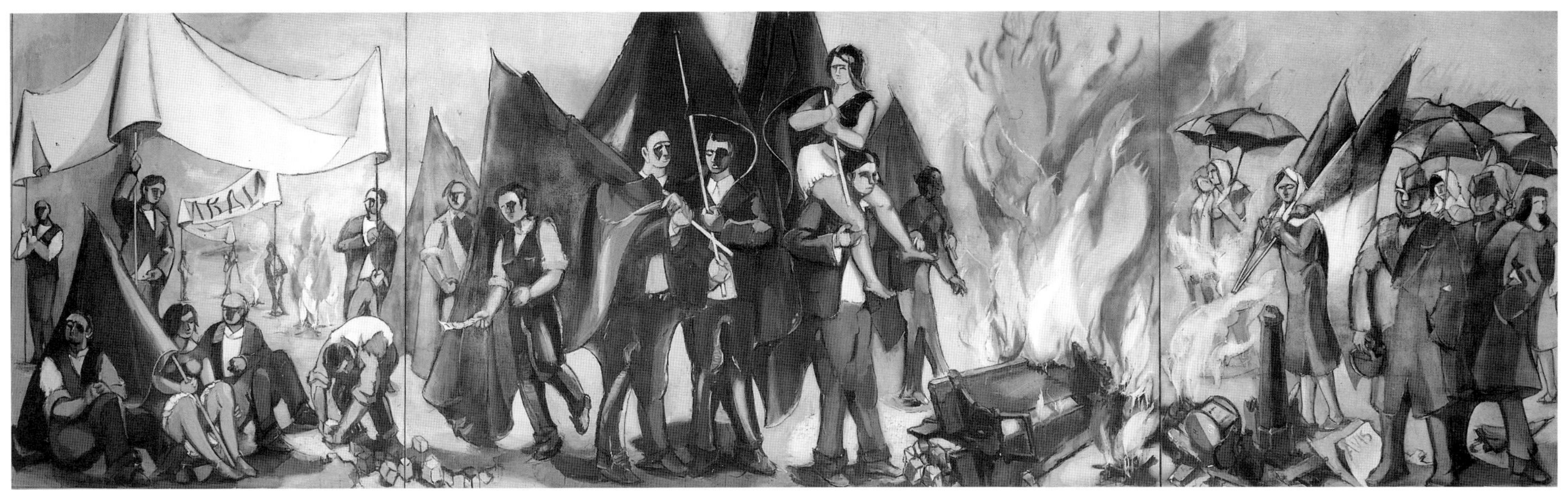

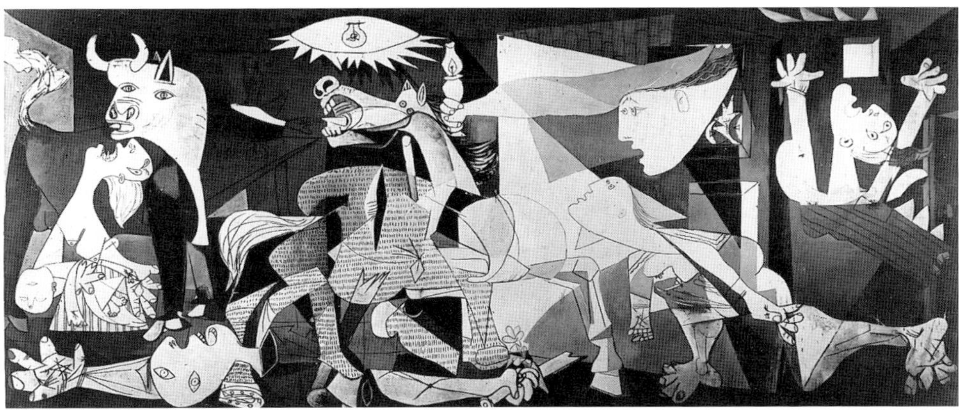

Jean Hélion
Things seen in May, 1969
Triptych, acrylic on canvas, 275 x 876 cm
Centre Pompidou, Musée national d'art moderne,
Paris, accepted in lieu of tax 1991

Pablo Picasso
Guernica, 1937
Oil on canvas, 349.3 x 776.6 cm
Museo nacional, Centro de Arte Reina Sofia, Madrid

JEAN HÉLION – THE WORLD AS PROSE

If there is one word which is particularly applicable to the figure of Jean Hélion, it is 'resistant'. All his life Jean Hélion was resistant to received and dominant ideas and, above all, to anything in any domain which he regarded as contrary to a certain morality of unfettered human fulfilment. All things considered he paid a heavy price for this fidelity to himself, for from the late 1930s onwards he was also one of the most controversial, misunderstood and neglected of painters. Hélion himself harboured as many doubts as strong convictions and was fully aware of the contradiction he carried within him. Perhaps more than any other painter of his generation, he was able immediately to integrate the consequences of this contradiction into the core of his work, putting it to good use, with all the power of his courageous, relentless independence, in a bold oeuvre which today retains its profound singularity.

To some extent the work resembles the events that marked Hélion's life, for one is initially struck by the diversity of the paths he took, paths which broke with, distanced themselves from or went *à rebours*, "the wrong way up", to dominant trends.[1] This he did with a freedom of attitude and an apparent indifference to ambient tastes (though not without personal suffering) which might pass for detachment, when in fact they reflect his close involvement with the preoccupations of his time. Hélion's particular paradox is that, with great courage and a sense of risk, he seems tacitly to have exploited failure (or pretended to do so), or at any rate accepted his difficulties and setbacks, pulling himself free and bouncing back all the more strongly to proclaim his own vitality loud and clear.

In addition to an uncommon intellectual lucidity, Hélion had a highly effective capacity for critical questioning. These two characteristics were expressed in carefully chosen and always trenchant words – he had consummate artistry as a speaker – backed up by a rare verbal ease. He was always alert, the brio of his language surpassed only by its intelligence, as has been noted.[2] Though lively and generous, he always strove for precision and, while humanity remained his prime concern, he never gave quarter. Around 1925, when Hélion dedicated himself entirely to painting, this speech took over from the poetry for which he had hitherto shown some talent. Afterwards his poetic qualities surfaced all the more powerfully here and there in his writings, conversations and oeuvre. Using concise, synthetic phrases, his language was particularly striking for its power of visual suggestion. It overflowed with the kind of formulations which also abound in his paintings and which, like all deeply felt assertions, accept that they may

not find favour. But this language was only the visible tip of uninterrupted and particularly dense thinking on painting and creativity. This thinking fed and accompanied an oeuvre which ultimately appears as its reflection, a kind of double, shedding another light on Hélion's central theme of correspondence, equivalence, kinship, duality, the passage from one world to another.

In this light (even though they have deservedly been much discussed owing to their pivotal position in his career), we can once again gauge the importance of the wording in the titles of two major works: *Fallen figure* of 1939 and *Wrong way up* [*À rebours*] of 1947. Almost despite themselves and beyond their metaphorical charge, these titles carry a negative inflexion, a meaning which hints at its other side, which ironically, but tacitly, tolerates an element of failure. Naturally this was deliberate. As many testimonies prove (notably Hélion's *Journal d'un peintre. Carnets*),[3] it was an integral part of the role played by these works in the gradual evolution in the painter's work at that time, in the steps directing his thinking.

Hélion paid meticulous attention to his titles,[4] which cannot ultimately be separated from the image they accompany. Together the two form a pair, an indivisible binomial. Departing from their usual – and fundamentally deceitful – function, they are worded to convey the subject, either through a hiatus effect or, conversely, through a slight redundancy; however they also play on a semantic fluidity, a flexibility of meaning that opens up unexpected, unrestricted horizons and interpretations. The variety of titling mechanisms or processes used by Hélion makes them worthy of study in themselves, so intrinsic are they to the very nature of the painter's pictorial project. Considering that this was a domain in which Hélion continually manifested his felicity of expression and revealed the inexhaustible resources of his imagination, it is well worth listing a few (remembering that, to appreciate their full piquancy, the titles should not be detached from their images – some are illustrated in the catalogue): *Brilliant figure* [*Figure brillante*] (1936), *Man with a red cheek* [*L'Homme à la joue rouge*] (1943), *Gothic figure* [*Figure gothique*] (1945), *Blue 'daily' man* [*Journalier bleu*] (1947), *Beautiful Etruscan* [*La Belle Étrusque*] (or *Pumpkin carrier* [*Le Porteur de citrouille*]) (1948), *Gold mannequin event* [*Mannequinerie d'or*] (1950–51), *The great plough* [*Le Grand Brabant*] (1957), *Dead man and the maiden* [*La Jeune Fille et le mort*] (1957), *Monument to a butcher* [*Monument pour un boucher*] (1963), *Auguste set alight* [*Auguste mis à feu*] (1969), *Cabbage duet* [*Duo en choux*] (1972), *Coat-tree and echoes* [*Le*

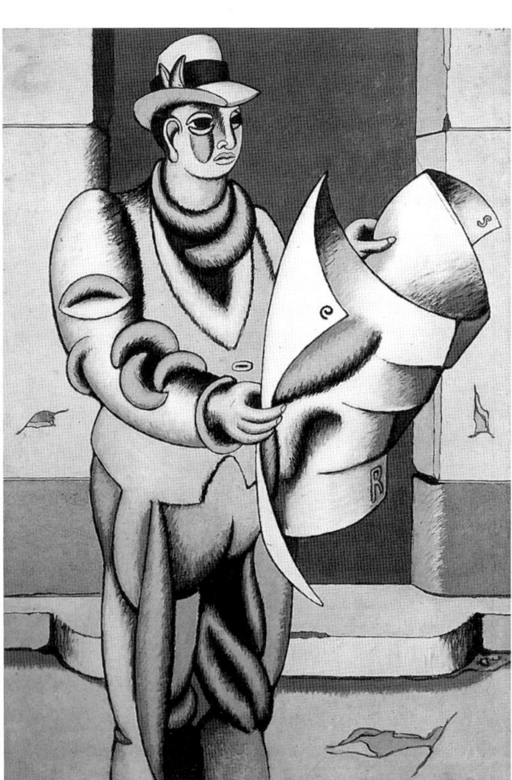

Jean Hélion
Blue daily man, 1947
Oil on canvas, 130 x 89 cm
Private collection, Japan

Perroquet et ses échos] (1975), *Rainy mechanical suite* [*Suite machinale pluvieuse*] (1977), *The Last Judgment of things* [*Jugement dernier des choses*] (1978–79), *Betrothal of the unknown squaddie* [*Fiançailles du poilu inconnu*] (1981), *Trumpet for a pumpkin* [*Trombone pour une citrouille*] (1983) and, lastly and wonderfully symbolic of the artist's thinking at the end of his life, *The Painter trampled by his model* [*Le Peintre piétiné par son modèle*] (1983). Using short forms in which poetry meets prose and humour combines with irony, like a long scroll these titles roll out parts of phrases, fragments of poems almost, which paradoxically mark out and reveal the thematic path traced daily by the painter in his work.

All these titles act as a foreword. They cast a particular light on the work which, perhaps even more than the image, enables us to grasp its complexity and meaning. They set us firmly on the right path. Hélion is always driven by his irrepressible need to "show",[5] to liberate the image from pretension or, conversely, its iconic exhaustion, to bring it closer to us without making it lose its power. Though he might flirt with a certain pictorial solemnity, or play – felicitously enough – on his own formulaicity and theatricality, for Hélion the title incontestably had a very serious role. It exalts the subject it so energetically submits for the viewer's attention, while at the same time undermining its specialness. To use an architectural metaphor that Hélion particularly liked to see applied to his work,[6] it is often there to make an ironic comment on the piece for which, in its own way, it acts as a pedestal, like an unexpected dedication on a monument or stele. Where necessary the title calls us back into line, back to life, to humour, to gravity – indeed to sight. Above all it saves us from being deceived by the implications of looking at the painting, by considering what the painting means both for Hélion himself as painter and for us as viewers. The title puts us back in our place, or leaves us there. Through this stratagem, like a negative image of some of Magritte's ploys, Hélion shelters us from any kind of deceit or blindness, resolutely placing his picture in full light. He warns us of everything that might lessen the value or effectiveness of the precious act of seeing. He literally signposts what he meant to express and what he wants to reveal, often despite the enigmatic or complex nature of the subject, helping us begin the process of "deciphering"[7] the work, gradually interpreting, each in turn, its different registers, the different strata of meaning, which build up the composition like some kind of tracking shot.

These titles are linked to each other by an invisible but continuous thread which, over time and almost despite Hélion himself, tells the story of the painter's approach, the "fables" that his painting works to illuminate. Referring to Francis Ponge,[8] Hélion went so far as to say that the list of his titles could in itself constitute an autonomous work, an endless book or poem, infinitely illustrating and commenting on his oeuvre, its long verbal phrases resembling the phrases of objects, motifs, graphic airs, accents and colours, that run through his paintings and give them a solid construction. In itself the "suite"[9] of titles encloses the territory within which the artist's pictorial world is erected. It numbers and lists the themes, subjects and forms which constitute that world, which provides the painted reflection of the boundless, intoxicating interaction of rhetorical figures and the playful resources of language. There is a constant movement back and forth between the image and the words it inspires, just as, in a different idiom, the phrases of objects, movements and poses comment on the image from within the composition they help to shape and, in turn, become purely visual phrases.[10]

Having set off, like some modern-day Ulysses, on an initiatory journey where shipwreck and wandering are combined with the happiness and pride of success, tirelessly travelling reality as though it were an unknown continent that his eye never wearied of exploring, Hélion seems to give voice in the wake of his images. He "sings" the world. As he had formerly done in his poems (in which we hear both Apollinaire and Prévert), he gets the better of the silence around him, his own solitude, by surreptitiously humming a tune which in its apparent simplicity always has something cheekily mocking about it, but which remains benevolent towards both reality and the painter himself on his dogged quest. In this he is almost certainly showing us that he has no illusions. On the contrary, with precision and humour, seemingly by chance, he makes the best of the paths down which he is driven, almost despite himself, by his own demands and dreams. This is reflected in the many neologisms ("-eries", for instance *mannequineries* [mannequin events], *lapineries* [rabbit events], *citrouilleries* [pumpkin events], *journalieries* [daily-eries – both 'newspaper' and 'everyday']) he readily forges; their ironic familiarity demonstrates his capacity to transform the world at will, subsequently drawing freely from it all the metamorphoses that lie dormant within it, as well as the imaginary dimension that feeds all of his work.

However, in Hélion's work this experimentation is carried out without the slightest affectation. If reality is really there before his eyes, it is not so that he can exploit its unexpected, selective, exotic aspects, artificially exalting its triviality, nor in order to stimulate blind curiosity, still less

1 The words in quotation marks are Jean Hélion's own, either because, as here, they repeat the title of one of his works, or because they are phrases invented by him or commonly used by him, whether orally or in his writings.
2 On this aspect of Hélion's personality see Jean-Dominique Rey's interesting account in *Hélion, la figure tombée*, Colmar, Musée d'Unterlinden/Paris, Adam Biro, 1995, pp. 115–16.
3 See Jean Hélion, *Journal d'un peintre. Carnets 1929–1962 et 1963–1984*, ed. Anne Moeglin-Delcroix, 2 vols., Paris, Maeght, 1992.
4 Henry-Claude Cousseau, *Hélion*, Paris, Éd. du Regard, 1992, p. 23.
5 *Ibid.* This theme is analysed in the first chapter, entitled "'Faire voir' ou le théâtre des apparences" ['Showing' or the theatre of appearances], pp. 11–21.
6 *Ibid.*, p. 23.
7 *Ibid.*, chapter entitled 'Tout est pareil' [Everything is alike], p. 157.
8 See J. Hélion, *Journal d'un peintre, op. cit.*, particularly 8 September 1975; and J. Hélion, *À perte de vue*, Paris, IMEC, 1996, p. 146.
9 The way that Hélion frequently uses the word *'suite'* in his titles (cf. H.-C. Cousseau, *Hélion, op. cit.*, p. 168) has some analogies with the musical form of the same name, signifying a chain of several parts that form the overall composition.
10 On the important question of the "picture as sentence" (Aragon) and the sentence as a system of signs and pictograms (see H.-C. Cousseau, *Hélion, op. cit.*, pp. 161, 168, 193), see Aragon's superb chapter 'Signs' [*Les signes*] in *Henri Matisse, roman*, vol. 1, Paris, Gallimard, 1971, pp. 147–57. His words can also be applied to Hélion's work.

11 See H.-C. Cousseau, *Hélion, op. cit.*, the chapter 'Tout est pareil', p. 155, of which the title is taken from a passage in the *carnets* dated 20 February 1975.
12 Francis Ponge, *L'Atelier contemporain*, Paris, Gallimard, 1977, pp. 88–89.
13 J. Hélion, *Journal d'un peintre, op. cit.*, Paris, 28 September 1947.
14 The reference is to Jean Dubuffet, *L'Homme du commun à l'ouvrage*, Paris, Gallimard, 1973.
15 On the relationship between triviality and modernism, see F. Ponge, *L'Atelier contemporain, op. cit.*, pp. 88–89.

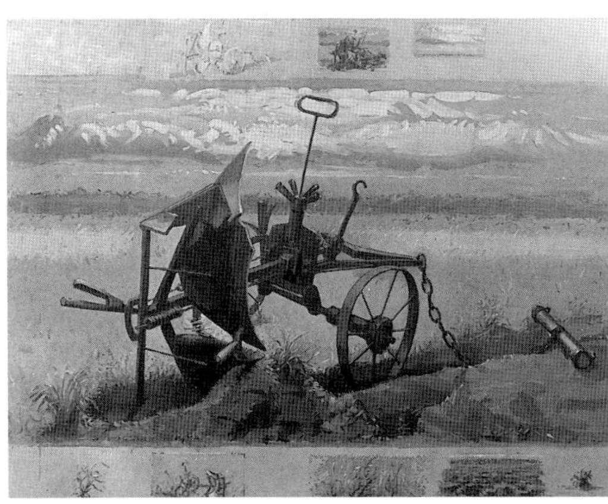

Jean Hélion
The great plough, 1957
Oil on canvas, 150 x 185 cm
Musée Zervos, Vézelay

to reduce or erase its lumps and bumps. On the contrary, Hélion keeps to a repertoire of objects, motifs, themes and genres that are as neutral and impartial, and thus also as true and raw, as possible. Shop-window mannequins, cigarettes, French bread and newspapers, nudes, still lifes, scenes, portraits and allegories have always belonged to the history of painting. However, rather than a faraway, cerebral world, Hélion uses them to translate the theatre of everyday life, the environment that is simply his and ours, without subjecting it to the distortions of an aesthete's distant, calculated vision. Above all he wants to celebrate a reality that is within reach of hand and eye, unaffectedly to reveal the magnificence hiding in a cabbage or the dazzling majesty of a pumpkin, the floral geometry of an umbrella, the calligraphic beauty of a trumpet, the perfect cadence of a violin, the tumescence of a hat, the great arpeggio of a stool, the eschatological sign of a crane. In his work we find no hint of a vision that might strip these objects of their flesh, their meaning or of their capacity to signify to us that we (who look at them, who "see" them) are at same level as they are, in the same world, the same reality, part of the whole that we form with them, swept along, as in our turn we are when we observe them, on the same adventure.

For Hélion, bard of reality and life, all these actors of the day-to-day must ultimately start to speak, in paint. The voice that Hélion lends them is in the image of his own – polished and sophisticated, yet direct, with no false affectations, readily familiar. This is what gives us the inimitable, pungent mix of apparently simple signs and complex figures, of the boldly pared-down, stylized sketch and the premeditation of clever and trivial formulations. Above all it is striking to note how he surpasses and transforms the pictorial conventions on which he nevertheless bases his work, referring more to the mechanisms and structural resources of language and speech than those of representation. This ability is manifested not so much in a desire to describe the world as to "write" it. There is something in Hélion's graphic approach that infallibly verges on the sign, but this is an archetypal sign, with a "coded" power that gives it the potential to express the "whole", or perhaps that first principle hiding behind the infinitely proliferating appearance of forms. From one point of view Hélion is searching, if not for a fantastical sign capable of revealing the meaning of appearances, then at least for the movement, the inflexion (of both hand and eye) that might suddenly get the better of his clairvoyance, the bedazzlement it provokes in him. It is only natural that for him drawing most closely resembles a form of writing. In the outlined

forms of the 1940s his line first espouses the sinuosity and inflexions of writing, and thereafter its modulations and rhythms, so that the fragments of bodies or objects become words, and these join together into sentences.[11]

Jean Hélion's originality also lies in his effective use of rhetorical figures, which certainly had no parallel in the twentieth century before him. The full diversity of the classical panoply is there in its entirety, from alliteration to antithesis, metaphor, metonymy, anagrams, chiasmus, contrast, synecdoche, repetition and embedded quotations or subtexts, providing his painting with a uniquely expressive and discursive arsenal. At the time only surrealism could boast a similar effectiveness, but in the opposite mode, with the text preceding the image. Hélion's work truly represents a new exploration of the possibilities of painting, once again looked at intuitively, from the angle of language. In this respect it can be seen as prefiguring the explorations pursued in the period 1960–70, notably in France, by the generations immediately following Hélion, who took advantage of developments in the semiological approaches then dominating the social sciences to carry out analytical deconstruction. Exploiting the elements of a "dialectic of opposites", as he liked to put it, playing with their tension, Hélion suddenly pushes the power, complexity and richness of speech and writing into painting. The iconographic arrangements that are so peculiar to him resemble the ploys and artifice specific to language. In borrowing them he emphasizes as never before the link between language and representation, their mutual dependency. But Hélion did not, of course, confine himself to purely discursive mechanisms, however rich these might be in effects and resources. He introduced them into pictorial language to make better use of their flexibility and their capacity to deal with a ceaseless exchange between reality and the imagination, to free unconscious forces more fully and to arm painting more effectively with the oneiric dimension that it bears within it. He did this even though, paradoxically, in his own work the dimension of the dream clings as closely as possible to what reality has to show, as though it were in the unreal distance of dreams that life can best be perceived, as though deciphering reality enabled one to decipher one's dreams more successfully.

However, the appetite for "seeing", the desire to "show" that lies at the heart of Hélion's project was conceivable only with a constant effort of belief. Ultimately it was through a degree of theatricality and its corollary, a certain form of declaration, that this project was able to reach fulfilment and attain its goals. Without being taken in by the artifices that such a practice imposed on him, Hélion was always willing to use deliberately oratorical devices such as suspense, mime, full-frontal figures and clever symmetries. Faithful to his admiration for that other wonderful director of painting, Philippe de Champaigne, and his consummate art of silent exposition, he quite naturally used expressive hand gestures and exploited the speech of movement. With Hélion we are in the presence of an unusual orator who, through powerful phraseology combined with poetic artistry, masterfully builds the visual and semantic structure of his pictures, maintaining an unshakeable control of his stratagems. Like a musician, he shapes the phrases and rhythms that irrigate his images with a dynamic fluidity, sounds the right chord at the right moment, finds the appropriate harmonies and brings in orchestral effects that destabilize the figurative organization and send reality veering towards imagination, the physicality of the image towards allegory, the everyday myth towards the parable that is invariably concealed within it.

In this sense Jean Hélion's position remains eminently singular. Even taking into account the political inflexion which to some extent underlies his open, generous aesthetic language and its concern to avoid any elitist divisions, the fact that he persisted in making images in such an independent fashion still raises questions. Ranged around him were Abstraction at its height, a dominant Surrealism, and imposing tutelary figures such as Picasso (often mentioned in the *carnets* – with Picasso, somewhat unwillingly, Hélion carried on a kind of personal sparring) and with Léger, still projecting their powerful shadows. Here we should note that, despite his natural activism and intellectual attachments, Jean Hélion's art remained untouched by any partisan spirit. The neutrality and hieratism he displays in his images can also in some ways be seen as expressions of a sense of propriety which held at bay all effects not derived from the sincerity and independence of his thought. Like Courbet, Manet and, in a different way, Cézanne – all of whom he greatly admired – and while remaining fully committed to his own activism, Hélion undoubtedly sought to keep his art at a distance from all constraints that were not its own, to confront it with itself on an ideal plane and to keep it independent of pressure from ideas that could only be contingent, so enabling its transcendence. This sharp sense of personal freedom also illuminates Hélion's aesthetic stances, which, as Ponge suggested, despite or because of the "hypnotic" power intrinsically linked to his painting, attain a neutral pictorial expression, stripped as far as possible of any "charm" or "taste".[12] In resolutely

open opposition to the dominant canons of the times, he sought to create an immediate quality of conviction and visual power. Far from exclusively asserting particular aesthetic principles, he based his work on the logic of synthesis (a recurrent theme in his thinking), on dialogue between a mental process of rigorous thought and strong sensual experience, and so managed to create something much broader. So he found what he called the "stumbling point",[13] which he defined as "the intersection of the seen and conceived, reality and the imaginary".

It was in this "meeting" – to use a key word – that he believed he would find a pictorial transcription that would be both free of the overly narrow constraints and limitations of realism and yet also faithful to the element of stability and utopia which reality invariably carries within it. In Hélion's work, as in that of Jean Renoir, Cartier-Bresson, Boubat and Doisneau at the same period, a joyful euphoria rises up from the theatre of the street; there is a happiness in his figures, in their poses and their noise, a need for cheery brotherhood reflected in the abundance of apparently anodyne motifs, such as mannequins in shop-windows, hats, umbrellas, walking-sticks, bread and pumpkins. All these things are the signs of a full and ordinary life without anxiety, the tangible guarantee of immediate happiness, sure of its own simplicity; they express a desire for enchantment which, in the aftermath of the war and its tragedies, suddenly contradicts not just history, but also the greyness of Sartrian existentialism.

In opting for prose, which he regarded as the only form capable of depicting the palpable, intense poetry of reality, and turning away from the deceptive conventions of distant, disdainful poetry, Hélion invented a true recitative that matched his project. He was not afraid of the banality at the heart of the prosaic. On the contrary, in it he found the challenge he had been looking for. At a stroke he had relieved painting of its aesthetic weight, condemning it to a certain bareness, but also showing it its own power, its own capacity for resistance; he freed it from the burden of its conventional, ancient charm. The same concern informs the work of many contemporary artists and writers, from Ponge to Queneau, Jean Dubuffet to Chaissac, Gruber to Giacometti, not forgetting Léger and Picasso. It is the praise of a certain banality, of the beauty inherent in commonplace things,[14] of their bareness, of the element of hitherto unexplored modernity contained precisely in their triviality and of the new territories that modernism opens up for conquest.[15]

Even today to speak of modernism is to return to the famous piece by Baudelaire, published late in 1863, *The*

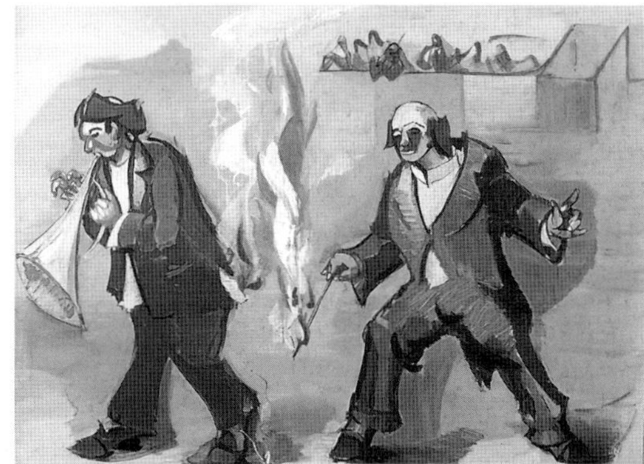

Jean Hélion
Auguste set on fire, 1969
Acrylic on canvas, 150 x 200 cm
Collection of David Hélion

16 The text of 1869 is reprinted in 'L'Art romantique', *Œuvres complètes*, Paris, Gallimard, La Pléiade, 1961, pp. 1152–92.

17 J. Hélion, *À perte de vue*, followed by *Choses revues*, ed. C. Paulhan and P. Fréchet, Paris, IMEC, 1996, particularly p. 273.

18 *Id., Journal d'un peintre, op. cit.*, 9 March 1948: "I am reading Baudelaire's *L'Art romantique* for the first time and in it I find, expressed far better than I ever did, many things I have often said or written".

19 *Ibid.*, 10 September 1975: "My undertaking – to rehabilitate the present in modern painting – is among the most profound of all".

20 H.-C. Cousseau, *Hélion, op. cit.*, pp. 163–64.

21 J. Hélion, *Journal d'un peintre, op. cit.*, between 14 and 17 June 1972, on the picture *Lady with cabbage [La Dame au chou]*.

Painter of Modern Life.[16] There is no doubt that, although Baudelaire is seldom cited in the *carnets*, despite odd notes recorded here and there, particularly in *Choses revues*,[17] the nineteenth-century poet was fundamentally important to the painter. Hélion had certainly read the text mentioned, as is revealed by a fragment in the *carnets* dated 9 March 1948.[18] He says he might have written these passages himself, so closely do they coincide with his vision, starting with Baudelaire's famous definition of modernism: "It is a matter … of extracting from fashion what it may contain of the poetic within the historic, of drawing out the eternal from the transitory"; "the duality of art is a fatal consequence of the duality of man". Even more disturbing is the fact that some of Hélion's quintessential grand themes, such as that of visual happiness, of the archetypal view of the everyday, the satirical vision of history, the morality drawn from the everyday or the allegorism of detail, seem already to have been suggested in the various chapter titles of Baudelaire's text, such as 'Beauty, fashion and happiness', 'A sketch of manners' and 'Pomp and solemnity'. 'The soldier' reminds us of *Suites for 11 November*, 'The dandy' refers back to the *Émile*s, the men in hats and their cold, monumental stiffness, 'Woman' to the very many, exclusively female nudes, and 'Carriages' to the telluric accidents of the 1980s.

Of course Hélion treats the 'Baudelairean' aspect of these subjects in a very different register, where humour gives rise to derision, lyricism and gravity. Nevertheless the "vain" theatricality of the world, displayed for example in the great triptychs of the late 1960s, where the futility and deceptive appearances of the things of life take on a moral dimension, provides a spectacular comment on Baudelairean ethics. The poet's evocation of the "bitter or heady flavour of the wine of life", the "pomp of life", and particularly his remarks on "the desire to see and to forget nothing" in the chapter entitled 'The mnemonic art', give some foretaste of the more unusual aspects of Hélion's thought. The link between seeing and memory, looking and remembering, light and darkness, inside and outside and the external and underground worlds are all recurrent elements of the painter's dialectics, as is his (literally and figuratively) pronounced taste for monuments, for sculptural monumentality, his propensity – sometimes tainted with sarcasm – for commemorations, applied not only to the doubtful, pitiful events that make up the human comedy, but also to the quintessentially anodyne, familiar things, the objects that fetishistically provide the reference points of a "decipherable" world. Where most of his contemporaries regarded such a return to realism as a dead end, a regression, today we see it as a different approach to modernism. But Hélion's was a modernism paradoxically concerned to maintain its distance from the doctrines and ideas of the period; their utopian dimension implied a form of progress the profoundly sceptical painter could not accept. His was a singular, independent modernism, seemingly focused exclusively on itself and deliberately anchored in the act of looking directly at reality, at the present.[19]

To speak of the world is to recall, with Baudelaire, the feeling of sensuous impulses passing through it. For Hélion, more explicitly still, the world is also the reflection, the consequence, the endpoint, of a vast erotic design. It is this that shapes the world, just as it also shapes the way we look at it. As a result sexual metaphors of both a visual and semantic order abound in his work, as do subjects which, implicitly or not, play on their allusive power to illustrate, or more often suggest, amorous exchanges. The objects themselves, including hats, umbrellas, pumpkins, trousers, gloves and other garments, are charged with erotic tension, or situated in a way that gives the compositions an implicit energy, irresistibly subjecting them to the dynamic of coupling which the painter ceaselessly evokes[20] and which is simply another variation on the theme of duality.

Hélion's first direct allusion to eroticism came very early, in 1939, in *With cyclist*. After this he explored the theme on a great many occasions. Overtly abandoning all interpretations linked to the workings of the unconscious then in vogue, notably among the surrealists, Hélion deliberately favoured a more naturalistic, playful vision. He shows the reality of the act of love, the tangible signs that reflect human erotic customs and the sociability to which they give rise. Unlike Picasso, Hélion is neither a voyeur nor an exhibitionist; his work does not compulsively substitute eroticism for the practice of painting. But for Hélion it is through eroticism that human beings identify with the world and fulfil part of their destiny. He therefore turns the triviality of his subject into a celebration, a serious yet jubilant eulogy, breathing into it the life of an allegorical vision. This renders his magnification of the ordinary more lively still; the pumpkins, bottles and umbrellas, cigarettes and newspapers, drums, trumpets and soup-dishes all become more powerfully archetypal; they not only "decipher" reality, but are invested with hidden power, capable of revealing the tales and fables that, in Hélion's eyes, they must possess and which he intends to disclose to us.[21]

Despite his laconic, lapidary style, Hélion was well-versed in the art of stories. He often liked to say that his pictures were "fables". Just as he liked to "sing", he also liked to recite, to "phrase". It is surprising that an art as silent as his, as stable in its components, should in fact be a vehicle for so many songs and dreams. But just as his sleepers are full of dreams which literally unfold before our eyes, so his images are alive with secrets, which they must both contain and reveal. This means that the image often appears to be in suspense, on the threshold of an imminent event or following one that has just taken place, caught between past and future, carrying within it a narrative charge heightened by being paused in this way. And yet, as we have noted, Hélion's language most favours dialogue, conversation. Within the picture all the elements that govern the composition, all the protagonists, even those most apparently indifferent and hieratic, invariably relate to each other and carry out iconographic, formal and semantic exchanges between themselves. The image is addressed in the first instance to its viewer. This impulse towards dialogue, this mutual attraction, should undoubtedly be seen in the light of the amorous project which Hélion regards as intrinsic to reality, the erotic tension underlying the construction of the world. After his comparatively respectful implementation of constructivist rules in the early 1930s – in which this dialectic is, however, already at work – everything subsequently attests to a desire for attraction, a centripetal force bringing forms together, leading them to move together towards the figure or towards a stage on which the theatre of life will soon unfold. All the parts have a relationship of dependency and meaning. Everything is linked in the movement of a phrase, carried along in the unfolding of a story, the construction of an allegory. The erotic project perceived by Hélion is in its turn no more than a metaphor, a parable of the inseparable character of things, proof that opposites attract, that oppositions are complementary, that we cannot escape the great, contradictory, antinomial cycle that governs our existence.

Above and beyond his desire to develop a pictorial language, day by day, almost laboriously, and the impressive longevity of his experience, persistence and tenacity, we may well wonder what space remained, when its creative processes seem to have been dominated by discursive impulses and intellectual motivations, for the wellspring of vigorous exuberance underlying Hélion's project. It is hard to forget Matisse's terrible judgment that Hélion should cut out his tongue, since his tongue's speech could shatter the speech of painting, or reduce its impact. For Matisse the world was transparent and a painting was a luminous window shedding light and opening the eye that looked at it. But for Hélion reality, the totality that makes up the world, was not necessarily visible from the outset. It seems to be more like a rebus, a collection of signs which holds the eye by its riddle. Only the painter's eye can decipher it and dissipate its fascination, but at the considerable risk of being blinded. So in Hélion's work the picture is the quintessential tool of an eye wielding its magic power as an intersection, a border between the real and the imaginary, inside and outside, image and speech, light and darkness, day and night – although ultimately this night merges and combines with the light and dazzle of jubilation.

A premonition of this feeling appears in the mid 1960s, around the time of the creation of the *Dragon Street triptych*. Here, in an effort of hitherto unachieved synthesis, a theme unfolds combining all those that had hitherto haunted the painter's work. Previously his pictorial writing had been firm, concise and ornamental in character (particularly in the 1940s), with an abundance of encircling. But after the deliberately realist episode of the 1950s, a return to tradition marked by a relish for pictorial fullness and density, Hélion's style threw off such constraints. In the decade of the 1980s his writing becomes exasperated, strained by a new necessity and awareness of time, overtaken by an urgent need to tell, to represent the episodes proliferating in full view. His rhythmical, strident, sonorous compositions seem to form an uninterrupted series of scenes illustrating everyday life, spooling the film of his life ever more rapidly through the filter of memories. The clearest proof of this is the title of a painting from this time, alluding to the novel by Marcel Proust, *Time regained* [*Le Temps retrouvé*]. As Hélion synthesizes his experience, retrospectively reviewing his entire output, the themes come in a rush, literally falling in a heap before our eyes, transformed by time but always the same, with little care either for him or for their own meaning. Together they form a unique pictorial narrative, reflecting the vagaries of dreams, memory and consciousness, unconcerned by time and its constraints, its conventions and laws, and giving a special place to the process of embedding, of painting within painting so often found in his work.

The blindness Hélion faced at the end of his life naturally had a major effect on his work during this last period. But, far from allowing it to paralyse him, he turned it to his advantage, as was his habit. Blindness became a different way of seeing; it revealed a different approach to reality,

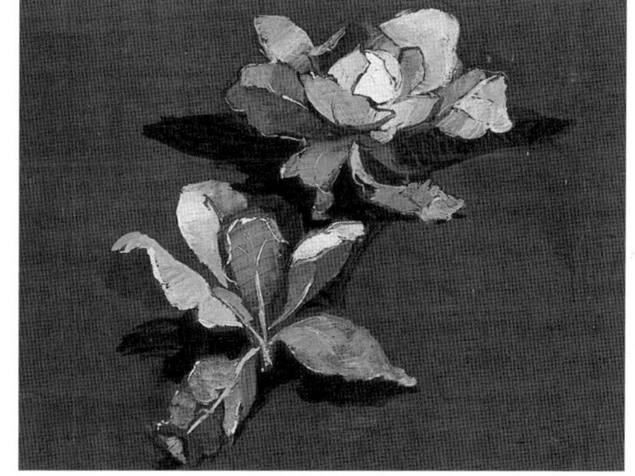

Jean Hélion
Cabbage duet, 1972
Acrylic on canvas, 65 x 81 cm
Private collection

22 *Ibid.*, 14 December 1982.
23 Jacques Derrida, *Mémoires d'aveugle, l'autoportrait et autres ruines*, Paris, Musée du Louvre/Réunion des Musées nationaux, 1990, p. 23.

led to a different perception and a different way of being dazzled. Returning to writing (dictating his words), the painter reinterpreted his life and work in his 'memories', the last of his abundant texts. The essential accounts are given in three magnificently illuminating pieces, *À perte de vue* [As far as the eye can see], *Choses revues* [Things seen again] and *Mémoire de la chambre jaune* [Memory of the yellow room], the titles of which play on words as usual, reflecting their author's semi-comical, semi-affecting approach, and again convey a meaning at once immediate and hidden. However Hélion was also driven by the need to find exclusively in painting something he had successfully achieved in his *carnets* – a counterpoint, a tight, indissoluble dialogue between writing and drawing. And through a natural, almost symmetrical return to his earliest creative impulses, Hélion as a painter became even more of a writer in his thinking. It is the intimacy of writing that he projects into painting, its improvisational vigour, its flexibility, its pulsations and vivacious sketchiness. At last he had won the freedom to unburden himself of the incessant effort to construct the arrangement of his world; now he could juggle with forms and colours, subjects and themes, metaphors and allegories, space and time, with no constraints, without worrying about pictorial conventions. This led him deliberately to distance himself from these conventions and, finally and happily, to confront and abandon himself to the hallucinations of which they had taken the place. Hélion's strength now lay in the way he assembled the scattered pieces (like words for a writer) that make up reality – his own reality – and in doing so, described an everyday world. But this description did not take the form of yet another representation, new interpretation or original visual construction; instead it led to a narrative, a kind of chronicle at last revealing how, between myth and lived history, fable and experience, the world was ultimately constructed for him, in its order, its episodes, its elements, in a rhapsody summoning the inventory of everything from which it was composed, of the "whole" it formed.

"It is said that Homer was blind." These familiar words, born of a humble rule of Latin syntax but fortuitously significant, suddenly find illustration here with all the splendour of legendary greatness radiating its mythical nobility. Hélion, too, had come to the end of his life. Blind and inspired by the grace of his sightlessness, he took as his guides two new avatars of Hermes who had continually haunted his pictures, the sewage worker and the blind man. In the heart of his night he tore into the opacity of the light flooding the world, summoned all that his eye had gleaned throughout his life, that he could no longer see, and fearlessly made his way through the depths of the darkness towards his truth. Superbly ignoring the tyranny of time, like the bard he was, he intoned a solitary, powerful incantation, celebrating a vision which ultimately ousted reality and made it burst. He "painted to see clearly",[22] with a "hand that went further than the eye".[23] Life had at last become a dream, and that dream was the painting he dreamed of.

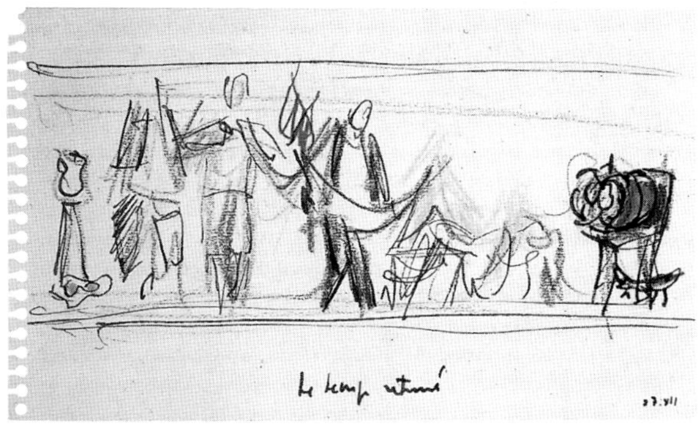

Jean Hélion
Study for *Time regained*, coloured chalk, 11 x 17.5 cm
***Carnets,* 27 December 1977**
Bibliothèque nationale de France,
département des Manuscrits, Paris

Matthew Gale

JEAN HÉLION AND BRITISH ART, 1933–1937

"We are a few with something in common»

In 1935 *Cahiers d'art* published an *enquête* on the questions facing contemporary art.[1] Towards the end of his introduction Christian Zervos raised the topic of the artist's ambiguous relationship with the *bourgeoisie*, at once attacked and sought-after as patrons. "Does this confusion", he asked, 'not run the risk of creating misunderstandings, especially in the United States and in England, countries in the process of adopting the researches of today's art?"[2] To illustrate such a "misunderstanding" he cited the decision of an English collector to sell his Cézannes in order "to replace them with mediocre, though allegedly very modern, works".[3] Zervos clearly felt a responsibility to protect such untutored collectors from their own inclinations. However, it is notable that he did not propose that these countries were places in which new artists were emerging. This is all the more striking because he knew of the international contacts that Jean Hélion and others had been developing and, in the particular case of Britain that concerns us here, Zervos had recently been approached by Ben Nicholson to promote the London-based group Unit One.

What was said (and left unsaid) in the *enquête* in *Cahiers d'art* provides one context for the cross-Channel exchange between Paris and London. The economic conditions that underlie the concerns it expressed were especially acute. Towards the end of the previous year, Hélion had listed the imminent closure or retrenchment of four avant-garde galleries. With bitter resilience, he told Ben Nicholson in his characteristic English: "The closing of the galleries will not indeed do much difference to me, but it helps a 'psychose' of decay, decadence, despair".[4] Though hardly unique, Hélion's poverty around this time was stringent; Winifred Nicholson reported that "Jean lives almost entirely on haricot beans".[5] Added to the wider economic collapse was the political tension across Europe, which stimulated the question of the political engagement of modernism. The flow of exiles from Germany and central Europe occasioned a shift in the cultural balance that would lead to the brief period of London's ascendancy as the centre of 'constructive' art.

Hélion contributed crucially to bringing about this broadening. He combined radical painting and thinking with a passionate and compelling eloquence. This made him a key advocate for the internationalization of abstraction, a restless role he seems to have inherited from his mentors Joaquim Torres García and Theo van Doesburg. For British artists and writers, Hélion provided a welcoming – and, crucially, English-speaking – introduction to the heart of Parisian modernism. In return, they contributed ideas and contacts with other artists, dealers and collectors. His network thus ensured that mutually beneficial contacts were made. He thrived – perhaps at times, relied – on the exchange.

Given his prominence at that moment, it comes as little surprise that Hélion was a respondent to Zervos's 1935 *enquête*. It is telling to set his position against that of the critic and author Herbert Read, the only British respondent. Their views divide over the reliance upon the collector and the social role of art. Hélion presented an idealist view familiar from previous pronouncements: "The artist has only one example, the world, and only one unity, himself". The social importance of the work emerges, Hélion suggested, through a process of absorption and communication: "If he clarifies circumstances for himself, he clarifies them for others".[6] In this view, the artist could be a medium for introducing a contemporary creativity into a wider social realm, and this closely follows his earlier attribution of a "power of social action" to the abstract or concrete work.[7] Read, drawing upon the programme of William Morris and the Bauhaus, favoured greater engagement. He urged that the artist should be "a link in the production and distribution of the necessities of life", and concluded: "It is the dilettante spirit in art, a legacy of capitalism and the system of patronage, which is the cause of all the malaises in contemporary art".[8] The fact that Hélion did not adopt such a functionalist position fits with his deep belief in a privileged role for the artist. In 1936, he expressed this memorably as a challenge to himself: "I am on course to remake the world beginning with myself: remake – reform".[9]

Hélion's contacts with Britain began to develop in 1932–34, as a result of his position as one of the founding committee members of Abstraction-Création. He edited the first of the group's yearbooks, published in 1932 with a contribution from only one British artist, Edward Wadsworth.[10] It was with the arrival in Paris of Winifred Nicholson, who settled there in September 1932 in order to distance herself from her husband's life with Barbara Hepworth, that a new generation of British artists made direct contact with their French counterparts. Although she had missed Hélion's first solo show (at the

1 I would like to thank Didier Ottinger, who invited me to write this text, Nicole Ouvrard and Maïa Muller for their help, and Julia Creed at the Tate archives, especially as regards documentation of the Pipers.
2 C[hristian] Z[ervos], "Enquête", *Cahiers d'art*, nos. 1-4, 1935, p. 8.
3 *Ibid.*
4 Jean Hélion to Ben Nicholson, 5-6 October 1934, Tate Archive, 8717.1.2.1571.
5 Winifred Nicholson to Ben Nicholson, postmarked 1934, Tate Archive 8717.1.1.1741. Myfanwy (Evans) Piper recalled the misery of artists in London in "Back in the Thirties", *Art and Literature: An International Review*, winter 1965, pp. 136-50 (also cited by Jane Beckett, "Circle : The theory and patronage of constructive art in the thirties", in Jeremy Lewison, ed., *Circle: Constructive Art in Britain 1934–1940*, exh. cat., Kettle's Yard Gallery, Cambridge, 1982, p. 14, n. 7.
6 J. Hélion, réponse à «Enquête», *Cahiers d'art, op. cit.*, p. 60.
7 *Id.*, «À Solder», *Abstraction-Création*, no. 1, 1932, pp. 17-18.
8 Herbert Read, réponse à «Enquête», *Cahiers d'art, op. cit.*, p. 70.
9 J. Hélion, *Journal d'un peintre: Carnets 1929–1962*, ed. Anne Moeglin-Delcroix, Paris, Maeght, 1992, 8 October 1936, p. 58.
10 It is not known exactly when Wadsworth was invited to contribute to *Abstraction-Création*, but he had numerous contacts in Paris, notably with Zadkine and the dealer Léonce Rosenberg, and he had stayed for long periods in the capital in 1928 and 1930. See Barbara Wadsworth, *Edward Wadsworth: A Painter's Life* [1975], Salisbury, 1989, pp. 154-58.

Galerie Pierre in June–July 1932) before his departure for Virginia that autumn, Winifred Nicholson's presence facilitated the growth of a new currency of ideas in contact with other Abstraction-Création artists such as Mondrian, Domela and Hans Erni. She did not join the association herself and kept her experiments with abstraction on its fringes; however it is clear that her seriousness about her art and her remarkably discerning sensibility to colour won admiration among these new friends.

The presence of his family in Paris soon brought visits from Ben Nicholson. It was either during his first stay (December 1932–January 1933) or during his visit in March–April 1933 that he and Hepworth were invited to join Abstraction-Création. It is often suggested that the invitation came from Hélion, but it now seems uncertain that their travels coincided, and the invitation may have come through Auguste Herbin.[11] Nicholson's interests at that moment were summarized by his enthusiasm at meeting Braque on both trips. The first work that he illustrated in the group yearbook, the abstract *1932 (painting)* (Tate, London), confirms this influence in its encrusted surface and cursive lines. Hepworth had already declared that her work was "tending to become more abstract", and she chose to publish the most radical of her recent carvings, *Pierced form*, 1931 (subsequently destroyed).[12] Of course 'abstract' was a relative term at this moment of rapid exploration. As Nicholson acknowledged of what he called "this abstract language": "Certainly I feel I discover something new about it each week & in my work what I felt to be abstract 2 months ago hardly seems so at all now & one continues like that."[13]

The inclusion of Hepworth and Nicholson in Abstraction-Création ran parallel with their involvement in two other groups in London. Throughout the latter part of the 1920s, Ben and Winifred Nicholson had been active within the 7 & 5 Society, a loose affiliation of modernist artists whose soft style of landscape and still-life painting has been dismissed as 'insular modernism'.[14] By 1933 Ben Nicholson, with support from Hepworth and Henry Moore, began to reshape this association in the image of his own increasingly abstract work. Among the new artists who joined that year was John Piper.

At the same time, Nicholson and Hepworth were enlisted into a new, more élite, Unit One, formed by Paul Nash and Wadsworth. Nash's public announcement came in June 1933 after a long period of debate about the constitution and nature of the group. Nash's purpose was to gather significant talents and present them to a wide British public (the exhibition in April 1934 would tour to six cities). The aspiration was to include painters, sculptors and architects (to an eventual total of nine) and to this end Moore and the architect Wells Coates (designer of Lawn Road flats, occupied by Gropius, Breuer and others) were among the prime-movers. The sense of exclusivity was confirmed when the artists contributed to an exhibition in October 1933 to mark the publication of Herbert Read's survey of modernism, *Art Now*, and this was followed by the publication of the Unit One volume in March 1934 (also edited and introduced by Read), that was in the mould of the Abstraction-Création yearbook.

It was an illustration of *Equilibrium*, 1933 (Bernard Galateau collection) in *Art Now* that introduced Helion's work to Britain. Read's survey was an introduction to general themes for the cultured reader, and he anchored his approach in examples from the past. The illustrations exemplified the new art. The section on abstract art, which opens with two Légers, included a 1923 Picasso still life opposite Nicholson's *Composition,* 1933.[15] Hélion featured opposite a painting by Sophie Taeuber.[16] In the (surprising) absence of Mondrian, these two paintings were the most pared-down of the abstract works. Read discussed the social significance of abstract art in his penultimate chapter, stating: "… there is no doubt that the modern artist, feeling himself no longer in any vital contact with society, performing no necessary or positive function in the life of the community, retreats upon himself and gives expression to his own states of subjectivity, limiting himself to this expression, and not caring whether expression is also communication".[17] This anticipates Read's statement in *Cahiers d'art* two years later, and the problem of isolated individualism remained the consistent challenge of the time. Though focussed on promoting specific individuals (it included nine contributors' statements, their photographic portraits, and those of their hands and their workplaces), the Unit One volume that appeared in the following spring was also an expression of faith in contemporary culture in the face of these challenges. Read returned to the theme in his contemporaneous *Art and Industry*, where he illustrated Hélion's *Abstract painting* as exemplary of the intuitive aspect that should continue to enliven industrial design.[18]

By the spring of 1934 the British artists had definitely made personal contact with Hélion. Nicholson paid his first visit to Mondrian's studio on 5 April 1934, but there is no direct confirmation of his meeting with Hélion.[19] However, when he got back to London, Ben wrote to Winifred in terms that may suggest a recent encounter: "I shall be most interested to hear if you like Hélion – and his new

11 See Jeremy Lewison, *Ben Nicholson*, exh. cat., Tate Gallery, London, and Musée d'Art moderne, St-Étienne, 1993–94, pp. 38–39. Merle S. Schipper (*Jean Hélion: The Abstract Years, 1929-1939*, PhD thesis, University of California, Los Angeles, 1974, p. 241), places the meeting in 1932 or 1933. Maïa Muller (in *Hélion, propagateur de l'abstraction aux États-Unis et en Angleterre*, mémoire de DEA, université de Paris I, Panthéon-Sorbonne, 2001, p. 39) puts forwards the hypothesis that Nicholson had been introduced to Hélion by Mondrian in 1933. On the possibility that they met in 1934, see further below.
12 Barbara Hepworth to Ben Nicholson, postmarked 2 October 1931, Tate Archive, 8717.1.1.56. See Matthew Gale and Chris Stephens, *Barbara Hepworth: Works in the Tate Gallery Collection and the Barbara Hepworth Museum St Ives*, London, Tate Gallery, 1999, pp. 13, 52. New research by Sophie Bowness suggests that the sculpture may have been executed in 1932 and dated earlier.
13 Ben to Winifred Nicholson, 3 May 1933, quoted in J. Lewison, *Ben Nicholson, op. cit.*, p. 39.
14 Charles Harrison, *English Art and Modernism 1900–1939*, New Haven and London, 1994, pp. 231–53.
15 H. Read, *Art Now*, London, 1933, pls. 65-73. The use of Picasso to make a flattering comparison recurs in the often noted juxtaposition of *The Crucifixion* by Francis Bacon (the unknown) with a Dinard *Bather* by Picasso (pls. 60-61).
16 *Ibid.*, pls. 74-77.
17 *Ibid.*, p. 117. In the artistic debate of the 1930s the word 'vital' had a special sense. Here, it means 'living', but in descriptions of works of art it denotes a creative energetic, positive drive, that is, in an immaterial sense, aesthetically right. In this sense it corresponds to aesthetic emotion as understood by Fry and Bell.
18 H. Read, *Art and Industry*, London 1934, reproduced p. 38; see also David Thistlewood, "Herbert Read: A New Vision of Art and Industry", in Benedict Read and David Thistlewood, ed., *Herbert Read: A British Vision of World Art*, exh. cat., Leeds City Art Galleries, 1993, pp. 95–101.
19 So J. Lewison (*Ben Nicholson, op. cit.*, p. 44) dates the visit to Mondrian's studio, citing a letter from Nicholson to John Summerson of 3 January 1944. In April 1934, Hepworth declared: "I would really like to meet Hélion» (letter to Nicholson, postmarked April 1934, Tate Archive, 8717.1.1.186); however, the meeting did not take place before Hélion's visit to London in June (Hélion to Nicholson, 26 July 1934, Tate Archive, 8717.1.2.1566).

20 Ben to Winifred Nicholson, 12 April 1934, in Andrew Nicholson, ed., *Unknown Colour: Paintings, Letters, Writings by Winifred Nicholson*, London, 1987, p. 146.

21 Winifred to Ben Nicholson, postmarked 26 April 1934, Tate Archive, 8717.1.1.1737.

22 Winifred Nicholson's admiration was made manifest by her quiet generosity. She bought a painting from Hélion (referred to in a letter to Ben [May 1936], Tate Archive, 8717.1.1.1762, in which she says she bought it for £25 "two years ago") and, seeing how badly off Hélion was, she would send him a canvas and a frame with her compliments (as Hélion noted in his *Journal d'un peintre*, *op. cit.*, 1992, p. 51).

23 The concept of the book was the object of much attention, but some of those involved thought that it did not meet European standards. Hepworth disliked it, perhaps because of the "respectable matt paper" (letter to Ben Nicholson, postmarked 23 March 1934, Tate Archive, 8717.1.1.173); Nicholson was almost equally reserved, though he found it better than he had thought, and, "for England" a sign of progress (letter to Winifred Nicholson, 12 April 1934, published in Andrew Nicholson, ed., *Unknown Colour ...*, *op. cit.*, p. 146). Winifred Nicholson was still more scathing: she found the images confused (letter to Ben Nicholson, postmarked 26 April 1934, Tate Archive, 8717.1.1.1737).

24 Winifred to Ben Nicholson, postmarked 26 April 1934, Tate Archive, 8717.1.1.1737.

25 Jean (Blair) Hélion to Nicholson, 17 June 1934, Tate Archive, 8717.1.2.1594.

26 J. Lewison, *Ben Nicholson, op. cit.*, p. 41.

27 On the vote at Unit One, see J. Lewison, *Ben Nicholson, op. cit.*, p. 47. Read proposed the idea of functionalism in a letter to Nash, 23 novembre 1934, Tate Archive, 9129.96.

28 Hélion to Nicholson, 18 June 1934, Tate Archive, 8717.1.2.1564.

29 Jean (Blair) Hélion to Nicholson, 17 June 1934, Tate Archive, 8717.1.2.1594.

30 Hélion to Nicholson, 18 June 1934, Tate Archive, 8717.1.2.1564.

31 Hélion to Nicholson, 26 July 1934, Tate Archive, 8717.1.2.1565.

32 Ede's visitor's book, Kettle's Yard Archive, University of Cambridge. I would like to thank Sebastiano Barassi for confirming these details. "Adrian" is probably Adrian Stokes; "John et Penelope" are not identifiable.

33 Hélion to Nicholson, 26 July 1934, Tate Archive, 8717.1.2.1566.

34 Hélion to Nicholson, 18 June 1934, Tate Archive, 8717.1.2.1564.

35 See M. Schipper, *Jean Hélion: The Abstract Years, op. cit.*, p. 243.

36 Hélion to Nicholson, 25 September 1934, Tate Archive, 8717.1.2.1569.

37 J. Hélion, *Lettres d'Amérique: Correspondance avec Raymond Queneau 1934–1967*, ed. Claude Rameil, Paris, IMEC, 1996, pp. 63–67, 70 (23 June 1937).

38 There is a recent analysis of *Axis* in Alan Powers, "The Reluctant Romantics: *Axis Magazine* 1935-37", in David Peters Corbett, Ysanne Holt and Fiona Russell, ed., *The Geographies of Englishness: Landscape and the National Past 1880–1940*, New Haven and London, 2002. See also Frances Spalding and David Fraser

work – I like his thought – it is most refreshing and has essentially all that clarity and 'clearness' that Erni talked of and am most interested to see his development – it will be a big contribution – it is already important."[20] In her response, Winifred agreed:

"I liked Hélion's work

1. because it is conscious as well as subconscious.

2. because the shapes are shapes, beautiful for painting not shapes that would be better sculpted.

3. because he is the only person I have seen who does abstract colour light using the same abstract idea for colour that other people have used for shapes."[21]

As she used the term "colour light" in relation to her own exploration of colour harmonies, this last point suggests a sense of shared purpose.[22]

The reception of Unit One in Paris seems to have been fairly favourable.[23] Certainly the presence of Ben Nicholson's new carved reliefs, which embodied such a departure in his work in early 1934, was remarked upon. In the same letter Winifred reported that Hélion had received a copy and passed it to the critic Anatole Jacovski, and as a consequence: "There was a lot of talk about your circles a sort of undercurrent of appreciation and understanding, like a little running brook …. Erni, Hélion and Jacovsky etc at Power's private view."[24] This thread of appreciation (whether or not exaggerated by Winifred's indefatigable admiration for Ben's work) did not quite spill over into *Cahiers d'art*. Hélion's American wife, Jean Blair, told Nicholson that Hélion had "tried several times to get you into their group exhibition chez Zervos".[25] Nicholson himself, visiting Paris in May, also tried to persuade the dealer to mount a Unit One exhibition.[26] Zervos put him off, and it came to nothing as events took a new turn in London. Abiding by a strict procedure for determining the Unit One membership in November 1934, only two (Nash and Moore) of the original nine members secured enough votes from their colleagues to continue. Although Nash talked much of unity, and Read proposed a functionalist purpose, this counter-productive process was the death-knell of the group.[27]

The collapse of Unit One in London followed that of the original structure of Abstraction-Création in Paris. Domela, Erni and Hélion resigned in June 1934, objecting to Herbin's and Vantongerloo's dominance and their financially driven determination to expand membership. Telling Nicholson, "I hope you won't stay", Hélion explained: "… they are doing exactly what we do not want. We want selection and quality. They want number and everything."[28] However, as Blair had made clear in her earlier letter, the resignations were more widespread: Arp, Taeuber, Fernandez and Paalen had also gone, and "as you know Mondrian resigned months ago".[29] Nicholson and Hepworth joined the exodus. It is characteristic of Hélion that he drew strength from this melt-down, immediately envisaging the next development:

"I think it is time for our generation to part from the others.

"We are a few with something in common: we love life, hate formulas; we are outside of cubism, foes of surrealism, and, if we receive a lesson from constructivism and neo-plasticism, we are already far beyond them, going towards a language, an expression of the whole man in his progressive sense. Is not this a real base for a group?"[30]

This admirably summarizes the fertility of his ideas, as – in a few lines – he moved persuasively from a general disgust with groups to the prospects for a new group. He seems to have felt a compulsion to unite and promote, despite continual disappointments.

At this moment the prospects were bright, because he was acting as a guide to the Paris studios for the American collector of abstract art A.E. Gallatin. The painter's infectious enthusiasm and privileged connections made him an extraordinary companion and, given the dire financial position of most of the artists, Gallatin must have seemed a godsend. The collector had also planned an excursion to London and, with days to go, invited Hélion as his guide. Nicholson, alerted by Hélion, made all the arrangements, annotating the letter with a Hampstead-based itinerary.[31] The appointments, reflecting Hélion's suggestions, included Nash and Moore, as well as H.S. 'Jim' Ede, the modernist-orientated assistant curator at the Tate Gallery and long-time friend of Nicholson. The entry in the Edes' guest-book confirms that they had a very cosmopolitan supper party on 6 July: "Gallatin + Hélion, Ben, Barbara, Adrian, Braque + Mrs Braque, John + Penelope, + after Mr + Mrs Piper".[32] Nicholson and Hepworth probably held a party at the Mall Studios, as Hélion's letter of thanks names "Read, Moore, Ede, your neighbours and all friends".[33]

During the extended period that they spent together, Hélion and Gallatin planned an American periodical "devoted to our art (those we like, Picasso, Léger, Braque, Gris)". The painter told Nicholson: "We are discussing the aims of such a thing, its attitude and its limits. It should be very strongly against surrealism and literature in painting."[34] Details of this scheme only just pre-date, but in many ways anticipate, Hélion's vision for the British periodical *Axis* planned by Myfanwy Evans in the autumn. This has led to the suggestion that he transferred his scheme and that *Axis* carried through the plan relinquished by Gallatin.[35] While this is certainly plausible, a slightly longer trajectory reveals Hélion's continual stream of proposals for periodicals and other publications. Thus, as he was having his first discussions with Evans and contributing to Anatole Jacovski's publication of a book of prints, Hélion could also report to Nicholson: "Arp, Fernandez and I met once already about the other publication, much stricter we have said, we should make to replace for us Abs. Création".[36] In the following years he would write to Raymond Queneau from America at length about the structure, details and possibilities of the latter's periodical *Volontés*.[37]

The pattern that emerges is that Hélion laid great importance on periodicals and he expressed his views on them with certainty. They were the primary means of producing good-quality reproductions for a wide market at a relatively low cost. It also seems that he relished the relationships thrown up by juxtaposing articles and the sense of immediacy in transmitting new ideas. As such, it may be argued that *Axis* was not so much the revived Gallatin project, but that it was one of many such projects. What distinguished *Axis* was the determination of Evans to put it into practice.

While this is not the place to attempt a survey of *Axis*, which emerged in January 1935, the periodical was the most public point of contact between Hélion and his British friends.[38] It is clear that he felt an immediate sympathy for John Piper and Myfanwy Evans. Piper and his first wife Eileen Holding had visited him in Paris before the middle of June 1934.[39] Through him they met Domela, whose reliefs would inspire their work. They met again in London and by late summer Hélion was impressed by Piper's constructions.[40] At this stage, the Pipers' marriage was unravelling and Evans was on the scene. She stayed in Paris through parts of August and September; "young and enthusiastic" and armed with Piper's introduction, she sought out the Hélions. Jean Blair captured the immediate affection that grew up, writing soon after to Evans of their need for "your gaiety, vim, vitality and pep".[41] It was at that fertile moment that the form of *Axis* was debated, as Nicholson was told soon after:

"I encouraged her to found an English magazine based on that group you practically constitute with Barbara, Moore, Piper, and a few others. Whatever will be the also proposed Gallatin's magazine, they could be very different and have an equal success."[42]

Piper, writing while she was still in Paris, was enthusiastic about the suggestion: "What a sensible man Jean Hélion is, hitting on the right idea straight away".[43] Many years later Evans recalled this encounter as exhilarating but also, in some sense, inevitable. Hélion's strengths lay in the certainty with which he expressed his ideas, and the fact that his network equipped him to make specific suggestions about contributors. Above all, as he revealed to Nicholson, he saw a periodical as an agitational tool:

"The aims of the magazine should be well defined: to help the movement of modern painting, its clarification, its development, its understanding; to encourage and criticize clearly the Tate Gallery, the organizations of show, the Galleries; to get in touch with the student art clubs such as the Oxford one, help them to organize shows, lectures; to encourage the good collectors and give publicity to their best acquisitions; to let know what interesting is made everywhere else etc."

For this resounding programme he concluded: "Our interests are the same everywhere, the movement must be developed, advertised everywhere, broadened; if not we shall starve and become either dry as paper or green with mould."[45] Amid the ideals lies an undertone of material desperation, a realisation that the vitality of contemporary art was under threat from the daily realities of life.

The first number of *Axis* appeared in January 1935. Its relatively swift production demonstrated Evans's considerable energy as well as the circle of connections upon whom she could draw. It was carefully planned, from the Gill Sans typography to the balance of articles. Among the contributors were Read, Ede and Nash. Artists were represented by a single illustration, an egalitarianism counterbalanced by the sequence, beginning Picasso, Kandinsky, Nicholson, Moore. Hélion's painting is the fifteenth of the nineteen illustrations, but his name is cited repeatedly. In her editorial, 'Dead or Alive', Evans wrote of Cézanne and Mondrian ("analysis perfected") but dwelt on Hélion. "He aims", she wrote, "at the complexity of nature without the object. Immense intersections and fine subtleties of forms without bastard memories, but no less expressive of experience." This is, in other words, the epitome of the vibrant but relevant art for which *Axis* had been created. Evans was followed by Read, who remade his case for the Platonic perfection of the new art and quoted Hélion's preference for the term 'concrete' over 'abstract'. For Geoffrey Grigson, Hélion ("who sees as sharply as any painter the need for a new biomorphic complexity") was among the Parisians whose influence was sweeping away the residual influence of Bloomsbury.

Anatole Jacovski simply called him "perhaps the one

Jenkins, *John Piper in the 1930s: Abstraction on the Beach*, exh. cat., Dulwich Picture Gallery, London, 2003.
39 Hélion to Nicholson, 18 June 1934, Tate Archive, 8717.1.2.1564.
40 Hélion to Nicholson, 17 September 1934, Tate Archive, 8717.1.2.1568.
41 Jean (Blair) Hélion to Evans, 30 September 1934, Tate Archive.
42 Hélion to Nicholson, 17 September 1934, Tate Archive, 8717.1.2.1568.
43 Piper to Evans, 5 September [1934], Tate Archive, quoted in F. Spalding and D. F. Jenkins, *John Piper in the 1930s, op. cit.*, p. 24. In the 1970s, Hélion made out that Nicholson, Hepworth and Piper were also present at his first meeting with Evans (see M. Schipper, *Jean Hélion: The Abstract Years, op. cit.*, p. 242, letter from Hélion, 12 April 1972), but it is more probable that their meeting took place at the time of his visit to Britain a year later.
44 Myfanwy (Evans) Piper, "Back in the Thirties", in *Art and Literature, op. cit.*, p. 139; see also Frances Spalding, "John Piper in the 1930s: 'Abstraction on the Beach'", in *John Piper in the 1930s, op. cit.*, pp. 20–21.
45 Hélion to Nicholson, 17 September 1934, Tate Archive, 8717.1.2.1568.

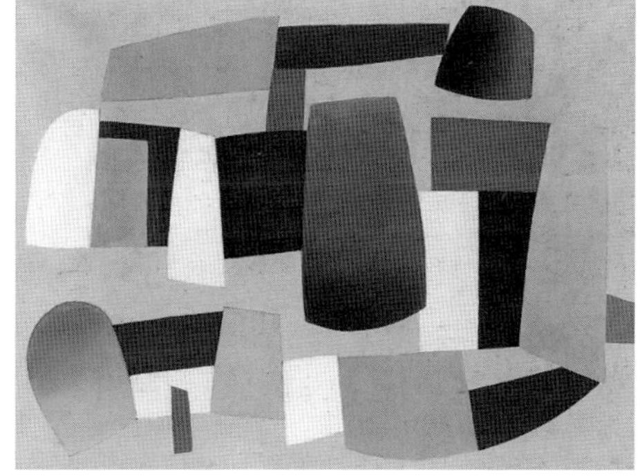

Jean Hélion
Abstract composition, 1934
Oil on canvas, 27.1 x 35 cm
(given by the artist to Evans and Piper, c. 1937)
Tate, London

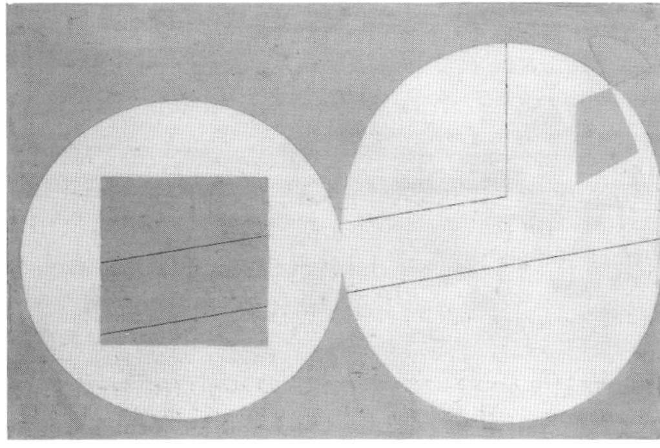

Winifred Nicholson
48 quai d'Auteuil, 1935
Oil on board, 67.6 x 100 cm
Tate, London

Ben Nicholson
1935 (White relief)
Painted, 101.6 x 166.4 cm (reproduced in *Axis*, no. 2,
April 1935, p. 15, as *Carved Relief in Wood*)
Tate, London

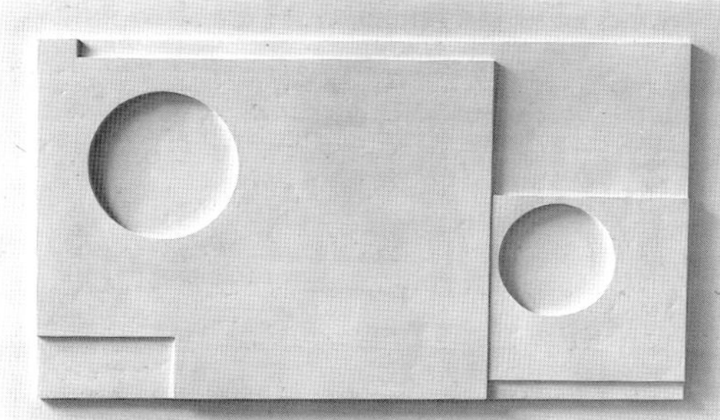

'genuine' among younger painters".[46] Although Hélion was not the only artist to be referred to so often, and he was discussed in many different ways, the fact that he formed an indispensable point of reference is a mark of his importance.

Evans seems to have had, probably from the start, a general structure mapped out for the opening issues of *Axis*. Between the scene-setting of the first number and the special sculpture issue that appeared in July lay the reinforcing concerns of *Axis 2*, published in April. The hierarchy of illustrations in *Axis 1* is repeated (with the insertion of Klee) in detailed articles – Picasso, Kandinsky, Nicholson.[47] Following these is Hélion's 'From Reduction to Growth', a substantial theoretical text tracing the development of contemporary art. It was the first of four essays for his new English audience published in quick succession during 1935–37. Although each explored different issues, they shared an underlying belief that the new art should be discussed in relation to the classical tradition. As he had told Nicholson in the previous autumn: "You know how keen I am about certain periods of ancient art and that I think that the so-called modern art should not be separated from those, but understood as their transformed continuation".[48] This use of the past to lead an audience to the present was his consistent theme.

Far from being a combative justification, 'From Reduction to Growth' was shot through with a disarming uncertainty. Hélion began by acknowledging the concern (so often addressed elsewhere) of the relation between the artist and society, and though he admired the artist who "can work in his corner" he was also suspicious of the unreality of this situation. The point of reference for those seeking engagement lay in the art of the past. "I try to understand how", he wrote, "in spite of the elevation of the preoccupations of the abstract tendencies, their realisations are smashed by any Raphael or Poussin".[49] Rather unexpected, in the context, was Hélion's view that – while acknowledging his own debt – Mondrian's "totally abstract position" was a "reduction of possibilities". This is, in fact, a public airing of the private difference (explained to Gallatin some time before) between Mondrian's view that "painting will end soon as a personal entity" and Hélion's belief that it would become "an exceptional thing expressing man".[50] In seeking to continue the tradition of Poussin, Hélion suggested in 'From Reduction to Growth' that the contemporary artist needed to embrace a paradox: "Simplification must be obtained on the way to growth, as a stage of that growth, instead of being obtained on the way to reduction, by suppression".[51] The tone of analysis is serious, and the diagnosis is "a confrontation of all terms, all degrees, of all positions, with permanent reference to all steps of the past and to our own steps; a slow process of assimilation, correction, and digestion, of which will be capable only supple, patient minds; humble enough to accept the re-discussion of the painfully got certitudes, and proud enough to think it worth while."

This was a dense and thoughtful text. In advising on a translation that Evans made of Hélion's writing (probably of this article), Jean Blair had acknowledged the propensity for "sentences of 116 words, with no subject and no predicate". It is difficult to judge how the painter's colleagues received this text. Not quite enough is conveyed by Hepworth's passing comment that the whole issue of *Axis* was "more mature than no.1, less amateur, but with a lot less clarity in many ways".[52] However, Hélion's more extended visit to Britain in September 1935 seems to have reinforced his influence. He stayed with Piper and Evans at Fawley Bottom, their rural home in Oxfordshire, reporting to Gallatin: "Axis is growing on a farm, beautifully located. If painting fails to sustain it, breeding of cows would pay, eventually."[53]

It was probably on this visit that they all met with Nicholson and Hepworth to debate the form of the periodical. One outcome would appear to be the presence of articles by Evans and Read on Hélion in *Axis 4* of November 1935. This prominence confirms that the sobriety of Hélion's views in 'From Reduction to Growth ' was admired. Evans was explicit about his inspiring role in her appreciation, while Read returned to the artist's role in society. He suggested that Hélion would "welcome a way back to social integration, to a functional art of some kind. But … it can only come through the inherent development of his strictly aesthetic ideals. It is for society to catch up with the artist – not *vice-versa*."[54] This view echoed the concern about the need for modernist artists to engage politically if they were to contribute to turning the tide on fascism. Read and Hélion shared the view that the artist's commitment to liberty did not require a propagandizing social realism of the sort that grew in strength over the following years.[55]

The articles on Hélion in late 1935 completed the main trajectory of his presence in *Axis* just as they served to raise his profile in Britain. In the summer of 1936, he slightly inverted his appreciation of the past in two articles published in London, 'Poussin, Seurat and Double Rhythm', his last contribution to *Axis*, and 'Seurat as a Predecessor' in *The Burlington Magazine* (edited by Read).[56] These articles cover closely related material, revealing the abstract structures that underlie all carefully composed paintings. It is typical that Hélion should write of Poussin in the first of these articles, as if describing one of his own works, "… progressions of corresponding colours and counter progressions of opposed colours accelerate the speed of the movements in such a composition".[57] He admired the compositional clarity of Seurat, which he contrasted with Cézanne's fragmentation. This led to an insight into the composition of his own work:

"Then, to equilibrate is to gather all elements, all groups of elements, all fragments of elements in such a position that there are never any symmetrical terms, that each term belongs to an accelerated progression. Whatever the order in which you penetrate and follow the picture, there is acceleration, continuity, infinity."[58]

The theoretical articles served as a counterpoint to the work itself, and the pattern of exhibiting in 1935–36 was especially complex. In February 1935, Nicholson and Hélion participated in Erni's group exhibition *Thèse, Antithèse, Synthèse*. They both made the trip to Lucerne, as did Nicholson's pupil (and Hepworth's cousin) Arthur Jackson.[59] The selection and Erni's subsequent discussion of the show in *Axis 2* seem to have been fraught with difficulties, but it remained a significant international survey.[60] In London, meanwhile, the disintegration of Unit One and the break with Abstraction-Création seem to have encouraged Nicholson and Hepworth to transform the 7 & 5 into an abstract association. This move was supported by Piper and Winifred Nicholson, and determined the character of the exhibition in October 1935. Although Nicholson also had plans to invite foreign participation, this proved to be the group's last show.[61]

The cross-Channel relationship reached a point of culmination in 1936 in the *Abstract and Concrete* exhibition, the title of which was indebted to Hélion's preferred terminology. Supported by Axis, it was organized by Nicolete Gray, who wrote in her brief catalogue introduction of her conviction that "the appearance of an abstract art today is most significant" and demanded attention.[62] The exhibition shared the Unit One desire to spread the word nationwide, beginning in Oxford in February and travelling to Liverpool, Newcastle, London and Cambridge. Its international scope made it the first significant exhibition of abstract art in Britain. Amongst the sixteen artists, it introduced new works by Calder, Domela, Gabo, Hélion, Mondrian, in company with Hepworth, Moore, Nicholson and Piper. The works were of high quality: Mondrian's *Composition B with red* and Hepworth's *Three forms* (both Tate, London) are exemplary. Hélion's three works included the two-metre wide *Île de France*. One of Jackson's surviving photographs shows that the exhibition space was rather cramped and intrusively panelled: two Mondrians were hung one above the other and over the dado rail, with *Île de France* resting on a mantlepiece.[63] Nevertheless, Hélion found *Axis 5*, which accompanied the exhibition, "excellent" and was happy with the photographs from Oxford.[64]

The exhibition appeared rather more spacious when it arrived at the Lefevre Galleries in London, where *Île de France* and Piper's *Forms on dark blue* (subsequently destroyed) dominated one large room. Winifred Nicholson was characteristically forthright: "What bad hanging I should have said to put 3 Mondrians so close to one another".[65] Despite (or because of) the exhibition's pioneering aspirations, only five works (two of them Mondrian's) were sold.[66] The architect Serge Chermayeff later bought

46 *Axis*, no. 1, January 1935: Evans, 'Dead or Alive», p. 3; Read, 'Our Terminology', p. 7; Grigson, 'Comment on England', p. 10; Jacovski, 'Inscriptions under Pictures', p. 17.
47 *Axis*, no. 2, April 1935: Evans, 'Beginning with Picasso'; Kandinsky, 'Line and Fish'; Evans, 'Kandinsky's Vision'; Jakovski, 'Wassily Kandinsky'; Will Grohmann, 'Klee at Berne'; Read, 'Ben Nicholson's Recent Work'; Jan Tschischold, 'On Ben Nicholson's Reliefs'.
48 Hélion to Nicholson, 29 October 1934, Tate Archive, 8717.1.2.1572.
49 Hélion, 'From Reduction to Growth', *Axis*, no. 2, April 1935, p. 19.
50 Hélion to Gallatin, 29 August 1934, A.E. Gallatin Archives, New York Historical Society, quoted in Joop M. Joosten, *Piet Mondrian: Catalogue raisonné of the Work of 1911–1944*, New York, 1998, p. 157.
51 Hélion, 'From Reduction to Growth', *art. cit.*, p. 23.
52 Hepworth to Nicholson, postmarked 4 May 1935, Tate Archive 8717.1.1.209.
53 Hélion to Gallatin, 6 November 1935, A. E. Gallatin Archives, New York Historical Society, cité dans M. Schipper, *Jean Hélion : The Abstract Years, op. cit.*, p. 243, n. 10.
54 *Axis*, n° 4, November 1935: Read, 'Jean Hélion', pp. 3–4; Evans, 'Hélion Today: A Personal Comment', pp. 4–9.
55 In 1938, Read participed in one of the debates on naturalism in English art; see Judith Collins, '"An Event of Some Importance in the History of English Art"', in B. Read and D. Thistlewood, ed., *Herbert Read, op. cit.*, p. 68–70.
56 Hélion, 'Poussin, Seurat and Double Rhythm', *Axis*, no. 6, summer1936, and 'Seurat as a Predecessor', *The Burlington Magazine*, July 1936.
57 *Ibid.*, p. 11.
58 *Ibid.*, p. 16.
59 Hélion to Nicholson, 18 February 1935, Tate Archive, 8717.1.2.1574.
60 See J. Lewison, *Circle: Constructive Art in Britain*, *op. cit.*, p. 2; Hélion referred to these difficulties in his letters to Nicholson of 18 June 1934 and 19 July 1935, Tate Archive, 8717.1.2.1564 and 1575.
61 J. Lewison, *Circle: Constructive Art in Britain, op. cit.*, p. 43.
62 Nicolete Gray, 'Introduction', *Abstract and Concrete*, exh. cat., Lefevre Gallery, London, 1936 [p. 2].
63 The photograph is reproduced in M. Gale and C. Stephens, *Barbara Hepworth, op. cit.*, p. 57.
64 Hélion to Nicholson, 20 April 1935, Tate Archive, 8717.1.2.1579.
65 Winifred to Ben Nicholson [May 1936], Tate Archive, 8717.1.2.1562.
66 Nicolete Gray, 'Introduction', *Helen Sutherland Collection: A Pioneering Collector of the 1930s*, exh. cat., London, Arts Council of Great Britain, 1970–71, p. 20.

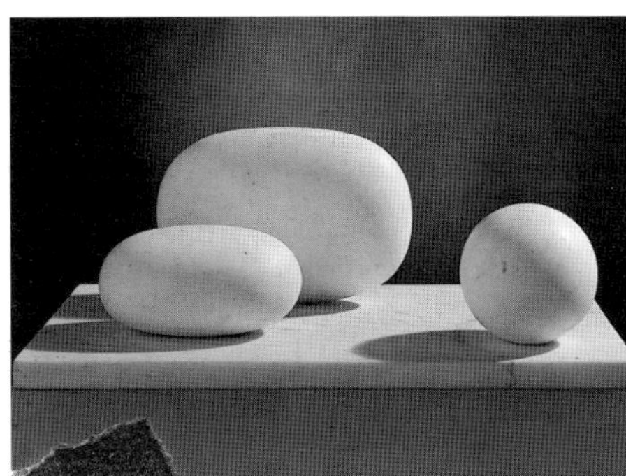

Barbara Hepworth
Three forms, 1935
Marbre, 20 x 53.3 x 34.3 cm
(shown in the exhibition *Abstract and Concrete*,
Lefevre Gallery, London, 1936)
Tate, London

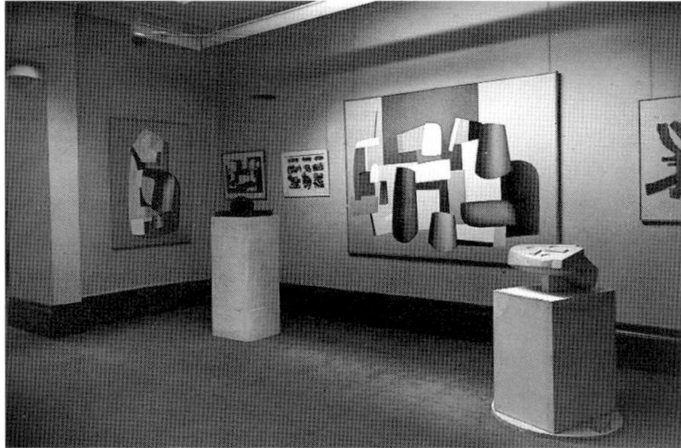

View of the exhibition *Abstract and Concrete*,
Lefevre Gallery, Londonn, 1936,
showing *Île-de-France* by Hélion
Tate Archive, London

Piper's *Forms on dark blue* and borrowed the large 1934 Hélion that had been illustrated in *Axis 1*; this was a significant development, given the status of Chermayeff's house Bentley Wood (built in 1937–38) as exemplarily modernist.[67]

It is typical of Hélion's commitment and productivity that at the same moment that *Abstract and Concrete* opened he held a solo show at the Galerie Cahiers d'art in February, his first in Paris since 1932. The uncluttered clarity of the space is shown in a photograph published with the review in *Axis 6*. It opened "with more success than I expected (even Picasso came)" and Arp, Mondrian and Giacometti were all enthusiastic.[68] Through this combination of events, Hélion seemed in command of the position towards which he had been building for some time. However, it was not long after, in early July, that he and his wife set out to return to America, effectively cur-

tailing the fertile exchange. Although the distance need not have determined the level of communication with his British colleagues, Hélion's move to rural Virginia brought with it an urge towards consolidation. His notebooks and letters to Queneau show him considering the broad sweep of his work as a project to be completed over a ten-year period. Feeling that this was the opportunity to concentrate on painting, he wrote and lectured less, making exceptions only when his finances demanded.

Superficially, this need to concentrate might explain the absence of a text by Hélion in *Circle*, the anthology edited by Nicholson, Gabo and the architect Leslie Martin in 1937, in which four of his paintings were illustrated. However, the fact that Hélion was represented by two texts, a reprint of 'Poussin, Seurat and Double Rhythm' and 'Opinions and Avowals', in Evans's contemporaneous anthology, *The Painter's Object*, suggests that he became the casualty of a growing division among his London friends.[69] This hinged upon dogmatism. As was demonstrated with the 7 & 5, Nicholson was perceived to be building a movement for abstract art with the European constructivist artists settling as exiles in London – notably Gabo, Moholy-Nagy and, eventually, Mondrian (who arrived in 1939). Piper was among those who dissented. Writing to Nicholson while *Abstract and Concrete* was still touring, he argued for individualism over "dull and deathly" movements.[70] Evans had already posited a more inclusive approach in *Axis* and, after the periodical's closure, this was the basis of *The Painter's Object*. Read and Moore contributed to both 1937 anthologies (just as they accommodated surrealism in 1936) but found it an uncertain balancing act. In his text, 'Lost, A Valuable Object', Piper disavowed abstraction and identified this desire in other contemporary artists. Among those seeking ways to replace the object, he cited Hélion "constructing complex object-symbols, new yet age-old, part-game and part-worship". Piper's conclusion was: "It all seems to me an attempt to return to the object, not escape from it".[71]

It is difficult to judge Hélion's position as this debate developed in Britain. The only hint is his comment (around the same time as Piper's dissention) about the 1936 International Surrealist exhibition in London: "But you are so many in England now, with the new comers, that you can resist the wave".[72] While this displays his natural inclination to groups, the inclusion of his articles in *The Painter's Object* may reflect his ultimate inclination towards individualism on the eve of his departure for America.

While Hélion obviously relished the connections that he had throughout the art world, there were times when he found the responsibility tiresome. On resigning from Abstraction-Création, he found himself at the hub of a new network associated with Britain. Reflecting on the trouble caused by his recommendations for the 1935 Lucerne exhibition he remarked: "The same happens with *Axis*, I am supposed to have distributed all the places. Often people come to me and ask how they could get in, suggesting that, because once I said encouraging things about their painting, or because I like them as people, I could introduce them."[73] The burden of expectation, especially in meagre times, was heavy.

That it was a thankless task was confirmed towards the end of 1936 in the pages of *Cahiers d'art*. In a bizarre comment on an artist whom he had just shown with considerable success, Zervos wrote: "Unfortunately Hélion has not avoided the fault of the majority of young artists – megalomania. Instead of working patiently to gain his stripes, he would run through the stages and set himself up as a master."[74] It is hardly surprising that the painter was outraged on a number of levels, given their recent collaboration and the hardships that he suffered for his art. Significantly, he interpreted Zervos's comment as an accusation of building a personal school. Writing to Queneau from America in 1937, Hélion looked back:

"As for the young people that I have encouraged and who also encouraged me through their enthusiasm and health, some English, some Swiss or some Americans from time to time passing through Paris … I do not think that they will be very concerned about his flippant remarks."[75]

Characteristically, Hélion expressed his confidence in the independence and creativity of those he had encouraged. This was symptomatic of a search for quality in others, so that, ultimately, his inclination always favoured the individual over the group.

67 Concerning Bentley Wood, the house that Chermayeff built for himself in 1937–38 and for which he commissioned Moore *Reclining figure* of 1937, see Alan Powers, *Serge Chermayeff: Designer, Architect, Teacher*, London, 2001, p. 129, n. 10.
68 Hélion to Nicholson, 26 February 1935, Tate Archive, 8717.1.2.1577. La photograph accompanied the article by Herta Wescher, 'New Work in Paris', *Axis* no. 6, p. 29.
69 M. Evans, ed., *The Painter's Object*, London, 1937.
70 Piper to Nicholson, 5 May 1936, Tate Archive, 8717.1.2.3403. There is a subtle analysis of this break-up in A. Powers, «The Reluctant Romantics», *art. cit.*
71 Piper, 'Lost: A Valuable Object', in M. Evans, *The Painter's Object*, *op. cit.*, reproduced in F. Spalding and D.F. Jenkins, *John Piper in the 1930s, op. cit.*, pp. 182–83.
72 Hélion to Nicholson, 29 May 1936, Tate Archive, 8717.1.2.1580, postcard.
73 Hélion to Nicholson, 18 February 1935, Tate Archive, 8717.1.2.1574.
74 Zervos, 'Hélion (Galerie Cahiers d'Art)', *Cahiers d'Art*, nos. 8–10, 1936. This text is also to be found in J. Hélion, *Lettres d'Amérique, op. cit.*, p. 58 (31 May 1937).
75 *Ibid.*, p. 59.

Debra Bricker Balken

JEAN HÉLION'S AMERICAN CONNECTIONS

A stay in a foreign country, foreign climate, foreign architecture, provoke opinions on colors and associations of colors rarely experienced at home. The narrow amount of free space in New York has made me conscious of other variations in my own balance of free space. After visiting any American show I have always felt by opposition a strict pupil of Seurat and Cézanne. Yet the dark ochres, the red bricks, the putties of your buildings, replacing the Parisian greys, have made me develop in my palette zones corresponding to them.
Jean Hélion, *Partisan Review*, 1938

... anyone who knows America can see that the tone and color contrasts are quite native, that the cumulative rhythmic organization resounds from an accent which has originated in America alone. With each succeeding show, the alien influences become more deeply integrated, more difficult to classify.
George L.K. Morris, *The American Abstract Artists*, 1939

In the mid 1960s, long after his various sojourns in America (from 1932 to 1946) had receded into memory, Jean Hélion wrote to his old friend George L.K. Morris, "I have not forgotten Gallatin and his seriousness, the 'gentility' with which he considered painting. An article certainly should be written about the early thirties in New York, the beginning of what was going to be so important in the United States: the Gallery of Living Art ...."[1] Hélion's fond reminiscences of Albert Eugene Gallatin, founder, director and patron of the Gallery of Living Art at New York University, in Washington Square East, frame a significant chapter not only in the renewal of abstract painting in New York during the decade of the Great Depression, but also in the ongoing development of the artist's own painting. In fact, the two are reciprocal, integrally linked and bound. In large part through Hélion's interaction with members of New York's proliferating community of artists, critics and curators during one of the most inauspicious and hostile moments in American cultural history, certain inroads were forged towards enhancing the receptivity to abstract art in the United States. Along the way, Hélion's work also subtly responded to and incorporated aspects of these exchanges.

Virtually from the outset of his career as an artist, Hélion revealed a deep preoccupation with the aesthetic language, forms and ethos of machine-age culture. In his earlier paintings this interest took the form of terse, geometric statements, such as *Orthogonal composition* and *Abstract composition*, both of 1930. These evoke an orderly, regulated, utopian world that echoes the emergence of the new building technologies that were rapidly transforming the built environment, particularly in the United States. A predisposition was there, then, to absorb New York, a city which had undergone drastic change and reconfiguration through the introduction of the skyscraper, along with manifold automation, in the 1910s and the 1920s. When Hélion met Joaquin Torres-García (an artist with whom he briefly shared an apartment) and John Xceron, both newly arrived in Paris from New York in 1926, his imaginings of the city and its dynamism were escalated, adding to an impassioned and idealistic belief in progressive modernism, however understated in his work.

Although Hélion would not travel to New York until 1932, he established numerous friendships and professional relationships with American artists before this date. Figures such as Alexander Calder, Katherine Dreier, John Ferren and Carl Holty, all of whom became members of his Abstraction-Création group, gravitated towards the French artist, discovering correspondences between his intel-

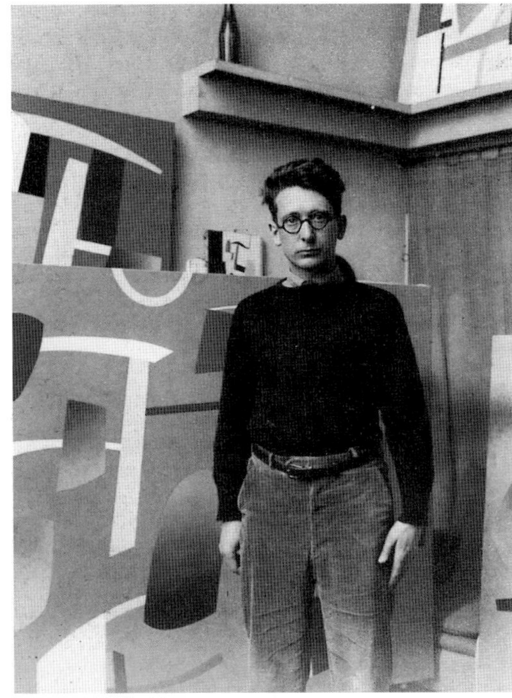

Albert Eugene Gallatin

Photographic portrait of Jean Hélion, 1934

18 x 12.8 cm

Philadelphia Museum of Art, Edgar Viguers Seeler Fund, Katharine Levin Farrell Fund

lectual and cerebral approach to abstraction and their own formalist leanings. Calder, especially, would become a life-long friend, someone whom Hélion would eventually hail as "the best artist living in the States".[2] In addition, Paul Nelson, an American-born architect who made his career in France, would prove a like-minded colleague, his ideas on the structural fundaments of architecture being akin to the conceptual basis of Hélion's early work.

Of all the connections that Hélion was to sustain with American artists and patrons, the one which proved the most pivotal was that with Gallatin. On the eve of travelling to Virginia to marry Jean Blair in 1932, on the occasion of his first one-person exhibition, at the Galerie Pierre, Hélion was introduced to Gallatin by Robert Delaunay. Their meeting was propitious. It led not only to the purchase by Gallatin of Hélion's *Composition*, 1932, but also to numerous subsequent encounters in Paris and New York and an extensive correspondence. Gallatin took pride in his illustrious Swiss-French namesake, Albert Gallatin, who had been Secretary of the Treasury under Thomas Jefferson and James Madison, and frequently travelled to Paris to acquire work for the Gallery of Living Art, founded in 1927. As the first showcase devoted exclusively to modernist art in the United States (the one-room facility preceded the emergence of the Museum of Modern Art in 1929 and the Whitney Museum of American art in 1930), the Gallery of Living Art provided many New York artists who lived in Greenwich Village with an introduction to the work of Pablo Picasso, Georges Braque, Juan Gris and Ferdinand Léger, as well as numerous others engaged in extending the pictorial possibilities of Cubist art. As such, the institution quickly played a critical role, whatever the modesty of its scale, in shaping and directing a still emergent modernism in New York.

While Gallatin had declared from the outset of his project that he "favored no particular cliques, made no special propaganda, and little known, or unknown, painters figured in the collection as well as internationally famous artists",[3] Hélion was able to convince him in short order that his array of painting required greater definition and focus. Whatever the initial *ad hoc* mandate for the Gallery of Living Art, under Hélion's guidance a once vague concentration on Cubist art became pronounced and distinct, so that, within the collection, it became by implication the aesthetic thrust of contemporary art. This dominant direction was achieved by culling and editing, by largely eliminating work within the Gallery's holdings that was preoccupied with figurative and narrative references, thus straying from the modernist will to the invention and elab-

oration of the formal constituents of art. Besides paring his collection to a "severe selection",[4] as Gallatin eventually called it, Hélion imparted a sense of historical continuity and a coherent thread to the paintings on view at the Gallery of Living Art.

On a subsequent trip by Gallatin to Paris in May of 1933, Hélion arranged for him to meet both Jean Arp and Piet Mondrian, prominent members of Abstraction-Création who were updating and renewing, albeit with differing compositional means, the varying trajectories of Cubist art. Visits to each artist's studio resulted in acquisitions that would become significant in the American context. Mondrian's *Composition with blue and yellow*, 1932, while diminutive in size, was the first painting by the artist to enter a public collection in the United States.[5] With this, and the two works by Arp that he purchased on the same trip, the collection was not only reinvigorated and

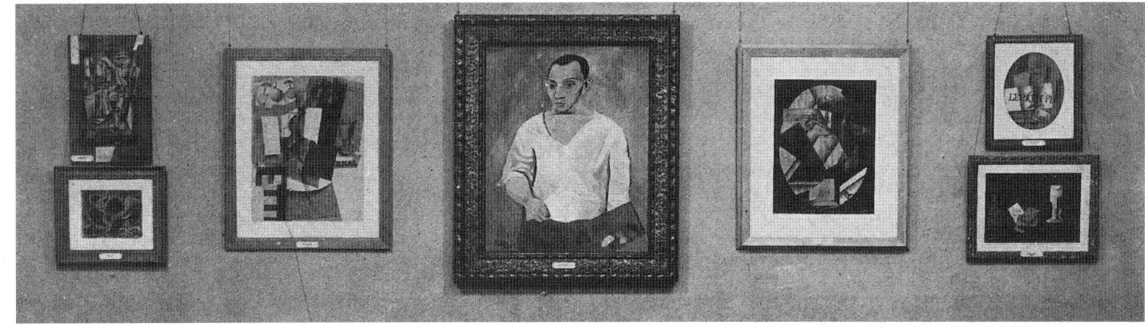

modified but its thematic identity was consolidated. As Hélion would note, "This pair of Arp and Mondrian had a very good influence through me on Gallatin because they both represent a complete form of art .... Both of them made a complete and very rich opposition .... I made him go frankly towards abstract art, where before it was a mixture of cubist, pre-cubist, and abstract, pre-abstract art .... My influence upon him is that he did clarify his collection. With the accent on Mondrian and Leger and Arp."[6]

The new acquisitions to the Gallery of Living Art included work by Hélion himself, enshrining his name in the historic scheme of this now narrowly delineated modernist script. Within months of visiting Arp's and Mondrian's studios, Gallatin added Hélion's *Composition,* 1933, from his *Equilibrium* series, to the collection. In it Hélion demonstrated a revised aesthetic outlook. Unlike the taut, rectangular, interlocking planes and lines which characterized

1. Jean Hélion to George L.K. Morris, 16 May 196[5?]: George L.K. Morris Papers, Archives of American Art, Smithsonian Institution, Washington, D.C.
2. Jean Hélion to Albert Eugene Gallatin, 24 April 1936: this and further citations below from A. E. Gallatin, Correspondence of Prominent People, Archives of American Art, Smithsonian Institution, Washington, D.C. .
3. A.E. Gallatin, 'Gallery of Living Art, New York University', *Creative Art*, no. 3, March 1929, p. XI.
4. A.E. Gallatin, 'The Museum of Living Art', *New York University Alumnus*, no. 18, March 1938, p. 11.
5. For a discussion of A.E. Gallatin's Gallery of Living Art and the impact which it had on American art during its fifteen-year history, see Debra Bricker Balken, 'The Park Avenue Cubists: Gallatin, Morris, Frelinghuysen and Shaw', in *The Park Avenue Cubists*, ed. D.B. Balken and Robert Lubar, exh. cat., Grey Art Gallery, New York University, 2003.
6. Jean Hélion, interview with Gail Stavitsky, 18 June 1986: quoted in Gail Stavitsky, 'The A.E. Gallatin Collection: An Early Adventure in Modern Art', *Bulletin of the Philadelphia Museum of Art*, 1994, p. 22.

Albert Eugene Gallatin and Jean Hélion on the terrace of a café,
1930s, postcard
Centre Pompidou, Bibliothèque Kandinsky, Paris,
fonds photographique A.E. Gallatin

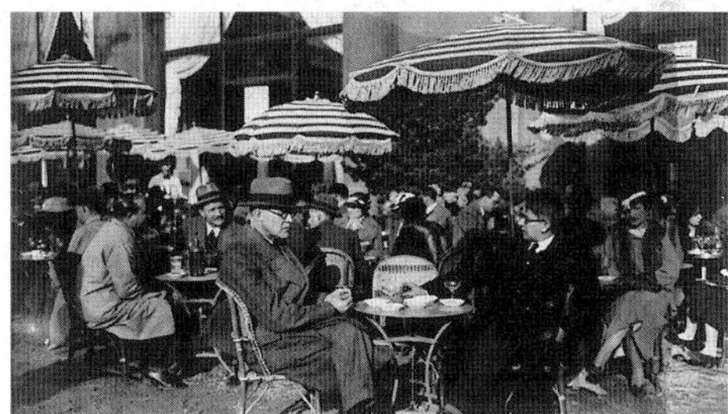

A wall of the Gallery of Living Art,
New York, reproduced in A.E. Gallatin, *The Gallery of Living Art,*
A. E. Gallatin Collection, New York University, 1933

7. Jean Hélion, 'From Reduction to Growth', *Axis*, no. 2, April 1935, p. 22.
8. Hélion, quoted in Stavitsky, *op. cit.*, p. 24.

paintings such as *Orthogonal composition,* 1930, this new body of work eased into fluid, free-floating shapes which were cast in various gradations of muted colour. While still non-mimetic and purged of any external reference, these works are imbued with a new naturalism, a relinquishing of the crisp geometries that had once ordered his work. Hélion's immersion in the ideals of machine-age culture and the prescriptions of movements, such as De Stijl, informed by them, were being superseded by the curvilinear and biomorphic forms of Arp, Léger and Joan Miró.

Hélion would adopt the word '*concret*' (concrete), a term jointly coined with Arp, to describe these elusive, hovering shapes, oddly suggestive and mysterious but devoid of any specific meaning. Although the *Equilibrium* series represented a distinct departure for Hélion, foregoing the

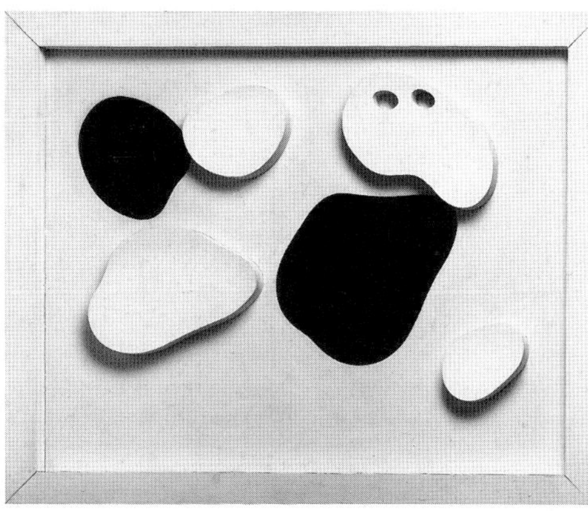

fixed and stable pictorial economies of *Orthogonal composition*, the stasis and calm associated with his *Orthogonal* paintings would always remain a feature of his work. However tumescent his new forms, they abide by the same symmetry and balance. An identical quality was ascribed by Gallatin to the overall content of his growing collection, which he believed showed a sense of constancy and permanency. The artist and his New York patron held similar beliefs in the transcendent possibilities of art, that its existence remained unbound by time.

While Hélion had moved on from Mondrian's rectilinear compositions to a more hybrid abstraction by 1933, he subsequently noted, "I, personally, owe a great deal to the influence of Mondrian, and I admire his works fully".[7] Upon Hélion's urging Mondrian would come to occupy a pro-

minent position in the Gallery of Living Art, when Gallatin later acquired a larger canvas, *Composition with blue*, 1926. Hélion, who frequently tired of Gallatin's notoriously parsimonious nature, admonished the collector on numerous occasions that he should purchase more monumental works: "I told him he should have important pictures. He really was a postage-stamp collector."[8] In 1934, as his debt to Léger became increasingly apparent in the *Equilibrium* series, Hélion coaxed Gallatin into trading a minor work by Léger, *Composition with figures*, 1931, for *Composition*, 1923–27, a more substantial canvas which elaborated more fully on the artist's combined mechanistic and biomorphic syntax.

Gallatin had made some major purchases for the Gallery of Living Art before meeting Hélion – Picasso's *Self-portrait*, 1906; Man Ray's *A.D. 1914*, 1914; Miró's *Painting (Fratellini)*, 1927, and *Dog barking at the moon*, 1926 – but the collection had been composed largely of works on paper and small-scale paintings. Gallatin subsequently acquired, besides Mondrian's *Composition with blue*, notable works such as Picasso's *Three musicians*, 1921 and Léger's *The city*, 1919, the latter through Hélion's persuasion in 1936. Hélion's influence, then, became felt not only through the revised aesthetic content of Gallatin's project at New York University, but through the occasional presence of large-scale paintings. Gallatin's core collection would continue to focus on the work of Braque, Picasso, Gris and Léger, the mainstays of Cubism, but these artists would become construed, through Hélion's shaping, as historic figures, the forerunners of more contemporary experimentation by Arp, Mondrian, Van Doesburg and others.

Gallatin had also, earlier, included in his purview the work of some of the American practitioners of Cubism such as Man Ray, John Marin and Charles Demuth, but as the Gallery of Living Art developed he made numerous excisions and updates in this area of the collection, too, with the upshot that, in the Gallery, New York painting was represented as the latter-day heir or New World extension of European formalism. Like George L.K. Morris, who would become a founding member of the American Abstract Artists (AAA) group in 1936, Gallatin believed that America was poised to inherit the cultural mantle of Paris, a destiny ostensibly manifest in the work of exponents of Cubism such as Charles G. Shaw, John Ferren and Morris himself. Hélion, though he actively encouraged the founding of the AAA, engineering introductions between artists such as Harry Holtzman, Albert Swinden, Balcomb and Gertrude Greene and Morris, whom he met variously

Albert Eugene Gallatin
Photographic portrait of Piet Mondrian, June 1934
Centre Pompidou, Bibliothèque Kandinsky, Paris,
fonds photographique A. E. Gallatin

Jean Arp, *Configuration with two dangerous points*, 1930
Painted and sculpted wood relief, 65 x 84.3 cm
Philadelphia Museum of Art, A.E. Gallatin Collection

in New York and Paris, remained mute on the issue of this nationalist codicil. He viewed the group (of which he had hoped to become a member)[9] more as an offshoot of Abstraction-Création. Even as Gallatin acquired work by artists who would become members of the AAA, however, he once again heeded Hélion's advice, adding to the collection a work of sculpture by Calder known as *Construction*, 1932. Of this stationary relief, Hélion wrote to Gallatin, "I am very glad that you got a Calder. The best artist living in the States had to be included in your collection, and will help the level of the others."[10]

Hélion's contribution to the Gallery of Living Art was not confined solely to advice. To announce the installation of his reformulated collection, in 1933 Gallatin published a short handbook, containing essays and reproductions of some of the more prominent works he had recently acquired. The publication included a noteworthy essay by Hélion, 'The Evolution of Abstract Art as Shown in the Gallery of Living Art', which proposed a binary view of art, its momentum and history caught in self-perpetuating but opposing stylistic dualities. The dynamic of this essentially formalist construction rested on the assumption that art offered two possible means of expression. In art, Hélion expounded, "... either ancient or modern, circulates a rhythm of evolution common to all periods: the effort to open, and the effort to close. Mantegna, Ingres, and Seurat illustrate the effort to close. Their works are compact, in both form and subject. Rubens, Delacroix, Matisse and all the Fauves illustrate the effort to open. Their works are spread out, their shapes burst open, they demolish."[11]

Within these polarities, Hélion noted that Picasso was capable of "running from one to the one other increasingly".[12] Clearly, the development of his own work from the *Orthogonal* to the *Equilibrium* series remained restricted within the 'closed or compact' model. But the reference to Picasso's ingenuity and versatility ironically anticipates the future meanderings of his aesthetics. Even if their abstract articulation would turn out to be relatively brief and episodic, as figuration ultimately supplanted non-referential composition in his work, Hélion would, nevertheless, always work with a tight and condensed vocabulary of forms. And through his various sojourns in New York from 1932 to 1943, it was Hélion's advocacy of abstraction that was instrumental, making a profound impact on the development of avant-garde art in America.

Shortly after the release of the 1933 handbook of the Gallery of Living Art, Hélion was invited by Gallatin to deliver a lecture at New York University. The event, which was attended by Calder, Marcel Duchamp, Arshile Gorky, Frederick Kiesler, Gaston Lachaise and Marin among many other notable downtown artists, was a prelude to his first solo exhibition in New York, in January 1934 at the John Becker Gallery. The project attracted wide response, and, in particular, a review from Henry McBride in the *New York Sun* who discerned Hélion's "ability to distinguish himself from the crowd".[13] While McBride did not venture any prophecy as to the position Hélion would ultimately hold within art, he did state that "it is important to note that he is willing to stand on upon his own mental experiences, and an artist who has arrived at that state of independence is more certain than most to make a definite contribution".[14]

The singularity of Hélion's work and his conviction in the cause of modernism were, in fact, being noticed in New York, and discussed by numerous artists, critics and curators. With his essay in Gallatin's catalogue, which was much read, his lecture at New York University and his show at the John Becker Gallery, Hélion became a highly visible figure in New York, sought out by the likes of art historians such as Meyer Schapiro, who by the time of his 1940 exhibition at the Georgette Passedoit Gallery – his fourth exhibition in New York – declared him to be the "outstanding abstract painter of the younger generation of American and European artists. Painters here and abroad follow his work as the most advanced and masterly of its kind."[15]

Not only through his methodical, deliberated ideas on abstract painting, and his commitment to the ongoing vitality of post-Cubist art, but also by virtue of his conviction of the artist's role Hélion was responsible for inspir-

9. Hélion had hoped to become a member of the American Abstract Artists after his application to become an naturalized American citizen in 1938 was approved. However, the Second World War intervened and Hélion's enlistment in the French army obviated this process. The AAA did, however, include Hélion in their 1942 annual exhibition as a symbolic gesture, a recognition of his place within American art.
10. Jean Hélion to Albert Eugene Gallatin, 6 November 1935.
11. Jean Hélion, 'The Evolution of Abstract Art as Shown in the Museum of Living Art' (1933), reprinted in *A.E. Gallatin Collection, Museum of Living Art*, Philadelphia (Philadelphia Museum of Art) 1954, p. 15.
12. *Ibid.*, p. 16.
13. Henry McBride, 'Jean Helion', *New York Sun*, 13 January 1934, p. 9.
14. *Ibid.*
15. Meyer Schapiro, quoted in Merle Schipper, *Jean Helion: The Abstract Years, 1929–1939*, Ph.D. thesis, Ann Arbor, Michigan, 1974, p. 231.

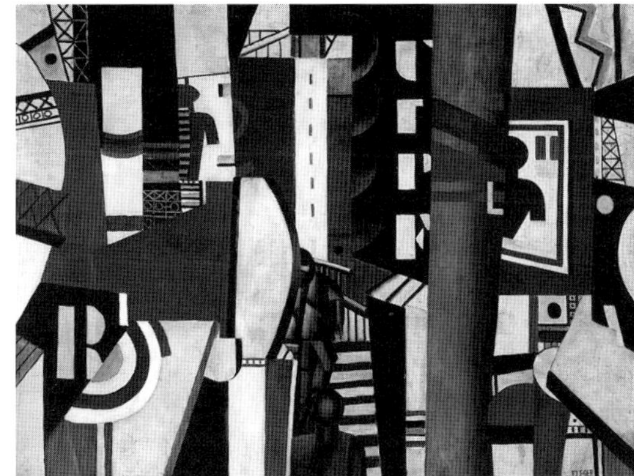

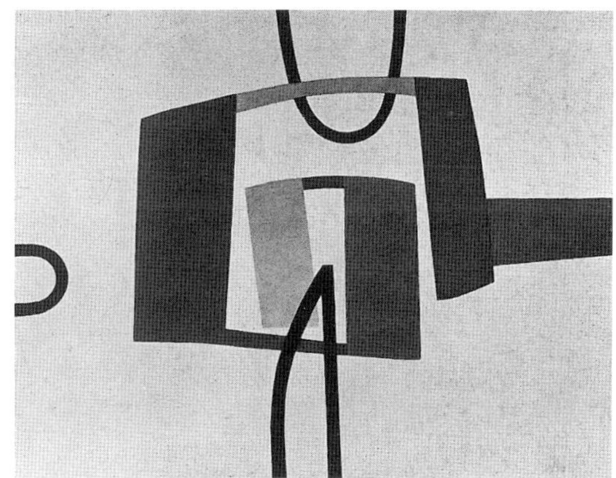

Fernand Léger, *The city*, 1919
Oil on canvas, 130 x 298 cm
Philadelphia Museum of Art, A.E. Gallatin Collection

Jean Hélion, *Construction*, 1933
Oil on canvas, 64.8 x 81.3 cm
Reproduced in A.E. Gallatin, *The Gallery of Living Art*,
New York, 1933, photo no. 50

16. Willem de Kooning, quoted *ibid.*, p. 195.
17. David Hare, quoted *ibid.*, p. 197.
18. Jean Hélion to Albert Eugene Gallatin, 26 March 1934.
19. *Ibid.*
20. Jean Hélion to Albert Eugene Gallatin, 21 November 1934.
21. Jean Hélion to Albert Eugene Gallatin, 15 September 1936.
22. Jean Hélion to Albert Eugene Gallatin, 21 November 1934.
23. Jean Hélion to Albert Eugene Gallatin, 24 April 1936.

ing a growing professional confidence in the still small circle of New York artists. Willem de Kooning observed, for instance, that "all the other European artists came here and we met them slowly and surely but Hélion went out of his way to see what was cooking".[16] David Hare, the New York School sculptor, corroborates this impression, noting that "... he in a sense symbolized the European artist ... Hélion was revolutionary. But he himself was very secure in what the artist's role was. The American artist was not at all secure in what the artist's role was. The American artist wanted to revolt and at the same time he was scared to death of revolting because he thought he didn't know enough .... He assured the American artist that there was a place in society, in world culture, for the avant-garde artist."[17]

Shortly after the opening of his show at John Becker Gallery, Hélion returned home to Paris for a period of more than two years. However enthralled he may have been by his protracted American trips, he wrote to Gallatin shortly after his return in 1934, "... Paris is the place where I work best anyway. I enjoyed very much my stay in the States but I am not pleased with my work over there."[18] Withstanding the idiosyncracies of place, the milieu of Paris, with its heady cultural scene, proved the more invigorating for Hélion, at least for the while. He would quickly become disaffected of Abstraction-Création, writing to Gallatin in the same letter that "too many second or third rate painters have been admitted. Arp and I are fighting to clear it up, if it is possible. I doubt it though."[19] Both Arp and Hélion would extricate themselves from the group long before its demise in 1936. In the process of disconnection, Hélion would become increasingly more aware of the potential for American art. He laboured tirelessly on Gallatin's behalf to find outlets and distributors in Paris for the 1933 catalogue of the Gallery of Living Art, a gesture that illustrates his recognition of a growing international artistic movement. In addition, he actively encouraged the inception of a new publication, which he entitled *Plastic*, to reinforce the increasingly formalist and theoretical bent of Gallatin's venture on Washington Square East.

Pursuing his belief in the necessity for a journal to elucidate the current reverberations of modernism, as well as its historic foundations and American extensions, Hélion developed a structure and a programme for the first five issues of *Plastic*. He proposed the writer (and later curator of the Museum of Modern Art) James Johnson Sweeney as editor of the publication and Morris as associate editor. He outlined articles and suggestions for pro-

files on artists such as Kiesler, Léger and Torres-García. But the template was never realised, at least not in the form Hélion envisaged. Citing financial constraints posed by tax difficulties, Gallatin backed away from the project. Hélion persisted, admonishing his patron, "I hope that you will not give up the idea for always and that when you meet better conditions, you will give America what it needs so badly, a periodical seriously and intelligently devoted to the manifestation of modern art, that can be developed into a total culture".[20]

An incarnation of *Plastic* would emerge, three years after Hélion's urging, albeit on foreign soil. In reaction to the widespread proliferation of veristic Surrealism in the mid to late 1930s, with all its Freudian overtones and emphasis on the sub-conscious as an agency for imagery, Gallatin, Morris and Charles G. Shaw were persuaded by Cesar Domela, Jean Arp and Sophie Taeuber-Arp to launch *Plastique* in 1937. The French-English journal, produced in Paris as a collaborative endeavour but financed by the American half of the team, ran through five issues without Hélion's involvement. Opposed to the elusive, rather than concrete or material, realisation of form – in other words to the private, corporeal and sometimes highly sexual content of Surrealist art – Hélion wrote to Gallatin on the eve of the appearance of *Plastique*, "It will be interesting to see the face of 'Plastic'. I regret it is not going to appear in America, where it is so much needed."[21]

By the time that Hélion returned to the United States, in summer of 1936, Surrealism had begun to vie for recognition with the purer expressions of abstract painting, displacing the inventive and progressive aspects of post-Cubism. Concomitant with the rise of fascism in Europe and the growing threat of another world war, Surrealist art presented internalized and subjective, illusory and sometimes horrific visions, circumventing the pictorial priorities pursued by modernist movements such as Art Concret and Abstraction-Création. Hélion, who had earlier stated, "I am convinced that art has nothing to do with politics"[22] – a position he would long uphold – now became "anxious", as he put it, "to work in New York (or near) in the atmosphere of one healthy country. I bear enough of France in my blood to supply what could be missing over there, that had helped art, so far, to develop everywhere."[23] Whatever contentment he had earlier felt working in Paris soon dissipated, as political circumstances changed.

During the two years during which Hélion had remained in Paris his painting continued to generate considerable attention in the United States. His first exhibition at the Valentine Gallery, in April 1936, gave rise to numerous favourable reviews. He was pleased, in particular, that MacBride pitted his work against emergent Surrealism, stating: "[He] did fine in opposing me to Freud and, by allusion, to freudian painters; I am glad that he noticed that I proved that life could be happy, clear and healthy .... This should encourage Valentine, help to sell more, and I to go to this country of America I am now longing for."[24] Hélion's 1936 trip to America was divided, again, between Virginia and New York city, in a contrast, as he characterized it, "between excessive machinery and overflowing nature".[25] While the reserved or "healthy" traits of his work could never have been defined as "excessive" – the word he projected on the metropolis of New York – certain correspondences now emerged between this description and the increasingly naturalized clusters of abstract forms that came to dominate his work in 1935.

The *Equilibrium* series, with its sparse shapes and luxuriant space, became supplanted by compositions such as *Île-de-France*, 1935, in which overlapping cylinders and volumetric designs are compressed within a limited ground. These packed pictures would soon ease into "figures", as Hélion called them, singular forms vaguely suggestive of the body but otherwise retaining all the opaque traits of abstraction, along with its reluctance to specify and to name. In *Standing figure*, 1936 and *Pink figure,* 1937, for instance, the centralized, rounded shapes congeal into a ambiguous presence, its identity withheld and unknown. In 1938–39, on the eve of the war, when he was living permanently in Virginia, Hélion abandoned abstraction entirely and introduced the figure into his work. On this seemingly abrupt transition, conditioned by the realisation that abstract painting was no longer viable in the face of a war, Hélion declared, "I feel I have always been doing the same thing in my work: this development has been merely a surface change, not an essential one. In fact, I still consider myself an abstract painter."[26]

However much the subject-matter of his work had been reconsidered, Hélion would be remembered in America above all for his ardent championing of Cubist and post-Cubist art. Even as the body began to resurface in his work, his *Equilibrium* paintings were being exhibited at various American venues. Alfred Barr, for example, included two of these works in his landmark *Cubism and Abstract Art* exhibition at the Museum of Modern Art in spring 1936. Duchamp, moreover, arranged at the Howard Putzel Gallery in Hollywood in 1936 and 1937 two exhibitions which drew from this series and from that of *Figure*. This venture provided Hélion with enough exposure on the West Coast to ensure that his work was subsequently in-

corporated in a large thematic exhibition of contemporary art at the San Francisco Museum of Art in 1938, an exhibition which later moved to Chicago.

Gallatin would also continue to tap Hélion's expertise for his collection and for the release of his 1936 catalogue, which reprinted Hélion's earlier essay, a mark of the influence it continued to exert on American art. The new publication was occasioned not only by new additions to Gallatin's collection, such as Picasso's *Three musicians* and Leger's *The city*, but by the renaming of the institution, now the Museum of Living Art – a change which Hélion wholeheartedly endorsed. Around the time of Hélion's second exhibition at the Valentine Gallery in 1938, George Morris, by now the art critic for the newly restructured *Partisan Review*, interviewed the artist for the periodical, the outcome of which further reinforced the ties between American and European art. Hélion noted in the interview, "Art is essentially something to continue, not to start ... it may vary enormously providing the evolution is homogenous; it is born of itself permanently, and cannot be born of anything else. Painting is what provokes painting. This is why I believe in museums. You have many of those and some are excellent."[27]

The construction of a formalist tradition in art, created by the innovations of numerous artists throughout history and now stretched to incorporate American developments, was deeply affirming to Gallatin and to Morris, and to numerous artists associated with the AAA. Morris, who would become the group's chief spokesman, adopted this aesthetic stance in his frequent essays and tracts as a means to lobby for the legitimacy of contemporary American abstraction, claiming its historic inevitability.[28] In fact, Morris, whose formalist interpretations pre-dated that of Clement Greenberg, his eventual successor at the *Partisan Review,* was profoundly indebted to Hélion's binary stylistic formation, taking his own methodological tack from its analysis of internalization and closure. Over and above the interview in *Partisan Review,* he quoted the artist in his article for the *American Abstract Artists Yearbook* in 1939,[29] evoking his authority as a theorist and his notion of art's self-perpetuating continuity and repetitions – the coherence of which was evident in the latest outcrop of abstract painting in New York.

The year 1939 was also that in which Hélion which Hélion enlisted in the French army. On the eve of his mobilization in 1940, resulting almost immediately in his capture by the Germans, he wrote to Gallatin, "Goodbye, farewell perhaps, to painting".[30] Painting was, of course, an activity that he eventually resumed after his return to

24. *Ibid.*
25. Jean Hélion to Albert Eugene Gallatin, 1 May 1938.
26. Jean Hélion, in 'Eleven Europeans in America', *Bulletin of the Museum of Modern Art*, no. 45, 1946, p. 28.
27. George L.K. Morris, 'Interview with Jean Hélion', *Partisan Review*, IV, no. 5, April 1938, p. 34.
28. For a discussion of George L.K. Morris's aesthetic position see Debra Bricker Balken, 'Interactions in the Lives and Work of Suzy Frelinghuysen and George L.K. Morris', in D.B. Balken and Deborah Menaker Rothschild, *Suzy Frelinghuysen and George L.K. Morris, American Abstract Artists: Aspects of Their Work and Collection*, exh. cat., Williams College Museum of Art, Williamstown, Massachusetts, 1992.
29. George L.K. Morris, 'The American Abstract Artists', *American Abstract Artists Yearbook*, 1939, n. p.
30. Jean Hélion to Albert Eugene Gallatin, 3 September 1939.

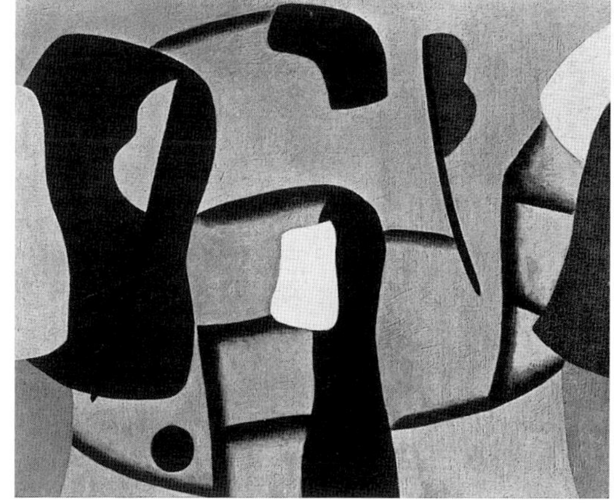

31. Edward Alden Jewell, 'An Alert Explorer', *The New York Times*, 14 February 1943, p. X7.

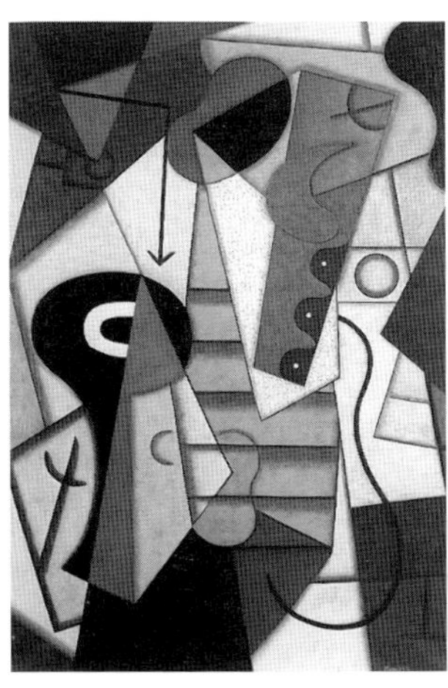

George L.K. Morris, *Nautical composition,* 1937–42

Oil on canvas, 129.5 x 88.9 cm

The Whitney Museum of American Art, New York

Piet Mondrian, *Composition with blue*, 1926

Oil on canvas, 61.1 x 61.1 cm (diagonal)

Philadelphia Museum of Art,

A.E. Gallatin Collection

Virginia in 1942, following his dramatic escape from imprisonment. The once non-referential compositions which made up his *Orthogonal*, *Equilibrium* and *Figure* series, however, had long since been permanently replaced by identifiable figures and known objects and settings. While retaining the same compositional rigour and dispassionate tone, Hélion would revoke abstract painting entirely from this juncture onwards. However, when in 1943 Peggy Guggenheim offered Hélion an exhibition of his work at her gallery, Art of This Century, the works shown were his earlier abstractions, prompting Edward Alden Jewell of *The New York Times* to herald Hélion "as a veritable leader in the non-objective field".[31]

As the burgeoning New York School began to draw on aspects of Surrealism – the unconscious being a particular wellspring – Hélion's Cubist elaborations, like much of the work of the AAA, came to be overlooked and dismissed by many critics as too hermetic and inconsequential, a now closed chapter in modernist history. Some artists, however, such as Nell Blaine, Leland Bell and Albert Kresch – members of the so-called Jane Street group – regarded Hélion's reconsideration of the late 1930s as exemplary. They followed suit and relinquished their own earlier investment in abstract painting for more recognizable forms. By the time Hélion left America in 1946 to live permanently in Paris, Abstract Expressionism had become the dominant movement, challenging and displacing the Hélion's notion of a "healthy" art, in so far as it was driven by subjective experience rather than by the rational engagement of visual components.

Besides George L.K. Morris and the AAA, whose influence was waning, there were few adherents left to perpetuate the formal ethos of post-Cubist art. Albert Eugene Gallatin's Museum of Living Art had disbanded in 1943, its collection re-located to the Philadelphia Museum of Art after New York University had determined that its space would be put to better use as a library processing centre. The considerable mark which Hélion left on New York culture remained crystallized within the period of the Depression and the prelude to the Second World War. It was a period in which a sense of artistic unity had arisen, and the avant-garde had been legitimized. Hélion's encounters with New York's artists, patrons and curators contributed not only to a new sense of community but to a national identity, to the realisation that American art could function on the world's stage. On their other hand, his own painting benefited from the new environment and from an expanded audience, and these indelibly shaped its ongoing development.

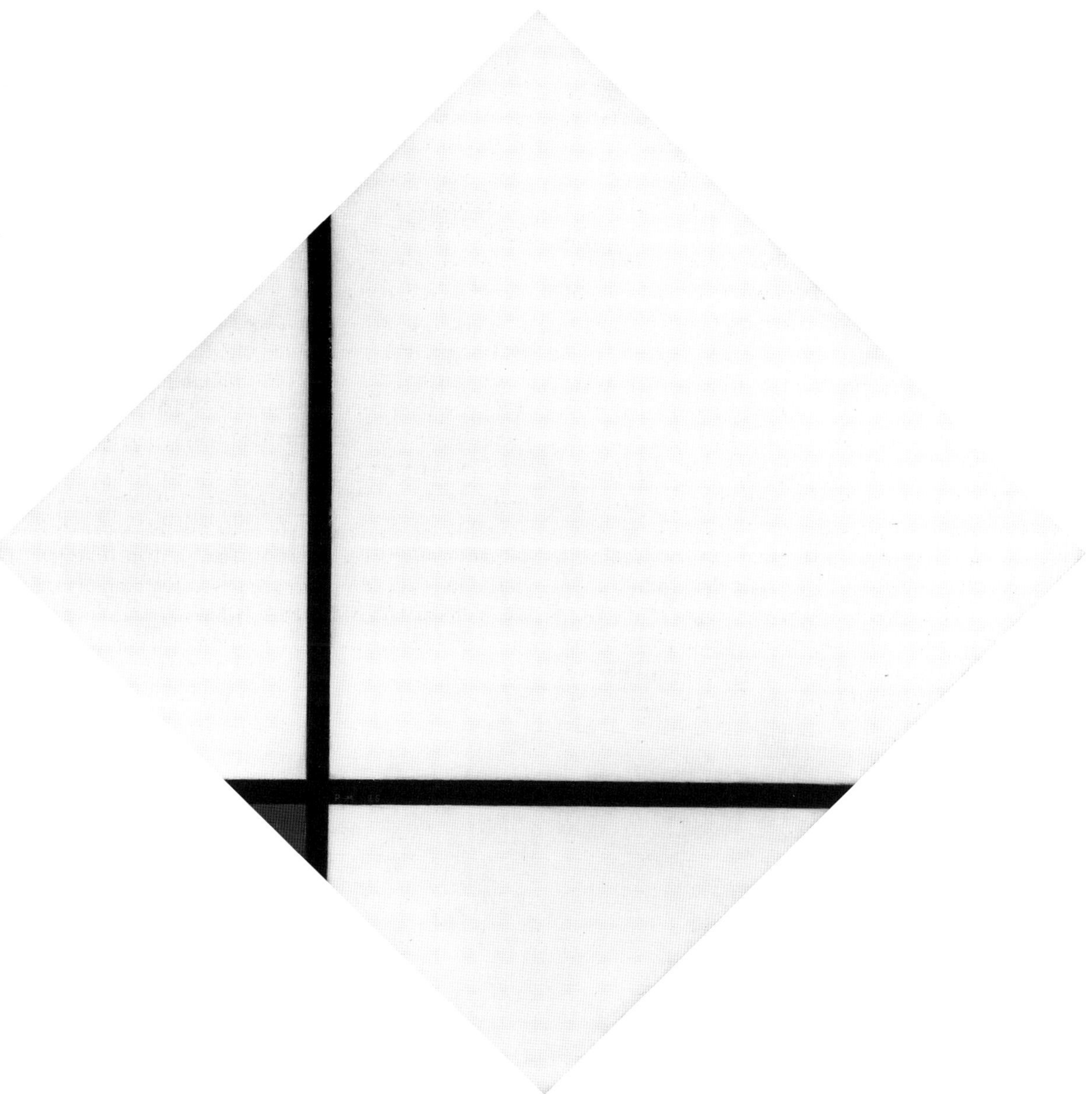

mais vivre est perdre le prestige de se tromper.

Pourtant en attaquant les objets sommaires et industriels de Raynaud, élégamment raréfiés, et les tableaux unicolores de Klein repoussant sensibles, mais aussi élégamment exploités, je ne voudrais pas me joindre à ceux qui les attaquent par en dessous, parce qu'ils préfèrent la confusion, la palette sale ou sentimentale, enfin tous les oublis merci au nettoyage. Partisan de l'air mais n'adorons pas le flacon de miroir et le tapis brosse, et l'écriteau Défense de Fumer.

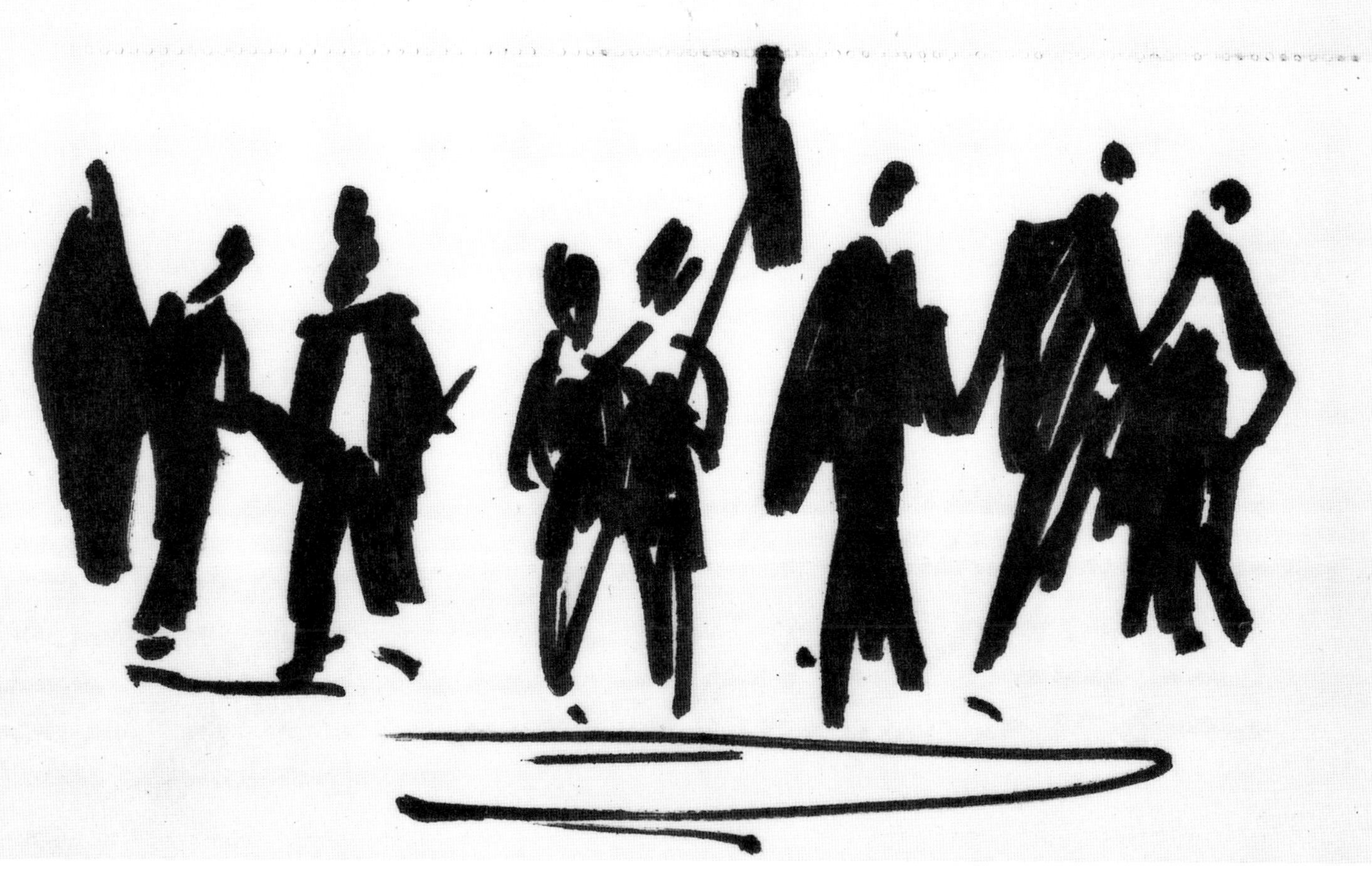

CATALOGUE
ŒUVRES EXPOSÉES

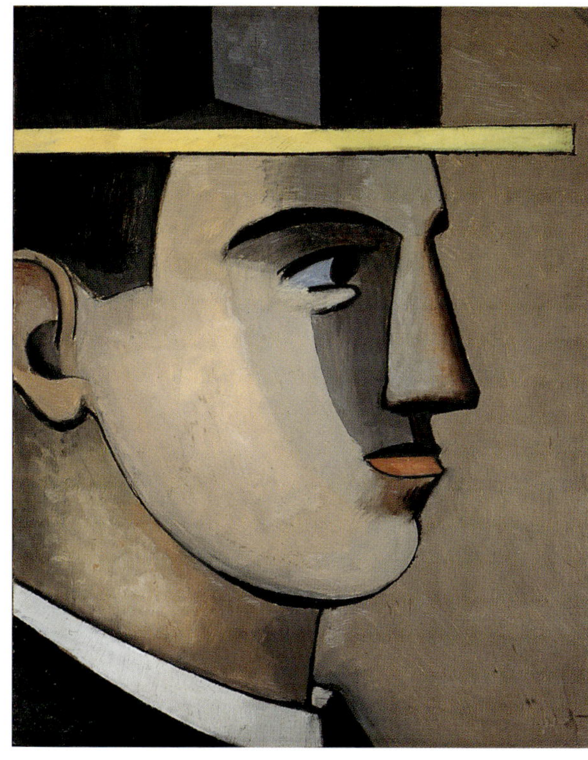

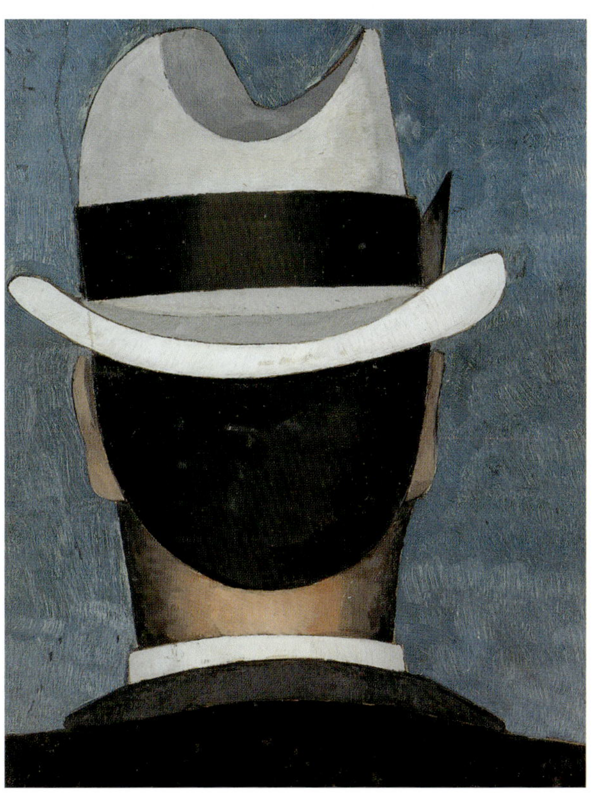

Charles, 1939
(Study)
Oil on Isorel
38.2 x 28 cm
Private collection

Édouard, 1939
Oil on board
33 x 25.7 cm
Private collection

A CONCRETE ART

"Art is universal, it transcends both period and personality.
Its place is in the domain of unchanging certainties, and it
is governed by logic."

« L'art est universel, il échappe
aux personnalités comme aux époques.
Il appartient au domaine des certitudes constantes,
est contrôlable par la logique. »

Jean Hélion, *Art Concret,* avril 1930, p. 5.

UN ART CONCRET

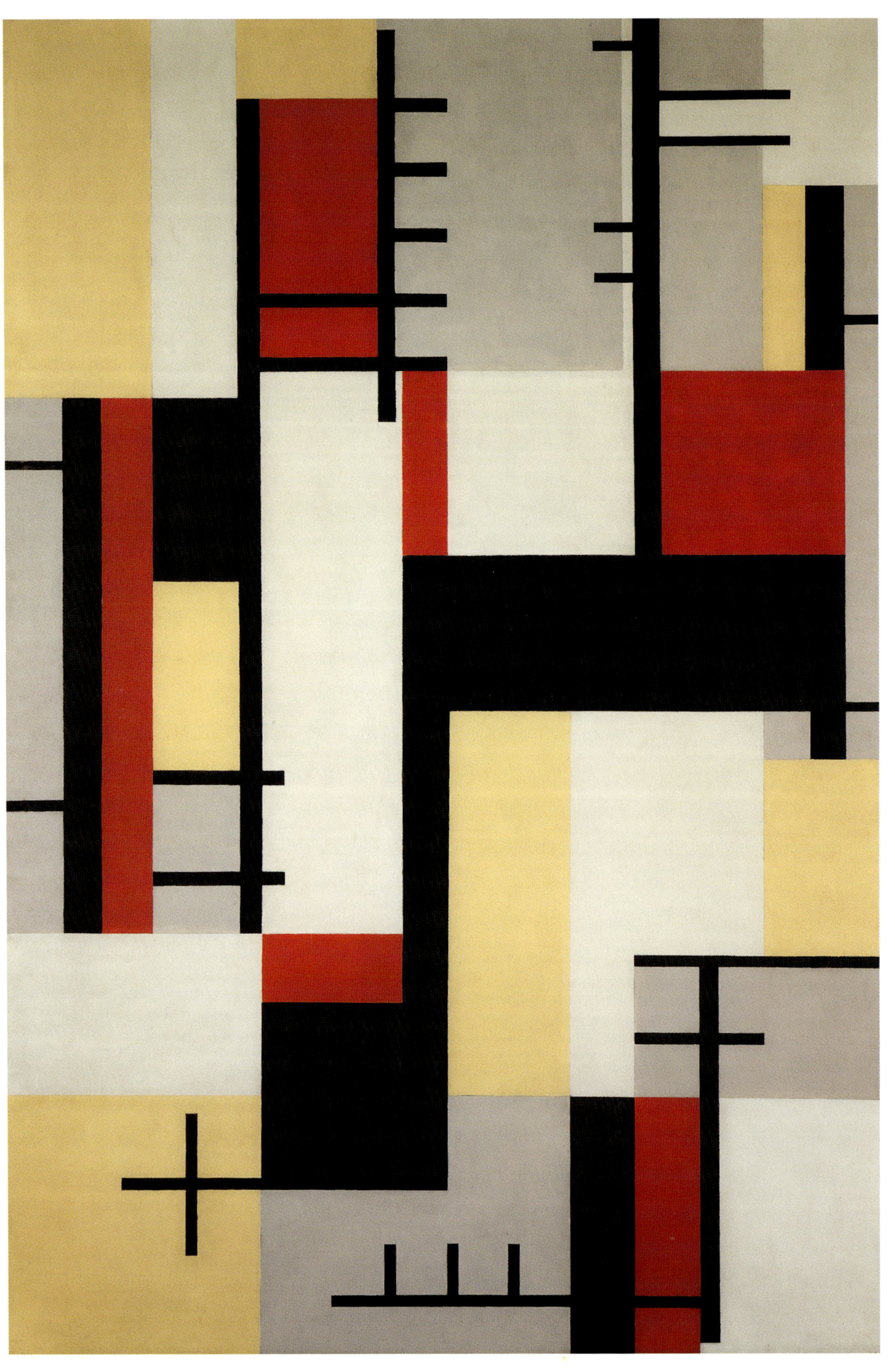

Orthogonal composition, 1929–30
Oil on canvas
146 x 97 cm
Private collection, Paris

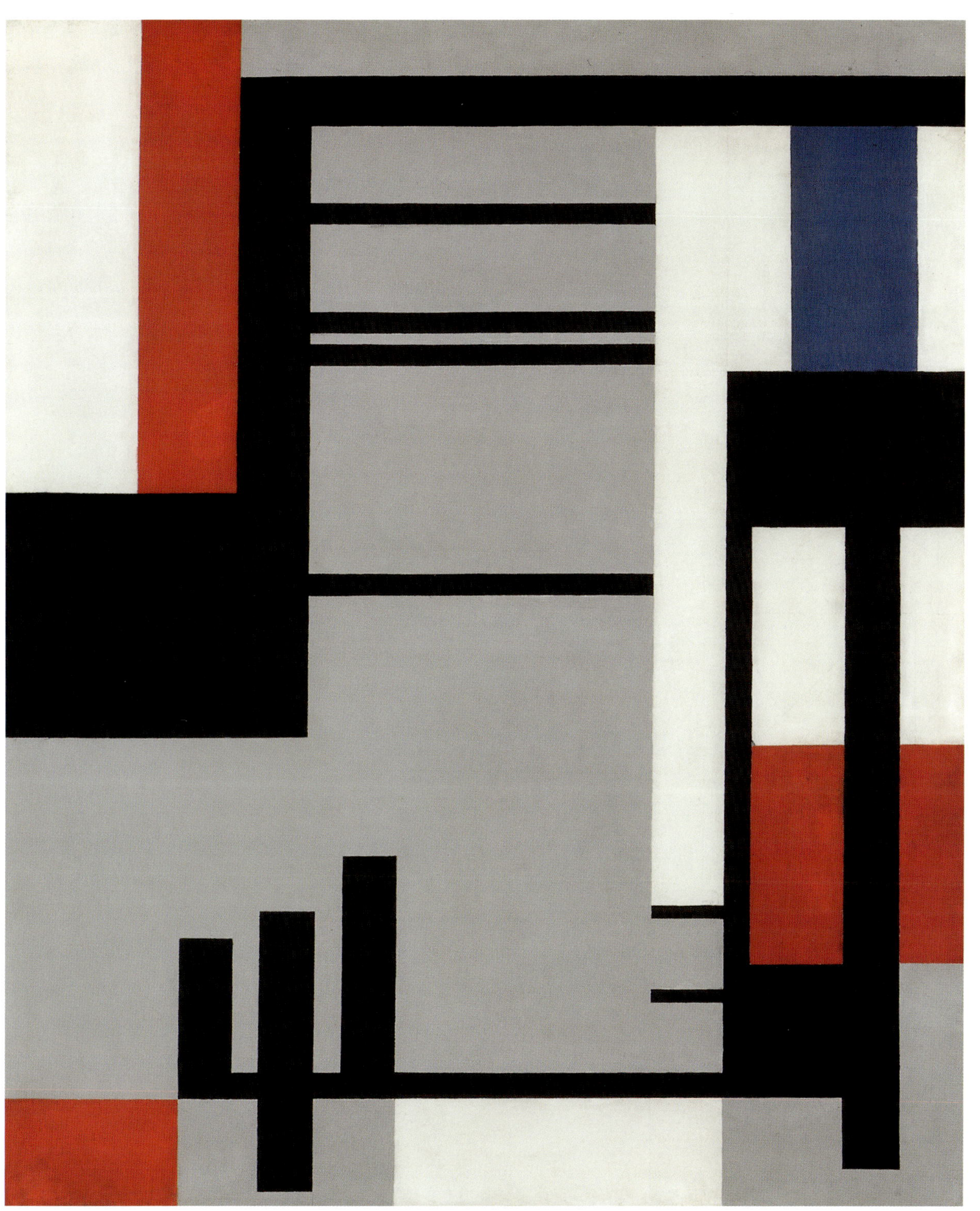

Orthogonal composition, 1930
Oil on canvas
100 x 81 cm
Centre Pompidou, Musée national d'art moderne, Paris,
purchase 1975

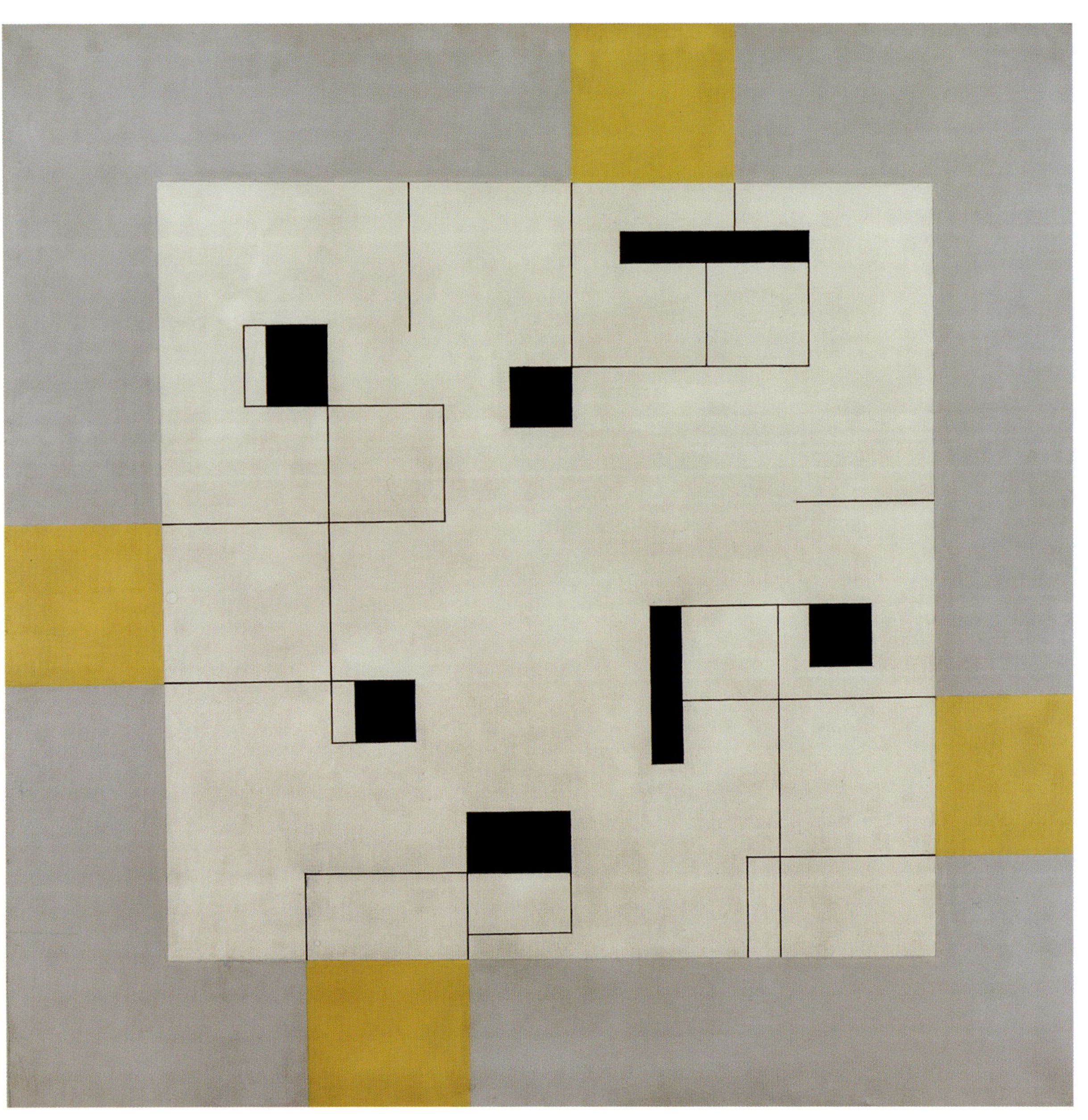

Complex tensions, 1930
Oil on canvas
90 x 89 cm
Private collection
Courtesy galerie Louis Carré

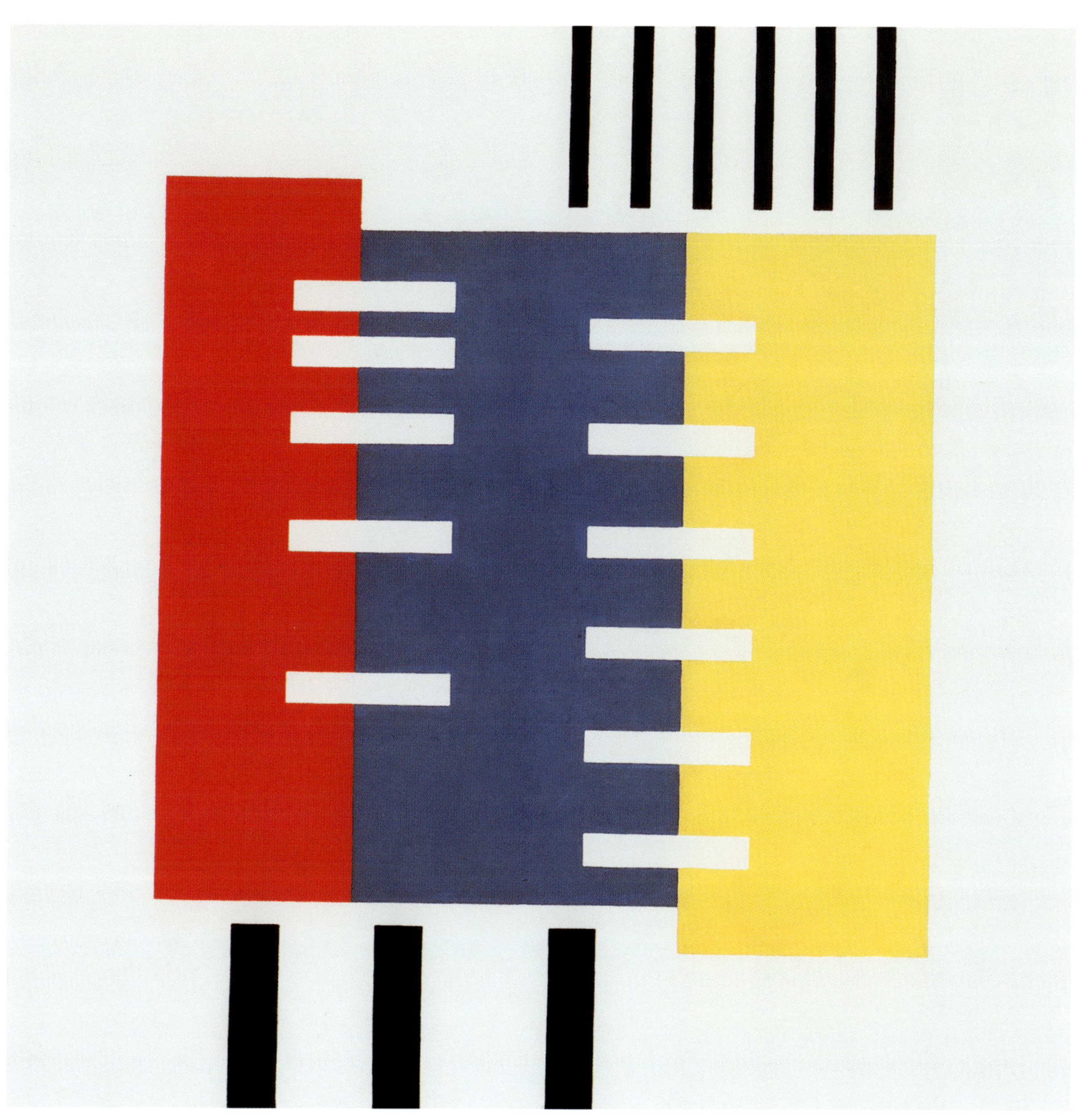

Abstract composition, 1930
Oil on canvas
89.5 x 89.9 cm
Collection Herta and Paul Amir, United States

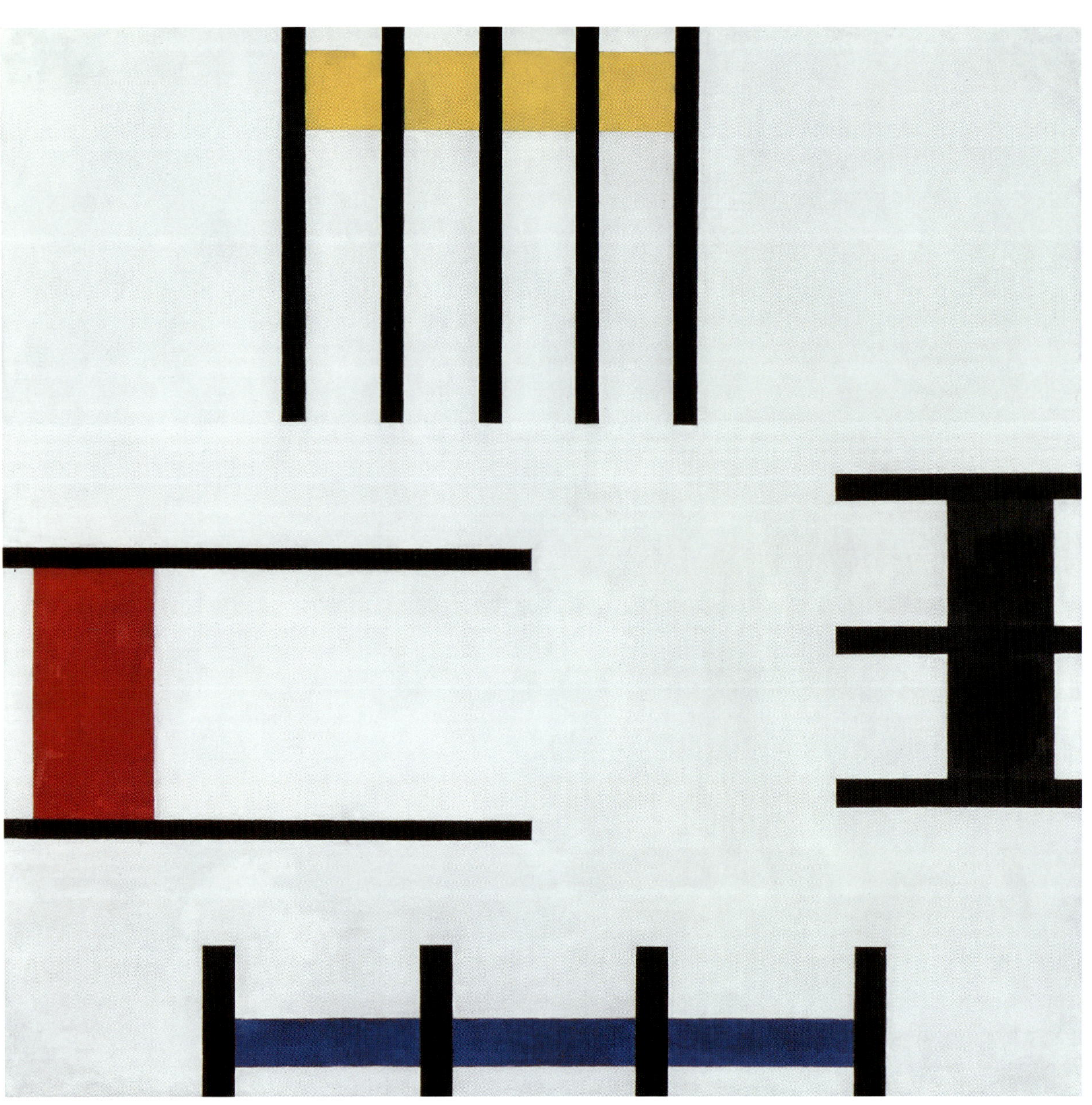

Composition, 1932
Oil on canvas
90 x 90 cm
Musée de Grenoble, Grenoble

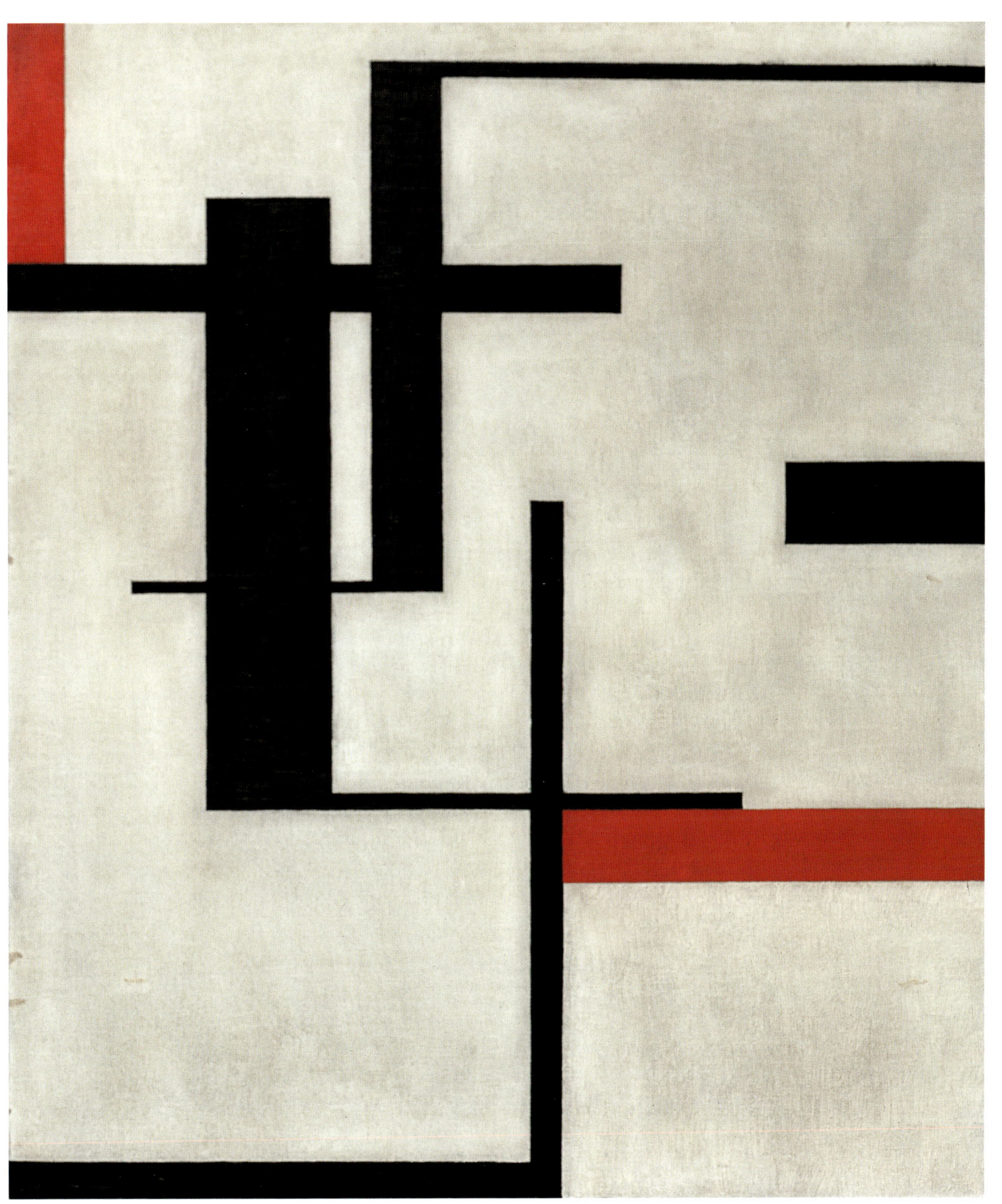

Tensions, 1932
Oil on canvas
73 x 60 cm
Musée Malraux, Le Havre

2

CURVES AND TENSIONS

"It seems to me that my paintings, which, from 1930 to
1932, were like dry seeds, are starting to swell, to take on
life. How they will flower I don't know."

« Il me semble que mes tableaux qui,
de 1930 à 1932, furent comme des grains secs,
se mettent à gonfler, à vivre.
Je ne sais pas comment ils fleuriront. »

Jean Hélion, *Carnets,* 24 mars 1933, p. 41.

COURBES ET TENSIONS

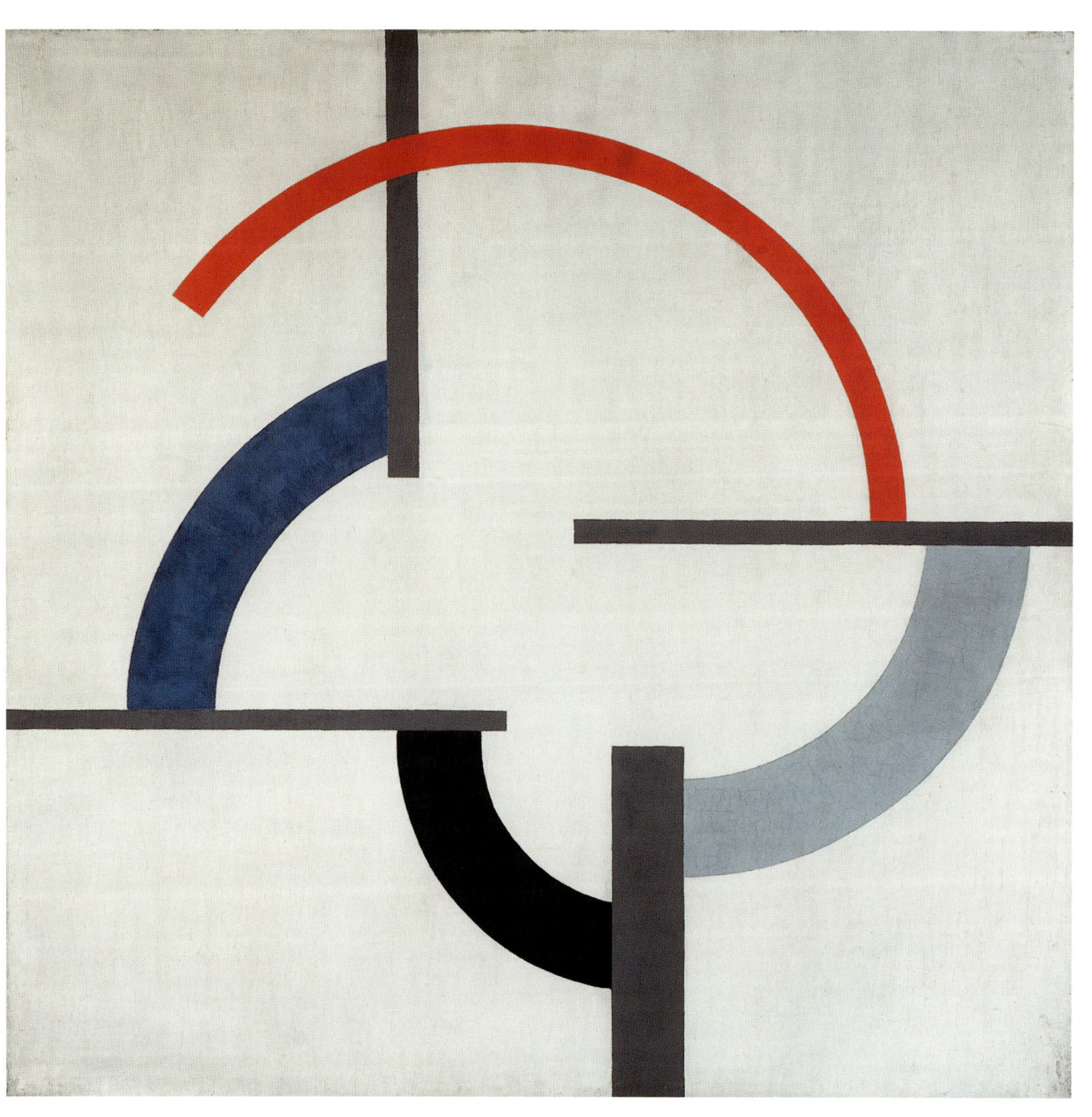

Circular tensions no. 1, 1931–32
Oil on canvas
75 x 75 cm
Private collection

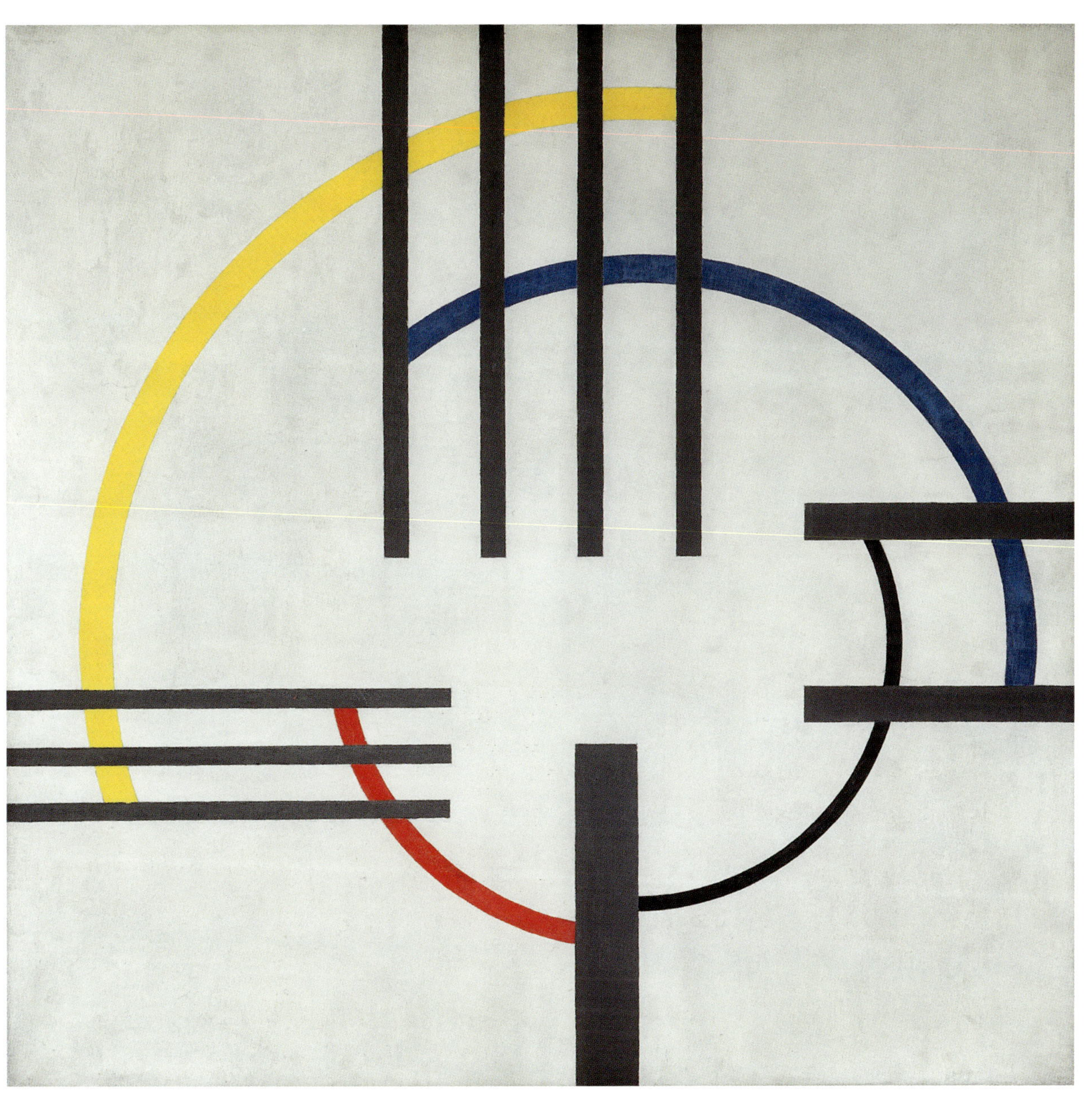

Circular tensions no. 2, 1931–32
Oil on canvas
75 x 75 cm
Private collection

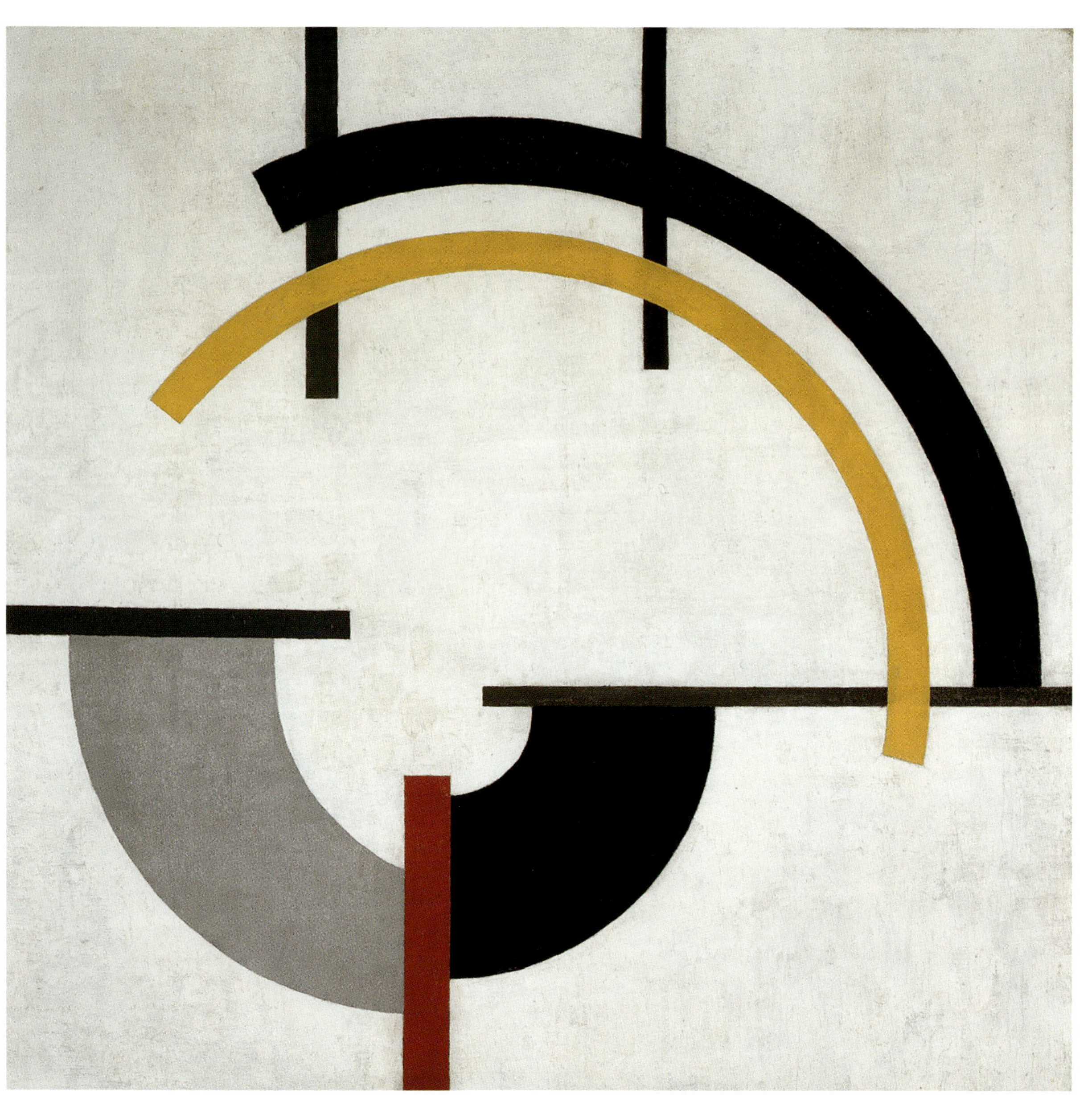

First curves, 1932
Oil on canvas
74.6 x 74.6 cm
Private collection, Germany

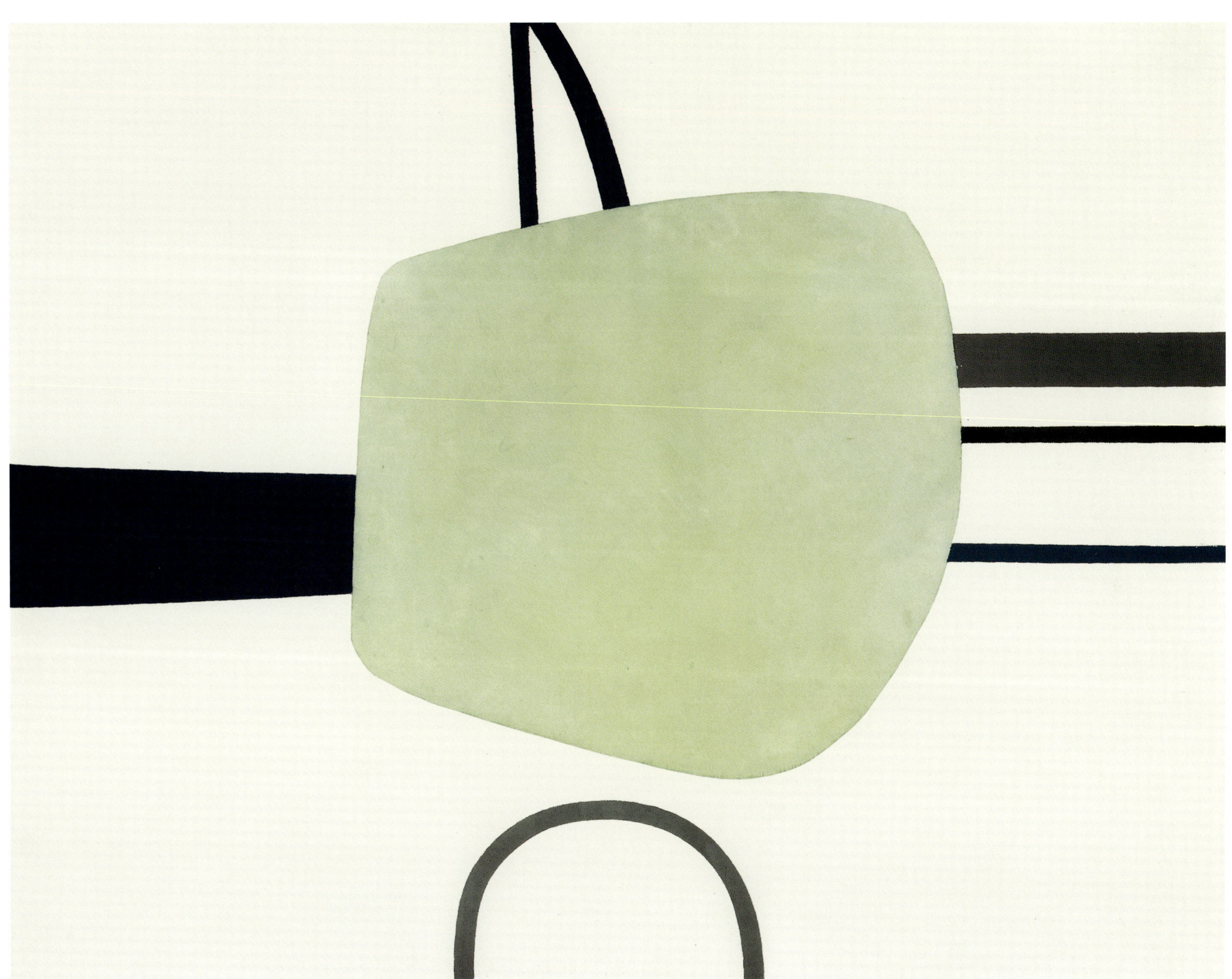

Abstract composition, 1933
Oil on canvas
72 x 91 cm
Musée d'Art moderne de la Ville de Paris, Paris

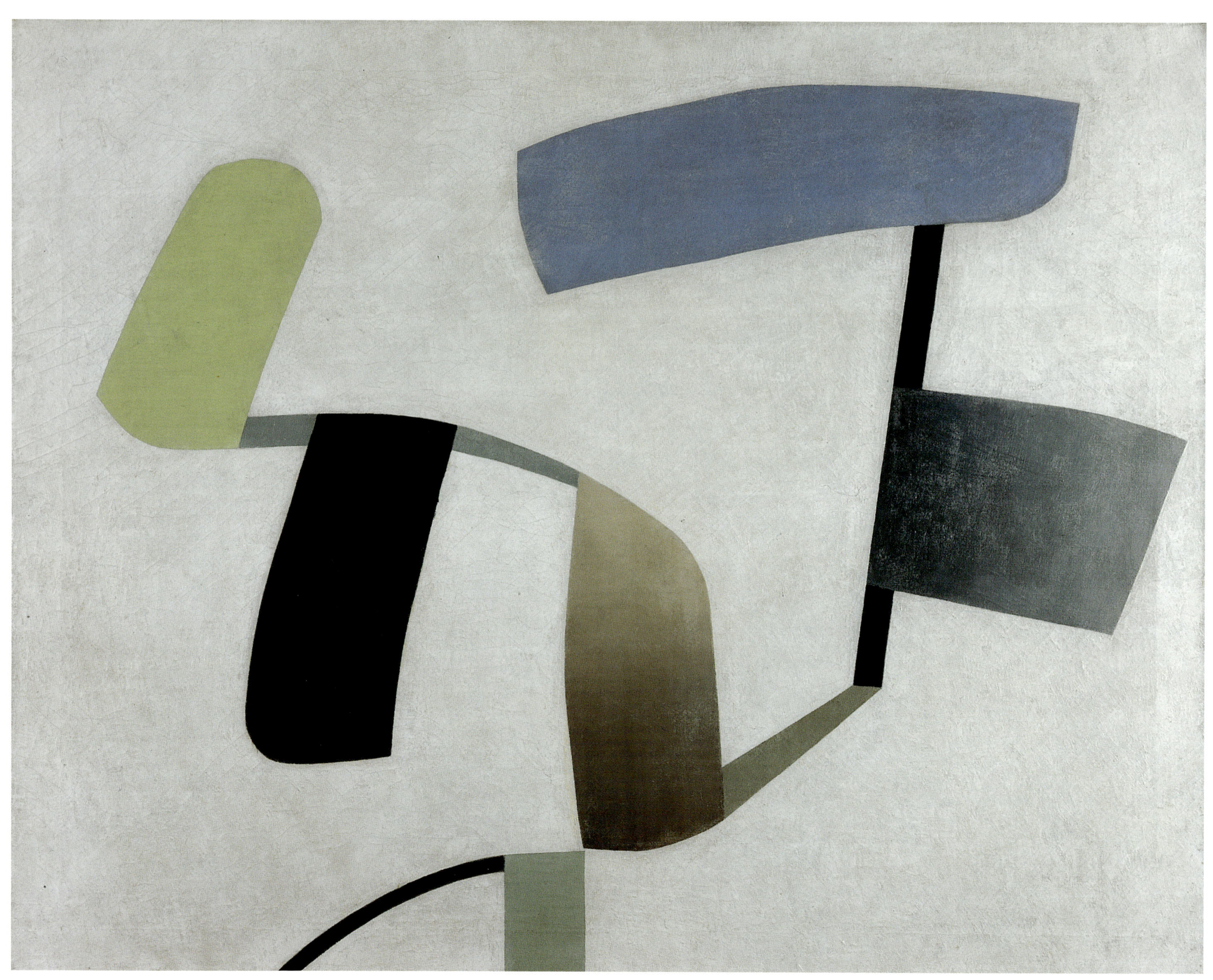

Equilibrium, 1933
Oil on canvas
74 x 91.5 cm
Collection of Louis Hélion Blair

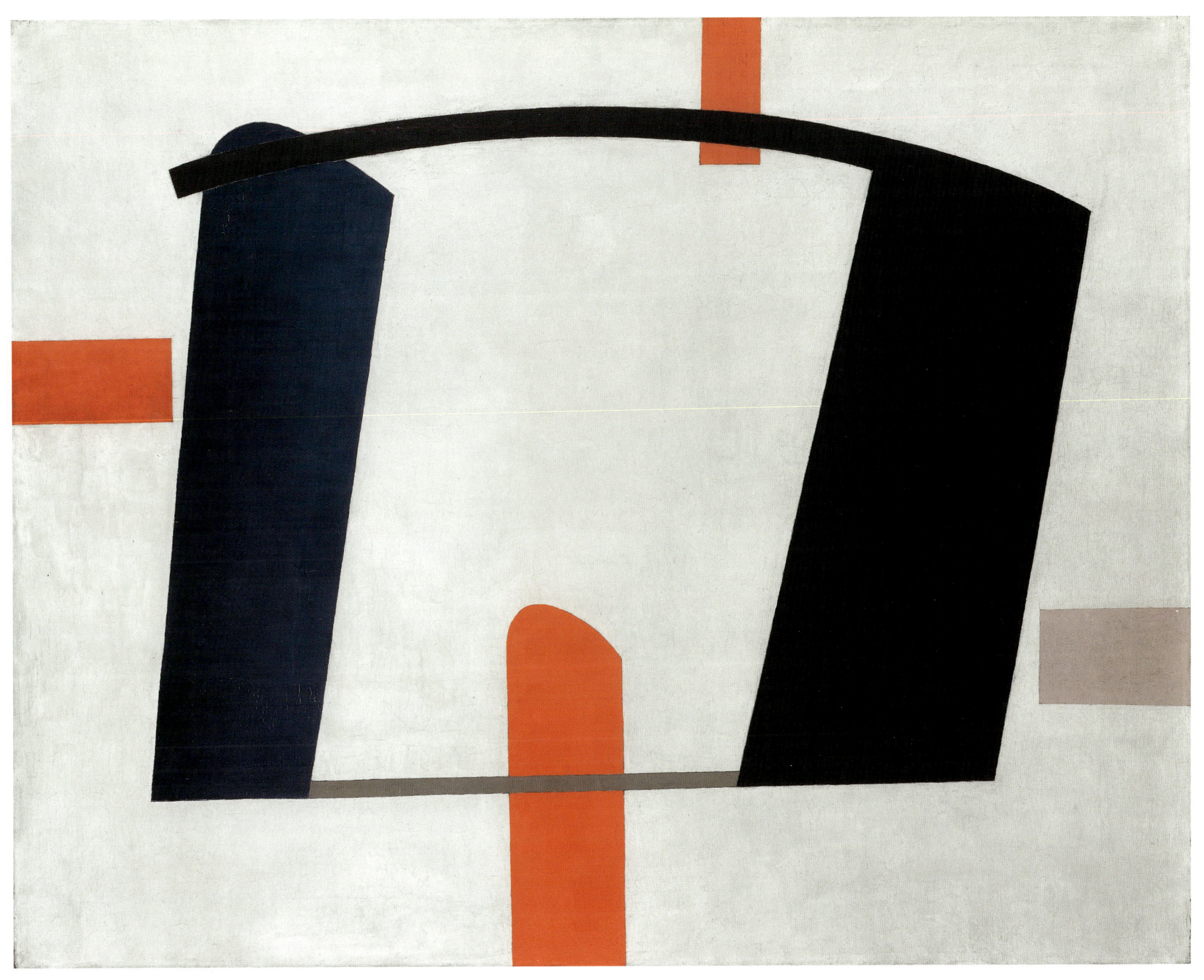

Equilibrium, 1933
Oil on canvas
81 x 100 cm
Hamburger Kunsthalle, Hamburg

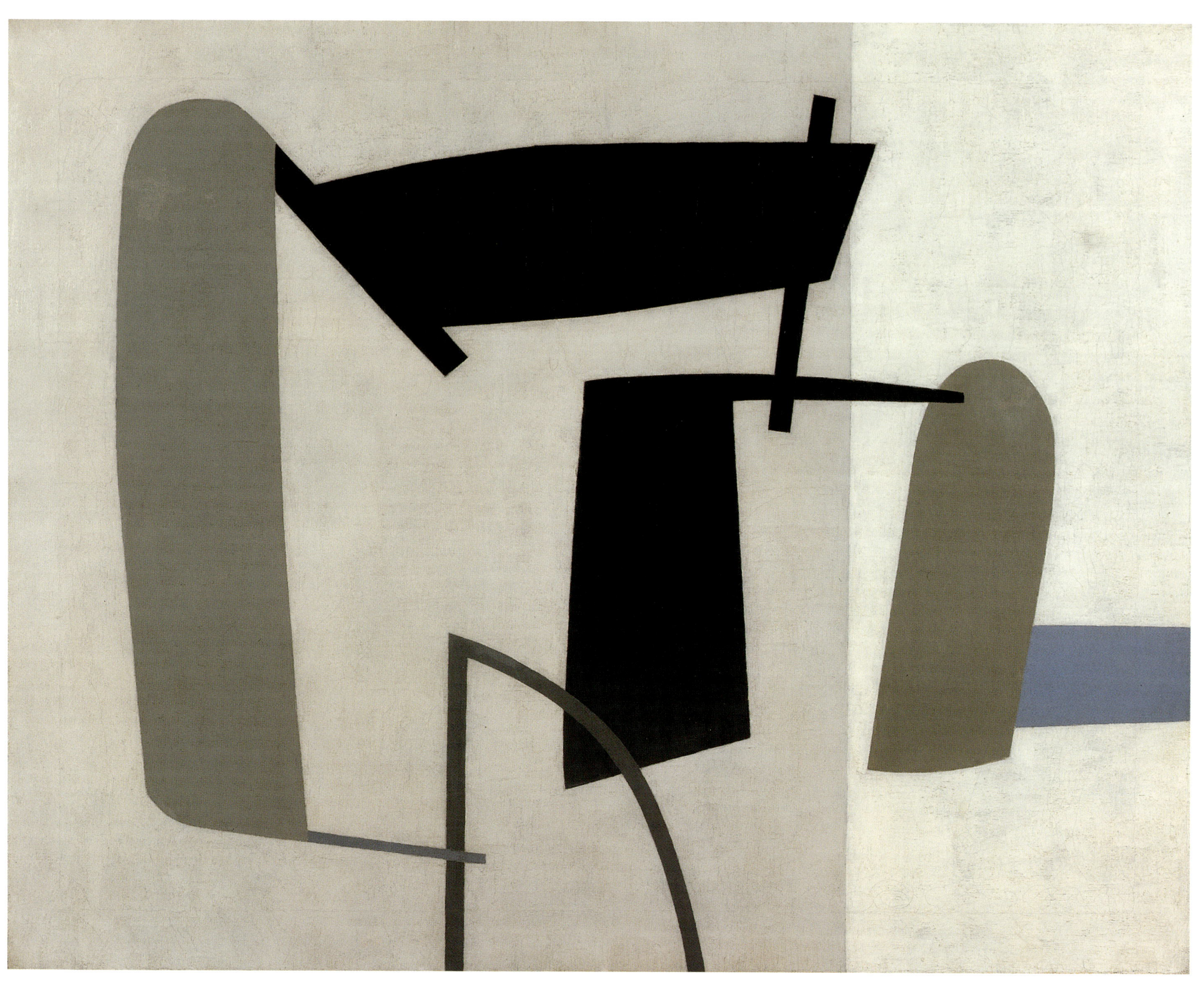

Equilibrium, 1933
Oil on canvas
63.5 x 78.7 cm
Courtesy Rachel Adler Fine Art, New York

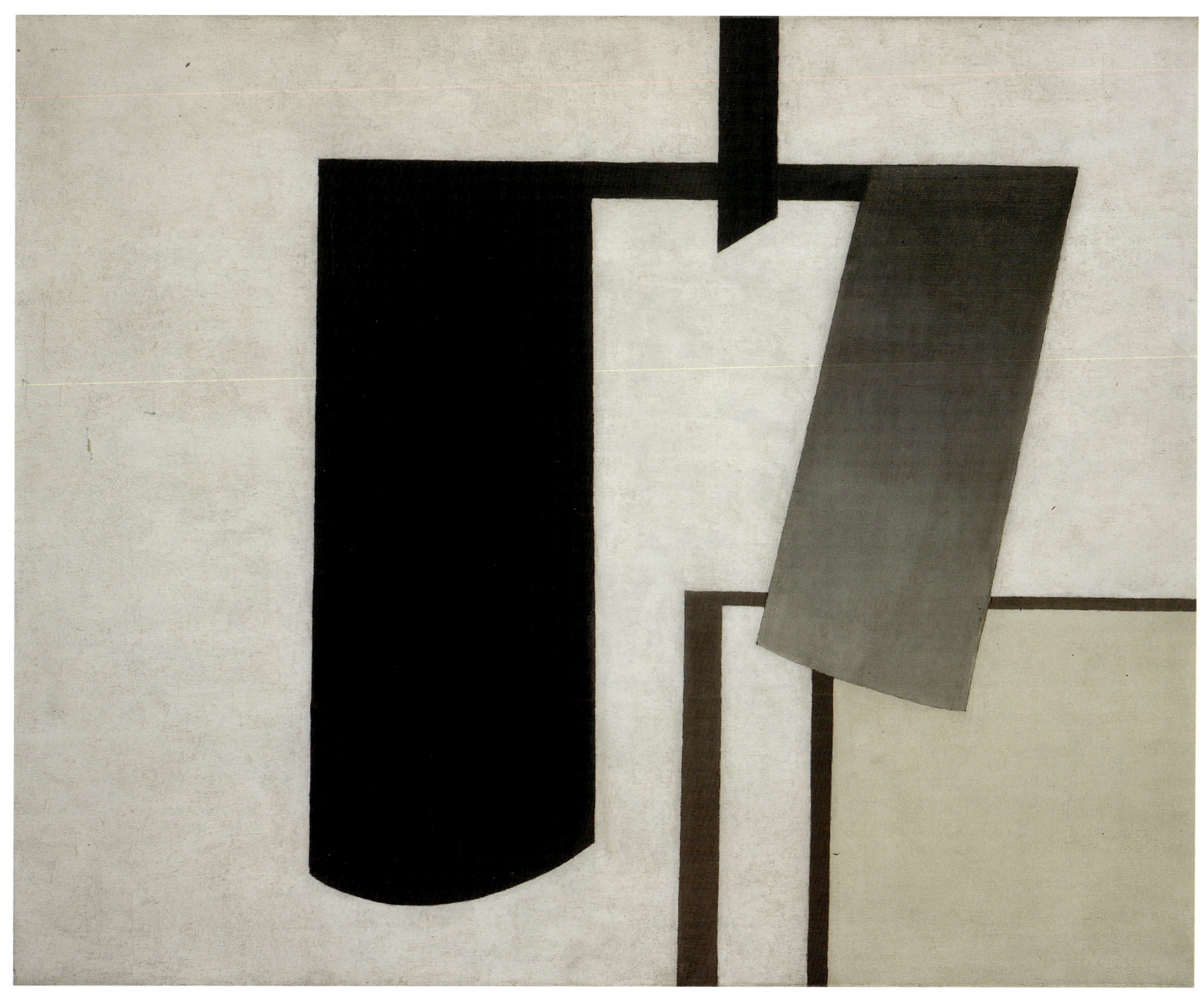

Equilibrium, 1933
Oil on canvas
59.6 x 72.6 cm
Private collection

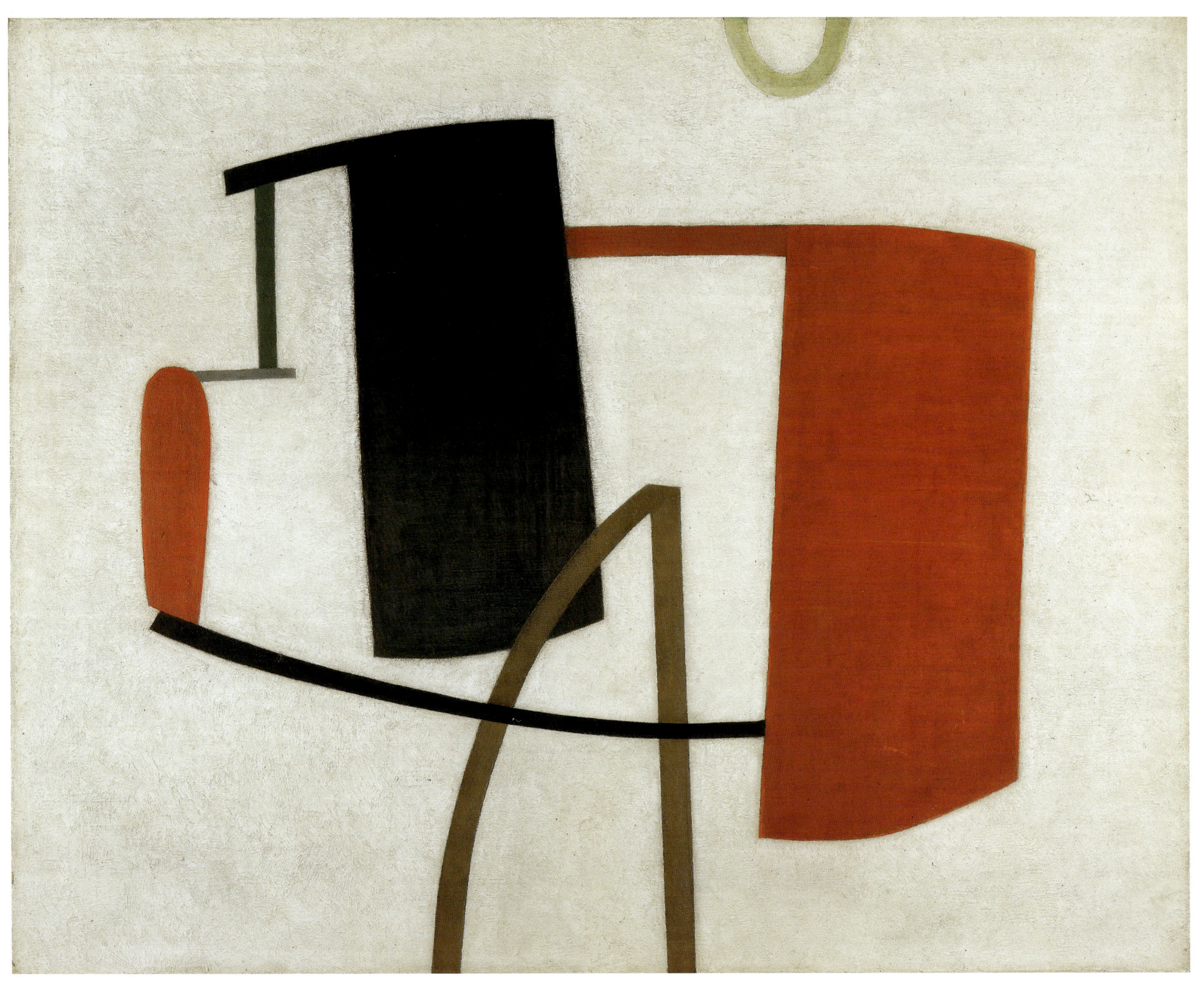

Equilibrium, 1933
Oil on canvas
60 x 73 cm
IVAM, Instituto Valenciano de Arte Moderno, Valencia
Generalitat Valenciana

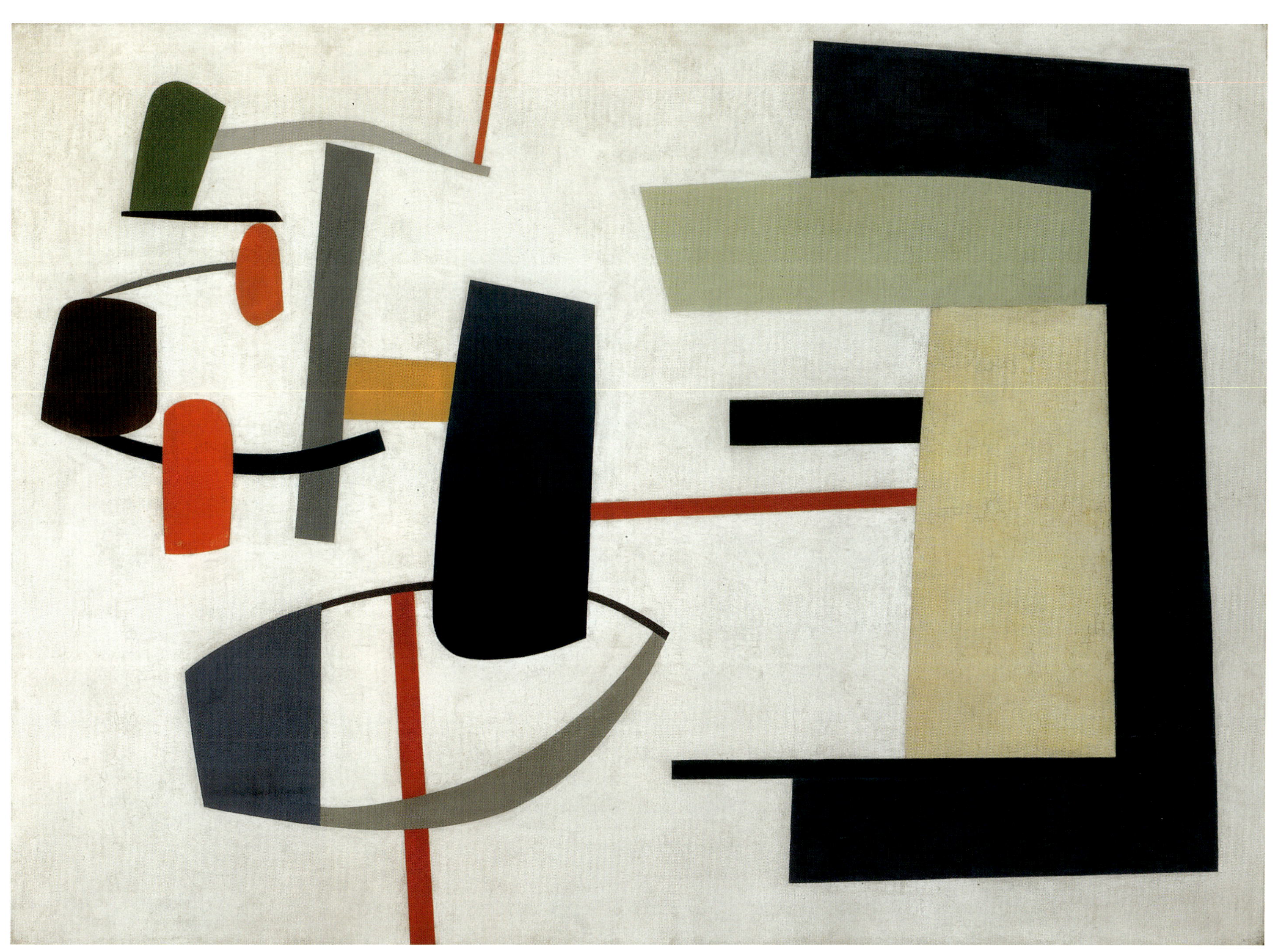

Equilibrium, 1933–34
Oil on canvas
97.4 x 131.2 cm
Peggy Guggenheim Collection, Venice
Solomon R. Guggenheim Foundation, New-York

3

MONUMENTS

"Painting definitely belongs to the world of the spirit, and
what I want from it is that it should be a plane of reality
where instincts, ideas and sensations conjoin. I unite into a
composition the brute facts of my instinct (taken in as
energy), more purely intellectual structures, and the colours
I amorously uncover on my palette."

« La peinture appartient définitivement au monde de l'esprit,
et j'attends d'elle qu'elle constitue un plan de réalité
commun pour les instincts, les idées et les sens.
Je compose les données brutes de mon instinct,
admises comme des énergies, avec des structures
plus purement intellectuelles, et avec des couleurs
amoureusement découvertes sur ma palette. »

Jean Hélion, *Carnets,* [30 ou 31 mars] 1937, p. 62.

MONUMENTS

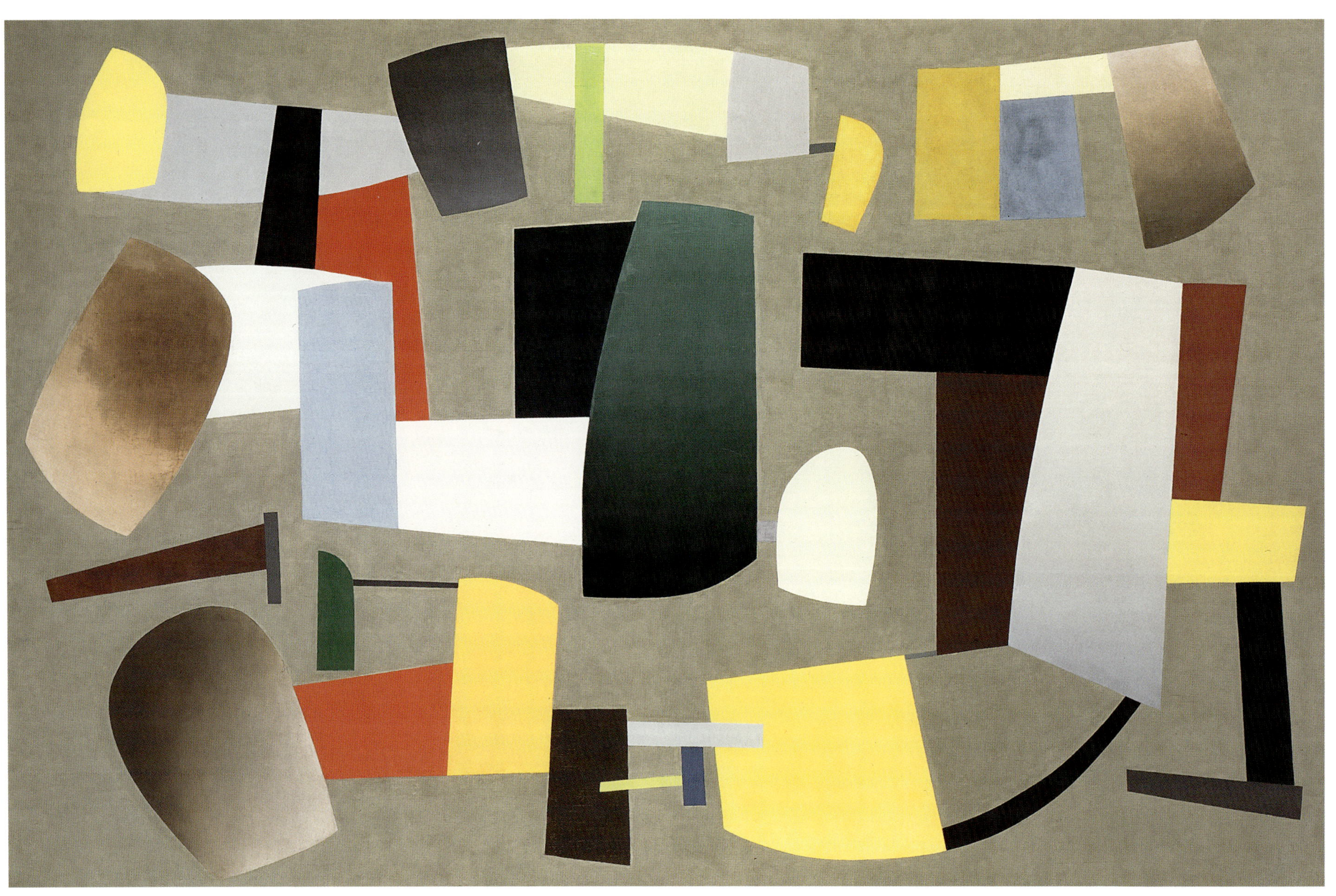

Composition in colours, 1934
Oil on canvas
128.6 x 194 cm
San Diego Museum of Art, California
Gift of Peggy Guggenheim

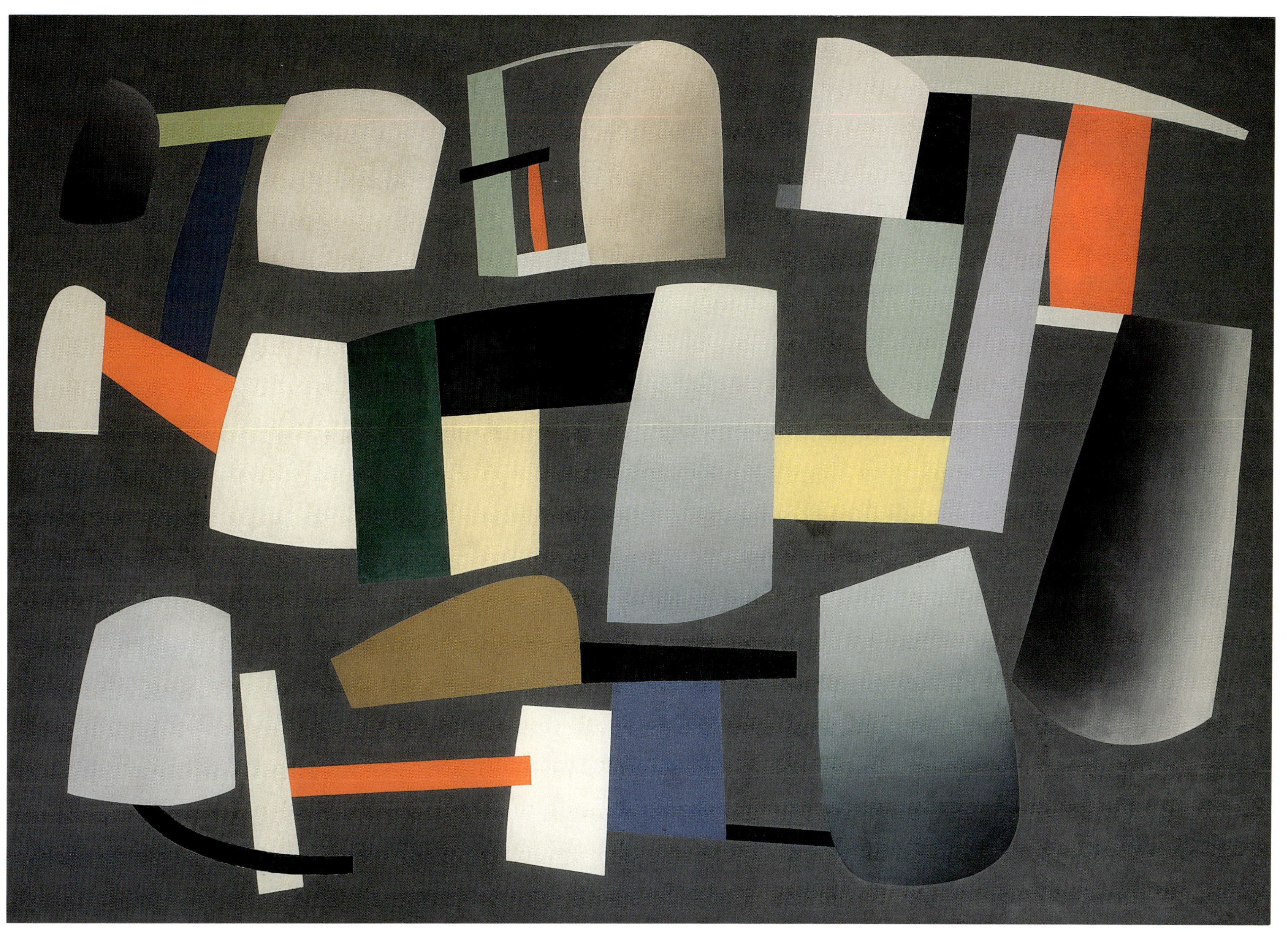

Composition, 1934
Oil on canvas
144.3 x 199.8 cm
Solomon R. Guggenheim Museum, New York

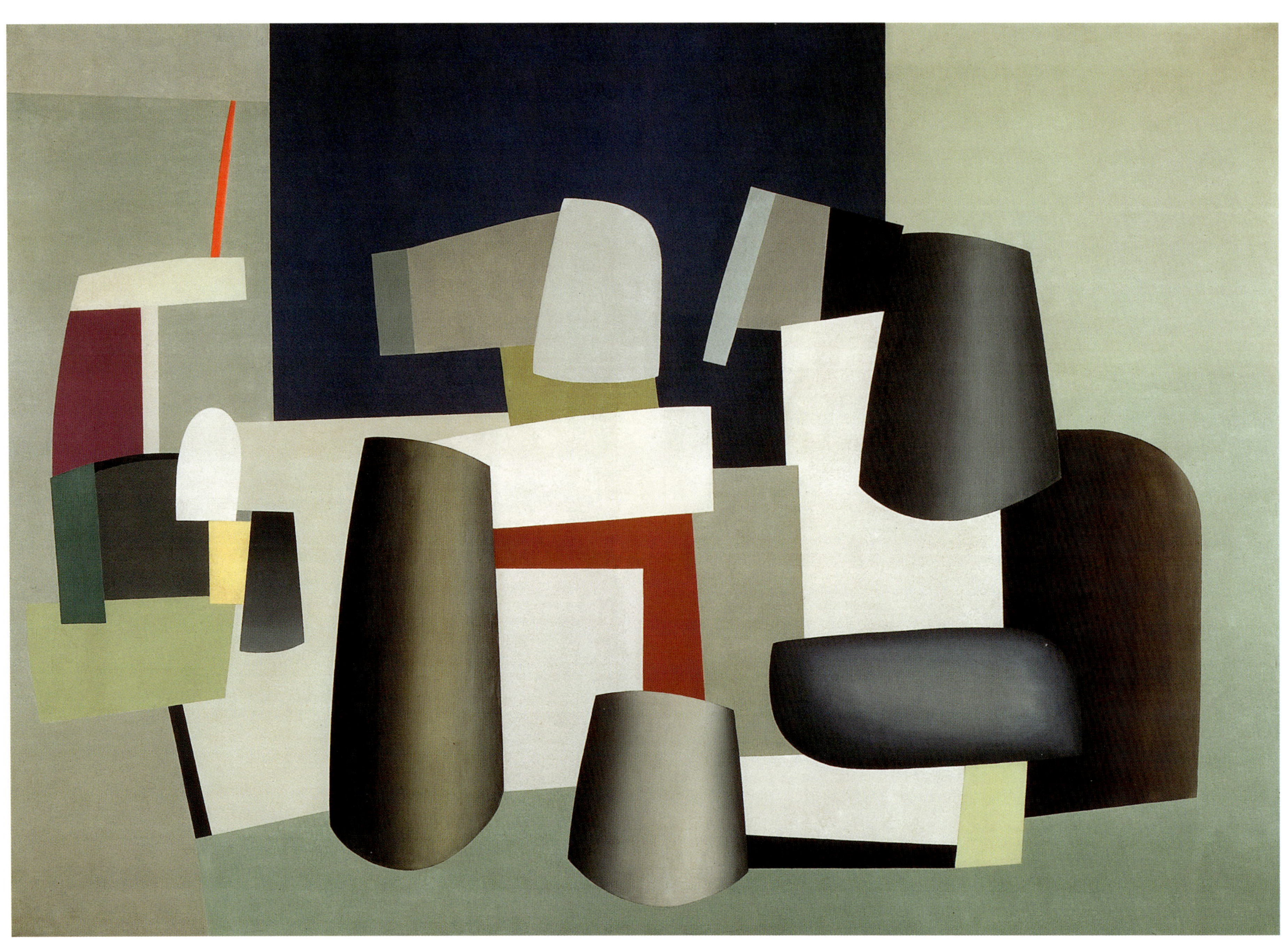

Île-de-France, 1935
Oil on canvas
145.4 x 200 cm
Tate, London

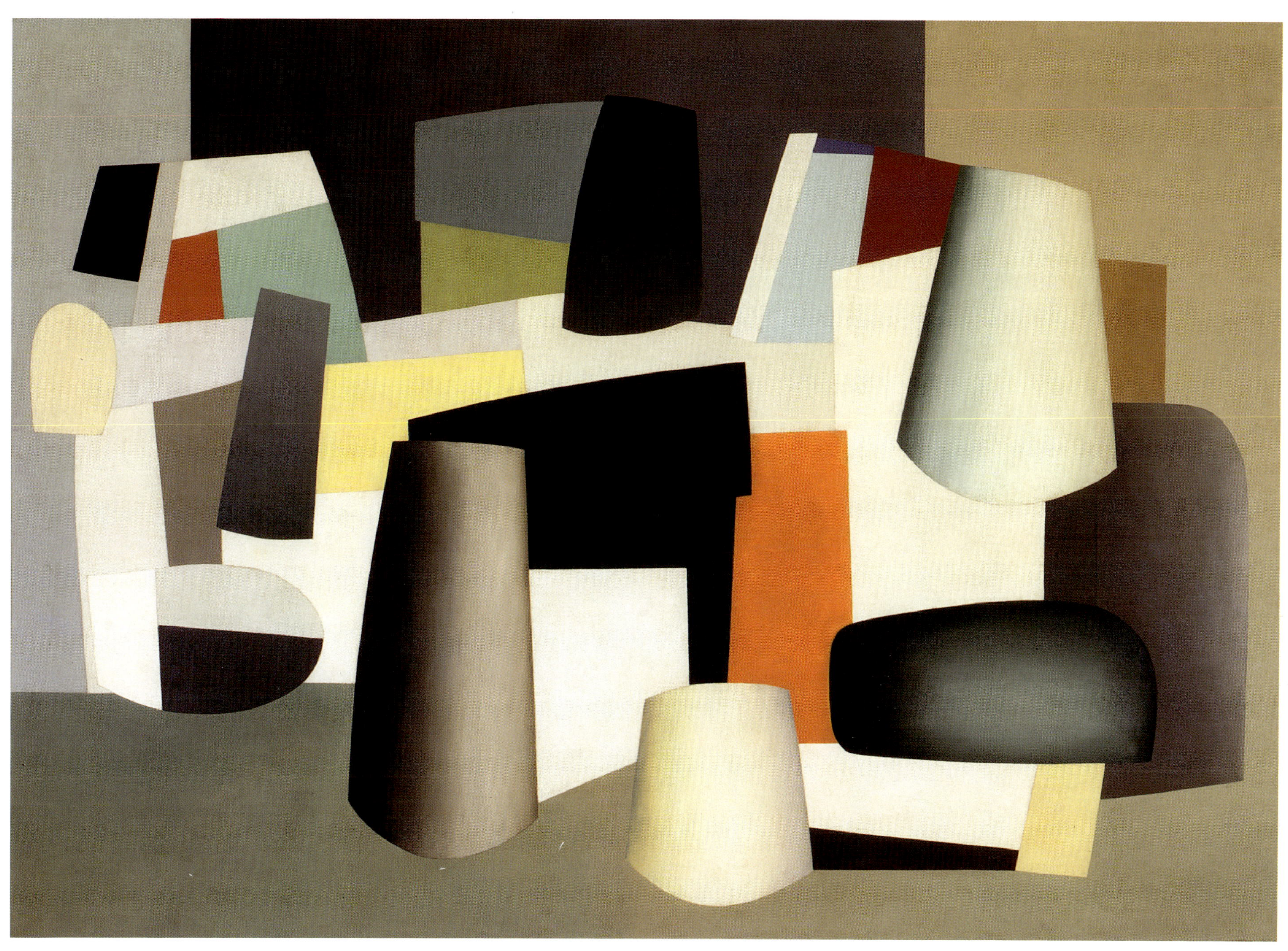

Abstraction, 1935
Oil on canvas
145 x 200 cm
Private collection

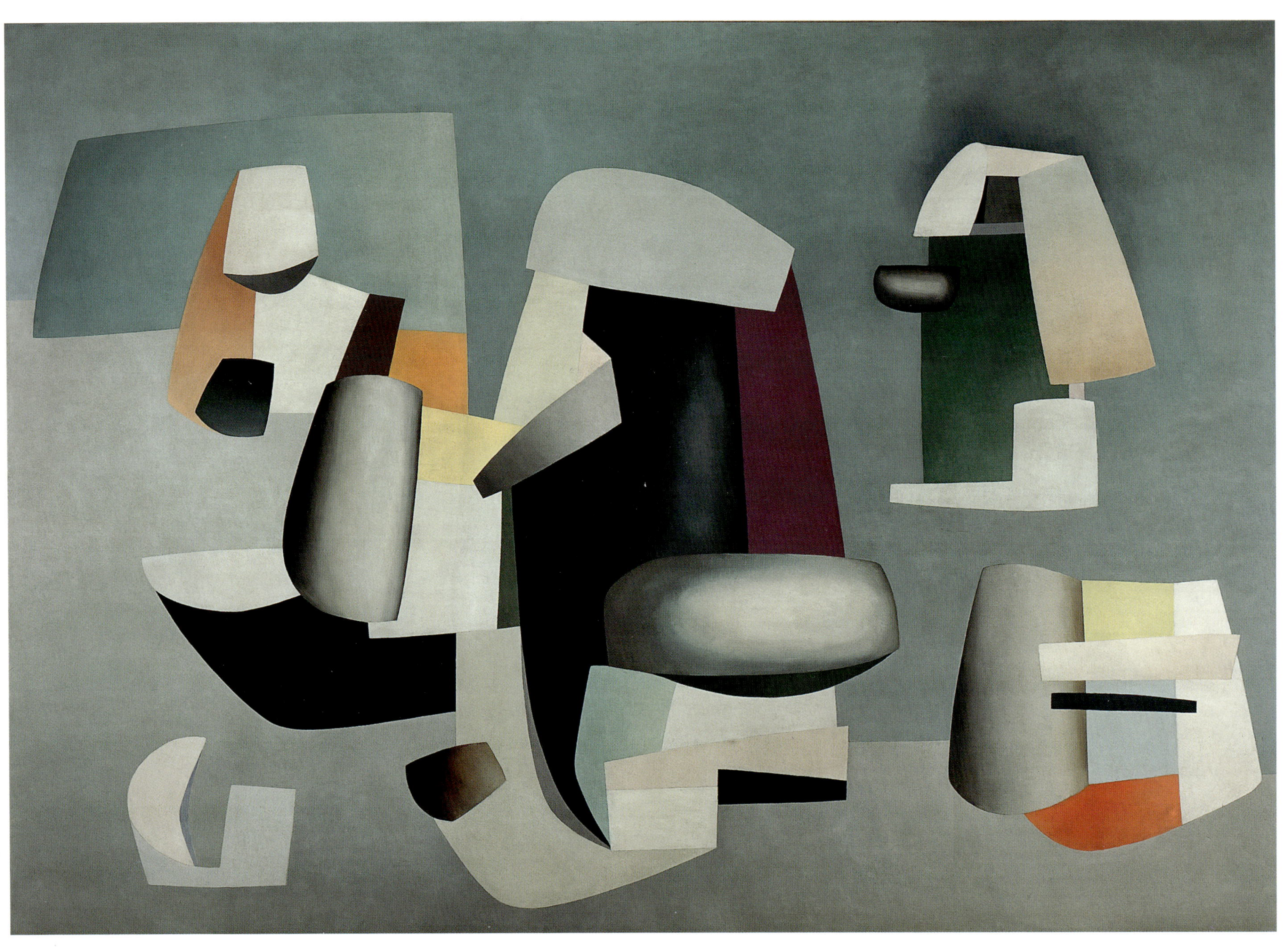

Blue spaces, 1936
Oil on canvas
200 x 276 cm
Musée national d'Histoire et d'Art du Grand-Duché
de Luxembourg, Luxembourg

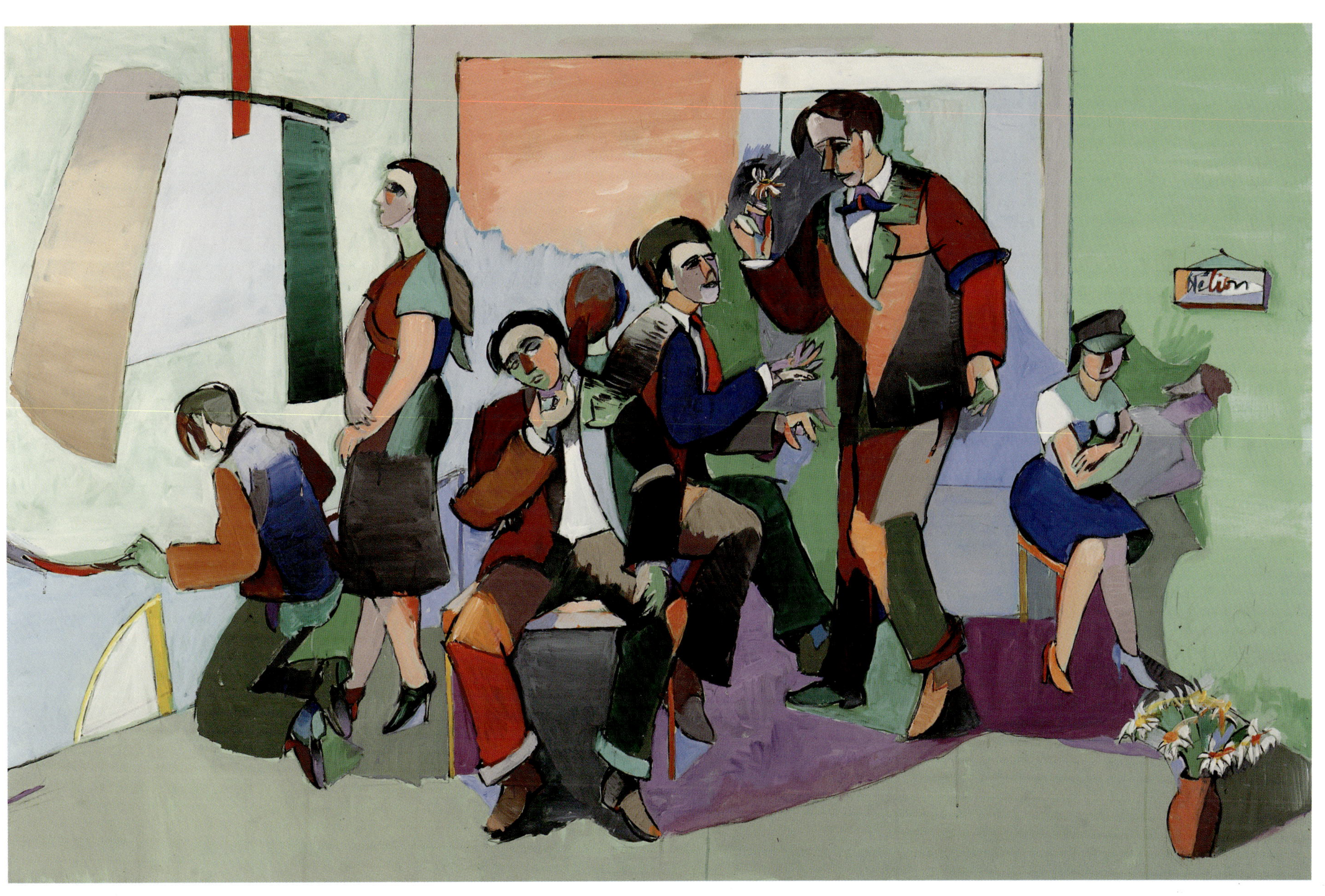

The exhibition of 1934, 1979–80
Acrylic on canvas
130 x 195 cm
Centre Pompidou, Musée national d'art moderne, Paris,
purchase 1981

4

"I was pushing my abstract signs as far as they could go. At
first I would combine them vertically to create sorts of standing
figures in conversation. In great curved monuments, they threw
themselves at cubes and triangles."

« Je poussais mes signes abstraits vers leur fin.
D'abord je les rassemblais verticalement pour créer
des sortes de personnages debout qui conversaient entre eux.
Dans de grands monuments courbes, ils se jetaient à la tête
des cubes et des triangles. »

Jean Hélion, *À perte de vue…*, Paris, IMEC, 1996, p. 67.

FIGURES
FIGURES

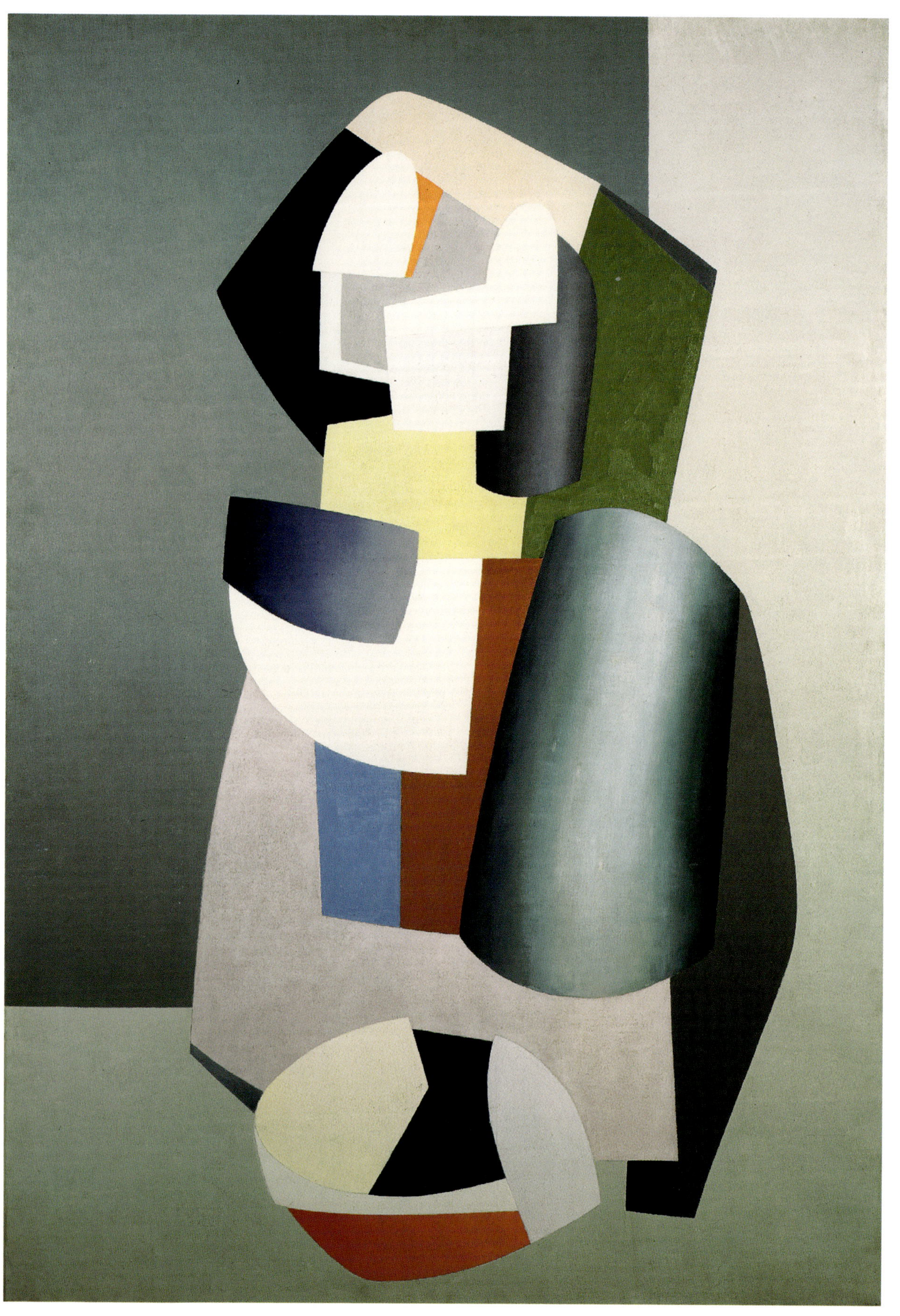

Standing figure, 1935
Oil on canvas
130 x 89 cm
Albright-Knox Art Gallery, Buffalo (New York)
Room of Contemporary Art Fund, 1944

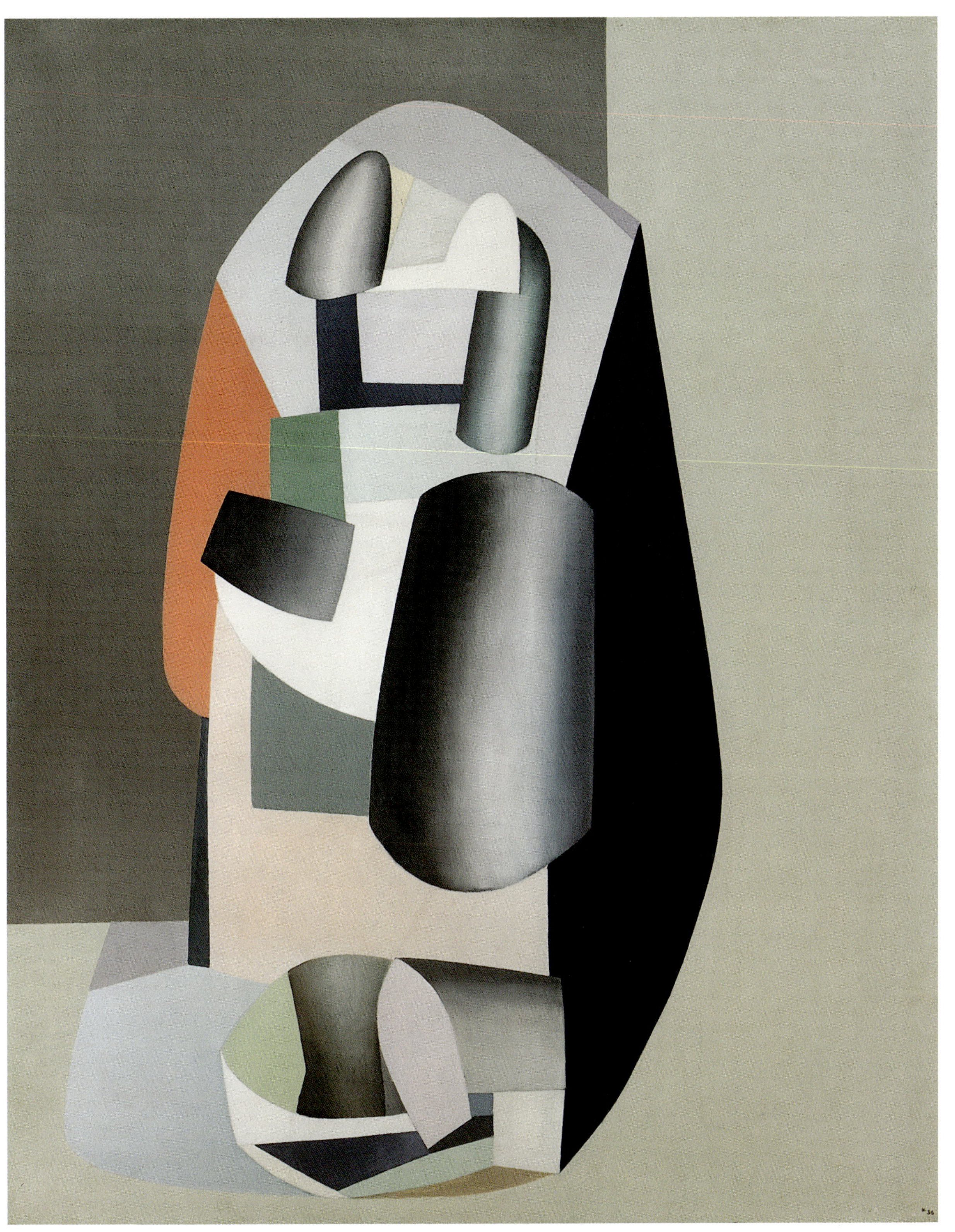

Standing figure, 1936
Oil on canvas
146.1 x 114 cm
The Metropolitan Museum of Art, New York
Gift of the Joseph Cantor Foundation, 1982

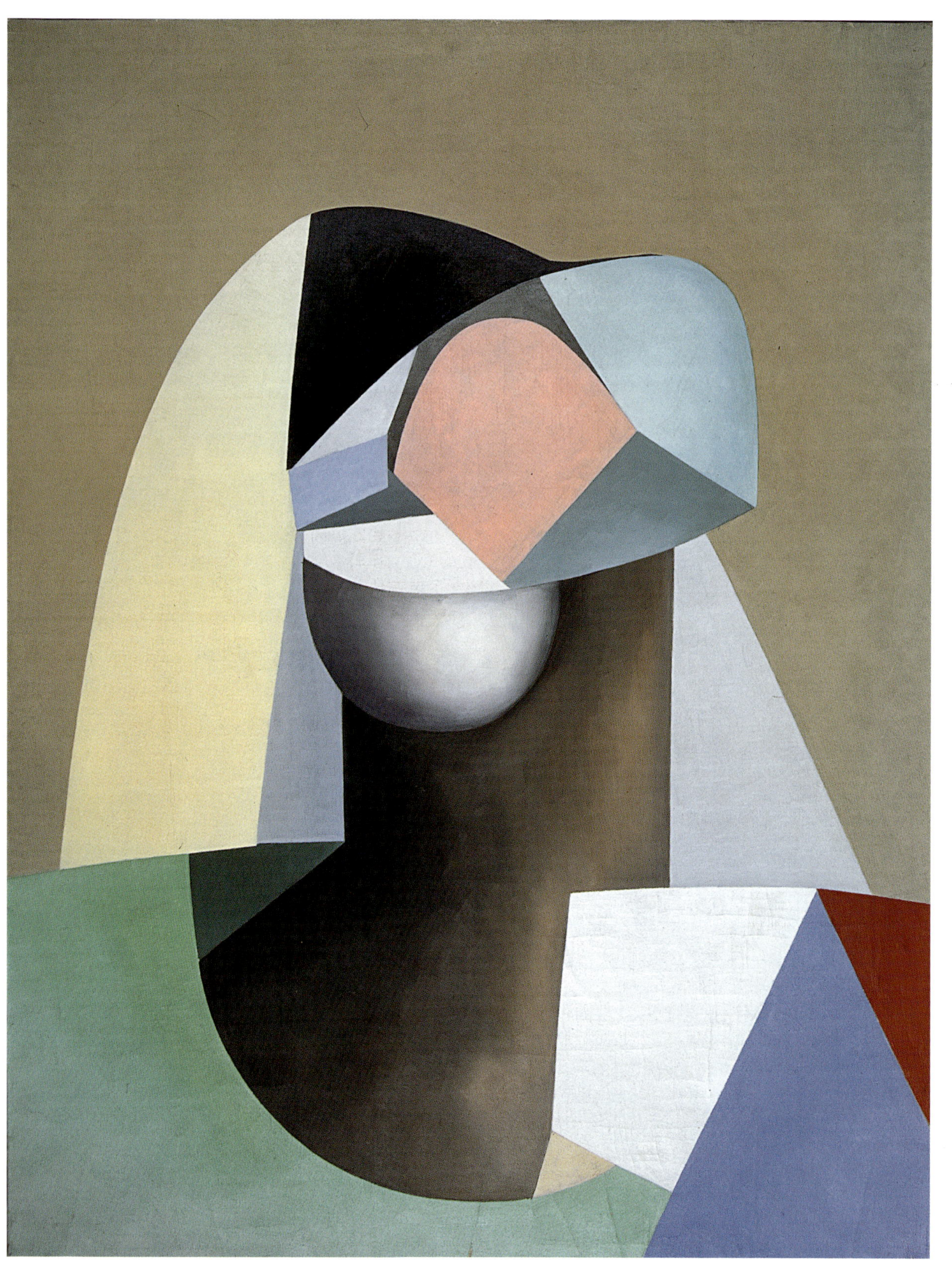

Hollow figure, 1936
Oil on canvas
112 x 84 cm
Private collection

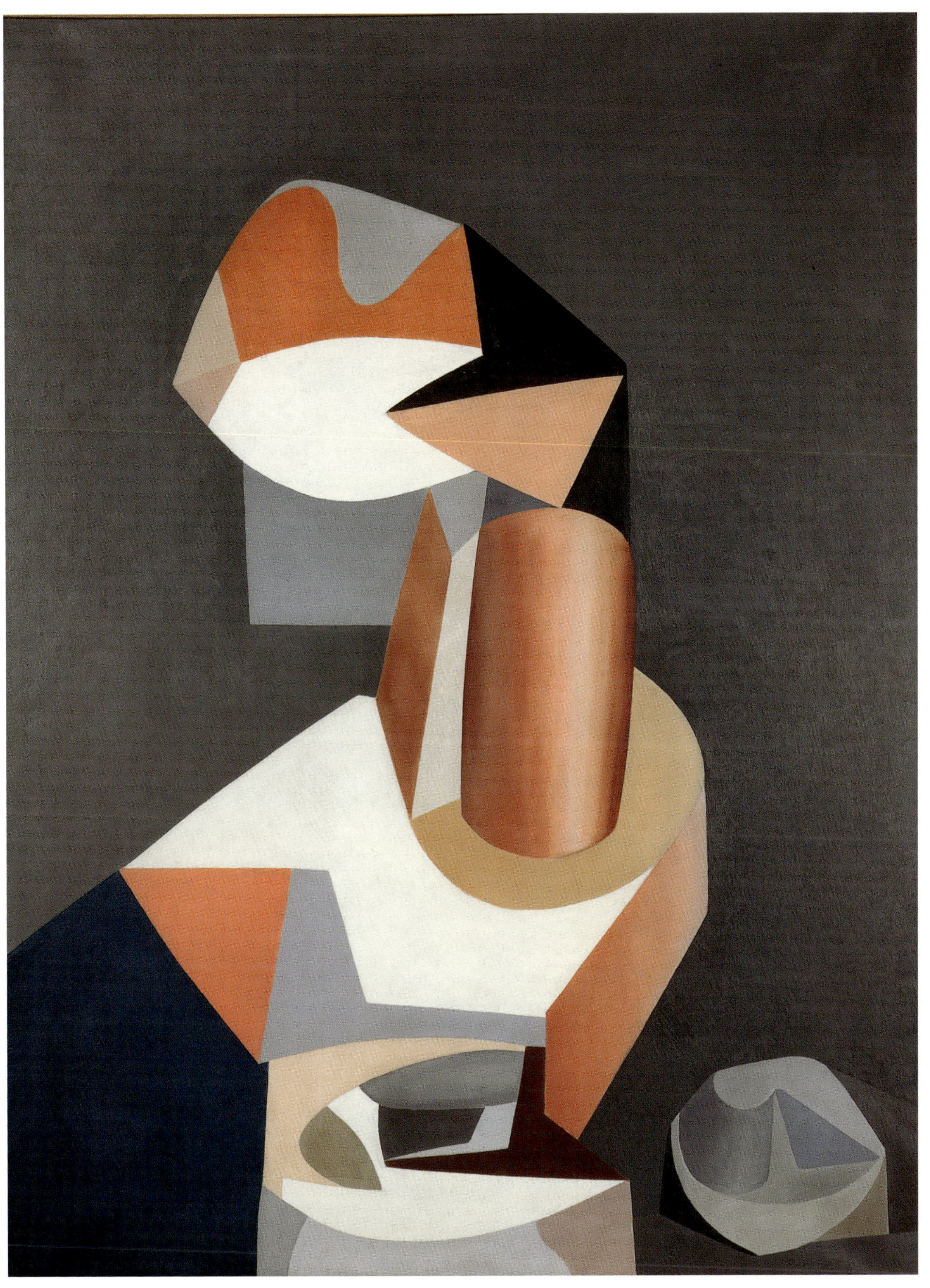

Pink figure, 1937
Oil on canvas
133 x 97 cm
Centre Pompidou, Musée national d'art moderne, Paris,
purchase 1963

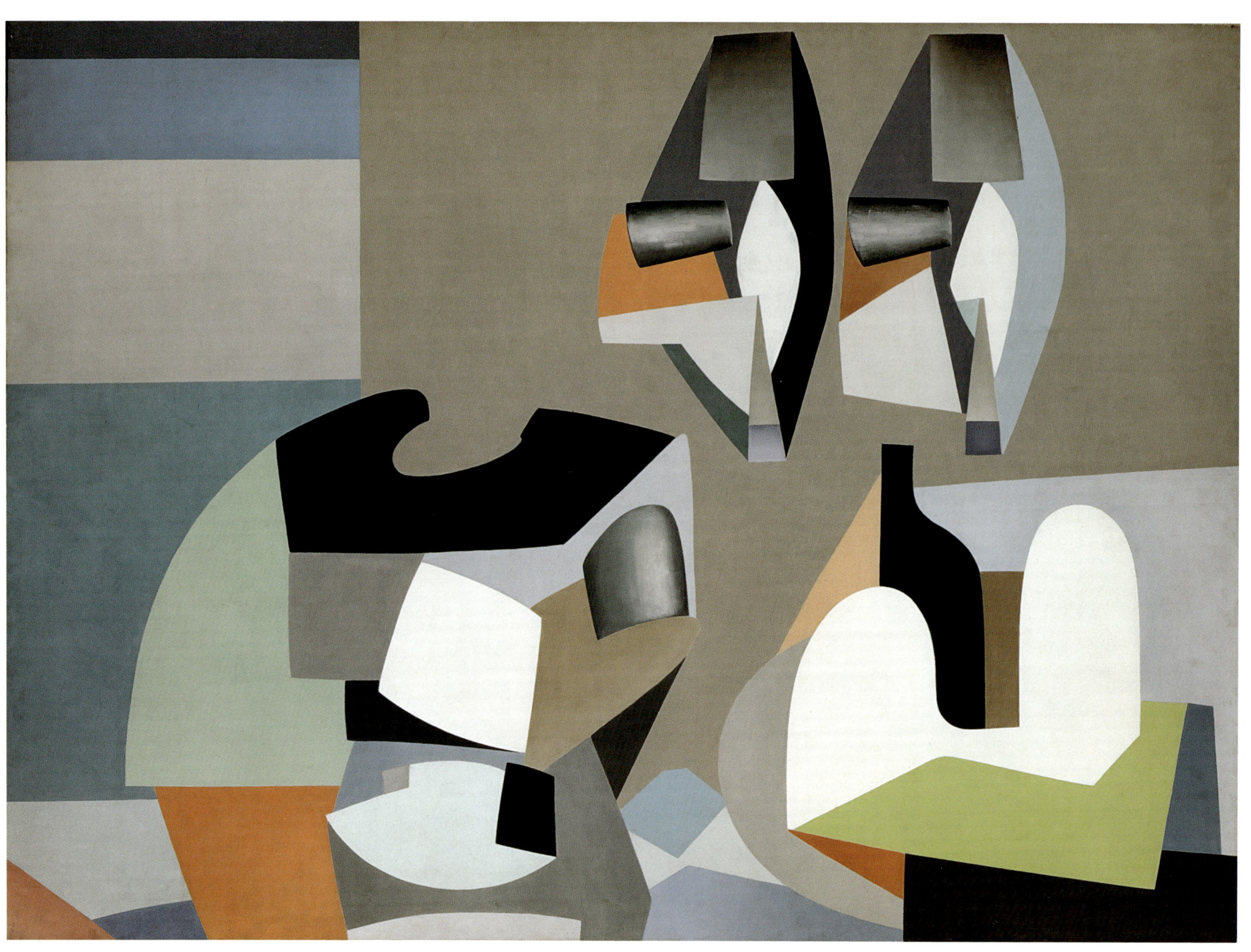

Twin figures, 1938
Oil on canvas
132.1 x 175.3 cm
The Art Institute of Chicago
Gift of Peggy Guggenheim, 1975

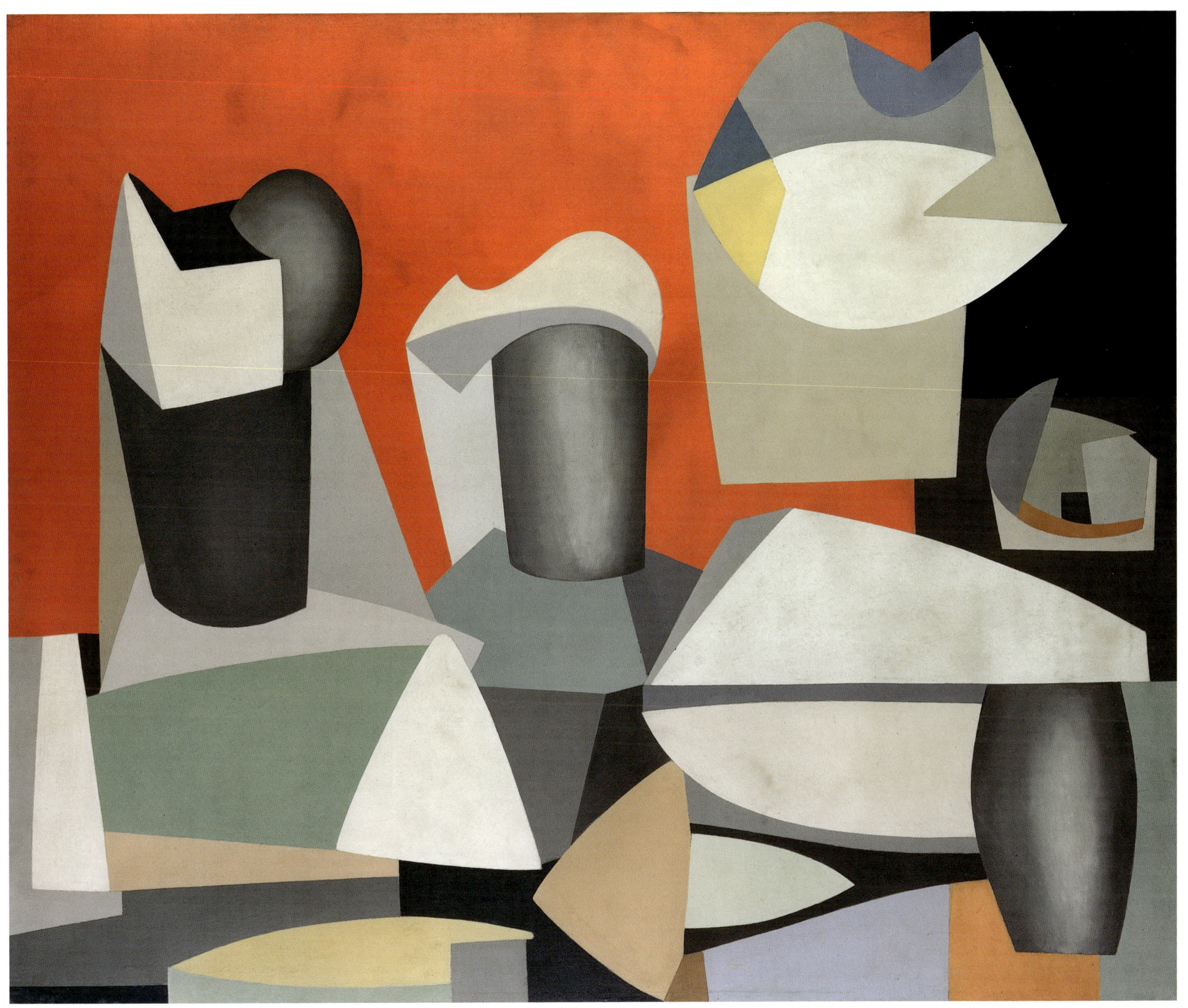

Three figures, 1938
Oil on canvas
112 x 152 cm
Private collection, Paris

DO NOT ...
DÉFENSE D'

Défense d', 1943
Oil on canvas
101.8 x 81 cm
Collection of Daniel Malingue

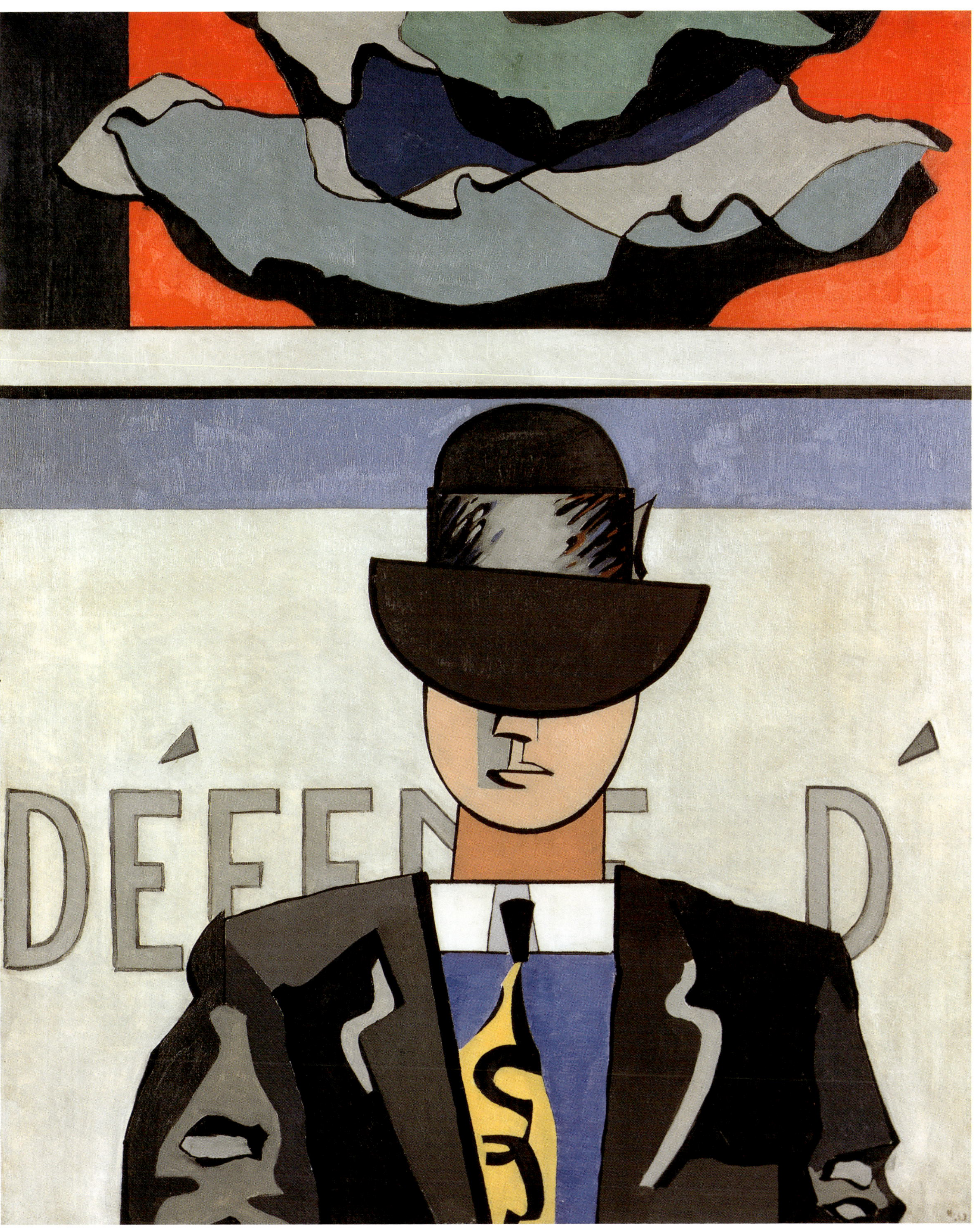

DÉFEN
D

5

"*Accident.* An accident is a self-contained event, as complete
as a person, taking its place in the crowd of other such. Use
the accidents of objects in the same way."

« *Accident.* L'accident est un événement en soi,
complet comme un individu, et qui prend une place
dans la foule des autres. Utiliser les accidents d'objets
de la même façon. »

Jean Hélion, *Carnets,* 27 juin 1942, p. 75.

TUMBLES
CHUTES

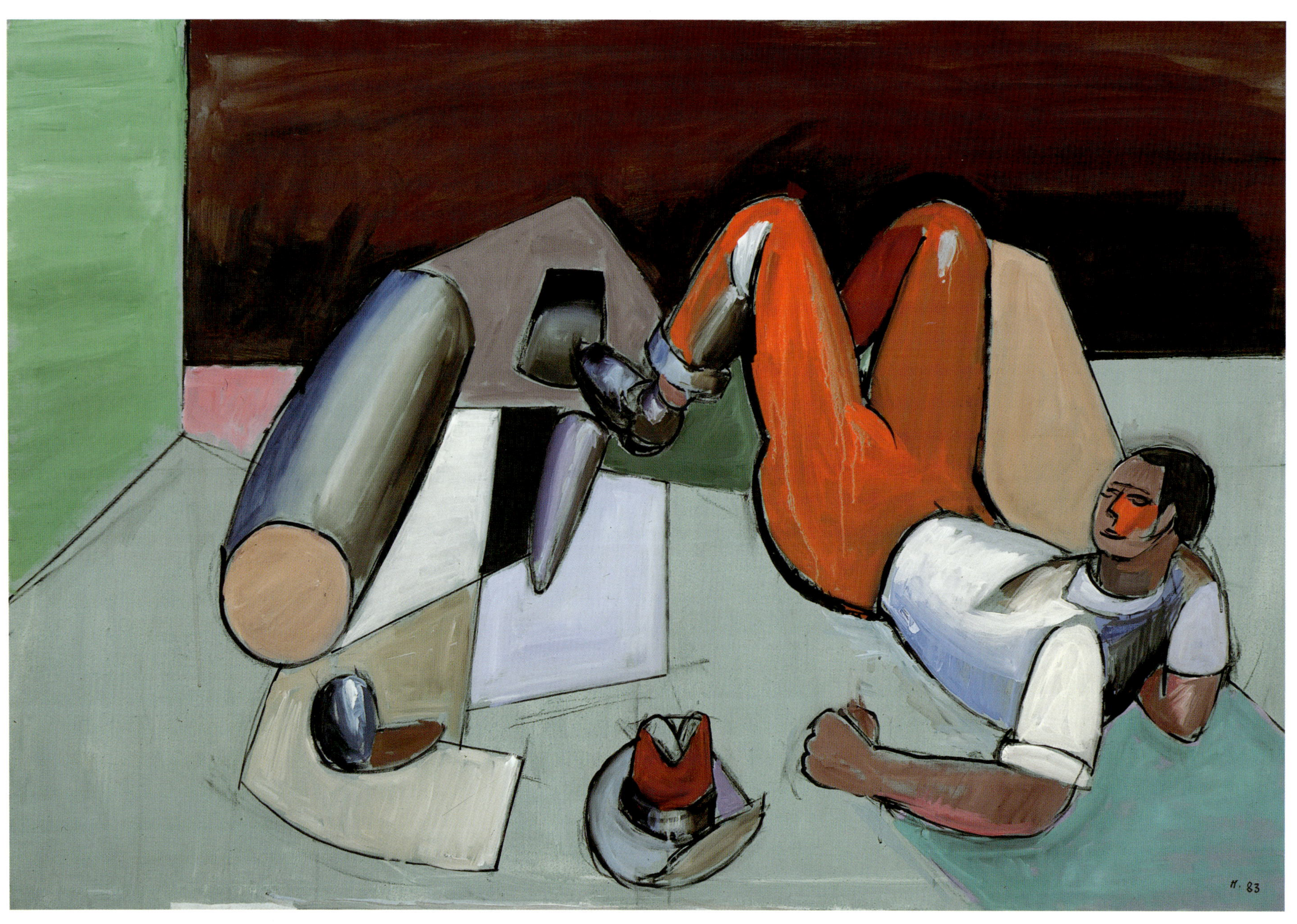

Upturns, 1983
Acrylic on canvas
114 x 162 cm
BNP/PARIBAS

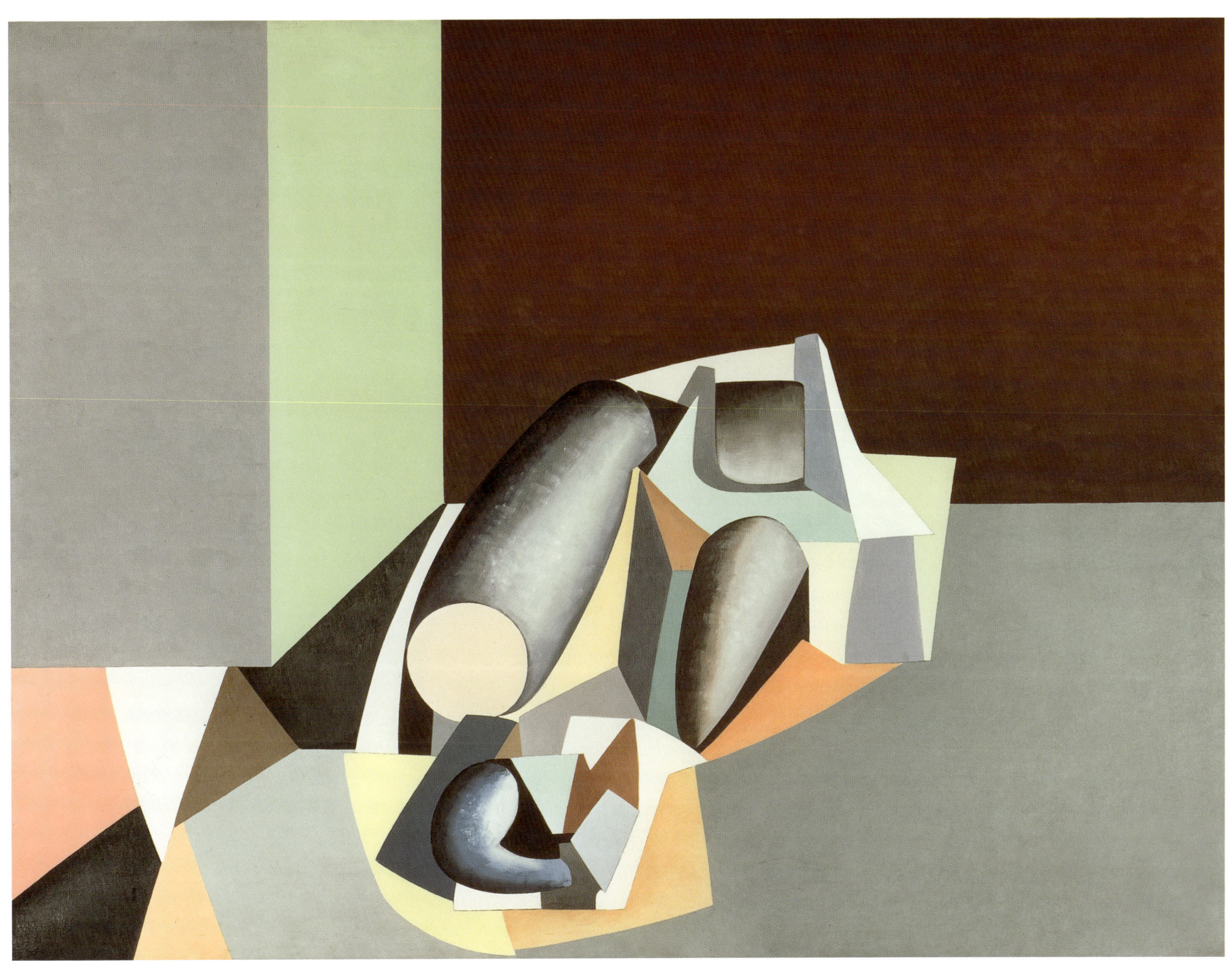

Fallen figure, 1939
Oil on canvas
126.2 x 164.3 cm
Centre Pompidou, Musée national d'Art moderne, Paris,
purchase 1987

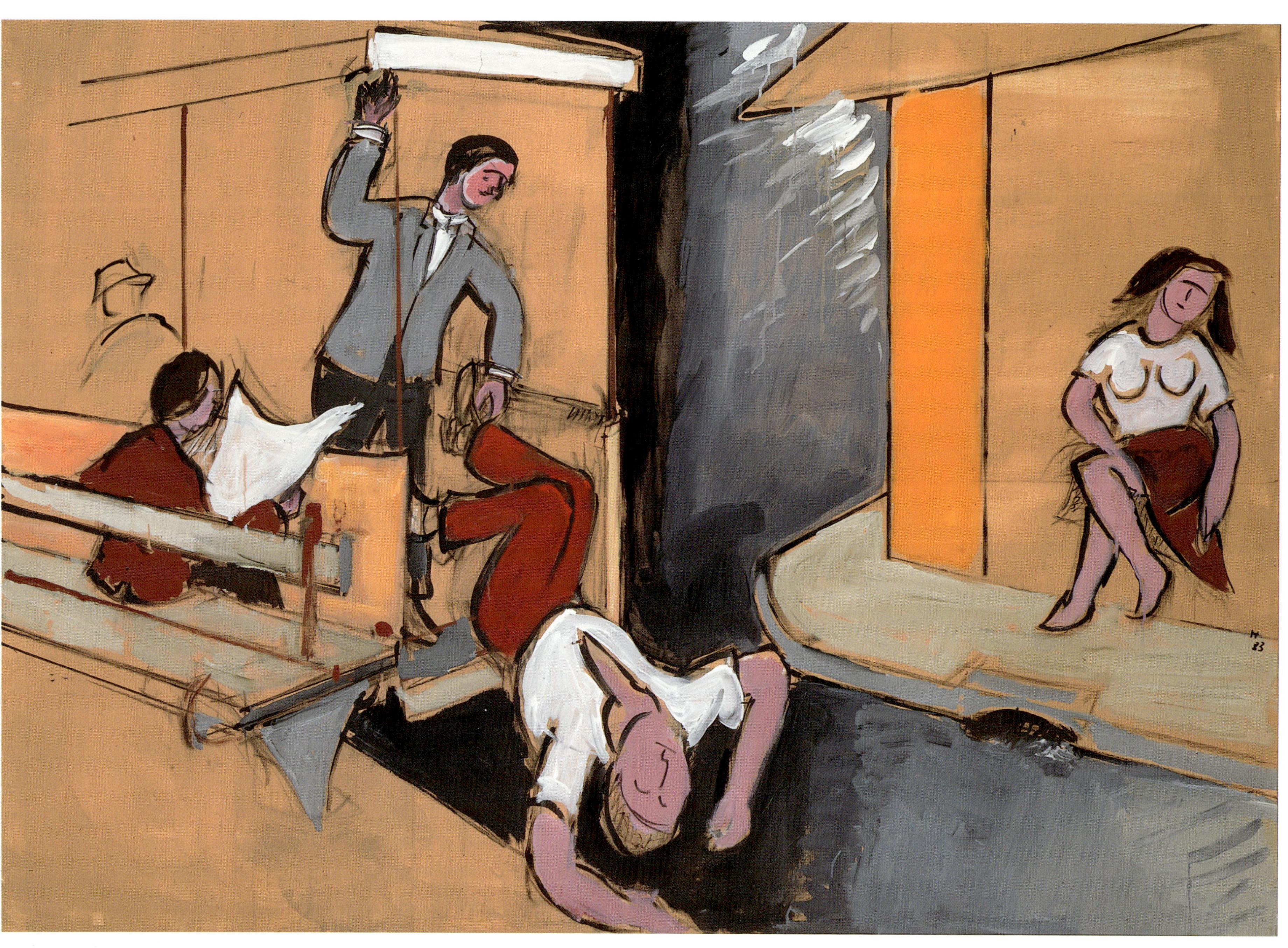

Last tumble, 1983
Acrylique on canvas
145 x 200 cm
Collection of Jacqueline Hélion

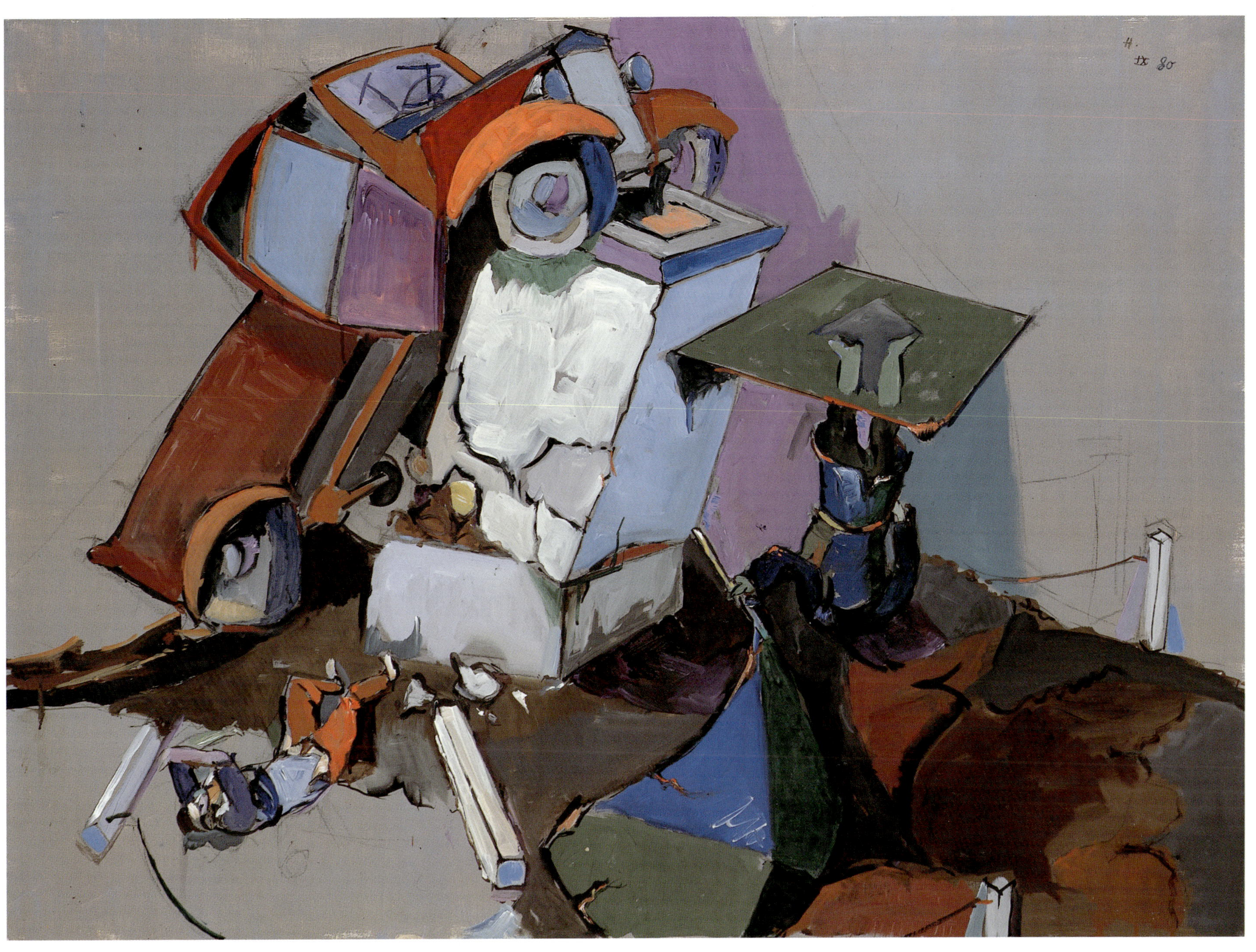

The accident, 1979
Acrylic on canvas
97 x 130 cm
Collection of Nicolas Hélion

THE STUDIO
L'ATELIER

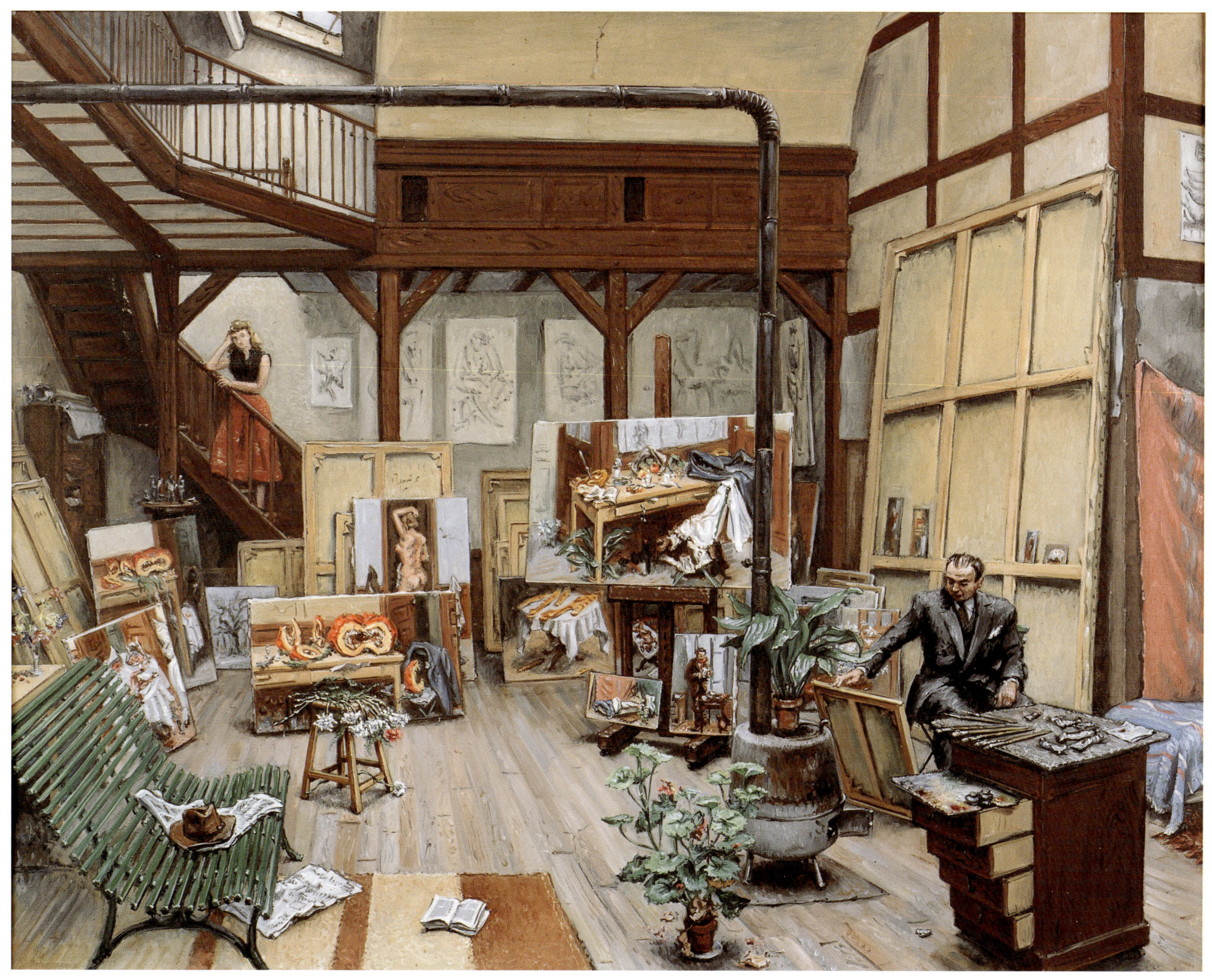

The studio, 1953
Oil on canvas
81 x 100 cm
Private collection

6

THE PAINTER ...

LE PEINTRE...

"Nudes. Flesh. Temple of the flesh. The limbs contain the
tender parts – breasts, sex. The flesh, hot and firm."

« Nus. Chair. Temple de chair.
Les membres contiennent les parties tendres :
seins, sexe. La chair, chaude et ferme. »

Jean Hélion, *Carnets,* 2 octobre 1948, p. 151.

AND HIS MODEL
ET SON MODÈLE

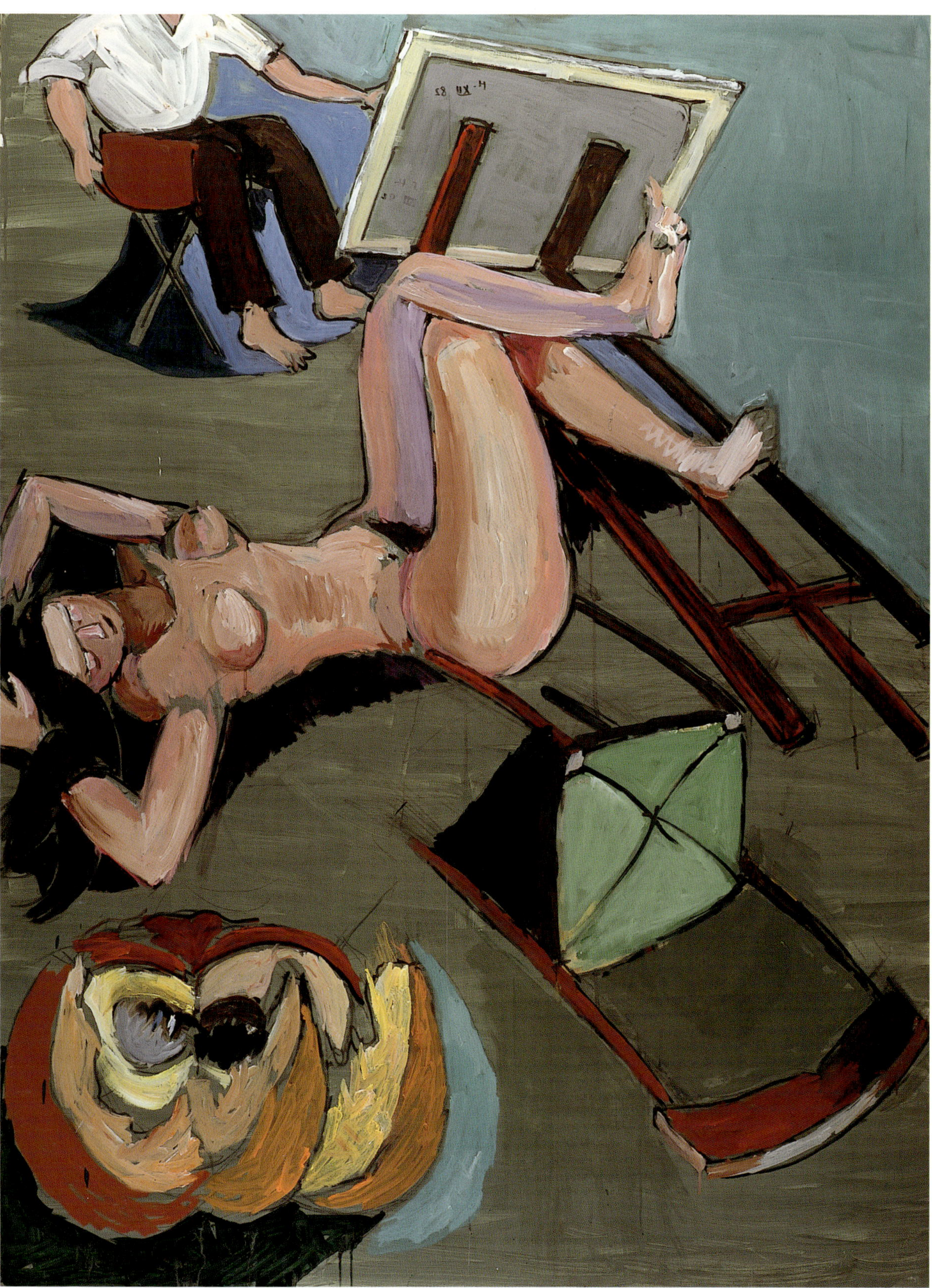

The moment after, 1982
Acrylic on canvas
200 x 145 cm
Collection of David Hélion and Jean-Jacques Bichier

The painter trampled by his model, 1983
Acrylic on canvas
200 x 145 cm
Fonds régional d'Art contemporain de Picardie

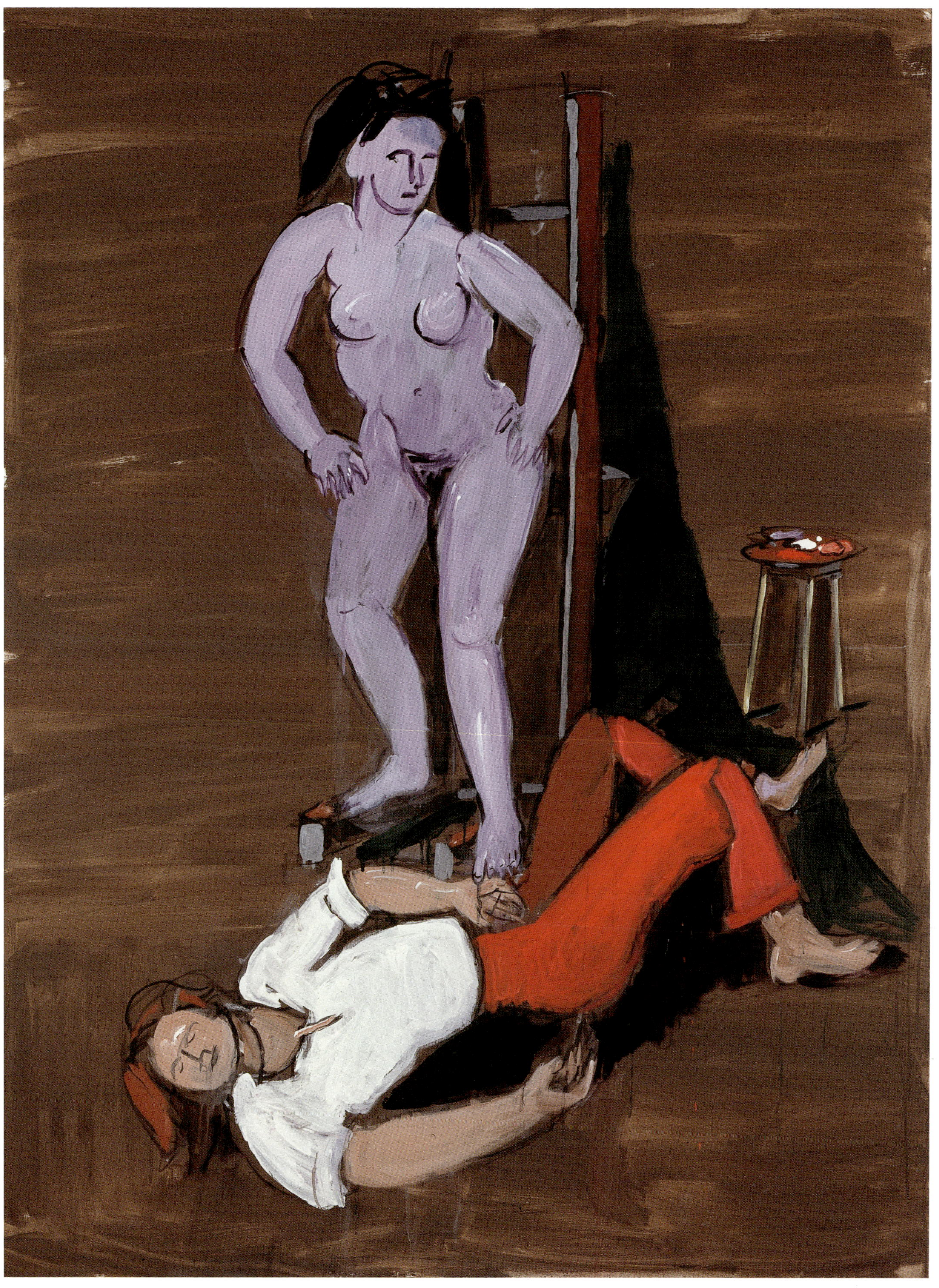

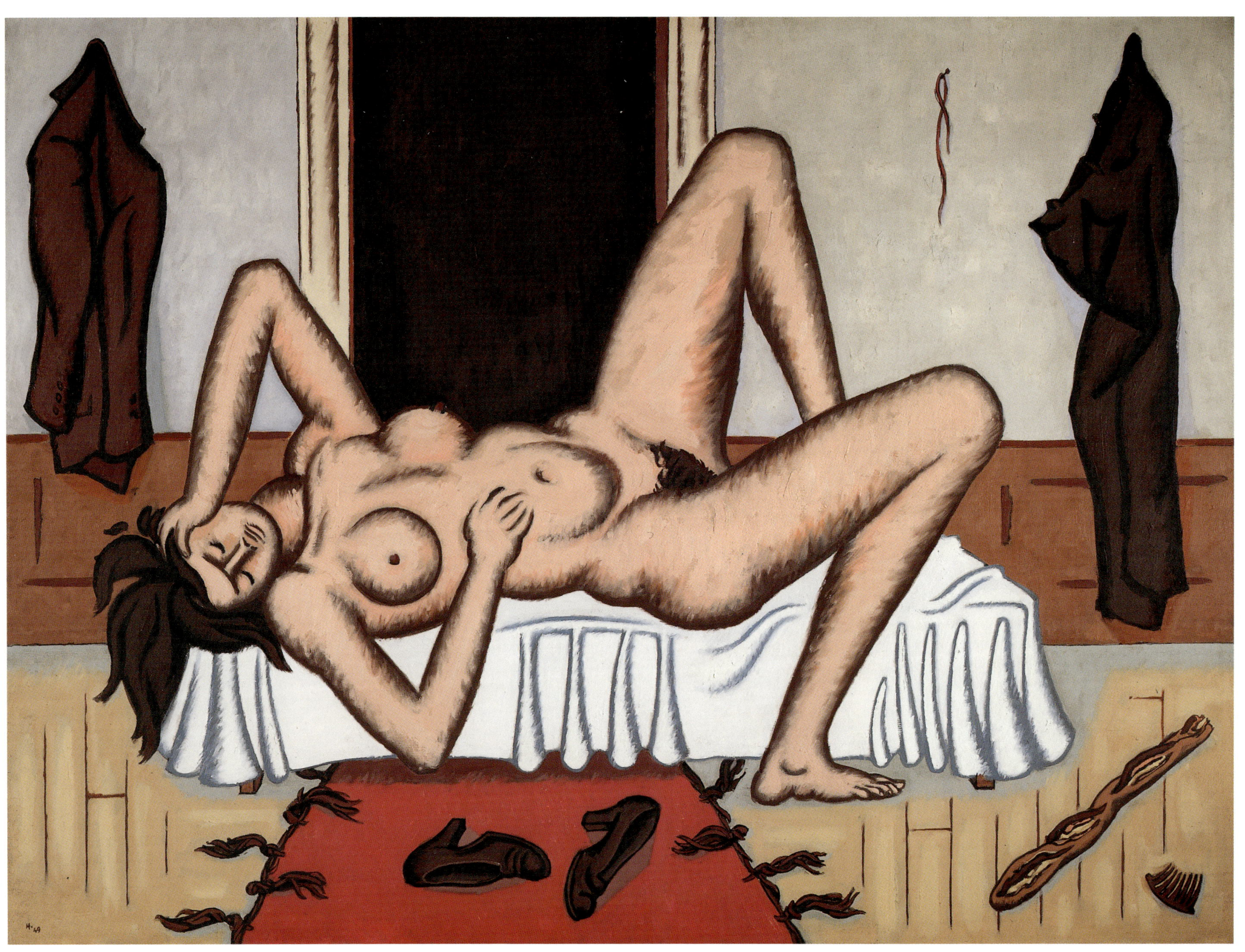

Star-nude with trousers, 1949
Oil on canvas
89 x 116 cm
Private collection

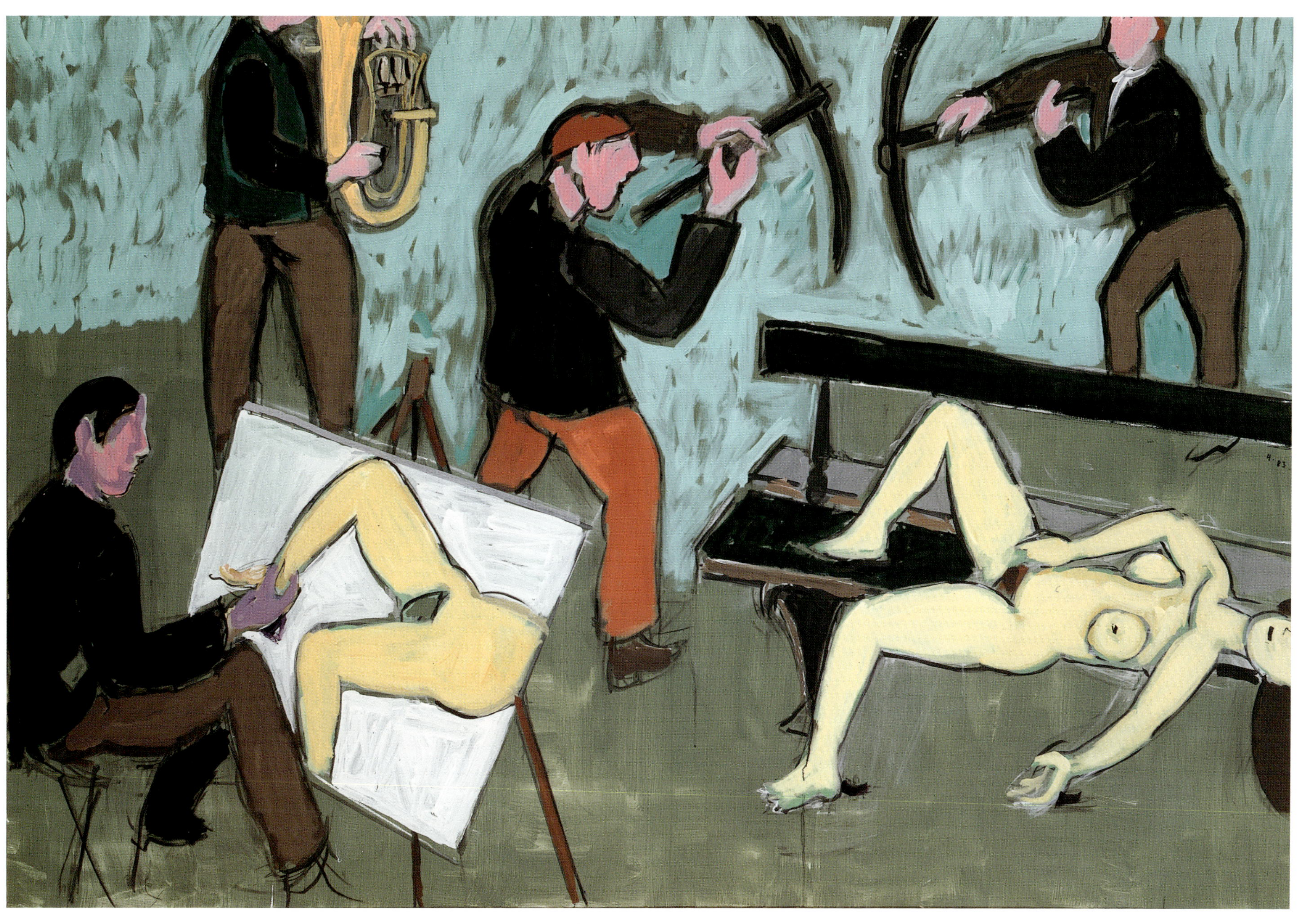

Trumpet for a painter, 1983
Acrylic on canvas
175 x 250 cm
Collection of Louis Hélion Blair, United States

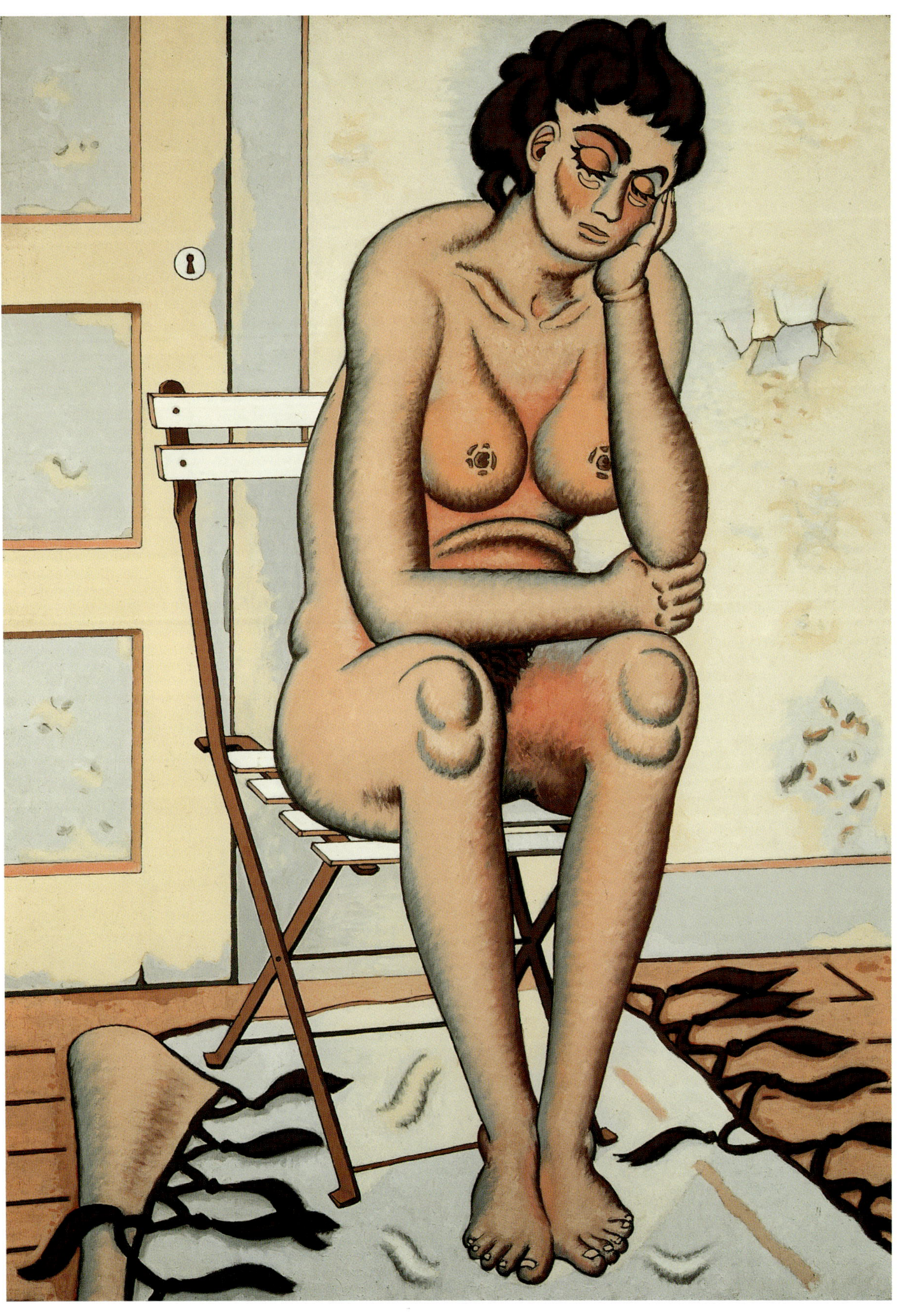

Nude leaning on elbow, 1948–49
Oil on canvas
116 x 81 cm
Collection of David Hélion

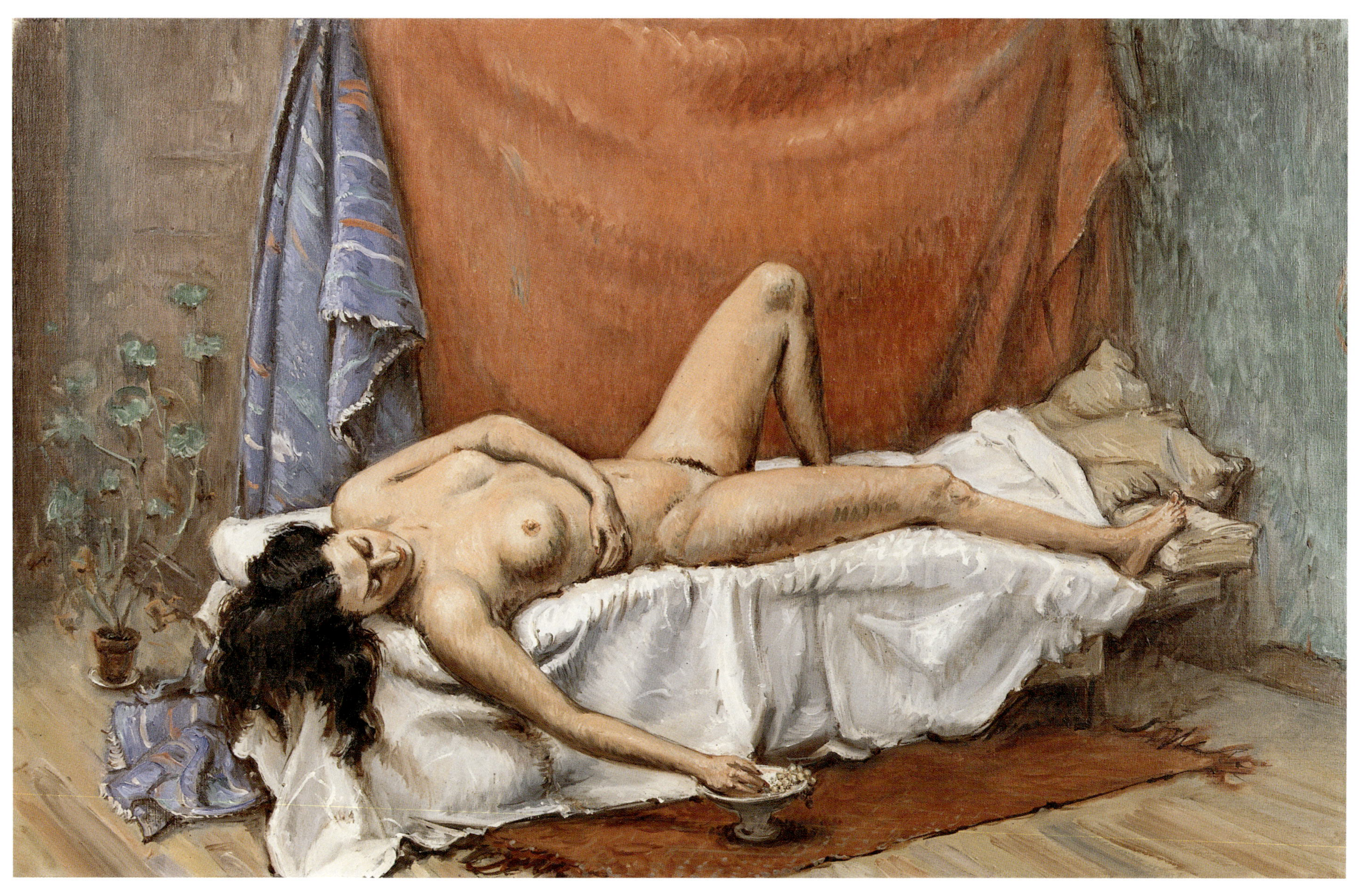

Odalisque, 1953
Oil on canvas
60 x 92 cm
Private collection

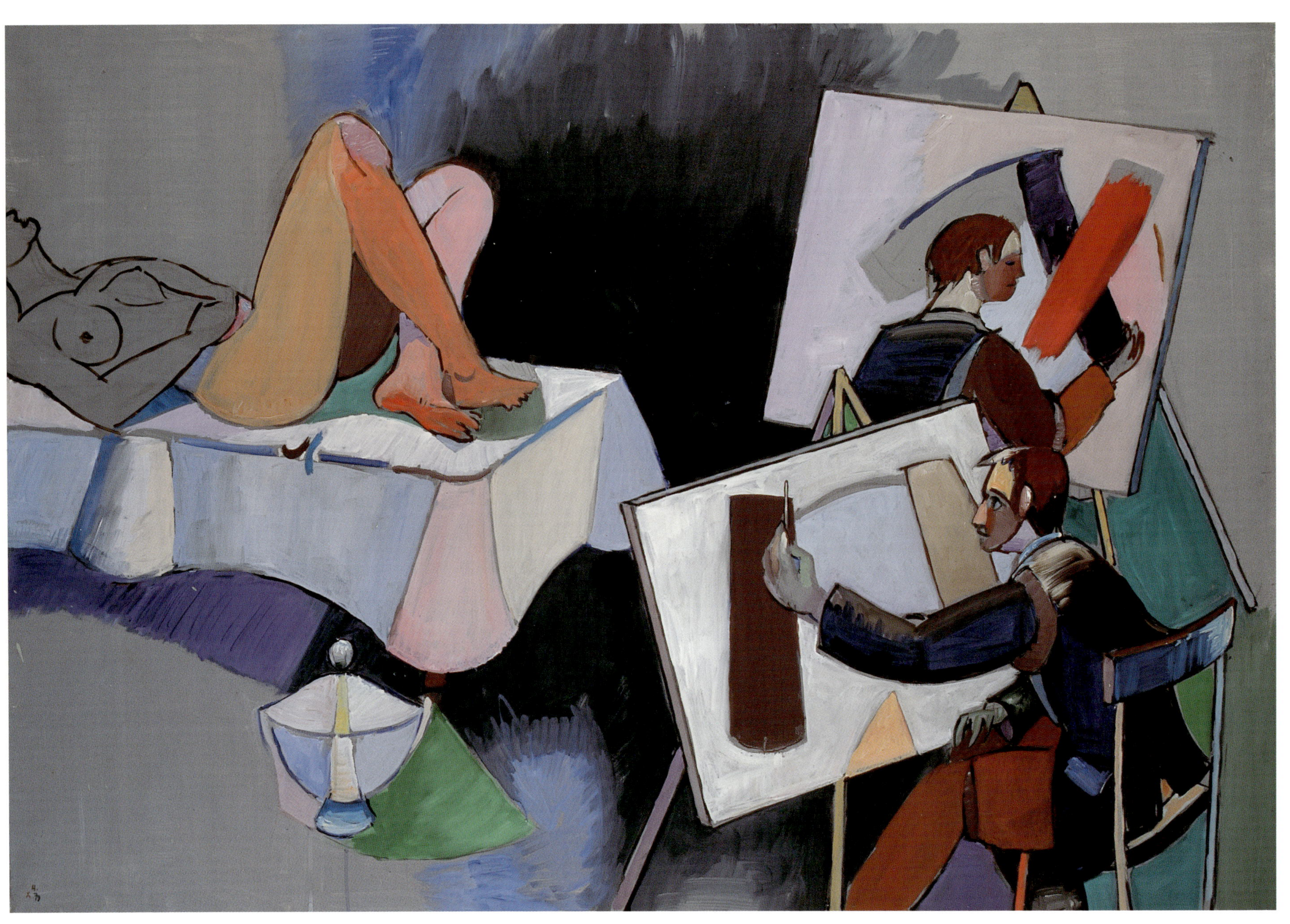

The real and the dream, 1979–81
Acrylic on canvas
114 x 162 cm
Private collection

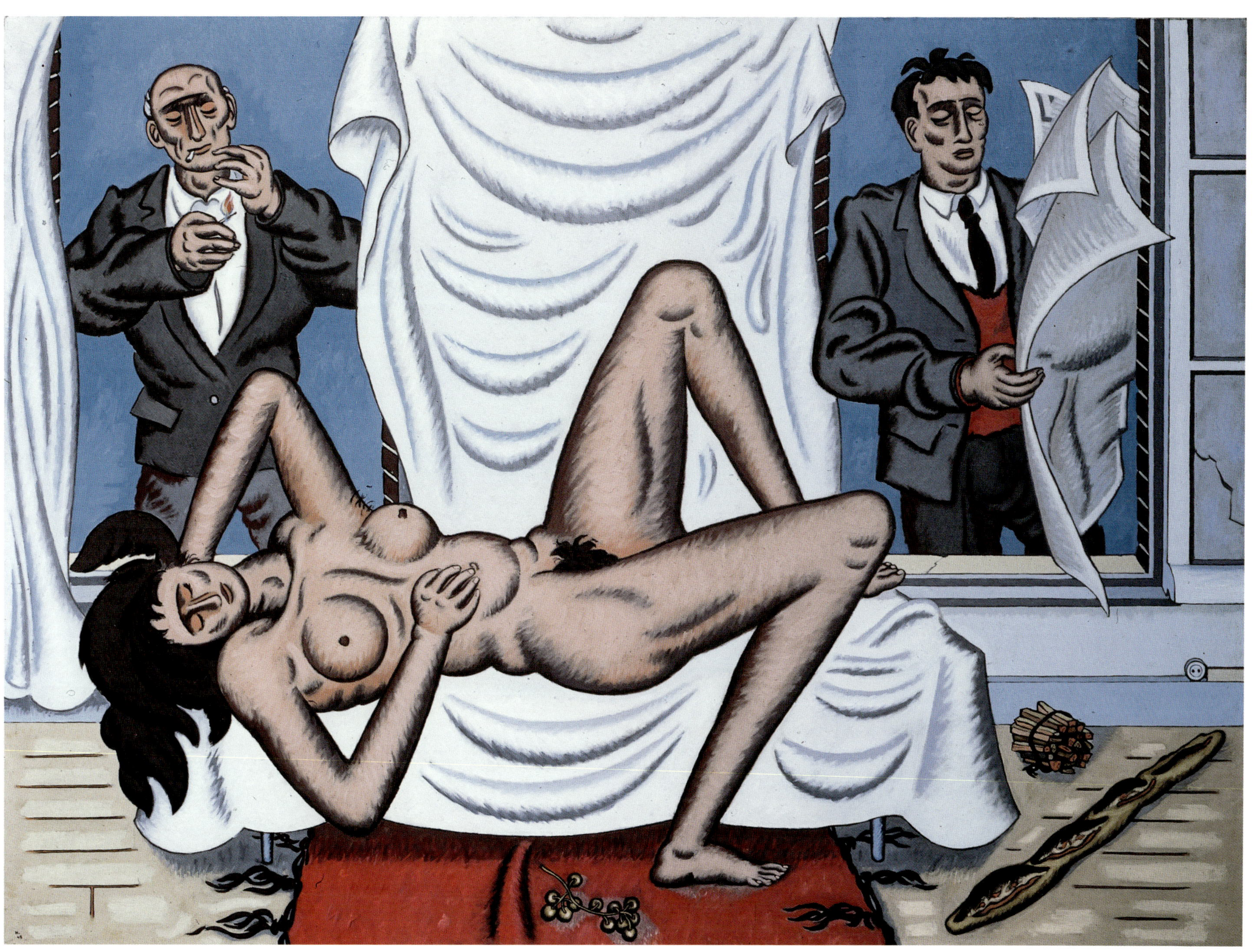

***Star-nude with smoker
and daily-reader***, 1949
Oil on canvas
155 x 200 cm
Private collection

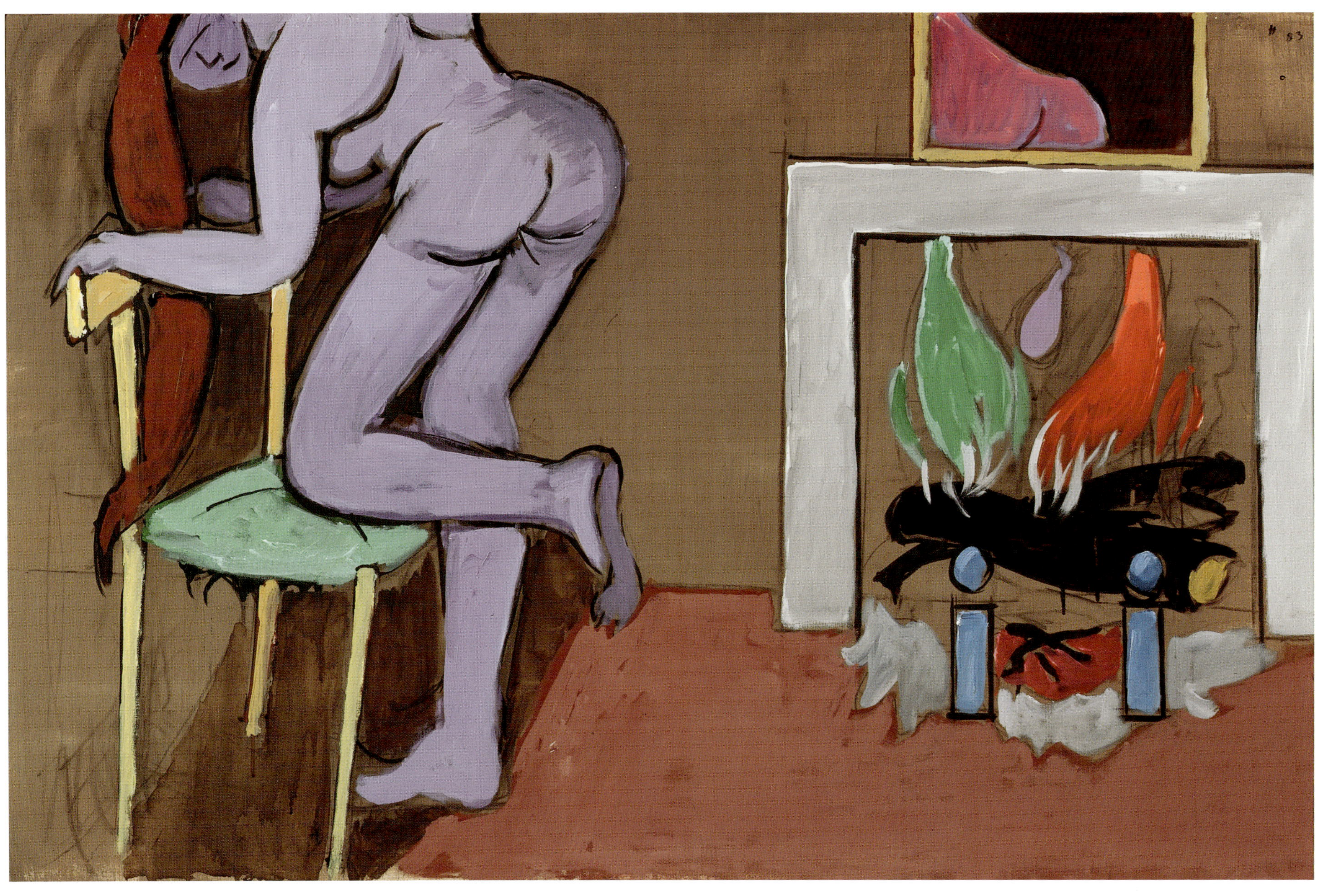

Fire with nude, 1983
Acrylic on canvas
97 x 146 cm
Centre Pompidou, Musée national d'Art moderne, Paris,
accepted in lieu of tax 1991
On deposit with the Musée des Beaux-Arts, Orléans

Back with breads, 1952
Oil on canvas
130.1 x 97 cm
Tate, London

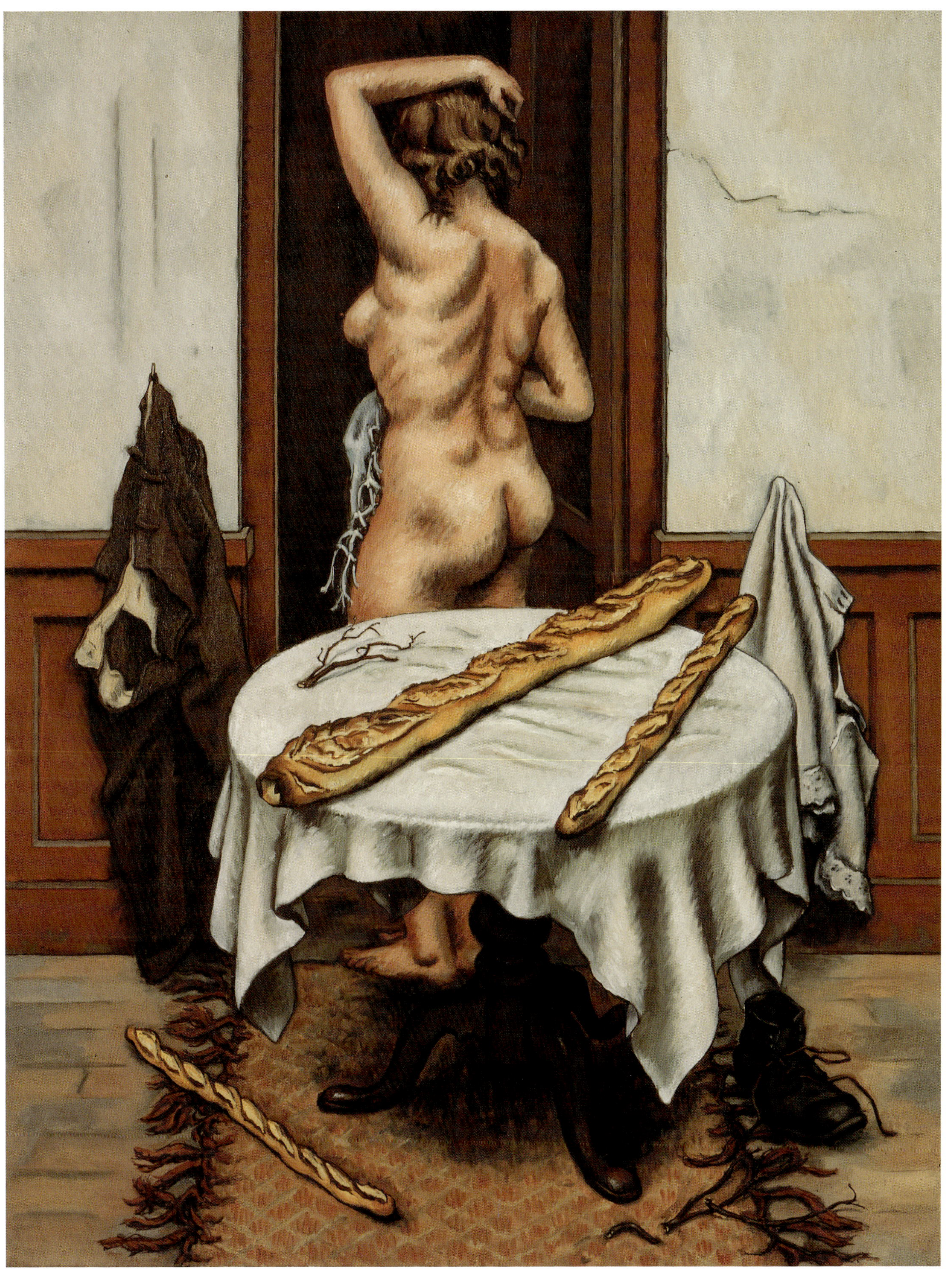

7

"An array of objects is a sentence that does not need to be
translated into language."

« Un alignement d'objets est une phrase
qui n'a pas besoin d'être traduite dans une langue. »

Jean Hélion, *Carnets,* [1re quinzaine de juillet] 1975, p. 189.

THE FLEA-MARKET
LE MARCHÉ AUX PUCES

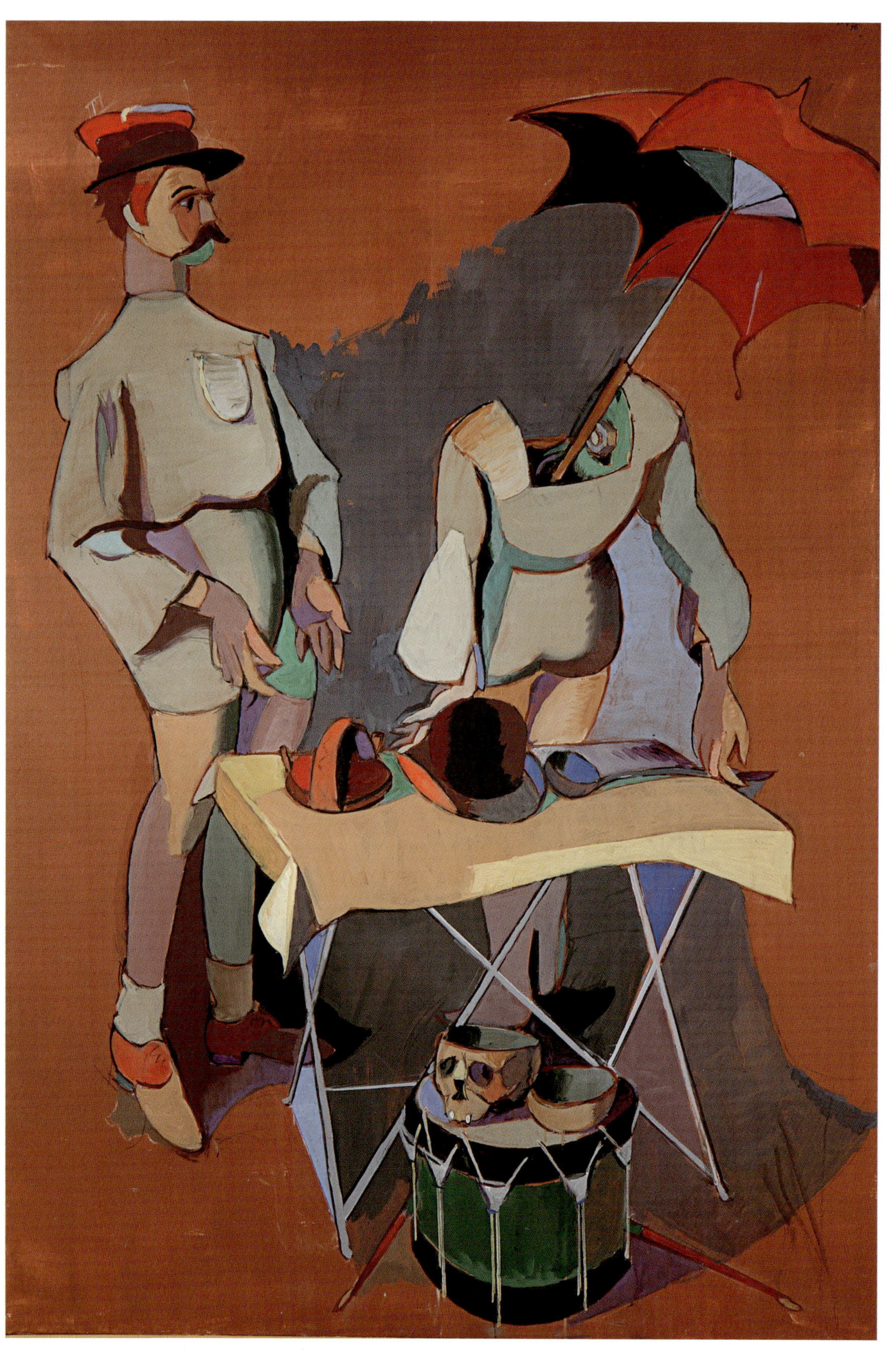

Mannequin event – sale, 1978
Acrylic on canvas
195 x 130 cm
Private collection
Courtesy galerie Art Attitude
Hervé Bize, Nancy

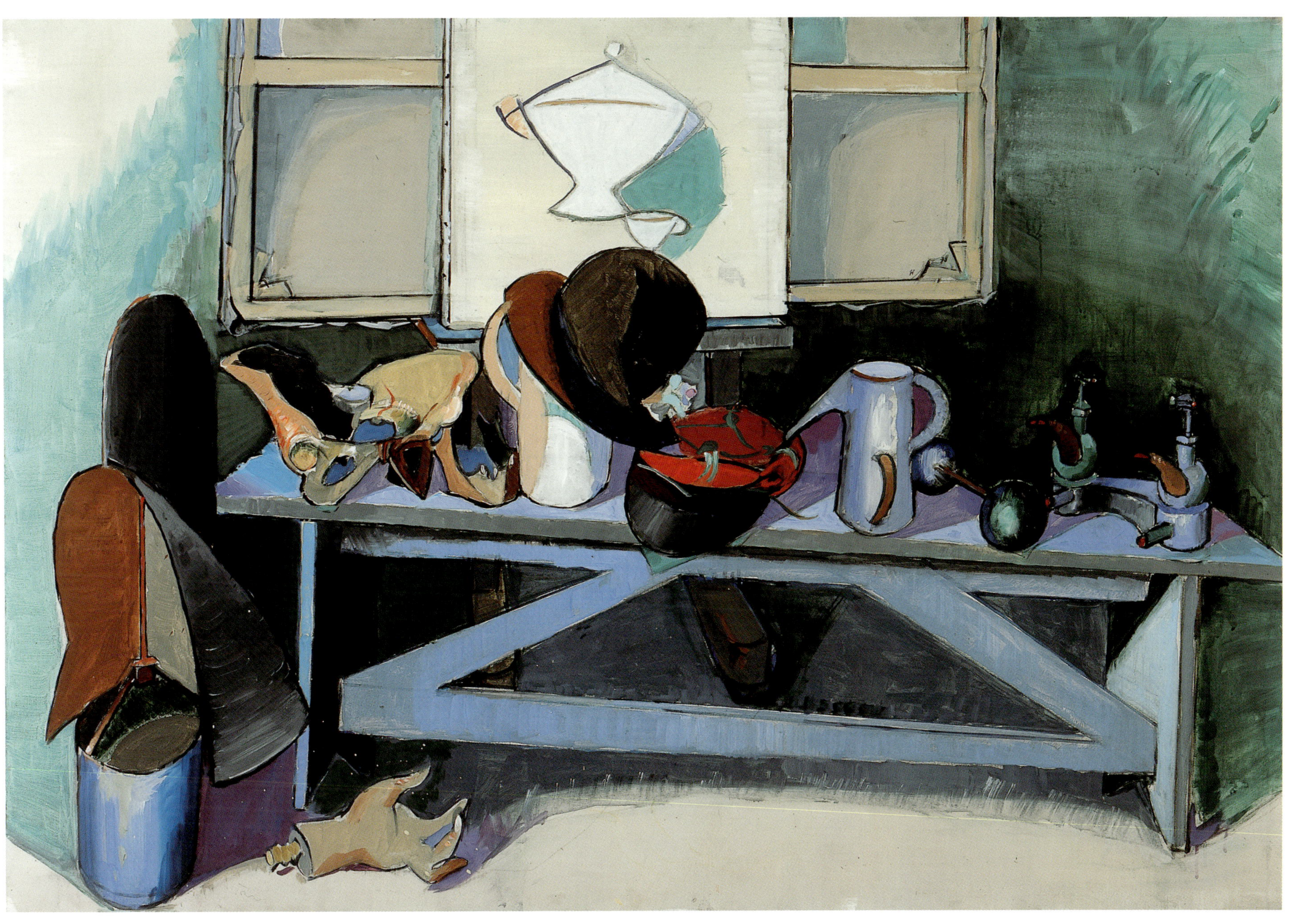

First flea-market collection in the studio,
1978
Acrylic on canvas
114 x 162.5 cm
Collection of the Grand-Ducal Court, Luxembourg

117

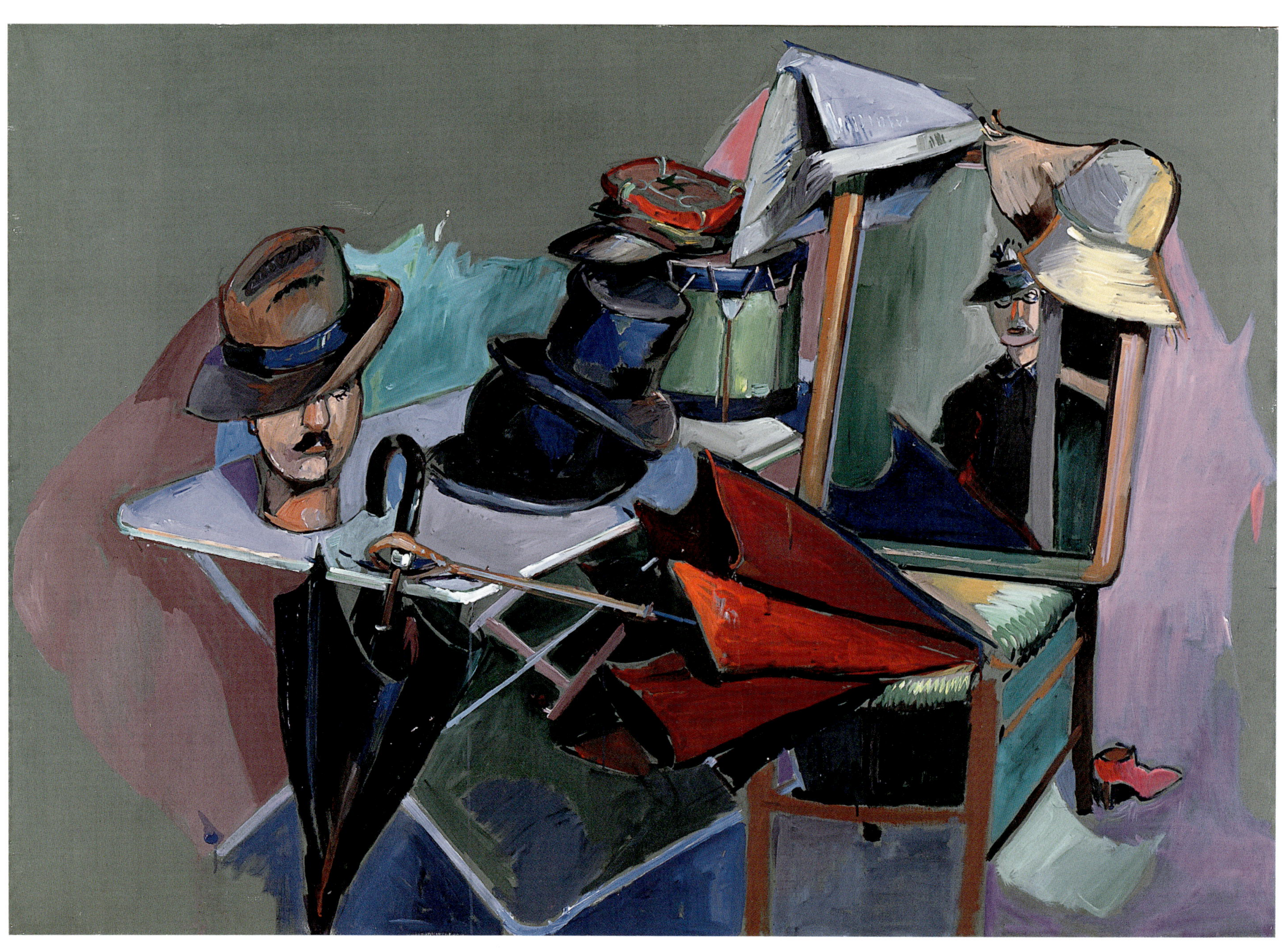

1 jumble for Émile, 1981
Acrylic on canvas
145 x 200 cm
Fonds régional d'Art contemporain d'Auvergne

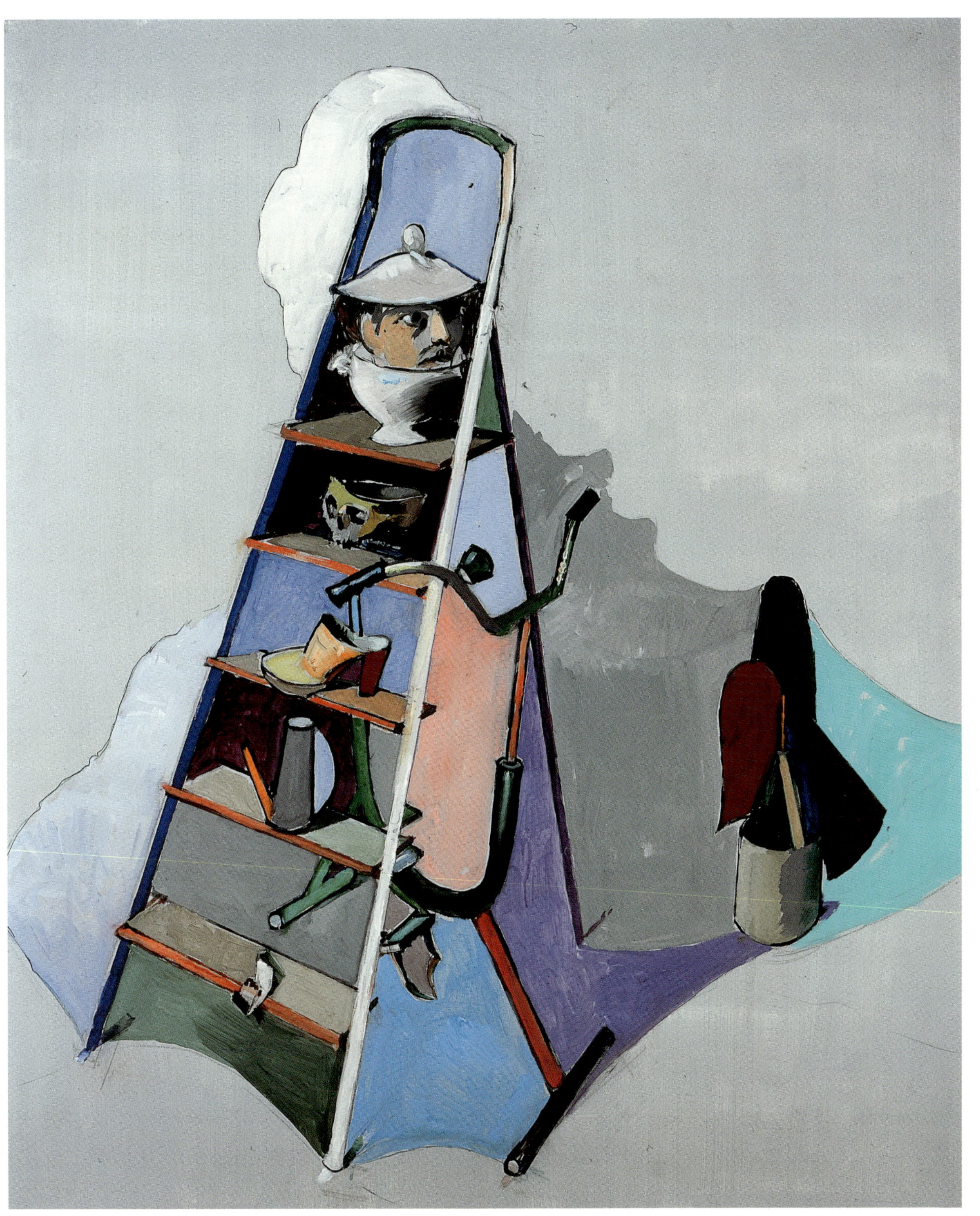

Find the cyclist, 1979
(Arpeggios)
Acrylic on canvas
162 x 130 cm
Musée national d'Histoire et d'Art du Grand-Duché
de Luxembourg, Luxembourg

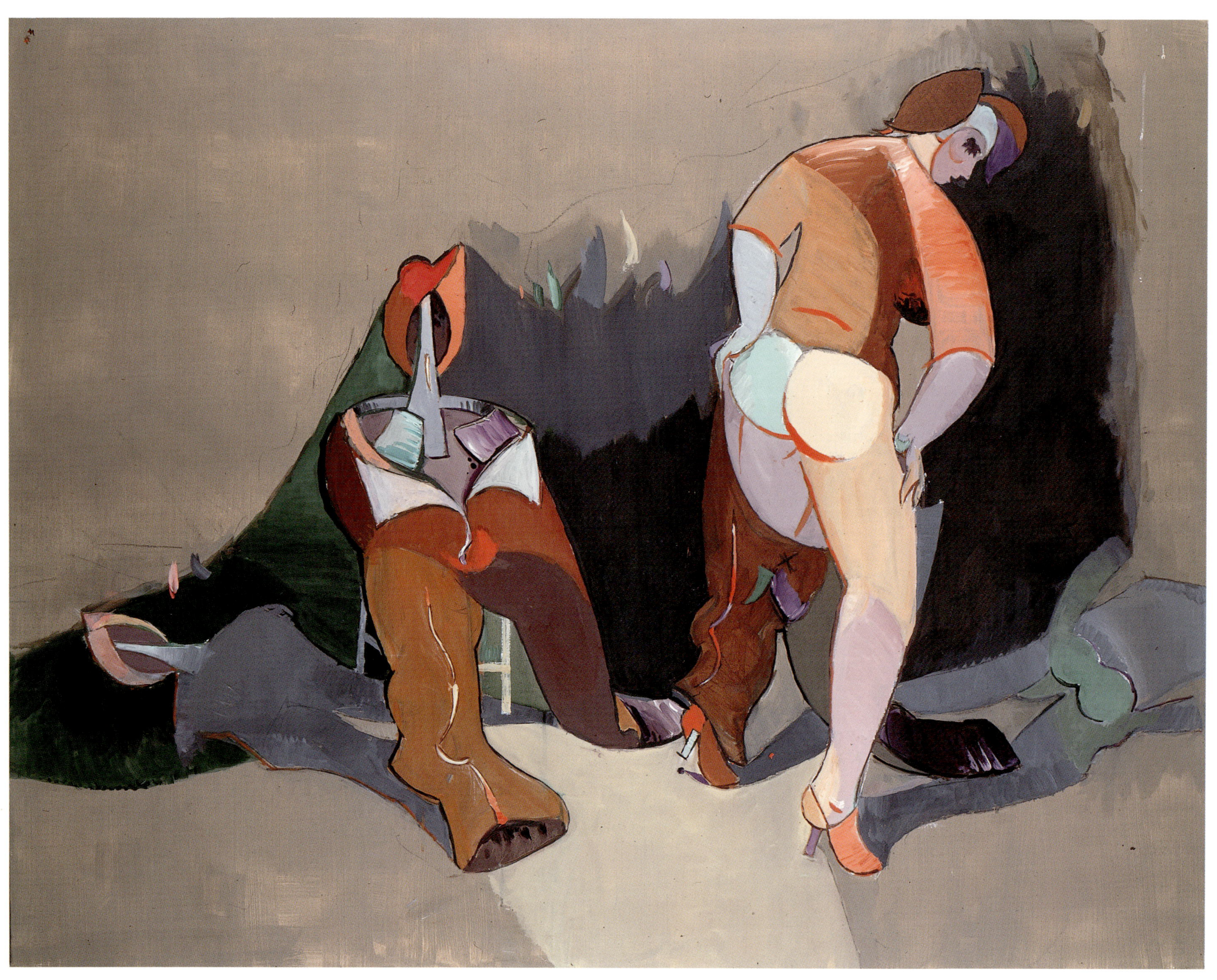

Leggery, 1977
Acrylic on canvas
132 x 163 cm
Collection of David Hélion

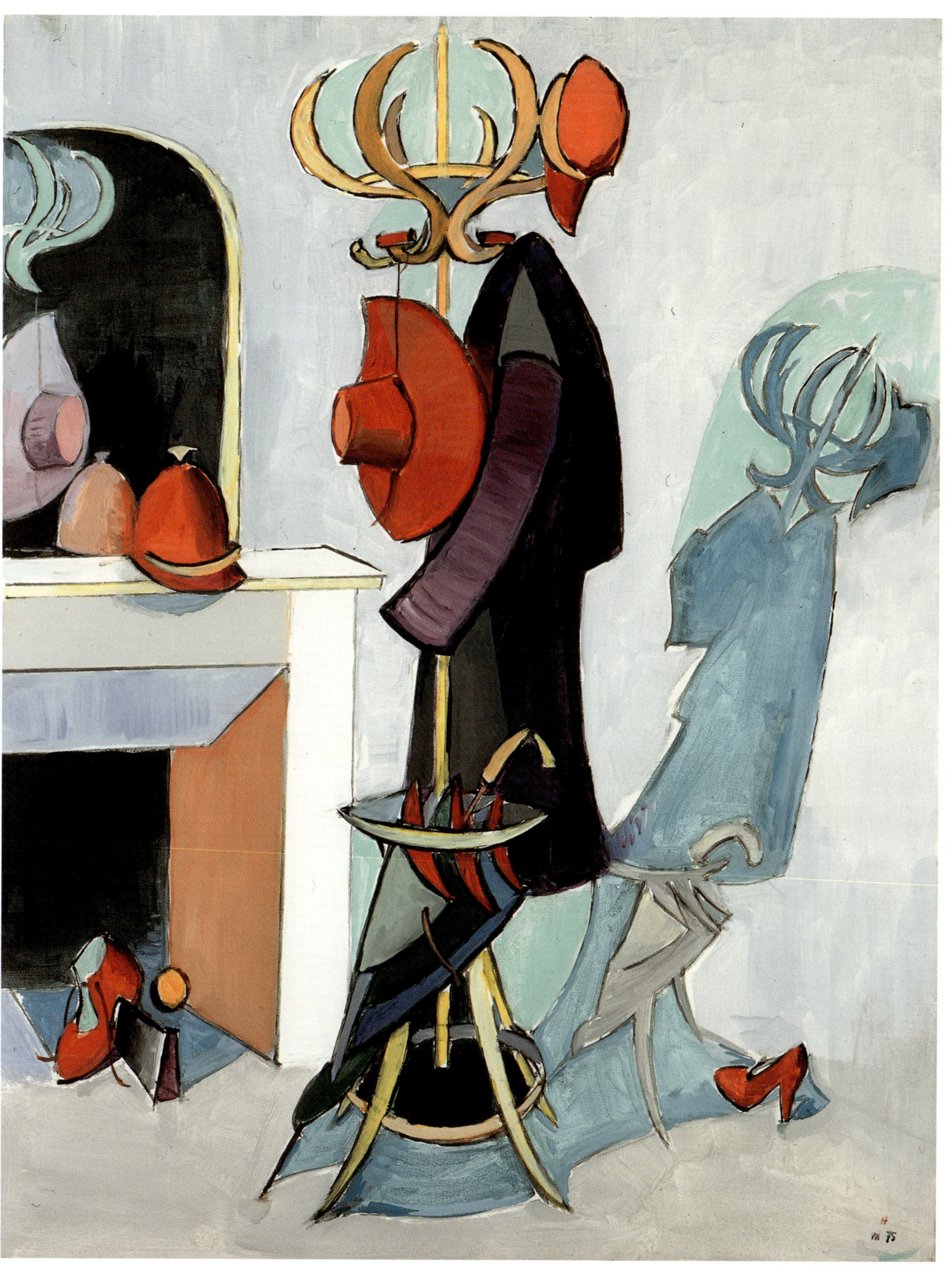

Coat-tree and echo, 1975
Oil on canvas
130 x 97 cm
Musée d'Art moderne, Saint-Étienne

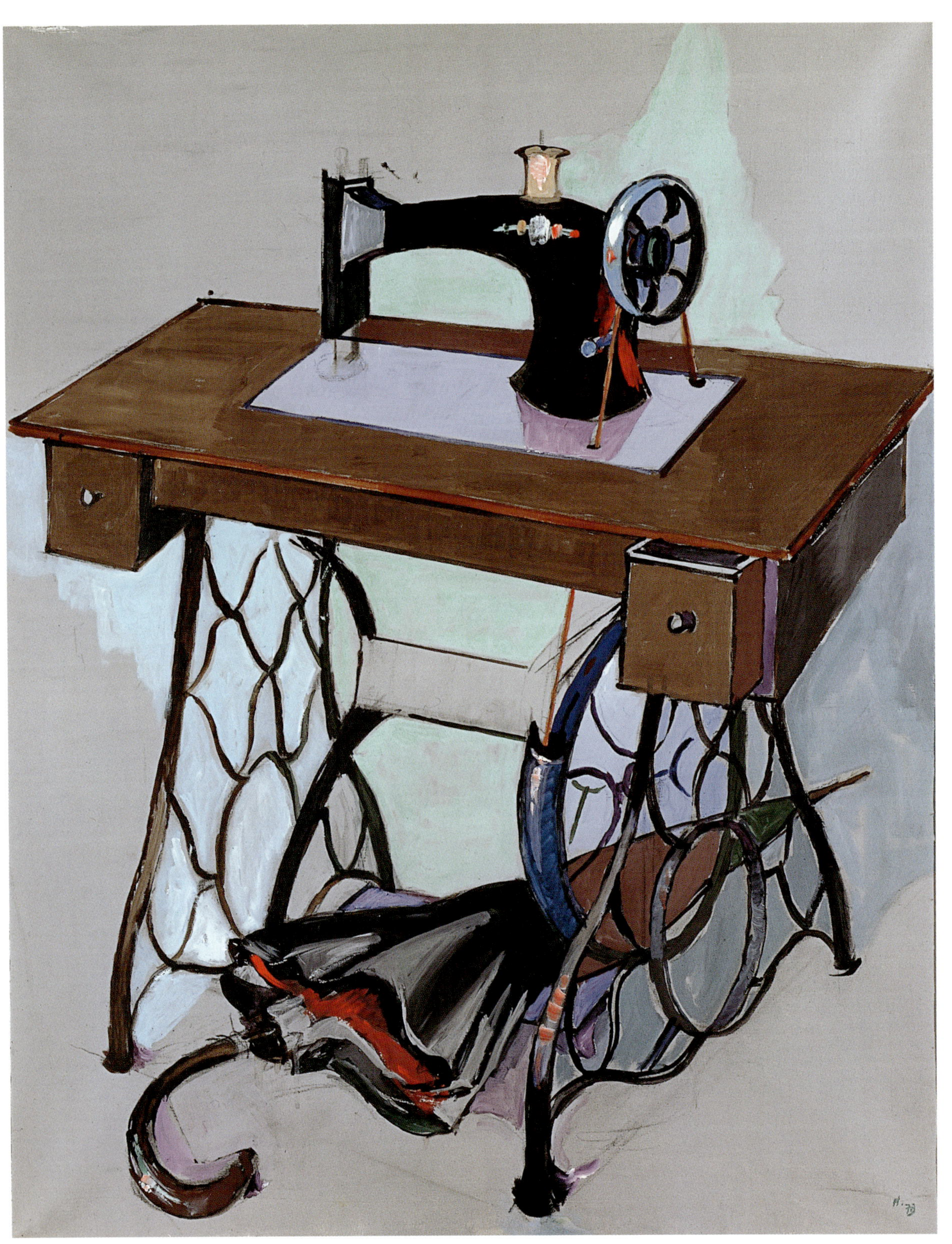

As beautiful as a ..., 1979
Acrylic on canvas
116 x 89 cm
Collection of Raphaël and Emmanuel Hélion

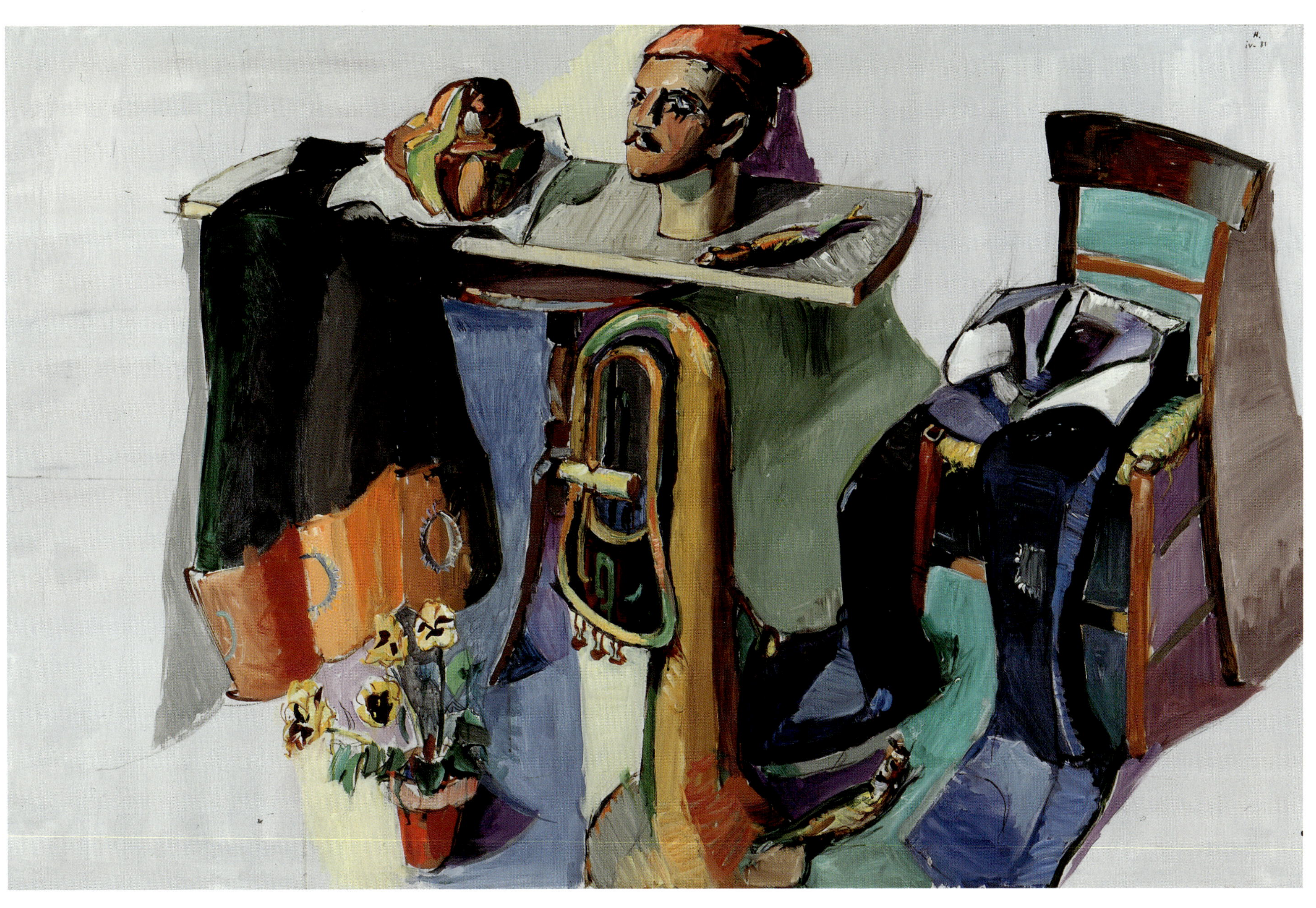

Best wishes to Richard Lindner, 1981
Acrylic on canvas
129.5 x 194.5 cm
Centre Pompidou, Musée national d'art moderne, Paris,
accepted in lieu of tax 1991

8

OFFERINGS ...
OFFRANDES...

"I'm beginning to feel that a bunch of radishes in itself says
everything about the world."

« Je commence à sentir qu'une botte de radis
exprime à elle seule le monde. »

Jean Hélion, *Carnets,* 7-8-9 juin 1973, p. 132.

AND STILL LIFES
ET NATURES MORTES

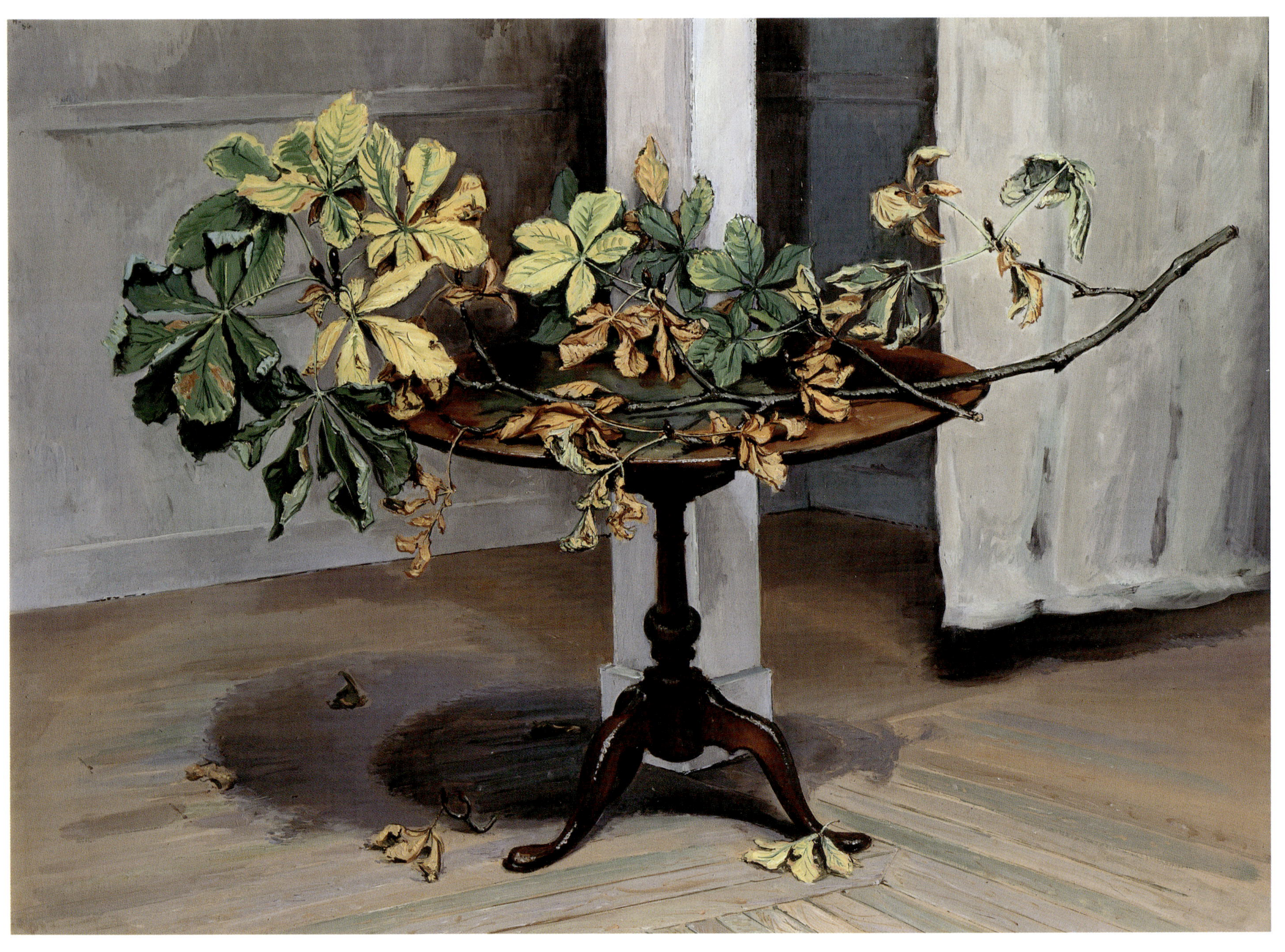

Autumn leaves, 1954
Oil on canvas
97 x 130 cm
Collection of Paolo Zanasi, Modena

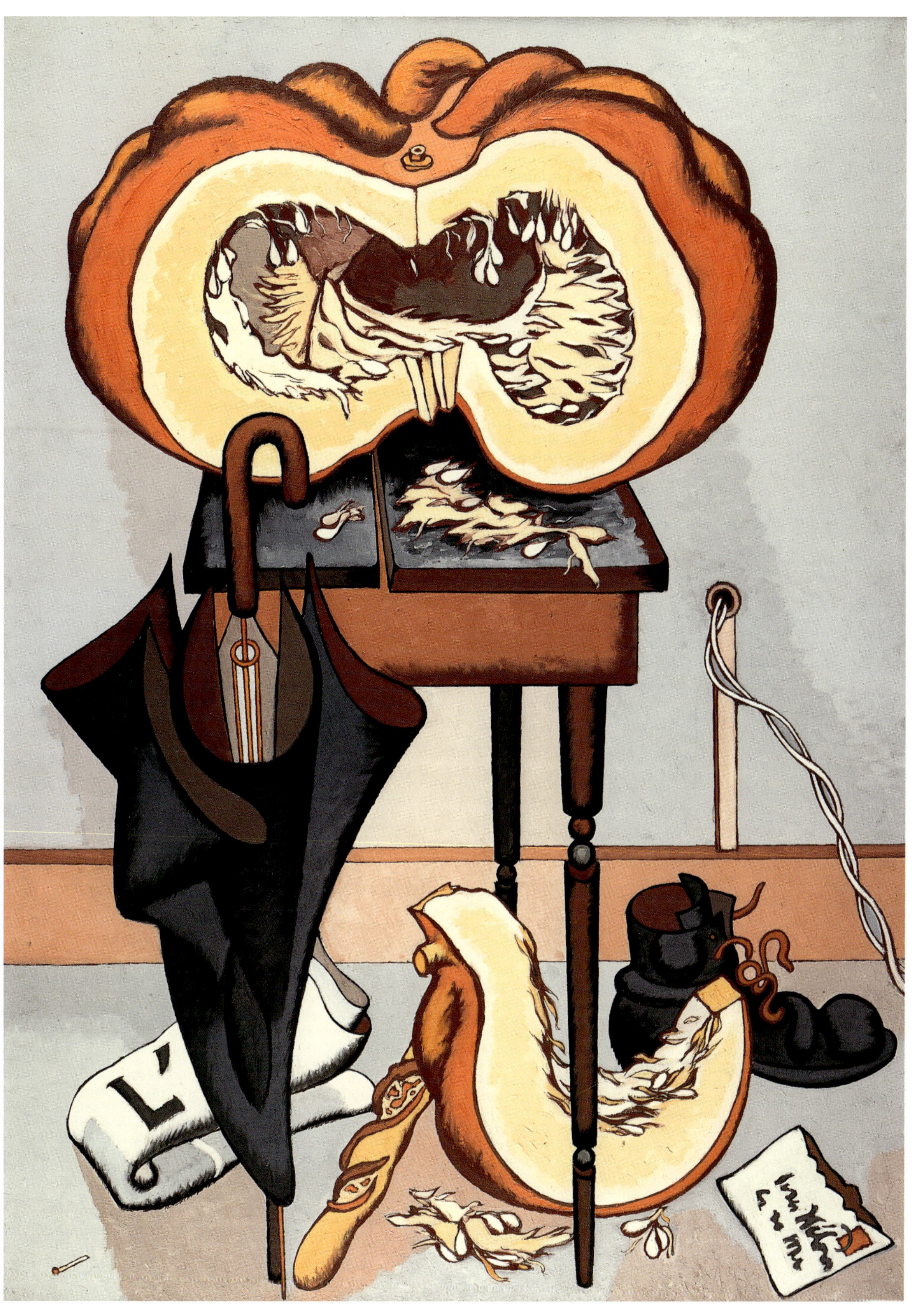

Still life with pumpkin, 1948
Oil on canvas
140 x 70 cm
Fonds national d'Art contemporain,
Ministère de la Culture et de la Communication, Paris
On deposit with the Musée des Beaux-Arts, Nantes

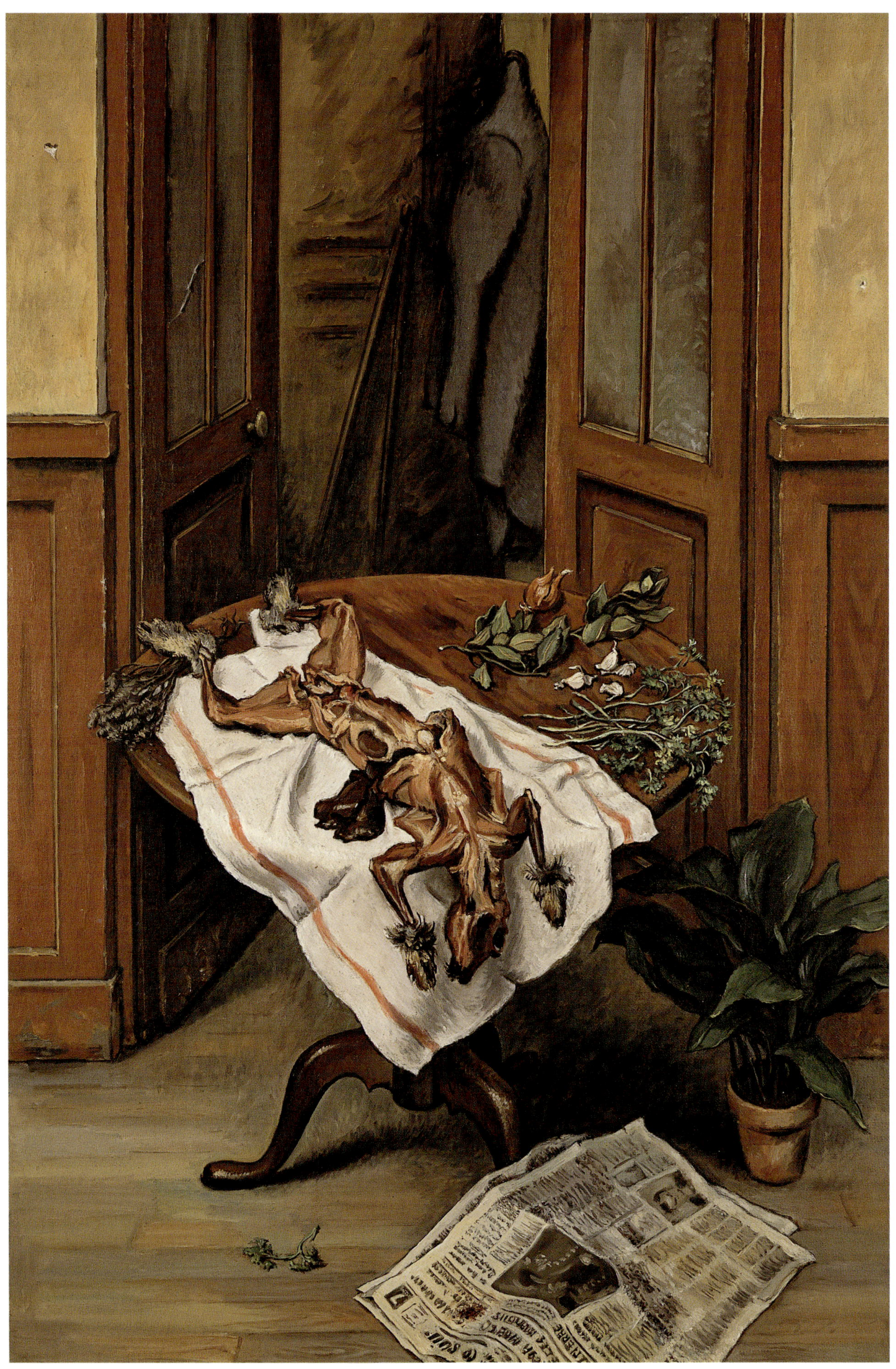

Rabbit event, 1952
Oil on canvas
92 x 60 cm
Private collection, Paris

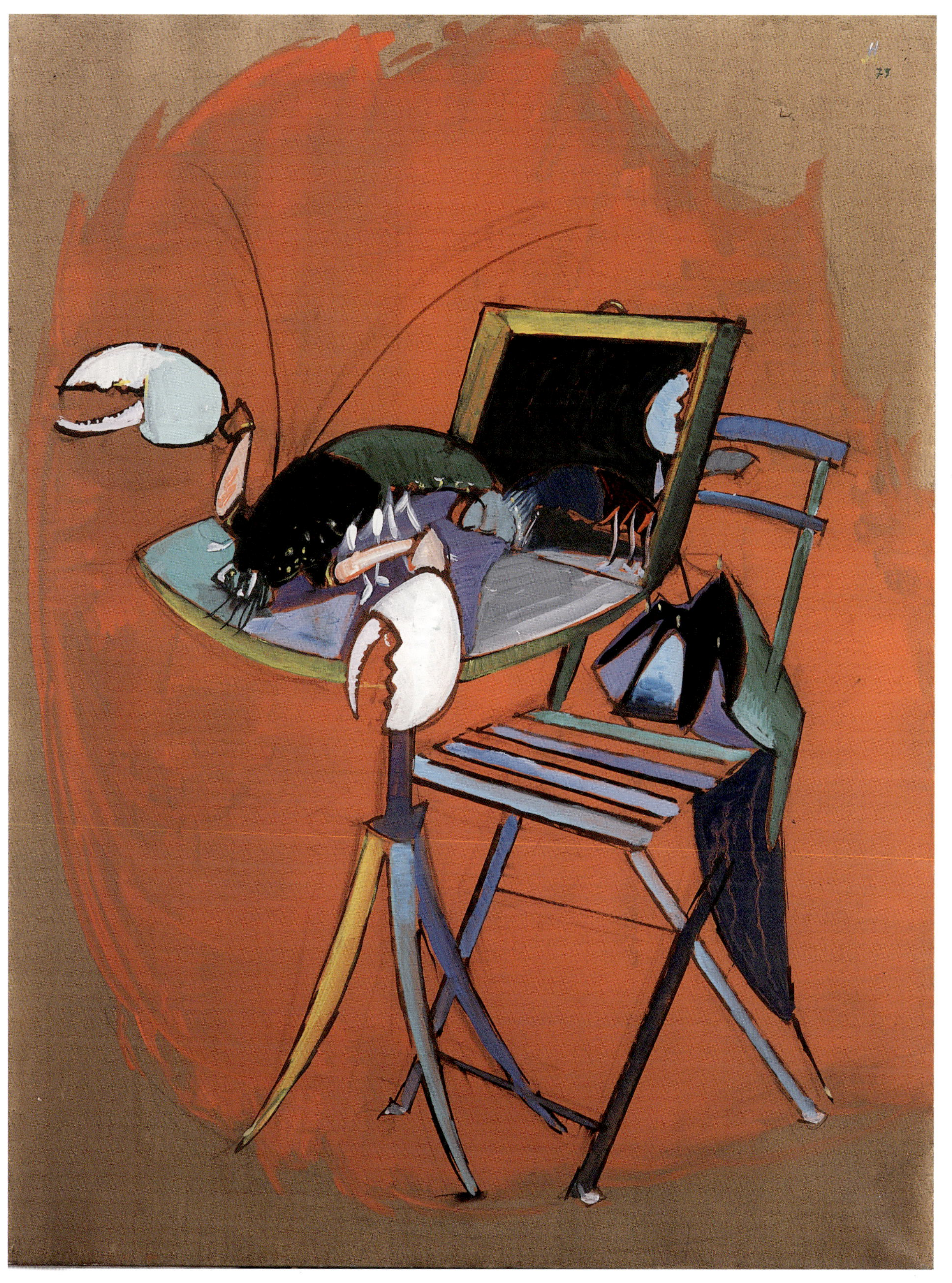

Lobster and its reflection, 1975
Acrylic on canvas
100 x 73 cm
Private collection, Mulhouse

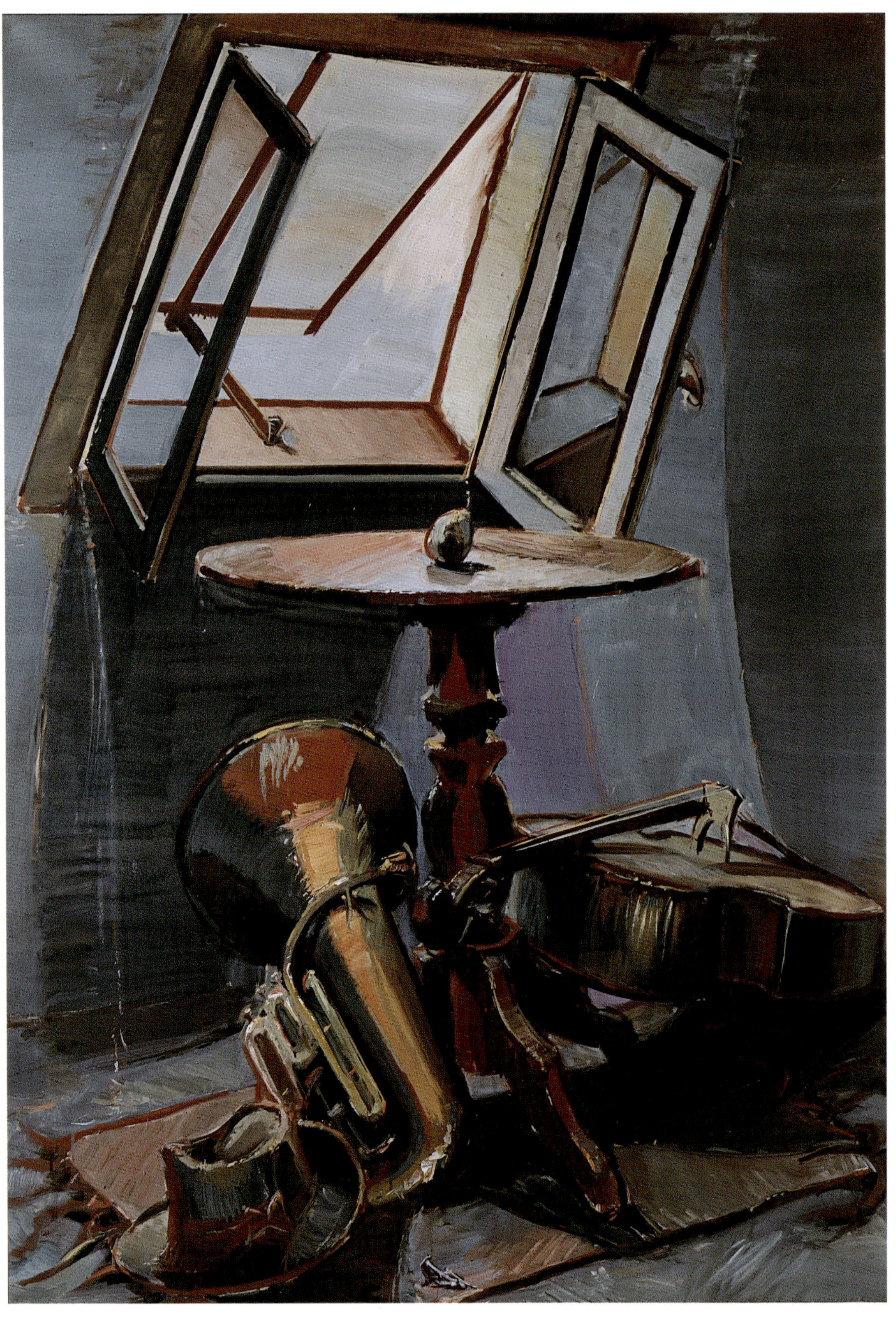

Chamber music, 1960
Oil on canvas
130 x 89 cm
Collection of Paolo Zanasi, Modena

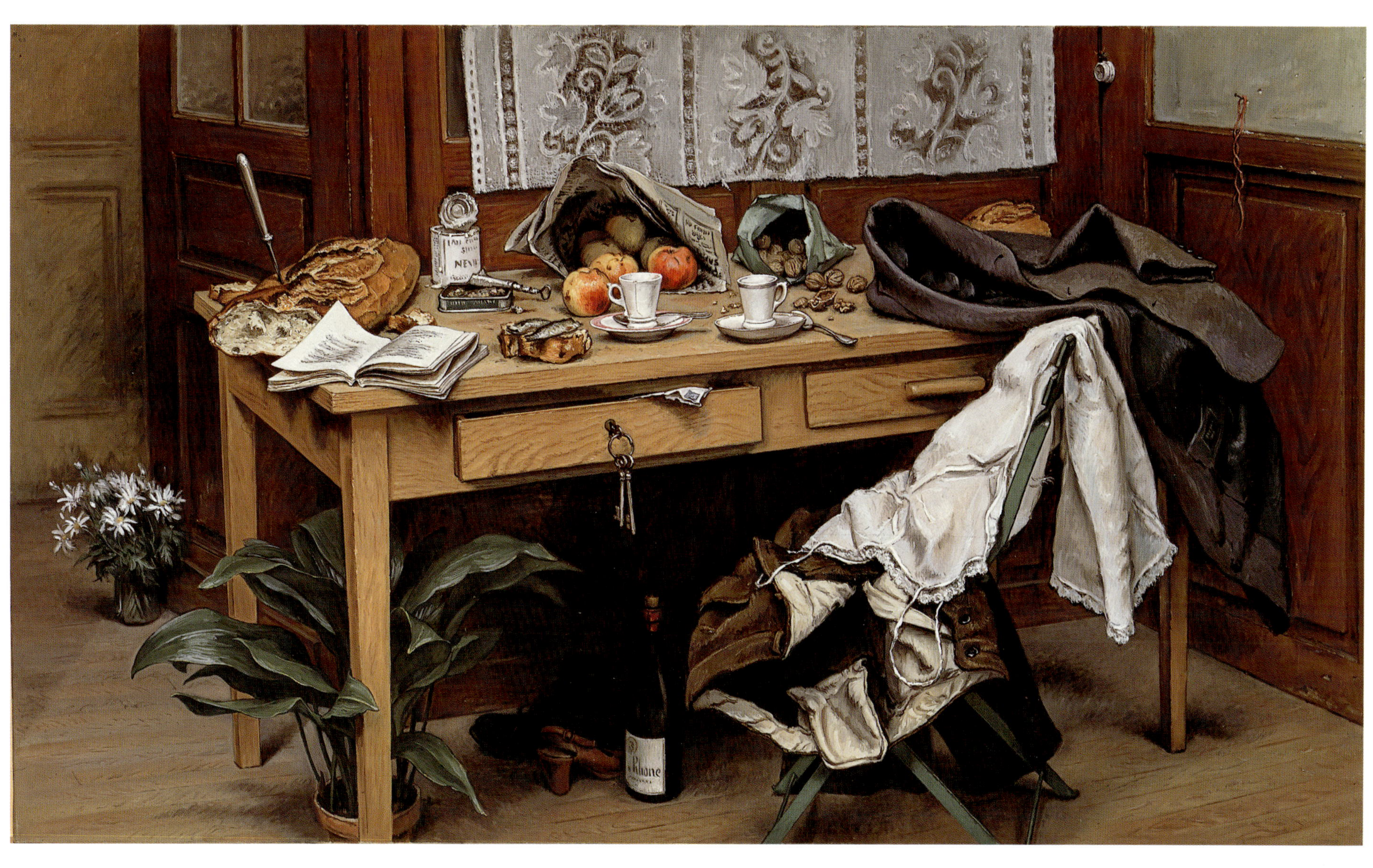

The snack 1953
Oil on canvas
89 x 147 cm
Private collection, Paris

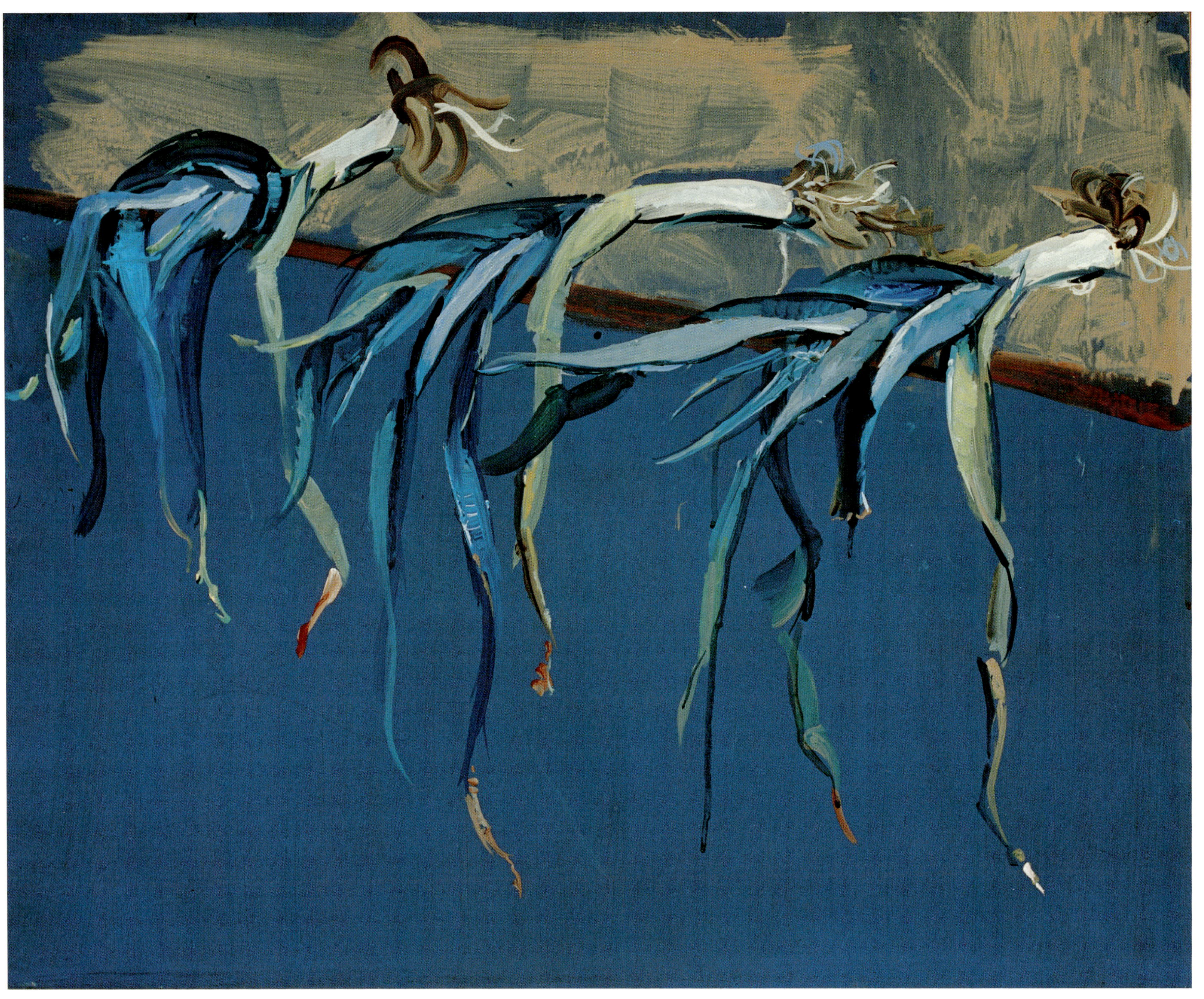

Leeks, 1973
Acrylic on canvas
60 x 73 cm
Private collection

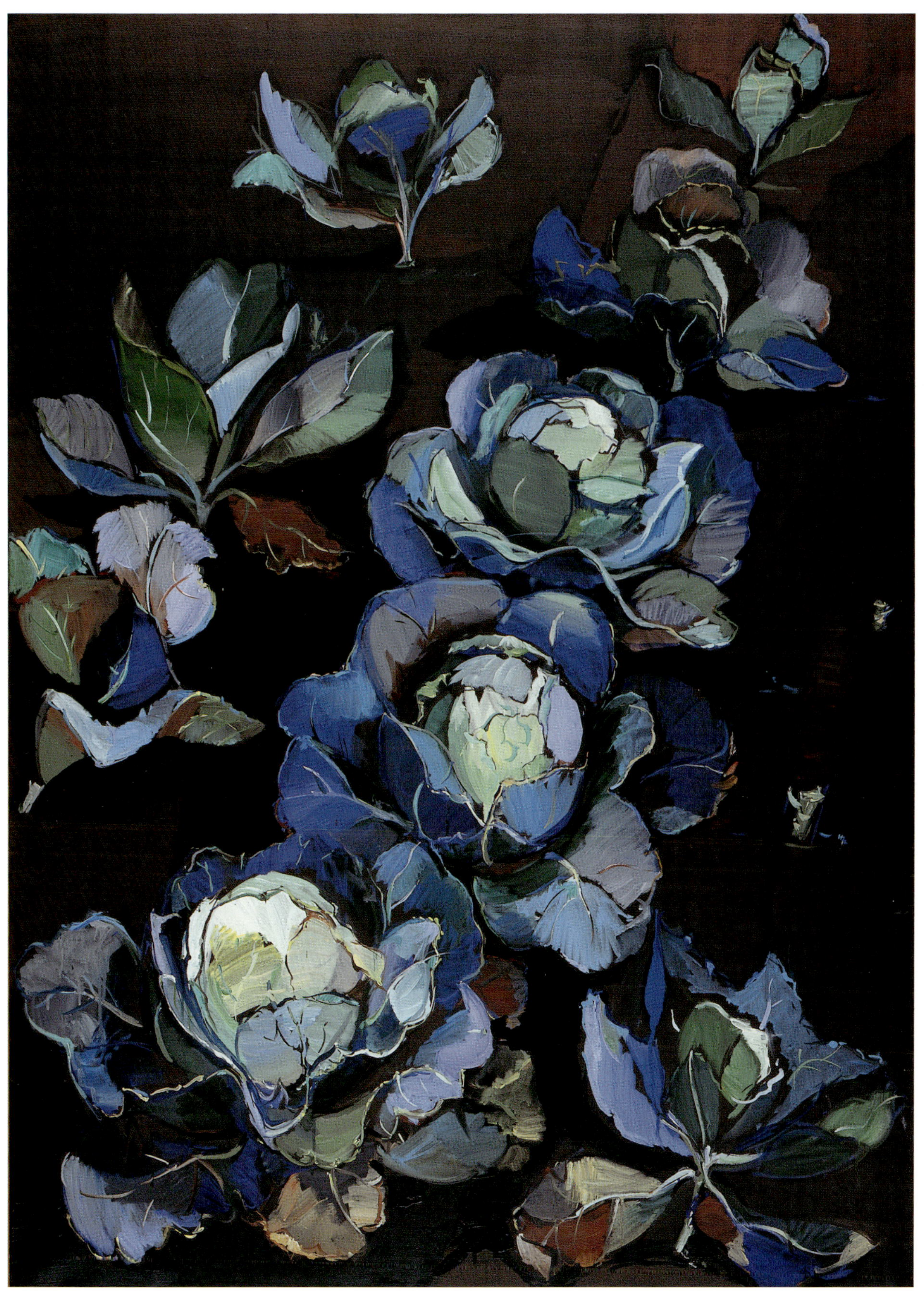

Cabbage patch, 1972
Acrylic on canvas
161 x 114 cm
Private collection

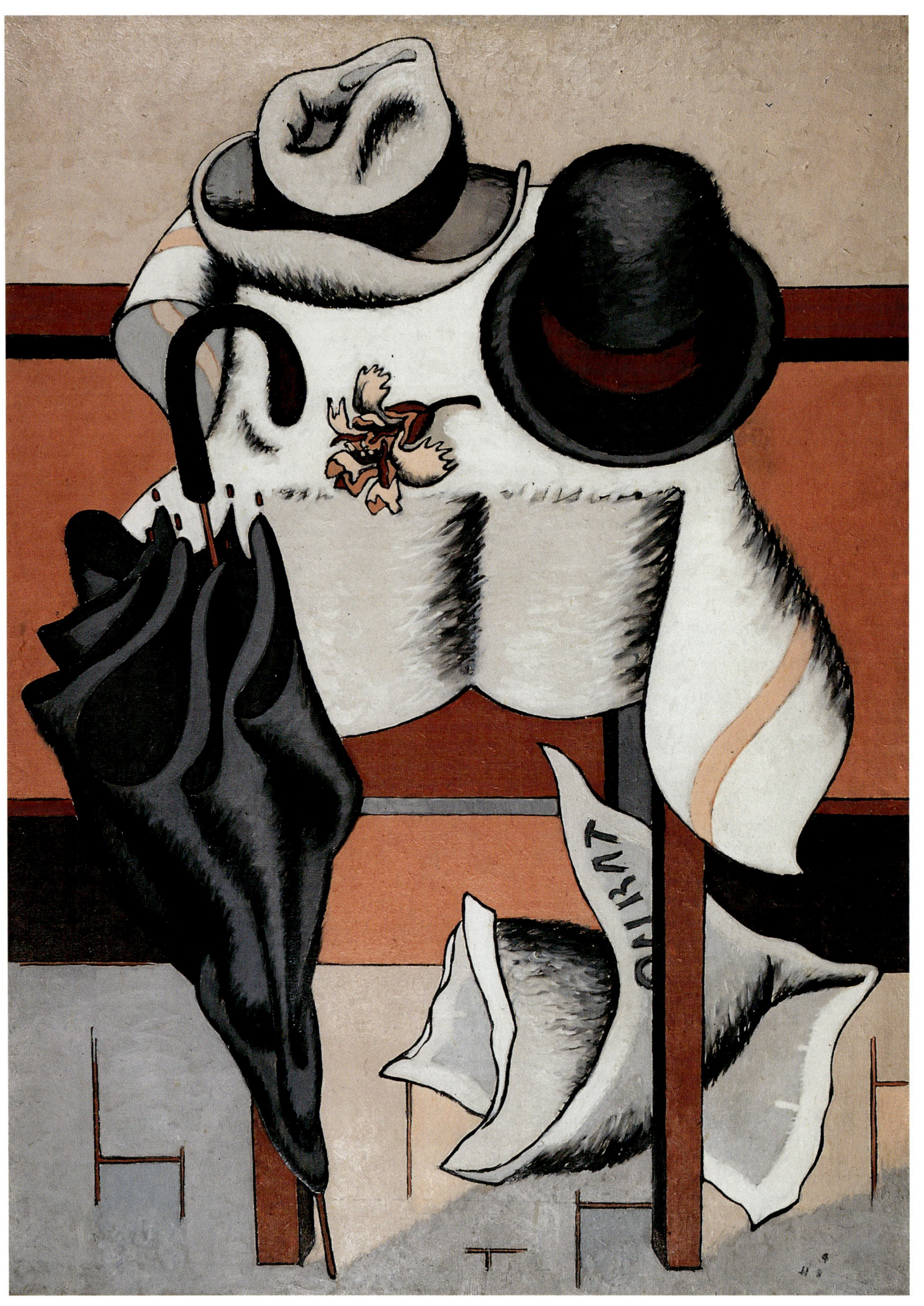

Still life with carnation, 1948
Oil on canvas
92 x 65 cm
Private collection

Ballet of chairs at Skyros, 1980
Acrylic on canvas
145 x 200 cm
Private collection, Paris

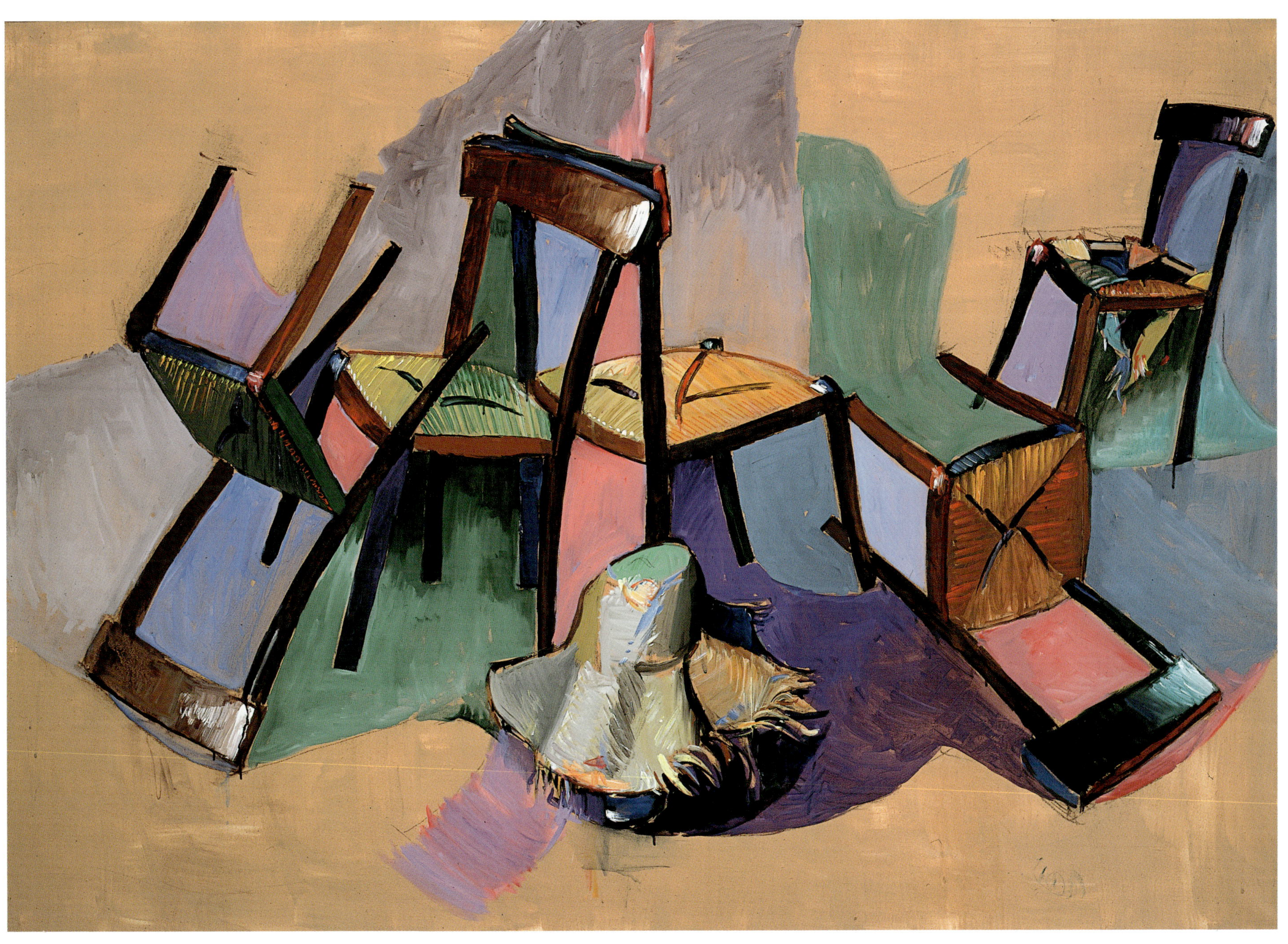

135

THE CITY
LA VILLE

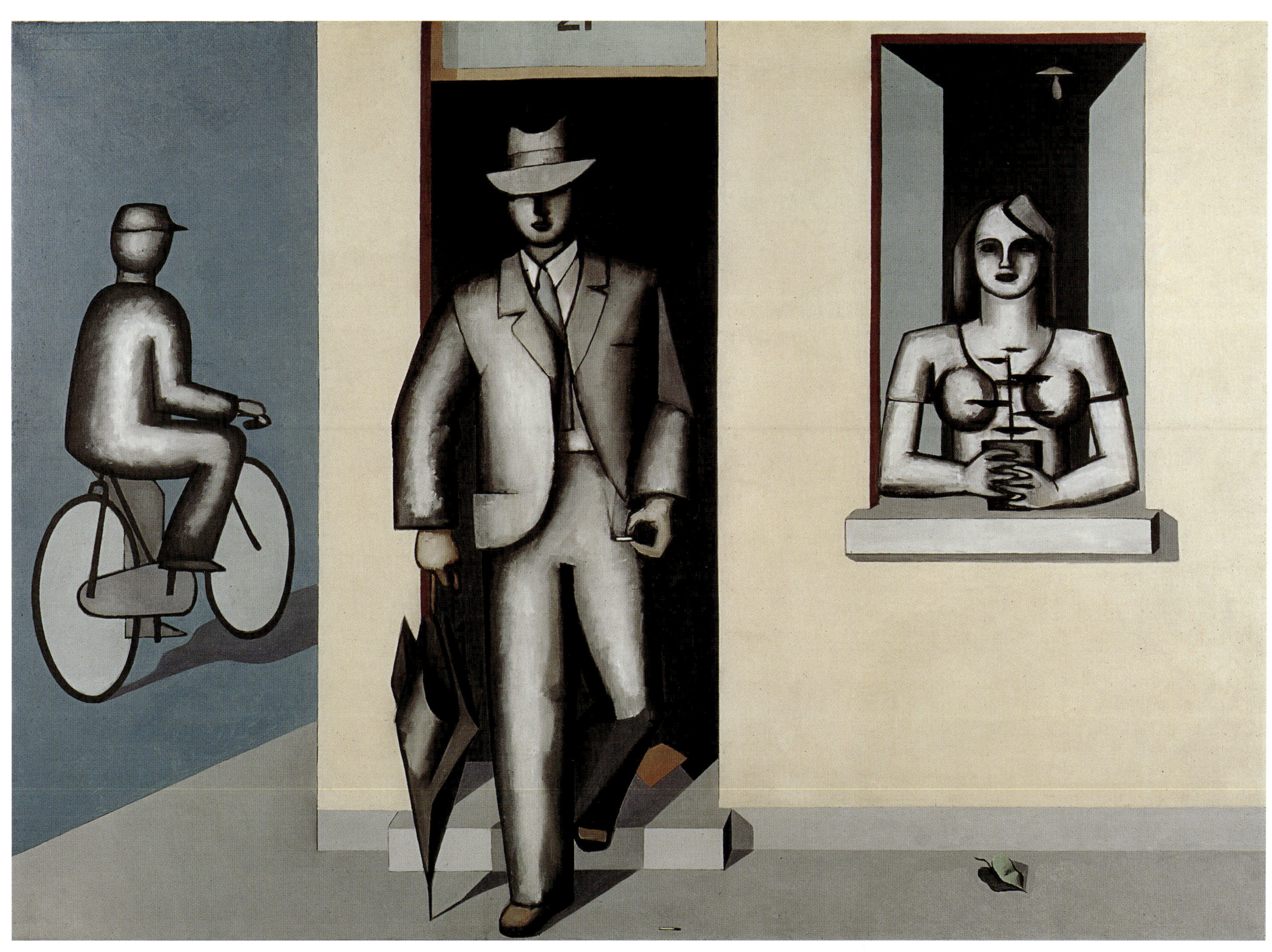

With cyclist, 1939
Oil on canvas
132 x 180.5 cm
Centre Pompidou,
Musée national d'art moderne,
Paris, purchase 1968

137

9

INSIDE/OUTSIDE

"Shop windows itemize the life of society – reassuringly,
clarifyingly …. It is also a spectacle we cannot do without.
Shops like stage sets. Same lighting – footlights, spotlights.

« Les vitrines présentent l'énumération
de la vie sociale : elle est rassurante, clarifiante. […]
C'est aussi un spectacle indispensable.
Les boutiques en forme de scène de théâtre.
Même éclairage de rampes et projecteurs. »

Jean Hélion, *Carnets,* 21 août 1950, p. 209

DEDANS/DEHORS

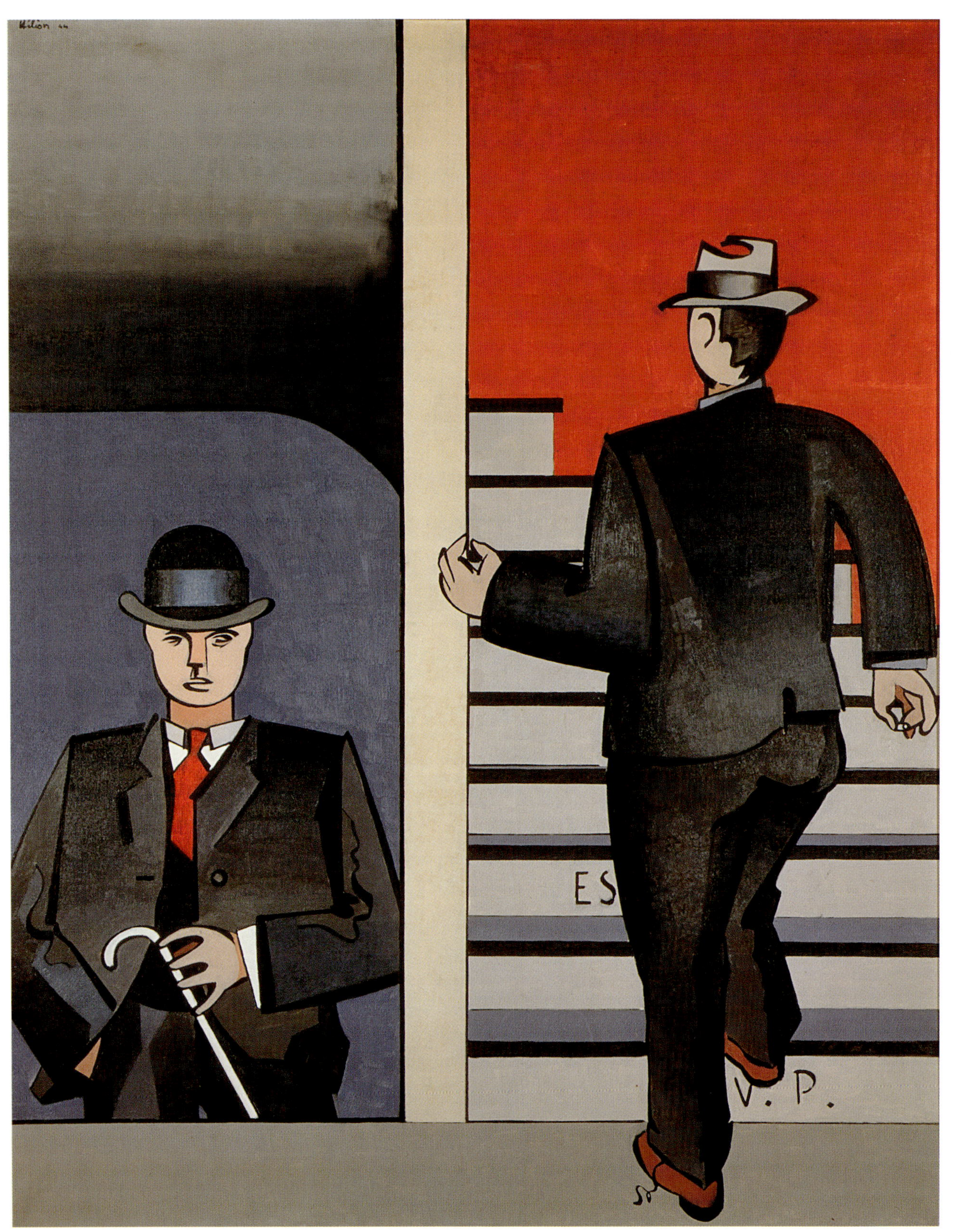

The stairs, 1944
Oil on canvas
130 x 97 cm
Private collection, Paris

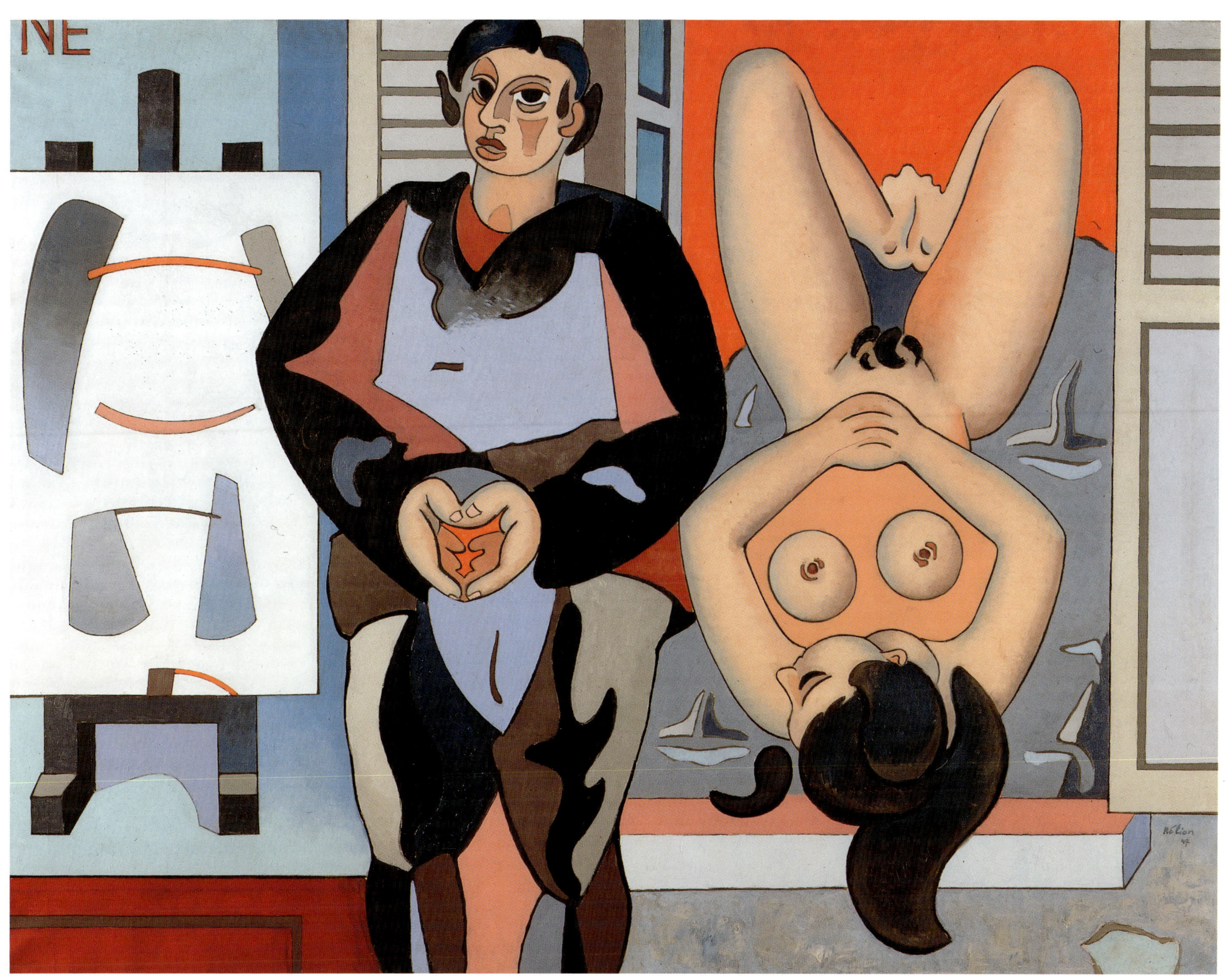

Wrong way up / À rebours, 1947
Oil on canvas
113.5 x 146 cm
Centre Pompidou, Musée national d'art moderne, Paris,
purchase 1975

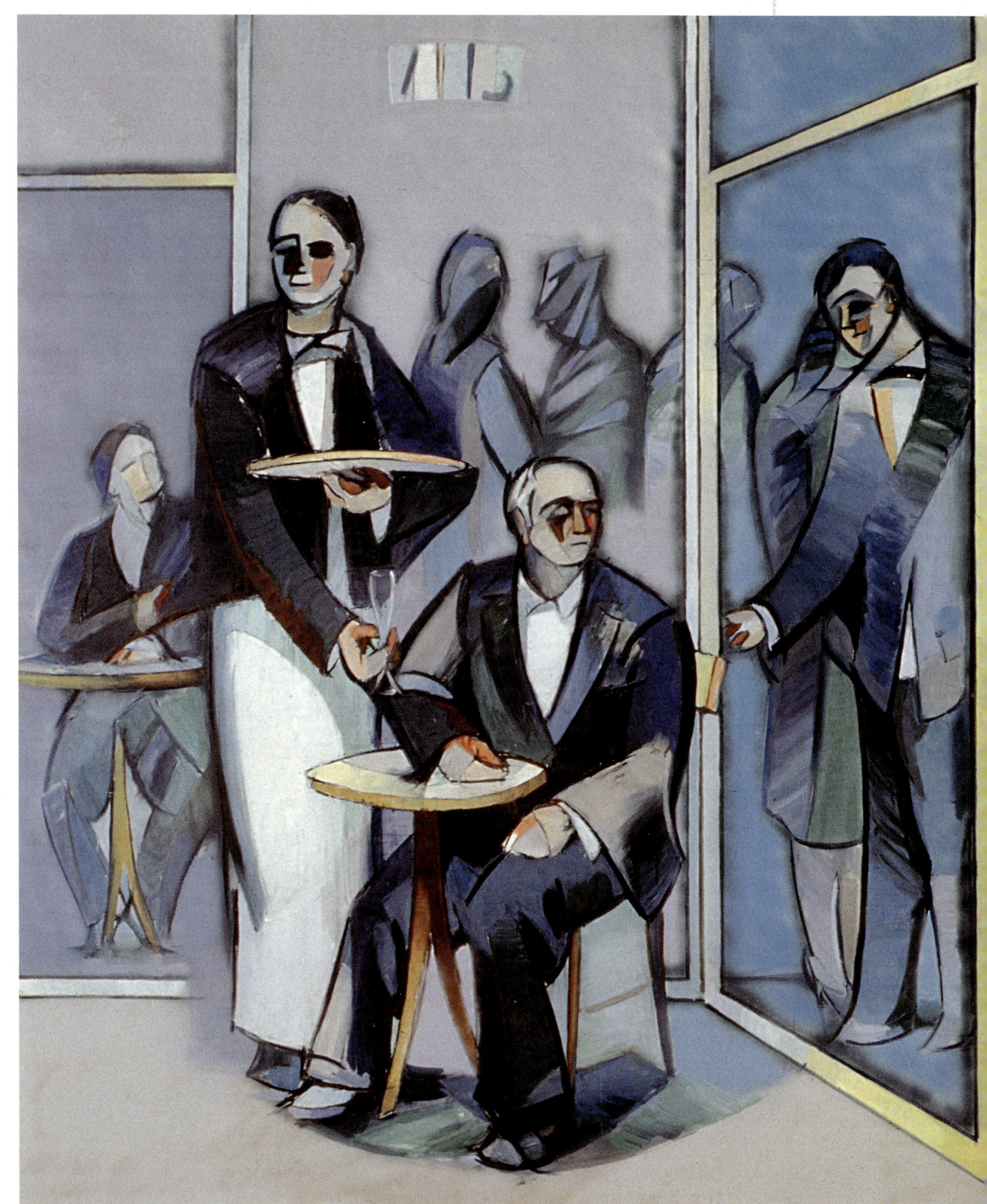

The Dragon Street triptych, 1967
Acrylic on canvas
275 x 875 cm (whole)
Central panel 275 x 425 cm,
side panels 275 x 225 cm
Fonds régional d'Art contemporain de Bretagne

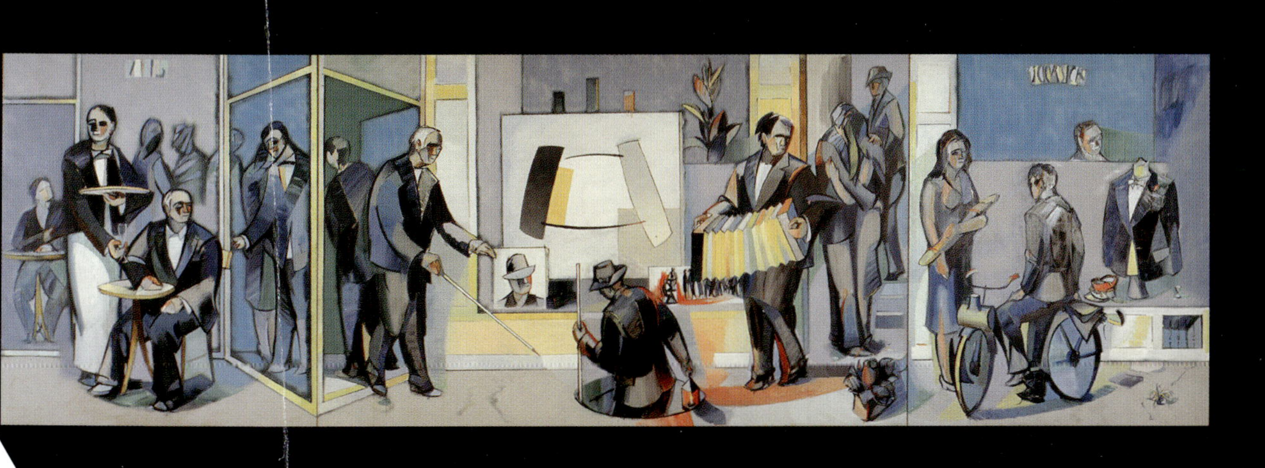

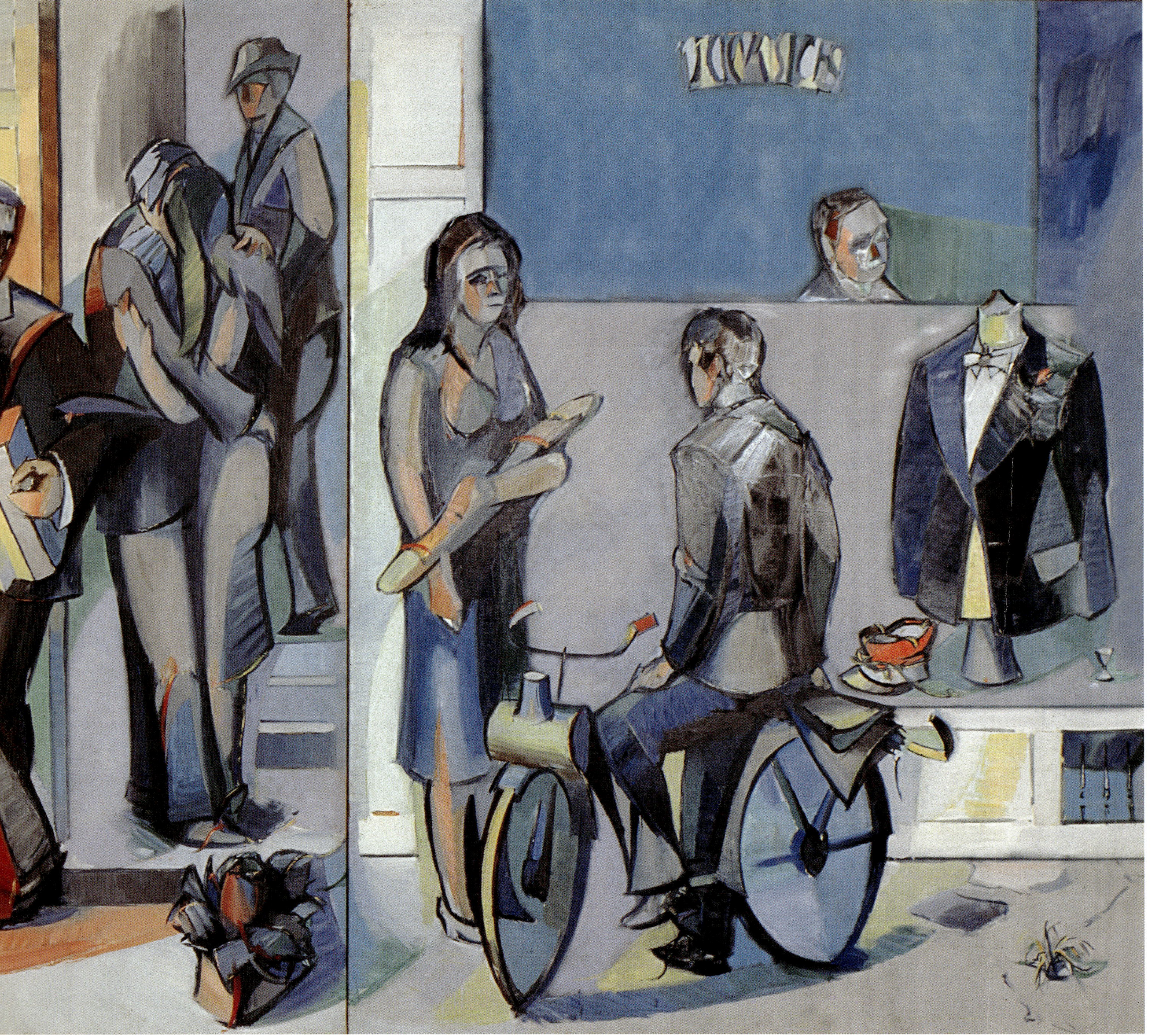

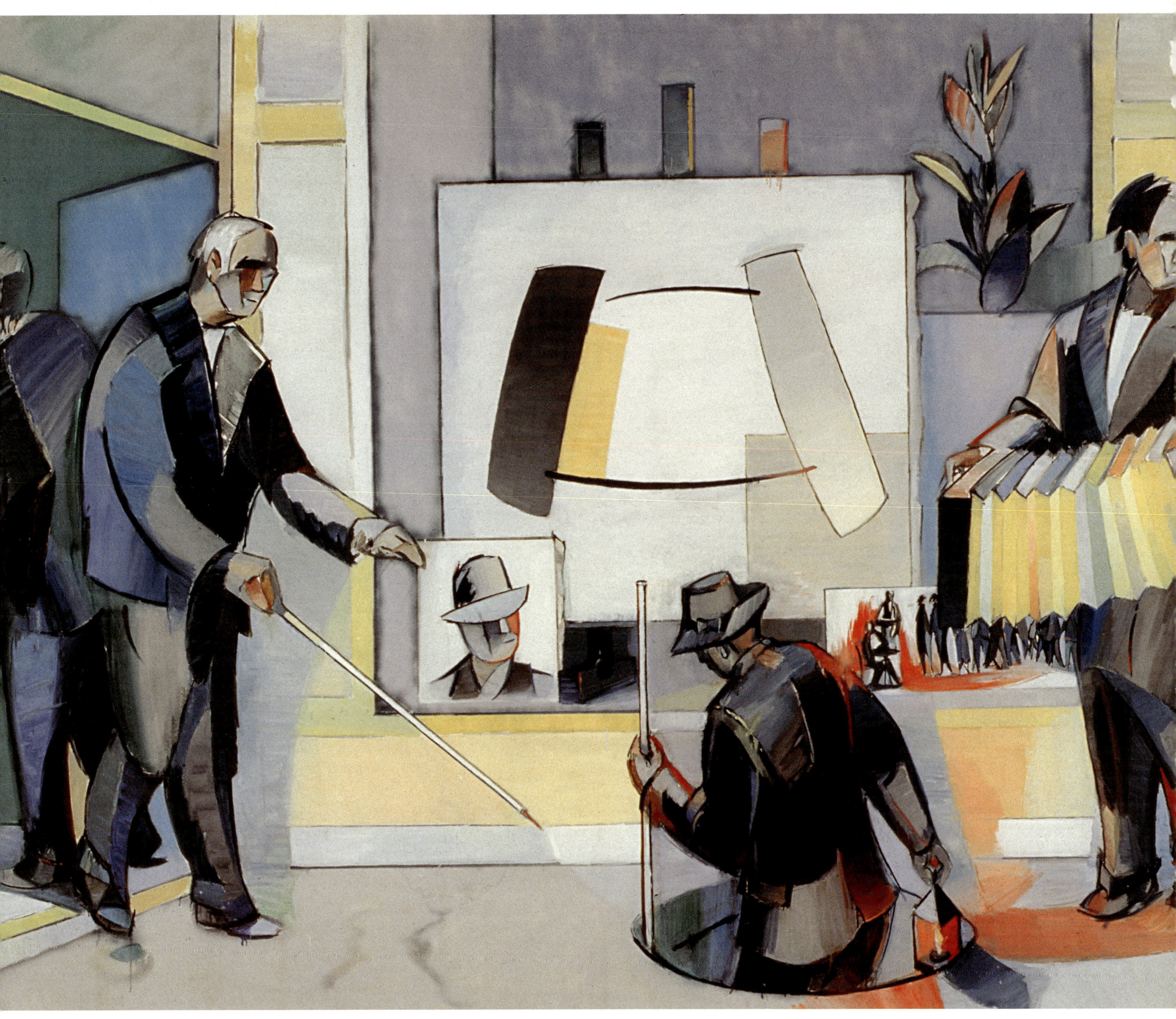

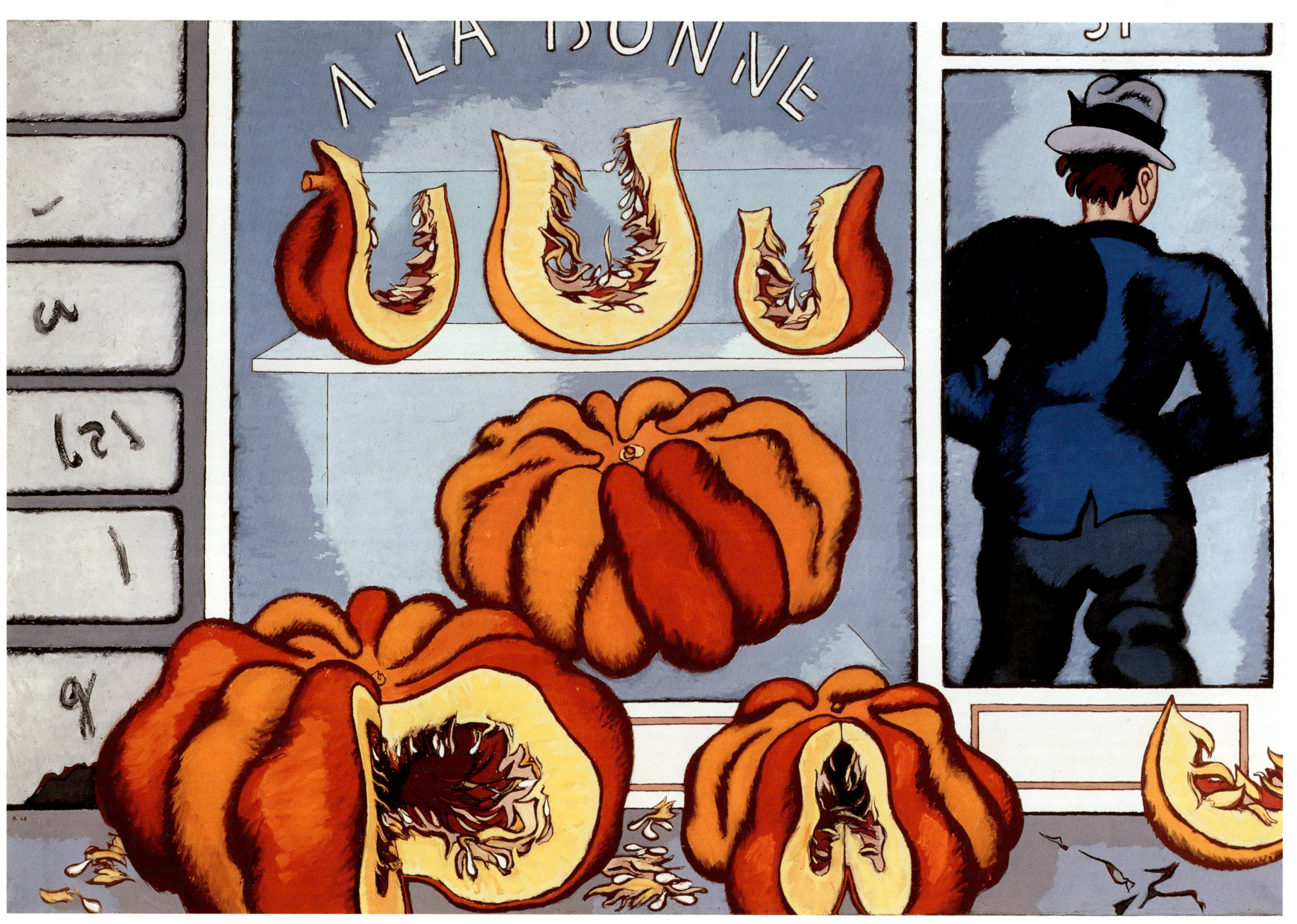

Big pumpkin event, 1948
Oil on canvas
114 x 162 cm
Private collection

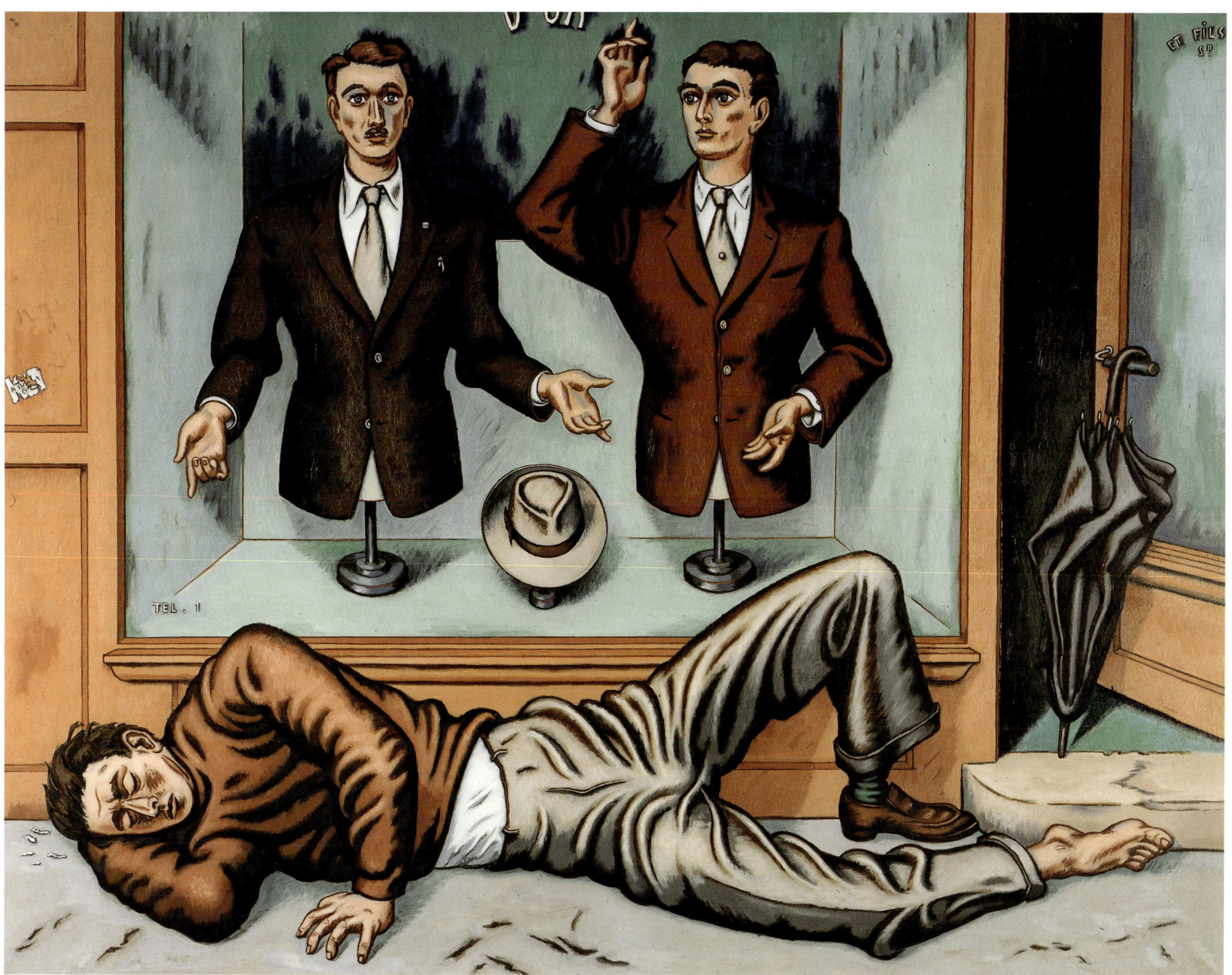

Big mannequin event, 1951
Oil on canvas
129.5 x 161.5 cm
Musée d'Art moderne de la Ville de Paris, Paris

147

10

DAILY EVENTS
SCÈNES JOURNALIÈRES :

“I thought I could find behind ordinary acts the sacred acts
that were their symbol”

« Je croyais trouver derrière le geste ordinaire
le geste sacré qui en était le symbole. »

Jean Hélion, *À perte de vue…*, Paris, IMEC, 1996, p. 89.

THE PROSE OF THE ORDINARY
LA PROSE DU QUOTIDIEN

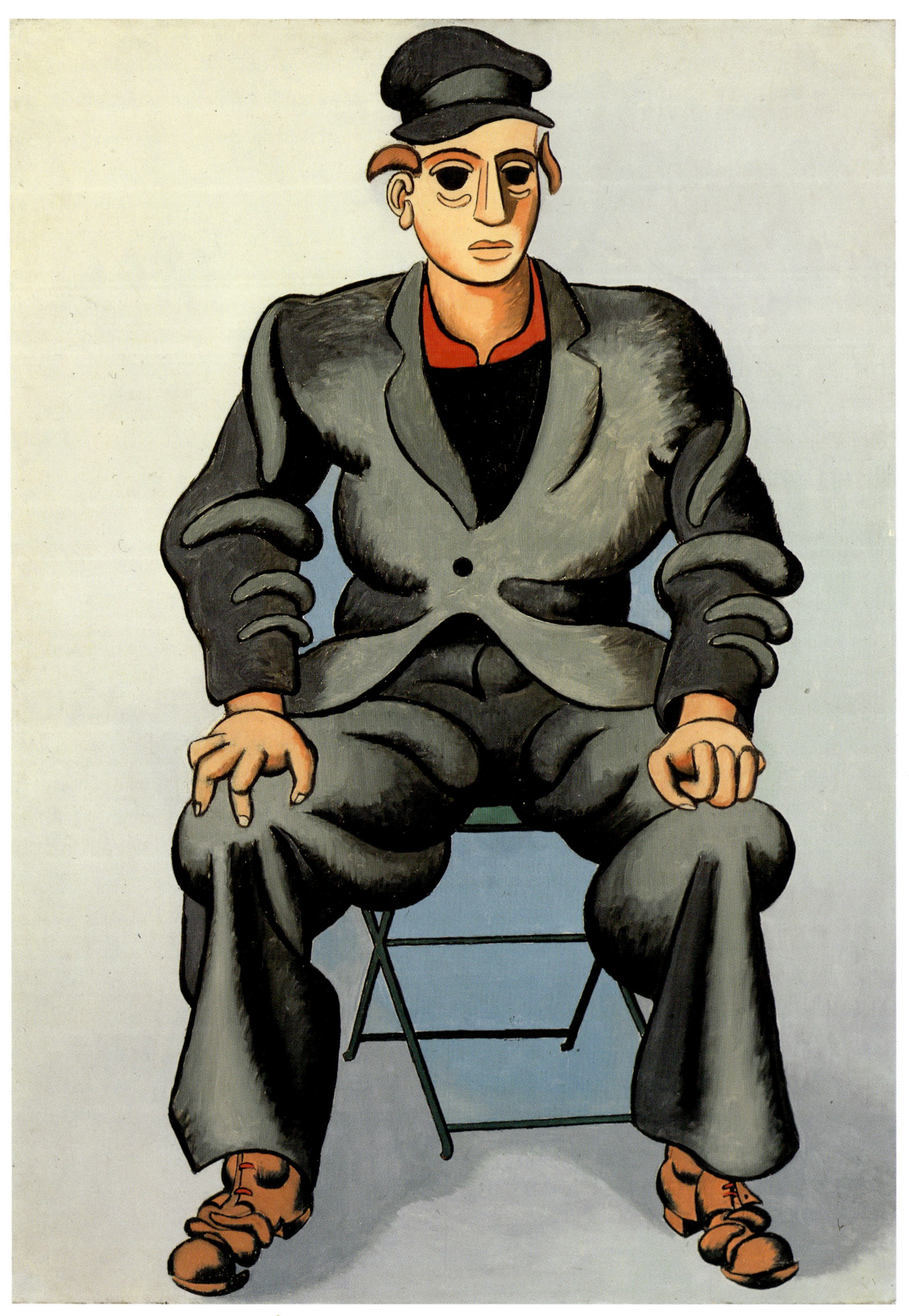

Man seated, 1947
Oil on canvas
117 x 81.5 cm
Städtische Galerie im Lenbachhaus, Munich

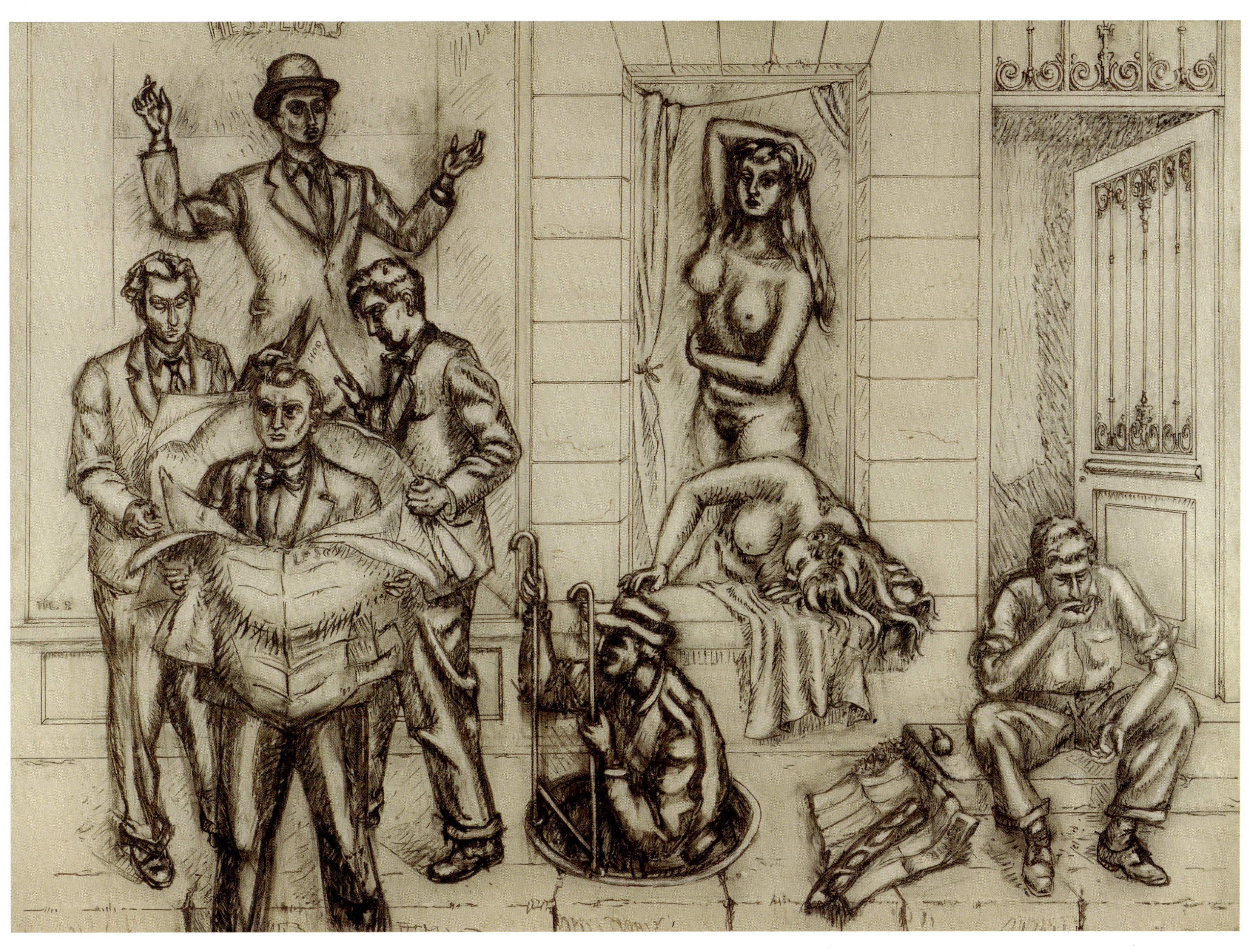

Daily allegory, 1951–53
Charcoal, paint and mixed media on canvas
194.7 x 259.6 cm
Musée Zervos, Vézelay

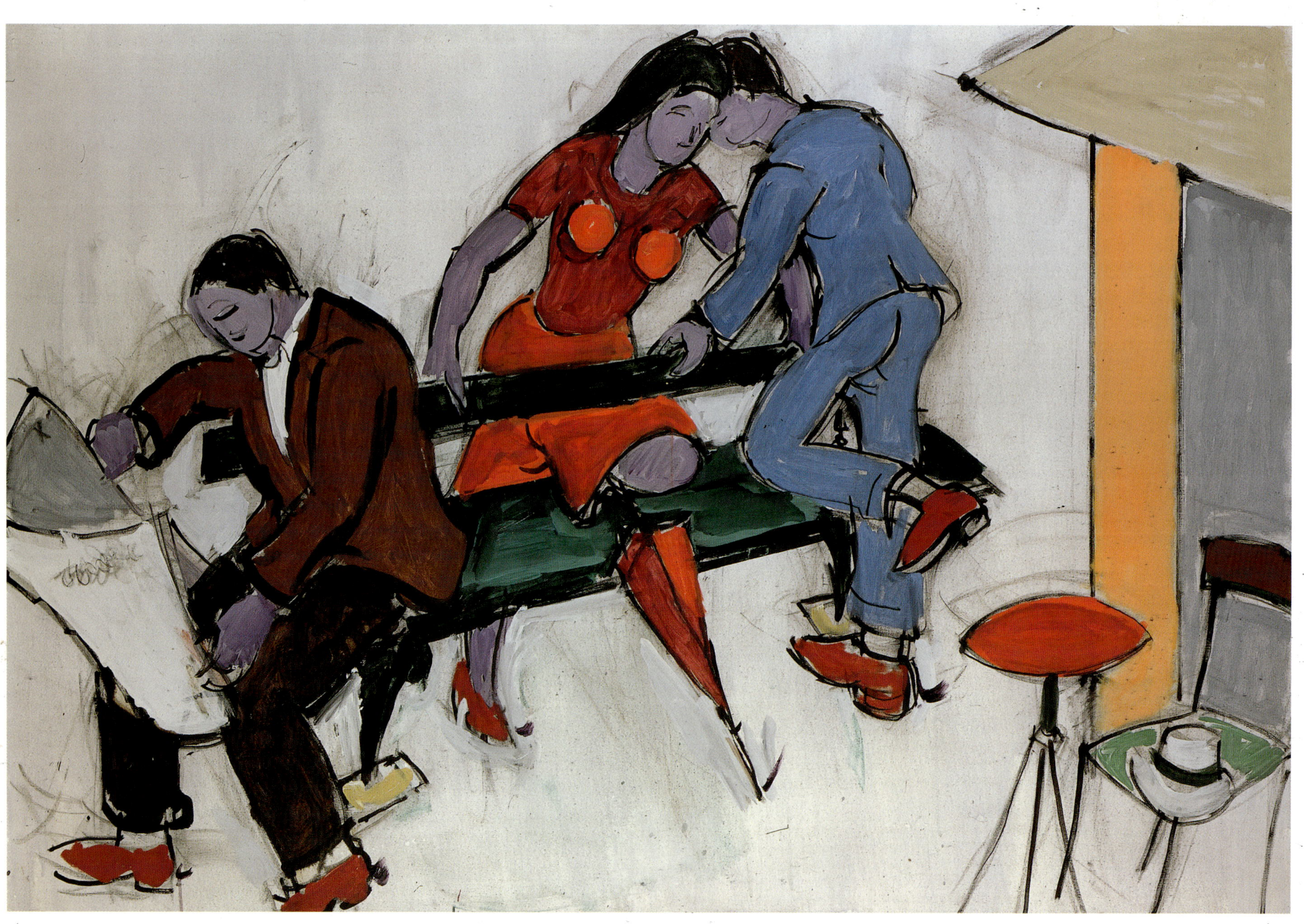

Bench scene, 1983
Acrylic on canvas
114 x 162 cm
Collection of Nicolas Hélion

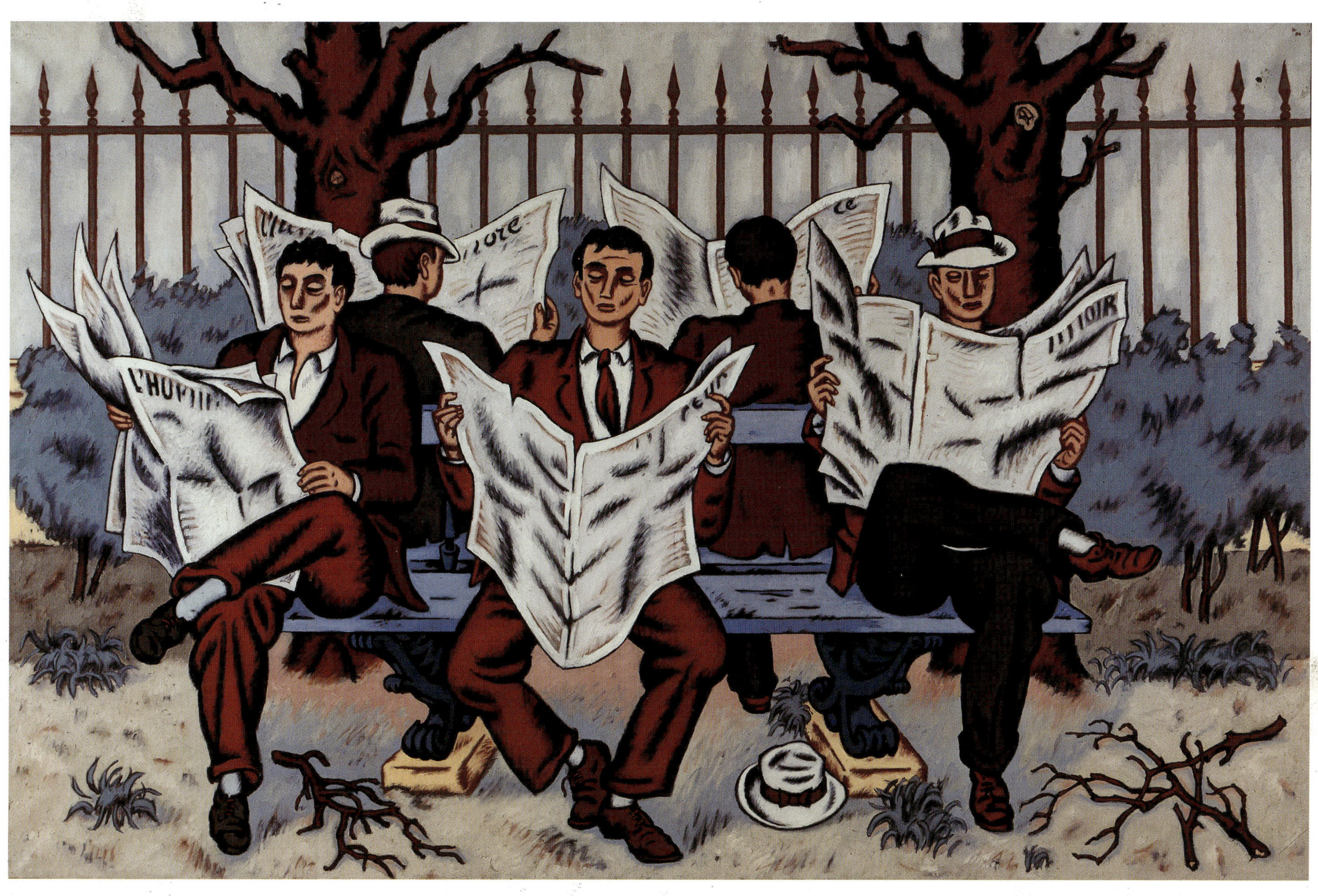

The big daily read, 1950
Oil on canvas
130 x 195 cm
Courtesy Robert Miller Gallery, New York

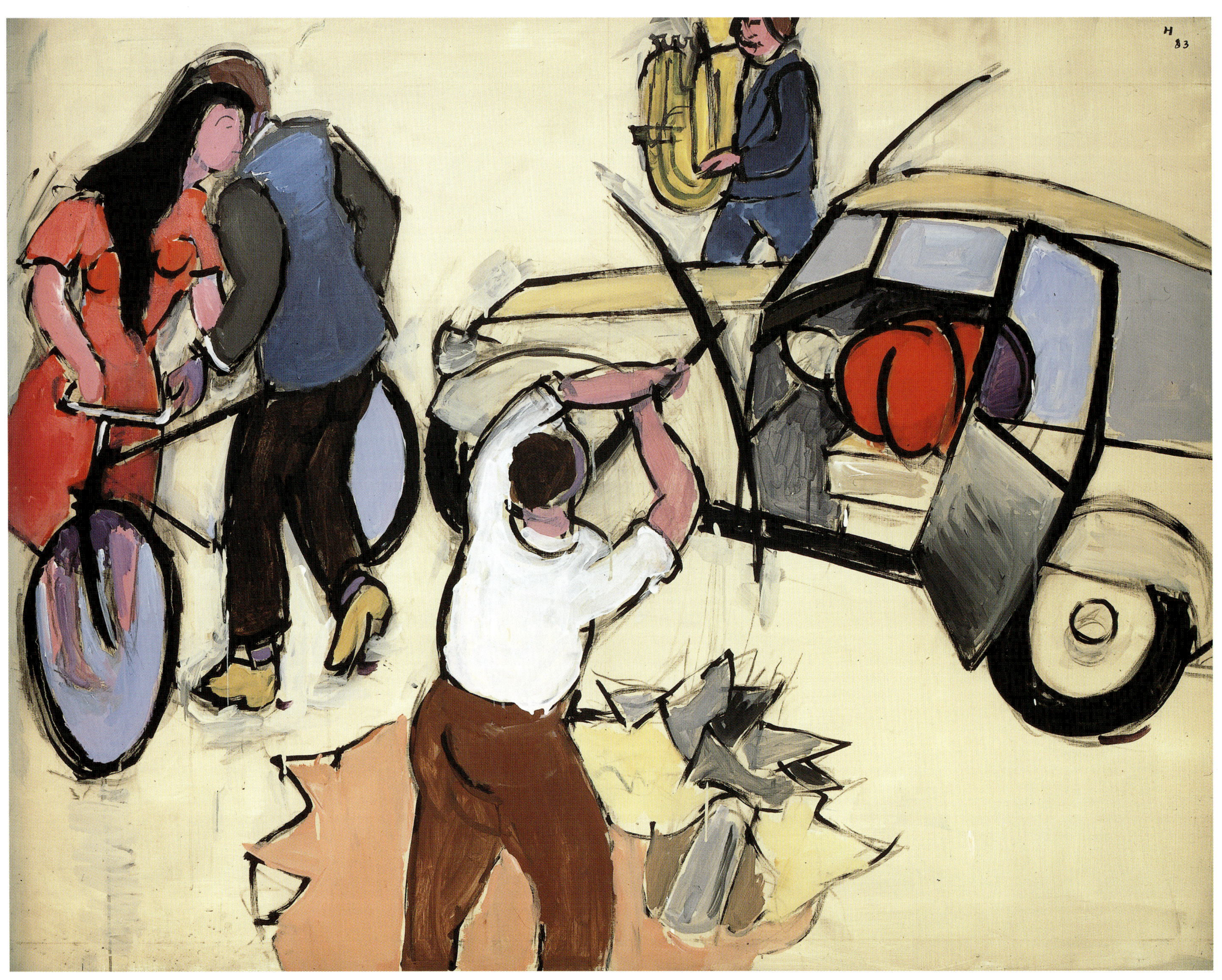

Trumpet for a pumpkin, 1983
Acrylique on canvas
130 x 162 cm
Private collection

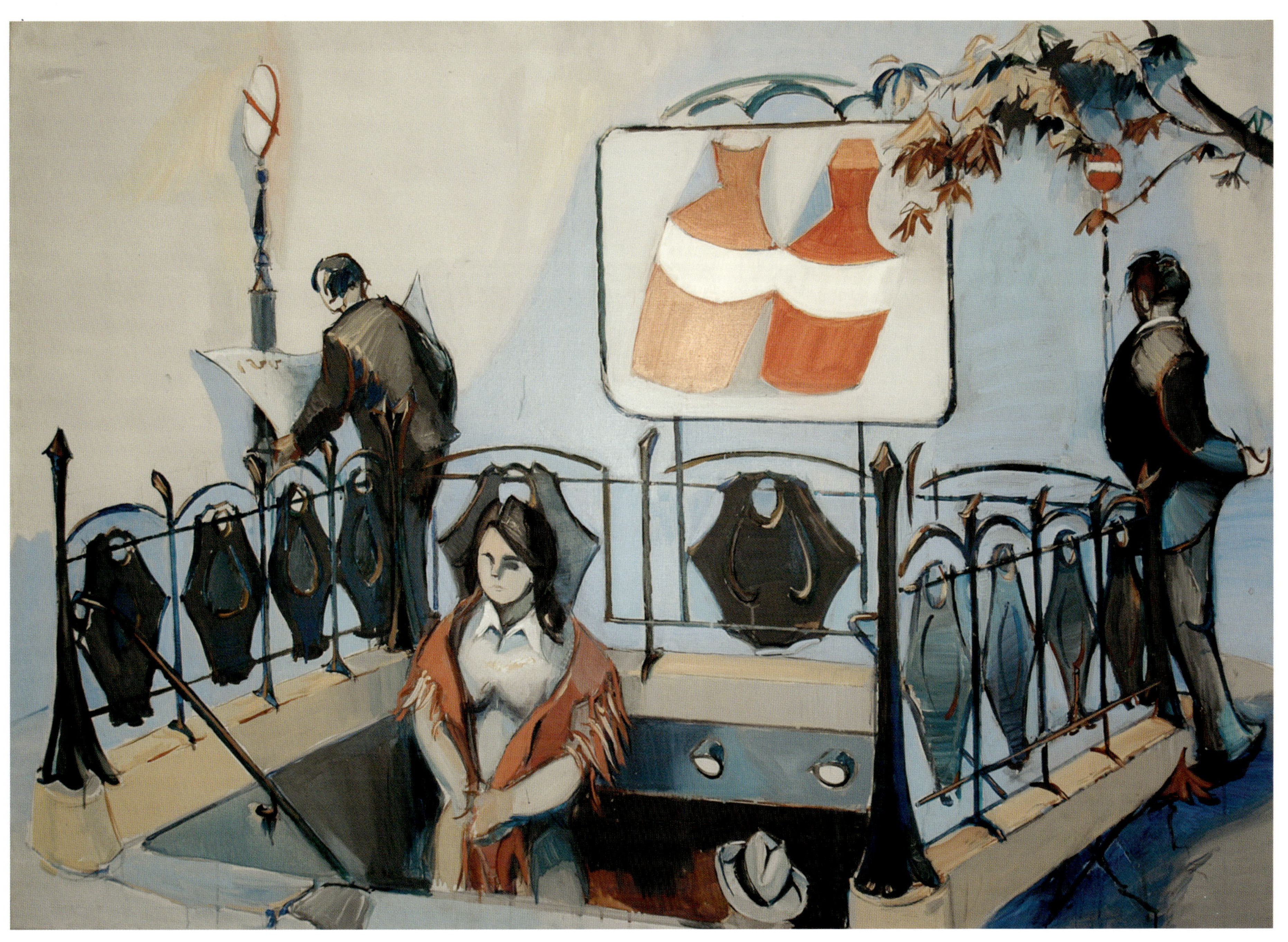

Métro exit, 1969
Acrylic on canvas
130 x 180 cm
Private collection

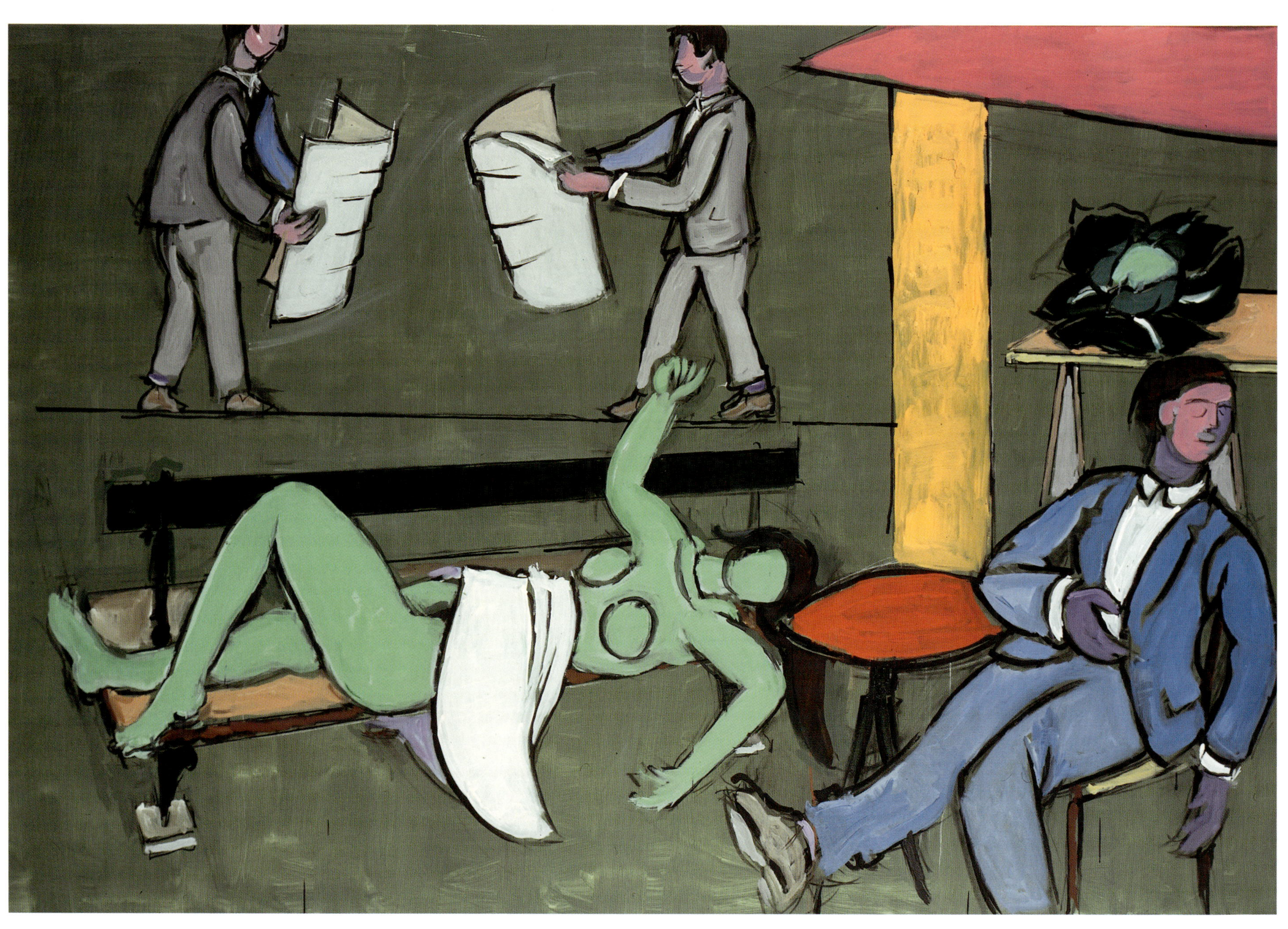

Another daily scene, 1983
Acrylic on canvas
175 x 250 cm
Private collection

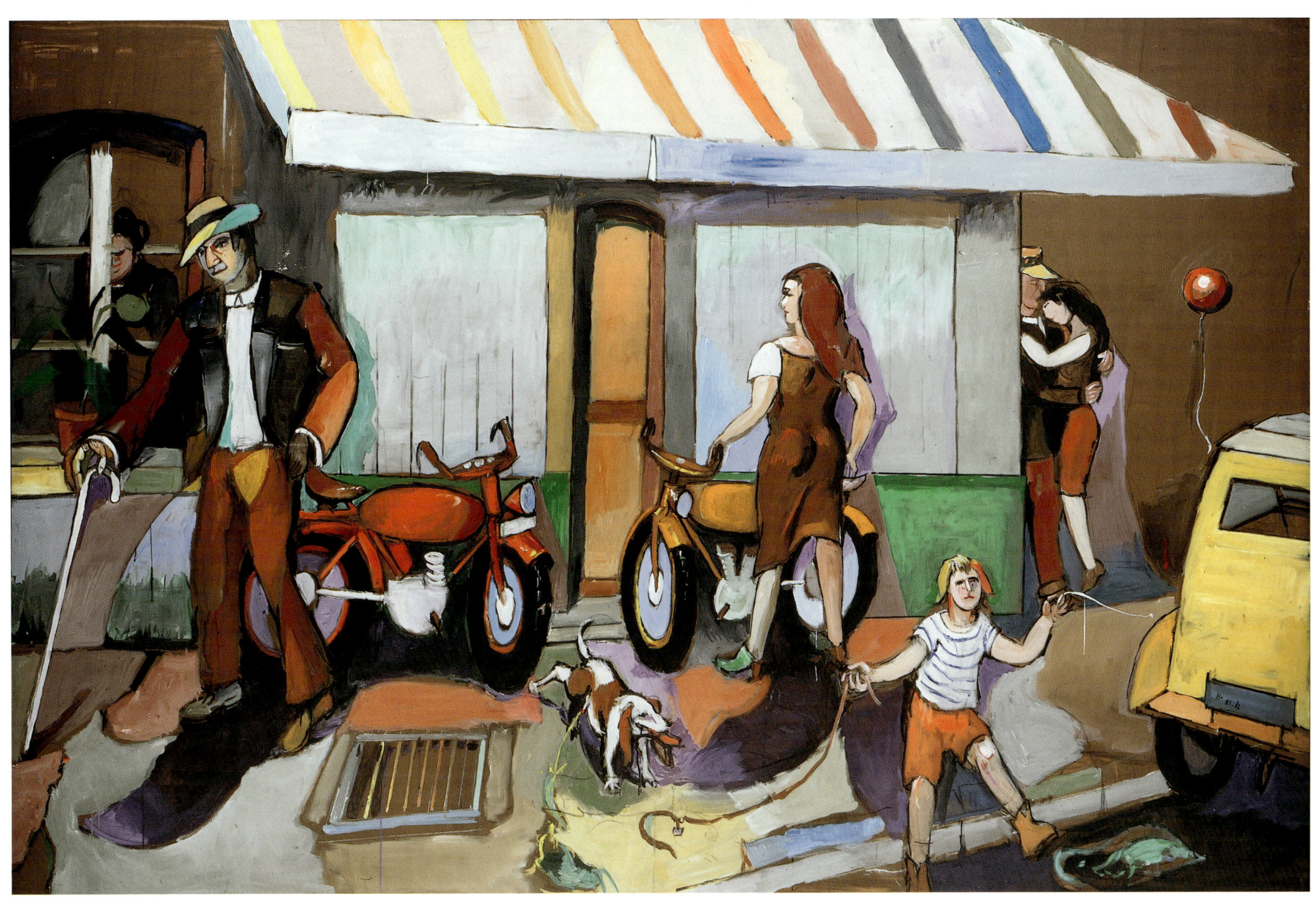

The day's events, 1982
Acrylic on canvas
200 x 300 cm
Private collection, Geneva

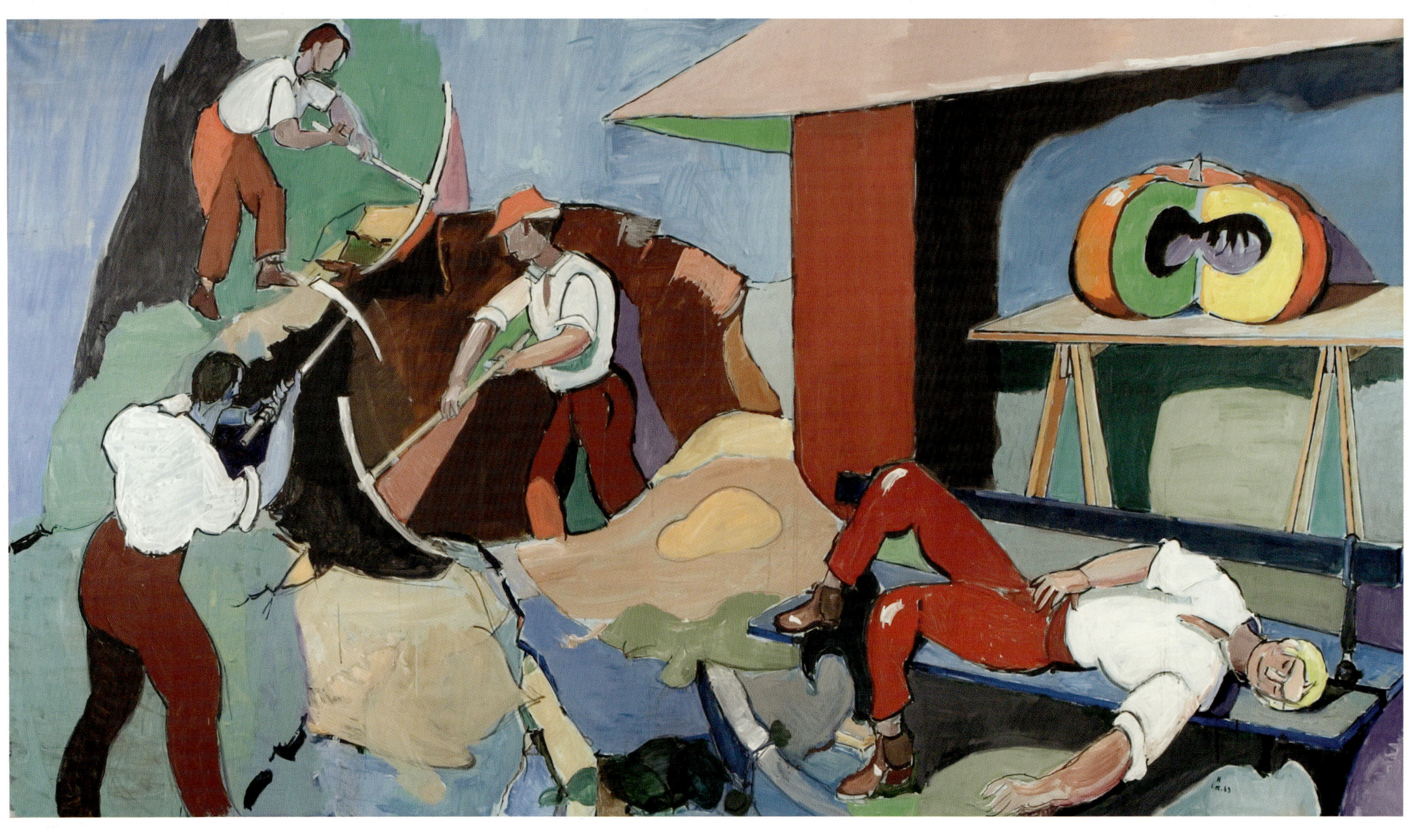

The city, 1983
Acrylic on canvas
200 x 350 cm
Galerie Piltzer

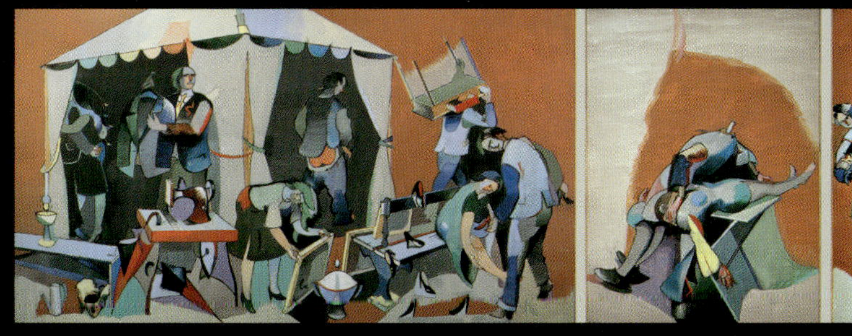
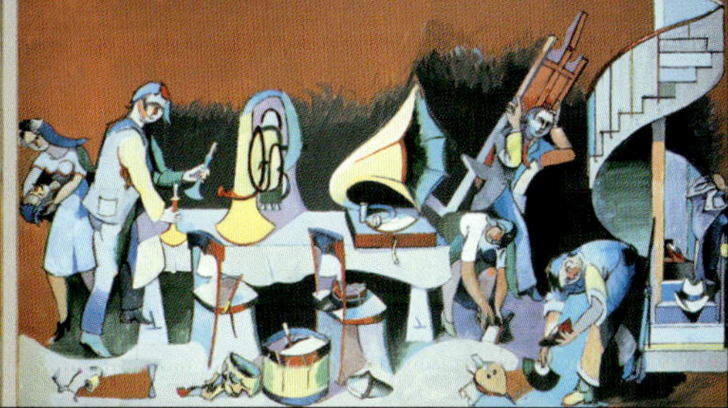

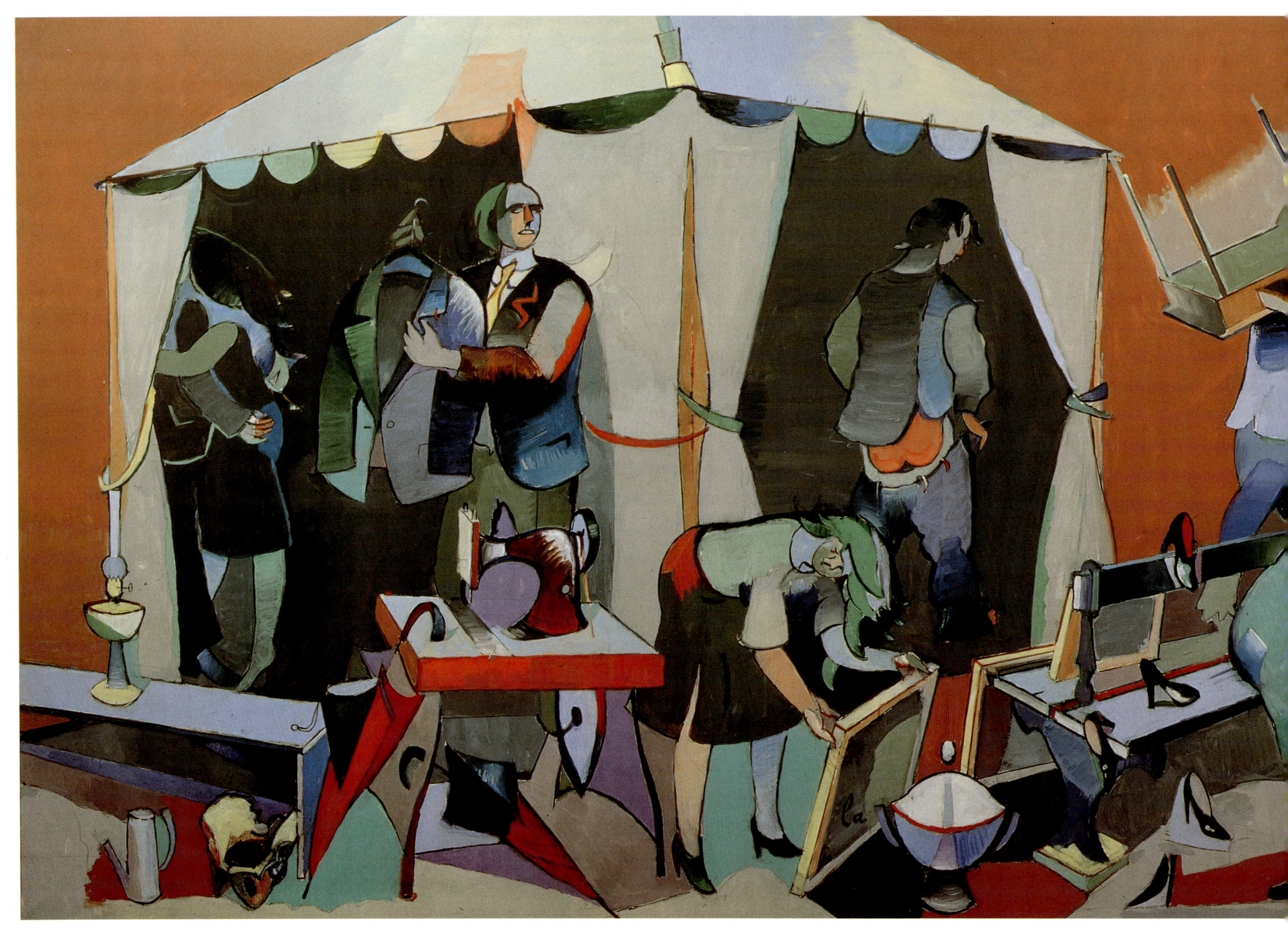

The Last Judgement of things, 1978–79
Triptych, acrylic on canvas
200 x 845 cm (whole)
Central panel 200 x 145 cm,
side panels 200 x 350 cm
Private collection

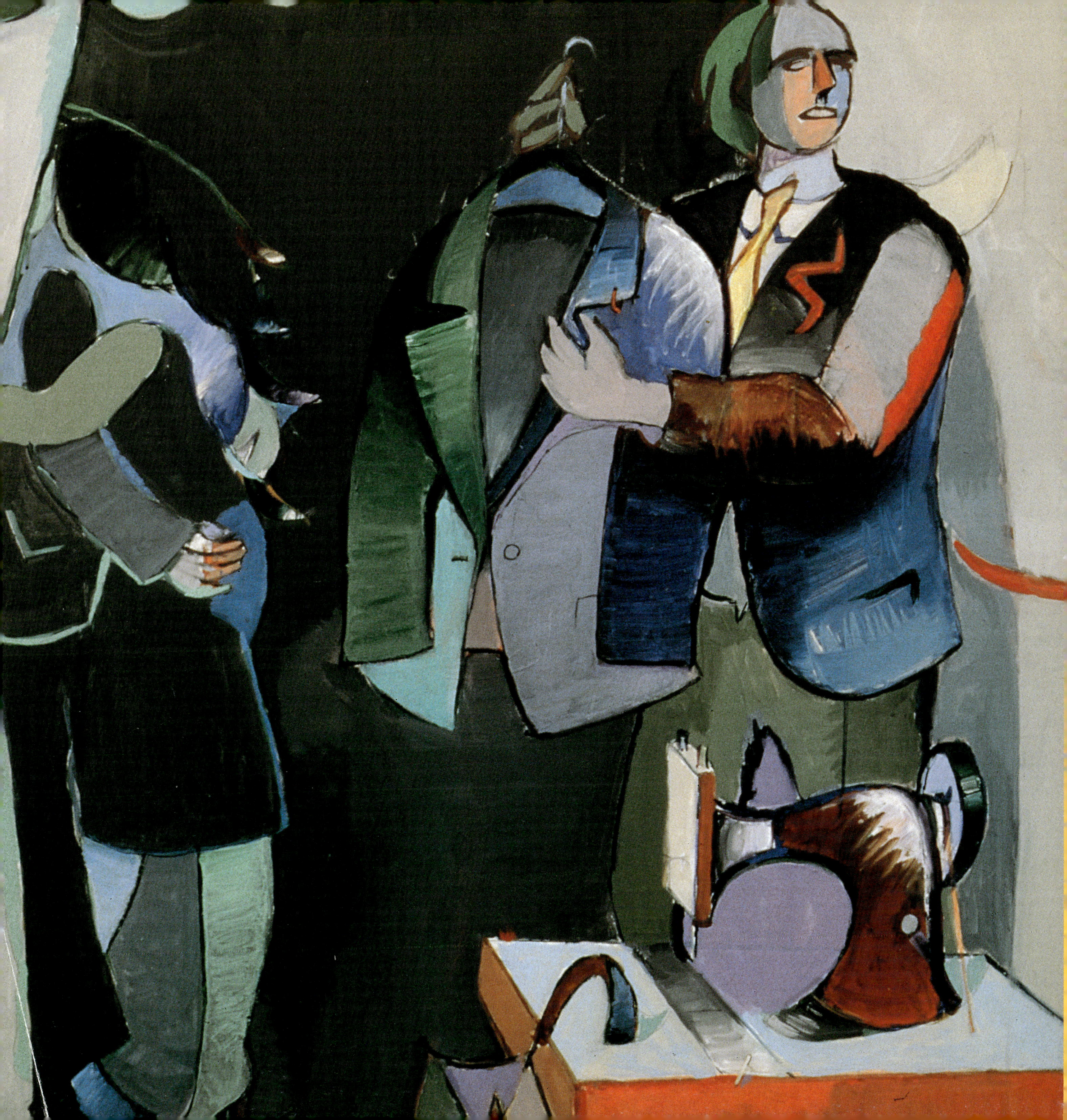

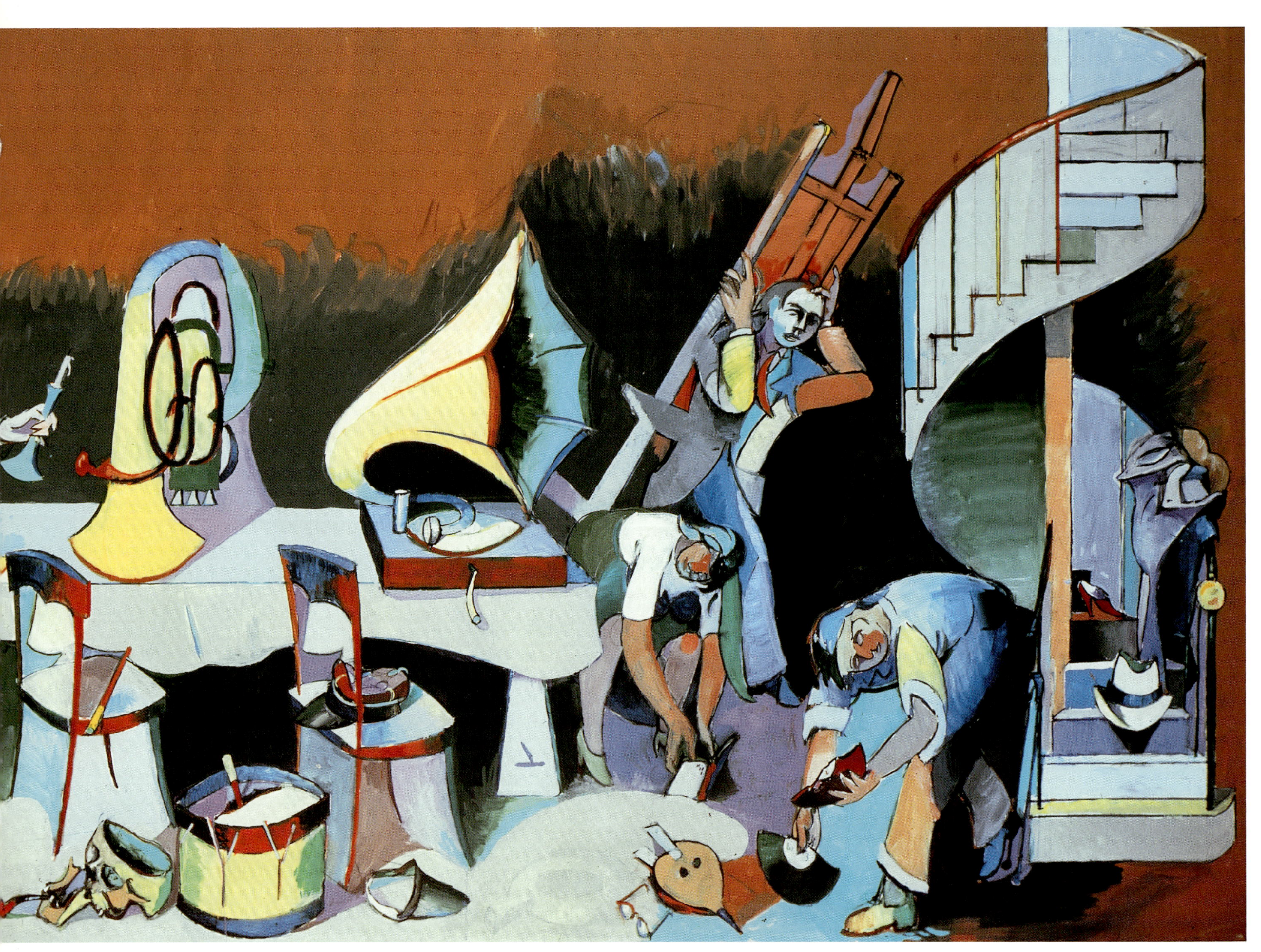

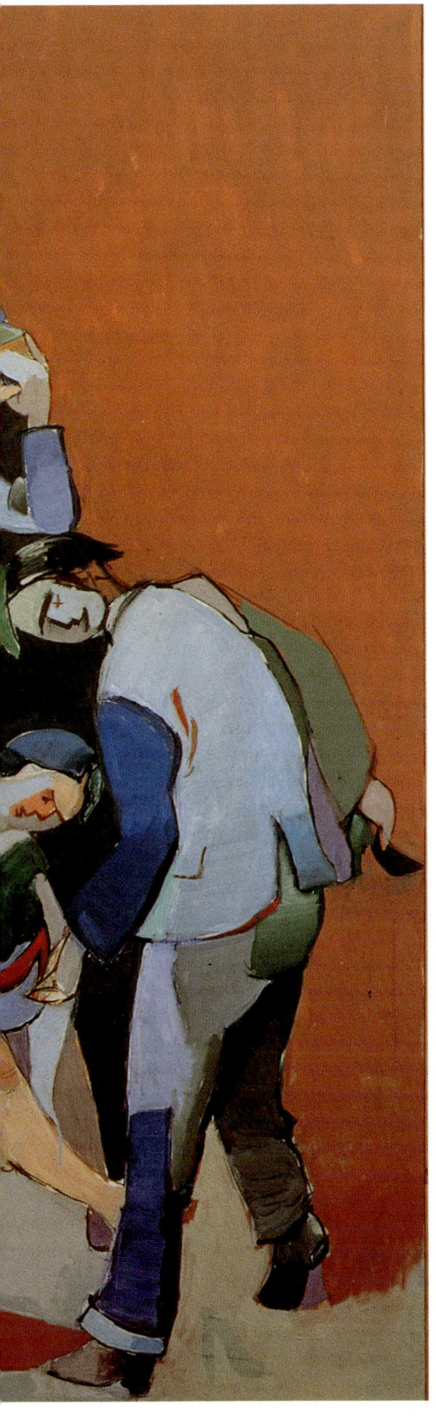
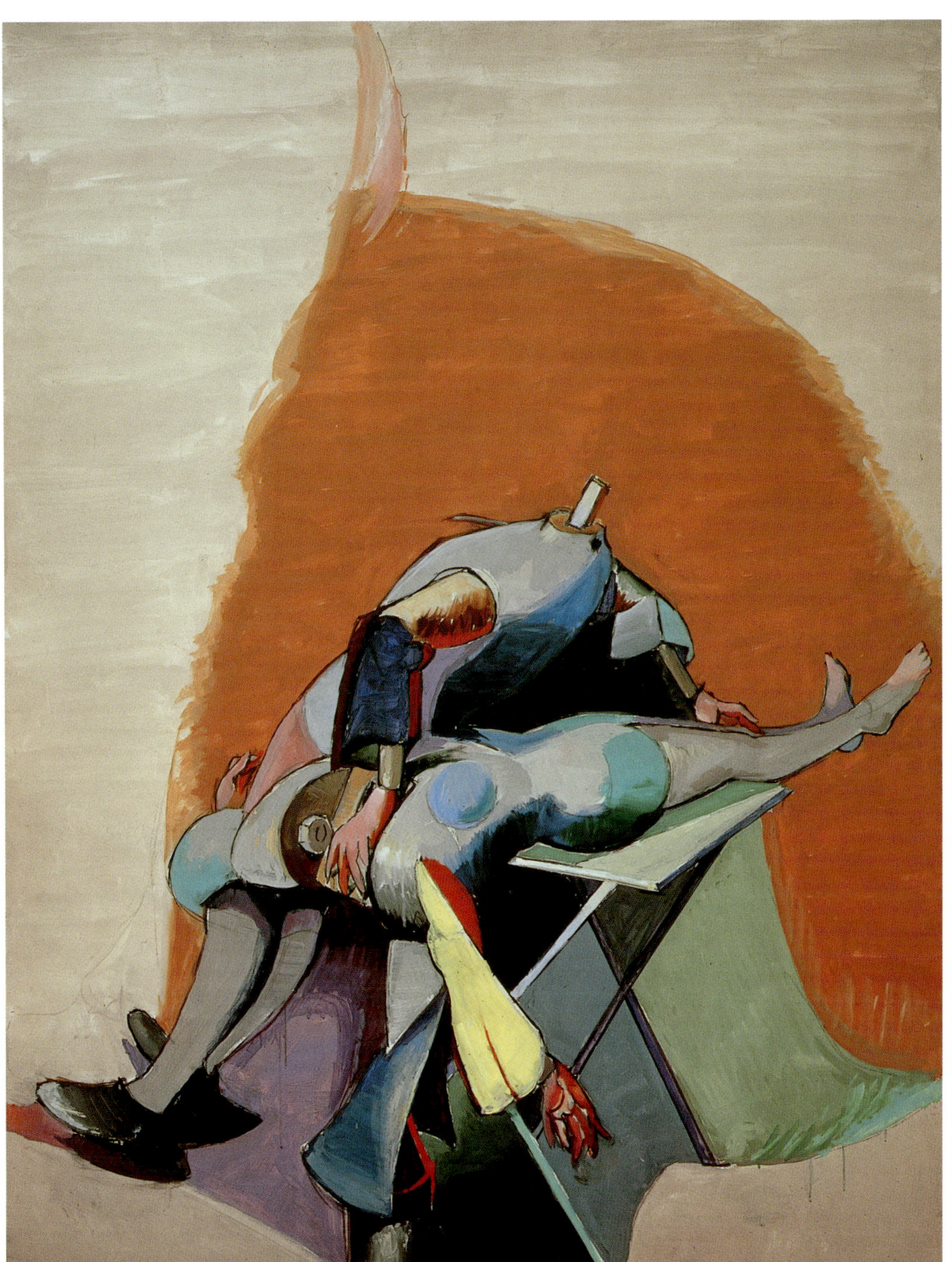
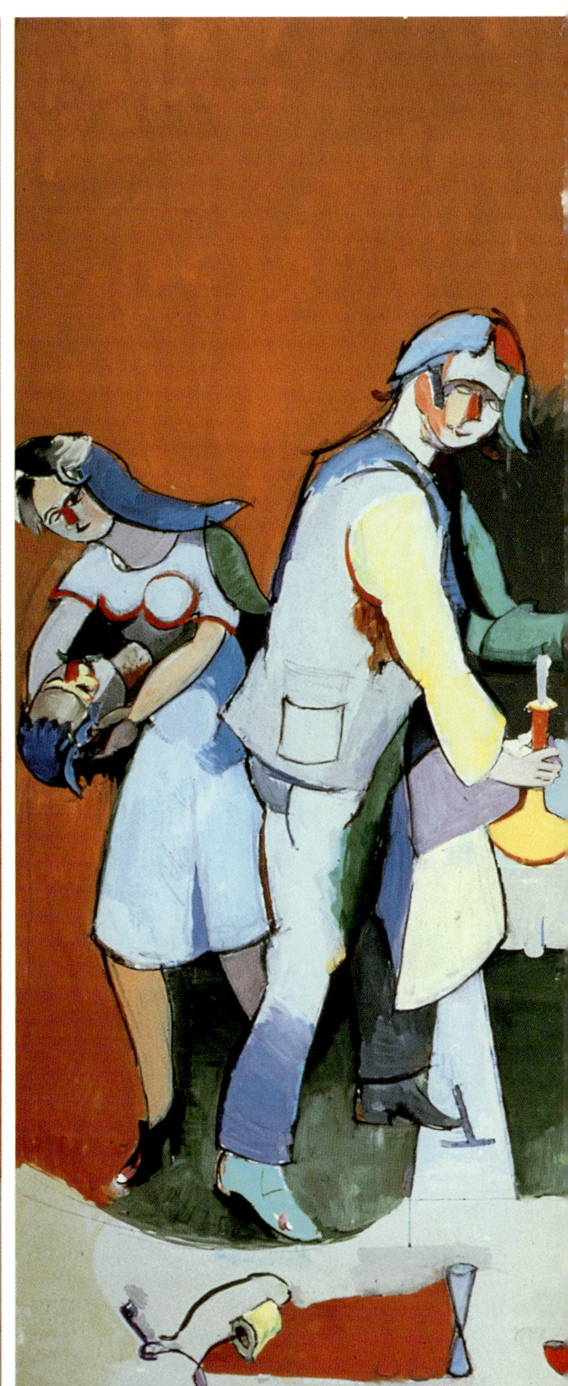

DRAWINGS
DESSINS

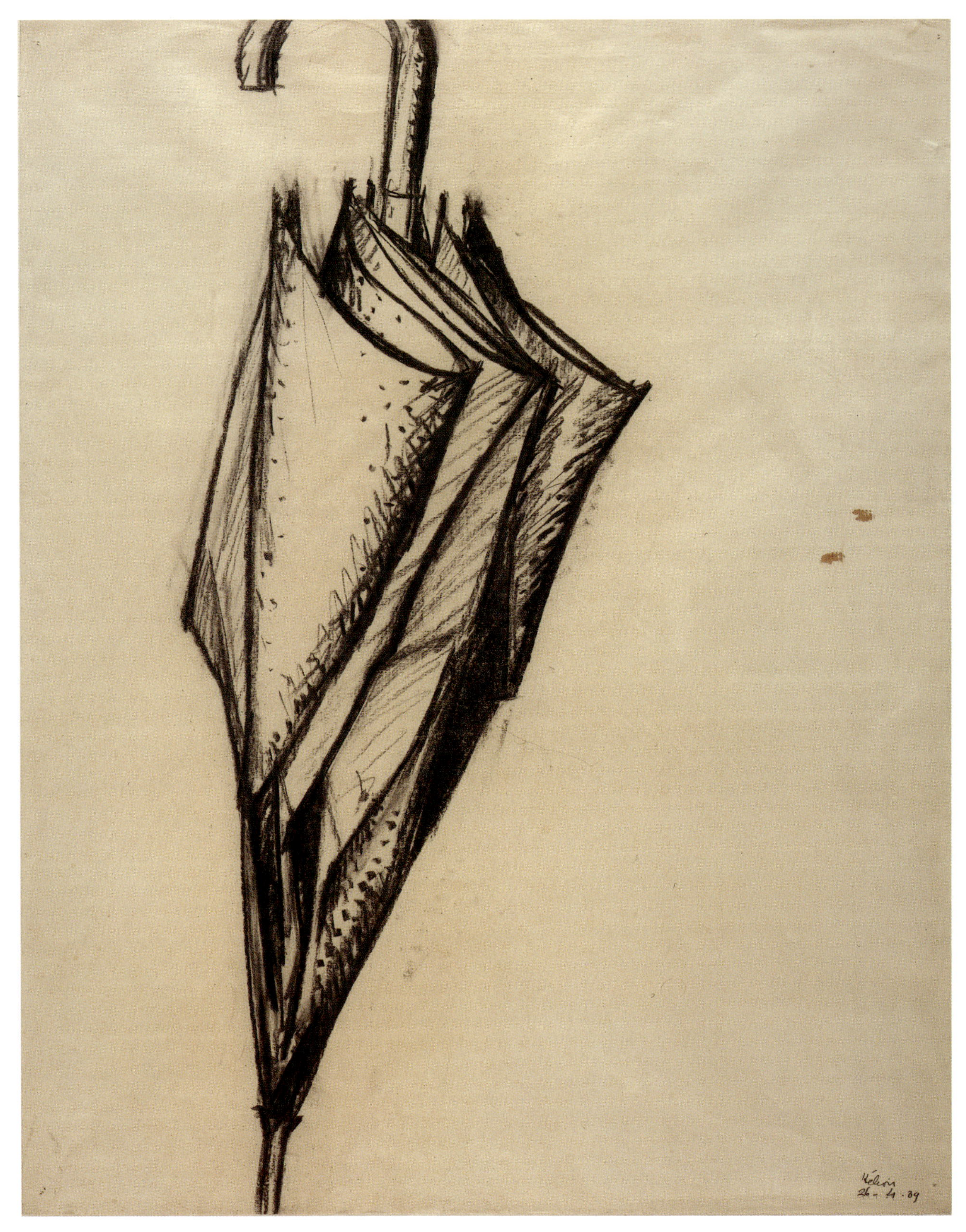

Umbrella, 1939
Charcoal on Ingres paper, 62 x 47.5 cm
Centre Pompidou, Musée national d'art moderne, Paris,
gift of the Société des Amis du Musée national d'art
moderne, 1980

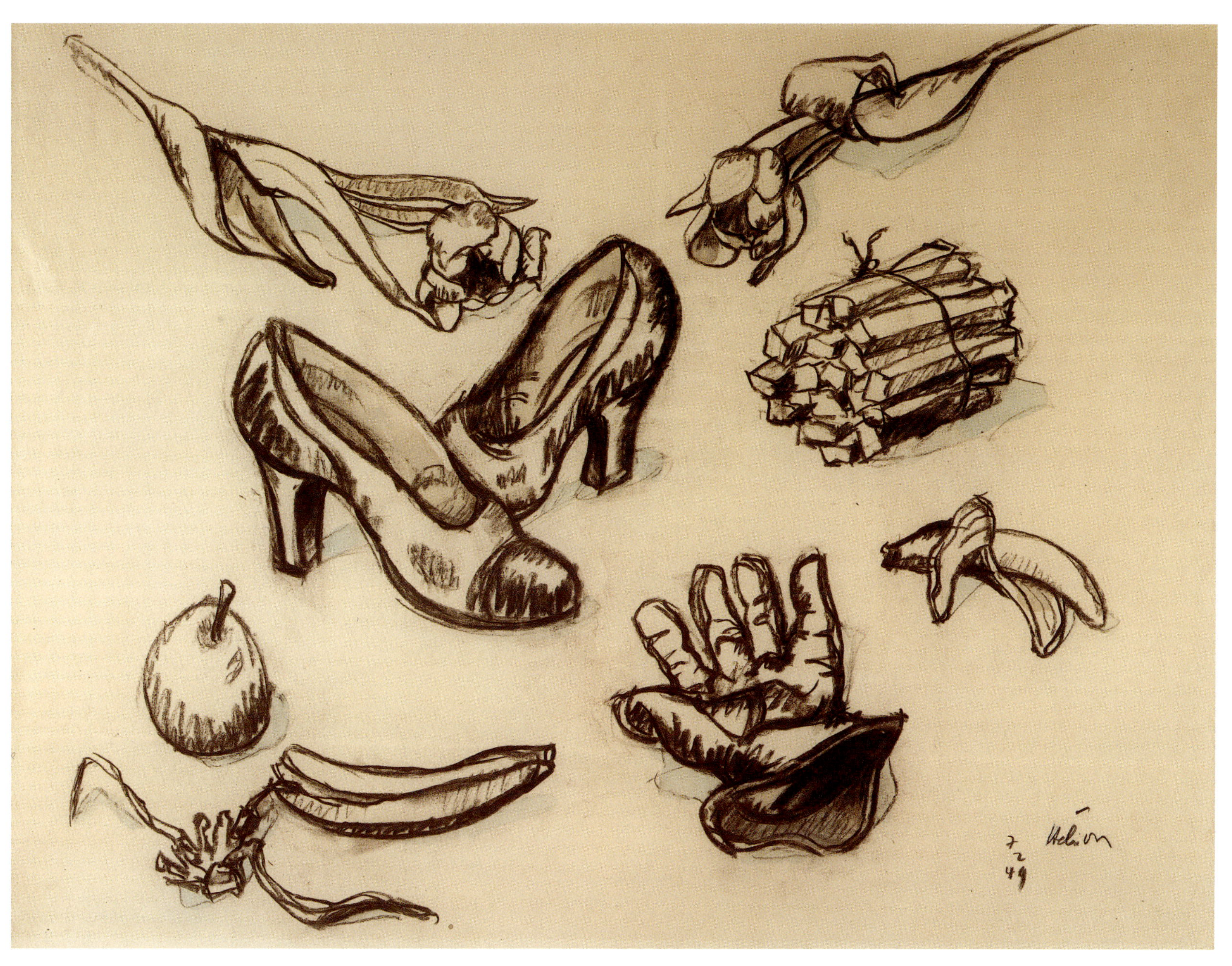

Items 21, 1949
Charcoal with watercolour heightening on paper,
49.7 x 64.7 cm
Centre Pompidou, Musée national d'art moderne, Paris,
gift of the Société des Amis du Musée national d'art
moderne, 1980

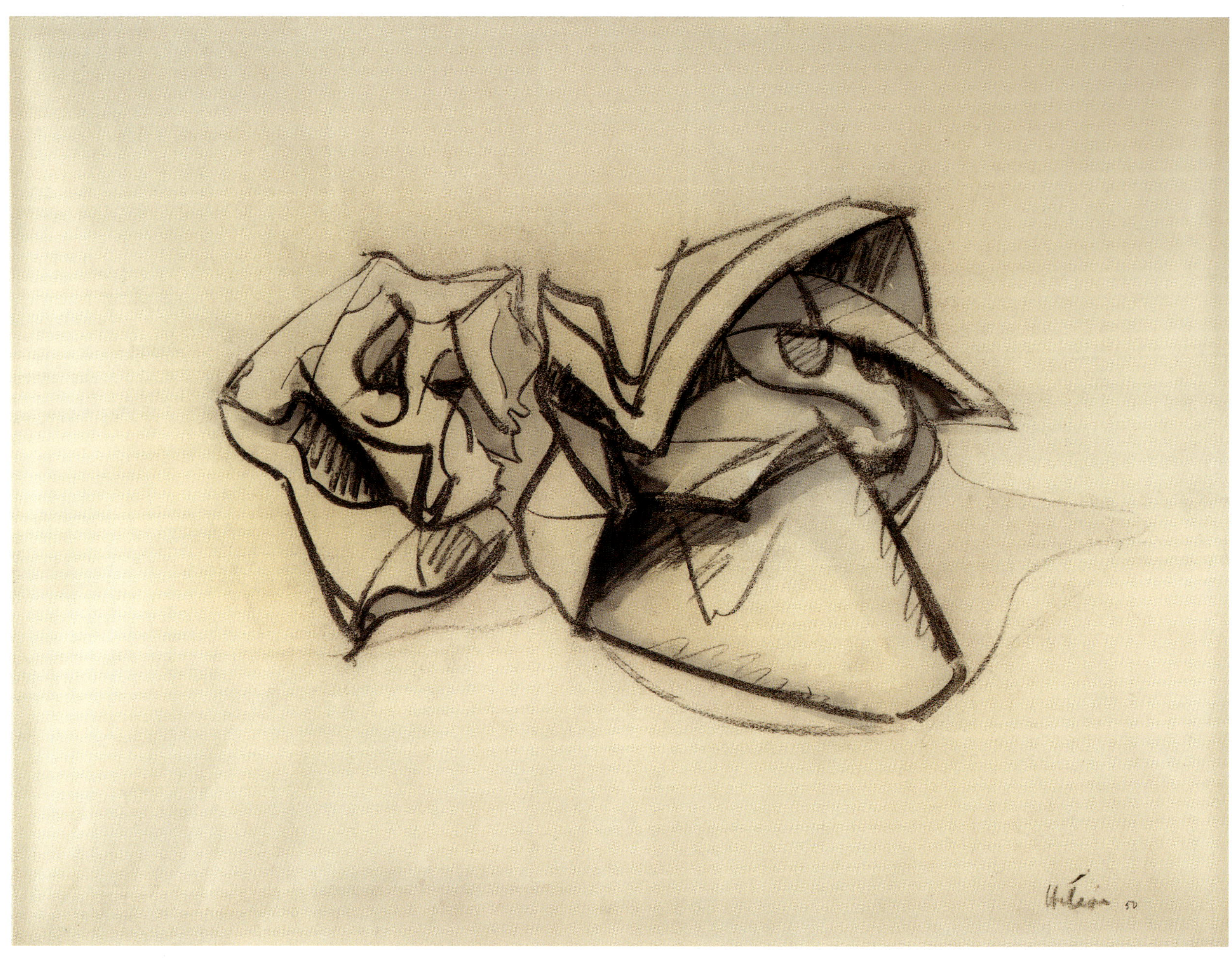

Crumpled newspaper, 1950
Charcoal with ink heightening on stuck-down paper
50.5 x 65.3 cm
Centre Pompidou, Musée national d'art moderne, Paris,
gift of the Société des Amis du Musée national d'art
moderne, 1980

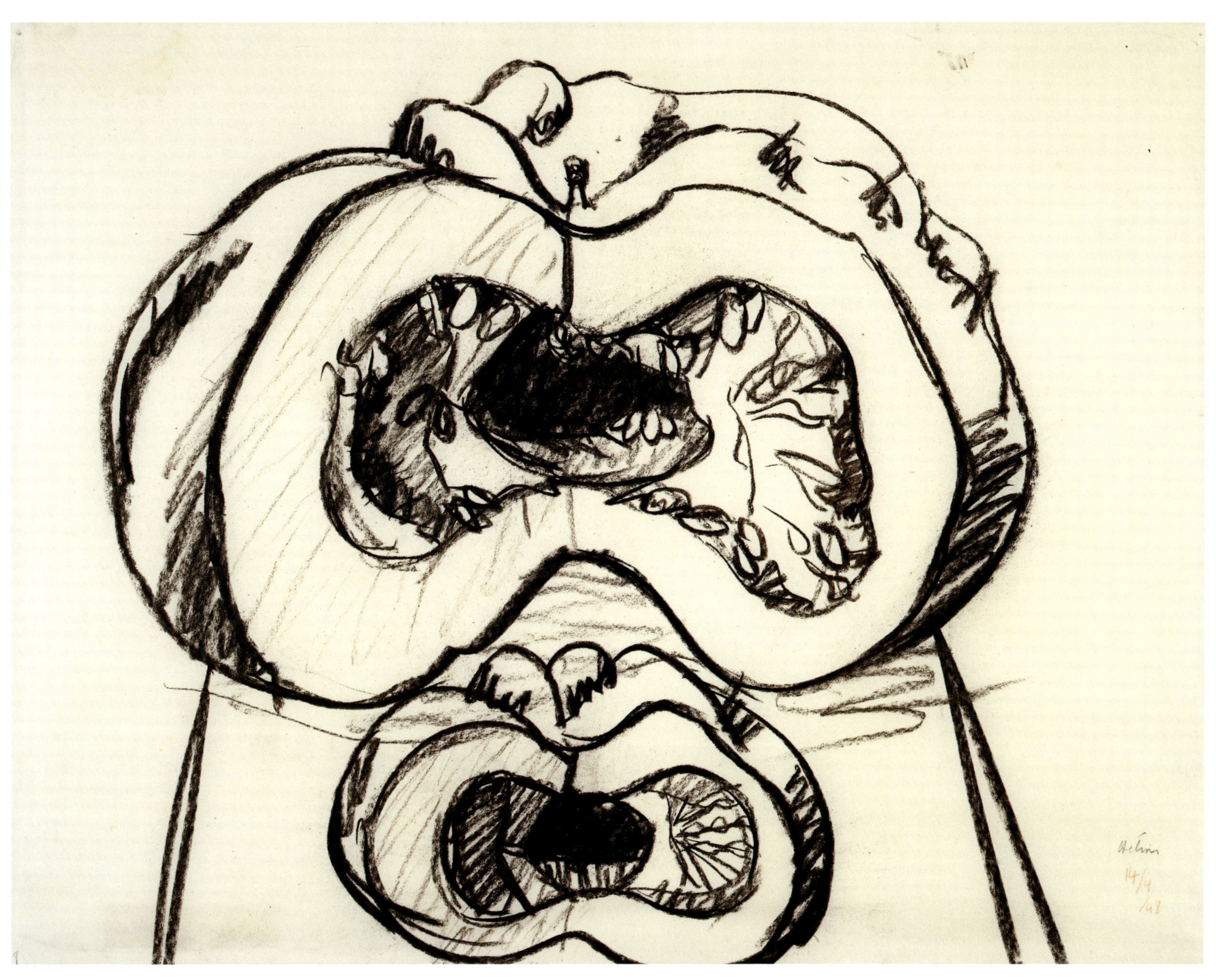

Mother and daughter pumpkin, 1948
Charcoal on paper, 44.2 x 56.1 cm
Centre Pompidou, Musée national d'art moderne, Paris,
accepted in lieu of tax 1991

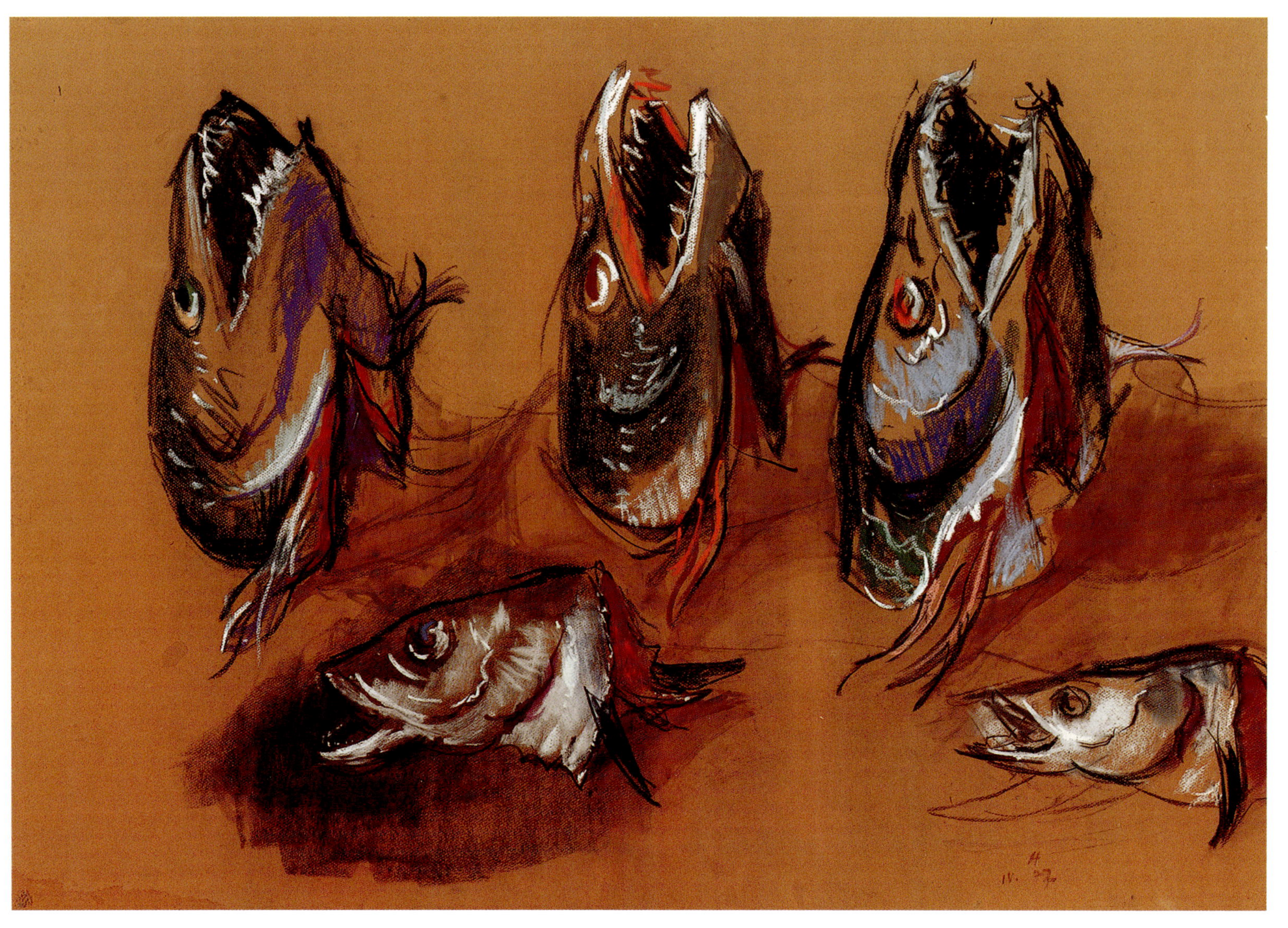

Sacrificial victims, 1977
Pastel and wash on brown Canson paper, 75 x 106 cm
Centre Pompidou, Musée national d'art moderne, Paris,
accepted in lieu of tax 1991

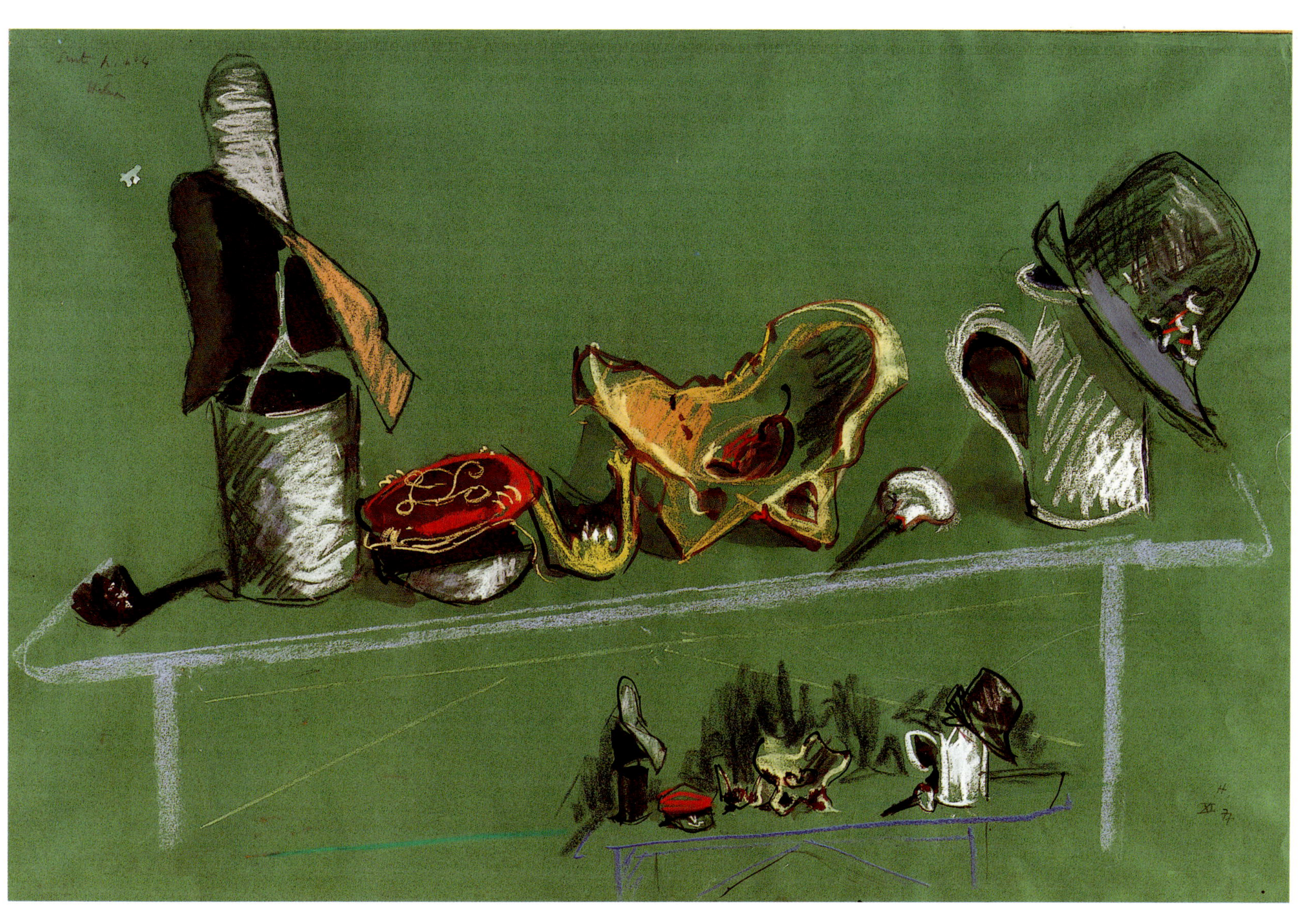

Flea-market stuff, 1977
Charcoal, pastel and inks on green Canson paper,
75.4 x 110.5 cm
Centre Pompidou, Musée national d'art moderne, Paris,
accepted in lieu of tax 1991

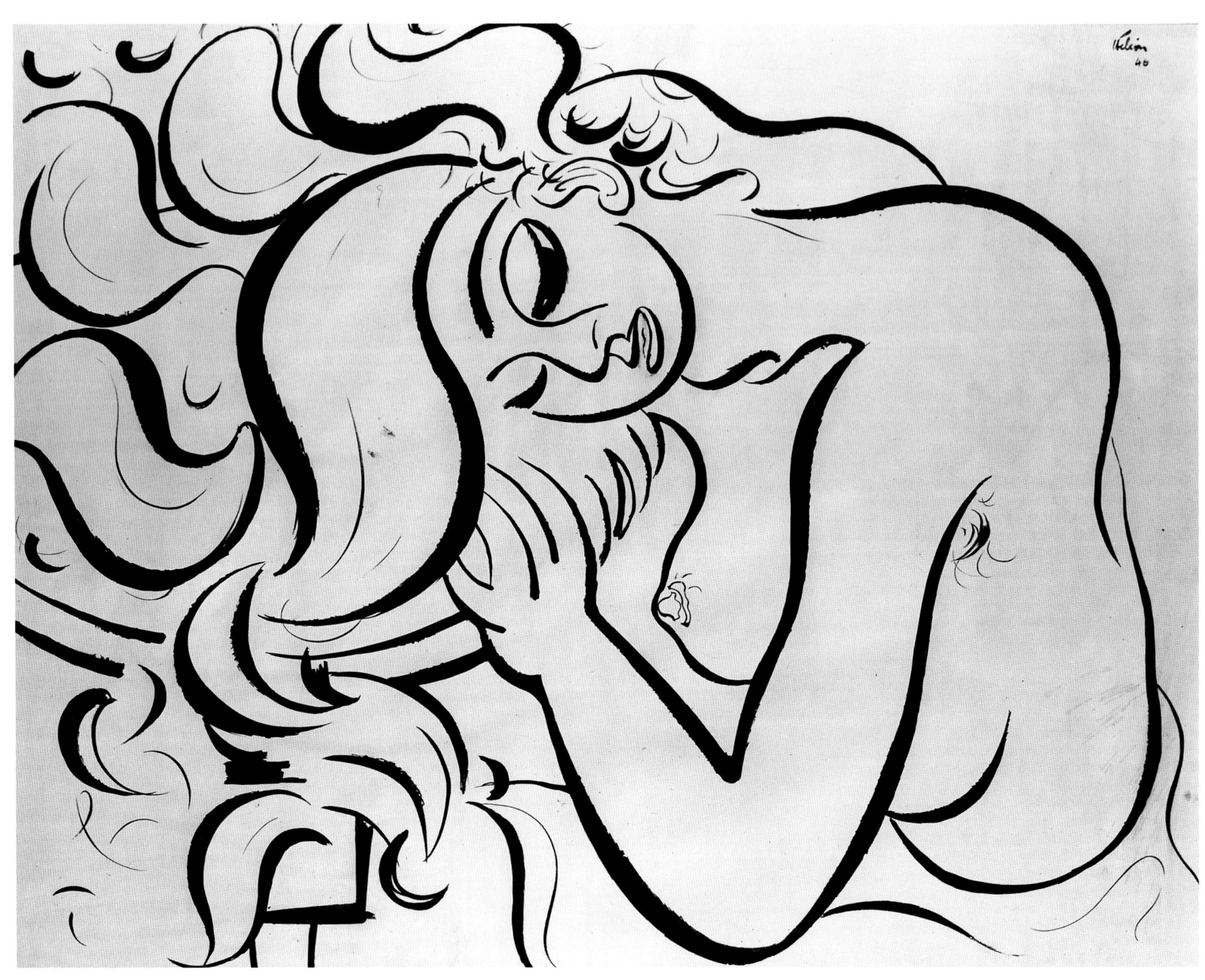

Girl with her hair undone, 1946
Brush and Chinese ink, 79 x 100 cm
Private collection, Paris

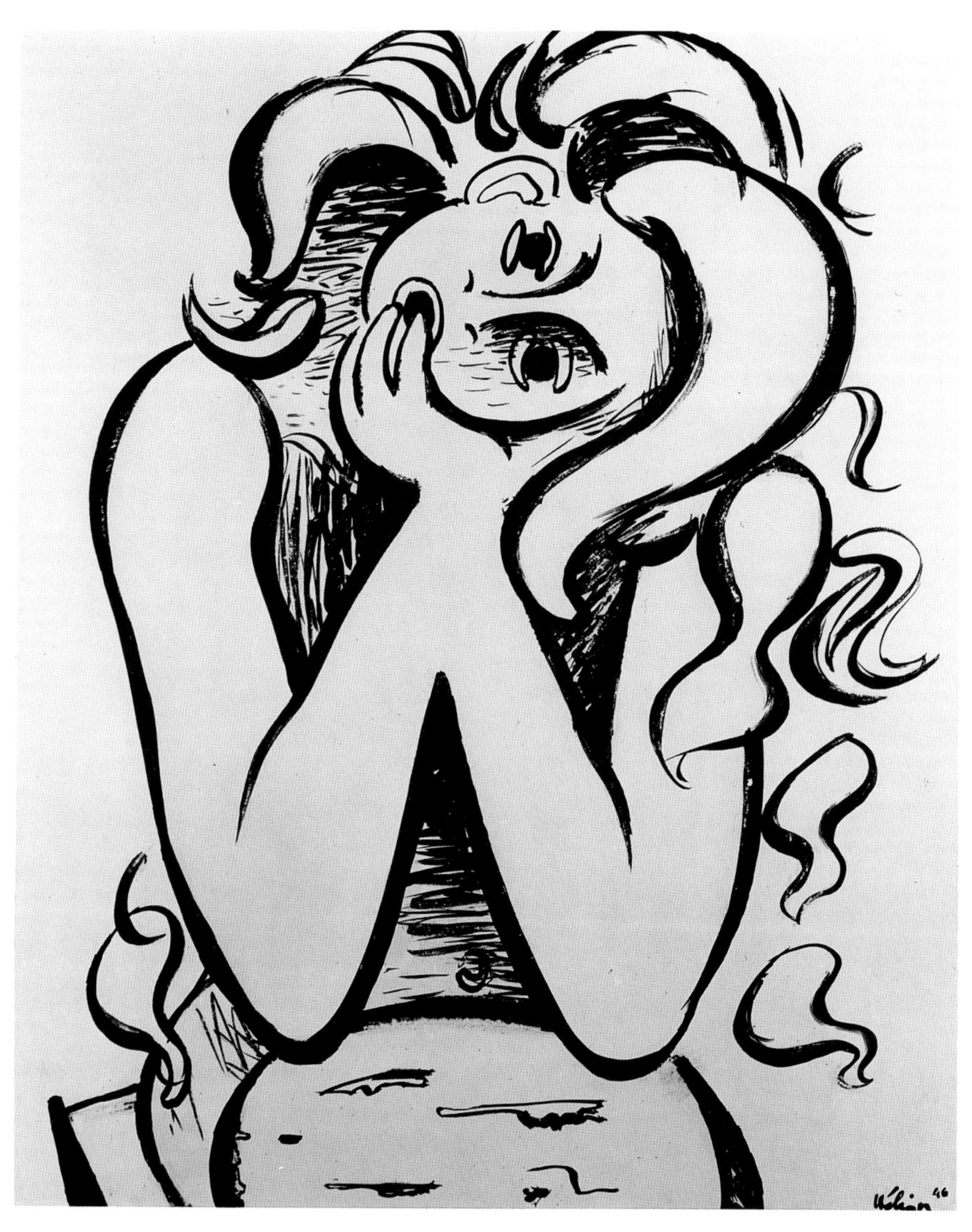

Woman leaning on her elbows, 1946
Brush and Chinese ink, 73 x 59 cm
Private collection, Paris

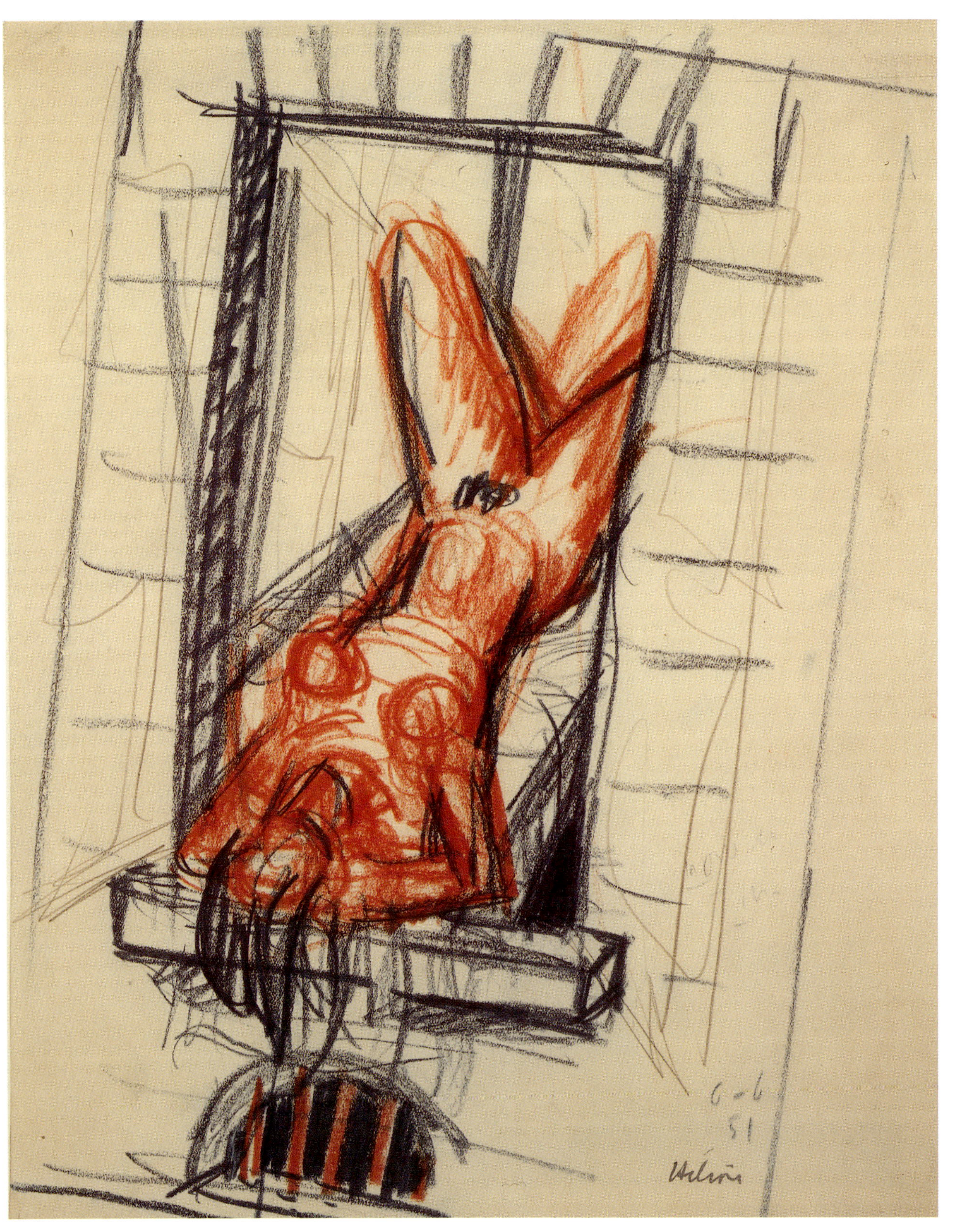

The Spring, 1951
(Inverted nude)
Chalks on paper, 30.5 x 24 cm
Centre Pompidou, Musée national d'art moderne, Paris,
purchase 1976

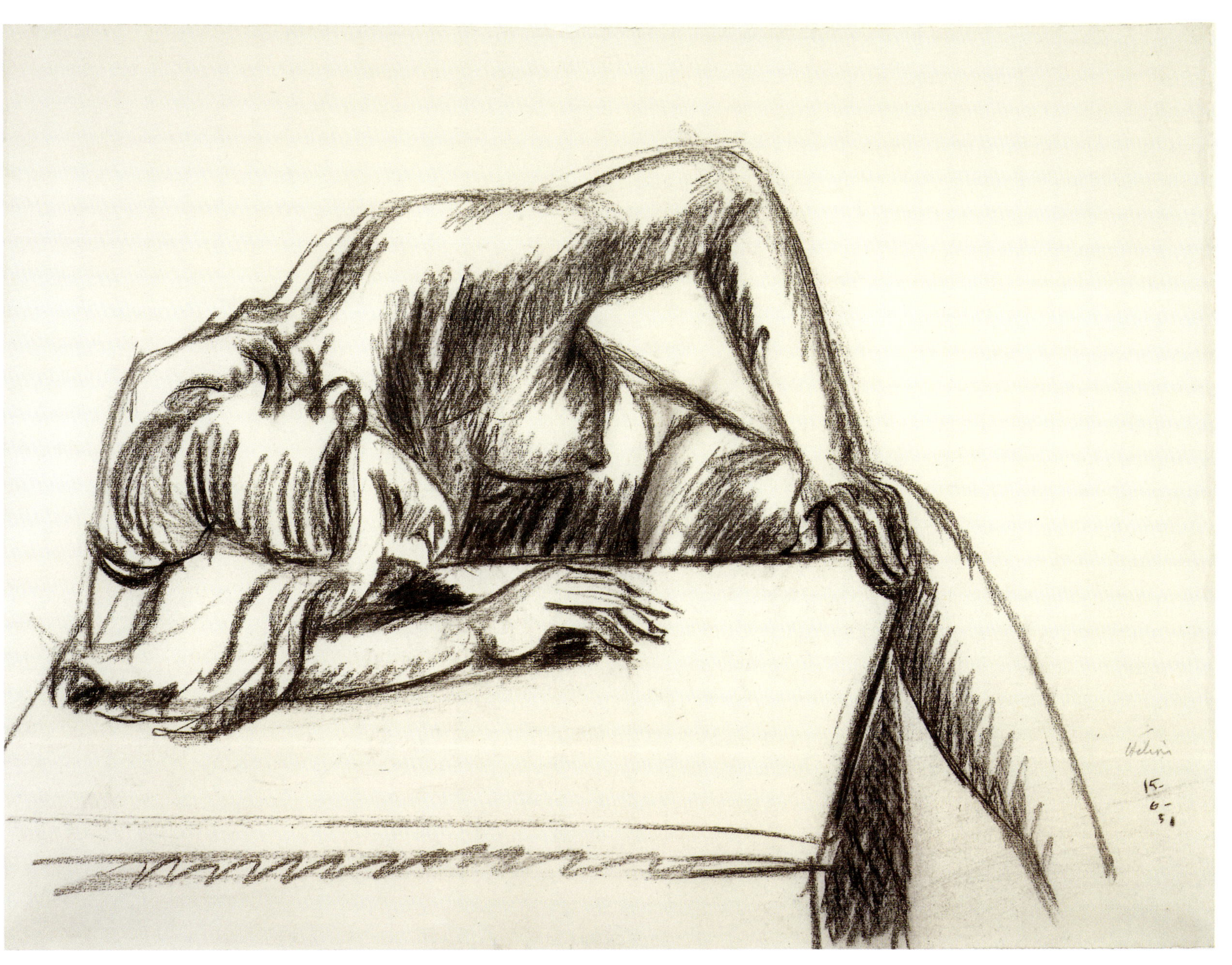

Nude slumped, 1951
Charcoal on laid paper, 48.2 x 63.1 cm
Centre Pompidou, Musée national d'art moderne, Paris,
accepted in lieu of tax 1991

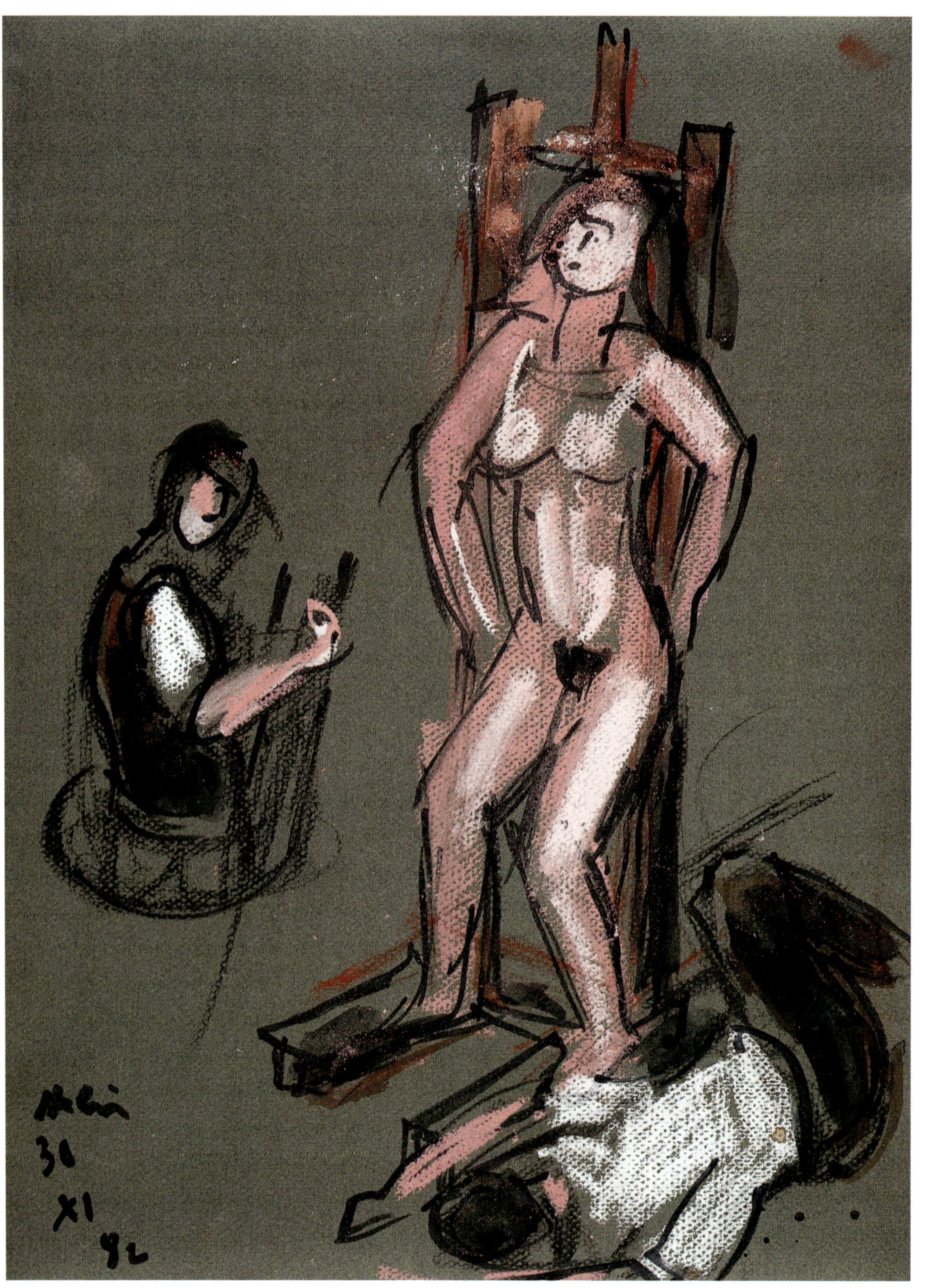

Last symbol, 1982
Pastel, charcoal and inks on green Canson paper,
44.2 x 31.8 cm
Centre Pompidou, Musée national d'art moderne, Paris,
accepted in lieu of tax 1991

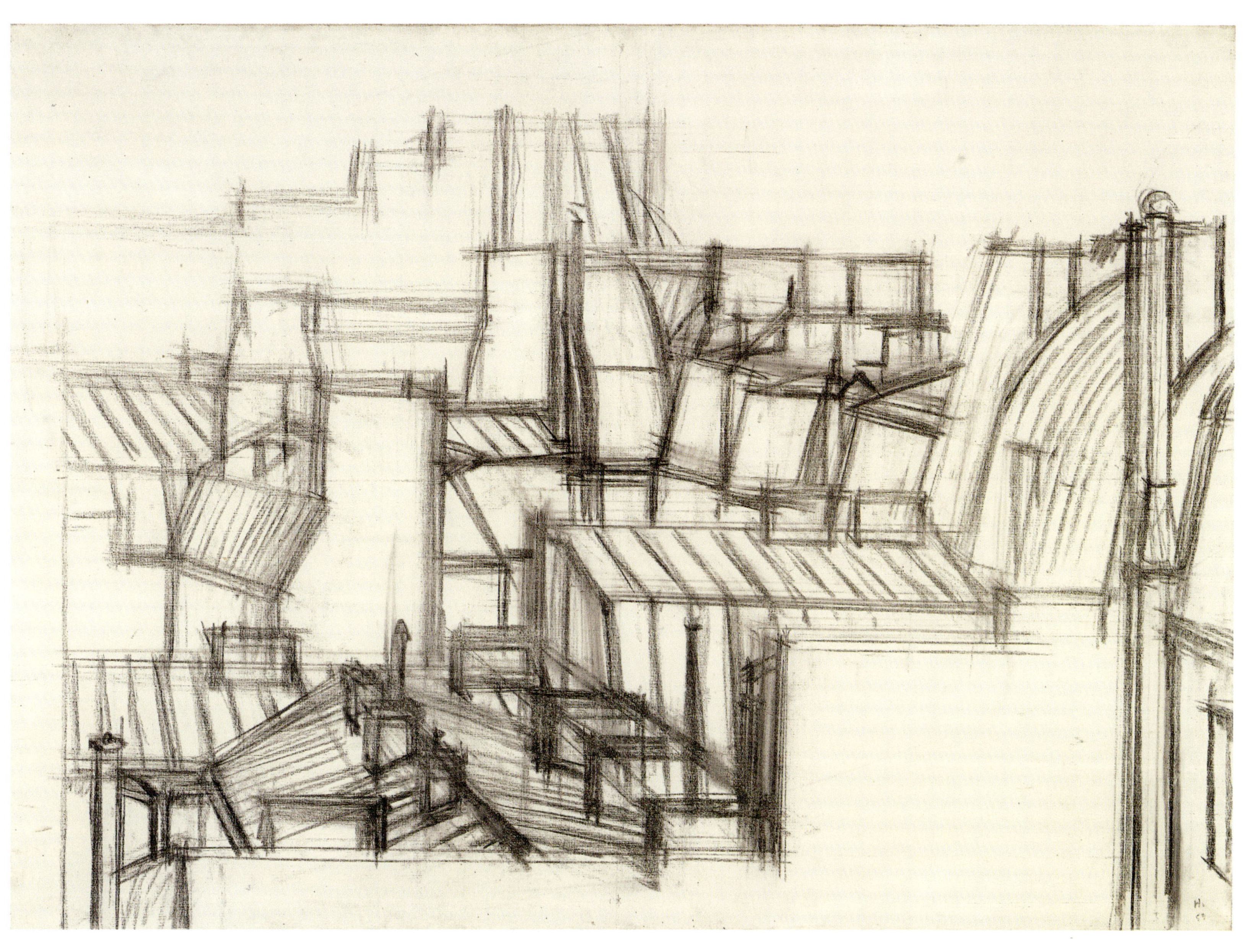

Roofs, 1953
(Study)
Charcoal on canvas, 96 x 128.5 cm
Centre Pompidou, Musée national d'art moderne, Paris,
accepted in lieu of tax 1991

CHRONO
ANTHO

1904

Jean Hélion (real name Bichier) is born at Couterne (Orne) on 21 April. He is brought up in Normandy by his grandmother until the age of eight: "After devoting all my life to Art, I now wonder what paths led me irresistibly in that direction from a young age. People did not talk about art at Couterne, where a grandmother and a great-aunt, both charming, brought me up, nor even of beauty. I heard people say things like 'what a beautiful rabbit', 'what a beautiful meadow', or even 'what a beautiful baby'. But that did nothing to separate the notions of beauty from the rest of the world."[1]

1912–17

Joins his parents in Amiens in 1912, where he attends primary school. His father, Louis, is a taxi-driver, his mother a dressmaker:
"I am the son of a taxi-driver of rural origins. On my mother's side, minor officials, turned small shopkeepers or poor manual workers. It would appear – but can one be sure? – that one of my great-great-grandmothers was St Elisabeth Bichier des Âges. To tell the truth, I am very much of common birth, of the people, though not of the rabble. I have large, rather clumsy feet; large hands, which would be attractive if the nails were not short and brittle. From all that I draw strength. I have the patience of a peasant farmer, the ingenuity and endurance of a manual worker. That can be useful. But working people do not recognize me as one of their own. Though unaffected, I have neither their tastes nor their manners. Neither have I the manners of the others, middle-class people and the rest of them."[2]
"My mother boiled our modest cooking-pot as best she could. Then we climbed a ladder to the attic, where my mother slept with my cousin Jeanne. The adjacent garret was for my grandmother and me. They had installed a mattress beneath the roof timbers. The four corners were full of bric-à-brac: poor people are reluctant to throw away things which might still come in useful, goodness knows when or to whom. They accumulate in attics, they end up here or there. From my bed I could see things which had lost all identity and the large rounded shapes of outmoded tailor's dummies. As I remember it, they were scattered around the attic. But when I picture them, they are standing upright like figures in the theatre, posing for my future mannequin shows, the performance of which fifty years later seems to have reshaped my memories. In another corner, there were some books, including a treatise on obstetrics. Where did it come from? It taught me the secrets of femininity. The illustrations were cold and impersonal. Piled flat, the books had slipped and turned as if to display their dog-eared corners. The dummy on the right was leaning at an angle against the wall, its tripod raised. Between one and the other there were intimate exchanges. These paper sexual organs were admirably suited to these canvas-and-cardboard ladies, their legs sawn at the rump. This was the preamble, or rather the preliminary plan, of a reality of which I already perceived the irresistible attraction…"[3]

In 1912, death of his elder sister Héliane. At junior school, he meets "… a boy full of character, Jean Vassal, who informed me that in a shop in town they were selling off paints at four *sous* a tube; I bought a tube of red lead and another of cobalt blue. I was fascinated by the harmony between them, which reminded me of the hussars' uniforms I had seen at the big parade of 14 July 1913 …. Vassal took me to his house, where, on a round dining-room table, he taught me to apply these paints to a piece of cardboard and make pictures. I was pervaded by a kind of drunkenness, from which I was never to recover."[4]

1918–20

Witnesses an air raid during the First World War: "[One night in 1918] flashes could be seen through the window, the Gothas were bombing Amiens and now and again flashes of light penetrated the attic. Was it really the case or did I imagine that at that moment the waxy body gleamed more brightly in the darkness? There rose in my a kind of song, lasting until dawn, in which I seemed to be expressing as a sense of *joie de vivre*, despite the bombs and the nearness of death, as well as the misery all around us. This song was given rhythm by the beating of my pulse and sometimes upset by the explosions. I have never been the same since. Art had begun in me, stimulated equally by all sorts of shocks, impulses, encouragements or scratches."[5]

In 1918, he returns to Normandy, to La Hubaudière, near Couterne, and works as an assistant in a pharmacy at Bagnoles-de-l'Orne: "Was it there that I got the idea of wresting from each thing the sign that it concealed? The love of chemistry I contracted at that time pursued me for several years. I had converted my bedroom at home into a kind of laboratory … which was really a little theatre, where I dreamed and was attracted by shapes and colours which proceeded from the reality of things and were their very essence. My passion for inorganic chemistry arose from my fondness for these shapes, these crystals, these colours, this analysis of a revealed truth."[6]

Admitted in 1920 to the Institut Industriel du Nord, he begins studying chemistry but does not complete the course: "The history of my life had led me to an industrial school – the Institut Industriel du Nord in Lille – to study chemistry. In fact, I very much liked the subject, but my fellow students very soon pointed out to me that I did not belong there. Their ambitions were not the same as mine and one of them, seeing me write poems during a maths class, said: 'Look, old chap, if I composed poetry I would not stay here, I would go to Paris!' And, in my naivety, I went."[7]

1921

Settles in Paris. Having read Arthur Rimbaud, Jules Laforgue and Tristan Corbière, he practises writing poetry: "Words flowed easily from my mouth and fastened on to things and feelings equally. Already I was mumbling poems, or rather verses, the phrases of which rhymed voluptuously. At primary school, a student teacher had already told me: 'Whenever you have a few pennies to spare, go to such-and-such a bookseller's and buy a book in the Calmann-Lévy, 'Les Meilleurs Livres' collection, they've got everything'."[8]

Apprentice draughtsman in an architect's office (Agence Bourlot), he goes all over town doing surveys. Visits the Louvre, where he discovers the works of Poussin and Philippe de Champaigne: "One day they decided to send me to the Louvre to decipher some apparently rather complicated tracery in a mosaic from Kabira, near Tyre. I deciphered it without any difficulty, then – and this was the great turning-point of my life – I ascended the grand staircase and, at the top, was the great room where, at that time, everything was crammed together, Poussin cheek by jowl with Titian or Philippe de Champaigne. I stood in front of Philippe de Champaigne's *Richelieu*, which seemed to me eloquent and clear, and I said to myself, excuse my pretension: 'Well, I could do that'. In comparison, the Poussins seemed amazingly profound. I did not know why, but they held my attention. I left the Louvre a different man."[9]
Decides to become a painter.

1922–23

Takes another draughtsman's job with an architect.
Birth of his first son, Jean-Jacques, in 1922. He moves with his companion, Andrée Jouart, to a two-room flat at 207 rue Saint-Martin, in the 3rd *arrondissement*: "The apartment was poverty-stricken but charming. Along two sides ran a leaded balcony with rusty railings, overlooking two courtyards. This was my first workshop. Every Sunday, I painted one courtyard or the other, using an easel designed for outdoor work. The view was one of extraordinary richness. On one side, a vast wall rose from the greenish depths of the courtyard to the sky, edged with chimneys and earthenware tiles. I wrote at the time that there were patches of light-coloured plaster like the flesh of a young girl, but what did I know about girls? Opposite, a broad roof discharged into a gutter. To the left, lean-to roofs cascaded downwards, punctuated by as many improvised skylights as they would support.

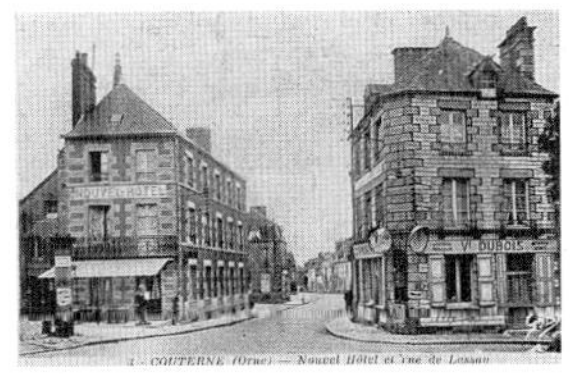

Postcard of Couterne (Orne) where Jean Hélion was born 21 April 1904

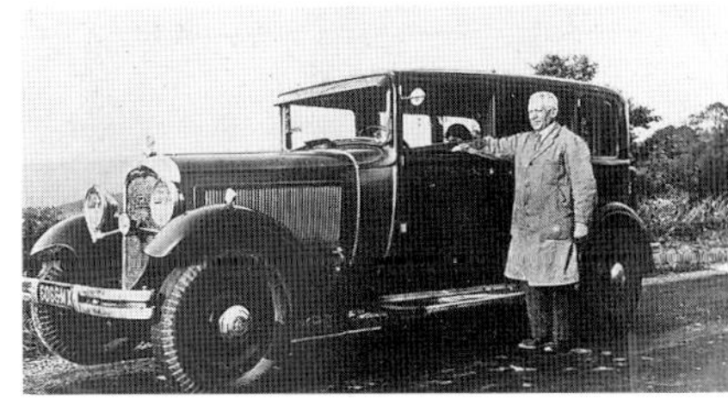

Louis Bichier, Jean Hélion's father

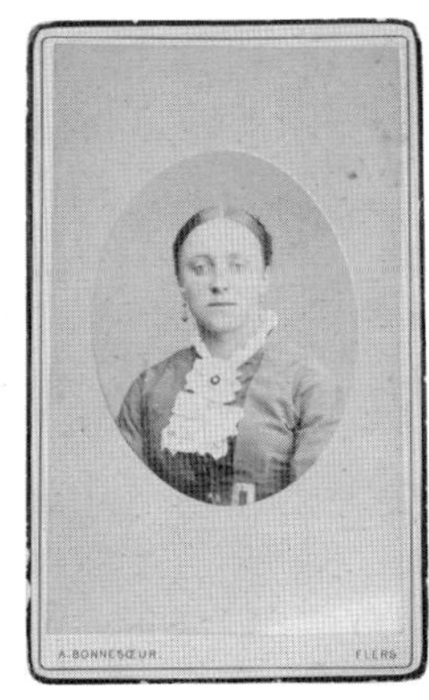

Jean Hélion's mother

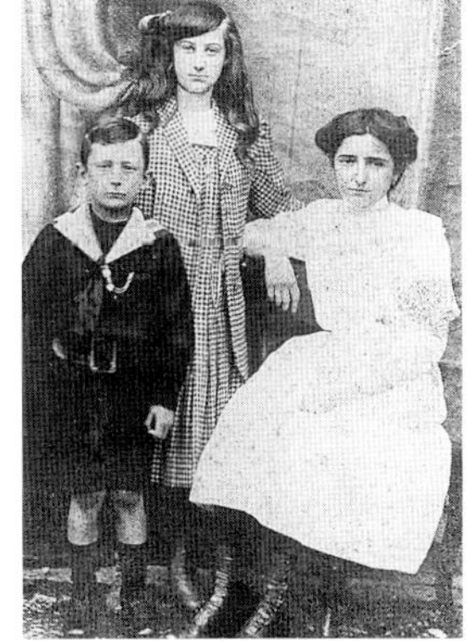

Jean Hélion (né Bichier), his sister Héliane Bichier and his cousin Jeanne Racouchot, 1910s

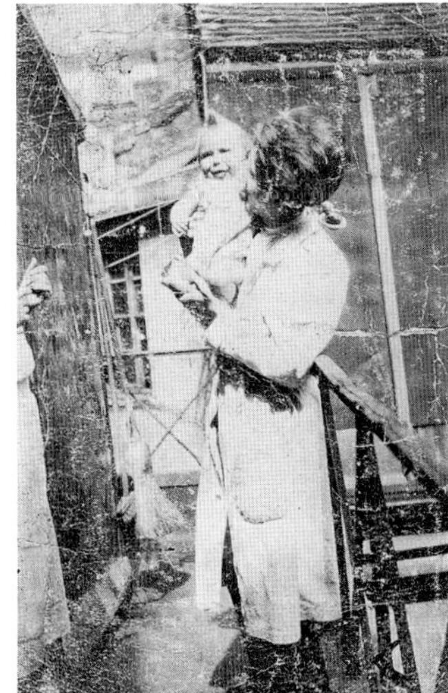

Jean-Jacques Bichier, Jean Hélion's elder brother, in the arms of his mother outside the Bichier apartment, rue Saint-Martin, Paris

LOGY

These were the components of the first courtyard. In the second, one corner was occupied by the well of the staircase, while tenements with attic and lean-to roofs filled the others. Dominating all else, chimneys sprouted in one corner or another, crowned with pink tiles and chimney pots conducting a thunderous semaphore as far as the eye could see …. Aware of its unheard-of richness, I first concentrated on elaborating the framework: the large vertical planes and the angles the mansards and roof made with them. In this crush of geometrical shapes, the roofs were a world apart."[10]

Produces his first paintings and watercolours – *Streets at night*, *Roofs at dawn*, *Staircases*, then portraits and landscapes.

1924
Meets the Belgian painter Luc Lafnet, with whom he exhibits at the Foire aux Croûtes in Montmartre: "A musician friend introduced me to a Belgian painter, Luc Laffnet [*sic*], a rather academic artist but really gifted, who always had something helpful to say, pointed you in the right direction. He was the one who told me: 'Go to the Louvre and see Rembrandt', a shock from which I have never recovered, a shock to end all shocks. This man, to whom I had been introduced as a poet, said, on seeing my poems, 'but you ought to be doing paintings, these contain nothing but colours and rhythms.'"[11]
Paints pots of flowers, views of the Seine, since lost, which constitute his 'Impressionist period': "When I met Lafnet, I painted, under his influence, but how much more violently – and clumsily – than him *The Tower of Babel* [*La Tour de Babel*] (60 F [130 x 89 cm]), unfortunately now destroyed, which I can still see in my mind's eye, some severe still lifes, and some views of my head in the mirror, which had their qualities, I would say, though one of the eyes was never completely finished. He had me exhibit alongside him at the Foire aux Croûtes, where I sold a few paintings, in particular some self-portraits, one of which was purchased by Engel-Pak."[12]
In Parisian galleries, Hélion becomes familiar with the painting of Cézanne, Matisse and Derain.

1925
At the Foire aux Croûtes, he makes the acquaintance of Georges Bine, who buys his still life *Jug and bread* [*Cruche et mie de pain*] and, in September, gets him to sign his first five-year contract.
Paints his first pumpkin: "Bored by the red carpets in his [Georges Bine's] sitting-room with its gilt mirrors where I was working (3 or 5, rue Grétry), I hacked open a pumpkin, shoved around a chair and some bottles and made them into a painting, which was fine to start with, but which subsequently I clumsily hardened and flattened."[13]
Gives up architecture to devote himself exclusively to painting. Attends courses in nude drawing at the Académie Adler.
Meets Tristan Rémy[14] and Otto Freundlich: "We got together frequently. He (Rémy) was then employed by the railways, working in some office or other, but with his friend Henri Poulaille had undertaken a series of novels referred to as 'populist'. He was a man of the people, in the true sense …. It was at his place, at one of the very modest soirées he held for his friends, that I met Otto Freundlich. Freundlich was the first abstract painter I had met, before seeing the engravings and drawings he had given to Tristan Rémy. At that time I had no idea there was such a thing as abstract art."[15]

1926
Married and father of a child, he moves to a workshop at 1 rue Marcel-Sembat (18th *arrondissement*), near the Porte de Clignancourt. For two months, he takes in the Uruguayan painter Joaquin Torres-García and his family. Torres-García introduces him to cubism and informs him of the development of the international avant-garde movement: "He spoke to me about cubism, of which he knew the leading exponents, and of surrealism. He took me to Pierre Loeb's to see the amazing works painted by Miró in 1926. This shook me to the core, though it was a year before these influences became apparent in my pictures, the cubist tradition gradually replacing that of Soutine. It was at Torres-García's that I met Van Doesburg, T.-G. having found a workshop nearby …. Complex, contradictory and dictatorial, he was not easy to get on with. We nevertheless worshipped him. Impressed by what Van Doesburg had to say, he began doing abstract work, in a limited way, while I threw myself into it head first."[16]
"He was undoubtedly very influential in getting me to dispense with descriptive imagery. It was at his place that I first saw a Mondrian, which he had borrowed for an exhibition in Barcelona. It left me reeling!"[17]

Paints more portraits, a series of self-portraits, red on a blue background, and some 'butchers'.

1927
Founds the journal *L'Acte* in conjunction with Luc Lafnet, Jean Réande and Jamblan. Torres-García also contributes. Only four issues are published: "In '27, we produced the journal *L'Acte* together, and with Jamblan, who later became a cabaret singer. For a time, his mistress was Laurette Achard, whom I was very fond of. To earn a living, Réande also directed a hairdressing magazine, *La Coiffure*, with the result that he got all sorts of adverts for combs and soaps for our little review."[18]
In the third number of *L'Acte*, he published one of his poems, 'Hâleur d'affiches' [Sandwich-board man]: "In some poems there were feelings which I still experience very keenly, as in 'Hâleur d'affiches'. Those sandwich-board men, carrying their posters around town, seemed like ships' captains sailing their boat up the street. This small picture with workmen digging holes and sailing through the tarmac with their shovels expresses emotions which I felt at a very early stage, but were really given flesh by the use of colour."[19]
Another of his poems, 'Contact' was published in April 1928, in the fourth and last issue of the review: "Man is a parasite conqueror of the mass.
To disappear all he need do is stop moving.
All life is movement.
Every gesture a fragment of vital force.
Every shape the outline of a gesture.
Every shape an essential mark of life.
Between the earth and man are the objects he had drawn from it and modelled according to the dual necessity of their original matter and the desire he has.
The object bears the sign of life. Its surface is the inner limit of all the gestures man has made around the raw material.

1. J. Hélion, *À perte de vue* followed by *Choses revues*, Paris, IMEC, 1996, p. 11.
2. Id., *Journal d'un peintre, Carnets 1929–1962*, vol. I, ed. A. Mœglin-Delcroix, Paris, Maeght, 1992, 1 November 1948, pp. 157–58.
3. *À perte de vue …, op. cit.*, pp. 179–80.
4. *Ibid.*, p. 15.
5. *Ibid.*, pp. 14–15
6. *Ibid.*, pp. 17–18.
7. J. Hélion, interview by Daniel Abadie, "Dialogue en guise d'ouverture", in *Hélion ou la force des choses*, Brussels, La Connaissance S.A., 1975, p. 9.
8. *À perte de vue …, op. cit.*, pp. 15–16.
9. "Dialogue en guise d'ouverture", as note 7, p. 10.
10. *À perte de vue …, op. cit.*, pp. 191–93.
11. "Dialogue en guise d'ouverture", as note 7, pp. 10–11.
12. *Journal d'un peintre*, vol. I, *op. cit.*, 6 November 1951, p. 222.
13. *Ibid.*, 5 April 1948, p. 117.
14. Tristan Rémy, today best known as an historian of the circus, was one of the leading figures in the movement promoting proletarian literature, .
15. J. Hélion, *Mémoire de la chambre jaune*, Paris, École nationale supérieure des Beaux-Arts, 1994, p. 18.
16. J. Hélion, *Journal d'un peintre, Carnets 1963–1984*, vol. II, Paris, Maeght, 1992, 5 January 1982, p. 371.
17. *À perte de vue …, op. cit.*, p. 33.
18. *Journal d'un peintre*, vol. II, *op. cit.*, 14 December 1981, p. 367.
19. "Dialogue en guise d'ouverture", as note 7, p. 9.

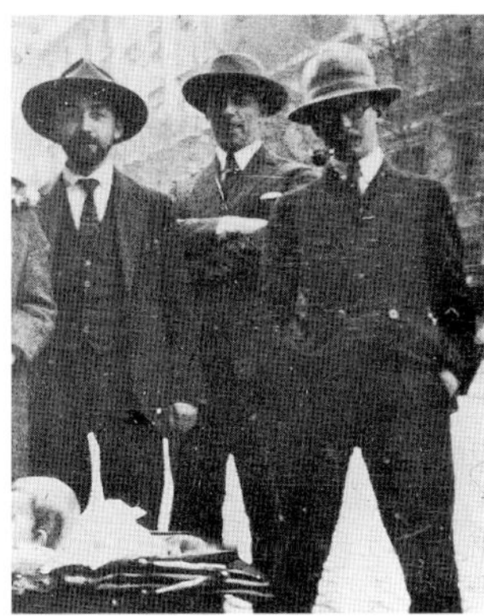

Luc Lafnet, Engel-Pak and Hélion at the Foire aux Croûtes, Montmartre, Paris, 1924

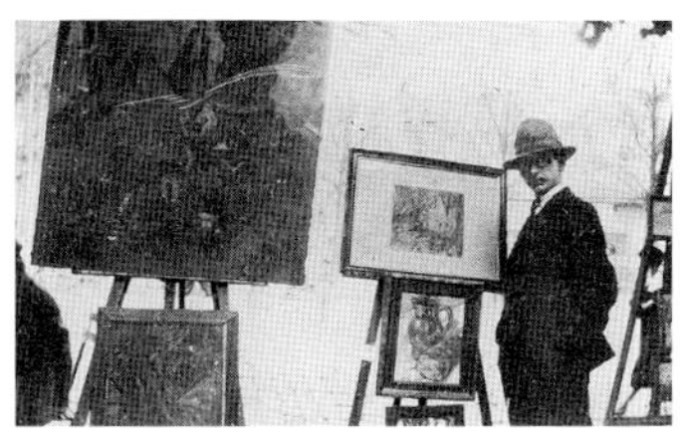

Jean Hélion at the Foire aux Croûtes, Montmartre, Paris, 1924

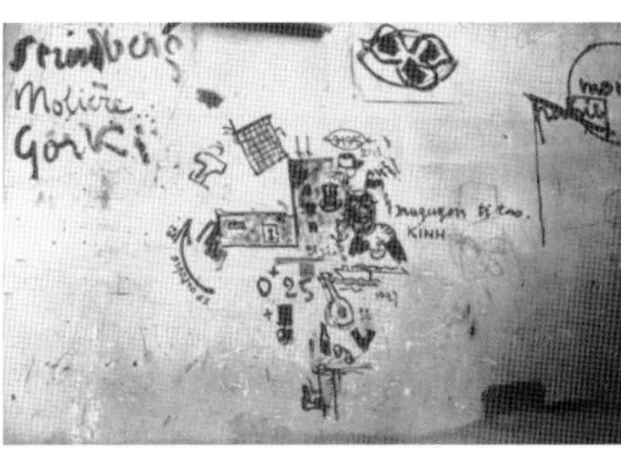

above and right
Jean Hélion's studio,
1 rue Marcel-Sembat, Paris, 1929

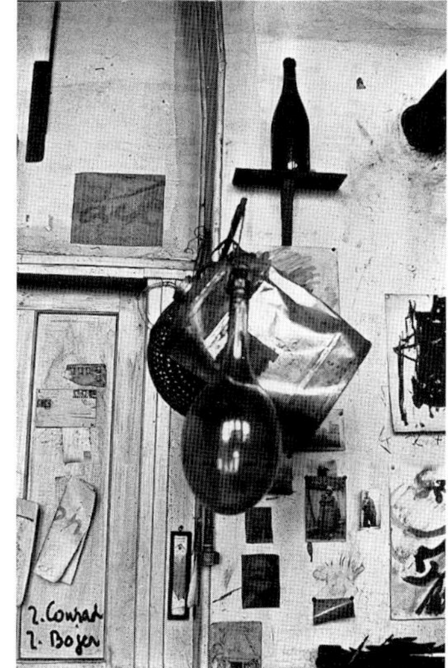

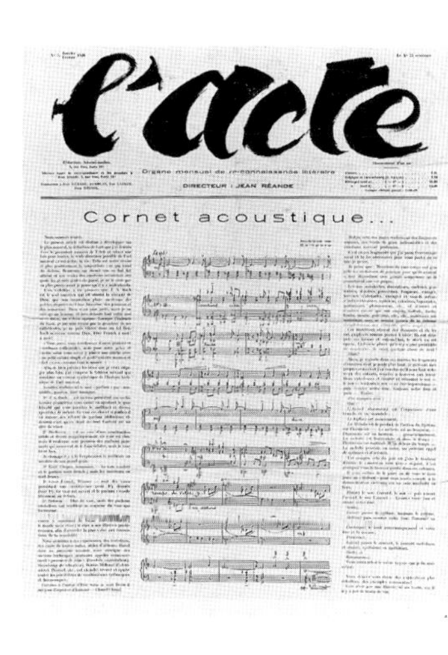

Cover of issue no. 3 of the review *L'Acte*, January–February 1928

The object is the crystal of a whole activity determined by man. Crystal or total.
The man disappears. The object remains on which the man is inscribed. With the projections on a plane of a few points of a solid body, descriptive geometry reconstitutes him in his entirety.
The object is the working drawing of a man."

1928

Between 1928 and 1929, he succeeds in "… grasping the image of nature in a form of writing. I was able to replicate a real spoon with a 'spoon-stroke' on the canvas, a glass with 'glass-strokes' summing up the object in the interests of speed of vision, clarification of rhythm and colour. The painting came to define a kind of balance between what I removed from nature on the pretext of clarifying its appearance and what I developed among the multiple possibilities of colours."[20]
Lives in precarious circumstances: "My life changed in this first period of adventure and poverty. I lost the semblance of family structure I had previously and entered a kind of solitude, in which only pots wanted to live with me. They were always posing for me; the elements of my lunch would pose for me: an apple, two fried eggs, which I painted passionately before eating them. One good thing about poverty is that it teaches you principles. One of the first architects who had persecuted me had given me a large oriental blanket which I hung on the wall because it was a fine red colour. Eventually, it had some nice holes in it, through which the wall was visible. I knew this was the truth, that one should not hide anything but see things through the holes.

The hole appeared to me as revealing the inner reality and, starting with the hole in my blanket, I admired the hole in pots, which was their very soul, and I ended up taking an interest in all the holes in my workshop."[21]

In January–February, he exhibits two paintings at the Salon des Indépendants. The critic Louis-Léon Martin reports favourably on them in *Le Crapouillot*: "I do not know M. Jean Hélion's age; neither do I know if he has exhibited before. But certainly his entries seem to herald a very real talent. He knows how to conduct a painting; his colour naturally obeys a dominant; the light is felicitously distributed; his exact vision bears witness to sure observation. Since the Indépendants, too, would fail in their task if he were not discovered, I am determined to record my little act of faith in M. Jean Hélion."[22]

Rejected at the Salon d'Automne, from 3 to 15 November he organizes an exhibition entitled *Les 5 refusés* at the Galerie Marck, featuring works by Torres-García, Engel-Pak, Aberdam, Pierre Daura and Hélion himself (portraits, landscapes, bouquets of flowers, still lifes and his first *Woman with an umbrella*). The critic André Salmon writes: "In M. Jean Hélion, we sense an ardent and generous nature, in a word, soul. The future may smile on him."[23]

1929

His painting develops in the direction of greater formalism. The American painter John Xceron, to whom Hélion is introduced in Paris in 1926 by Torres-García, bears witness to this development: "According to Hélion's latest views on aesthetics, painting of the future

will be completely separated from objectivism and tradition and will become an abstract art, pure form like music and architecture. Much of modern art that is called 'modern' today, says Hélion, is already past and classical. In his opinion, art must be in accord with our mechanical and industrial age, and the artist, the creator of rythms and forms, [must] perpetuate on canvas the spirit of modernity."[24]

Begins writing jottings in his first *carnets* [notebooks]: "I have begun to abbreviate, accelerate the schema so rapidly that the objective image has disappeared. Colour-writing has encountered object-writing, and my paintings have become abstract."[25]

Moves to Montparnasse: "The first thing I did at that time was to leave Montmartre and come and live in Montparnasse, where abstraction could thrive. Montmartre was the home of a passionate form of art, not abstraction."[26]

He meets the Armenian painter Léon Tutundjian: "Forced to flee Armenia by the Turkish massacres, he had travelled through Greece, where he learned decoration, and arrived in Paris, coming from the south and east, whereas I came from the north. Our dates coincided. We soon became friends. His painting, composed of thin lines and subtle gradations, seemed to depict a cosmos, a world of spheres oscillating on their trajectories. It conveyed extraordinary authority …. Léon Tutundjian spoke admirably a quite different language from Torres-García or Lafnet. Something oriental, in which reasons circulated obliquely, unexpectedly, not up and down after the fashion of Descartes.

I could identify with everything he said, I was not there myself but I understood. This was the other truth I had been so long wanting to find. Like a high priest from another race and another church, Léon was preaching it to me. He, too, identified with my first attempts at almost geometric abstraction."[27]

In the summer, Georges Bine takes him to the Pyrenees, in particular to Pau, where he produces his first abstract works.
Writes articles on modern art for the monthly journal *Pyrénées*, "… a newspaper which called itself *L'Ami du Peuple*, well produced in the most conservative possible way. Its art critic was Camille Mauclair, the man who had described Cézanne as an artist with a disease of the retina. I sent him a history of art which had appeared under my name in a journal entitled *Pyrénées*. He replied saying it was the first time he had understood anything at all about modern art, hitherto 'defended by the precarious humbug of Gleizes and Metzinger' (I quote)."[28]

Makes his first trip to Spain, to Barcelona. Returns to Paris in the autumn.

In November, the Dalmau Gallery in Barcelona shows his first abstract works (two compositions) in its *Exposición de arte moderno nacional y extranjero*.
In the course of the year, he makes the acquaintance of Jean Arp, Serge Charchoune, John Graham, Antoine Pevsner and Georges Vantongerloo.

1930

With Theo van Doesburg, Otto Carlsund and Léon Tutundjian, he founds the Art Concret group: "Art

Concret was born of my meeting the Swede Otto Carlsund, a bearded romantic, drunkard, generous and devilishly intelligent, who, having fallen for my painting, revealed to me aspects of it of which I was not aware. I already knew Tutundjian and Van Doesburg and, in 1930, around a table, drinking beer or tea, what were four men of that kind to do but found a journal. Such was the mentality of the time. Van Doesburg was a jack-of-all-trades and I was very prepared to get involved. I was immediately appointed general secretary of Art Concret. Van Doesburg was undoubtedly the guiding spirit, but it would be true to say it was the two of us who created the journal."[29]

Publication in April of the first and last number of *Art Concret*. Hélion contributed 'Les problèmes de l'art concret – Art et Mathématiques': "If art is universal, it is above personalities and periods. It belongs to the realm of constant certainties, is controllable by logic. The search for constants, by logic, is the essential aim of mathematics. Mathematics establishes constant certainties by means of formulae; painting does so with colours. Mathematics and painting are therefore essentially related. No further demonstration is needed."[30]

Makes the acquaintance of Piet Mondrian: "Arp had come to see the Art Concret group. He was not involved, could not join, but he encouraged us. He was seeing Mondrian, with whom Doesburg was on bad terms, as he was with everybody. I immediately liked Mondrian very much, his kind of innate nobility, his wonderful detachment, the sense he retained all his life of being on a summit, on a high

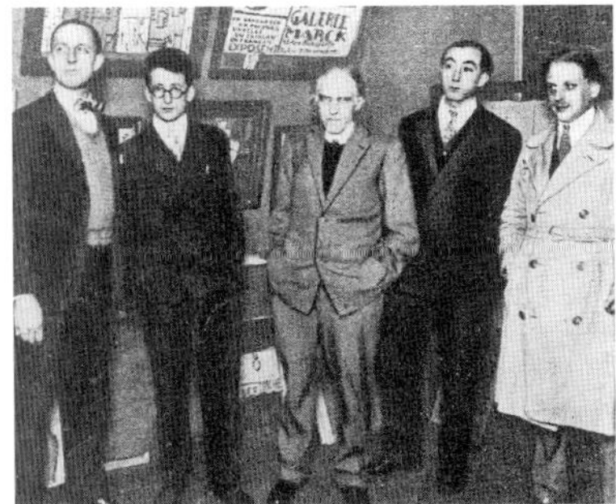

The five 'refusés' from the Salon d'Automne:
from left to right: Engel-Pak (Rozier), Hélion, Torres-García, Pierre Daura, Aberdam
Press cutting, from the illustrated supplement to *Alès-Journal*, 15 December 1928

Poster, designed by Torres-García, for the exhibition *Les 5 refusés*, 1928

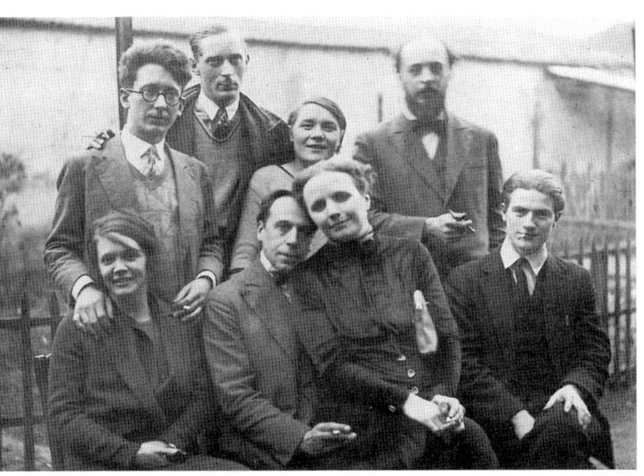

The Art Concret group:
standing, on the left: Jean Hélion,
on the right, Otto Carlsund
seated, from left to right: Jean Blair,
Theo and Nelly van Doesburg, Marcel Wantz

point. He was totally different from Van Doesburg, who was an intellectual adventurer, in the best sense of the word, ready to take any risk. Van Doesburg was Dada, Mondrian was a classicist."[31]

Increasingly he associates with members of the American community in Paris. In his workshop, young artists are able to meet the key figures on the Parisian scene: Mondrian, Arp, Joan Miró, Fernand Léger and Alberto Giacometti. His American 'coterie' includes Alexander Calder, John Ferren, John Graham and the architect Frederick Kiesler. For these artists, he plays the role of disseminator of avant-garde ideas. Convinced that the cause of abstraction would be strengthened by a group project, he urges the American artists, in particular Harry Holtzman, to set up an organization, which will finally come into being in 1936 as American Abstract Artists (AAA).

Gives French lessons to a diplomat from the Soviet Embassy, Vladimir Barkov, who introduces him to two Soviet writers, Kirshon and Afinoguenov: "To these children of Russian futurism, whom I admired very much, I hopefully showed my orthogonal experiments. They both broke into almost Homeric laughter and refused to listen to my pleadings in favour of freedom of thought and expression."[32]

In the autumn, he takes part in the exhibition *Kubism, Purism, Konstructivism* organized by Otto Carlsund in Stockholm. Among other contributions, the catalogue includes an introduction by Otto Carlsund and a preface by Jean Hélion.

1931

Is involved in the founding of the Abstraction-Création group with Arp, Gleizes, Herbin, Kupka, Tutundjian, Valmier and Van Doesburg; they appoint him to manage the first issue of the new review: "There was a fairly large and arbitrary meeting of artists, known as Cercle et Carré [Circle and Square], in which I did not take part, organized by Seuphor. Quite apart from that, we were then meeting at Van Doesburg's, who had been publishing *De Stijl* for ten years. By 'we' I mean Carlsund, Tutundjian, Shwab, Wantz and me. It was because De Stijl was moribund that we set up Art Concret, which was published only once, and it was because this journal made little impression – being, unlike Cercle et Carré, very rigorous – that we invented a grouping of fundamentally abstract artists, the name of which was debated among the founders, who were Van Doesburg, at whose new house in Meudon we met; Arp, his neighbour; Herbin, who was immediately very energetic and dictatorial; Delaunay, spectacular but cautious; Kupka; Tutundjian; Valmier; and myself, who took on the secretaryship."[33]

"It was only when we set up the Abstraction-Création grouping that I came into contact with practically all the world's abstract painters …. There was already Freundlich, who had his own completely irregular form of abstraction, which some people were to cultivate twenty years later, and others who were puritans, very strict, very serious people. All kinds of tendencies began to emerge. Abstraction-Création was fairly representative of a wealth of styles, extending to the fringes of surrealism with Seligmann, and of cubism with Gleizes and Valmier …."[34]

Death of Theo van Doesburg in March; Vantongerloo joins Abstraction-Création.
Spends time with Julio González, forms a friendship with Calder: "In Montparnasse there was also Alexander Calder, a magician with wire, who would go to friends' homes with a roll of wire and pliers to do their portraits, then suspend them on a string so that they would turn in the slightest breeze and cast shadows on the walls. He was won over to abstraction at about the same time as me, disowning the portraits of Léger and Ozenfant for which he was already known. He began working on cosmogonies composed of wire circles with straight vectors ending in small wooden balls. The whole thing insolently mounted on a tray, like a bust. He very soon found that these vectors could be made to move obliquely, backwards and forwards, up and down, and that some curved lines could also move, anticipating the mobiles that made him famous two or three years later."[35]

Gets to know Fernand Léger, Michel Seuphor, Amédée Ozenfant, Jean Gorin, and the Swedish poet Gunnar Ekelöf.

Accompanied by the American painter William Einstein, he undertakes a two-and-a-half-month trip to the USSR: "When, at the beginning of Abstraction-Création, I met the painter William Einstein, who was a to some degree a pupil of Ozenfant's and, as a friend of Mondrian, was turning to abstraction, he told me: 'For years I've been trying to go to the USSR, but cannot get a visa'. Without thinking, I said I might be able to help him. I spoke about it to Vladimir Barkov, who laughed and said, 'If he brings you, I'll grant him a visa immediately'."[36]
In Berlin, they visit Naum Gabo. In the Soviet Union, Vladimir Tatlin is the only artist Hélion manages to meet. At the suggestion of Carlsund and Ekelöf, they stop off in Sweden before returning to Paris.
"The USSR was like a kind of Christmas story, the grandiose rubbing shoulders with the most down-to-earth …. All of that, though, was leading to the Gulag. What was one to believe? But at that moment, Herbin and I thought the world had at last found the way of justice and one could never again depart from it. In the news, things were beginning to go wrong. There were sinister rumours. In 1937, they assassinated the very people I had taken for heroes. Of course, I did not remain a communist sympathizer."[37]

Later, in the United States, the American painter George L.K. Morris was to question him about his trip to the U.S.S.R.: "When you visited the Soviet union, did you find indications that a strong plastic expression might emerge from its system of society?"
J.H.: "In U.S.S.R. seven years ago, painting did not seem to play much part in anything but helping propaganda. Perhaps I was unable to find the men who were painting freely …. If a strong plastic expression might emerge from U.S.S.R. was not to be seen yet, but could only result from a very permanent activity in all branches of art kept on for many more years. Logically, in the very fact that it would be supported at first by the minority of people whose evolution has led to deve-

20. *Journal d'un peintre*, vol. I, *op. cit.*, 4 May 1933, p. 43.
21. "Dialogue en guise d'ouverture", as note 7, p. 14.
22. L.-L. Martin, "Le Salon des indépendants", *Le Crapouillot*, February 1928, p. 23.
23 A. Salmon, *La Revue de France*, 1 December 1928.
24 J. Xceron, "Who's Who Abroad: Jean Hélion", *Chicago Tribune*, European Edition, Paris, Wednesday 5 June 1929, p. 4.
25. *Journal d'un peintre*, vol. I, *op. cit.*, 4 May 1933, p. 45.
26. "Dialogue en guise d'ouverture", as note 7, p. 21.
27. *À perte de vue …*, *op. cit.*, pp. 41–42.
28. *Ibid.*, p. 39.
29. "Dialogue en guise d'ouverture", as note 7, p. 20.
30. Jean Hélion, *Art Concret*, April 1930, p. 5.
31. "Dialogue en guise d'ouverture", as note 7, p. 19.
32. *À perte de vue …*, *op. cit.*, p. 40.
33. *Journal d'un peintre*, vol. II, *op. cit.*, [between 17 and 19 March] 1981, pp. 357–58.
34. "Dialogue en guise d'ouverture", as note 7, p. 21.
35. *À perte de vue …*, *op. cit.*, pp. 51–52.
36. *Ibid.*, p. 61.
37. *Ibid.*, p. 64.

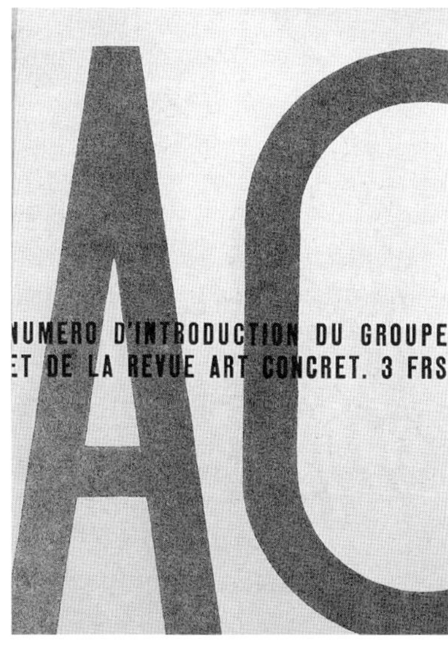

Cover of the only issue of **Art Concret**, April 1930, and (**right**) the manifesto of the Art Concret group

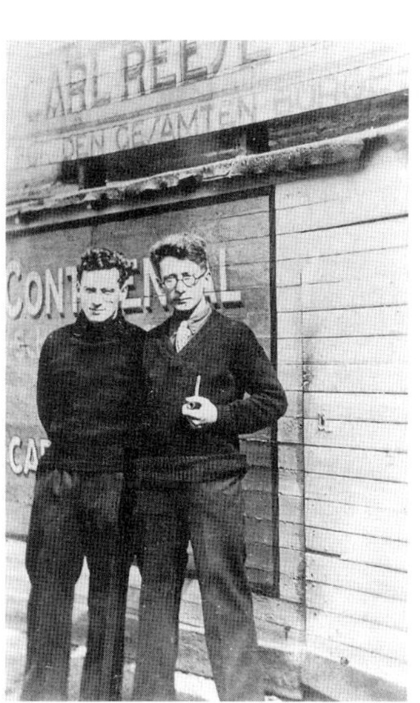

William Einstein and Jean Hélion in Kiel during their voyage to the U.S.S.R., 1931

loping their plastic taste to a great degree; thus propably hard to find, for it is gratuitous to claim that this minority is sure to be influential. I believe it is too early."[38]

In November, on returning to Paris, he earns his living by giving drawing lessons and writing articles: "On the advice of Georges Simenon, whose reputation was growing, I had written for *Paris-Plaisirs* (!) seventeen risqué if not lightweight stories, of which I sold three or four, under the pseudonym of Jean Golaud or Jean Bernier. I also wrote some 'serious' tales: *Un bouquet à la mer*, *Cravates*, etc."[39]
Moves to a studio at 19 rue Daguerre, in the 14th *arrondissement*.
At the end of the year, he meets Max Ernst, Tristan Tzara and Marcel Duchamp.
Death of his mother, at Couterne, in November.

1932
His abstract painting undergoes its first metamorphosis: "Finally I arrived at curves and oblique lines …. In searching for the effect of space and movement on the elements, that is to say in constructing a work in movement, or rather in creating equilibrium out of movement, my images have become more pliant, more permeable and at the same time my world has taken on colour. To establish relations between surfaces as complex as those defined by curves, it is necessary to arrange nuances. That is why my colours have again become light. So my pictures have again begun to be in touch with nature, and I myself, under their influence, have again begun to desire it ardently, but without conceiving how I might encounter it."[40]

Directs the first issue of Abstraction-Création, to which he contributes '*À solder*' [To settle the balance]: "The frame is not a pot for containing the image; it is a provisional means of defence against the disorder of surrounding objects, but this image, like a wave, must extend through it into the whole of space. The work may be considered as the prolongation of a piece of architecture, the crystallization of its 'sign'. Inscribed on walls, it is the prolongation in a single plane of the spirit which architecture develops in space. One can for a moment envisage the 'transportable picture' as a 'model cell' to be introduced into all the defective environments of everyday life, to serve as a yardstick for their reconstruction, a benchmark, a formulary ….
Mathematics provides the keys to a series of mental attitudes we need to adopt in order to realize that everything is the same, to find the way in everything, the constancy of each thing."[41]

In Paris, in June–July, he has his first solo exhibition at the Galerie Pierre [Loeb], featuring his *Orthogonal* paintings and his *Circular tensions*. Here he meets the American painters George L.K. Morris and Arshile Gorky, the art critic James Johnson Sweeney, and Albert E. Gallatin, founder of the Gallery of Living Art in New York, the first approach to a modern art museum in the United States. He also makes the acquaintance of Christian Zervos, director of *Cahiers d'Art*.

At Couterne during the summer.
In the autumn, having divorced his first wife, he sets off for the United States, where he marries Jean Blair, a native of Virginia: "This stay in America was to prove an important

development", wrote Jean-Jacques Lévêque. "Not only because Hélion met Kiesler, Arshile Gorky and Sidney Janis, but because he anticipated by several years the wave of émigrés fleeing Nazism who, through friendships and exchange of experience, would weld the European stream of experimental art (a mixture of geometric abstraction and surrealism) to the youthful forces of American art, rescuing the latter from its provincialism and conformist tranquillity and hustling it to the front of the international stage."[42]

In December, he returns to Paris and moves to a new workshop at 9 impasse Nansouty, in the 14th *arrondissement*.
Meets Victor Brauner. Forms friendships with Arp, Giacometti and Mondrian.

With Paul Vaillant-Couturier, he founds the Association des Écrivains et Artistes Révolutionnaires (AEAR): "Under the leadership of Paul Vaillant-Couturier and Léon Moussinac, some of us had some epic discussions. Herbin, who courageously defended total abstraction, spoke of odious interference on the part of communist leaders – Jdanov, Plekhanov – and demanded freedom for art to develop in its own way."[43]

1933
Publication in the second number of Abstraction-Création of his answer to a series of question from the editorial committee:
"1. Why do you not paint nudes?
2. What do you think of the influence of trees on your work?
3. Is a locomotive a work of art? Why or why not?
4. Does the fact that a work has the appearance of a machine or techni-

cal creation detract from or add to its artistic effectiveness?
5. Does the fact that a work has the appearance of an animal detract from or add to its artistic effectiveness?"
Hélion: "Compare paintings to trees? It is high time we did. It has been all too easy to use big words to justify ourselves. The universal, the general, the permanent, and so on, have no really clear meaning. Let us set them aside for a while.
The tree is the archetype of any work. It begins in the ground, an opaque heavy mass. It grows in space, a transparent light mass. It is born from a tiny seed which contains the modulus and schema of what it will become. It sprouts, explores the surrounding soil, feels its way and nevertheless gathers pace, breaks out, climbs, spreads out and, in space, follows all kinds of attractions and repulsions which rectify its primitive form.
It strives to face up to space on as wide a front as possible. It stops growing when it has achieved equilibrium between the projecting force it received from the seed and the inertia of the ground.
Does this image not convey the adventure of a painting?
The soil is both the surface and the paint; space is what the painter manages to elaborate between boxes of chocolates, colours, creams, pastes and melt-in-the-mouth candies.
There are painters whose mouths water at the thought of these candies and whose works are like Christmas trees.
At the water's edge, in the shade of a poplar tree, with a charming woman, tenderness works itself out, stiffness turns to flaccidity, and we sleep. Or maybe it is better to do some fishing."[44]

László Moholy-Nagy visits his workshop in impasse Nansouty.
In May, on Hélion's initiative, Gallatin comes to Paris to meet Arp and Mondrian, and buys from them.

In June, group exhibition at the Galerie Pierre, featuring works by Arp, Calder, Hélion, Miró, Pevsner and Kurt Seligmann.

In July, Hélion makes another trip to the United States. In New York, he becomes the *éminence grise* of the Gallery of Living Art. He encourages A.E. Gallatin to form a collection of abstract works, urging him to acquire works by Arp, González, Hartung, Magnelli, Mondrian, Pevsner and the British abstract artists Barbara Hepworth, Henry Moore and Ben Nicholson. Establishes himself as the theoretician of the Gallery of Living Art, and writes a preface for the catalogue, 'The Evolution of Abstract Art as Shown in the Gallery of Living Art':[45]
"With its recent acquisitions, the Museum of Living Art presents a clear definition of the denaturalisation of the subject, and its progressive transformation in free elements, neither men nor pipes, neither apples nor Venuses for rent."[46] At Gallatin's request, he gives his first lecture at the University of New York, explaining "… what goes on in the mind of a painter as he seeks to conceive and create a work which does not resemble nature".[47] Many artists, including Calder, Duchamp, Kiesler, Gaston Lachaise and John Marin, and the critics James John Sweeney and Henry McBride, attend.
In December, Calder visits him in Virginia and discovers his compositions based on the balancing of opposing forms: "My body must have itched, making me discover

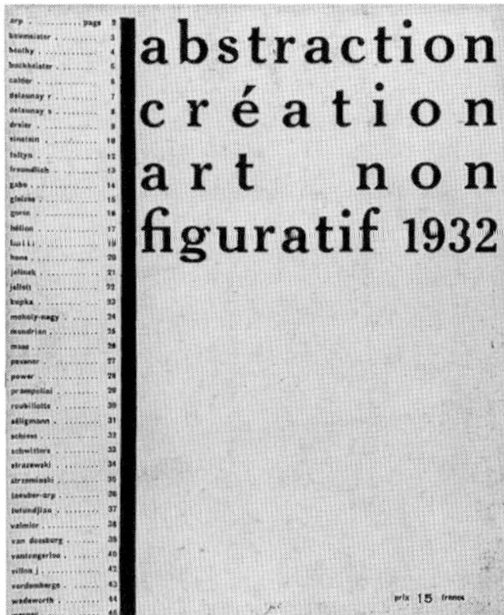

Cover of the first issue of *Abstraction-Création*, 1932

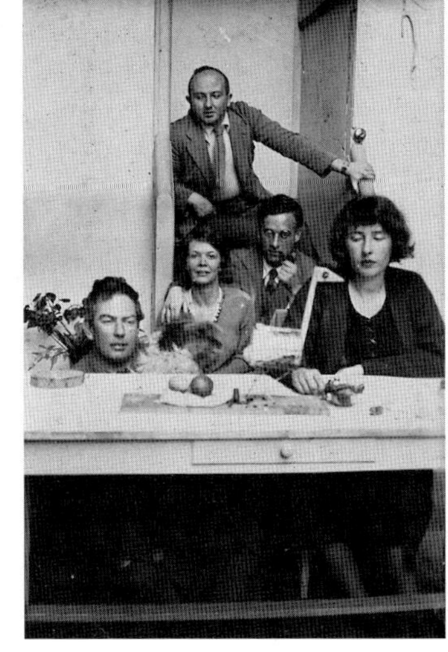

In the studio at impasse Nansouty, Paris, about 1934
standing: Anatole Jakovsky
from left to right in the foreground:
Alexander Calder, Jean Blair, William Einstein, Louisa Calder

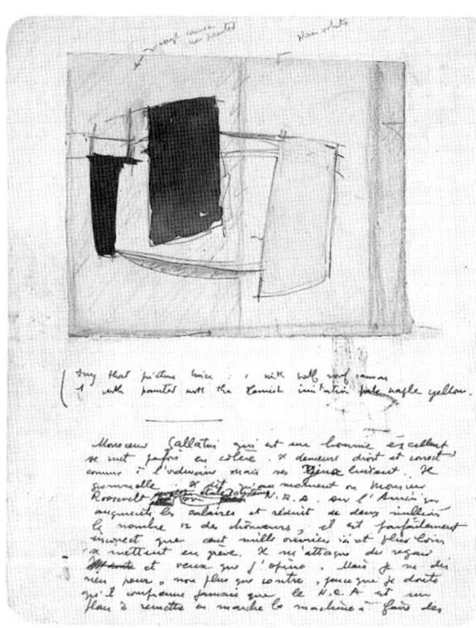

From the *Carnets*, 1933
Bibliothèque nationale de France, department des Étampes et de la Photographie

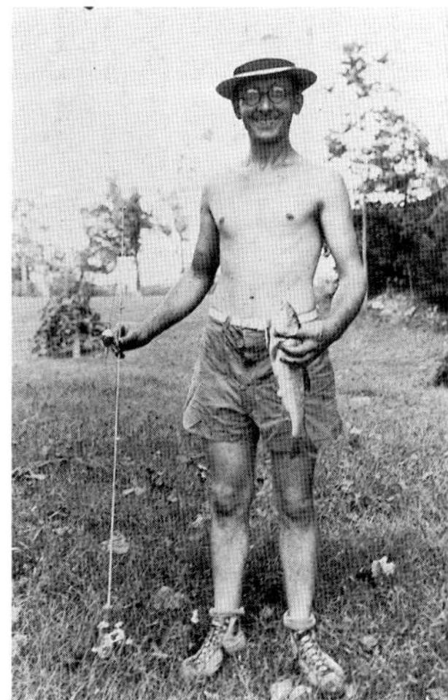

Jean Hélion in Virginia, U.S.A., late 1933

between the fundamental lines an element, an 'organism', a 'being', circulating, swinging, complex, a cell. I immediately found my way back to forms. I had to transform the lines into reacting elements."[48]

1934

In January, he has his first one-man exhibition in the United States, at the John Becker Gallery in New York. Here he gets to know the art dealer Sidney Janis and the critic Henry McBride.

Returning to Paris in February, he meets Miró, Lipchitz and Pierre-Georges Bruguière, who is beginning to collect his work, as well as works by Arp, Giacometti, Léger and Miró. Also forms a friendship with Hans Hartung.
He is introduced by Calder to the architect Paul Nelson. Later, in the 1935 issue of *Cahiers d'Art*, Hélion publishes 'Termes de vie, termes d'espaces', an article about Nelson's design for a surgical facility in Ismailia (Egypt). In 1936–37, during his stay in New York, he keeps in touch with the architect.
Some time around March, at the home of Georges Ribemont-Dessaignes, he meets Raymond Queneau, beginning a friendship sustained by exchanges of letters and meetings: "This, he said, is the author of Chiendent, which has just been published and which you absolutely must read. I started the book that very evening and have read it many times since. I was then committed to Abstraction, but secretly troubled by a nostalgia for the Real, already. Raymond could sense this and soon wrote that eyes were half-opening in my paintings. I now realize that his poems and novels did in fact help me to get back to daily life."[49]

In June, he leaves the Abstraction-Création group: "Was it Mies van der Rohe who said at the Bauhaus 'We must do more by doing less'? That is how abstraction began; by cutting out detail, artists gave greater quality to their compositions, and simplified to the point of putting a white square on a white background. After that, the history of painting rebounded behind the white canvas and began all over again in the opposite direction: from simple to complex. This seemed inevitable to me as early as 1934, when all my friends were rejoicing at having reached the end of the line with the white canvas and were staying there. I flattered myself that I could initiate the reverse movement of growth. This gradually resulted in my falling out with all concerned."[50]
He also resigns from the AEAR.

Makes his first trip to London with Gallatin, where he meets Barbara Hepworth, Henry Moore, Ben Nicholson, John Piper and his wife Myfanwy Evans and the art historian Herbert Read.

In July, he exhibits at the Cahiers d'Art alongside Arp, Sophie Taeuber-Arp and Ghika.

Publication of the article '*La réalité dans la peinture*' in *Cahiers d'Art*: "The eyes light up only one small side of the head, edged by the eyelids and eyebrows. The rest of the head is full of memories, dreams and imaginings fringed with night. It is necessary, by process of thought, to produce a strange amalgam of bits of shapes perceived one by one, of bits of the world which combine any old way. It is only by study and practice that one succeeds in conceiving the continuity of objects, adding the back which the eyes have not seen. Reality, then, is a matter of conception."[51]

1935

In February, he goes to Switzerland for the exhibition *Thèse, Antithèse, Synthèse* organized by Hans Erni in Lucerne. Four of his works are on show: "We have become very strong, since Cézanne, on pictorial fact, the palette event, impossible elsewhere, local, exceptional. The aim is to draw from it a renewable generality, to develop its fundamental contradictions, to discover in it the totality of the world. Painting has been very much felt, but insufficiently thought about. Whatever one lazily claims, it can give body to the clearest ideas without taking the roundabout route of descriptive explanations. The mere idea of totality as opposed to specialized fragmentariness immediately assumes a formal sense; it sets up possibilities. But is important that everything should go via the eyes, without being reduced to them. The artist must think in the order of forms and colours, in the very field of their possibilities, with the dual concern of following and leading them."[52]
Contributes to *Axis*, the first British journal devoted to promoting abstract art, six issues of which appear in the years 1935 and 1936. In April, in the second issue of the review, appears his theoretical essay 'From Reduction to Growth', which sketches out the development of contemporary art in relation to the classical tradition.
In November, in the fourth number, two articles are devoted to him, 'Hélion to-day: a Personal Comment', by Myfanwy Evans, and 'Jean Hélion', by Herbert Read. The latter presents him as "… one of the most mature leaders of the modern movement, in the direct line of descent from Cézanne, Seurat, Gris and Léger. His particular preoccupation has been to carry Cubism from the static condition which was the inevitable result of its analytical approach to nature, forward to a dynamic condition, which condition still retains the essential features of the discoveries made by Picasso, Kandinsky, Gris and Léger."[53]

In September, he makes a second trip to England, where he meets Henry Miller, Kandinsky and Hartung.

Moves to a new workshop in Paris, in the boulevard Saint-Jacques, where he paints monumental abstract compositions, including *Île-de-France*: "My painting is on the move. Until now I have tried to think as much as possible in the field of the elements at my disposal. Now I am trying just to think and to allow to grow on the initial structures another structure, emotional, unconscious, my unregistered baggage. But without it coming unstuck. It is almost a matter of allowing the framework to sprout so that it becomes a framework-tree. This is a process of change requiring infinite adaptability, infinite patience, flexible reasoning. The whole future of my painting is now at stake.
Oppositions develop, colours are refined, spaces becomes more pliable, but the further I advance, the more evident the demands of nature become. The space is provisionally, miraculously filled with light, but the volumes will have to become complete – objects, bodies. Inevitably, nature will soon shove its nose in, and we shall pass on to a new naturalist era."[54]

38. "Interview with Jean Hélion" (by George L.K. Morris), *Partisan Review*, New York, April 1938, pp. 35–36.
39. *Journal d'un peintre*, vol. II, *op. cit.*, 28 July 1973, p. 138.
40. *Journal d'un peintre*, vol. I, *op. cit.*, 4 May 1933, p. 45.
41. Jean Hélion, "À solder", *Abstraction-Création*, no. 1, 1932, p. 18.
42. J.-J. Lévêque, "Hélion", *Cimaise*, no. 122, January–April 1975, p. 16.
43. *Mémoire de la chambre jaune*, *op. cit.*, p. 176.
44. Jean Hélion, *Abstraction-Création*, no. 2, 1933, p. 22.
45. Id., "The Evolution of Abstract Art as Shown in the Gallery of Living Art", catalogue of the Gallery of Living Art, New York University, New York, 1933, n. p.
46. *Ibid.*
47. Letter from Hélion to George L.K. Morris, 11 October 1933, George L. K. Morris Papers, Washington, D.C., Archives of American Art, Smithsonian Art Institute.
48. *Journal d'un peintre*, vol. II, *op. cit.*, 15 February 1934, p. 49.
49. Jean Hélion, "Pratique de Chêne et Chien", *L'Herne*, spécial Raymond Queneau, Paris, December 1975, p. 272; Jean Hélion, *Lettres d'Amérique. Correspondance avec Raymond Queneau 1934–1967*, Paris, IMEC, 1996, p. 172.
50. *Mémoire de la chambre jaune*, *op. cit.*, p. 93.
51. *Cahiers d'art*, nos. 9–10, 1934, p. 256.
52. J. Hélion, text in exhibition catalogue, Paris, February 1935, p. 9.
53. H. Read, "Jean Hélion", *Axis*, no. 4, November 1935, p. 3.
54. *Journal d'un peintre*, vol. I, *op. cit.*, 28 April 1935, p. 45.

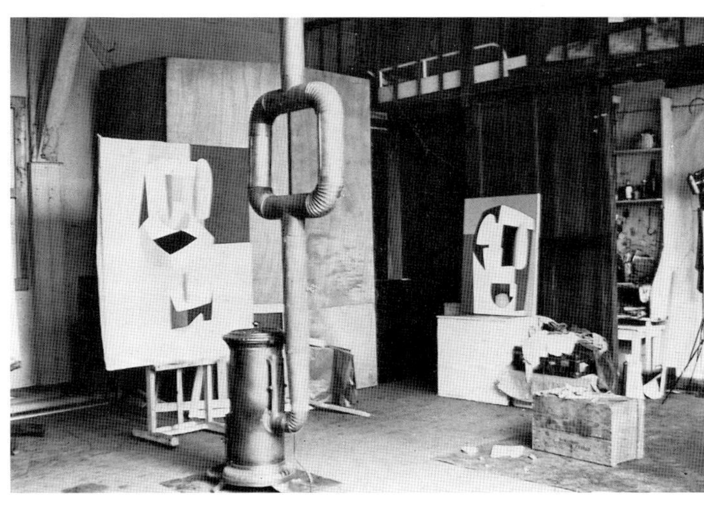

Hélion and Pierre-Georges Bruguière, impasse Nansouty, Paris, 1935

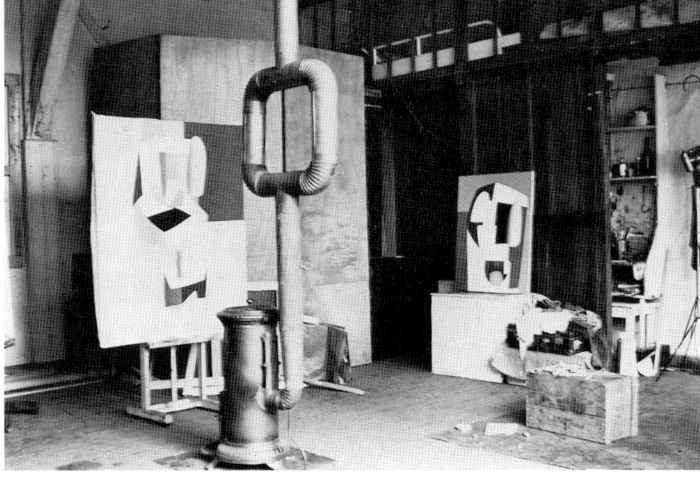

The studio in boulevard St-Jacques, Paris, 1936

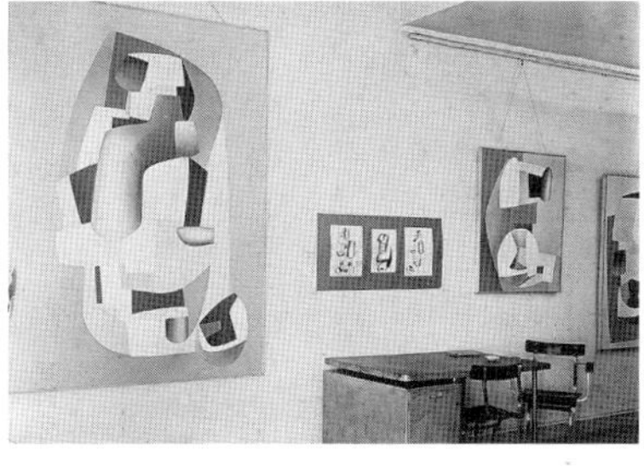

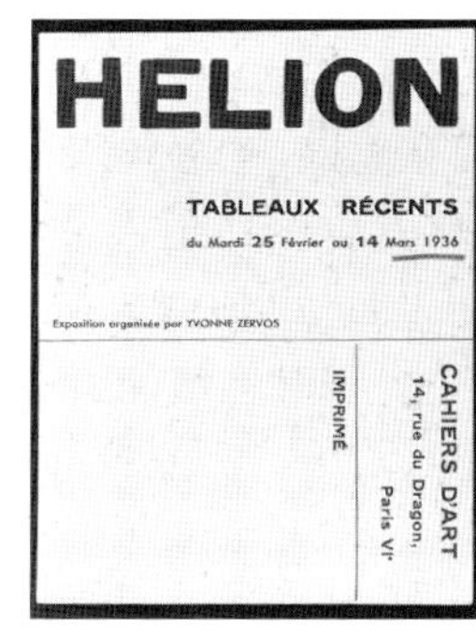

View (*left*) of the exhibition *Hélion. Tableaux récents* at the Galerie des Cahiers d'art, Paris, 25 February–14 March 1936

Invitation (*above*) to the exhibition

1936

"Around 1935, I succeeded in establishing a dialogue between modern art and the Renaissance (Raphael, Poussin); my friends wanted to have a dialogue only with the primitives. That led to my large-scale abstract works: *Île-de-France*, *Blue spaces* [*Espaces bleus*], etc., and my standing figures (*Figure debout*). But also to the end of abstract art!"[55]

In February–March, he holds his first solo exhibition at the Galerie Cahiers d'Art. It opens with "un-hoped-for success (even Picasso came), and Arp, Mondrian and Giacometti are enthusiastic", he comments. In the *Nouvelle Revue française*, Raymond Queneau compares the works on show to the development of a living being: "Surprise follows surprise, but with a sense of certainty; and in his most recent paintings, we see his 'characters' open their eyes – eyes which until now our blindness prevented us from discerning, just as one does not suspect what wonderful plumage a little feather-less chick will be clothed in when it grows up."[56]

In April 1938, in an interview with George L.K. Morris, he is to comment on the way New York influenced his development:
"In what ways do you find that the year you have spend in America has influenced the quality of your work? or has it failed to influence you in any way that you can discern?"
J.H.: "One reason for coming here was to isolate myself from the milieu I have developed in, and reconsider everything. New York, so different in every respect, has shown me how much I have been influenced by the architecture of my own country, its

density in the cities, the proportion between free space and built space, solid and fluid, curve and straight lines, light and dark, hard and soft, and the amount of human motion composed with it. However free one believes to be in front of the canvas, one always handles opposition of any factors according to a scale of proportions learned through daily experiences, and varying very slowly …. A stay in a country, foreign climate, foreign architecture, provokes opinions on colors, and associations of colors rarely rarely experienced at home. The narrow amount of free space in New York, has made me conscious of other variations in my own balance of other variations in my own balance of free space and occupied space. After visiting an American show, I have always felt, by opposition, a strict pupil of Seurat and Cézanne. Yet the dark ochres, the red bricks, the putties of your buildings, replacing the Parisian greys, have made me develop in my palette zones corresponding to those. No doubt also that the violent light of New York has led me to sharper oppositions of values and colors."[57]

The New York critic Henry McBride reports on his solo exhibition, organized in April by the city's Valentine Gallery: "Designed, no doubt, to synchronize with the great show of abstract art at the Modern Museum, a number of one-man modernist exhibitions have recently taken place, culminating with Jean Hélion's appearance in the Valentine Gallery. 'Culminating' seems to be the correct word for it, since Hélion has more abstract graces that might prove attractive to American eyes than have the other practicing non-realists. Jean Hélion is a young

French man who has married an American wife but who remains, I believe, a Frenchman for all that. He is an extreme purist. There is a sanctity, a kind of Quaker elegance in his use of color, that is astonishing just at first but in the end is very gratifying …. Evidently he has no prurient curiosities. He is not like the late Samuel Butler, who immediately upon discovering that we were in the midst of 'The Machine Age', proceeded to write an essay called 'Love among the Machines'. Jean Hélion is not like that. Seeing that the Old World System of handmade things – the system upon which the old type aesthetics had been founded – was dropping away from us, he, quite, quite undismayed, soared immediately, like Emerson, to the realms of the oversoul, where nothing is foul, where dross is eliminated and where only beauty reigns."[58]

Before leaving, in July, for the United States, where he stays until April 1938, he makes the acquaintance of André Breton.

From the winter of 1936 to the end of May 1937, he is installed at 1 Sheridan Square, New York, "… in this small workshop, very well-lit, satisfactory …. A vast view of New York, uncluttered to the left, in full view to the north, and looking towards Washington Square to the right. We are on the edge of Greenwich Village."[59] He receives many American artists, in particular Ilya Bolotowsky, Harry Holtzman, George L.K. Morris, Charles Shaw, the sculptor David Hare, and the art critic Meyer Schapiro. According to Hare, Hélion represented "something … that is missing in this country. He was a professional. In saying that, I do not mean a professional

painter, as was the case of many people. I mean he was a professional revolutionary. Not from a political point of view, you know, but in terms of independent mindedness, believe me …. He conveyed to American artists that there was a place in society, in world culture, for the avant-garde artist."[60]
Forms a friendship with Meyer Schapiro; urges Gallatin to foster the development of the first phase of American abstract art.

Attends a lecture by Salvador Dalí at the Museum of Modern Art in New York: "He said in particular that surrealism could find expression in all languages, all idioms, all styles, from the most childlike, as in the case of Miró, to the most sophisticated …. I had been as offended as the most narrow-minded bourgeois by the deliberately shocking aspect of some surrealist images, which seem to be schoolboy pranks, but I was also very aware that our geometrical seriousness was frightfully scholastic, lacking at its heart a roar of laughter to scandalize people. Though not attracted by the worldly, provocative side of surrealism, I was aware of its liveliness, its ability to come spurting up out of sleep and intuition, Freudian science and the cataracts of politics."[61]

Publication in July of the article 'Seurat as a Predecessor' in *The Burlington Magazine*: "Seeing is perceiving intelligibly, in an order allowing the faculties to seize elements, place them, make their existence possible inside …. I cannot let nature just enter me, because nature does not offers any structure visible or intelligible from one point of view, from one side. Nature is true only from all points of view, by the sum of perceptions,

which is endless. I only see bits of it, framed by the eye-lids. The rest perpetually fades around.
But Seurat's picture goes entirely through my eyes."[62]

In the summer, his essay 'Poussin, Seurat and Double Rhythm' appears in *Axis*, pointing out the guiding principles of a form of abstract art structured according to the conventions of cubism: "If one believes, as I do, that painting is to be continued as one best way for man to accomplish his potentialities, compose them and satisfy himself, it is hard to stand a certain amount of control. It cannot be let loose. It has to stay clear. The way Poussin, Mantegna, Ucello, the Chaldeans have been clear. This is calling for tradition, but to do so, after having understood what Cézanne, Picasso, Mondrian did (to name only three clear stages), has another meaning than to consider the past without admiring their work. Poussin, through them, looks greater than ever, and much clearer." He then adds: "There must be composition in two direction: the whole, the inside. The whole, the part. And each may also be organized in many ways. The egg-structure constitutes an aspect of the double rhythm; unity, totality, continuity. But every part, like the whole, must be both compact, closed, and opened, like a tree. Second aspect. A tree, holding space, embracing it. The composition of those two opposed qualities produces a resulting force, the solidity of the painted, its true and only reality."[63]

Takes part in many collective exhibitions – in Paris, at the Galerie Pierre, with Arp, Ferren, Giacometti, Hartung, Kandinsky, Nelson, Paalen and Sophie Tauber-Arp; at the

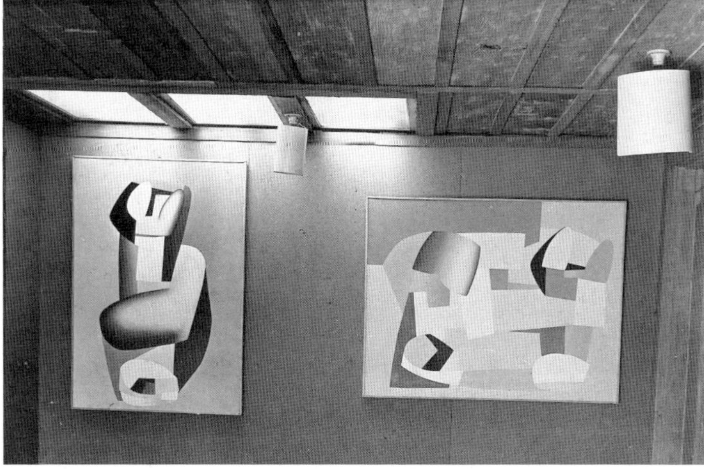

The exhibition *Jean Hélion* organized by Marcel Duchamp, Howard Putzel Gallery, Hollywood, February 1937

Galerie Diana Castelucho, with Fernandez, González, Magnelli and Picasso; in England, in the travelling *Abstract & Concrete* exhibition, organized in collaboration with the journal *Axis*.

1937
From summer 1937 until April 1938 Hélion lives at Rockbridge Baths, Virginia: "Some galleries were already opening up to me. I was lionized to some extent, which soon weighed on me. It was for this reason that I left New York [during the summer] and took refuge in the mountains of Virginia, where I had already built a workshop out of Californian redwood. I wanted to be able to think, far from all influences. I wanted to let my abstract art develop towards its end, which I accepted, towards a magnificent concordance of the modern and classicism …. But in this workshop at Rockbridge Baths, I experienced some sumptuous moments; I pushed my abstract symbols towards their end."[64]

Emergence of naturalistic forms in his compositions and implicit return of the human figure: "The lines curved bit by bit, and as soon as they started to curve they took on figurative capabilities, they conjured up things that existed elsewhere. This trend gained ground in my work, starting in 1937 and then accelerating."[65]

Revival of interest in drawing "… that has to be gone into in detail, in depth, has to be required to give a very clear definition of the design".[66] "Moreover I've started (keep this strictly between ourselves, please) studies after my wife, drawings that are still awkward because I'm out of practice in this genre, which I never adequately mastered in any case in my too rapid career, but they have an odd resemblance to my abstract pictures, which is the best sign of hope. I'm concentrating on reading elements, and on natural ways of assembling those elements; then on varying their composition within the bounds of objectivity. All that still feeling my way, without hurrying, to give substance to my thoughts, and with absolutely no idea of separation from what I paint daily." [67]

Draws after the illustrations in *La Magnifique Histoire de l'architecture* by Choisy, studies Egyptian history, reads *The Iliad*: "Of course I've been dipping into the *Iliad* for fifteen years, but I'd never set about creating it as a spectacle that entered my head, using all my imagination; that helps me too." [68]

Sends Queneau a drawing which the writer uses as a frontispiece for his collection *Chêne et chien* [Oak and dog] published by Denoël: "Influence of *Chêne et chien* on my abstraction in 1937 in New York when in 1935 I'd been unable to accept his kind invitation to illustrate it. My dreams of grandiose illustrations for *Chêne et chien* in keeping with old records of the family house, with collages of pillow lace. Let all that stuff, scribbled in the corner of the studio, that was only dreamt – not finished, soon carried off by the war – be given to him in complete friendship. *Chêne et chien*. I knew many parts of it off by heart. I entertained my friends in New York with it, Meyer Schapiro, among others."[69]

Death of his father Louis in December.

1938
In April, returns to France, to Couterne, then in May settles in Paris, where he works in a new Paris studio at 152 rue Broca in the 13th *arrondissement*.
Makes friends with Yves Tanguy.

In autumn, another stay at Rockbridge Baths in Virginia. Carries out large abstract compositions including *Twin figures* [*Figures jumelles*].

Taking stock, and start of a new cycle: "I'm working all day, a lot. In May or June I expect to have finished five or six canvases (not started but got ready) which should round off the past ten years of my efforts. A sort of converging and culminating point, from which I hope to set off for a wider, deeper, lighter zone."[70]
His plan to teach at the New Bauhaus in Chicago, suggested by Moholy-Nagy, comes to nothing. Reads Proust, Balzac and Montaigne.
On 29 November he gives a lecture at the Brooklyn Institute of Arts and Sciences in New York .

1939
His work develops inexorably towards the figurative. He writes to Pierre-Georges Bruguière: "I can tell you of my amazement; of my powerlessness to resist such a genuine trend which is at the bottom of what I've been looking for. By drawing from life I proved to myself that I could do it like anyone else; but what I produced never appeared true to me like these things that come out of my head and my heart. I think that now I won't stop drawing from life, but it will always be in relation to the concept."[71]

From 4 January 1939 to the end of April 1939 he produces *Kaleidoscope* for the journal *Volontés*, a series of linocuts recapitulating fifty-six stages of his progression from 1929 to 1939 (in the end these works are not published): "All of a sudden I started to finish off six drawings for linocuts, and I engraved them in three and a half days of hard graft. Go and see them at Pelorson's [director of the journal]; I sent them straight off, with a proof printed as best I could; they form a small series I'd like to publish under the title Kaleidoscope, a fragment, in the order indicated. They're violent, good I think, rather cursory in the treatment, but that suits linoleum, a soft material that has to be shaken up, and a magazine."[72]

9 February, birth of his second son, Louis.

Final abstract compositions, ending with *Dramatic composition* [*Composition dramatique*] and *Fallen figure* [*Figure tombée*].
"Dramatic composition. Started on 13 April 1939 at Rockbridge Baths. Completed on 14 September 1939 at Rockbridge Baths.
In a watercolour from late autumn 1938: Second romantic or dramatic composition: reclining figure. An element looking like a cloth on the ground. Flying element above it …. This picture has become (or come) like a funerary symbol that I'd be happy to dedicate to defeated Loyalist Spain."[73]

On *Fallen figure*, begun 15 April 1939, completed 25 September 1939 at Rockbridge Baths: "On the canvas I put up a sort of monument to my adventure. That is, the abstraction took the form of a collapse into a space. This picture is now

55. *Journal d'un peintre*, vol. II, *op. cit.*,
21 January 1970, p. 92.
56. Raymond Queneau, "Jean Hélion aux Cahiers d'art", *Nouvelle Revue française*, no. 271, April 1936, p. 627.
57. "Interview with Jean Hélion" (by George L.K. Morris), as note 38, p. 33.
58. H. McBride, "Abstractions by Jean Hélion. Purity in art especially acceptable to American Taste", *New York Sun*, 11 April 1936, p. 32.
59. *Lettres d'Amérique*, *op. cit.*,
20 November 1936, p. 19.
60. Comments collected by Merle Schipper, in *Jean Hélion: The Abstract Years, 1929–1939*, PhD thesis, University of Los Angeles, 1974, p. 197.
61. *À perte de vue …*, *op. cit.*,
pp. 56 and 58.
62. Jean Hélion, "Seurat as a Predecessor", *The Burlington Magazine*, no. 69, July 1936, p. 4.
63. *Axis*, no. 6, summer 1936, p. 14.
64. *À perte de vue …*, *op. cit.*, p. 67.
65. "Hélion l'Amérique" (interview with Jean Hélion), *L'Art vivant*, July–August 1984, p. 61.
66. *Journal d'un peintre*, vol. I, *op. cit.*,
5 April 1948, p. 118.
67. Unpublished letter to Pierre-Georges Bruguière, Rockbridge Baths, 9 October 1937.
68. J. Hélion, Rockbridge Baths, 23 or 24 November 1937, in *Lettres d'Amérique …*, *op. cit.*, p. 81.
69. *Journal d'un peintre*, vol. II, *op. cit.*,
17 April 1972, p. 117.
70. J. Hélion, Rockbridge Baths, 26 December 1938, in *Lettres d'Amérique …*, *op. cit.*, p. 116.
71. Unpublished letter from J. Hélion to Pierrre-Georges Bruguière, Rockbridge Baths, Va., 26 May 1939.
72. J. Hélion, Rockbridge Baths, Va., 15 January 1939, in *Lettres d'Amérique …*, *op. cit.*, pp. 118–19.
73. *Journal d'un peintre*, vol. I, *op. cit.*, [between 13 April and 14 September] 1939, pp. 70–71.

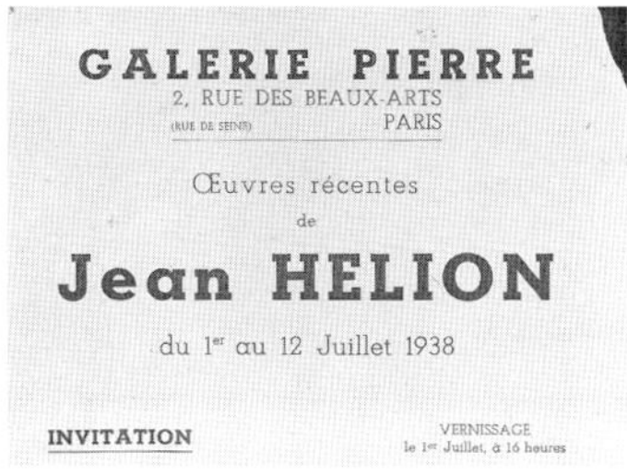

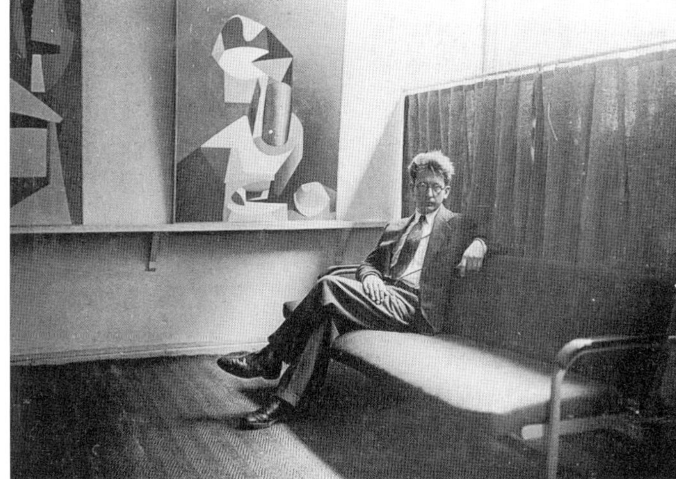

Jean Hélion (*right*) at the exhibition *Œuvres récentes* organized by the Galerie Pierre [Loeb], Paris, July 1938

Invitation (*above*) to the exhibition

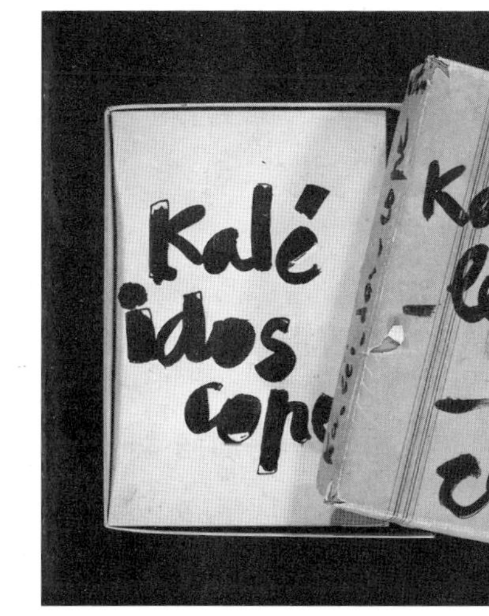

Cover of *Kaléidoscope,* 1938–39
Chinese ink on paper, 21 x 16.7 x 3.5 cm
Centre Pompidou, Musée national d'art moderne, Paris, gift of the artist 1977

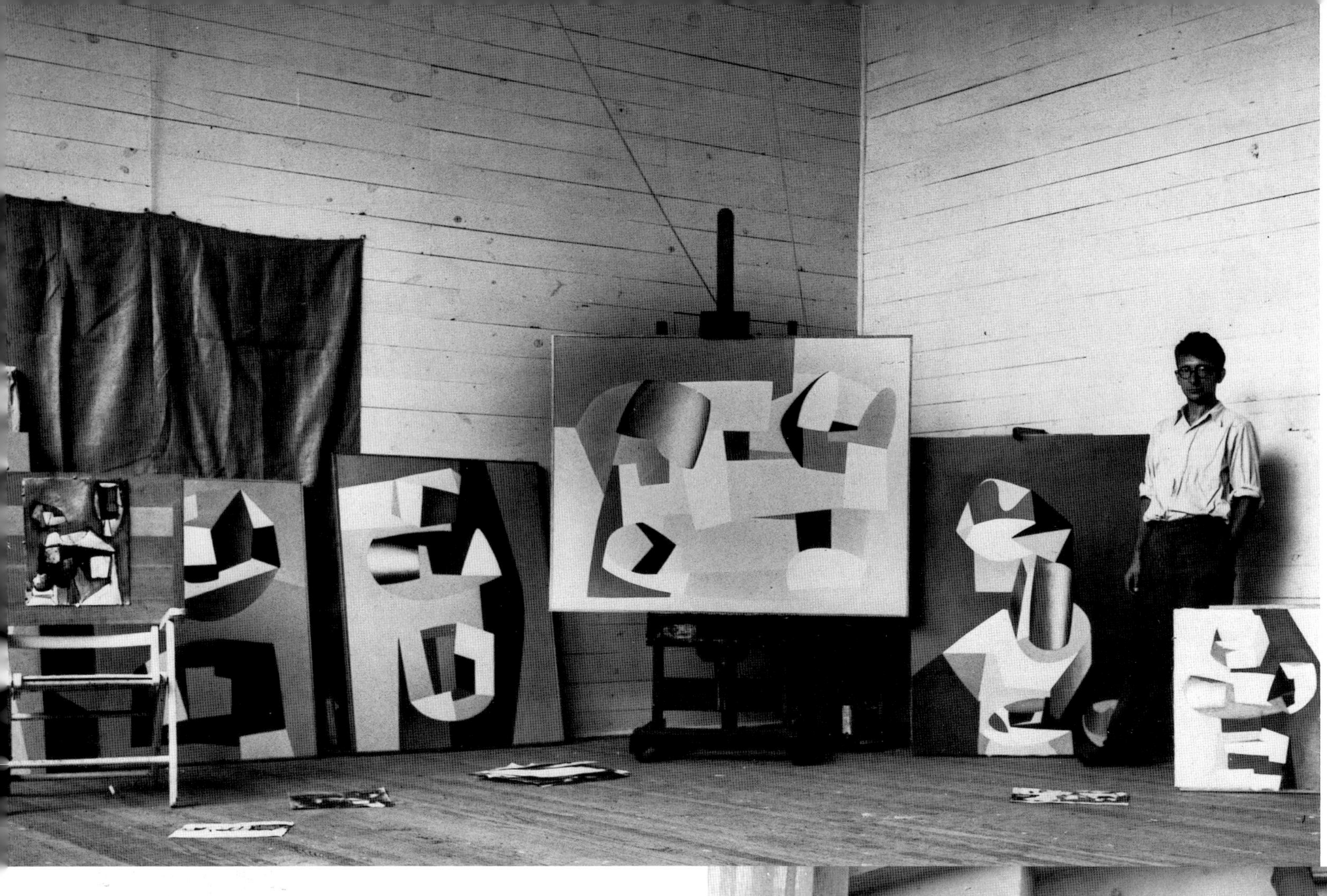

Jean Hélion in his studio at Rockbridge
Baths, Virginia, about 1937

Hélion's personal, 'cult' objects in his studio
in the rue Michelet, Paris, 1947

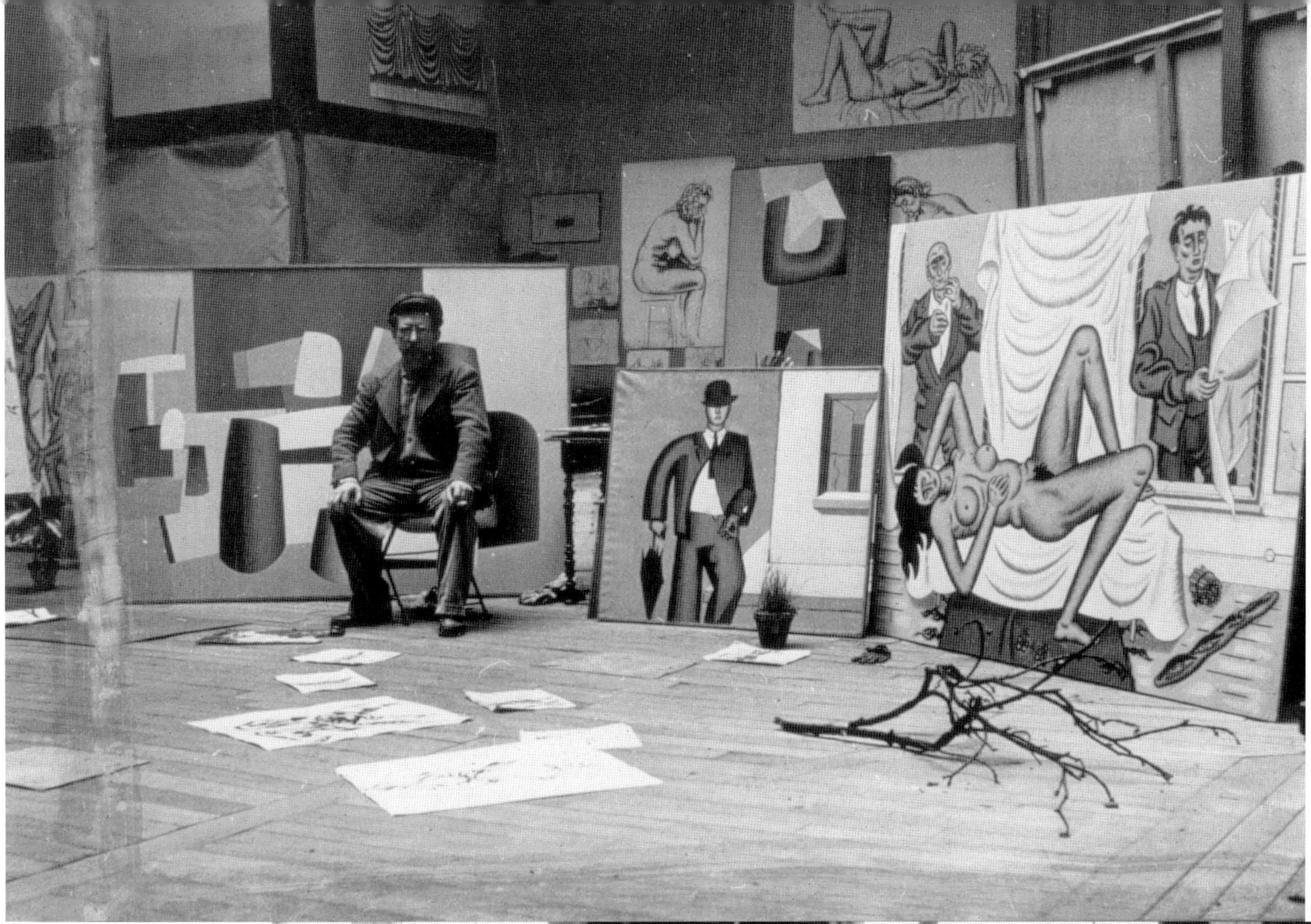

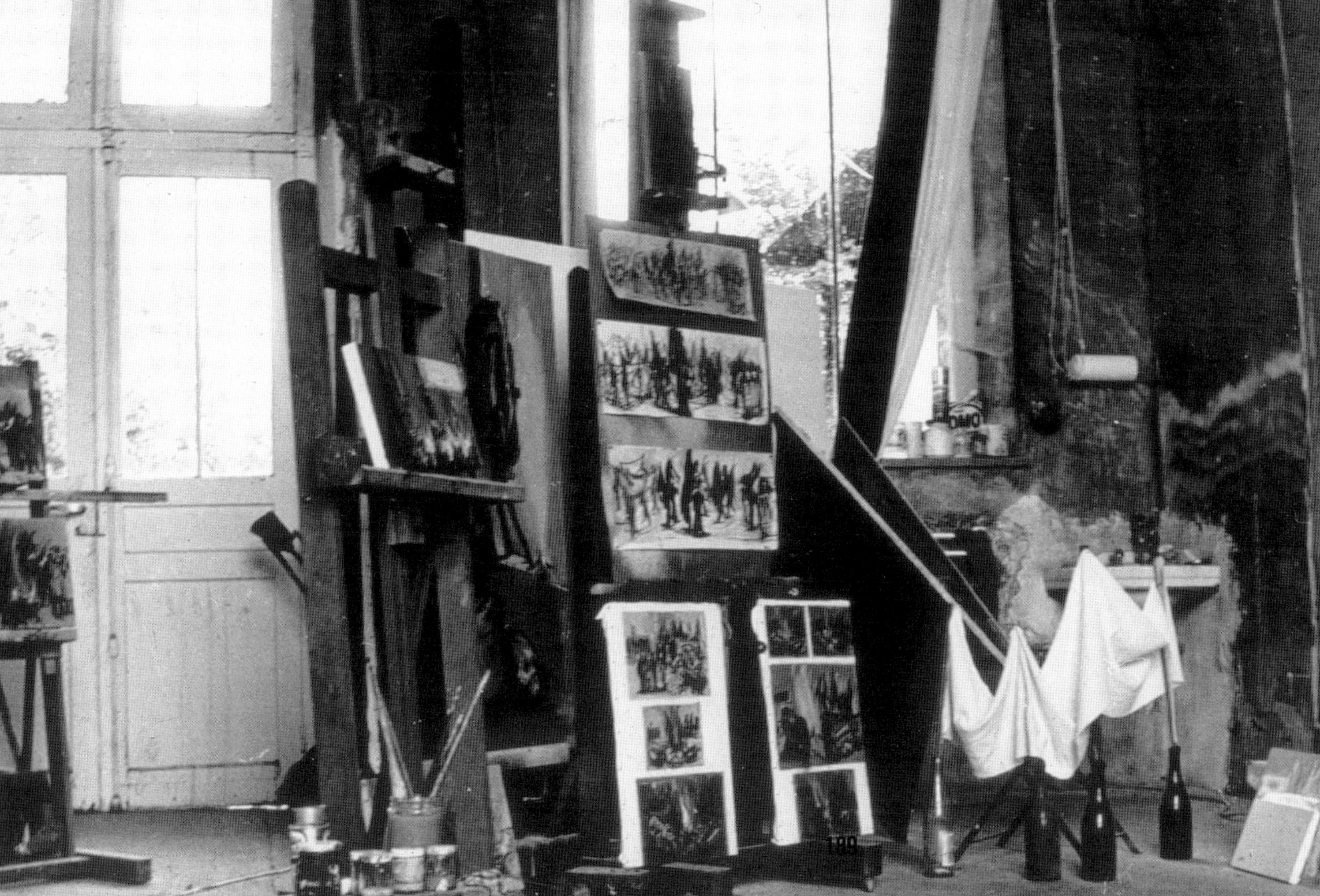

Jean Hélion in his studio,
avenue de l'Observatoire,
Paris, 1950

The studio at Bigeonnette,
1968, with materials serving as
preparation for the triptych
Things seen in May (1969)

called *Fallen figure* and I can say that it's famous. But in parallel, other manoeuvres, other revolutions, other troubles were shaking up the world and demolishing it as I had myself destroyed my abstraction. On the pretext of maturing, it was itself collapsing. The noise of boots could be heard. Hitler was thundering; the radio was already reporting his rambling speeches as fiery words. Everyone had a presentiment of the approaching fall. As for me, in the silence of my studio, I was hastening slowly. I was trying to complete my work, *i.e.* to rediscover the uncoded world: and to name it boldly."[74]

From spring onwards devotes himself to naturalistic studies that culminate in twelve watercolours: "The most beautiful of all the watercolours depicts a street (a Paris street, always Paris, my city of birth, the archetypal place, special in type, for which I nurture a growing passion). A pavement. On the pavement a café door, a table, a seated man, looking, who resembles you. A glass and a soda siphon. In the dark of the door a waiter who is also dark. In the street a cyclist falls off his bike. The seated man looks a bit like you. The waiter is perhaps called Alfred. The street is blue like a river. On the wall: *Défense d'A* [Stick no b(ills)]."[75]

In May, starts work on the first large-format figurative canvas, *With cyclist* [*Au cycliste*]: "This extremely austere, extremely concentrated painting I was doing then led me to an irresistible, imperious need to open the window, to speak to nature at very close quarters, to call it by its first name in a kind of way. I painted a man on a bike and that men went to the things, the flowers, the landscapes, towards women."[76]

In his *carnets* he admits he is trying to strike a balance, "… that of the figurative representation that I am capable of realising on the one hand, and which my ideas and tastes can put up with on the other. Drawn in tempera: man reading a newspaper, man falling, cyclist."[77]

Reports to the French consul in Philadelphia on 24 August 1939: "I prefer to go to war and remain a Frenchman than to become an American citizen, no offence to America and though I can become one next November. This exile has taught me a lot about myself, my needs and my potential. And then History has turned, in a manner of speaking. It's no longer possible to take temporary flight. It's necessary to choose and stay put. It's wiser to remain where you are born, to love in the place where you have roots, to measure your efforts against traditions that you feel and know. I'm convinced it's better to be a patriot in the present state of the world than an internationalist, as I thought I was. That feeling was imaginary; it was based on the influence of the Soviet Union, which seemed to be the start of a worldwide regime; but I want nothing to do with that regime, black as it has turned out to be."[78]

In November, paints the first heads, *Édouard, Émile* and *Charles*: "*Émile* … I name this character as he emerges from these eleven studies *Émile*. He is Émile. And not someone who might have posed for these studies. This is the way in which I expect to name the individuals I will perfect one after the other. *Édouard*: head in absolute profile; wearing a boater; orange-coloured bow tie.
Charles: head seen from behind, soft pale grey hat."[79]

Leaves several large abstract compositions and the drawings for several figurative painting projects at sketch stage.

1940–41
Called up in January, leaves New York on the *De Grasse* on 16 January to travel to Dreux, his mobilization centre, then on to the non-commissioned officers' class at Mézières-en-Drouais: "I was approaching from the low point, I recognized myself there, I was at the same rank as the humblest, in my place, to start again. The tiniest village where we manoeuvred appeared sublime to me, the houses were perfect volumes, the people walking in the street made gestures, downstrokes, of unparalleled and very simple complexity. I admired the crevices, the folds of the shutters, the fine cracks and behind the houses the wild gestures of the trees; it was winter, they were begging the sky that all this misery might finish, and that we might at last recover enjoyment in living."[80]

Taken prisoner on 19 June, he is sent to a camp in Pomerania, then to a prison-ship anchored in the harbour of Stettin an der Oder (now Szczecin, Poland). As he has a rudimentary knowledge of German, he acts as interpreter for his fellow prisoners and endeavours to set up a resistance network.

Reads *Nadja* by Breton: "Hardly had I arrived at the barracks in 1940 when I was put on duty in an office. Harnessed and girdled, I was tremendously bored and I started rummaging through the drawers. In the first one I found a copy of *Nadja* …. Throughout my life I've found objects, pebbles from who knows what imaginary Tom Thumb, that marked my path. I recognized them. So I was on the right path, going the right way. *Nadja* was one of those pebbles."[81]

In the preface to the catalogue of his solo exhibition, *Jean Hélion. Works 1935–1939*, organized in New York by the Georgette Passedoit Gallery (25 March–6 April) the American critic Meyer Schapiro writes: "Jean Hélion is the outstanding abstract painter of the young generation of American and European artists. Painters, here and abroad, follow his work closely as the most highly esteemed and best controlled of its genre. When abstract art in pursuit of purity became increasingly bare and flat, Hélion was the most successful in finding a return path to the fullness of nature within the framework of abstract art. His forms preserve the properties of objects in their solidity, their depth, the plentiful contrasts, the complex links, inside a realm with strict forms where everything has been weighed and perfected. I admire his thoughtfulness and his severity, his sober harmonies, the concentrated, precise, often powerful forms, clear but for all that evasively constructed. These qualities belong to all periods and more particularly to the present day. Devoid of ornamental attractions, sugary charm, brilliant brushstrokes or amazing motifs, his work is made to be thought about for a long time; the constructive mind is there in front of you, beautiful and imperturbable."

The exhibition is favourably received by American critics, particularly by Henry McBride: "The Passedoit Gallery is presenting a show of the work of Jean Hélion, one of the leading younger abstractionists of the French school. Hélion has had earlier shows here and is well liked by the devotees of purism. It is as a purist in fact, and as a colorist, that he seems to stand out among other practitioners. Mr Meyer Shapiro, in an appreciatory note, claims something of a miracle for Hélion, whom he poses as a prophet 'finding a return path to the fullness of nature within the framework of abstract art'. There isn't a trace of 'nature' ordinarily in Helion's view of art; in fact, he would be an admirable candidate for baroness Rebay's Gallery of non objectives or Mr Gallatin's 'Museum of Living Art', where he is doubtless already represented. The pictures, in bright individual patterns, are quite accurately explained by their titles, which themselves imply no mystery other than, for the most part, a frank love of color."[82]

1942
Escapes from Stettin on 13 February. On 17 February regains Paris, where he hides with the help of his friend Mary Reynolds. Travels clandestinely to the south, arrives in Marseilles, becomes a telephonist in a camp of 'displaced' persons. He meets up with Duchamp, Tristan Tzara, Victor Brauner, Nelly van Doesburg, Jacques Hérold and the Paris gallery owners Henriette and André Gomès: "I'm still between two places, almost gone, if I'm to believe the latest news, but far from arriving if I believe experience, constantly extended by new difficulties …. In fact, I know that my Portuguese visa has been granted by Lisbon, but the consulate has still not been informed."[83]

Purchases a new sketchbook in which he sets down what he calls his "attempts to re-engage with the world, freed first from the Stalag and then from abstraction."[84] "The

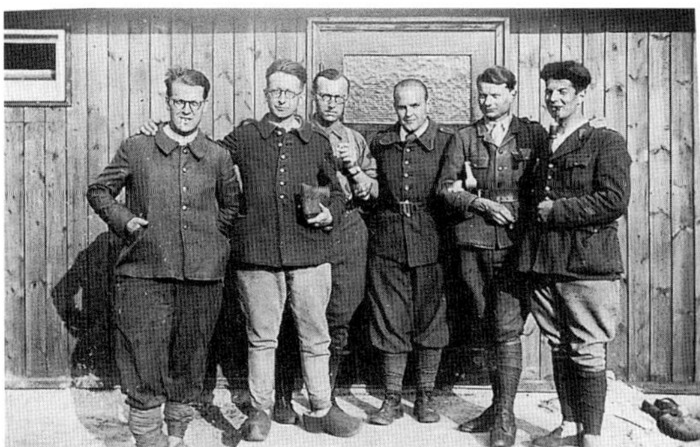

Jean Hélion and his companions in captivity in Stalag II C, Stettin, Pomerania [10 June 1941] from left to right: René Gaude, Jean Hélion, Paul Hostel, unknown, Paul Poitier, Paul Martin

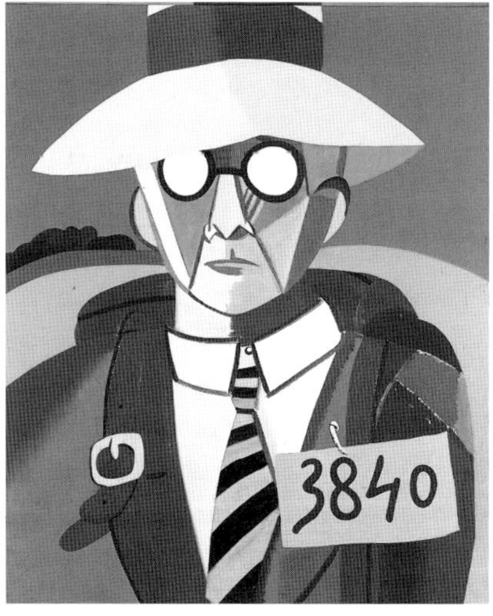

Eduardo Arroyo
Jean Hélion after his escape, en route from Pomerania towards Paris (frontal), 1974
Oil on canvas, 100 x 81 cm
Centre Pompidou, Musée national d'art moderne, Paris
purchase 1977

first object I'd bought in the free zone was a sketchbook, and all puffed up with my regained freedom, I drew my first motifs – a half-blocked ventilator which perhaps for me conjured up the oubliette from which I had luckily emerged. Then some trees, boles which were conceived as cylinders but which swayed out and separated into branches. In the streets full of notices prohibiting this or that, a man quite naturally stood in front of a prohibition sign. You see what followed …"[85]

Obtains an American visa and returns to Baltimore in October. Back in Virginia, writes *They Shall Not Have Me*, the story of his captivity. He embarks on a series of lectures on the same subject across the East Coast of the United States and on radio in support of Free France: "Eight months later I was in America, back at work in the studio I'd left in 1939 with the first *Émiles*, the first *Édouards*, the first *Charleses*. But first I was urged to write a book describing my adventures, which was published in English, then I was dragged from radio station to lecture hall to speak for hours on end about my captivity."[86]

In May the exhibition *Hélion–Daura* shown at the Virginia Museum of Fine Arts in Richmond provokes lively interest: "His paintings are not paintings of anything – they are solidly conceived fantasies in color. Looking at them for the first time is like hearing Stravinsky for the first time – you feel the same dismay and bewilderment. Just as you feel anyone could have written the groans, thumps and thuds of 'Sacre du Printemps' so you get a first impression that anyone with a palette

could have turned out an Hélion oil. It's not true. The longer you study Hélion's works, the more quality you find. What appears at first to be the simplest sort of poster brushwork becomes a delicate and effective technique upon closer examination: what looks like flat color is actually very subtle modulation. A first impression is that Hélion tosses paint with indiscriminate abandon. A longer look convinces you that he has mastered the art of fine discrimination. At any rate, the Hélions are interesting pieces. They are the higher mathematics of art. The painter has gone into the science of color harmony with the same intellectual enthusiasm of a calculus student plotting up a fourth dimension, or a Bach writing mathematical variations on a theme. Instead of calling his paintings 'Paris' or 'Printemps', they might properly be identified by opus numbers."[87]

1943
Publication of *They Shall Not Have Me* by Dutton & Co., Inc. New York. This story of captivity becomes a best-seller immediately it appears in the United States.
Resumption of work: "In my studio on the table I found piles of sketches left there before I went to war (as they say). This involved a double effort, that of filling in the gaps in my abstraction and the seemingly contrary one of rejoining the world. I wanted to grasp figures by the middle, wanted to dig out holes, and yet had the opposite desire to travel into an undefined space."[88]
"It happens that for me abstraction came to an end with the war which was a great upheaval of ideas, the advent of nameless misfortunes and catastrophes. Through all these misfortunes they [other artists] were

able to carry on doing the same thing. Coming back from the war to which he went and where he suffered, Hans Hartung resumed the picture he had started and continued to improve it. That's all well and good. But I couldn't do the same. I was in a turmoil. I had identified my life or rather life in general with my art. If there was a war going on outside, well my art had to respond to it. I'm not saying it wages war, but perhaps it makes up for it. Because the world outside had been turned upside down my art was turned upside down, and I felt that this was right. I felt at ease with it. I looked at my pre-war abstract pictures: they seemed very successful to me, but I couldn't have done them in this state. It isn't so much a desire to tell my story as a desire to be right, to be in tune with this world." [89]

In February–March, a solo exhibition, *Jean Hélion. Paintings 1933–1939*, at Peggy Guggenheim's New York gallery, Art of this Century, curated by Max Ernst, which emphasizes the importance of the impact of his work on modern European art: "A mature leader of the modern movement in direct line with Gris and Léger, Hélion is shown at his best with this selection of 35 examples of his distinctive compositions."[90] "At Art of this Century", Robert M. Coates writes, "they are showing oils and water colors by Jean Helion, most of them done in the period 1936–1939. His, I think, is a style that derives primarily from Léger's work in the early Dynamist days, but from this beginning Hélion has gone on to develop a design that is strongly personal and that also combines grace, dignity, and deep suggestiveness in a way that few other contemporary abstractionists can equal. I liked particularly his

'Rouge Brillant', with its curiously lip-like forms, as well as the darker 'Figure Bleue', and the really swell 'Figure debout' with its grave greens and grays and generally cool tonality."[91]

In April, produces a series of abstract gouaches conceived in 1939, then in October his first *Man with umbrella*. Paints *Défense d'* [Do not …], a work in which a version of the *Émile* for which he had done a study in 1939 is embedded.

1944
At the end of January, departs Rockbridge Baths, leaving his wife and his son Louis, and moves to New York: "In 1944, Pegeen [Vail][92] entered my life, bringing me woman. I composed man and woman, Pegeen and me, in street scenes. Then I tackled a few gestures – smoker, person waving, walker, male or female porter, man sleeping, woman sleeping, person with one leg. Woman carrying an umbrella. And I composed them. 1944–45."[93]

In New York meets up again with Breton, Calder, Chagall, Max Ernst, Léger, Mondrian, Ozenfant, Seligmann and Tanguy, refugees in the United States.

Produces the series of *Lighters up* [*Allumeurs*], *Smokers* [*Fumeurs*] *Girls with yellow hair*, [*Filles aux cheveux jaunes*]: "… in 1944 in New York Breton recognized a surrealist impulse in my first figures, my men with lowered hats and my dishevelled nudes. It seems to me that there is as little point in saying what is happening as in denying it. I understood surrealism as a level of attention beyond boredom and ordinariness, as an act of life and not as a distinguished suicide." [94]

74. *À perte de vue …*, *op. cit.*, pp. 67, 69.
75. Jean Hélion, Rockbridge Baths, Va., 18 August 1939, in *Lettres d'Amérique …*, *op. cit.*, p. 147.
76. Remarks collected by Maïten Boisset, "C'est l'heure d'aller voir Hélion", *Le Matin*, 22 June 1984, p. 34.
77. *Journal d'un peintre*, vol. I, op. cit., 27–28 September 1939, p. 72.
78. Jean Hélion, Rockbridge Baths, Va., 18 August 1939, in *Lettres d'Amérique …*, *op. cit.*, pp. 141–42.
79. *Journal d'un peintre*, vol. I, *op. cit.*, [October] 1939, p. 72.
80. *À perte de vue …*, *op. cit.*, pp. 77–78.
81. *Mémoire de la chambre jaune*, *op. cit.*, p. 165.
82. H. McBride, *New York Herald Tribune*, 31 March 1940.
83. J. Hélion, Camp de la Blancarde, Marseilles, 25 August 1942, to Henriette and André Gomès, G. Heytens archives.
84. *À perte de vue …*, *op. cit.*, p. 259.
85. *Ibid.*, p. 80.
86. *Ibid.*
87. J.K., "Neat Contrasts in Works of Jean Hélion, Pierre Daura", *American New York Journal*, 24 May 1942.
88. *Mémoire de la chambre jaune*, *op. cit.*, p. 12.
89. Conversation with Jean Hélion, "L'indécence d'aimer", from the journal *ArTitudes*, nos. 21–23, published on the occasion of *Hélion, cinquante ans de peinture* at the Galerie Karl Flinker, 22 April–30 June 1975, p. 79.
90. "Hélion abstractionist", *The Art Digest*, New York, 15 February 1943.
91. R.M. Coates, *New Yorker*, New York, 27 February 1943.
92. Pegeen Vail, the daughter of Peggy Guggenheim, whom he married in 1945.
93. *Journal d'un peintre*, vol. I, *op. cit.*, 3 September 1949, p. 196.
94. *À perte de vue …*, *op. cit.*, p. 59.

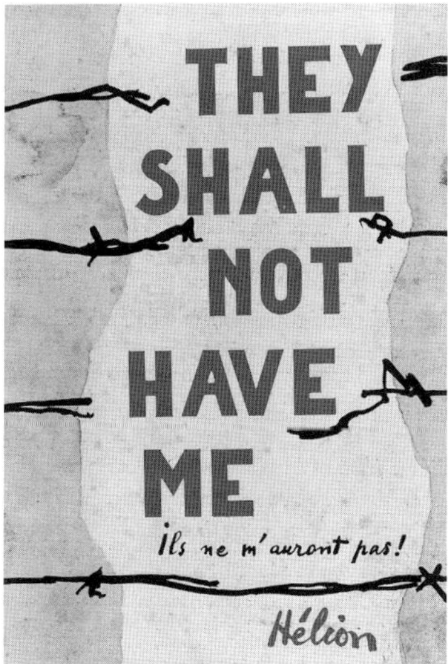

Dust jacket of Jean Hélion's book *They Shall Not Have Me*, New York, E.P. Dutton, 1943

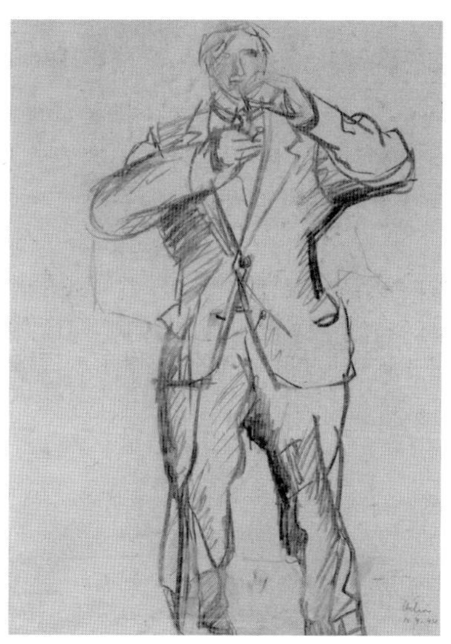

Lighter up, 1944
Charcoal on paper, 60.5 x 45 cm
Centre Pompidou, Musée national d'art moderne, Paris
Gift of the Société des Amis du Musée national d'art moderne, 1960

In March, writes the article 'How War Made me Paint' for the journal *ArtNews*, in which he analyses his painting method: "My share of the war has been sordid, yet rich. I have come back, after three years, feeling hurt and muddy, from feet to soul, yet strangely happy and alive. And my work has advanced one step that has changed his appearance entirely. The war has not given me any new idea. But it has produced a new balance among my various ideas and some of these, compressed until then in the back of my head, have now come forward …. While passionately painting abstractions, I had dreamed about recognizable forms and a responsible subject-matter; only a distant reflection of these actually materialized in my work. They came to life mainly when I talked. Now, I do not want to talk, nor write any more. I'm trying to express myself fully in a form of painting that would need neither poetic nor technical comments. When, at times, I despaired of ever coming out of the hole which I had fallen a captive, I realized that the sharpest abstraction could not embody the two major emotions now shaking me: a violent passion for life, as a whole, as it was denied to me, the streets, the people, the things. And without illusions about their weak sides, a devoted admiration for my comrades, who had shown me that men behave much better under hardships than under happiness."[95]

In March–April Paul Rosenberg organizes an exhibition of his recent works in his New York gallery, which is badly received by the critics: "My first exhibition at his gallery was a catastrophe. People arrived and soon left; even Léger, who is always so friendly, seemed not to under-

stand. Chagall, insistent and quarrelsome, was about the only person to study all my pictures carefully and show a real interest in them. The reviews were terrible. Insults and abuse were heaped on me, such as: 'We had a first-rate abstract painter, what are we left with now?', etc. I had just become part of a family the name of which is synonymous with superb collections of abstract, futurist and surrealist art both in America and Europe. I was going in the completely opposite direction. People didn't understand me."[96]

In a letter he wrote to Pierre-Georges Bruguière, he describes the keen interest he takes in his new motifs: "I've never felt so vibrant. I'm trying with all my being, all my senses, all my ideas, and all my dreams too, to produce a completely human body of work. I'm mixing the abstract with the real, things thought with things witnessed, all that in a quite obvious way: that's where the shoe pinches. My characters raise a hat or a leg; they smoke or they read the paper. They turn this way and that. The folds on all their clothes are abstractions. The women have their hair on their shoulders and are dazzling. I sing in praise even of objects that have fallen into the gutter, and I emphasize how abstract dream and reality coincide."[97]

In October, death of his second wife, Jean Blair.

1945
In January, his recent works are exhibited at the Caresse Crosby Gallery in Washington: "It is hard to keep up with a man as clever as Jean Helion. The critics had this gifted French artist neatly pigeonholed as an abstractionist. Then he

confounded them by turning up with a whole series of canvases representing men and women in bold outline and brilliant colour walking up and down stairs, smoking a cigarette or just standing still …. After a first view, we left wondering what there was behind the smart façade and whether we really were supposed to look."[98]

Starts work on *Greeters* [*Salueurs*], *Walkers* [*Promeneurs*], *Figures in the rain* [*Figures de pluie*]. "On 50 M [canvas size 116 x 73 cm] upright have painted man on crutches,[99] three-quarter view, quite good, but needs to be looked at again. Am on a second man on crutches,[100] 60 P [canvas size 130 x 89 cm], frontal view, much better. Haunted by an ogival feeling, a feeling of cathedrals, flying buttresses, which has led me to stained-glass colours, in this second one-legged man: the cathedral between the legs."[101]

Between early June and late July paints *Girl with her feet in the water* [*La Fille aux pieds dans l'eau*]: "The contrast of the soft, heavy body with the hard, slender chaise-longue (an object clearly belonging to the 19th century) is brutal. I've thought of the space comprised by the limbs as an environment with a special atmosphere and light – a cathedral of flesh. Consequently the sand between the legs is more luminous than elsewhere. Is that acceptable? They'll moan. To emphasize that sensation-idea, I've marked the area of sand contained between the feet of the chair, on the left and the right, in a similar way."[102]

From 2 September to 5 October travels across America with Pegeen Vail: "Colorado, the Rockies, Salt

Lake Desert, Yosemite Park, San Francisco, the coast to Big Sur, Los Angeles (had lunch with Stravinsky, spent evening with Faulkner), Death Valley, Bryce Canyon, Painted Desert, Petrified Forest, etc., 15,000 km."[103]

Embarks on *Couple with the umbrella* [*Couple au parapluie*] in November: "While working on it, I realised that my uppermost emotion-sensation right now is the spatial gesture (i.e. the definition of the gesture by the spaces it contains or divides). I have to colour the spatial gesture first – emphasize it, and leave the remainder (solids, flat washes, grounds, etc.) to develop around it, in second place, as subsidiaries. That's always where I go wrong. I allow myself to be carried away and colour the object first, and I make it beautiful and bright, but in doing so I lose my real motif (this interplay of spatial gestures)."[104]

In November, marries Pegeen Vail, who has been his companion since 1944: "Perhaps you've had news of me from this person or that? My news can be summed up like this: I've remarried, and my new wife Pegeen Vail, Peggy Guggenheim's daughter, and I are going to bring our happiness back to France as soon as possible. We've just requested our return visas, and expect to set sail after my next exhibition at Rosenberg's, scheduled for February …. Léger tells me by letter that he's requested his documents, too. Even Marcel Duchamp is talking of going back."[105]

His exhibition of works on paper, presented in November at Paul Rosenberg's New York gallery, meets with a lukewarm reception: "Yesterday, opening of my third exhibition at Rosenberg's –

gouaches and watercolours from 1935 to 1945 …. Some people, including Bouchard, the photographer, who wants to make a film about me, are enthusiastic.[106] Others are saying nothing, i.e. they hate them. The press, as it always has been since my first exhibition at Rosenberg's, is very fiercely anti. Isamu Noguchi, the sculptor, said to me yesterday evening at the Sandor concert I'd taken him to at Carnegie Hall[107] that what people didn't like about my figures was that they expressed feelings!"[108]

1946
Starts work on his series *Nudes leaning on elbows* [*Nus accoudés*]: "Finished *Girl leaning on her elbows* [*Fille accoudée*], 50 P [canvas size 116 x 81 cm] – which will be called *Sleeping girl leaning on her elbows* [*La dormeuse accoudée*]? I wonder! I don't like my titles much. *Fille accoudée* is better, less witty, but also very ordinary. *Painting* can designate anything. I detest mysterious titles – or pretentious ones – or theoretical ones. This is woman as temple. Temple of the arms, temple of the legs, where the altar of life lies. But if I've been successful, people should see that without an explanatory title. So I use a minimal title to designate the picture and distinguish it just enough from others."[109]

Before his final return to France in April burns a large part of his *carnets*, writings and papers.
In May, signs a contract with Colle & Renou and Paul Rosenberg (50/50).
Spends the summer at Cagnes-sur-Mer, where he paints naked and semi-naked figures: "Through drawing Pegeen, and thinking, I'm beginning to know what a nude is,

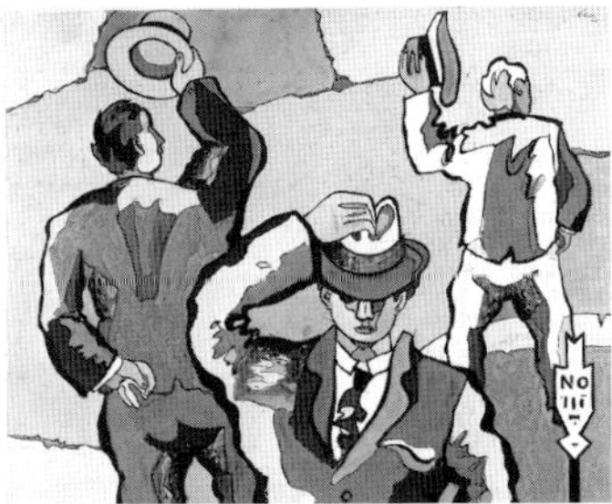

The greeters, 1945
Gouache and watercolour
58 x 71 cm
Private collection

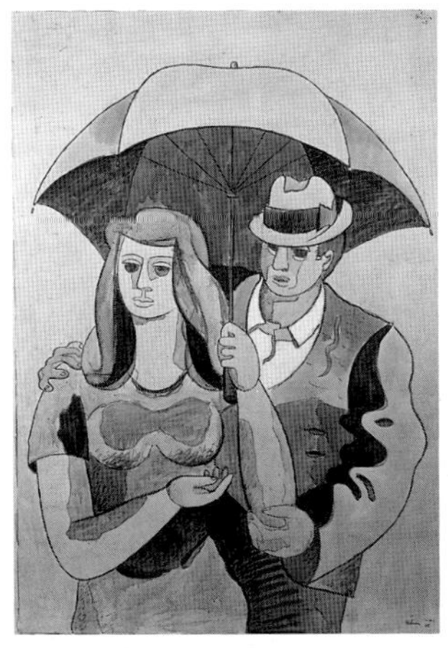

Couple with umbrella, 1946
Grey wash, watercolour on stuck-down paper
138 x 90 cm
Centre Pompidou, Musée national
d'art moderne, purchase 1971

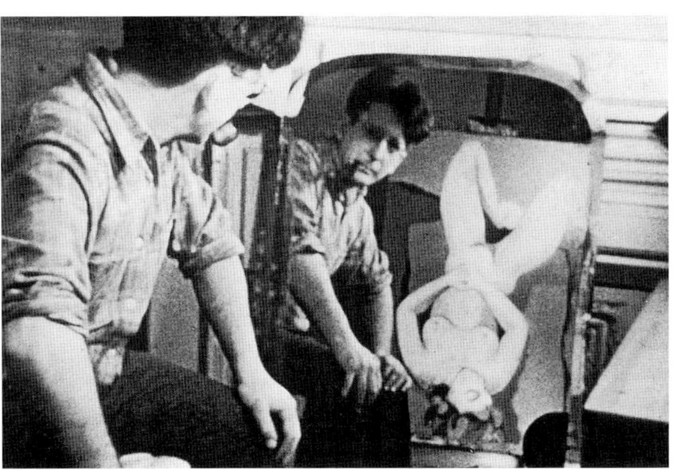

Jean Hélion in his studio in the rue Michelet,
about 1947–48

and to find enough in it to satisfy my imagination fully. I'll show you the drawings that prove that the surface of this subject trodden over for thousands of years has barely been touched. Every day I discover and note gestures that seem completely new to me and this gives me that enthusiasm only experienced when advancing on to *terra incognita*."[110]

In September writes to Pierre-Georges Bruguière: "Now I'm doing nude after nude, I'm rediscovering what I knew so well in the abstract period – the power of slow variations. I'm beginning to do nudes … that speak intensely as such. I'm going into the being in passionate depth – the only being, the naked being – and in it I'm discovering the successive layers you've enumerated so well."[111]

In October, sets up home in Paris at 4 rue Michelet in the 6th *arrondissement*, where he will remain until the end of his life: "Jean Hélion lives and paints", writes John Ashbery, "in a large, irregularly shaped penthouse apartment near the Jardin du Luxembourg in Paris …. Hélion, who is invariably at work behind the enormous studio window looks up to see the visitor emerging onto the roof and comes out to greet him and watch him look at the view, which is superb."[112]

Meets up with Tristan Rémy again: "He was now passionate about the circus and was gradually becoming a renowned specialist on it, but he was no longer a communist. Neither was I. Yet we both felt nostalgic for a time when we had believed that it would be possible to organize a world that favoured everybody and that it would be responsive to art and poetry. More modestly, we've

each of us started to work for himself and for a few friends."[113]

1947

Sums up his development in one of his notebooks: "A summary of my history is as follows:
In 1929, demolished the world I lived in.
In 1930, cancelled this world reduced to three lines.
From there, rebuilt a universe: 1932. Then restarted populating it with abstract beings, 1932–33, etc., complete beings, 1935–36 (standing figures) and collapsed ones (fallen figures), 1939– before the war.
In 1939, the war: destroyed my world yet again. On my return restarted populating a new world with characters that had the soul of the abstract standing figures of 1936, etc.
Then, when these characters had grown up, undertook to make gods out of them and bring together the important movements of the flesh and of thought, according to a new mythology."[114]

The *carnet* for the year is entitled *Journal des Hommes assis, des journaliers, des natures mortes* [Journal of seated men, 'daily' men, still lifes]: "Starting from a drawing of myself seated in front of the mirror, I arrived at a series of ever larger drawings in which I want to explore the reality of THE SEATED MAN, to feed into my SEATED READERS at a later stage."[115]

On 5 February, completion of *Wrong way up* [*À rebours*], a major work that sums up his evolution since his abstract phase. This work heralds two major themes for development, the characters of his 'daily' [*journalier*] scenes and the motif of the nude upside down: "You know *À*

rebours, in which there is an abstraction, a standing figure and a woman the wrong way round in a window. I had exhibited that picture in 1947. A critic at the time, René Guilly, wrote in the journal *Paru* that he had never seen painting insulted in such a way. The more I think about it, the more I think that he paid me the finest compliment and that he probably did so wittingly. He was revolted. Probably years later he started to love it. But long live indecency, as I said to you a short time ago."[116] "You would have to have had your eyes put out not to be aware of the abstract hovering over paintings like *À rebours* (1947), which does not bear the title of the major work by J.K. Huysmans, the pope of mystical naturalism, for nothing. The painter, his painting and his model form a sort of triptych which is simultaneously powerfully realistic and put together like a machine."[117]

On 19 April, birth of his third son, Fabrice.
In late May, cancellation of his contract with Paul Rosenberg.
Spends the summer in Brittany.

1948

"Hélion paints portraits only of his friends. Like Jean-Pierre [Burgart], many of Hélion's friends – René Char, Francis Ponge, André du Bouchet, Yves Bonnefoy – are poets, and his work has always had a special attraction for writers. He is a poet's painter, as Ponge (who has written on Hélion) is a painter's writer. Both have invented a new kind of description, poetic without being rhapsodic, which treats the outside of things as though it were their soul, and in which the avoidance of all metaphysical temptations becomes itself a kind of religion."[118]

First series of *Daily men* [*Journaliers*] and still lifes with his fetish objects as motifs – newspapers, loaves of bread, pumpkins, umbrellas, hats.

"I've never studied anything as hard to draw as an open newspaper. I can only manage it if I mark the folds of the new newspaper (folded in two, then in three, then in two) firmly with red and so once again find the simple polyhedron in the very complex figure of the open newspaper."[119]

"The loaf that carries sexual openings, the wounded loaf, climbs while swaying its hips. Relatedness of wound – mouth – lips, of the labyrinth-lips-heart of the carnation and the genitals of the soft hat. Without my being hypnotized solely by the sexual language and reality of objects, I find it a very revealing aspect of their existence."[120]

"At present all the carnal meaning, the dazzling heaviness, the setting sun, the recumbent flesh, the open belly, the streaming gold of this common, poor man's vegetable dazzle me. Have already done three rapid watercolours where the pumpkin reigns supreme."[121]

"I love the object [the umbrella], the form of which is animated by the hand that holds it. I like its petticoats pressed tightly on to the stick, the fat handle, the fine tip, the chapel it forms above the people it shelters. Slender, but capable of a huge space …. They're damned fools, the people who see the motif as foolish. Playing with it, my soul sounds like a cello."[122]

New canvases devoted to shops: "The pumpkin shop, the bread shop,

95. *ArtNews*, vol. XLIII, no. 3, 15–31 March 1944, p. 17.
96. *À perte de vue …*, op. cit., p. 85.
97. Unpublished letter from J. Hélion to Pierre-Georges Bruguière, 531 Hudson Street, New York City, 29 November 1944.
98. Jane Watson, "New Helion Exhibit Impressive", *Washington Post*, Sunday, 14 January 1945.
99. The reference is to *Gothic figure* [*Figure gothique*].
100. The reference is to *One-legged man* [*Unijambiste*].
101. *Journal d'un peintre*, vol. I, op. cit., 6 November 1945, p. 86.
102. *Ibid.*, 29 July 1945, p. 82.
103. *Ibid.*, 13 October 1945, p. 84.
104. *Ibid.*, 21 December 1945, p. 89.
105. J. Hélion to Henriette and André Gomès, 25 July 1945, 531 Hudson Street, New York, G. Heytens archives.
106. Thomas Bouchard, director and producer of the film *One Artist at Work*, 1946.
107. A Hungarian pianist, pupil of Bartók.
108. *Journal d'un peintre*, vol. I, op. cit., 6 November 1945, p. 85.
109. *Ibid.*, 6 January 1946, p. 92.
110. J. Hélion, Cagnes-sur-mer, to Pierre-Georges Bruguière, 5 August 1946.
111. To Pierre-Georges Bruguière, Cagnes-sur-mer, 18 September 1946.
112. J. Ashbery, "Hélion paints a series of portraits", *ArtNews*, New York, vol. 58, no. 10, February 1960, p. 32.
113. *Mémoire de la chambre jaune*, op. cit., pp. 19–20.
114. *Journal d'un peintre*, vol. I, op. cit., 14 October 1947, p. 105.
115. *Ibid.*, 30 September 1947, p. 101.
116. In conversation, as note 89, p. 80.
117. Michel Tournier, "Les entrailles roses de la citrouille", *Le Nouvel Observateur*, 30 November 1984, p. 96.
118. J. Ashbery, as note 112, p. 34.
119. *Journal d'un peintre*, vol. I, op. cit., 17 November 1947, p. 109.
120. *Ibid.*, 24 March 1948, p. 116.
121. *Ibid.*, 5 April 1948, p. 117.
122. *Journal d'un peintre*, vol. II, op. cit., 25 March 1980, p. 344.

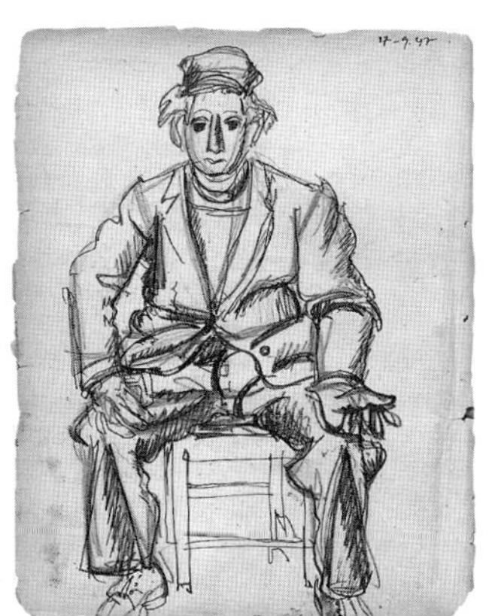

From the *carnets*: 'Journal of seated men' [*Journal des hommes assis*], 1947
Bibliothèque nationale de France, department des Étampes et de la Photographie

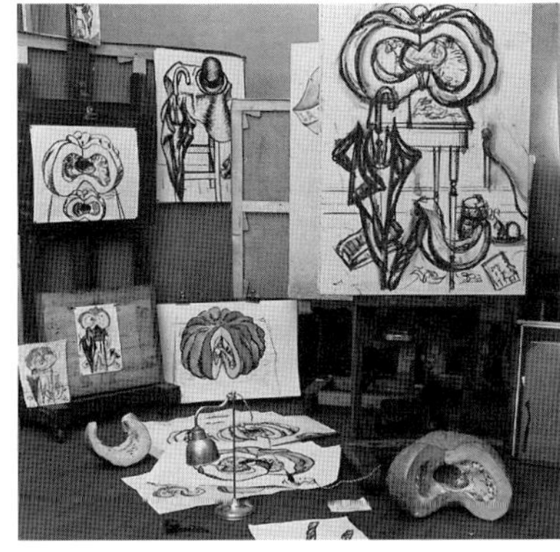

Pumpkin events [*Citrouilleries*] in the studio in the rue Michelet, Paris, 1947

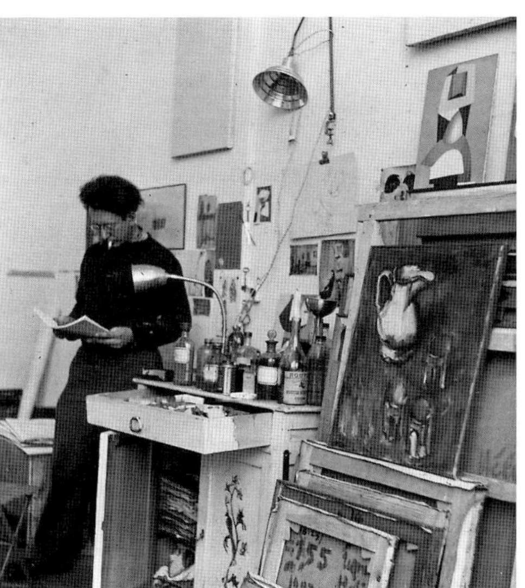

Jean Hélion in his studio in the rue Michelet, about 1947–48

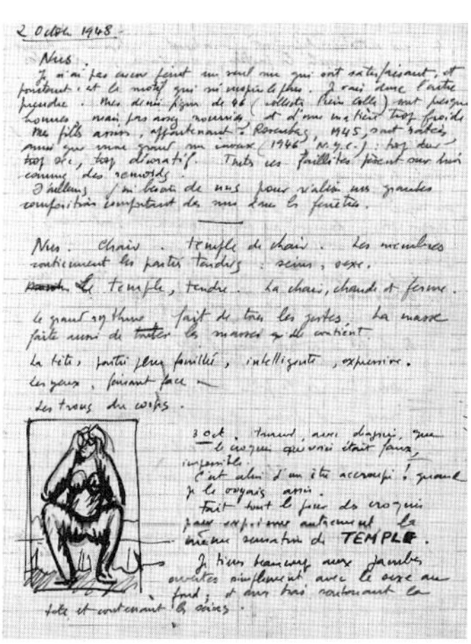

From the *carnets*: 'Journal of nudes' [*Journal des nus*], 1948
Bibliothèque nationale de France, department des Étampes et de la Photographie

the hat and umbrella shop. I'm quite aware of the 'comical' side lurking round my compositions. I'm Shakespearean in that. Delacroix would not have approved at all. But the times I live in are more ridiculous than his period. The modern hero is Charlie Chaplin. Only he is acceptable. The seriousness of others reminds us of 'Hitler' or 'De Gaulle' (not that I think De Gaulle is Hitler, but they have unbearable mannerisms in common)."[123]

Regular reading of Delacroix's *Journal*, Baudelaire's *L'Art romantique*.
In May, visit from Fernand Léger: "He totally approved of my efforts and left quite stirred, and impressed, too, by the fact that I'm daring 'to swim against the current all on my own'."[124]
Associates with Francis Ponge, Pierre Guéguen, Hans Hartung, Georges Limbour, Roland Penrose, Henri Michaux and Victor Brauner. End of June–July, spends holidays at Bandol (Var), where he reads André Malraux's *Musée imaginaire*. First visit to Italy, to Venice and Genoa, where he discovers Magnasco among others. Returns with Raymond Queneau after stopping at Vézelay.
In October begins *Journal of the Nudes* [*Journal des Nus*]: "Nudes. Flesh. Temple of flesh. The limbs contain soft parts – breasts, genitals. The temple, soft. The flesh, warm and firm. The great rhythm makes every kind of gesture. Also the mass made by all the masses it contains. The head, a more elaborate, intelligent, expressive part. The eyes looking out. The holes of the body."[125]

Chairs Front Humain, a group "resisting political and social decadence" founded by Robert Sarrazac, a former officer in the Resistance. Meets Gary Davis there.[126]
Reads poems by García Lorca and *Degas, Danse, Dessin* by Paul Valéry.

1949
Moves to a new studio at 15 avenue de l'Observatoire (6th *arrondissement*), where he will work until 1957. In January, paints female nudes (*Seated nudes* [*Nus assis*], *Girl Temple* [*Fille temple*]), and combinations of nudes and recumbent figures: "In 1949: seated nude, reclining nude, composition of the two. Good elements, strong, dense, beautiful, well placed, which fire me with enthusiasm. I've begun the set of larger compositions, including readers, seated men, seated nudes, reclining nudes in an architecture that locates them and brings them together – the street. OK. This time I've gone beyond the facts. There are hardly any nudes in windows or at doors, normally. I put them there. I construct, with everyday elements, because they matter to me and I know them. I construct a palace, a cathedral, from crucial everyday things – love, meditation, reading, the group, solitude, sleep, etc. I compose – spontaneously to start with, and then thinking about it – all these elements that interest me passionately. That satisfies me."[127]

On 10 January, birth of his fourth son, David.

Frequent visits to flea markets: "To the Porte de Vanves flea market in the morning. Objects sparsely set out on carpets, beside the gutter. A woman sitting in front of them. A subject belonging to me. Moreover I've been thinking about it for twenty-two years. Made a bad little picture of it in 1928. Subject to be inserted in the series of shops!"[128]
"Brief visit to the St-Ouen flea market yesterday to think about my subject – still life – shop – exposed to the wind. Decor: sky – fence – pavement – gutter …. Flea market: the stall holder is really a guardian. A vestal virgin. A goddess. The guardian of found objects. Her naked feet offered for sale on the carpet, too."[129]

In February, visit to André Breton's studio; in April, to Jean Bazaine's. Goes regularly to the Louvre and the Petit Palais: "Yesterday, enthralling visit to the Louvre: nudes through the periods. How did they model? How did they give interest to the nude in itself? Too often by cutting across it with clothes. Then to the French school installed in the wedding cake that is the Petit Palais: greatness of Fouquet, density of the figure; perfection of his formulation. Fine primitive from Avignon: Christ leaving the tomb. Fine Fontainebleau [School], the two nudes in the bathtub, modelled with no details, superb.[130] The frightening decadence, room by room, up to Impressionism … to look again at the Manets the clumsiness of which strikes me as brotherly – I admire his ultimate victory over the inadequacy of his as often as not truly bumbling means – like mine. Dear Manet."[131]

In April takes a three-day trip during which he visits Chartres, Couterne, Briouze, Falaise, Lisieux, Honfleur, Dieppe, Rouen and Les Andelys. During the summer, stays in Italy: "What I saw this summer has confirmed my efforts. Riffling through the photographs of my nudes, after seeing Cimabue, Duccio, Giotto, the Sienese painters, Raphael, the Sistine Chapel, and here, the Venetians, they appear to me to be those of excellent works."[132]
Then spends part of the month of September in Venice at the *palazzo* of Peggy Guggenheim, his mother-in-law.

1950
Themes of the year: groups of *Daily men* [*Journaliers*] and *Recumbents* [*Gisants*], series of large and small *Mannequin events* [*Mannequineries*]: "In shop-windows I'd always admired the models which made gestures and carried labels on the tips of their stiff fingers, a bit like the way musical instruments in bands carry musical scores perched on a little music stand. These models always appeared to me to enact a whole drama behind the window, a theatre of elegance and manners. There was also a kind of sermon accomplished by their gestures. If I lay recumbent figures down on the pavement at their feet, they were never tramps, but dreamers, protesters. I've always given the gesture of lying down a protest value. Perhaps it dates from 1931 when I was travelling by boat (a *doubok*) among the reefs on the River Dnepr, parallel with the land of the Zaporogue Cossacks. A former soldier who happened to be on board told me through an interpreter that when the Turks or the Tartars used to invade these regions, the men escaped to the woods and the women stretched out across the roads, their legs open, to stop the invaders. However comical or saucy such an image may be, I saw only grandeur and tragedy in it. The splendour of the nudes stopping the brute beasts. In my nudes practising this gesture, there has always been this secret proclamation: 'No through way'."[133]

"The shop windows present a catalogue of the accessories of social life: it is reassuring, elucidatory. So this is what we live with. It is also an indispensable show. Shops as theatre. Even lighting from the footlights and projectors …."[134]

1951
In spring starts work on a *Daily allegory* [*Allégorie journalière*] which he will complete in 1953.
In autumn, paintings from life of chrysanthemums: "… at the end of summer 1951, after the failure of several exhibitions in five capital cities, I decided yet again on a fresh start, restarting from a lower point. This was the chrysanthemums series – I painted twenty or thirty versions of them. I sang on these chrysanthemums as on violins and they responded to my touch like an instrument to a sensitive bow. It was very satisfying. On the one hand you bought a very beautiful chrysanthemum for 10 francs and it told you so many things that I liked to repeat them, to magnify them to the point of yelling them, going so far as to find that all human experience was fixed there, that there was all of life in the vigour of this stem down to the thin strips of the petals …. At that period I lived only chrysanthemums."[135]

In October, in his *carnets*: "Since I started on flowers, my pre-'51 pictures seem dry to me, a little staged – in the manner of Racine, whom I'm glancing through at the moment – and I'm pleased to be progressing towards a mellower and fuller way of conceiving and realising."[136]

For a long time the verism of his new manner sets him apart from the Parisian artistic scene, dedicated to abstraction.

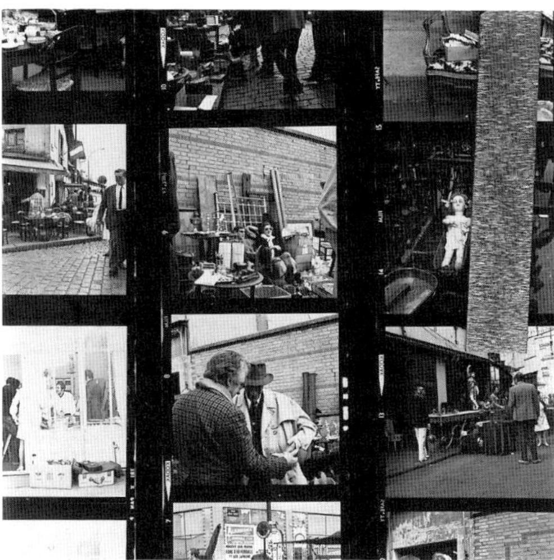

Jean Hélion at the flea-market

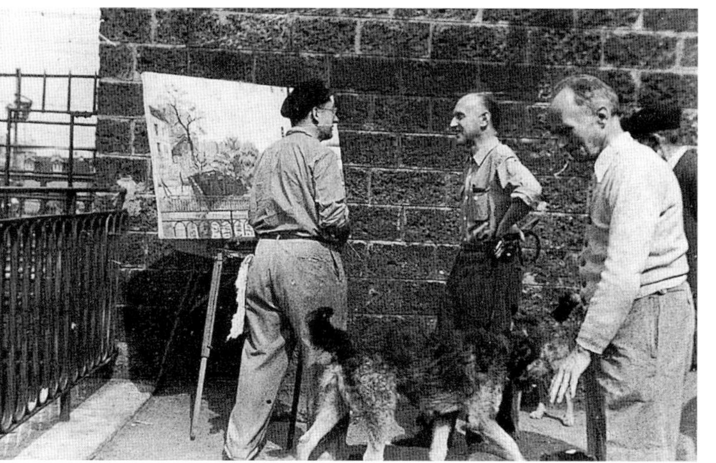

Hélion painting in the rue Blottière (Paris, 14th *arrondissement*) with Victor Brauner, 1952

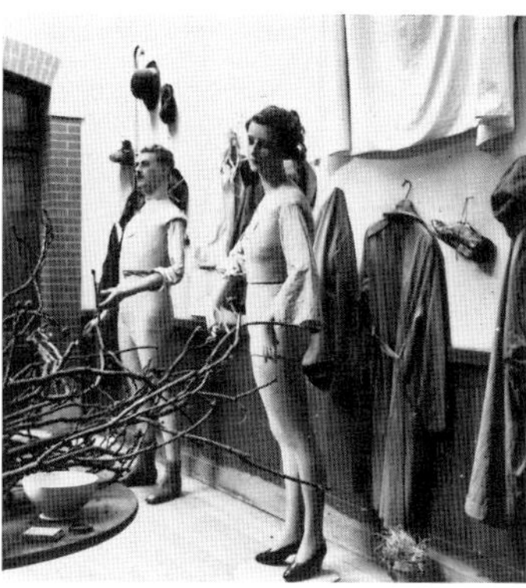

Mannequins in the studio in the avenue de l'Observatoire, Paris, 1953

Reverts to the motif of the loaf of bread: "One of the most wonderful themes. I'm dealing with long loaves, *baguettes* and *ficelles*, that form a line on the round table, under which the three feet of a single leg are dancing, in the middle an attractive shadow, soft at the edge, where the notion of the large folds of the hanging tablecloth is palpitating. Horizon of the plinth.[137] With this round table in the middle of the room, with this great void that it shelters, underlined by the shadow cast, I am again more in a deep space than with the chrysanthemums, and passionately eager to explore it."[138]

First series of six lithographs on the theme of *Daily men* [*Journaliers*].

1952

In the studio at avenue de l'Observatoire, still lifes with loaves of bread, rabbits and pumpkins: "I've always loved this vegetable, this golden fruit, this setting-sun fruit, this Ali Baba's cave directly you slit it open. Having achieved through the chrysanthemums a new realism that allowed me to recount the thing seen in detail, I set up several displays of pumpkins. They had every merit in my eyes. On the one hand they were vulgar like myself ('*homme de petite extrace*' – man of lowly extraction; François Villon); they lived in my past, the past of rue Grétry in 1925. I had rediscovered it in 1948. Now in 1952 I'll go to the very end; I now had the means to withhold nothing of its beauty. On the wooden temple of a very ordinary table, I set up a splendid pumpkin slit open to reveal all the treasure of its entrails, its bunches of seeds, its filaments, its golden glazes."[139]

Series of nudes from a model. The loaf of bread and the nude are combined in the composition *Back with bread* [*Dos aux pains*]: "The nude and the bread. From the rear, because from the front it would be a person, and the relationship between flesh and soft bread would no longer be established except very remotely. The male and female relationship is once again expressed by the antinomy of dark/white, heavy/light, the hanging trousers and petticoat. Carpet with fringes, for the nude offers the fringe of her hair."[140]

On 16 May, birth of his fifth son, Nicolas.
During the summer reads the work of Zola.

In October starts work on *The pumpkin event* [*La Citrouillerie*], which he completes in November: "It is conceived as a sonata, in three movements – the triumphant allegro of the pumpkin shop, the adagio of the jacket and the napkin, the largo of the green plant and the shade …".[141]

1953

 "What do I have in view? Equalling the greatest masters of all times. What am I going to paint? Quite simply, the Life of my time."[142]

New series of still lifes, including *The snack* [*Le Goûter*]: "Apple bag (newspaper), walnut bag (green), balls bag (trousers), breasts bag (slip), feet bag (shoes), and it can be said that the book is a poem bag."[143]
"*Still life with scattered objects* [*Nature morte aux objets épars*].[144] Here they are on the same rather hard, ugly, badly made oak table, so typical of the "pretend sturdy" ob-

jects at the Bazar de l'Hôtel de Ville. Shifted towards the right, to have the door opening on the left. Placed on it the things for breakfast, or a snack between meals, with men's and women's clothes mixed together on the chair and table, as if they had been left there to make love."[145]

Giacometti (in February) and Balthus (in March) visit him at the studio and react enthusiastically to the painting.

Growing interest in the Old Masters, Ingres, David, Rembrandt, Raphael, the Spanish painters, and Caravaggio: "I'm preoccupied with Caravaggio right now. Pegeen had given me a very beautiful book about him – I knew almost nothing about him and in the things he excels in he's becoming supremely important to me. A fault: his characters pose and don't live their gestures. They don't feel much. But what smoothness, what roundness of colour and form, what suppleness, what variety in the composition. What marvellous arrangement of shade and light, I'm stunned by it."[146]

In May, starts work on *The studio* [*L'Atelier*]: "'Why don't you paint the whole studio? Why don't you turn round the picture that Bruguière is studying?' Du Bouchet asks me. And here I am setting off on this horse. Watercolour yesterday of my whole studio, around Bruguière getting to grips – a grip on my painting, or in gear like an engine? – with a picture. Pegeen, a figurine on the stairs; Du Bouchet, to pay him back for starting me off on such an ambitious work, on the green bench, and he will just have to pose for a while.[147] A tremendous project that I'm trying to arrange today as a 40 F [canvas size 81 x 100 cm]."[148]

Reads Paul Eluard's poems from *Au rendez-vous allemand*.
Goes to Belle-Île-en-Mer for the first time during the summer.

In November–December, solo exhibition at the premises of the painter Mayo: "This exhibition, without too much fuss, breaks the ice of a long silence: the last was held in 1947 at Renou's and (the late Pierre Colle's) …. So far reviews in the press that set out to be laudatory, and speak of my almost surrealist realism, or the almost abstract *trompe-l'œil*."[149]

1954

Paris, January: finishes *The Painter* [*Le Peintre*]:[150] "In drawing the painter I hadn't grasped his mythical sense: there are three easels, like three guillotines that make a kind of 'cross'. The sliding part – what's its name – that holds the edge of the canvas, perched upside-down at the top of the easel's middle vertical bar, looks like a 'foot-rest' for the crucified man. It's a minor martyrdom that the painter endures: I'd like to be able to express it without it being grotesque. So in my new version, having got rid of the round table, I'm starting out with the intention of highlighting the way the painter is hooked on his three easels, how he's 'seized' by the spirit of the painter, his possession by the god he has created for himself. Meanwhile the panelling of the studio makes a temple above the scene."[151]
Arum lilies [*Les Arums*] contains echoes of two abstract paintings, a *Composition* from 1934 and a *Fallen figure* from 1939: "The *Arums* will suggest an underlying abstraction, a theme of balance that's quite similar to my best *Equilibrium*s of 1933, and then the greedy reality of the flower; then the

123. *Journal d'un peintre*, vol. I, *op. cit.*, 6 May 1948, pp. 120–21.
124. *Ibid.*, 12 May 1948, p. 124.
125. *Ibid.*, 2 October 1948, p. 151.
126. A young American who had renounced his nationality of his own free will, he proclaimed himself a citizen of the world and tried to form a global government.
127. *Journal d'un peintre*, vol. I, *op. cit.*, 3 September 1949, p. 197.
128. *Ibid.*, 7 February 1949, p. 175.
129. *Ibid.*, 15 February 1949, pp. 175–76.
130. Gabrielle d'Estrées and the duchesse de Villars.
131. *Journal d'un peintre*, vol. I, *op. cit.*, 30 April 1949, p. 187.
132. Unpublished letter to Pierre-Georges Bruguière, 701 San Gregorio, Venice, 7 September 49.
133. *À perte de vue …., op. cit.*, p. 107.
134. *Journal d'un peintre*, vol. I, *op. cit.*, 21 August 1950, p. 209.
135. *À perte de vue …., op. cit.*, pp. 110–11.
136. *Journal d'un peintre*, vol. I, *op. cit.*, 26 October 1951, p. 220.
137. The reference is to *The loaves* [*Les Pains*].
138. *Journal d'un peintre*, vol. I, *op. cit.*, 24 November 1951, p. 227.
139. *À perte de vue …., op. cit.*, p. 112.
140. *Journal d'un peintre*, vol. I, *op. cit.*, 6 March 1952, p. 234.
141. *Ibid.*, 26 November 1952, p. 249.
142. *Ibid.*, 20 January 1953, p. 257.
143. *Ibid.*, 5 March 1953, p. 259.
144. Initial title of the work.
145. *Journal d'un peintre*, vol. I, *op. cit.*, 10 January 1953, p. 253.
146. *Ibid.*, 12 January 1953, p. 255.
147. In the end André du Bouchet did not appear in the finished painting.
148. *Journal d'un peintre*, vol. I, *op. cit.*, 8 May 1953, pp. 260–261.
149. *Ibid.*, 30 November 1953, p. 266.
150. Second version of *The studio*.
151. *Journal d'un peintre*, vol. I, *op. cit.*, 2 January 1954, p. 271.

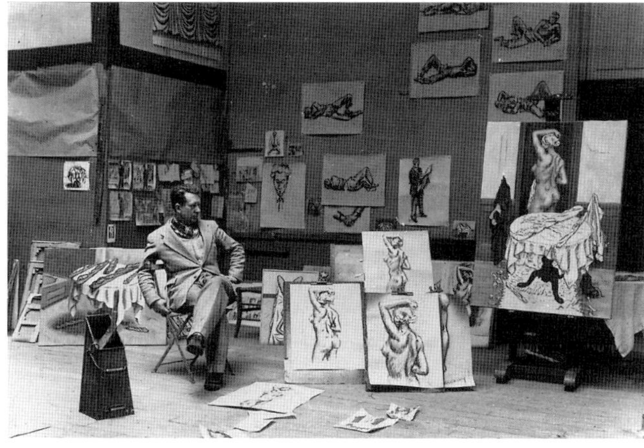

Jean Hélion with studies of nudes in the studio of the avenue de l'Observatoire, Paris, 1952

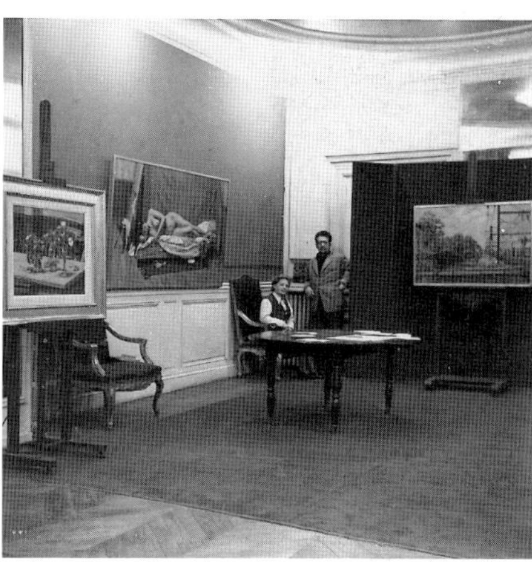

Jean Hélion with Henriette Gomès at his exhibition at the premises of the painter Mayo, Paris, 1953

unbelievable (yet familiar) contrast of flowers and abstract paintings."[152]

Reading Heidegger: "Nowhere else have I found anything that enlightens me so precisely. It's so much better than my own thinking, yet so much in the same direction, that I use it without effort."[153]

Buys a house at Belle-Île: studies of landscapes and objects of nature.

October: starts work on a monumental composition (*Le Grand Luxembourg*) based on the Luxembourg Gardens in Paris – numerous studies of people out walking, statues, dead leaves: "Yesterday sketch with figures in the colours of my studies from nature. Taking two girls on the bench: Pegeen, blonde, seen from the front, holding autumn leaves in her hand and almost certainly with her eyes closed. Jacqueline [Ventadour][154] on the other side of the bench, but turning towards the readers, each one's hair, autumn brown and blonde. So the time of this picture will really be that of my being, me, alone and dreaming at the foot of a tree to the right."[155]

1955

Rereading Delacroix's *Journal*: "The year 1853 … the finest and most useful pages, particularly concerning rough sketches and the completion of paintings; the particular way of painting a tree, starting from what he calls, without quite defining it, the reflected half-shade. Reflecting what? the sky? or other elements in the painting?"[156]

Studies of Pegeen: "Pegeen and I had already split up, but we had agreed that she would come back to live at the house to endure an analysis …. Each time her face was distraught in a new way, as though the things the doctor had drawn out of her were running down her face, and I, prey at that time to a desire to create a fine face, I took advantage of her torments to follow their twists and turns …. In a way I tried to heal her by painting a good picture, by harmoniously combining the brushstrokes along her features. But her distress swept into my painting. From time to time, above and beyond that face, I still saw one that could have made for a happy picture, but it always slipped away."[157]

Endlessly retouches *Le Grand Luxembourg*: "Zervos told me my large gouache has a certain 18th-century air, and now I see what he means. There is a grace that's unusual in my work. As for the figures, whom I'm starting to sketch on paper, in oil, or rather in turpentine, with colours just mixed in pots, and the first elements, the statue and a tree nearby, they have a peculiar size and force."[158]

Series of interiors and still lifes. Spring: visit to Italy, first trip to Masaccio.

1956

Trip to Holland, Amsterdam and Haarlem; particular attention to works by Rembrandt and Hals. Returns to old themes: "So I have just – yesterday – managed to take up – to rediscover – the theme of the nude again, the man and the pumpkin, once hostile, but now brought together in a feeling of bacchanalia; today I rediscovered the man lying on the pavement, the man sitting in the door, the nude in the window, once antinomical, now brought together in the happiness of a hot morning in Provence."[159]

Makes five plates illustrating André Du Bouchet's *Au deuxième étage*.

1957

January: "*Le Grand Luxembourg* has been finished for a week. What shall I call it? *Autumn and Time*? This picture is as profound as any picture ever painted; but I know of a great many that are brighter, more welcoming. To me it is wonderful because it authentically opens a window on to a real life, a bedazzlement. I think it has failed to the extent that it is too severe and a bit enclosed like a Beethoven quartet. To successfully complete a large undertaking like this with the freshness of my Belle-Île landscapes and the flesh of my nudes from last June, that's what I must try to do."[160]

February: a new motif, 'Skulleries' [*Crâneries*]: "The Skull. Seashell. Human object. Stone-object, related to flint and chalk …. Ovoid, full and hollow, open and closed. Constructed in its unity. Tendency to turn gold like a dead leaf and a flint. To roll like a pebble."[161]
"What painter has not been fascinated by these? The best subject for my studies came from the Cochin hospital, whence a doctor friend of mine had taken it, a skull that no longer had any use. It had long ago had its autopsy, the top had been sawn off, its grimace was yellow, its apophyses were worn, its teeth had almost all fallen out, its jawbone was not connected. I had to keep lifting the skull and setting it on the jawbone, leaning it backwards. I never had any macabre meditations about it. Without being in any way cheerful, to me it seemed a sign of permanence rather than death; wasn't it this that had outlived a man's flesh?"[162]

Interviewed by Alain Jouffroy on Mondrian:
J.H.: "From the beginning of my abstract period Mondrian declared that I was in the naturalist tradition. He was leaving forms behind in all his pictures; I, in pictures apparently as abstract as his, I was looking for forms."
A.J.: "What was Mondrian like in real life? Did he pay great attention to the approach of a painter as different from himself as you were? Did he give you advice?"
J.H.: "For me Mondrian became the exemplary artist, in both his life and his work. He went to the limits of what he believed and he lived as he painted. Of all the artists I've known he was the purest, the simplest and the kindest. He believed in the eye. When people talked to him about calculations and aesthetic science, he would softly snigger. He felt himself to be a painter, like Rembrandt and Van Gogh. He despised anything mathematical in art."
A.J.: "Why were you fascinated by his pictures?"
J.H.: "Because they seemed to me to be the opposite of all painting, whereas he, in every aspect of himself, was clearly subtle, sensitive, impassioned – tyrannically so. Mondrian used to say: 'Art is always interesting in all its forms'. He was a great admirer of Léger, for example. He took an interest in my development and gave me detailed advice on the arrangement of the image on the surface. He wanted the image always to possess the entire surface. He would say things like, 'It's too long' or 'It's too wide'. He would look for the universal image in everything."[163]

The revelation of Japanese art: "In it I find the support I was lacking. Besides the rich use of flat colours and shaded tones, which have always been congenial to me, it offers me a wonderful example of the integration of the real and the imaginary, present and past, the serious and the fantastical, all the more stimulating because, Japanese iconography being very different from my own, it leaves me completely free. Also very successful – the integration of figures in landscapes or interiors. In the work of Sesshu, for example, the religious side – the admiring examination of creation and recognition of divine order give me a sublime example without affectation. I feel extremely grateful."[164]

1958

Nudes in the studio, *Pumpkins* and still life paintings.
Autumn: begins work on *The great plough* [*Le Grand Brabant*]:
"Near a village called Borchudan, Jacqueline, who lived not far away, told me about a superb object that we went to identify that evening. It was in the corner of a field, digging into the last furrow, a half-turn plough. That type where the ploughshare is turned at the end of a furrow to dig the next in the same way. This agricultural object really looks like an abstract construction. There are two large symmetrical blades like wings and then a kind of iron bicycle linking them to a shaft where a horse is harnessed …. I worked on the plough *in situ*. I took some drawings home and turned them into pictures. From the ones I took to Paris I made *The great plough*, in the Zervos collection, which seems a fine thing to me. It is a large picture, the edge of which I lined a series of small studies of every possible variation, like a kind of predella – different lights, different angles, ideas,

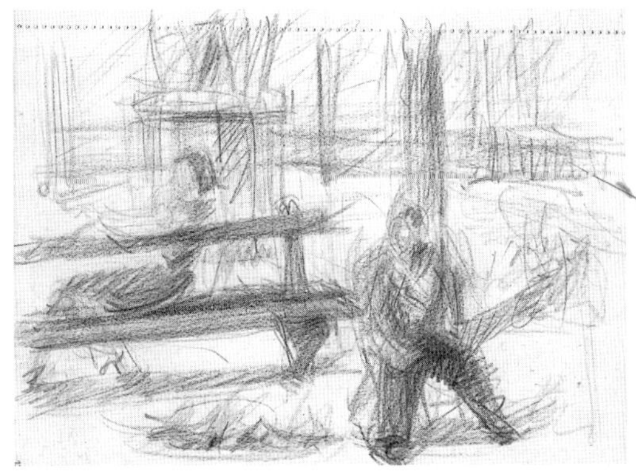

From the *carnets*: study for *Le Grand Luxembourg*, 1954
Bibliothèque nationale de France, department des Étampes et de la Photographie

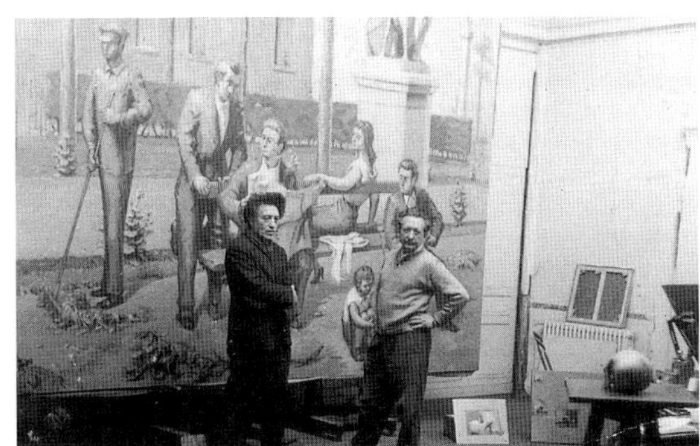

Jean Hélion with Alberto Giacometti in rue Michelet with **Le Grand Luxembourg** (1954–57) in course of execution, Paris, 1956

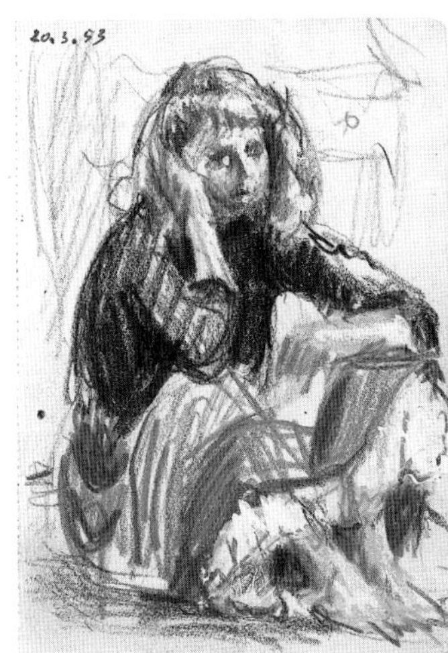

From the *carnets*: *Pegeen*, 1953
Bibliothèque nationale de France, department des Étampes et de la Photographie

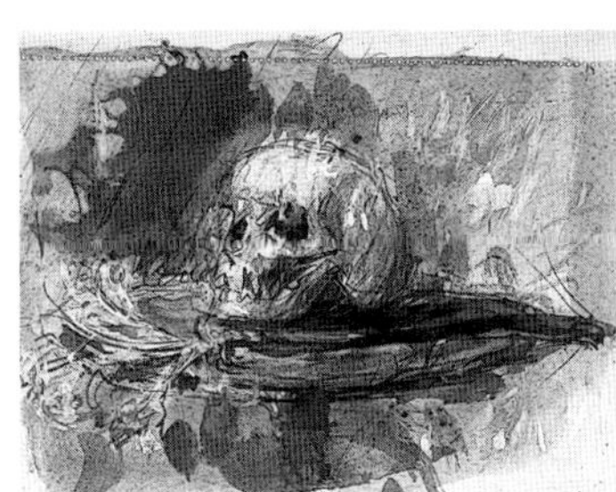

From the *carnets*: *Skullery* [*Crânerie*], 1957
Bibliothèque nationale de France, department des Étampes et de la Photographie

dreams. Then I started on the ploughed earth."[165]

Late October: separates from his wife Pegeen; leaves rue Observatoire studio for the studio in rue Michelet.

1959
Series of portraits of friends, Georges Bine, Yves Bonnefoy, André Du Bouchet, Pierre-Georges Bruguière, Jean-Pierre Burgart and Charles Duits: "I've decided to do eleven seated portraits of my friends. I feel them inside me with the violence and certainty I felt in 1935 when I began the abstract series of *Standing figure*, which I said would be family portraits …. To paint a portrait is, for a time, to reduce all of humanity, and all of painting, to this one incarnation of being."[166]

September: travels to Holland with Jacqueline to see Hals and Rembrandt again.

1960–61
Still lifes with musical instruments and a return to views of roofs and the Luxembourg theme in his rue Michelet studio.
"All in all, two kinds of still life in these *Chamber music* paintings [*Musique de chambre*] – those that are painted slowly and where I dispense my knowledge; and those that are painted quickly, in which I suddenly invent visual solutions, with a cry of joy.
Singing or shouting at the top of my voice – two modes that never manage to merge, but something seems to leap back and forth from one to the other and gains new vigour with each leap."[167]
"The theme of roofs is the hardest of all, because the roofs have already been drawn by the architects.

One must reach the point of seeing them as mountains and craters, beyond the rules of their construction, while retaining the best aspects of their order.
Roofs:　　The town's masks
　　　　　Sky traps
　　　　　Hats for all walls."[168]

February: paints another version of *Le Grand Luxembourg, Autumn Luxembourg* [*Luxembourg d'automne*]:[169] "This Luxembourg doesn't 'copy' the garden of that name but draws on its atmosphere. I started a group in my imagination, based on visual memories. Then I had the Luxembourg trees grow up around this group. Their mission is not so much to describe this lovely park as to support my figures, to illuminate them, to frame them, to join them in rendering the accord of a harmonious universe in which sleeves and branches, heads and leaves reflect each other. I have the chairs cut, I transplant the bushes and I build new monuments in the spirit of the Luxembourg. I was unable to attain this freedom and this understanding when I painted the first *Grand Luxembourg*, and that held up my work a great deal."[170]

1962
"Behind my window the roofs are posing. On a stool the skull teaches. The heap of recent drawings projects this year of work."[171]
Returns to the theme of nudes: "Here I am once again with this cycle of nudes defined by their power of gesture, of contrasting forms, of lively plenitude: but in a climate of happiness, of joyful sensuality, which makes all the difference. My pictures of 1949, so close to Romanesque or Byzantine art, had a climate of austere effort, solitude, opposition to my times. I no

longer feel any of that. On the contrary I feel at ease in my period, justified by it, well accompanied. I can paint easily and these 'gestural nudes' will create a happy song."[172]

Scenes of life at Les Halles market.

June–July, major exhibition at the Louis Carré gallery (*Peintures de 1929 à 1939*): "It was at that point in my life that a major dealer, Louis Carré, decided to put all my abstract works together in a superb exhibition. I have always thought my pictures are valid from one end of my career to the other and I agreed to exhibit them in whatever order was proposed. If my abstract works were wanted, so be it. They came down my stairs, they got into lorries and went off to be housed superbly on the avenue de Messine, while I went on with my roof scenes, which were giving me far more concern and going wrong. That exhibition was successful enough for me to buy Bigeonnette and find a fine studio there, which I first took for a tractor garage, and that is where I have worked ever since. At that time I was spending all my summers in Belle-Île, in a little house where I would spend my afternoons painting scenes I had come upon in the morning by the port. Of course that produced only small pictures, but after the holidays they were easy to sell and I lived off them. Belle-Île was primarily a port full of fishing smacks bobbing in rows."[173]

1963
Marries Jacqueline Ventadour.
In Paris, paints hieratic figures at Les Halles market, including *Monument to a butcher* [*Monument pour un boucher*]: "Butcher's, zoo of bovine flesh, exhibition of muscles and innards. My first flayed

bullocks in 1926; watercolours at La Villette; there's still a photo of a bit of picture, 60 or 80 P [canvas size], of a butcher hugging a bullock. The latest thing is a street, where the meat is on show, revealed, carried; which will join the series of pictures and drawings of this kind: shops selling pumpkins, bread, everyday allegories. I go to Les Halles, I quickly pencil the 'lads' carrying enormous loads of bullocks, calves and sheep. I go on with them in the studio.
This motif is one of the most perfect I've ever tried. First of all it's a problem of balance, which makes me uneasy balancing my figure. Then a problem of contrast in similarity. Body on body.
No sentimentality. Beauty that is perhaps tragic. Death feeds the living. Grandeur and gaiety.
Besides, the butchers sing between two loads. They hurl abuse at me. They use a familiar tone with me."[174]
Women with *cabas* (shopping bags) in Parisian markets he calls *cabassières*.
In Belle-Île, paints motifs of the port, fishermen and fishing-boats.

1964
Series of faces, self-portraits, portraits of Jean-Pierre Burgart, Pierre-Georges Bruguière, Georges Bine, Paul Nelson, and of his wife Jacqueline: "The face in the 'emergent' state, not contained in the rigid bowl of the drawing, but bearing it within it."[175]

Creates sets and costumes for Shakespeare's *King Lear* for French television.

December: exhibition of drawings at the Yvon Lambert gallery in Paris: "Hélion's persistence, by turns going with and against his gifts, is

152. *Journal d'un peintre*, vol. I, *op. cit.*, 16 January 1954, p. 277.
153. *Ibid.*, 18 May 1954, p. 283.
154. Jacqueline Ventadour-Vail, whom Hélion married in 1963.
155. *Journal d'un peintre*, vol. I, *op. cit.*, 17 November 1954, p. 292.
156. *Ibid.*, 9 March 1955, p. 294.
157. *Mémoire de la chambre jaune*, *op. cit.*, pp. 84–85.
158. *Journal d'un peintre*, vol. I, *op. cit.*, 9 March 1955, p. 294.
159. *Ibid.*, 24 January 1956, p. 303.
160. *Ibid.*, 25 January 1957, p. 324.
161. *Ibid.*, 24 February 1957, p. 324.
162. *À perte de vue …*, *op. cit.*, p. 143.
163. "Mondrian un figuratif devenu abstrait vu par Hélion, un abstrait devenu figuratif", interview with the artist by Alain Jouffroy, *Arts*, no. 611, 20–26 March 1957, p. 13.
164. *Journal d'un peintre*, vol. I, *op. cit.*, 12 October 1957, p. 336.
165. *À perte de vue …*, *op. cit.*, pp. 133–34.
166. *Journal d'un peintre*, vol. I, *op. cit.*, 9 January 1959, p. 359.
167. *Ibid.*, 23 March 1960, p. 376.
168. *Ibid.*, 21 May 1959, p. 370.
169. *Ibid.*, 10 October 1960, p. 380.
170. Definitive title: *Indian summer* [*L'Été de la St-Martin*].
171. J. Hélion, *Journal d'un peintre*, vol. I, *op. cit.*, 15 January 1962, p. 394.
172. *Ibid.*, 19 November 1962, p. 402.
173. *À perte de vue …*, *op. cit.*, p. 125.
174. *Journal d'un peintre*, vol. I, *op. cit.*, 16 February 1963, p. 5.
175. *Ibid.*, 28 January 1964, p. 13.

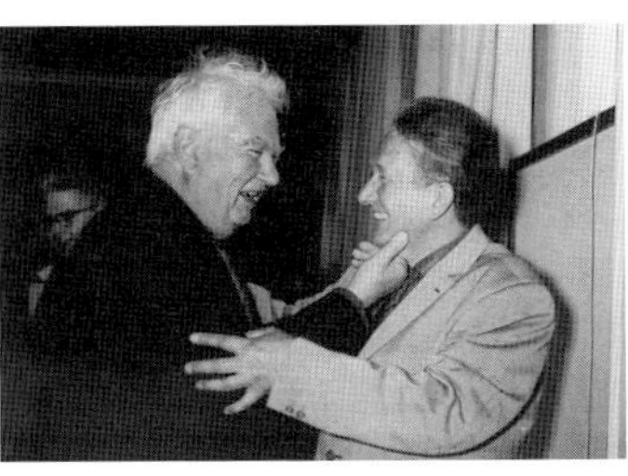

Alexander Calder and Hélion at the opening of the exhibition at the Galerie Louis Carré, Paris, June 1962

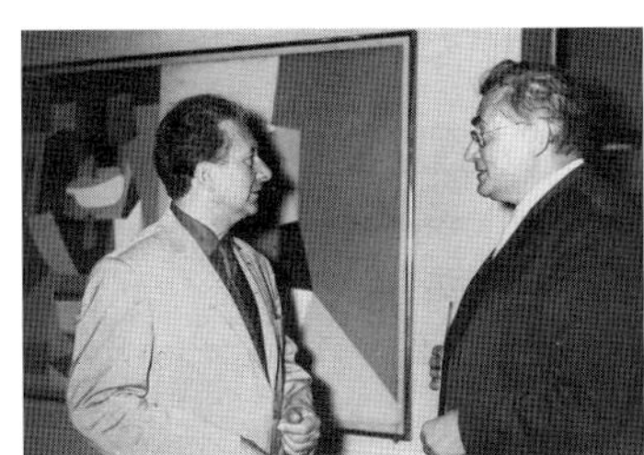

Jean Hélion and Raymond Queneau at the opening of the exhibition in the Galerie Louis Carré, Paris, June 1962

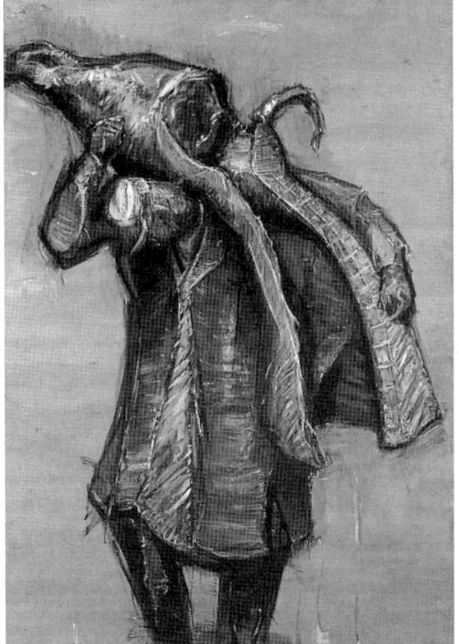

Monument for a butcher, 1963
Acrylic on canvas, 195 x 129.5 cm
Centre Pompidou, Musée national d'art moderne, Paris,
accepted in lieu of tax 1991

of unusual interest," writes André Chastel. "At a time when New York's Colombus Circle has just held a major exhibition of his work, and even though the choice of twenty-five pieces is too small to represent thirty years of unceasing practice, it is good to see a modest recapitulation of his graphic capacities in Paris. Even thirty-five years after it was painted, the wash drawing of *Lemons* (1928) offers the starting point for research that was to become as determined in the re-touched ink drawings from before 1939 as in the grasp of the implacably captured trivial forms – hat, seated man, 'daily', of the years from 1947. Since *Roofs*, a romantic fresco of 1960, bitterness has taken over, with the blood-soaked porters (1963) and the strong notations in gouache and pastel, attesting to the vigorous attack and capacities of this open-minded painter for whom one has such expectations."[176]

1965

Becomes increasingly interested in scenes of urban life: "Ultimately the city is a labyrinth of corridors through which men pass, distractedly. Corridors of walls and trees, and cars, and even corridors of individuals. That is precisely the idea of my work at present. There's enough there to absorb the days I have left."[177]

These scenes include *Greenwich Meridian* [*Le Méridien de Greenwich*]: "I obtained two 4 x 3 m frames from Lefèvre-Foinet. Brown paper was stretched over the first. I didn't feel up to taking on such a vast canvas without preparations and I put a gouache over it to define the place where my figures were to meet. I never thought it desirable for a landscape to be the subject in itself. It was waiting for figures. I

was going ahead of them in a way, but a park is at once countryside and town, the trees may grow there like anywhere else, but they are cut to make avenues. They are interspersed with monuments. Those of allée de l'Observatoire mark out the passage of the Paris meridian, which I at first took for the Greenwich meridian, which I knew passed near London. Rue Michelet cut across allée de l'Observatoire and the cars would line the pavements, some continuing the line of trees. One day a 2CV was stopped there with its bonnet up, while the driver groped around inside. This struck me as a divine subject. A few silhouettes in the avenue seemed to be moving towards him. I used it for a series of pictures which I wrongly named *Greenwich Meridian*."[178]

June: one-man show in London: "I've never had such success as at the exhibition now open at the Leicester Galleries. Abundant, generous press coverage, praise from visitors, etc. But all this is not followed by sales."[179]

"This year 1965 is one of the most filled with worry I have had in my whole life. But it also contains one of the best events, the publication and my reading of Ponge's *Malherbe*. I have never heard an artist's voice ring out so loudly! Here is a mind in which I see myself, in my prouder moments. Here I'm not extolling the virtues of his opinions on Malherbe, though they are valid, so much as the demanding nature of his thought; his awareness of every aspect of his art; rigour and nobility. Let those who take this nobility for vanity begin on page 212 of the first edition by Gallimard; I don't know whether to describe it as humbly superb or proudly humble."[180]

Lithographs for Jean-Pierre Burgart's poem *Force de la mer*.

1966

Kleine Nachtmusik [*Petite Musique de nuit*] on a canvas 3 x 5.50 m: "Night celebration. Idea of night transfigured. Light night; *verklärte Nacht*. Which rids us of the imitation of night. Of its darkness. It must be night in a light, shining, spiritual way. But this idealization must flow from a sensation that is coloured, sensually experienced, looking at the night, in Belle-Île."[181]

Series of streets and cafés.

Project for a *City of stars* (2.50 x 6 m): "We would have passed between the stars as in streets. Figures would have gestured to each other from one canvas to the next, memory of Venice and Veronese where, in some church – I no longer remember which – an angel gestures to the Virgin, across the emptiness of the chapel, that she is pregnant. For lack of space and money, I managed only to make a draft of one of these canvases on paper. Inspired at once by the local butcher on boulevard Saint-Michel and the one on rue Daguerre where I had a studio in 1932 and 1935."[182]

1967

January: *Aquarium*s series, "… in other words the café windows with the shadows swimming in them. The manner of realising it must be freshly conceived."[183]

March: begins work on his first triptych in the Bigeonnette studio: "Having been unable to realise the project of twelve canvases forming a city, I fell back on a new idea for me, the triptych. The first I started is perhaps the most important.

Because it found space in an exhibition on rue du Dragon, it was simply called *The Dragon Street triptych* [*Triptyque du Dragon*]. The left panel is a kind of café in which reside the witnesses to the scene. In the corner there is a booth, or glass-sided airlock, from which a blind man is emerging, brandishing his white stick. In front is a seated man who looks like my friend Matthew Josephson and a tall waiter is serving him with a drink. There I was overtly thinking of Raymond Queneau's hero in his novel *Les Derniers Jours*, where the café waiter is something of a prophet. Here he serves a drink as a priest says mass. The middle panel is occupied by a shop selling modern paintings, in which different stages of my work are on offer. First the abstraction of 1933, which became the key to all my figures. Starting this, I was thinking of the one in the museum in Denver, but as I worked, in order to harmonize with the other pictures, it altered. Below the window there is a crowd of figures crossing, unfolding across the canvas just like an accordion arranges its folds on the pavement. On a staircase to the right, because one should always indicate what is happening above the picture, is a pair of lovers and then someone climbing. The same thought in the other direction has a sewage-worker emerging from a hole in the pavement, but is he emerging or going down? I'm not sure, he's the man from below, the man from inside, the soul of things.
In the right panel, another shop, a memory of New York, in which a headless dummy is all dressed up, a flower in its buttonhole. Above, in the window, the shopkeeper's head seems ready to fit on to the dummy. In the street a boy who could be my

son David sitting on a moped, which he did in fact have at the time, is chatting to a girl carrying a loaf of bread. At her feet a magnificent *cabas* [shopping bag] hangs open. To the right, under the shop window, there's a cellar window, which is a memory of the one I saw after my arrival in the unoccupied zone in Châteauroux in 1942, one of my first drawings as a free man. Different periods of my life mingle in this way in a recent picture. In this triptych the side panels can be joined to the middle one however you like, at 90° or 30°, so that a kind of opening governed by the image can be created in space. This triptych is the closest I could get to my dream of a city in pictures."[184]

In his preface to the catalogue for the retrospective exhibition held in Paris in 1970–71 entitled *Hélion, cent tableaux, 1928–1970*, Roger Caillois devoted a chapter to this monumental work: "More recently, Hélion has taken on a strange undertaking: he paints part of the street with its real size ….
Reproducing a street life-size in the street being represented is aberrant – an insane pleonasm …. While Hélion's canvases may pretend to reproduce a real street, they do not seek to create the illusion of that street. There is no use of *trompe-l'œil*. The pictures seem to have been painted in haste, as though sketched for a stage with many sets, which is what a street ultimately is. On the garden side is a café, in the centre an art gallery, on the courtyard side a tailor's shop …. We can see nothing but ordinariness. At the same time, on reflection, everything has been composed in a quite unexpected way to draw the eye towards the central figure, the bogus sewage-worker, who is

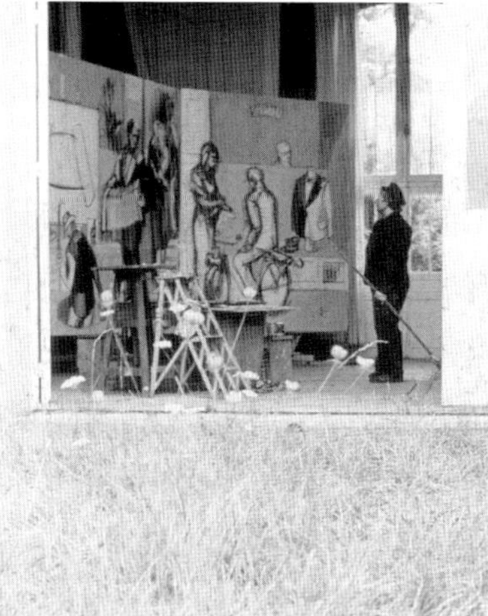

Hélion painting **The Dragon Street triptych** in the studio at Bigeonnette, 1967

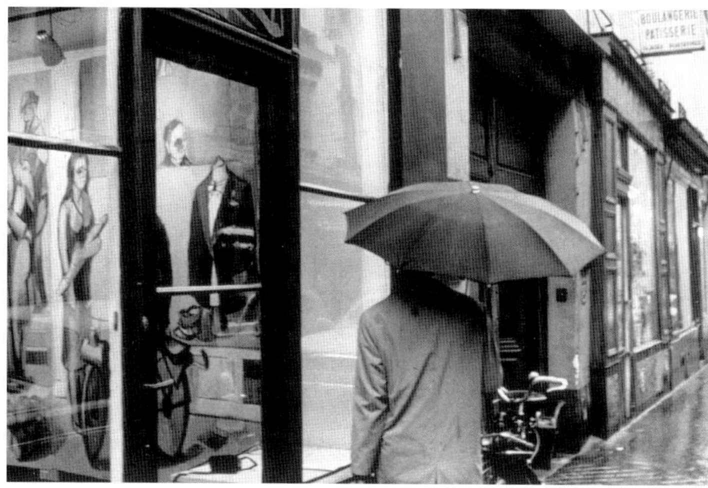

Hélion with **The Dragon Street triptych** (1966–67) during the exhibition *Au niveau de la rue.*
Le triptyque du Dragon. Suites , at the Galerie du Dragon, Paris, 19 October–18 November 1967

plunging into the ground in front of the gallery window with a lantern in his hand. Apart from a canvas lying on the ground, half hidden by the busker's accordion, it contains only two paintings, which could be, which probably are by Hélion himself – a large abstract composition and, at ground level, one of those men's faces he was painting around 1938, whose eyes are hidden by the lowered rim of the hat. It is, however, apparent that the portrait is looking in the direction of the fake sewage-worker and indeed that he is staring at him. The latter is wearing a precisely similar felt hat and, as he lowers his head to see where he is putting his foot on the ladder of the manhole, the figure in the painting looks like his reflection in a mirror.

To sum up, in the triptych mirroring the street, an earlier canvas, presumed to be by the artist who has also painted the whole, inexplicably reflects the invisible face of a figure in the new composition. I do not attribute any meaning to such exchanges or comings and goings, to this affirmation of, or challenge to, the received hierarchy of the real and the imaginary within the work itself, in other words in the place where their boundaries normally become blurred. However, the fact remains that the picture forcefully invites us to do so, not just through the main scene, but through the impression of unreal power, of theatrical grandiloquence emanating from a set painted on the scale of reality, which borrows all reality's elements and so ostensibly disdains to provide its likeness.

Too precise an interpretation would turn the picture into allegory. I cannot prejudge the painter's intention. I assume he sought merely to weight it with doubt, to manifest the

essential and general ambiguity that long experience has gradually taught him to perceive in everything, clear or obscure, which it falls to us to feel or to imagine we are creating."[185]

December: visit to the Médrano circus with Tristan Rémy: "*Coup de foudre*, once again. I could end my life at the circus, all that it signifies. All human gestures are presented here, where the vernacular meets pathos, in a smile!"[186] A few days later he writes, "I thought I was going to the circus alone. My characters came with me. They became clown acrobats."[187]

December: trip to Tunisia. Becomes friendly with Gilles Aillaud and Eduardo Arroyo.

1968
After a season devoted to the winter circus, disturbances in the Paris street occupy him:
"From 13 to 19 May 1968. Is it a revolt? Is it a revolution? While its army and general sit on benches, this country is trembling. From the young comes the breath of air that awakens the old union machines. From the students comes a fresh spirit, a generous, broad light, far in advance of what was expected. But what will come of all this?
Beautiful new faces: Cohn-Bendit, Sauvageot, Geismar. An old face lit up, Pierre Mendès France. The rest, very dark. Fluster and mediocrity of the ministers in power.
Senility of the general who went off to make speeches in Romania when the student revolt was beginning. Lack of clarity and spark from Mitterrand. Ambiguous position of the communists. General strike today, Monday 20 May. What a circus! I mean what I say. I shall work on my circus today. Life is a circus!"[188]

There follows the triptych *Things seen in May* [*Choses vues en mai*] and two still lifes (from May and July) intended as pendants to the triptych: "It was natural", writes Jean Duvignaud, "that Hélion's painting should have been set alight in May '68: here long figures sliding along the walls envelop burning cars and strangely lit Métro entrances. But also the world order changes. For a little while the internal structure of things is altered. Exactly as it does in this painting: the engine of human activity is related to other hidden – and truer – justifications than the justifications acknowledged so far. It is not often that the world starts looking like what a painter seeks to make of a world without likeness."[189]

1969
Trip to Czechoslovakia and Germany.
In Paris, 4 September, final touches to the *Thiongs seen in May* triptych; of the right-hand panel he wrote, "This woman with the two flags seen on boulevard Montparnasse (see my *carnets* May–June 1968) has become, against my will, the Republic, one *cabassière* among many on whom, that day, it was raining. I did my best, without however managing to avoid similarities with Roty's *La Semeuse* or Millet's *Angelus*. It really is the same woman, suddenly made symbolic. I didn't want that to happen, but it would be arbitrary to expel her from the picture."[190]
New *Métro exit*s and circus scenes.

1970
March: studies for "a funerary August-ery" which would lead to *Red trickery* [*Supercherie rouge*] and *Yellow trickery* [*Supercherie jaune*]: "I had forged something resembling friendship with Baba

Fratellini and his comrade Footit, both descended from famous clowns. To my great pleasure, they had a new trick. Baba ran after Footit, a lighted torch in his hand, caught him and quite simply set his arse on fire and Footit pretended to burn. When he was 'dead' he was put on a red carpet and some boys came and dragged him into the wings. That was the thing as it was seen, but the thing as it was painted was cranked a notch further."[191]

Jean Duvignaud wondered, "What gives such a fantastical aspect to these canvases collected in the rue Michelet which the painter shows with a smiling frenzy, as though he was having fun setting out such disquieting painting? When you look attentively at these canvases, you realise that the strange impression they produce comes from the way that their figuration is constructed like non-figuration. The dichotomous arrangement of the fine, large abstraction of 1938 (horizontal blue and grey bands separating an architecture resting on the ground to the left of a superimposition of isolated objects and caught in an immobile movement of conjuring) is the same as that of *Wrong way up* in 1947 (a bare-headed woman at the bottom and a man with clasped hands) or the *Red mannequin event* of 1951 (a man lying on the ground and a mannequin bent right over in the tailor's window). The same arrangement can also be seen in *August set alight* [*Auguste mis à feu*] between the clown on the right, alert and carrying a flaming torch, which he is waving at the bottom of the clown on the left, who is stupidly imprisoned by his trumpet."[192]

December: trip to Chad and Cameroon.

176. André Chastel, "Destin d'Hélion", *Le Monde*, 11 December 1964, p. 10.
177. *Journal d'un peintre*, vol. I, *op. cit.*, 14 May 1965, p. 28.
178. *À perte de vue*, *op. cit.*, pp. 138, 141.
179. *Journal d'un peintre*, vol. II, *op. cit.*, 24 June 1965, p. 30.
180. *Ibid.*, 6 October 1965, p. 35.
181. *Ibid.*, 7 August 1966, p. 46.
182. *À perte de vue*, *op. cit.*, pp. 93–94.
183. *Journal d'un peintre*, vol. II, *op. cit.*, 4 January 1967, p. 47.
184. *À perte de vue ...*, *op. cit.*, p. 98.
185. Roger Caillois, "Trois étapes d'un adieu à la géométrie", preface to the catalogue for the exhibition *Hélion. Cent tableaux, 1928–1970*, Grand Palais, Paris, 11 December 1970–1 February 1971, Centre National d'Art Contemporain, "Archives de l'Art contemporain, 15", pp. 7–8.
186. *Journal d'un peintre*, vol. II, *op. cit.*, 11 December 1967, p. 54.
187. *Ibid.*, [December] 1967, p. 55.
188. *Ibid.*, 20 May 1968, p. 60.
189. Jean Duvignaud, "L'homme d'Hélion", *Chroniques de l'art vivant*, Paris, no. 10, April 1970, p. 26.
190. *Journal d'un peintre*, vol. II, *op. cit.*, [summer] 1969, p. 82.
191. *À perte de vue ...*, *op. cit.*, p. 164.
192. J. Duvignaud, "L'homme d'Hélion", as note 189, p. 26.

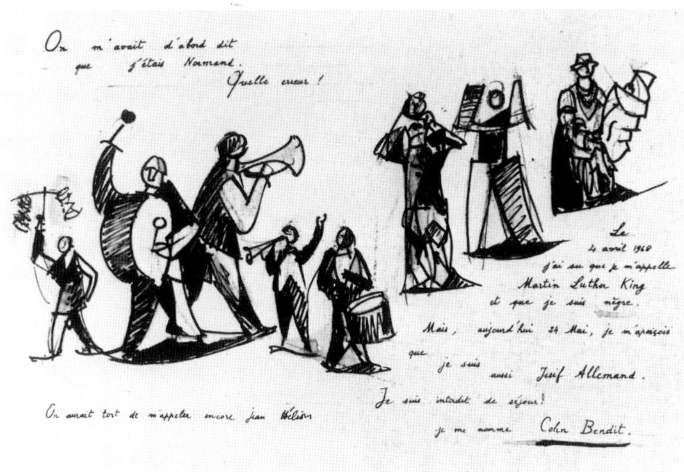

May litho, 1968
Lithograph heightened with watercolour, 37 x 57 cm
Collection of David Hélion

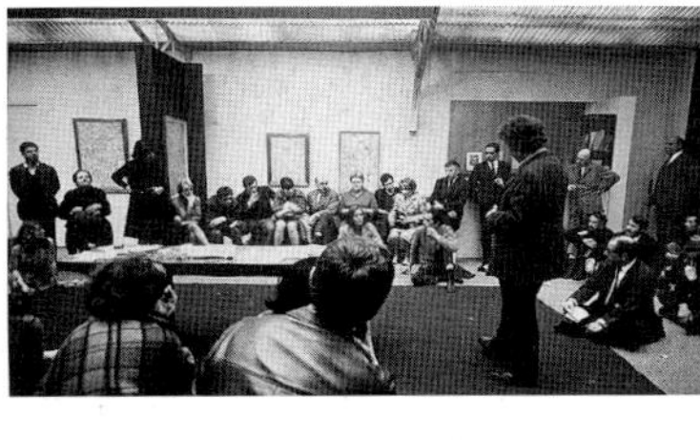

Gathering of artists at the Galerie Jeanne Bucher, Paris, 1968; on the right, standing, seen from behind, Jean Hélion

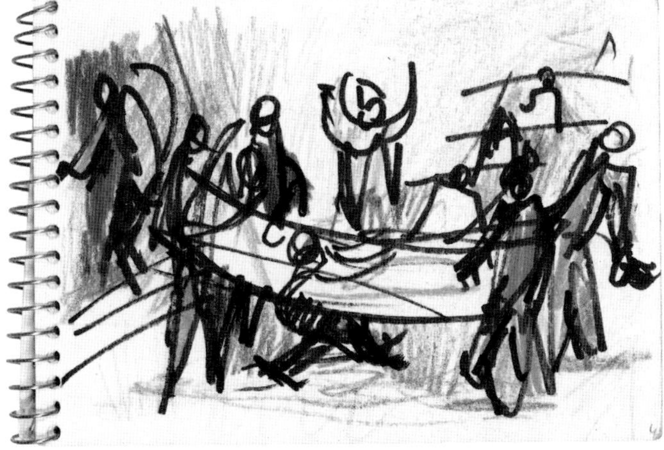

From the *carnets*: *Trickery* [*Supercherie*], 1970
Bibliothèque nationale de France, department des Étampes et de la Photographie

Retrospective exhibition *Cent tableaux 1928–1970* held at the Galeries Nationales du Grand Palais in Paris, 11 December–1 February 1971. Also two travelling exhibitions, *Hélion. Dix ans de peinture*, organized by the Centre National d'Art Contemporain, and *Hélion. 40 ans de dessins 1903–70*.

1971
May: retinal haemorrhage.
Late July, *Hippies in the city, Pause at the bridge* [*Hippies dans la ville, Halte au pont*]: "Independents have grouped together under a bridge in a musical way. In these groups there were often people playing the flute or the guitar, as though to say to everyone, 'Where are you going? Stay with us, we're happy here singing'."[193]
Late in the year, cataract operations on both eyes.

1972
Series of *Street orchestras* and *Jumbles*.
April: starts work on *Monument on the lawn* [*Monument sur l'herbe*]: "… when the demonstrations by the art school students led them on to the normally forbidden lawn of the Observatoire gardens, in which I walk every day. Act of freedom which matches my imagination. I'm working on erecting a monument to it. As always I am assailed by a range of ideas and solutions, into which I must carve. Be ascetic with my riches."[194]

June: series of studies of cabbages: "Jacqueline came to the studio clutching a cabbage to her breast. It was so beautiful I made a pastel of it at once. *Woman with cabbage*.[195] Perhaps even *Nude with cabbage*, for all kinds of reasons – first because I think it's beautiful; and right, be-cause of the petticoatish aspect of the cabbage and perhaps the plant aspect of the woman's body, its members like petals and, be-tween them, that rare flower, also all petals. I should have liked to paint that motif in the spirit of the azaleas of last year and the irises of this summer. From nature."[196]
"I really hope that one day these cabbages will be exhibited along-side my *Equilibrium on a white ground* [*Équilibre à fond blanc*] (1933). With no further explanation."[197]

September: trip to Germany (Nuremberg, Dresden, Berlin) and Czechoslovakia (Prague).

1973
At Bigeonnette, Hélion has a studio sufficiently large for his monumental projects. At Châteauneuf-en-Thymerais the market gives him the inspiration for many of his subjects: *March for a market* [*Marche pour un marché*]: "To the right, the 'theatre of dresses', to the left the cabbage seller. A wine porter passes a *cabassière*, in the centre. A blind man is getting lost in the night of the theatre of dresses, while, front right, a child is settling everything with the spinning of his top. Began painting yesterday. Noticed that beginning a painting with an invented rather than a de-scriptive definition of its space always stimulates me. From the outset this distancing defines a free-dom in relation to the motif, which I need in order to express it. In a way you have to grasp the space with passion rather than submission. Same with the colour. By painting a cabbage in red, in one of the pre-paratory panels (*Market garden suite with red cabbage and dress* [*Suite maraîchère au chou et à la robe rouges*]), I felt my work free itself and I soon escaped the un-believable swamp of hesitations through which I had been wading since my first market drawings from early June in Châteauneuf."[198]

September: trip to Ireland, to Dublin.
October: starts work on the *Market triptych* [*Triptyque du marché*].

1974
April: starts work on *Mathilde, her shadow and her reflection* [*Mathilde, son ombre et son reflet*].
May: stays in Belle-Île.
Late June: completes the *Market triptych*: "At a certain level on the completion of the picture this hap-pens: the rhythm swallows part of each object that it brings in. I leave it freely to itself on condition that the presence of the object is now ob-vious, if not integral. *E.g.* right panel of the *Market triptych*, couple in centre. The vertical rhythm in the girl as in the boy swallows and directs the heel of the shoe, while confirm-ing the shoe's function of keeping the figure on its base. It's this rhythm singing through the whole canvas that I colour and that also, in passing, dissolves the local tone while recalling it."[199]
July: a new theme, embraces.
"Mouth to mouth. Body to body. A monument to an embrace! With the ambivalently comforting impression that it will occupy the last years of my life. I hollow and I hammer this embrace and these consequences with a fervour that I think, in the whole history of painting, has been surpassed only by Picasso, whom I feel to be inhabiting my studio these days, as Poussin inhabited it during my years of abstraction."[200]

September: new Parisian scenes: "In Paris, on the corner of rue Michelet and boulevard St-Michel, there's a service station where I have often seen young men kneeling in front of their motorcycles, wor-shipping the flat tyre that must be revived. This banal act has always seemed sacred to me. I have dreamed of composing an image in which it would appear in triumph. A simple mental, abstract subject, everyday and eternal."[201]

Autumn: trip to East Germany (GDR), visits the museums of Dresden.
Start of a twelve-year working rela-tionship with the Paris gallery of Karl Flinker.

1975
Drawings of boulevard St-Michel.
At Bigeonnette, *Cloakroom at Bigeonnette* [*Vestiaire de Bigeonnette*], *Nude with coat-tree* [*Nu au perroquet*], *Blue coat-tree* [*Perroquet bleu*].
"*The coat-tree, the old clothes and the shadow*, second attempt 60F:[202] I know that, on a vertical wall, the shadow of a coat-tree is also verti-cal. Yet, irresistibly, it becomes oblique. The shadow is a being re-lated to the figure, but it emanci-pates itself, though in the direction of that being."[203]

May–June: the Galerie Flinker mounts the exhibition *Cinquante ans de peinture 1925–1975*.
Interview in *ArTitudes*: "In May, at the Galerie Karl Flinker, you are going to have an exhibition to be called 'Fifty years of painting'. What effect will it have on you to review this output? How do you regard this work?"
J.H.: "I have always wanted to do the same thing. So I shall see whether I am wrong or not. I have always run in the same direction, and I have often been surprised that that wasn't obvious. So I hope that together these fifty years of works will show that it's a coherent effort. That there are no contradictions."[204]

July: *Lobster and reflection* [*Homard et son reflet*]: "For example, at this time (4 pm) this meeting between a half-cooked lobster, a pedestal table, a folding metal chair and an umbrella is taking on a meaning. In other words it's shedding light on the ambiguity of today, like a song, like a fable …. Looking at the drawing I'm doing on this 40P canvas, it looks as though the lob-ster's reflection is committing sui-cide in the parasol's starry hollow. Am I going a little mad here? Anyway it's pleasant, liberating – an echo of Dada against the thick wall of reality."[205]

August: draws two figures undress-ing: "Working this 'buttock to but-tock' (100 F) which will be called *Back to back* [*Dos à dos*], the rest being obvious and back to back rhyming with *Tête à tête* (1972; just before the accident that caused me to lose the sight in my left eye): the arsey rhythm is hard to perfect and yet I feel it very strongly. A little more rhythm and it would become abstract; a little softer and it would be sensual. There is a perfect point for a sharp but sober visual fondling. I'm searching for it. Groping."[206]

In Belle-Île, gouaches of lobsters and fishmongers, and several pic-tures on the lobster theme: *Lobster with apples* [*Homards aux pommes*], *Little lobster sale* [*Petit marché aux homards*], *Lobster stall* [*Boutique aux homards*].
November: begins *Large lobster sale* [*Grand marché aux homards*]: "By analysing the realities of this

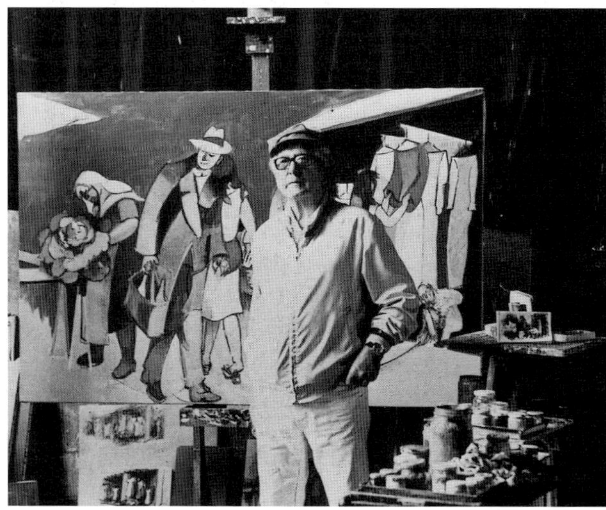

Jean Hélion in front of **March for a market**, Bigeonnette, 1973

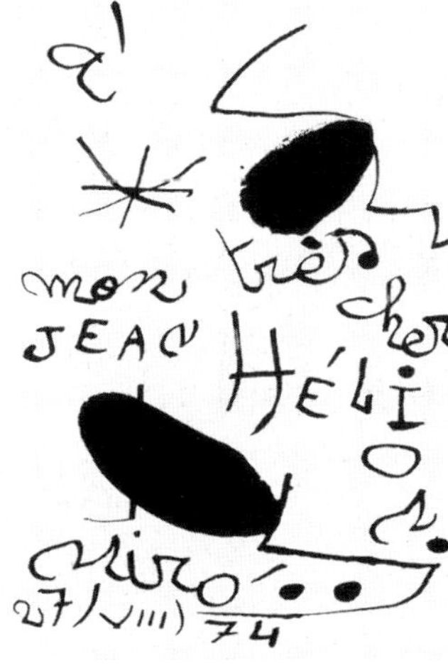

Letter from Joan Miró to Jean Hélion, 27 August 1974

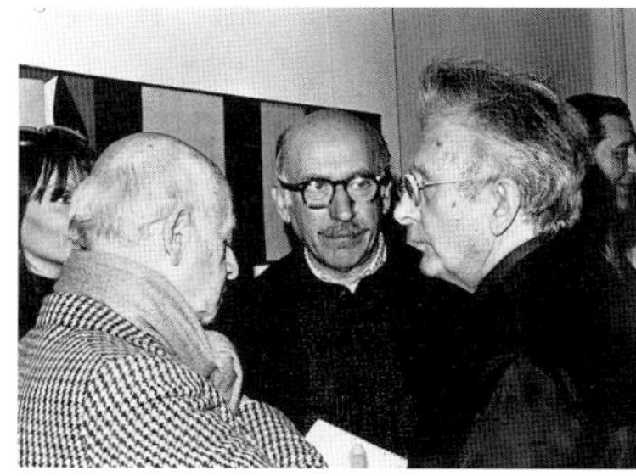

At the exhibition **Jean Hélion** at the Spencer Samuel Gallery, New York, 7 April–22 May 1976
from left to right: Denise and Richard Lindner, Saul Steinberg and Jean Hélion

last *marché*, mark my words, what I'm putting on sale are the lobsters that I grabbed from the trap of blue, red, green, violet, and the shoes of women I have loved, shoes thrown on the ground and sticking out from the bed. Sale of my idols."[207]

1976

February: begins the triptych *11 November* [*11 novembre*], exhibited at the Venice Biennale that year. April–June: one-man exhibition at the Spencer Samuel Gallery in New York. Nicolas Calas writes, "Helion's recent exhibition at the Spencer A. Samuels Gallery is his first one-man show held in New York since 1964 …. The exhibition included a sufficient number of early works for the attentive viewer to realize how consistent Hélion's development was from 1929 on. Thus *Equilibre* (1933), which could only be perceived as irregular abstract structure, took on the aspect of a man in a slouch hat (1943)."[208]

Visit to New York for this exhibition. Makes numerous sketches in the streets (inside and outside Sweet's), which will be used in works such as *New York seen* and *Tramps in the city* [*Les Clochards dans la ville*], inspired by a tramp who was "enormous, sitting on the wing of a smart car and cleaning his toe-nails. His gear on the ground. New York seen: the refined tramp."[209]

Reads Félix Vallotton's *Journal 1914–21*, finishing it in March. Back in Paris, subjects inspired by café terraces and urinals, which stimulate him to paint a vast composition, *The city is a dream* [*La ville est un songe*]: "At this moment, 12.30 pm on 24 December, my studio is so beautiful: the big urinal scene (shall I call it *Allégorie pissotière*?) well sketched in the three green, blue and red pastels surrounded by *pastels gouachés* on red, green, blue, grey 'grand aigle' sheets."[210]

"One night, when I was coming back from the theatre at midnight, there was a big crowd not far from the kiosk, it looked as though some society was meeting there. One character still haunts me, leaning against the garden gate. He was a blind man with his white cane, all dressed up with his shirt open and a light-coloured hat, he seemed to be blindly waiting for some adventure or other. For a moment I feared the worst for him, then I stopped thinking about him. That's another picture I should like to have painted, but later I had my public urinals period, those little circular metal temples around an enclosed pavilion. I even painted a version of it, which I think is admirable and which is called *The city is a dream*."[211]

1977

March: drawings and studies of *Pantalonnades* [Trouseries] and *Jambages* [Leggeries]: "Noting, three weeks ago in the Prado, that in Goya's 18th-century fantasies his best qualities appear in the background and that you could see that this painter of *courtisaneries* would one day become very vigorous, it came to me that my two 'misapprehensions' (Leggeries) 60F and 80F, a little too eloquent concerning recent things as a whole, have something of Louis XVI or XV which, in that way, relates my adventure to Goya. He was a man of the people who had been precious. Could it be said that I, who am so much of the people, have always had an underlying, or lateral, tendency for preciosity? I've fought against it, but it appears in some works. It was the same at the time of abstraction, but then it could have been defined as the excessive influence of Ingres, in whom the precious side often appears."[212]

November: first *Fleamarket suite* [*Suite pucière*]: "The objects-phrase, uttered by chance, into which I am now inserting the 'meeting' (Lautréamont!) includes a skeleton's pelvis I was brought twenty years ago by Dr Gabriel Illouz …. This human object has been knocking around since then in my studio. It hadn't yet found its rightful place in a picture …. But its interest today lies in its tubby structure, very manual, a bit vegetal, too, which relates it to the iron structures of the sewing-machine frame. This object, found inside the body, in the impulses of growth, has the qualities of a sketch. I am going to link it to the sign of a jawbone and to the dilapidation of the cap I have been using for a long time; and also to the interlaced pattern of the taps that Jacqueline brought me."[213]

October: trip to Spain. Hélion gives his series of drawings *Kaléidoscope 1929–39*, made in 1938 and 1939, to the Musée National d'Art Moderne.

1978

26 January–4 March: exhibition of works on paper at the Galerie Karl Flinker: "Around a hundred works all told", writes Jacques Michel. "They cover almost a half-century of the life of the painter – Jean Hélion, seventy-four years old. The older he gets, the more youthful his painting becomes, and the more he takes liberties with preconceived ideas and lets himself paint 'as it comes'. The miracle is that it does come. Straight from the fountainhead. Particularly in these pastels, where the French Hélion meets his eighteenth-century ancestors. He has their openness, warmth and mastery, but not their affectation …. His sight is failing, but he has everything in his head. His painting, more baroque and sensual than ever, is becoming mental. His drawing can only be a design. Hélion reinvents, composes these requiems for a pumpkin, unfurls these tables of carrots or leeks, hangs blue fish in space like daggers, pairs a solitary pansy with a fetish boot. Hélion in Bigeonnette is a bit like Monet with half-closed eyes looking at the waterlilies. The same way of looking, veiled by an inner reverie. And in these pastels of his advanced age, the admirable freedom and authority of his movement schematically tracing the look of a figure or nurturing the surface of a fruit."[214]

26 March: starts work on *Mannequinerie en solde* [Mannequin sale]: "These are the ones I used in 1950 and 1951 for the *Mannequinerie* of the time. I like this idea very much – sales at the studio. I've tried to indicate that moving objects in accordance with the perceptible imagination brings about a function of thinking. That thinking can unfold according to traditional processes, developing as it goes. Something like $2 + 2 = 4$. Or it can circulate in waves, in echoes, in reflection that becomes reflective thought. So to arrange the objects in this *Mannequinerie in the studio* is to articulate a vision of the world that is refreshed by the new order of the objects; plunging the fist of a red sunshade into the hollow heart of the female dummy seems delicious and joyful, like plunging my hand into a beloved breast and bringing with it, moreover, the vision of a kite setting off like a beating of red

193. *À perte de vue …*, *op. cit.*, pp. 99–100.
194. *Journal d'un peintre*, vol. II, *op. cit.*, 17 April 1972, p. 115.
195. Definitive title: *The lady with the cabbage* [*La Dame au chou*].
196. *Journal d'un peintre*, vol. II, *op. cit.*, [between 14 and 17 June 1972], p. 122.
197. *Ibid.*, 28 August 1972, p. 127.
198. *Ibid.*, 19 July 1973, p. 136.
199. *Ibid.*, 26 June 1974, pp. 165–66.
200. *Ibid.*, 29 July 1974, p. 167.
201. *Mémoire de la chambre jaune*, *op. cit.*, pp. 117–18.
202. Definitive title: *Coat-tree and echoes* [*Le Perroquet et ses échos*].
203. *Journal d'un peintre*, vol. II, *op. cit.*, 15 May 1975, p. 179.
204. Conversation with J. Hélion, *ArTitudes*, as note 89, p. 74.
205. J. Hélion, unpublished note of 16 July 1975.
206. *Journal d'un peintre*, vol. II, *op. cit.*, 19 August 1975, p. 198.
207. *Ibid.*, 27 November 1975, p. 228.
208. N. Calas, "Jean Hélion", *Arts*, June 1976.
209. *Journal d'un peintre*, vol. II, *op. cit.*, 16 May 1976, p. 247.
210. *Ibid.*, 24 December 1976, p. 259.
211. *À perte de vue …*, *op. cit.*, p. 155.
212. *Journal d'un peintre*, vol. II, *op. cit.*, 1 November 1977, p. 285.
213. *Ibid.*, 16 November 1977, p. 289.
214. J. Michel, "Desseins au pastel de Jean Hélion", *Le Monde*, 10 February 1978, p. 21.

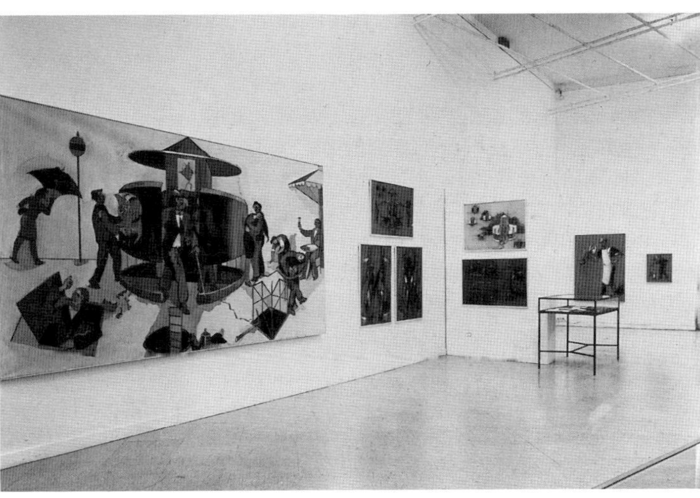

View of the exhibition *Hélion. Les marchés*, Musée d'Art moderne de la Ville de Paris, March–April 1977
on the left: *The city is a dream*, 1976

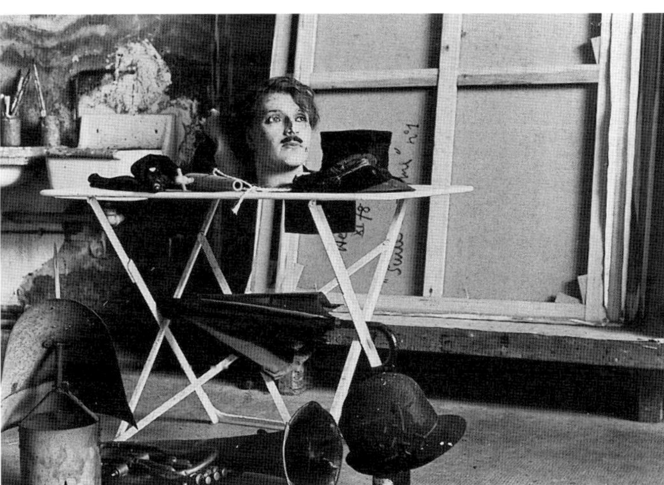

In the studio at Bigeonnette: preparations for *Anonymous suite no. 1*, 1978

wings, in unison with the joyful sensation I was talking about earlier."[215]

New triptych, *The Last Judgement of things* [*Jugement dernier des choses*]: "All in all, I shall end up with a 'motif market'. The objects I have met in my life will line up with the types of figures I have loved, men and women, apparently arranged in the disorder of a flea-market and, in reality, condensing a series of themes from my whole life, all put forward together, revealing (5.11.77) the meaning of their appearance, which is initially random, but leading to this parade. Will it also be 'time regained'?"[216]
"At last I am freely handling the gesticulations of the central panel of the planned triptych, *Last Judgement of things*. Important: from one end to the other across the three panels, at the bottom, runs a line of different objects including Esther's slipper in the middle.[217] Objects as close as possible to signs. Hieroglyphs. Shorthand – or telegram – of objects at the bottom."[218]

July: trip to Tuscany to see the early Sienese school and Piero della Francesca.
Takes part in the *Abstraction-Création* exhibition at the Musée d'Art Moderne de la Ville de Paris.

1979
February: Jacqueline's reading of his letters to Raymond Queneau stimulates him to paint *Grave parody* [*Parodie grave*]. Of the letters he writes, "They are good, I think, but with a certain old scent of Christianity which these days I am precisely perfecting with *Parody with easels* [*Parodie aux chevalets*].[219] In this three men are carrying an easel away on their backs, as I did in 1925, in St-Ouen.

The comical and serious side of my memory is very precisely expressed here. The comical corrects the sentimental, without denying it, which is exactly my attitude in relation to this hereditary religiosity that I carry within me like a minority which, though subjugated, still makes itself heard in the assembly of my thoughts."[220]
July: trip to Karl Flinker's house on Skyros. "Back from Skyros, where I fell in love with Karl's broken-down chairs– in his little house by the sea – I continue the play of bars and dishevelled straws, half after my Greek sketches, half after the intact chairs of Bigeonnette."[221]

10 December: the jury of the Beaux-Arts de la Ville de Paris awards him the Grand Prix de Peinture.

1980
January: *Portrait of the artist as an old man*: "I suddenly saw an old man looking at me. With his green and blue eyeshield, he made me think of Chardin. I at once captured him with the delicious mix of pastels, Lefranc Indian inks and charcoal that I've found. How can this old painter with a face peopled with shadows contain the young thoughts that inhabit him?"[222]
February–March: commission from Michel Guy, former Minister of Culture, for the Autumn Festival poster.
September: trip to Beijing for the exhibition in China.

1981
January: completes *Hat suite* [*Suite chapelière*]; starts work on *Jumble for Émile* [*Un Borsalino pour Émile*]: "A rainy hat suite [*suite chapelière et pluvieuse*] in which perspective is indicated by the regression of realism (maximum with

the black umbrella) into abstraction, or rather into realism summed up in abstraction until the red shoe. Perspective of writing, all in all. In the end I called this picture *A jumble for Émile*."[223]

Represents French painting, alongside Balthus, in the *New Spirit in Painting* exhibition at the Royal Academy of Arts in London, 15 January–18 March. One critic offered the following classification: "The artists who have been included can be split into three groups: Grand Old Men, Expressionists and Minimalists …. The Grand Old Men make an interesting group. Among them are Balthus, too seldom seen in England, with a series of paintings done since his memorable retrospective exhibition at the Tate; the academic Cubist Jean Hélion, an extraordinary survivor from the days of the Section d'Or; and the veteran American Abstract Expressionists Willem de Kooning and Philipp Guston."[224]

Completes *The real and the dream* [*Le Réel et le songe*]. Richard Crevier writes, "A strange detail figures in this picture – a soup tureen, neoplasticist in form, previously presented in *The Last Judgement of things*, which the painter seems to be visually assessing while he paints the recumbent nude over whose upper part passes the grey shadow of a plane of the picture, thereby integrating the figured form with the background. In fact the painter, split in two, is painting two abstractions from his period in the 1930s, seeming to signify by this that at every point in his oeuvre he has been engaged on the same path, with the everyday utensil, the nude and the abstract motif. At all times he is trying to invent, and so restore, the

musical fabric of things by their mental and formal metaphorization. This picture allows us to look at Hélion's 'studio'. He was making sketches from nature, surrounding himself with found objects from different moments in his own life and allowing associations to arise which of necessity would create the picture through the process of its composition. He was in a dream surrounded by his motifs, capturing his dream's reflection in paint. The concept 'dream' in his work signifies an enlargement of the object beyond realist detail towards its 'global' definition. Thus the eroticism of a nude's crotch takes on all its meaning only through the capture of its kinship with the soup tureen, whose knob seems to be opening out, like a rosebud or something else."[225]

Homage to Richard Lindner: "In *Fable for Richard Lindner*,[226] March–April, two versions 120P, I placed a brioche loaf on Jacqueline's dress to the left, and a kipper to the right of the mannequin's head in Richard's hat, near my jeans. Overall the brioche and the head with the hat look like each other and the superb kipper is like an arrow fired from the moon at the setting sun."[227]
Works without respite on large-format reinterpretations of his old motifs.

November: *Paintings and Drawings 1939-1960* exhibition at the Robert Miller Gallery in New York. Review in *Le Point* magazine: "The West is about to be won again! But peacefully, setting out from Paris this time, with two weeks of French painters. First the 75-year-old Hélion, whose exhibition of paintings at the Bob Miller gallery opens in October.

Then, next February, in several other New York galleries, painters of the new generation, including Martial Raysse, Viallat, Cane, Aillaud, Bioulès, Pincemin and Boltanski. Hélion has established his reputation, but the Americans had yet to hear about it. The moment has been well chosen since, after minimalist art and hyperrealism, the 'avant garde' crisis is now even more serious over there than it is here."[228]

1982
April: *One Sunday 59 years ago* [*Il y a 59 ans, un dimanche*]: "In 1923, on Sunday, on the balcony around my attic at 207, rue St-Martin, I was beginning, on an initial canvas, to formulate the sign that could decode the universe stretching away all around me. The roofs that together formed angles crowned by bunches of cowls from which rose jets of smoke in the shape of a five, more white than black (according to Verlaine). And skylights, windows full of beauties. In them you could see thighs, limbs, hair and tits. But, in front of a muslin curtain through which the wind played, I had the confused feeling that all this made a pattern of stiff and curved angles and that I, alone before it, might one day be able to sing it. In chorus. With one voice. These days I'm getting there, it seems to me. But I am almost blind and so old that I have become clumsy."[229]

Summer: long stay in Andalusia. Travels to the United States in August, at the invitation of the Showhegan Academy in Maine: lecture and discussions with students.

1983
Returns to one of his recurrent motifs with *The city* [*La Ville*]:

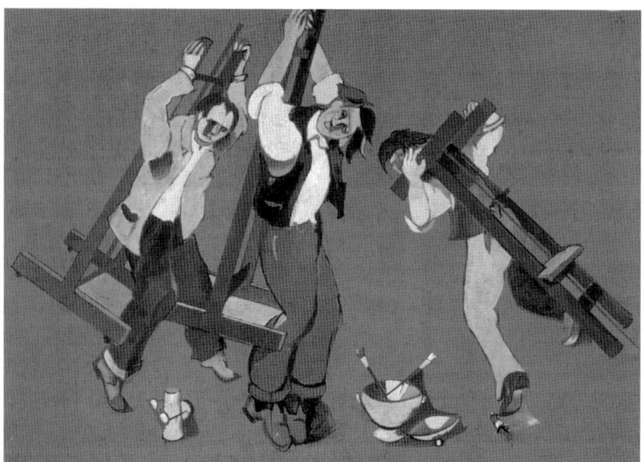

Grave parody, 1979
Acrylic on canvas, 145.5 x 200 cm
Centre Pompidou, Musée national d'art moderne, Paris, accepted in lieu of tax 1991

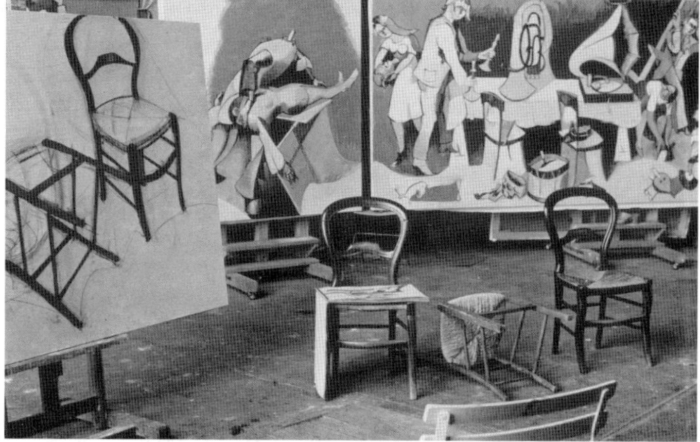

In the studio at Bigeonnette, 1978:
in the foreground: *Ballet of chairs at Skyros* (1978) in course of execution;
behind: the triptych *The Last Judgment of things* (1978–79) in course of execution

Richard Crevier writes: "'The city's murmur is appalling. The front of the newspapers discouraging …. Yet, I confess, I like the vulgar, solar splendour of the pumpkins', says Hélion. The painter dreams surrounded by the destruction of the city, of which Baudelaire once said, 'the heart of a man changes more slowly'. The man with the pickaxe had already become a central motif in Hélion's work, in opposition to the painter, who was frequently shown at that time painting in the same environment. In his paintings the hole becomes a leitmotiv that should be seen and understood as the inverted image of the Women at the window that are so numerous in his work, represented here by the sexual display of the pumpkin. In this way the picture makes an opening in the city, its reflection and parallel reality: art has a function of redeeming the wounds of modernism using the means of modernism itself. It is in pictures like this that we can gauge the extent to which Hélion is a 'critical' artist. He places the dream, the artistic utopia, at the heart of the reality which he thus shows without redundancy."[230]

Hélion never leaves his studio, his sight worsening from one day to the next.
Return to the nude between open shutters above a recumbent figure, painted in 1947 in *The sleeper and the nude*.

Hélion stops painting in October. From late 1983 to 1985, he dictates critical commentaries on the unfinished or "failed" paintings stored in a room in the attic at Bigeonnette. This *Mémoire de la chambre jaune* [Memory of the yellow room] is followed by three essays relating his childhood and the crucial encounters of his life as a painter.
"This yellow room is the refuge of many mistakes, many things that were never finished. But they did not seem lethal to me, and here and there I have been able to show, in a few works that, by definition, are not there, that it was possible to think with open eyes and to exist on every level at once. Perhaps an intelligible exhibition of all my works should show the path, through geometries, of the mental towards the living, the conceived towards the known. I can only hope that these solitary debates will one day help some young painter with an alert mind to find the right point in the hullaballoo which puts the emotion of art into the head – into the head and the body at the same time, like a dance at once sacred and profane, the profane becoming a shadow precisely carrying sacredness, like the shadows in which, in my diminished sight, my unfinished pictures take refuge."[231]

1984–85

Retrospective of his work in Munich and Paris. The critics say: "This time Hélion equals those he has taken as models, the masters of 'complete' painting, the painting of which Baudelaire announced the disappearance on the death of Delacroix, and which, he wrote, had been killed by Ingres and Courbet. The painting which the Cézanne of the still-life pictures despaired of reviving. 'Great' painting, in simple terms."[232]
"One of the reasons that led Hélion gradually to detach himself from the avant-garde and modernism is that they imposed a break with social reality. In the end, the marxism of his youth and his humanism of all ages led Hélion to place himself outside the avant-garde and the trans-avant-garde. Resolutely elsewhere, he seeks only to assert his sole vocation of giving back to art the power to speak of man, of life and the things around him."[233]

1986

Visits major exhibitions in Paris, with the help of descriptions by his wife Jacqueline.

1987

27 October 1987: Jean Hélion dies in Paris.
"With Jean Hélion dies one of the freest minds of his period ….
Around 1958 Hélion's work found its true dimension. By constantly looking at the world, trying to see beyond academic habits with the new eye he was given by abstraction, Hélion's approach became visionary. He returns to the lessons and spirit of the great masters in works that echo the canvases of Frans Hals and Manet and in which the brushstroke, suddenly asserted, no longer describes the object but sums it up in a sign. Alone from then on in the world of contemporary art, stripped even of the encounters and meetings of minds which, from Mondrian to Arp and from Léger to Giacometti, marked (albeit against the grain) his earlier painting, for twenty-five years Hélion piled boldness on audacity, scuppered the old taboos of painting … until, in the mid 1970s and, at first, on simple sheets of paper, then on many canvases, he discovered a totally new implementation of colour, a freedom which is, paradoxically, that of the very young painters who are contemporary with him and who, alone at the time, took him seriously. Gradually falling victim to blindness, in the last canvases his weak sight permitted him to paint Hélion sought to show that, rather than being a succession of periods, his oeuvre had a real consistency, that, in the time regained to which his pictures lead, characters and abstract figures had always had the same value of nullifying all conventions the better to convey the sense of the world's richness and diversity."[234]

215. *Journal d'un peintre*, vol. II, *op. cit.*, 26 March 1978, p. 301.
216. *Ibid.*, 5 November 1977, p. 288.
217. Name of Hélion's female mannequin.
218. *Journal d'un peintre*, vol. II, *op. cit.*, 29 May 1978, pp. 305, 307.
219. Definitive title: *Grave parody [Parodie grave]*.
220. *Journal d'un peintre*, vol. II, *op. cit.*, [around 10 February 1979], p. 322.
221. *Ibid.*, 9 August 1979, p. 328.
222. *Ibid.*, 11 January 1980, p. 341.
223. *Ibid.*, 20 January 1981, p. 354.
224. Edward Lucie-Smith, "A New Spirit in Painting?", *Pictorial News*, London, p. 68.
225. R. Crevier, "Jean Hélion", Paris, Galerie Piltzer, 1995, p. 4.
226. Definitive title: *Best wishes to Richard Lindner [Amitiés à Richard Lindner]*.
227. *Journal d'un peintre*, vol. II, *op. cit.*, 10 April 1981, p. 360.
228. [Anonymous], "Art : verdict sur la 5e avenue", *Le Point*, 6–12 April 1981, p. 109.
229. *Journal d'un peintre*, vol. II, *op. cit.*, (day before Easter, 10 April 1982), pp. 373, 375.
230. R. Crevier, as note 225.
231. *Mémoire de la chambre jaune*, *op. cit.*, p. 111.
232. Philippe Dagen, "Saisir Hélion", *Le Quotidien de Paris*, 19 November 1984, p. 35.
233. Gladys C. Fabre, "Paris Jean Hélion", *Beaux-Arts*, December 1984, p. 91.
234. Daniel Abadie, "Jean Hélion, chapeaux bas", *Libération*, 29 October 1987, p. 38.

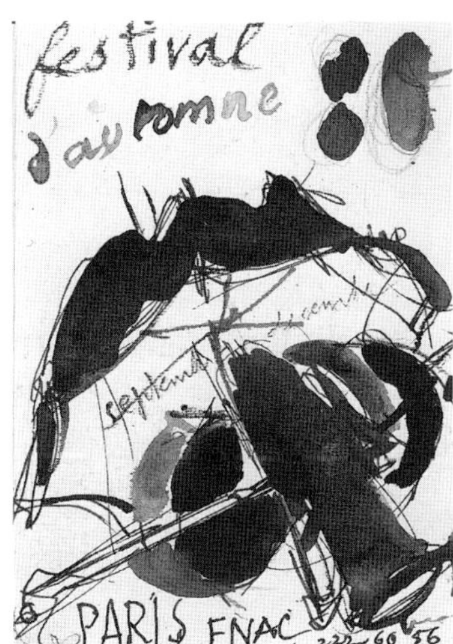

From the *carnets*: study for the poster for the Festival of Autumn, 1980
Bibliothèque nationale de France, department des Étampes et de la Photographie

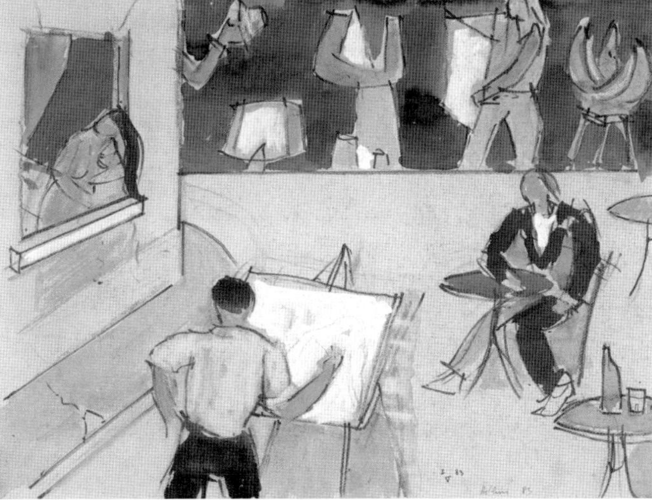

***Memory street [La Rue de souvenirs]*, 1953**
Charcoal, felt pen, acrylic, various inks, pastel on paper, 49.6 x 64.5 cm
Centre Pompidou, Musée national d'art moderne, Paris, accepted in lieu of tax 1991

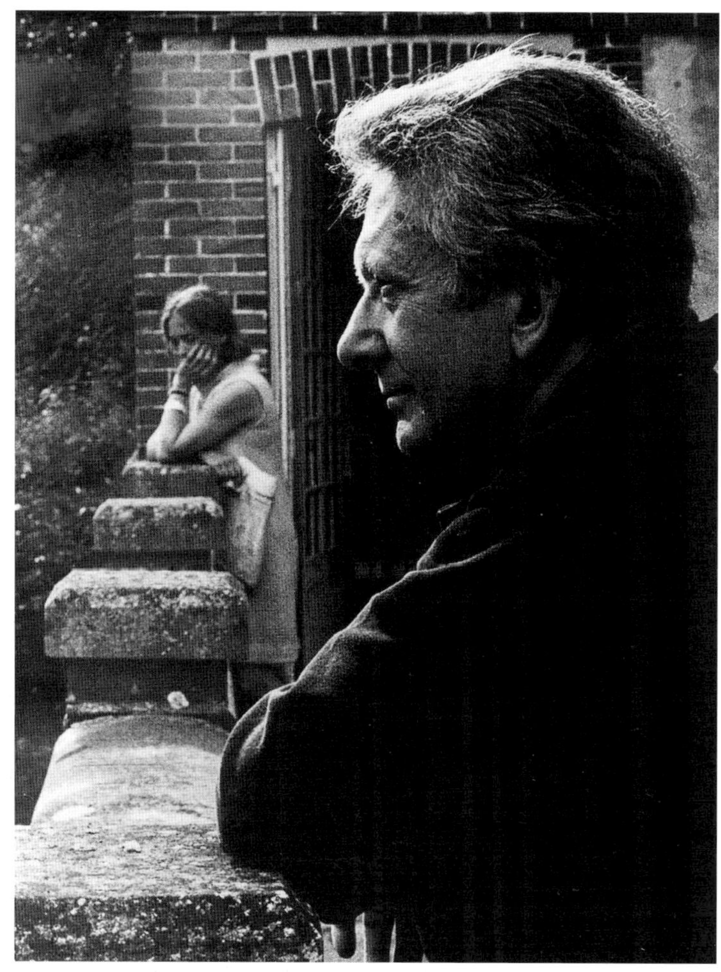

Jean and Jacqueline Hélion
at Bigeonnette, 1963

An asterisk following a bibliographical entry indicates the text could not be consulted.

Writings by Jean Hélion

Books
They Shall not Have Me
(*Ils ne m'auront pas*), New York,
E.P. Dutton, 1943
*Journal d'un peintre. Carnets,
1929–1984,* (vol. I: *1929–1962*;
vol. II: *1963–1984*), ed. Anne Mœglin-
Delcroix, Paris, Maeght, 1992
Mémoire de la chambre jaune,
ed. Marie-Anne Sichère, Paris, École
nationale supérieure des Beaux-Arts, coll.
"Écrits d'artistes", 1994
À perte de vue followed by *Choses
revues,* ed. Claire Paulhan and Patrick
Fréchet, Paris, IMEC, 1996
*Lettres d'Amérique. Correspondance
avec Raymond Queneau, 1934–1967,*
ed. Claude Rameil, Paris, IMEC, coll.
"Pièces d'archives", 1996
Duchamp Lettres Hélion, ed. Claude
Rameil, Cognac, Les Autodidactes, 2000
Écrits, a new and revised edition of
À perte de vue followed by *Choses
revues* and of *Mémoire de la chambre
jaune,* Paris, École nationale supérieure
des Beaux-Arts, coll. "Écrits
d'artistes"/IMEC, 2004

Articles (press and periodicals)
"Hâbleur d'affiche" (poem), *L'Acte,*
Paris, no. 3, January–February 1928, n. p.
"Vivants, usuriers et fuyards", *L'Acte,*
no. 3, January–February 1928, n. p.
"Contact", *L'Acte,* no. 4, April 1928,
n. p.
"[Histoire de l'art moderne]",
Pyrénées, 1929*
"Art et mathématiques", *Art Concret,*
Paris, April 1930, pp. 5–10 // Facsimile
in the review *16 Rue de Lille,* no. 1,
April 1976
"Préface", exh. cat. "Kubism – Post-
Kubism – Konstruktivism – Neoplasticism
– Sur-Realism – Sur-Impressionism",
Stockholm, August 1930, pp. 7–9
"À Solder", *Abstraction-Création.
Art non figuratif,* Paris, no. 1, 1932,
pp. 17–18 (reprint: New York, Arno
Press, 1968)
[Untitled], *De Stijl,* Amsterdam,
"last issue", January 1932, pp. 57–59
"Comparer les tableaux aux arbres?
…", *Abstraction-Création,* no. 2, 1933,
p. 20
"The Evolution of Abstract Art as
Shown in the Gallery of Living Art",
preface to the catalogue *The Gallery of
Living Art. Albert E. Gallatin Collection,*
New York, New York University, 1933,
n. p. // *The Museum of Living Art*
(catalogue of the A.E. Gallatin collection),
Philadelphia, Philadelphia Museum of Art,
1954, pp. 15–19
"La réalité dans la peinture", *Cahiers
d'art,* Paris, nos. 9–10, 1934,
pp. 253–260
"Étrange séparation. On ne saurait
intégrer la forme dans le fond …"
(Réponse à l'enquête sur l'art
d'aujourd'hui), *Cahiers d'art,* nos. 1–4,
1935, pp. 60–61
"Il s'agit d'agrandir la peinture …",
preface to the catalogue of the exhibition

"Thèse – Antithèse – Synthèse", Lucerne,
Kunstmuseum, 24 February–31 March
1935, pp. 8–9
"From Reduction to Growth", *Axis:
A Quarterly Review of Contemporary
Abstract Painting and Sculpture,* London,
no. 2, April 1935, pp. 19–24 (reprint:
New York, Arno Press, s. d.)
"Termes de vie. Termes d'espace"
(December 1935), (stufy for a kind of
surgical facility for the medical services of
the Compagnie du Canal de Suez,
Ismailia, Egypt, by the architect Paul
Nelson), *Cahiers d'art,* nos. 7–10, 1935,
pp. 268–73
"Poussin, Seurat and Double Rythm"
(Paris, December 1934), *Axis,* no. 6,
summer 1936, pp. 9–17 // *Painter's
Object,* ed. Myfanwy Evans (Piper),
London, Gerald Howe Ltd, 1937 //
New York, Arno Press, 1970, pp. 94–107
"Seurat as a Predecessor",
The Burlington Magazine, London,
no. 69, July 1936, pp. 4–14 //
The League, New York, vol. 8, no. 4,
April 1937, pp. 10–19
"Avowals and Comments", in *The
Painter's Object, op. cit.,* pp. 31–37
"Tableaux en cours, abstractions",
Volontés, Paris, no. 8, August 1938,
pp. 3–6 // *Two Cities,* Paris, no. 9,
autumn 1964, pp. 52–54 (French version
of "Avowals and Comments")
"Ten Frenchmen on a Prison Farm",
The Yale Review, A National Quarerly,
vol. XXXII, no. 4, summer 1943,
pp. 642–67
"Escape Through Germany",
The Atlantic Monthly, Boston, vol. 172,
no. 2, August 1943, pp. 41–51
"How War Has Made Me Paint",
ARTnews, New York, vol. XLIII, no. 3,
15–31 March 1944, p. 17
"Un artiste et la guerre", *Le Monde
libre,* New York, vol. II, no. 1, May 1944,
pp. 50–52 // *Présence* (the review for
French combatants in Italy), no. 17,
8 October 1944
"The Making of a Picture",
The Listener, London, no. 29, 4 June
1945, p. 857*
"Propos", in "Eleven Europeans in
America", *Bulletin of the Museum of
Modern Art,* New York, no. 45 [1946],
p. 28
"Fin ou commencement" (on ruins),
Technique et architecture, Paris,
nos. 5–6, 1948, p. 3
"Pour un art mondial", *Arts,* no. 197,
14–20 January 1949, p. 5
"Pierre Mabille", *Éducation et Théâtre,*
Paris, no. 15, December 1952,
pp. 45–48
"Un abstrait devenu figuratif. Jean
Hélion: 'J'avais la nostalgie des formes
du monde'", *Arts,* no. 727, 17–23 June
1959, p. 9
"Propos", *Dædalus (Journal of the
American Academy ot Arts and
Sciences),* Harvard University,
Cambridge, winter 1960, special no.:
"The Visual Arts Today", pp. 100–04
"Jean Hélion: La peinture n'est jamais
achevée", *Preuves,* Paris, no. 57, March
1964, pp. 47–48
"Figurer", *Mercure de France,* Paris,
June 1964, pp. 337–42. English version
in *Art and Literature,* Lausanne/Paris,

no. 1, March 1964, pp. 161–72, entitled
"Figure", translated by John Ashbery
"Portraits. Notes de travail" (Paris,
1959–60), *Two Cities,* Paris, autumn
1964, pp. 55–58
Remarks on "L'exposition du
XVIIIᵉ Congrès du Parti communiste" by
Michel Troche, *France nouvelle,* Paris,
no. 1108, 11 January 1967, p. 17
"Art concret 1930" (January 1966),
Art and Literature, no. 11, winter 1967,
pp. 128–40
"Jean Hélion", in exh. cat. *Artistes en
exil 1939–1946 U.S.A.,* American
Center, Paris, 16 May–6 June 1968,
p. 26
"Un témoignage d'Hélion" (forming
part of the *enquête:* "La querelle des
abstraits et des figuratifs"), *La Galerie
des Arts,* Paris, no. 54, June 1968,
pp. 25–27
"Vive la rue!" (réponse à l'enquête de
Françoise Choay "La ville et
l'imaginaire"), *Preuves,* nos. 209–210,
August–September 1968, pp. 46–47
"Carnet d'atelier" (extracts from the
Carnets of 1968), *Chorus,* Paris, no. 2,
winter 1968–69, pp. 10–12
Text in the catalogue *Hommage
à Yvonne Zervos,* Palais des Papes,
Avignon, 1970, n. p.
"Christian Zervos", *Les Lettres
françaises,* no. 1352, 23–29 September
1970, p. 26
"Carnets de travail 1968–69–71»,
Nabuchodonosor, Bellevue, no. 24,
March 1971*
"Les débuts de Engel-Pak", sale
catalogue *Ernst Engel-Pak Rozier,* Paris,
hôtel Drouot, May 1972
"Hélion: dynamite ou sirop?", *Gulliver,
Forum des lettres, des arts et de la vie
quotidienne,* Paris, no. 3, January 1973,
pp. 32–33
"À bas la censure", *Gulliver,* no. 4,
February 1973, p. 4
"Individus" (December 1972), exh. cat.
Raymond Queneau, Bibliothèque
municipale, Le Havre,
3 February–3 March 1973, n. p. //
Les Amis de Valentin Brû, Levallois-
Perret, no. 24–25: "Raymond Queneau
et la peinture", November 1983, p. 21
"Un mariage de raison", *ArTitudes
International,* St-Jeannet, nos. 9–11,
April–June 1974, pp. 32–33
"Courbet le paya très cher", *Le Figaro
littéraire,* Paris, no. 1473, 10–16 August
1974, pp. 1 and 13
"Pratique de 'Chêne et Chien'",
Cahier de l'Herne Raymond Queneau,
Paris, Éd. de l'Herne, 1975, pp. 272–74
// *Les Amis de Valentin Brû,* nos. 24–25,
op. cit., pp. 22–25
"Mon cheminement à New York …"
(May 1977), exh. cat. *Paris–New York,*
Centre Georges Pompidou, Paris,
1 June–19 September 1977,
pp. 505–50
"Kandinsky et l'antisémitisme", *Art
Press International,* Paris, no. 11,
October 1977, p. 4
"Pharmacies d'hier et d'aujourd'hui",
Le Pharmacien de France, Paris, no. 1,
January 1978, pp. 36–37
"Hélion critique du *Chiendent* et
illustrateur (critique) de *Chêne et Chien*"
(cinq lettres de Jean Hélion à Raymond

Queneau), *Temps mêlés*, Verviers, no. 6–7, January 1980, pp. 7–26

"Discours de Pékin" (10 September 1980), in Paris, galerie Karl Flinker (FIAC 81), taken in part from the review *Cimaise*, nos. 153–54, October–November 1981, pp. 14–15

"Extraits de carnets de 1981" and "Premier essai de 'Lexiquélion' de A à Z", taken in part from the review *Cimaise*, ibid., pp. 10–11

"À la rédaction de *Révolution*", *Révolution*, Paris, no. 190, 21–27 October 1983, pp. 10 and 15

"Lettres de Jean Hélion à Raymond Queneau". Extraits des *Lettres d'Amérique* … (see Books by Jean Hélion, above), *Les Amis de Valentin Brû*, Levallois-Perret, nos. 24–25: "Raymond Queneau et la peinture", November 1983, pp. 27–85

"D'un carnet" (extracts from the *carnets*), *Sixième Liasse*, no. 6, March 1984, pp. 23–28

"Notre-Dame de l'abstraction", *Le Nouvel Observateur*, 21–27 December 1984, pp. 70–71

"La découverte de Francis Ponge", *Cahier de l'Herne Francis Ponge*, Paris, Éd. de l'Herne, 1986, pp. 262–63

Monographs and special issues of periodicals devoted to the work of Jean Hélion

(in alphabetical order of author)

Daniel Abadie, *Hélion ou la force des choses*, Bruxelles, Éd. de La Connaissance, coll. "Témoins et témoignages / Monographies", 1975

Hervé Bize, *Jean Hélion*, Paris, Éd. Cercle d'Art, coll. "Découvrons l'art", 2004

Pierre-Georges Bruguière, *Jean Hélion*, Paris, SPEI Éd., 1970

Henry-Claude Cousseau, *Hélion*, Paris, Éd. du Regard, 1992

Philippe Dagen, *Hélion*, Paris, Hazan, 2004

Bernard Dahan, *Jean Hélion, peintre au confluent de la peinture, de la sémiologie et de la littérature*, thèse de 3e cycle, Paris, Université Paris III, December 1983 (unpublished)

René Micha, *Jean Hélion*, Paris, Flammarion, coll. "Maîtres de la peinture moderne", 1979 //English edition *Jean Hélion*, Naefels, Bonfini Press, 1979

Frances Morris, *Jean Hélion: Abstraction to Figuration 1930–1950*, M.A. thesis, London, Courtauld Institute University, May 1983 (unpublished)

Didier Ottinger, *Jean Hélion*, Paris, Éd. du Centre Georges Pompidou, coll. "Jalons", 1992

Merle S. Schipper, *Hélion, the Abstract Years: 1929–1939*, Los Angeles, PhD thesis, UCLA, 1974 (unpublished)

Silex, Grenoble, no. 29, 1er trimestre 1985 (textes de Francis Ponge, Pierre Mabille, Raymond Queneau, Gilbert Lascault, René de Obaldia, Georges Limbour, Jean-Pierre-Arthur Bernard, Jean-Charles Gateau, Pierre Gaudibert, Christian Limousin)

Articles and reviews

Daniel Abadie, "Jean Hélion ou l'exercice de la liberté", *Études*, May 1969, pp. 689–694, followed by extracts from Hélion's *carnets*, pp. 695–701 // Exh. cat. *Hélion, cent tableaux, 1928–1970*, Grand Palais, Paris, 11 December 1970–1 February 1971, pp. 9–11

D. Abadie, "L'œuvre de Jean Hélion, le précurseur", *Art international*, vol. XIX, no. 5, 15 May 1975, pp. 27–33

D. Abadie, "Les banalités épiques de Jean Hélion", *XXe Siècle*, Paris, no. 44, June 1975, pp. 99–104

D. Abadie, "Hélion (galerie Flinker, FIAC)", *Cimaise*, no. 155, December 1981–January 1982, p. 74

D. Abadie, "Jean Hélion. Le désir de dire" (interview), *Beaux-Arts Magazine*, no. 3, June 1983, pp. 26–30

D. Abadie, "Jean Hélion, chapeaux bas", *Libération*, 29 October 1987, p. 38

Cécile Agay, "L'artiste et son modèle", *Art d'aujourd'hui*, Boulogne-sur-Seine, nos. 10–11, May–June 1950, p. 16

Robert Altman, "Mas alla de la pintura", *Estudios*, July 1950*

R. Altman, "Hélion el fundator del objeto sobre el mar", *Islas*, April 1961*

Julien Alvard, "Des groupes de fantômes", *Le Nouvel Observateur*, no. 105, 16–22 November 1966, p. 50

J. Alvard, "Hélion's Parachute", *ARTnews*, vol. 65, no. 9, January 1967, pp. 25 and 64

[Anonymous], "Triangle, with Pendants", *The New Yorker*, 17 March 1945

[Anonymous], "'Prima' in Italia del pittore Hélion", *Il Gazzettino*, Venice, 26 August 1951

[Anonymous], "Hélion à la galerie Cahiers d'art", *Combat*, 17 November 1958

[Anonymous], "Hélion Looks at Paris's Art Crisis", *New York Herald Tribune*, 29 September 1964

[Anonymous], "Hélion Retrospective, 1928–1964", *Pen and Brush*, December 1964, pp. 9 and 12

[Anonymous], "La rue est le lieu privilégié pour le peintre Jean Hélion", *Le Maine libre*, 22 July 1970

[Anonymous], "Hélion et son œuvre au musée Ingres", *La Dépêche du Midi*, Toulouse, 29 June 1976

[Anonymous], "Art: verdict sur la 5e avenue", *Le Point*, 6–12 April 1981, p. 109

[Anonymous], "Bon anniversaire, Hélion !", *Connaissance des Arts*, no. 393, November 1984, p. 28

[Anonymous], "Hélion d'après nature", *Galerie-Jardin des Arts*, no. 226, November–December 1984, pp. 12–13

[Anonymous], "Jean Hélion à L'Isle-sur-la-Sorgue", *L'Œil*, Lausanne/Paris, no. 398, September 1988, p. 81

[Anonymous], "De la gravure et de ses techniques. Gravures sur bois, sur lino …", *Les Nouvelles de l'estampe*, Paris, no. 100, October 1988, p. 33

[Anonymous], "Prova d'orchestra", *Connaissance des Arts*, Paris, no. 507, June 1994, p. 42

[Anonymous], "Au 16 de l'avenue Matignon", *Connaissance des Arts*, no. 520, September 1995, pp. 102–07

Robert Aribout, "Jean Hélion: un grand peintre 'libre'", *La Dépêche du Midi*, 25 October 1971

Martine Arnault, "Jean Hélion. Les carnets ou l'entre-deux œuvres", *Cimaise*, no. 222, January–March 1993, p. 60

John Ashbery, "Hélion Paints a Series of Portraits", *ARTnews*, New York, vol. 58, no. 10, February 1960, pp. 32–35 and 59–61

J. Ashbery, "Avant-Gardist Jean Hélion at Galerie Cahiers d'Art", *New York Herald Tribune*, 14 June 1961

J. Ashbery, "Hélion (Cahiers d'art)", *Art International*, Zurich, vol. V, no. 8, 20 October 1961, pp. 91–92

J. Ashbery, "Art in Paris: Hélion" *New York Herald Tribune*, 6 June 1962

J. Ashbery, "Paris Letter: Hélion …", *Art International*, Zurich, vol. VI, no. 7, 25 September 1962, pp. 64–65

J. Ashbery, "Paris: Looking Backward", *New York Times*, 23 June 1980, p. 52

Pierre Astier, "Hélion: peintre-philosophe", *L'Actualité littéraire*, no. 19, May 1979, pp. 23–33

Georges Auclair, "Hélion ou la vicissitude de l'espoir en peinture", *La Nouvelle Revue française*, Paris, no. 277, January 1976, pp. 121–23

G. Auclair, "René Micha: Hélion", *La Nouvelle Revue française*, 1 October 1979, pp. 160–61

Giles Auty, "Hen of the North", *The Spectator*, 22 September 1990

H.B., "Hélion Abstractionist", *The Art Digest*, New York, 15 February 1943

R.B., "Hélion à la galerie des Cahiers d'Art", *Paris Presse*, 17 June 1961

Jacques Baron, "Les rencontres de Jean Hélion", *Preuves*, no. 190, December 1966, pp. 60–65

René Barotte, "Un grand peintre témoin de son temps, Jean Hélion", *L'Aurore*, 9 September 1964

Eduard Beaucamp, "Form und Folklore der Grosstadt. Ein Ausstellung des Maler Jean Hélion in Paris", *Frankfurter Allgemeine*, 24 June 1980

Leland Bell, "Jean Hélion", Paris–New York, *Arts Yearbook*, no. 3, 1959, pp. 141–142

L. Bell, "Hélion Paints the Impossible", *ARTnews*, vol. 63, no. 7, November 1964, pp. 36–37 and 66

Matteo Bellinelli, *I colori della libertà*, Lugano, Ed. Pantarei, December 1977*

Mondher Ben Milad, "À travers les galeries", *Combat*, 1 February 1971, p. 10

Jean-Pierre-Arthur Bernard, "Vanité de Mai", *Silex*, no. 29, 1er trimestre 1985, pp. 65–68

Florence B. Berryman, "Hélion's Paintings at Crosby Gallery", *Washington D.C. Star*, 28 January 1945

Anne Bertrand, "À la lumière d'Hélion", *Libération*, 5 March 1993, p. 16

Laurence Bertrand, "Le voyage en Allemagne" (remarks by artists collected in "L'offensive contre l'art moderne à Paris. 1940–1945"), *L'Écrit-Voir*, Paris, no. 1, May 1982, p. 18

L. Bertrand and Myrielle Hammer (compilers of artists' remarks), "Réponse à l'enquête 'Paroles d'artistes sur l'histoire de l'art et la critique'", *L'Écrit-Voir*, no. 5, 1984–85, pp. 65–66

Hervé Bize, "Jean Hélion. Where is a Will, There is a Way", *BAC Magazine*, no. 2, winter n.p.

Alain Bosquet, "Jean Hélion: notre folklore", *Le Quotidien de Paris*, 26 December 1985, p. 18

Georges Boudaille, "Situation de la figuration", *Les Lettres françaises*, no. 1190, 5–11 July 1967, p. 30

Roger Bouillot, "Hélion, l'aventure de la liberté", *L'Œil*, no. 352, November 1984, pp. 50–55

Maïten Bouisset, "Les dessins de Jean Hélion. Le regard accroché", *Le Matin de Paris*, 11 February 1978, p. 39

M. Bouisset, "Jean Hélion: peintre à contre-courant" *Le Matin de Paris*, 15–16 April 1978, p. 16

M. Bouisset, "Jean Hélion: 'J'ai voulu tutoyer la nature'" (propos de l'artiste), *Le Matin de Paris*, 2 June 1980, p. 28

M. Bouisset, "Jean Hélion à la conquête de la Chine", *Le Matin de Paris*, 8 October 1980, p. 21

M Bouisset, "Le monde sens dessus dessous de Jean Hélion", *Le Matin de Paris*, 28–29 May 1983, p. 27

M. Bouisset, "C'est l'heure d'aller voir Hélion", *Le Matin de Paris*, 22 June 1984, p. 34

Renée Boullier, "Jean Hélion", *La Nouvelle Revue française*, no. 170, 1 February 1967, pp. 346–47

R. Boullier, "Le Triptyque de Jean Hélion", *La Nouvelle Revue française*, no. 181, 1 January 1968, pp. 157–58

Jean Bouret, "Sept jours avec la peinture", *Les Lettres françaises*, no. 1365, 23–29 December 1970, p. 28

Camille Bourniquel, "Réponse [d'Hélion] à 'Réalisme et réalité. Enquête sur la peinture'", *Esprit*, Paris, no. 168, June 1950, pp. 937–43

Geneviève Breerette, "Jean Hélion en question. Leçon de peinture", *Le Monde*, 16–17 April 1978, p. 11

G. Breerette, "Hélion, l'humaine proportion", *Le Monde*, 29 June 1983, p. 16

G. Breerette, "Hélion, la peinture à bras-le-corps", *Le Monde*, 26 December 1984, pp. 1 and 8

G. Breerette, "Hélion, défroqué de l'abstraction", *Le Monde*, 30 October 1987, p. 26

G. Breerette," Sur la piste mystérieuse de 'Figure tombée' d'Hélion", *Le Monde*, 18 August 1995, p. 27

G. Breerette, "La 'Saga des homards', une bonne pêche des peintures de Hélion à Vannes", *Le Monde*, 27 August 1999, p. 27

Pierre-[Georges] Bruguière, "Notes sur les nus de Jean Hélion", *Cahiers d'art*, 1949, p. 289

P.[-G.] Bruguière, "Une nouvelle querelle des images", *Cahiers du Sud*, no. 305, 1er semestre 1951, pp. 119–26

P.[-G.] Bruguière, "L'homme se découvre dans une condition", *Numero*, Florence, vol. 5, no. 3, May–June 1953, pp. 16–17*

P.-G. Bruguière, "Figures de Jean Hélion", *Cahiers du Sud*, Marseille, no. 324, August 1954, pp. 247–54

P.[-G.] Bruguière, "Jean Hélion. Cinquante ans de souvenirs", in *Art & Représentation*, Paris, Éd. de la Maison des Sciences de l'Homme, 1987, pp. 134–41

P.[-G.] Bruguière, Françoise Woimant, "Hélion Kaléidoscope, 1939: linogravures et textes inédits", *Nouvelles de l'Estampe*, Paris, no. 98, May 1988, pp. 16–44

Jan Brzekowski, "Les quatre noms: Hans Arp, Ghika, Jean Hélion, S.H. Taueber Arp", *Cahiers d'art*, nos. 5–8, 1934, pp. 197–200

J. Bumpus, "Jean Hélion at 81" (interview), *Arts & Artists*, no. 225, June 1985, pp. 19–22*

Jean-Pierre Burgart, "Survivre à l'imaginaire", *Two Cities*, Paris, no. 9, autumn 1964, pp. 59–62

Scott Burton, "Cool and Concrete from the Thirties", *ARTnews*, vol. 66, no. 2, April 1967, pp. 34 and 69–71

D.C. "Jean Hélion", *Arts*, no. 115, 16 May 1947, p. 4

Pierre Cabanne, "Pourquoi Hélion peint", *Elle*, 13 February 1978

P. Cabanne, "Les années 50' d'Hélion. La magie de l'ordinaire", *Le Matin de Paris*, 2 June 1980, p. 28

P. Cabanne, "Hélion: L'art se fait en dépit de tout", *Le Matin de Paris*, 22 November 1984, p. 23

Nicolas Calas, "Hélion's Authenticity", *The Village Voice*, New York, 19 November 1964

N. Calas, "Jean Hélion", *Arts Magazine*, New York, vol. 50, no. 10, June 1976, p. 9

Colette Canty, "Quand le peintre Jean Hélion fait l'éloge du chou, du potiron, du poireau et de la botte de radis", *L'Espoir*, 12 April 1974, p. 10

Carmen de Carlos, "Jean Hélion o el enganche del arte", *ABC de las artes*, [June] 1990*

David Carrier, "American Apprentices: Thirties Abstractions", *Art in America*, New York, no. 2, February 1984, pp. 109–14

Jean-Paul Chambas, "80 ans, un âge suffisant pour être fou" (interview with the artist), *Les Nouvelles littéraires*, no. 1, December 1984, pp. 124–29

Raymond Charmet, "Hélion: reconversion", *Arts*, no. 826, 14–21 June 1961, p. 6

André Chastel, "Destin d'Hélion", *Le Monde*, 11 December 1964, p. 10

Yves Chèvrefils-Desbiolles, "'Ce qui dépasse'. Le projet scriptural de Jean Hélion", *Les Écrits d'artistes depuis 1940. Actes du colloque international, 6–9 March 2002, Paris et Caen*, Paris, IMEC, 2004, pp. 277–90

Y. Chèvrefils-Desbiolles, "Je ne cours plus depuis longtemps les galeries" (Deux lettres d'André Chastel. Une réponse de Jean Hélion), *Histoire de l'Art*, Paris, no. 53 ("Affinités: l'artiste et son public"), November 2003

W. Christlieb, "Jean Hélion à la galerie Karl Flinker", *Abendzeitung*, Munich, 22 May 1984*

Robert B. Coates, "Hélion", *New Yorker,* 27 February 1943*

Raymond Cogniat, "L'œuvre d'Hélion: une méditation", *Le Figaro,* 21 January 1971, p. 19

Michel Conil-Lacoste, "L'itinéraire d'Hélion", *Le Monde,* 22 June 1956

M. Conil-Lacoste, "Conséquence d'Hélion", *Le Monde,* 4 November 1966, p. 12

Pierre Courcelles, "André Masson, Jean Hélion", *Révolution,* no. 401, 6–12 November 1987, pp. 40–41

Jean-Paul Crespelle, "Hélion, abstrait du premier jour, revient au figuratif", *Le Journal du Dimanche,* 1 July 1956

J.-P. Crespelle, "Jean Hélion déclare: 'l'art abstrait est ma base, il est normal que je m'assoie dessus'", *Le Journal du Dimanche,* 10 June 1962

Richard Crevier, "Au-delà de l'abstraction: le pouvoir de la figure", *France nouvelle,* Paris, no. 1543, 9 June 1975, pp. 26–27

R. Crevier, "Échanges avec Jean Hélion, peintre" (interview), *France nouvelle,* 9 February 1976, pp. 25–27

R. Crevier, "Le défi de Hélion", *Révolution,* no. 15, 13–19 June 1980, p. 43

R. Crevier, "Hélion", *Eighty Magazine,* Paris, no. 3, June–July 1984, pp. 4–5

Lucien Curzi, "Les façons de voir de Jean Hélion", *L'Humanité,* 8 January 1971, p. 13

P.D., "Hélion et la traversée de l'abstraction", *Le Quotidien de Paris,* 2 July 1992, p. 18

Philippe Dagen, "Saisir Hélion", *Le Quotidien de Paris,* 19 November 1984, p. 35

P. Dagen, "À l'Isle-sur-la-Sorgue, Hélion le Grand", *Le Monde,* 10 August 1988, p. 9

P. Dagen, "Figures construites. De l'abstraction à la représentation: l'itinéraire paradoxal de Jean Hélion", *Le Monde,* 9 June 1992, p. 11

P. Dagen, "La citrouille et le vieux képi", *Le Monde,* 25 December 1992, p. 9

P. Dagen, "La chronique du xxᵉ siècle dans les tableaux de Jean Hélion", *Le Monde,* 28 December 1996

Bernard Dahan, "De tu à vous", *Les Amis de Valentin Brû,* Levallois-Perret, nos. 24–25 ("Raymond Queneau et la peinture"), November 1983, pp. 13–16

B. Dahan, "Clefs pour la V …", *Sixième Liasse,* no. 6, April 1984, pp. 29–35

Philippe Dejean, "Jean Hélion à la sortie du purgatoire", *Le Quotidien de Paris,* 22 May 1980

Christian Derouet, "Le Nouveau Réalisme de Fernand Léger: la modernité à contre pied", Paris, *Cahiers du Musée national d'art moderne,* no. 19–20, June 1987, pp. 136–45

Pierre Descargues, "Un des premiers partisans de Gary Davis est un peintre", *Arts,* no. 197, 14–20 January 1949, p. 1

P. Descargues, "Jean Hélion", *Arts,* no. 199, 28 January–3 February 1949, p. 4

P. Descargues, "La sopravvivenza della realtà", *Base,* no. 3, November–December 1949, pp. 2 and 6

P. Descargues, "Jean Hélion", *Les Lettres françaises,* no. 492, 26 November–3 December 1953, p. 6

P. Descargues, (enquête sur "L'exposition à faire"), Jean Hélion: "Une exposition Poussin", *Les Lettres françaises,* no. 581, 18–24 August 1955, p. 6 (the full text of this *enquête* was published in the August and September issues of the periodical).

P. Descargues, "Les amours de Jean Hélion", *La Tribune de Lausanne,* 15 July 1962

P. Descargues, "L'avantage des biographies", *Les Lettres françaises,* no. 1371, 3–9 February 1971, p. 30

John Devoluy, "Jean Hélion biographies", *New York Herald Tribune,* 16 May 1947

Howard Devree, "Hélion", *New York Times,* March 1940

H. Devree, "Seeking New Light on Abstraction Was Art", *The New York Times,* 23 July 1944

Gaston Diehl, "La solitude d'Hélion en 1950", *Nouvelles de France,* no. 76, June 1980, pp. 27–28*

Robert Droguet, "Découverte d'Hélion", *Résonances. Le Spectateur lyonnais,* July 1969, pp. 38–39

André Du Bouchet, "Visage altéré de la peinture de Jean Hélion", *Cahiers d'Art,* Paris, 1956–1957, pp. 371–378

A. Du Bouchet, "La peinture de Jean Hélion", *Mercure de France,* no. 1138, June 1958, pp. 240–243 // Exh. cat. *Hélion, cent tableaux, 1928–1970,* Grand Palais, Paris, 1970–71, pp. 64–65 (reworked extracts from "Visage altéré de la peinture de Jean Hélion", *Cahiers d'art,* Paris, 31–32ᵉ année, 1956–57, pp. 371–78)

Charles Duits, "Jean Hélion, l'objet dans le jardin", *Critique,* Paris, no. 145, June 1959, pp. 515–23

Jean-Marie Dunoyer, "Jean Hélion et les autres ruses de l'abstraction", *Le Monde,* 31 May 1975, p. 30

J.-M. Dunoyer, "Les vraies valeurs", *Le Monde,* 5–6 February 1978, p. 16

J.-M. Dunoyer, "Jean Hélion à la BN. Gravures et Carnets", *Le Monde,* 26 October 1988, p. 14

Marie-Pierre Dupuy, "Jean Hélion au musée ou le voyage d'un artiste peintre, de l'abstrait au figuratif", *Ouest-France,* 7 January 1970

Jean Duvignaud, "L'homme d'Hélion", *Chroniques de l'Art vivant,* Paris, no. 10, April 1970, pp. 26–27

C.E., "Hélion. Renou et Colle", *Combat,* 14 May 1947

John Elderfield, "Geometric Abstract Painting and Paris in the Thirties", *Art Forum,* New York, June 1970, pp. 70–75

J. Elderfield, "American Geometric Abstraction in the Late Thirties", *Art Forum,* December 1972, pp. 35–42

Patrick d'Elme, "Aux Sables-d'Olonne: Jean Hélion", *La Galerie des Arts,* no. 85, 1 February 1970, p. 16

P. d'Elme, "Jean Hélion. La peinture est une question", *Politique-Hebdo,* no. 11, 17 December 1970, pp. 16–17

P. d'Elme, "Hélion. Cette réalité qu'il faut regarder et peindre en face…" (propos de l'artiste), *Opus international,* no. 47, November 1973, pp. 25–27 (reprinted in *Peinture et politique,* Paris, Mame, 1974)

Charles Estienne, "Hélion ou la vérité à contre-fil", *Les Lettres françaises,* no. 1156, 10–16 November 1966, p. 31

Myfanwy Evans, "Hélion To-Day: a Personal Comment", *Axis,* no. 4, November 1935, pp. 4–9 (see also under the name Piper).

Gladys C. Fabre, "Paris. Jean Hélion", *Beaux-Arts Magazine,* no. 19, December 1984, pp. 90–91

L.P. Favre, "Hélion ou la vie quotidienne", *Combat,* 7 December 1953, p. 7

André Fermigier, "Hélion dans les années 50. L'énuméré des choses", *Le Monde,* 1–2 July 1980, pp. 1 and 15

Jean-Louis Ferrier, "Hélion, les années cinquante", *Le Point,* no. 400, 19–25 May 1980, p. 31

J.-L. Ferrier, "L'abstrait repenti", *Le Point,* no. 638, 10 December 1984, p. 145

Catherine Flohic, "Hélion", *Eighty Magazine,* no. 3, June–July 1984, pp. 2–3

Simone Frigerio, "Hélion: peintures 1929–1939", *Aujourd'hui,* Boulogne-sur-Seine, no. 37, June 1962, pp. 20–23

Michele Fueco, "Jean Hélion: pittore tra astrazione e figurazione", *Il Giornale di Modena,* 12 April 1981

Max Fullenbaum, "La liberté de Jean Hélion", *Univers des arts,* Paris, no. 1, November 1994, pp. 64–67

Julián Gállego, "Hélion y Léger", *Goya,* April 1971

Gérald Gassiot-Talabot, "Tout art est minoritaire", *Opus international,* no. 8, October 1968, pp. 39–40

G. Gassiot-Talabot, "Hélion", *Opus international,* no. 21, December 1970, p. 12

G. Gassiot-Talabot, "Les métamorphoses de Jean Hélion", *Les Annales Conferencia,* Paris, February 1971, pp. 47–50

Jean-Charles Gateau, "Il y a une femme coupée en deux par la fenêtre", *Silex,* no. 29, 1ᵉʳ trimestre 1985, pp. 79–80

Pierre Gaudibert, "Actualité d'Hélion" (interview with J.-P.-A. Bernard), *Silex,* no. 29, 1ᵉʳ trimestre 1985, pp. 82–86

Hervé Gauville, "La force d'Hélion", *Libération,* 17 August 1988, p. 26

Emily Genauer, "Two Brushes – Points of View, *New York World Telegram,* 10 March 1945

E. Genauer, "Jean Hélion Art Shown by Museum", *New York Herald Tribune,* 3 November 1964

Michel Georges-Michel, "Les deux évasions de Jean Hélion", *France-Amérique,* 25 February 1945

M. Georges-Michel, "Les deux évasions de Jean Hélion », *Aux Écoutes,* Paris, 15 June 1962

Alain Germoz, "Jean Hélion dans sa propre lumière", *Spécial,* 6 December 1967, pp. 69–70

Jo Gibbs, "Hélion Cannot Escape the Human Values", *The Art Digest,* New York, 15 March 1945

Michael Gibson, "Hélion", *Herald Tribune,* 21–22 June 1975

M. Gibson, "[Hélion]", *Herald Tribune,* 1 March 1978

Mark Glazebrook, "Jean Hélion", *Modern Painters,* vol. 11, no. 2, summer 1998, pp. 108–09

Virgilio Guzzi, "Manierismo di Hélion", *Tempo,* 24 May 1968*

Paul Haesaerts, "Nouvelles acquisitions au Musée de Liège", *Les Arts plastiques,* Bruxelles, no. 4, September–October 1950, pp. 250–74 (Hélion: p. 268)

Otto Hahn, "Jean Hélion, le peintre aux trois manières", *L'Express,* no. 981, 27 April–3 May 1970, p. 93

O. Hahn, "Hélion", *L'Express,* 11–17 January 1971, p. 16

Myrielle Hammer see L. Bertrand, 1984–85

Elizabeth Hayt-Atkins, "Jean Hélion (Rachel Adler)", *ARTnews,* vol. 88, no. 6, summer 1989, pp. 166 and 168

Katharina Hegewisch, "Ein Maler, der die Gegensätze des Jahrhunderts zu vermitteln suchte", *Frankfurter Allgemeine,* 27 September 1984, p. 27

K. Hegewisch, "Jean Hélion", *Das Kunstwerk,* Baden-Baden, vol. 37, no. 6, December 1984, pp. 66 and 77

Armelle Héliot, "Hélion, l'art et les manières", *Le Quotidien de Paris,* 9 August 1988, p. 17

Luce Hoctin see A. Jouffroy, 1955

Dan Hofstadter, "The Art World, Jean Hélion", *The New Yorker,* 6 January 1986*

France Huser, "Les objets de la vie", *Le Nouvel Observateur,* 27 May–2 June 1983, p. 14

A. J., "Hélion", *Arts,* 13–19 June 1956

Anatole Jakovski, *Arp, Calder, Hélion, Miró, Pevsner, Seligmann: six essais* (pamphlet organized by Hans Arp), Paris, Jacques Povolozky [1933], pp. 18–24 // Exh. cat. *Hélion. Cent tableaux 1928–1970,* Grand Palais, Paris, 1970–71, p. 21

A. Jakovski, "Inscriptions under Pictures" (October 1934), *Axis,* Londres, no. 1, January 1935, pp. 14–20

A. Jakovski, "La situation actuelle de la peinture", *Renouveau esthétique,* Paris, no. 1, 1936*

A. Jakovski, "L'imprevedibile Hélion", *Arte Rama,* Milan, February 1971, pp. 14–15

A. Jakovski, "Belle-Île-en-mer", *Nouvelles de France,* no. 18, September 1977, pp. 31–34*

Merlin Ingli James, "Jean Hélion at Louis Carré", *The Burlington Magazine,* vol. CXXIX, no. 1014, September 1987, pp. 616–17

M.I. James, "[Hélion at the Tate Gallery, Liverpool]", *The Burlington Magazine,* vol. CXXXII, no. 1051, October 1990, pp. 731–32

Raoul Jean-Moulin, "Les recherches et les contradictions de Jean Hélion", *Les Lettres françaises,* no. 1365, 23–29 December 1970, pp. 23–24

Matthew Josephson, "Jean Hélion: The Return from Abstract Art", *Minnesota Review,* vol. I, no. 3, April 1961, pp. 341–55

Alain Jouffroy, Jean-José Marchand, Luce Hoctin [réponse d'Hélion à une enquête sur l'enseignement des Beaux-Arts]: "L'École est un lieu de rencontre", *Arts spectacles,* no. 546, 14–20 December 1955, pp. 12–14

A. Jouffroy, "Mondrian un figuratif devenu abstrait vu par Hélion un abstrait devenu figuratif" (interview with the artist), *Arts,* no. 611, 20–26 March 1957, p. 13

A. Jouffroy, "Jean Hélion, peintre abstrait devenu figuratif" (interview with the artist), *Arts,* Paris, no. 662, 19–25 March 1958, p. 15

A. Jouffroy, "Une révision moderne du sacré", *XXᵉ Siècle,* no. 24, December 1964, pp. 89–98

A. Jouffroy, "Réponse à l'enquête sur l'expérience", *Mise en page,* Paris, no. 1, May 1972, pp. 22–23*

A. Jouffroy, "Jean Hélion: l'inacceptable", *XXᵉ Siècle,* no. 45, December 1975, pp. 146–47

Klaus Jürgen-Fischer, "Der gebrochene Stil", *Das Kunstwerk,* vol. 40, no. 1, February 1987, pp. 5–39*

J. K., "Neat Contrasts in Works of Jean Hélion, Pierre Daura", *New York Journal Americain,* 24 May 1942

Gyorgy Kepes, "Jean Hélion. Objects for a Painter", in *The Man-Made Object,* New York, George Braziller, 1966, pp. 148–71

Daniel Klébaner, "Notes sur Jean Hélion", *Rémanences,* no. 1, March 1993, pp. 56–60

Hilton Kramer, "Hélion – Returning from the Absolute", *The New York Times,* 26 March 1967

H. Kramer, "Jean Hélion's Uncertain Shift to Representation", *The New York Times,* 25 April 1976

H. Kramer, "Revisiting Hélion", *Art and Antiques,* New York, vol. 19, no. 6, June 1996, pp. 88–89*

René Lacôte, "Idées et problèmes d'aujourd'hui" (débat "Réalisme et réalité" en réponse au numéro de June 1950 de la revue *Esprit*), *Arts de France,* Paris, no. 31, October 1950, pp. 65–73 (Hélion: p. 70)

Bernard Lamarche-Vadel, "Jean Hélion. La crise de la peinture", *Art Press,* Paris, July–August 1975, p. 21

Luc Lang, "Jean Hélion: Unfashionable Figuration", *Art International,* no. 4, autumn 1988, pp. 27–32

Susan C. Larsen, "Going Abstract in the '30s" (interview with Ilya Bolotowsky), *Art in America,* New York, September–October 1976, pp. 71–79

Gilbert Lascault, "Mannequinerie d'or et saga des homards", *Silex,* no. 29, 1ᵉʳ trimestre 1985, pp. 20–27

François Lauris, "Hélion dans la rue. Il était abstrait, il a redécouvert l'homme en le regardant vivre", *Arts Loisirs,* Paris, no. 57, 26 October–2 November 1966, p. 9

Sylvie Lecoq-Ramond, "Jean Hélion, peintre de la réalité: à propos des sources picturales et littéraires de *L'Allumeur* (1944)", *La Revue du Louvre et des musées de France,* Paris, June 1997, pp. 76–84

Jacques Leenhardt, "Le retour de la réalité", *Le Journal de Genève*, 16 January 1971

Dominique Le Reun, "Les symphonies pour citrouilles et poireaux de Jean Hélion" (remarks by the artist), *Télérama*, Paris, no. 1474, 12–18 April 1978, pp. 19–21

Jean-Jacques Lerrant, "Jean Hélion", *Le Progrès*, Lyon, 21 June 1969

Jean-Jacques Lévêque, "Hélion ou le remords du réel", *Arts*, no. 872, 6–12 June 1962, p. 10

J.-J. Lévêque, "Hélion", *La Nouvelle Revue française*, no. 147, March 1965, pp. 551–52

J.-J. Lévêque, "Hélion le voyant", *La Galerie des Arts*, no. 71, 15 May 1969, pp. 13–15

J.-J. Lévêque, "Hélion et l'absolu", *Les Nouvelles littéraires*, 18 February 1970, p. 10

J.-J. Lévêque, "Hélion, la fascination du réel", *Le Nouveau Journal*, Paris, 19 December 1970

J.-J. Lévêque, "Hélion", *La Quinzaine littéraire*, 1–15 February 1971, p. 14

J.-J. Lévêque, "Coup de chapeau à Jean Hélion", *Cimaise*, Paris, no. 122, January–April 1975, pp. 10–21 (offprint from the exh. cat. "Jean Hélion, cinquante ans de peinture 1925–1975", galerie Karl Flinker, Paris, May–June 1975)

J.-J. Lévêque, "Hélion, pour ne pas mourir idiot", *Les Nouvelles littéraires*, 10–17 March 1977, p. 16

J.-J. Lévêque, "L'œil fertile. L'atelier d'Hélion", *Les Nouvelles littéraires*, no. 2740, 5–12 June 1980, p. 7

Stanley Lewis, "Realism is Alive and Well and Living in Paris", *ARTnews*, vol. 70, no. 4, summer 1971, pp. 34–37 and 68

Charlotte Lichtblau, "Abstract Qualities of Realism", *Enquirer*, 15 November 1964*

Christian Limousin, "Jean Hélion ou l'esprit de suite", *Silex*, no. 29, 1er trimestre 1985, pp. 87–93

Aline B. Louchheim, "Hélion in Transition", *ARTnews*, vol. XLIV, no. 3, 15–31 March 1945, p. 18

Pierre Mabille, "Jean Hélion et l'homme quotidien" (20 February 1949), *Éléments*, Paris, no. 1, January 1951, pp. 79–85 // *Conscience lumineuse, conscience picturale*, Paris, Éd. José Corti, 1989, pp. 177–96 // extracts in exh. cat. *Hélion. Cent tableaux…*, Grand Palais, 1970–71, Paris, pp. 57–58

Henry McBride, "Jean Hélion", *The New York Sun*, 13 January 1934, p. 9*

H. McBride, "Abstractions by Jean Hélion", *The New York Sun*, 11 April 1936, p. 32

H. McBride, "Jean Hélion's Paintings", *The New York Sun*, 4 January 1938*

H. McBride, "Jean Hélion", *The New York Sun*, 30 March 1940

H. McBride, "Jean Hélion", *New York Herald Tribune*, 31 March 1940

Robert Mahoney, "The Last Work at Rachel Adler", *Arts Magazine*, vol. 66, no. 5, January 1992

Anne Manson, enquête: "10 peintres répondent à la question: 'Pourquoi l'automobile est-elle absente de vos œuvres ?'" ("Hélion: un objet à répétition"), *Arts*, no. 793, 26 October–1 November 1960, p. 10

Jean Marcenac, "L'entretien dans l'atelier: Fernand Léger et Jean Hélion", *Les Lettres françaises*, Paris, no. 382, 13–20 November 1952, p. 5

Jean-José Marchand *see* A. Jouffroy, 1955

Louis-Léon Martin, "Le Salon des indépendants", *Le Crapouillot*, February 1928

Giorgio Mascherpa, "Diventò pittore per guarire della poesia", *Gente*, 9 April 1969*

Georges Mauclair, "Hélion ou les vicissitudes de l'espoir en peinture", *La Nouvelle Revue française*, January 1976, pp. 121–23

Pierre Mazars, "Hélion, le Queneau de la peinture", *Le Figaro littéraire*, no. 1283, 21–27 December 1970, p. 36

P. Mazars, "Hélion: la course d'un peintre solitaire", *Le Figaro*, 27 January 1978, p. 30

Robert Melville, "Proto-Pop", *New Statesman*, London, 18 June 1965, p. 977

R. Melville, "The Victimized Figure", *Architectural Review*, Londres, vol. 138, no. 823, September 1965, pp. 201–03

René Micha, "La quête d'Hélion", *Chroniques de l'Art vivant*, Paris, no. 57, 1 May–15 June 1975, pp. 7–9

R. Micha, "Jean Hélion: les années cinquante", *Les Cahiers obliques*, Nyons, no. 2, 1er trimestre 1980, pp. 29–33

R. Micha, "Jean Hélion: la nature et l'atelier", *Art International*, vol. 24, nos. 1–2, September–October 1980, pp. 191–94

R. Micha, "Le Hélion des années cinquante", + *ou − 0*, Genval-Lac (Belgium), no. 31, December 1980, p. 12

R. Micha, "Jean Hélion [80th Birthday]", *Art International*, vol. 27, no. 4, September–November 1984, pp. 48–49

R. Micha, "Hélion boucle la boucle", *Colóquio Artes*, Lisbon, vol. 28, no. 75, December 1987, pp. 18–23

Jacques Michel, "L'itinéraire de Jean Hélion", *Le Monde*, 15 June 1962, p. 13

J. Michel, "Le dragon de Jean Hélion", *Le Monde*, 3 November 1967, p. 14

J. Michel, "Hélion et ses desseins", *Le Monde*, 16 December 1970, p. 19 (with an interview with the artist: "Peindre, c'est trouver au-dehors ce que l'on porte en soi …")

J. Michel, "Les deux vérités de Jean Hélion", *Le Monde*, 19 June 1975, p. 17

J. Michel, "Le peintre au marché", *Le Monde*, 30 March 1977, p. 22

J. Michel, "Desseins au pastel de Jean Hélion", *Le Monde*, 10 February 1978, p. 21

J. Michel, "Hélion avant et Hélion après", *Le Monde*, 28 April 1979

Anne Mœglin-Delcroix, "Jean Hélion. Les années d'apprentissage (*Carnets 1929–1946*)", *Revue de la Bibliothèque nationale*, no. 1, September 1981, pp. 37–45

A. Mœglin-Delcroix, "Jean Hélion: la maîtrise", *Revue de la Bibliothèque nationale*, no. 7, March 1983, pp. 27–38

A. Mœglin-Delcroix, "Jean Hélion. Carnets, dessins et desseins", *Libération*, 29 October 1987, pp. 38–39

A. Mœglin-Delcroix, "Lux æsthetica (Hélion)", *Revue d'Esthétique*, Paris, no. 16, 1989, pp. 97–104

A. Mœglin-Delcroix, "Y a-t-il un dilemme abstraction/figuration", *Critique*, Paris, no. 510, November 1989, pp. 819–33

Bernard Moninot, "Sur lui la porte ne s'est jamais refermée" (remarks complied by Brigitte Paulino-Neto), *Libération*, 29 October 1987, p. 39

Duilio Morosini, "Jean Hélion: pittore allo sbaraglio", *Paese Sera*, 31 May 1968, p. 3

George L.K. Morris, "Interview with Jean Hélion", *Partisan Review*, New York, vol. IV, no. 5 [April 1938], p. 33–39

Edwin Mullins, "Age of Craftsmen", *The Sunday Telegraph*, 6 June 1965*

Bernard Murphy, "Jean Hélion", *News-Sentinel*, 23 March 1967, p. 9

Harry J. Naar, "A Natural Thing: Jean Hélion's Representational Paintings", *Arts Magazine*, vol. 58, no. 8, April 1984, pp. 104–06

Bernard Noël, "Jean Hélion: le raccourci", *XXe Siècle*, Paris, no. 51, December 1978, pp. 137–38

B. Noël, "Hélion-Kaléidoscope, 1939", *Journal du regard*, Paris, P.O.L., 1988*

René de Obaldia, "Les feux de Bigeonnette", *Silex*, 1er trimestre 1985, pp. 28–32

Heinz Ohff, "Der fehlende Seziertisch. A[usstellun]g Jean Hélion in der Galerie Poll", *Der Tagesspiegel*, 6 February 1980

Wolfgang Paalen, "*They Shall not Have Me*, by Jean Hélion", *Dyn*, Mexico, December 1943, n. p.

André Parinaud, Enquête "Où en est l'abstraction ?" (interview with the artist), *Arts*, no. 883, 26 September–2 October 1962, p. 15

A. Parinaud, "Hélion ou le lyrisme", *Tonus*, Paris, 28 May 1969, n. p.

Brigitte Paulino-Neto, "Lâchez l'Hélion et sauvez la peinture", *Libération*, 25 December 1984, p. 25 (*see also* B. Moninot)

Jérôme Peignot, "Hélion. Un rébus", *Opus International*, no. 21, December 1970, pp. 15–17

Jed Perl, "Hélion. The Last Judgment of Things", in *Paris without End. On French Art since World War I*, San Francisco, North Point Press, 1988, pp. 104–21

J. Perl, "Jean Hélion and the Evolution of Style", *Vogue America*, March 1988, vol. 6, pp. 48–56*

J. Perl, "Obituaries and Retrospectives", *The New Criterion*, New York, vol. 6, no. 9, May 1988

J. Perl, "Hélion's Optimism", *The New Criterion*, vol. 10, no. 2, October 1991*

J. Perl, "The Saint-Germain Story", *Modern Painters*, London, summer 1993, pp. 34–37

J. Perl, "Psycho Show", *Modern Painters*, autumn 1995, pp. 35–37

Philippe Piguet, "Jean Hélion, un monde peuplé d'images", *L'Œil*, Lausanne, no. 527, June 2001, p. 100

P. Piguet, "La réalité saisit par son trou", *Cimaise*, nos. 218–19, June–August 1992, pp. 101–04

Myfanwy (Evans) Piper, "[Hélion]", *Harper's Bazar*, Londres, summer 1962

Hans Platschek, "Jean Hélion", *Tendenzen*, no. 119, May–June 1978

Gilles Plazy, "Hélion. La peinture et la vie", *Le Quotidien de Paris*, 26 May 1975, p. 15

G. Plazy, "Les marchés d'Hélion", *Le Quotidien de Paris*, 25 April 1977, p. 11

Marcelin Pleynet, "Jean Hélion" dans "Lettre de Paris", *Art International*, vol. XV/2, 20 February 1971, pp. 49–51

François Pluchart, "Hélion a-t-il une importance comparable à celle de Léger?", *Combat*, 5 July 1965, p. 7

F. Pluchart, "Hélion ou la réalité inaccessible", *Combat*, 28 December 1965, p. 7

F. Pluchart, "L'art concret de Carlsund, Doesbourg, Hélion et Tutundjian a-t-il eu raison du surréalisme?", *Combat*, 28 February 1966, p. 9

F. Pluchart, "La synthèse de Hélion", *Combat*, 30 October 1967, p. 11

F. Pluchart, "L'indécence d'aimer" (dialogue with the artist), *ArTitudes*, St-Jeannet, nos. 21–23, April–June 1975, pp. 73–80

[F. Pluchart], "Hélion, l'Amérique" (interview), *L'Art vivant*, Paris, July–August 1984, pp. 58–61

Francis Ponge, "Hélion", *Cahiers d'art*, Paris, 1949, pp. 281–88 // Exh. cat. *Jean Hélion. Dix-neuf tableaux, 1937–1966 …*, Paris, galerie du Dragon, 1966, n. p. // Exh. cat. *Hélion, cent tableaux 1928–1970*, Grand Palais, Paris, 1970–71, pp. 47–48 // *Le Grand Recueil: Lyres*, Paris, Gallimard, 1961, pp. 65–70 // *Œuvres complètes*, vol. II, Paris, Gallimard, coll. "Bibliothèque de la Pléiade", 2002, pp. 575–78

Stuart Preston, "Jean Hélion's Works Cover 1928–1964", *The New York Times*, 3 November 1964*

Laurence Pythoud, "Hommage à Jean Hélion", *L'Œil*, no. 444, September 1992, pp. 103–04

Raymond Queneau, "Jean Hélion aux Cahiers d'Art", *La Nouvelle Revue française*, no. 271, April 1936, p. 627 // Exh. cat. *Jean Hélion, peintures 1929–1939*, galerie Louis Carré, Paris, 6 June–13 July 1962, n. p. // Exh. cat. *Hélion. Cent tableaux 1928–1970*, Grand Palais, Paris, 1970–71, p. 34

M.R., "Hélion Paints People", *The Art Digest*, New York, vol. 18, no. 12, 15 March 1944, p. 9

Robert Radford, "Journal d'un peintre, vol. 1, carnets 1929–1962, vol. 2, carnets 1963–1984'", *The Burlington Magazine*, vol. CXXXVI, no. 1100, November 1994, pp. 778–79

Carter Ratcliff, "Post-Abstract Hélion: Style as Meaning", *Art in America*, September–October 1976, pp. 93–96

Herbert Read, "Jean Hélion", *Axis*, London, no. 4, November 1935, pp. 3–4

H. Read, "Jean Hélion", in *A Coat of Many Colours* [1945], London, Faber and Faber, 1952, pp. 244–47

Jean-Dominique Rey, "Jean Hélion", *Jardin des Arts*, no. 123, February 1965, pp. 74–75

J.-D. Rey, "Jean Hélion", *Jardin des Arts*, no. 146, January 1967, pp. 72–73

J.-D. Rey, "Jean Hélion ou le dialogue retrouvé", *Jardin des Arts*, no. 195, February 1971, pp. 14–21

Maurice Rheims, "Jean Hélion: les figures de la modernité", *Le Figaro littéraire*, 9 June 1992, p. 8

Paul-Louis Rinuy, "*À perte de vue*, suivi de *Choses revues* et *Lettres d'Amérique* …", *Revue de l'Art*, no. 116, 1997, pp. 113–14

Claude Rivière, "Un nouveau monde? … Non, un rappel d'antan", *Combat*, 11 November 1964, p. 7

Bryan Robertson, "How to Be Flexible and Consistent too", *The Spectator*, 11 June 1965*

B. Robertson, "Hélion", *Manchester Guardian*, September 1990*

B. Robertson, "The Modernity of Bellini", *Modern Painters*, autumn 1995, pp. 26–29

Edouard Roditi, on the theme "Art Evens in Review", *View*, vol. 2, summer 1944, p. 58

Jean Rollin, "Jean Hélion, peintre du réel", *L'Humanité*, 8 January 1971, p. 12

Michel Roquebert, "Hélion, ou comment ne plus être abstrait", *La Dépêche du Midi*, 6 December 1965

Deborah Rosenthal, "Jean Hélion at Rachel Adler", *Art in America*, December 1985, pp. 132–33

D. Rosenthal, "Hélion", *Art and Antiques*, New York, January 1992, vol. 9, p. 86

Madeleine Rousseau, "Hélion", *Le Musée vivant*, nos. 23–24, 3e–4e trimestres 1964, p. 522

Pierre Rouve, "Hélion", *The Arts Review*, Londonn, May–June 1965, pp. 5–7

John Russell, "Abstraction Stays in the Balance", *The Sunday Times*, 13 June 1965, p. 9

Joseph Rykwert, "Hélion et Giacometti", *Domus*, September 1965*

André Salmon, [Le Salon d'automne], *Revue de France*, 1 December 1928

A. Salmon, "Hélion", *Journal de l'amateur d'art*, Paris, no. 121, 10 December 1953, p. 11

Wolfgang Sauré, "Jean Hélion. Retrospektive", *Die Kunst und das schöne Heim*, Munich, 6 June 1975*

W. Sauré, "Jean Hélion", *Die Weltkunst*, Munich, 15 February 1978*

W. Sauré, "Einheit von Abstraktion und Gegenständlichkeit …", *Die Kunst*, no. 2, February 1985, pp. 118–23*

Martica Sawin, "Jean Hélion: the Recent Decades", *Arts Magazine*, vol. 56, no. 3, November 1981, pp. 72–76

Merle S. Schipper, "Jean Hélion: The Abstract Decade", *Art in America*, September–October 1976, pp. 88–92

M.S. Schipper, "Jean Hélion", in *Abstract Art in America, 1927–1943*, New York, Abrams, 1983*

Pierre Schneider, "Jean Hélion", *Paris Review,* Paris/New York, no. 20, winter 1958–59, pp. 58–65

P. Schneider, "L'envers du figuratif", *L'Express,* no. 574, 14–20 June 1962, pp. 25–26

P. Schneider, "Art News from Paris", *ARTnews,* vol. 61, no. 6, October 1962, pp. 48 and 55

Summer Sinclair, "Jean Hélion's Forest of Symbols", *New York Herald Tribune,* 8 November 1966

Werner Spies, "Hélion oder die Rückkehr zum Baum", *Frankfurter Allgemeine Zeitung,* 25 July 1975

Gail Stavitsky, "Jean Hélion" (interview, 18 June 1986), in Gail Stavitsky, "The A.E. Gallatin Collection: An Early Adventure in Modern Art", *Bulletin,* Philadelphia Museum of Art, 1994, p. 22*

David Sylvester, "Portrait of the Artist no. 59: Jean Hélion", *Art News and Review,* London, vol. III, no. 7, 5 May 1951, pp. 1 and 5

Jean-Marie Tasset, "Hélion ou la réalité rêvée", *Le Figaro,* 16 May 1974, p. 22

J.-M. Tasset, "Hélion, à chacun sa réalité", *Le Figaro,* 3 November 1995

Werner Thuswaldner, "Zeuge und Mitgestalter einer grossen Zeit", *Salzburger Nachrichten,* 21 April 1981

Horace Titus, "Jean Hélion: the Complete Circle", *Esquire,* vol. XLVII, no. 1, January 1957, pp. 95, 30 and 132

Michel Tournier, "L'énigme Hélion. De l'abstrait au figuratif: l'itinéraire de Jean Hélion", *Le Point,* Paris, no. 141, 2 June 1975, p. 128 // Expanded version in exh. cat. *Jean Hélion. Dessins récents,* Les Sables-d'Olonne, 1977, n. p.

M. Tournier, "Hélion. Œuvres récentes", *Cimaise,* Paris, no. 153–54, October–November 1981, p. 7

M. Tournier, "Les entrailles roses de la citrouille", *Le Nouvel Observateur,* 30 November 1984, p. 96

Lorenza Trucchi, "Hélion al Fante di Spade", *Momento Sera,* 25 May 1968*

René Tusses, "La nature d'Hélion", *L'Humanité,* 2 February 1985, p. 8

G.V., "Hélion", *Il Messagerio,* 18 May 1968*

Dora Vallier, "Éléments pour une lecture", *Cimaise,* Paris, nos. 138–39, October–December 1978, pp. 53–57

Luc Vezin, "Le peintre Jean Hélion dévoile les mystères de la chambre jaune", *Info matin,* 1 April 1994

Cesare Vivaldi, "La chimera del reale nella pittura di Hélion", *Avanti,* 26 May 1968*

Patrick Waldberg, "La ville rêvée & la ville vécue", *XXᵉ Siècle,* Paris, no. 26, 1966, pp. 49–59 (Hélion: pp. 56 and 58)

Waldemar–George, "Hélion", *Le Peintre,* 1ᵉ July 1956*

Jeanine Warnod, "Hélion: le parcours d'un pionnier", *Le Figaro,* 12 December 1984, p. 25

J. Warnod, "France – Danemark: chassé-croisé de peintres et d'orfèvres", *Le Figaro,* 15 September 1987, p. 39

Pierre Wat, "Jean Hélion, après l'abstraction", *Beaux-Arts Magazine,* no. 191, April 2000, p. 36

Jane Watson, "New Hélion Exhibit Impressive", *Washington D.C. Post,* 14 January 1945

Gerhard Weber, "Maler Hélion", *Artis,* Constance/Berne, no. 11, November 1975, p. 21*

Gilbert A. Wehr, "Mr Hélion's Exhibit", *Baltimore M.D. Evening Sun,* 26 February 1945

Herta Wescher, "New York in Paris", *Axis,* London, no. 6, summer 1936, pp. 27–29

Carol Wharton, "Hélion", *Baltimore M.D. Morning Sun,* 25 February 1945*

Sheldon Williams, "Early Pop", *New York Herald Tribune,* 31 March 1964*

S. Williams, "Hélion – the Double Artist", *Contemporary Review,* vol. 206, May 1965, pp. 257–61

S. Williams, "Hélion Retrospective: from Abstract to Realist", *New York Herald Tribune,* 1 June 1965*

S. Williams, "Jean Hélion Now", *Studio international,* vol. 169, no. 866, June 1965, pp. 268–69

S. Williams, "Hélion – Before and After", *The Guardian,* 3 June 1965, p. 6

Sara Wilson, "Hélion, 'Distracted' French Abstractionist, Views Art", *Baltimore M.D. Evening Sun,* 19 February 1945

Françoise Woimant *see* Pierre-Georges Bruguière, 1988

F. Woimant, "Portraits et carnets", *Nouvelles de l'Estampe,* no. 122, April–June 1992, pp. 30–31

S. John Woods, "Time to Forget Ourselves", *Axis,* London, no. 6, summer 1936, pp. 19–21

Max Wykes-Joyce, "Hélion", *Arts Review,* no. 39, 25 September 1987, p. 636

John Xceron, "Jean Hélion", in "Who's Who Abroad", *Chicago Tribune* (European edn), 5 June 1929, p. 4

Christian Zervos, "Position actuelle de Jean Hélion", *Cahiers d'art,* Paris, 1951, pp. 171–180

Filmography

One Artist at Work
directed and produced by Thomas Bouchard, New York, 1946, 28 min. With Lionel Abel, Thomas Bouchard, Jean Hélion, Pegeen Guggenheim

La Palette de Jean Hélion
directed by Frédéric Czarnès, O.R.T.F.

Les Chemins de Jean Hélion
directed by Philippe Joulin, 35 min. Presented in the series "Banc d'essai", broadcast by Manuel Rainoird, 7 January 1971, Paris, O.R.T.F. With Georges Auclair, Michel Lonsdale and Manuel Rainoird

Parti de New York – Partie de New York – New York Party
directed by Daniel Abadie (interview with the artist), Bigeonnette, July 1976, 52 min. Production by Service audiovisuel du Centre Pompidou

I colori della libertà
directed by Matteo Bellinelli, 28 min. Italian-Swiss television, Lugano, 24 June 1977

L'Homme en question: Hélion
directed by Pierre-André Boutang et Philippe Collin, Paris, FR3, 16 April 1978

Jean Hélion. Portraits d'artistes.
directed by Liliane Thorn-Petit. Luxembourg television, 11 November 1979

L'Atelier de Jean Hélion
directed by Patrick Barberis for the Ministère des Affaires étrangères (département des Échanges culturels), 16 min 32 s. Production: Image-Information, Paris, 1981

Jean Hélion. Petits ronds … potirons
directed by Charles Chaboud-Davidis, 1986. With the Centre national des Arts plastiques, the Musée-Galerie de la S.E.I.T.A. and Nadine Muste.

Jean Hélion, l'inclassable
directed by Paul Bonnetain and Pierre Lepetit, 26 min. Production: Interfilm (Paris), May–June 1987

Jean Hélion
directed by Mme Haas, 3 min.

The presence of an asterisk indicates that the catalogue could not be consulted

1932

Jean Hélion, Paris, Galerie Pierre, June–July

1934

Jean Hélion, New York, John Becker Gallery, 9–31 January
Jean Hélion, University of Chicago*

1936

Hélion. Tableaux récents, Paris, Galerie Cahiers d'art, 25 February–14 March
Ten Abstract Paintings by Jean Hélion, New York, Valentine Gallery, 6–25 April
Jean Hélion, Hollywood, Howard Putzel Gallery, October

1937

Jean Hélion, Hollywood, Howard Putzel Gallery, February. Exhibition organized by Marcel Duchamp
Jean Hélion, San Francisco, San Francisco Museum of Art

1937–38

Jean Hélion. Paintings 1936–1937, New York, Valentine Gallery, December 1937–15 January 1938

1938

Jean Hélion. Abstractions, Chicago, The Arts Club of Chicago, 4–18 February
Œuvres récentes de Jean Hélion, Paris, Galerie Pierre, 1–12 July
Masters of the Bauhaus, Grand Rapids (Minnesota), Grand Rapids Art Gallery

1939

Abstract Paintings by Hélion, Washington, The Whyte Gallery, 6–30 November. Preface by M. Donald Whyte
Jean Hélion, Lynchburg (Virginie), Lynchburg Art Club, November–December

1940

Jean Hélion. Recent Paintings, New York, Gallery Georgette Passedoit, 25 March–6 April. Preface by Meyer Schapiro

1942

Hélion – Daura, Richmond, The Virginia Museum of Fine Arts, 12–30 May. Prefaces by Marie Piétri and Carolyn Smith

1943

Jean Hélion. Abstract Paintings, Chicago, The Arts Club of Chicago, 6–27 January
Jean Hélion. Paintings 1933–1939, New York, Art of this Century, 8 February–6 March. Preface by James Johnson Sweeney
Paintings by Jean Hélion, San Francisco, San Francisco Museum of Modern Art, 11 June–8 July
Jean Hélion, Los Angeles, Stendhal Art Gallery, August*

Jean Hélion. Gouaches, Bennington (Vermont), Bennington College, November*

1944

Recent Paintings by Jean Hélion, New York, Paul Rosenberg & Co., 14 March–8 April. Preface by Jean Hélion
Jean Hélion, Hollins (Virginia), Hollins College, March

1945

Paintings by Jean Hélion, Baltimore, Museum of Fine Arts, 6 February–4 March
Jean Hélion, Washington, Caresse Crosby Gallery, 11–30 January
Recent Paintings by Jean Hélion, New York, Paul Rosenberg & Co., 5–31 March
Gouaches and Watercolours by Jean Hélion (1935–1945), New York, Paul Rosenberg & Co., 5–24 November

1946

Paintings and Watercolors by Jean Hélion, San Francisco, San Francisco Museum of Modern Art, 10 September–6 October

1947

Jean Hélion. Œuvres récentes, Paris, Galerie Renou et Colle, 7–24 May

1951

Jean Hélion. Paintings (1947–1951), London, The Hanover Gallery, 10 April–5 May. Preface by Francis Ponge
Hélion. Pitture dal 1928 al 1951, Venice, Sala degli Specchi, Palazzo Venier dai Leoni, 24 August–September. Presentation by Peggy Guggenheim, extract from text by Christian Zervos (*Cahiers d'art*, 1951)
Hélion. Opere recenti, Milan, Galleria del Milione, 27 September–9 October. Text by Christian Zervos
Jean Hélion (Works of 1947–1951), New York, Feigl Gallery, 3–20 October
Jean Hélion. Opere recenti, Rome, Galleria San Marco, 23 October–1 November

1953

Jean Hélion. Œuvres récentes, Paris, Chez Mayo (10 rue de Seine), 25 November–15 December

1956

Jean Hélion. Peintures, Paris, Galerie Cahiers d'art, 5–30 June

1958

Jean Hélion. Peintures récentes, Paris, Galerie Cahiers d'Art, 14 November–6 December

1961

Jean Hélion. Peintures, Paris, Galerie Cahiers d'Art, 9–30 June

1962

Jean Hélion, peintures 1929–1939, Paris, Galerie Louis Carré, 6 June–13 July. Text by Raymond Queneau

1964

Paintings by Jean Hélion 1928–1964, New York, Gallery of Modern Art, 3 November–27 December. Preface by Forrest Selvig. Texts by Pierre [-Georges] Bruguière and Christian Zervos
Hélion. 30 ans de dessins, Paris, Galerie Yvon Lambert, 4–24 December. Preface by Francis Ponge

1965

Jean Hélion. Paintings 1929–1965 and Drawings 1933–1964, London, The Leicester Galleries, 1 June–1 July. Preface by Stephen Spender, text by Pierre[-Georges] Bruguière
Les Tableaux de petits formats de Jean Hélion, Toulouse, Galerie René Andrieu, 25 November–12 December. Preface by Pierre[-Georges] Bruguière

1966

Jean Hélion. Dix-neuf tableaux de 1937 à 1966, Paris, Galerie du Dragon, 21 October–18 November. Texts by Jean-Pierre Burgart, Pierre[-Georges] Bruguière, Alain Jouffroy, Francis Ponge, André Du Bouchet and Christian Zervos

1967

Jean Hélion. Paintings 1929 to 1939, New York, Willard Gallery, 21 March–22 April. Preface by Katharine Kuh
Jean Hélion. Au niveau de la rue. Le triptyque du Dragon. Suites, Paris, Galerie du Dragon, 9 October–18 November
Jean Hélion. Œuvres de 1951 à 1967, Bruxelles, Galerie Arcanes, 24 November 1967–13 January 1968. Texts by Raymond Queneau, René Micha, Maurits Bilcke, Pierre[-Georges] Bruguière and Georges Limbour

1968

Jean Hélion. Opere dal 1936 al 1967, Rome, Galleria Il Fante di Spade, May // Modène, Galleria Mutina, June. Texts by René Micha, Gilles Aillaud and Eduardo Arroyo

1969

Jean Hélion. Opere dal 1936 al 1967, Milan, Galleria Eunomia, March. Texts by Alain Jouffroy, Raymond Queneau, Pierre[-Georges] Bruguière and Francis Ponge
Hélion. Rétrospective 1926–1969, Lyons, Galerie Verrière, 6 June–10 July. Antipréface by Louis Guilloux

1970–71

Hélion. Cent tableaux 1928–1970, Paris, Grand Palais, 11 December 1970–1 February 1971. Prefaces by Francis Ponge and Roger Caillois, texts by Daniel Abadie, Anatole Jakovski, Raymond Queneau, Francis Ponge, Pierre Mabille, André Du Bouchet, Christian Zervos and Pierre[-Georges] Bruguière
Jean Hélion. 40 ans de dessins 1930–1970, Paris, Maisons des Jeunes et de la Culture, December 1970–January 1971. Travelling exhibition organized by the Centre national d'Art contemporain and the Service de la

Jeunesse, des Sports et des Loisirs de Paris. Text by Jean-Jacques Lévêque
Hélion. Dix ans de peinture (présentation de 20 œuvres des 10 dernières années). Antipréface by Louis Guilloux, texts by Daniel Abadie, André Du Bouchet, Alain Jouffroy, Jacques Baron, Francis Ponge, Edmond Humeau, Romain Weingarten, Jacques Blot, Georges Limbour, Paul Valet, Louise Herlin, Raymond Queneau, Jean Laude, Stephen Spender, Guillevic et Jean-Pierre Burgart. Travelling exhibition organized by the Centre national d'Art contemporain: Les Sables-d'Olonne, Musée municipal, 10 January–2 February 1970 // Rennes, Musée des Beaux-Arts, February // Nantes, Musée des Beaux-Arts, March // Rouen, Musée des Beaux-Arts, April // Beauvais, Musée départemental de l'Oise, May. Brest, Musée municipal, June // Vivoin (Sarthe), Centre culturel du Prieuré, 13 July–September // Caen, Théâtre municipal, October // Saint-Omer, Hôtel Sandelin, November // Arras, Musée municipal, December 1970–January 1971 // Auxerre, Musée du Tourisme, 5–28 February 1971 // Amiens, Maison de la Culture, March–April 1971 // Saint-Étienne, Maison de la Culture et des Loisirs, May // Cognac, Musée municipal, 23 June–August 1971 // Saint-Lizier (Ariège), Festival, September 1971* // Toulouse, Centre culturel, October 1971
Paris, Galerie Le Point*

1971

Jean Hélion. Peintures de 1928 et de 1929, Paris, Galerie Weiller, 14 January–27 February
Jean Hélion. Peintures 1952–1962, Paris, Galerie Henriette Gomès, 20 January–20 March. Invitation featuring text by Pierre [-Georges] Bruguière
Jean Hélion. 40 ans de dessins, Montpellier, Galerie Pops Gaibrois, 4 September–10 October*

1972

Jean Hélion. Peintures récentes, Toulouse, Galerie René Andrieu, February
Sochaux, Maison des Arts et Loisirs*
Paris, Galerie Armand*

1973

Hélion, œuvres récentes, Paris, Galerie Saint-Germain, 3 May–2 June. Preface by Daniel Abadie, texts by Jean Hélion
Lyons, Galerie Le Lutin*

1974

Hélion. Aquarelles 1930–1939, Paris, Galerie Jean Chauvelin, 6–23 March
Jean Hélion, Pontoise, Musée Tavet, 27 April–10 June. Preface by Pierre [-Georges] Bruguière

1975

Hélion. "Le Marché de Bigeonnette", Saint-Étienne, Maison de la Culture et des Loisirs, 4 April–26 May. Texts by Jean Hélion
Jean Hélion, cinquante ans de peinture 1925–1975, Paris, Galerie Karl Flinker, 23 May–30 June. Occasion of the publication of the book by Daniel Abadie, *Hélion ou la force des choses*

and of the texts *Coup de chapeau* by Jean-Jacques Lévêque (partly taken from the review *Cimaise*, nos. 122–23, May–June) and *L'indécence d'aimer* (dialogue with the artist) by François Pluchart (taken in part from the review *ARTitudes*, nos. 21–23, April–June). See Bibliography.
Hélion. Zeichnungen und Bilder, Cologne, Galerie Der Spiegel, 12 December 1975–end January 1976
Paris, Galerie Armand Zerbib*

1976

Jean Hélion, New York, Spencer A. Samuel Gallery, 7 April–22 May. Preface by John Ashbery
Milan, Galerie Il Matiglio*
Lyons, Galerie Le Lutin*
Brussels, Galerie Lauzenberg*
Turin, Galerie Documenta*

1977

Jean Hélion. Dessins récents, Les Sables-d'Olonne, Musée de l'Abbaye Sainte-Croix, February. Preface by Henry-Claude Cousseau, texts by Michel Tournier, Jean Hélion
Hélion. Les Marchés (1972–1977), Paris, Musée d'Art moderne de la Ville de Paris, 18 March–17 April. Preface by Jacques Lassaigne, texts by Françoise Marquet, Jean Frémon and Daniel Abadie
Jean Hélion. Choses vues, œuvres sur papier 1975–1977, Paris, Galerie du Centre, 15 April–2 July. Preface by Patrick d'Elme, texts by Jean Hélion

1978

Hélion. Dessins et desseins. Œuvres sur papier depuis 1939, Paris, Galerie Karl Flinker, 26 January–4 March.
Hélion, Nice, Galerie Sapone, 21 April–14 May
Jean Hélion. L'œuvre figurative de 1928 à 1978, Montauban, Musée Ingres, 24 June–10 September. Preface by Pierre Barousse, texts by Alain Jouffroy, Bernard Noël, Francis Ponge and Jean Hélion
Paris, Galerie Albert Loeb*

1979

Jean Hélion. Bilder und Zeichnungen, Cologne, Galerie Thomas Borgmann, 26 April–16 June // Munich, Galerie Michael Hasenclever, 27 September–2 November
Jean Hélion. Dessins, pastels et gouaches, Athens, Athens Gallery, 22 May–June
Jean Hélion ('présentation des œuvres appartenant aux collections du Musée national d'art moderne à l'occasion des 75 ans du peintre'), Paris, Centre Georges Pompidou, 9 May–11 June
Hélion. Dessins 1930–1978, Paris, Centre Georges Pompidou, Musée national d'art moderne, April // Athens, National Gallery, [summer] // Angers, École régionale des Beaux-Arts, 6–27 October. Travelling exhibition organized by the Musée national d'art moderne de Paris. Preface by Pontus-Hulten, text by Daniel Abadie
Hélion, peintures et dessins, 1929–1979, Saint-Étienne, Musée d'Art

et d'Industrie, 22 September–
30 October // Strasbourg, Musée d'Art
moderne (Ancienne douane),
16 November–31 December. Text by
Richard Crevier
Jean Hélion. Marché au poisson,
Saint-Priest, Galerie municipale,
[December]

1980

*Jean Hélion. Bilder und Zeichnungen
1929–1980*, Berlin, Galerie Poll,
4 February–29 March. Preface by Hans
Platschek
*Jean Hélion. Zeichnungen und
Aquarelle*, Wuppertal, Van der Heydt-
Museum, 16 March–27 April
Hélion, les années 50, Paris, Galerie
Karl Flinker, 8 May–28 June. Preface by
Karl Flinker, texts by Jean Hélion, Gilbert
Lascault, Pierre Astier, Alain Jouffroy,
Pierre[-Georges] Bruguière, Francis
Ponge
Hélion. Peintures, Peking, Palace of
Fine Art, 8–28 September // Shanghai,
Museum of Fine Art, 8–28 October //
Nanchang, Museum of Fine Art,
7–24 November. Exhibition organized by
the Musée national d'art moderne-Centre
Pompidou and the Association
française d'Action artistique. Preface
by Pontus-Hulten

1980–81

Hélion, dessins (1930–1978),
Amiens, Maison de la Culture,
31 May–29 June // Rennes, Musée des
Beaux-Arts, Cabinet d'art graphique,
18 December 1980–15 February 1981
// Liège, Musée de la Boverie, Cabinet
des estampes, 14 March–26 April 1981.
Travelling exhibition organized by the
Musée national d'art moderne with the
collaboration of the Galerie Karl Flinker

1981

*Jean Hélion. Œuvres autour du
"Triptyque du marché"*, Caen, Musée des
Beaux-Arts, February
*Jean Hélion. Astrazione e figurazione
1929–1949*, Modena, Galleria Fonte
d'Abisso, 11 April–30 May. Texts by
Paolo Fossati, Jean Hélion
*Jean Hélion. Bilder aus fünfzig
Jahren*, Salzbourg, Galerie Academia,
14 April–end May
Hélion. Œuvres récentes, Paris,
Grand Palais (FIAC, Galerie Karl Flinker),
16–23 October. Texts in part from the
review *Cimaise*, nos. 153–54,
October–November, by Michel Tournier
and Jean Hélion (*Discours de Pékin*
extracts from *carnet* of 1981)
*Jean Hélion. Paintings and Drawings
from the Years 1939–1960*, New York,
Robert Miller Gallery, 3–28 November.
Introduction by Lawrence Alloway
Jean Hélion. Arbeiten 1960–1900,
Wolfsburg, Kunstverein, 24 May–14 June
Jean Hélion, Helsinki, Galerie Bronda*

1982

Jean Hélion, Dreux, Nouvelle
Chapelle, February*
Hélion, tableaux 1929–1982,
Luxembourg, Musée de l'État,
24 September–24 October. Text by Jean-
Luc Koltz

1983

*Hélion. Œuvres récentes
1982–1983*, Paris, Galerie Karl Flinker,
19 May–5 June. Preface by Karl Flinker,
texts by Pierre Astier, Jean Hélion

1984

*Jean Hélion. Peintures des années
40*, Paris, Galerie Karl Flinker, 22 May–
30 June
Jean Hélion (5ᵉ Quinzaine des arts en
pays mêlois), Le Mêle-sur-Sarthe (Orne),
Salle des fêtes, 1–15 August. Text by
Roger Eskenaz
*Hélion. Œuvres provenant du legs
Zervos*, Vézelay, Salle gothique
de la mairie, 4 August–14 October.
Preface by Blaise Gautier, interview
with Jean Hélion by Christian Limousin,
texts by Christian Zervos
*Jean Hélion: Von der Abstraktion
zur Figuration, Bilder und Zeichnungen
1933–1983*, Berlin, Galerie Poll,
3 September–14 October. Texts by
Jean Hélion and Werner Spies //
Bremen, Galerie in der Böttcherstrasse,
26 November–31 December

1984–85

*Jean Hélion. Abstraktion und Mythen
des Alltags. Bilder. Zeichnungen,
Gouachen 1925–1983*, Munich,
Städtische Galerie im Lenbachhaus,
29 August–21 October. Preface by
Armin Zweite, texts by Merle S. Schipper,
Armin Zweite, Pierre-Georges Bruguière,
Bernard Dahan // *Hélion. Peintures et
dessins 1925–1983*, Paris, Musée d'Art
moderne de la Ville de Paris,
16 November 1984–6 January 1985.
Preface by Bernadette Contensou,
presentation by Aline Vidal, texts
by Pierre[-Georges] Bruguière,
Anne Mœglin-Delcroix and Jean Hélion

1985

Hélion. Rétrospective, Tarbes,
Bibliothèque municipale, January //
Bagnères, February. Exhibition organized
by the Fédération des œuvres laïques
des Hautes-Pyrénées. Texts by Alain
Jouffroy, Jean Hélion*
Jean Hélion. Les marchés, Thionville,
Centre culturel Jacques Brel,
20 April–24 May. Text by Jean Frémon
*Jean Hélion. Abstraction into
Figuration, 1934–1948*, New York,
Rachel Adler Gallery, 27 April–1 June.
Text by Donna Stein
*Jean Hélion, œuvres des années
1978 à 1983*, Issoire, Centre culturel
Nicolas Pomel, 30 June–31 August. Text
by Jean Hélion
Hélion. Les années soixante, Paris,
Galerie Patrice Trigano, 14 December
1985–8 February 1986. Notes by Pierre
Cabanne

1986

*Omaggio a Jean Hélion. Opere
recenti/ Homage to Jean Hélion.
Recent Works*, Venice, Fondazione
Solomon R. Guggenheim, March–April.
Texts by Thomas M. Messer, Jean Hélion
et Fred Licht
*Jean Hélion. Gemälde und
Zeichnungen*, Munich, Hasenclever
Galerie, 24 April–14 June

*Jean Hélion. Aquarelles, dessins
et estampes*, Paris, Galerie Berggruen
& Cie, 19 November–20 December

1987

*Jean Hélion. Peintures de 1929 à
1983*, Paris, Galerie Louis Carré & Cie,
21 May–25 July. Text by Luc Lang.
*Jean Hélion, maleri og tegning
1923–1983*, Aarhus (Danemark),
Kunstmuseum,
[5 September–25 October]. Preface
by Jens Erik Sørensen, biography and
interview with the artist by Daniel Abadie,
text by Nina Damsgaard.
*Hélion. Paintings in Oil and Acrylic
since 1960. Works on Paper since 1930*,
London, Albemarle Gallery, 10 September–
8 October. Letter from Myfanwy (Evans)
Piper to Jean Hélion, texts by
Sarah Wilson and Jean Hélion
Jean Hélion, peinture, Niort, Centre
d'action culturelle, 18 December
1987–21 February 1988

1988

En hommage à Jean Hélion, Paris,
Galerie Art of this Century,
28 January–12 March
Hélion. Mai 1968, Paris, Galerie
Patrice Trigano, 18 May–9 July
*Jean Hélion. Arbeiten auf Papier
1929–1983*, Berlin, Zentrum
für Kunstaustellungen der D.D.R.,
Nationalgalerie der Staatlichen Museen
zu Berlin. Texts by Gerd Gruber and
Gunther Rieger
Jean Hélion, L'Isle-sur-la-Sorgue, hôtel
Donadei de Campredon, 23 July–
30 October. Preface by Jacques Woliner,
texts by René de Obaldia and Jacqueline
Hélion
*Hélion. Kaléidoscope 1929–1939 –
Carnets 1929–1984*, Paris, Bibliothèque
nationale, 6 October–5 November

1989

*Hélion. Abstract Paintings of the
1930s*, New York, Rachel Adler Gallery,
11 February–11 March. Preface by Jed
Perl
*Jean Hélion. Peintures et dessins
1948–1950*, Paris, Galerie Art of this
Century, 18 October–18 November

1990

Jean Hélion, Valence, IVAM – Centro
Julio González, 27 March–3 May //
Liverpool, Tate Gallery, 5 September–
21 October. Presentation by Carmen
Alborch, introduction by Henry-Claude
Cousseau, texts by Clément Rosset,
Gilles Aillaud, Anne Mœglin-Delcroix
andJean Hélion
Hélion. Pinturas y dibujos, Valence,
Galeria Fandos, 15 May–June. Texts
by Anne Mœglin-Delcroix
[*Jean Hélion*], Madrid, galeria Levy*

1991

*Jean Hélion, œuvres des années
1960 à 1980*, Paris, Galerie Strouk,
2 March–13 April
*Jean Hélion, autour du Triptyque
du Dragon*, Quintin (Côtes-d'Armor),
château de Quintin, 15 March–20 May.
Exhibition organized par FRAC-Bretagne

*Jean Hélion. The Last Work,
1976–1983*, New York, Rachel Adler
Gallery, 28 September–26 October.
Preface by Bryan Robertson
Dation, peintures et dessins, Paris,
Musée national d'art moderne,
September–October

1992

Hélion et la traversée de l'abstraction,
Paris, Galerie Marwan Hoss. Salle 1:
*Jean Hélion "des abstractions".
49 œuvres sur papier 1929–1939*;
Salle 2: *Deux amis autour de Jean
Hélion: Julio González et Joaquín Torres-
García. 20 œuvres sur papier
1929–1939*, 3 June–17 July and
1–30 September. Preface by Pierre Daix
// *Jean Hélion. De la traversia de
la abstraccion*, Saragossa, Centre for
exhibitions and conventions,
27 October–27 November // *Hélion y la
travesía de la abstracción*, Logroño, Sala
Amós Salvador, 5–27 December
Hélion. De la géométrie aux mythes,
Royan, Centre d'Arts plastiques,
5 June–27 September. Text by
Maryvonne Georget

1993

Jean Hélion. Deux triptyques,
Cherbourg, Galeries du théâtre,
18 March–2 May

1994

Jean Hélion "Quartier libre",
Paris, Galerie Pierre Brullé,
7 June–23 July
Jean Hélion, Istres, Centre d'Art
contemporain, 15 September–
12 November. Text by Luc Vezin
Hélion, 20 Équilibres: 1932–1939,
New York, Linda Hyman Gallery*

1995

Jean Hélion, Orléans, Musée des
Beaux-Arts, 28 January. 'Œuvres
déposées par le Musée national d'art
moderne dans le cadre de la dation
Hélion faite à l'État et par le Fonds
national d'Art contemporain'.
Hélion. Quartier libre, Sallaumines
(Pas-de-Calais), Maison de l'Art et
de la Communication, 14 April–2 June.
Text by Richard Crevier
*Jean Hélion. Tableaux de la
succession*, Paris, Galerie Gérald Piltzer,
28 September–22 November. Leaflet
with text by Richard Crevier
Hélion, la figure tombée,
Colmar, Musée d'Unterlinden,
3 June–3 September // Les Sables-
d'Olonne, Musée de l'Abbaye Sainte-
Croix, 14 October 1995–7 January
1996. Texts by Sylvie Lecoq-Ramond,
Clément Rosset, Didier Ottinger,
Jean-Dominique Rey

1996

Jean Hélion. Paintings, New York,
Salander-O'Reilly Galleries, 2–27 April
*Jean Hélion. L'art des villes et des
campagnes*, Paris, Galerie Gérald Piltzer,
3 October–16 November

1996–97

Jean Hélion. À perte de vue, Caen,
Abbaye-aux-Dames, 13 December
1996–15 February 1997 // Paris, Galerie
Gérald Piltzer, 5 November–6 December
1997. Exhibition organized by IMEC.
Occasion of the publication of Jean
Hélion's *À perte de vue* followed by
Choses revues

1997

Jean Hélion, Bad Homburg v.d. Höhe
(Netherlands), Galerie Scheffel,
19 January–8 March

1998

Jean Hélion 1904–1987, London,
The Mayor Gallery, 1 June–4 September.
Text by Mark Glazebrook

1999

Jean Hélion. La saga aux homards,
Morlaix, Musée des Jacobins, 3
April–31May // Vannes, Musée de la
Cohue, 5 June–10 October. Texts by
Marie-Françoise Le Saux, Patrick
Jourdan, Henry-Claude Cousseau
Jean Hélion. Retrospective, Utrecht,
Galerie Quintessens, 10 April–3 July.
Texts by Mark Glazebrook and Dick
Adelaar

2000

Hélion, ou l'invention de l'autre,
Principauté de Monaco, salle du quai
Antoine Iᵉʳ, 4 March–24 April. Texts by
Martine Fresia, Didier Ottinger, Claude
Fournet and interviews with David Hélion,
Jacqueline Hélion

2001

Jean Hélion. Œuvres de 1929 à 1958,
Paris, Galerie Marwan Hoss,
26 April–13 July. Text by Gilbert Lascault

2002

Jean Hélion. Charles Lapicque, Paris,
Galerie Ileana Bouboulis,
24 September–19 October

2003

Jean Hélion, Gaillac, Musée
des Beaux-Arts, 29 June–15 September

I. Paintings

Orthogonal composition, 1929–30
Oil on canvas
146 x 97 cm
Private collection, Paris
p. 58

Abstract composition, 1930
Oil on canvas
89.5 x 89.9 cm
Collection of Herta and Paul Amir, United States
p. 61

Orthogonal composition, 1930
Oil on canvas
100 x 81 cm
Centre Pompidou, Musée national d'art moderne, Paris, purchase 1975
p. 67

Complex tensions, 1930
Oil on canvas
90 x 89 cm
Private collection
Courtesy galerie Louis Carré
p. 60

Circular tensions no. 1, 1931–32
Oil on canvas
75 x 75 cm
Private collection
p. 66

Circular tensions no. 2, 1931–32
Oil on canvas
75 x 75 cm
Private collection
p. 67

Composition, 1932
Oil on canvas
90 x 90 cm
Musée de Grenoble, Grenoble
p. 62

First curves, 1932
Oil on canvas
74.6 x 74.6 cm
Private collection, Germany
p. 68

Tensions, 1932
Oil on canvas
73 x 60 cm
Musée Malraux, Le Havre
p. 63

Abstract composition, 1933
Oil on canvas
72 x 91 cm
Musée d'Art moderne de la Ville de Paris
p. 69

Equilibrium, 1933
Oil on canvas
81 x 100 cm
Hamburger Kunsthalle, Hamburg
p. 71

Equilibrium, 1933
Oil on canvas
74 x 91.5 cm
Collection of Louis Hélion Blair
p. 70

Equilibrium, 1933
Oil on canvas
59.6 x 72.6 cm
Private collection
p. 73

Equilibrium, 1933
Oil on canvas
63.5 x 78.7 cm
Courtesy Rachel Adler Fine Art, New York
p. 72

Equilibrium, 1933
Oil on canvas
60 x 73 cm
IVAM, Instituto Valenciano de Arte moderno, Valencia
Generalitat Valenciana
p. 74

Equilibrium, 1933–34
Oil on canvas
97.4 x 131.2 cm
Peggy Guggenheim Collection, Venice
Solomon R. Guggenheim Foundation, New York
p. 75

Composition, 1934
Oil on canvas
144.3 x 199.8 cm
Solomon R. Guggenheim Museum, New York
p. 79

Composition in colours, 1934
Oil on canvas
128.6 x 194 cm
San Diego Museum of Art, California
Gift of Peggy Guggenheim
p. 78

Abstraction, 1935
Oil on canvas
145 x 200 cm
Private collection
p. 81

Standing figure, 1935
Oil on canvas
130 x 89 cm
Albright-Knox Art Gallery, Buffalo (New York)
Room of Contemporary Art Fund, 1944
p. 86

Île-de-France, 1935
Oil on canvas
145.4 x 200 cm
Tate, London, purchase 1965
p. 80

Blue spaces, 1936
Oil on canvas
200 x 276 cm
Musée national d'Histoire et d'Art du Grand-Duché de Luxembourg, Luxembourg
p. 82

Hollow figure, 1936
Oil on canvas
112 x 84 cm
Private collection
p. 88

Standing figure, 1936
Oil on canvas
146.1 x 114 cm
The Metropolitan Museum of Art, New York
Gift of the Joseph Cantor Foundation, 1982
p. 87

Pink figure, 1937
Oil on canvas
133 x 97 cm
Centre Pompidou, Musée national d'art moderne, Paris, purchase 1963
p. 89

Twin figures, 1938
Oil on canvas
132.1 x 175.3 cm
The Art Institute of Chicago
Gift of Peggy Guggenheim, 1975
p. 90

Three figures, 1938
Oil on canvas
112 x 152 cm
Private collection, Paris
p. 91

With cyclist, 1939
Oil on canvas
132 x 180.5 cm
Centre Pompidou, Musée national d'art moderne, Paris, purchase 1968
p. 137

Charles, 1939
(Study)
Oil on Isorel
38.2 x 28 cm
Private collection
p. 55

Édouard, 1939
Oil on board
33 x 25.7 cm
Private collection
p. 55

Fallen figure, 1939
Oil on canvas
126.2 x 164.3 cm
Centre Pompidou, Musée national d'art moderne, Paris, purchase 1987
p. 97

Défense d', 1943
Oil on canvas
101.8 x 81 cm
Collection of Daniel Malingue
p. 93

The stairs, 1944
Oil on canvas
130 x 97 cm
Private collection, Paris
p. 140

Wrong way up / À rebours, 1947
Oil on canvas
113.5 x 146 cm
Centre Pompidou, Musée national d'art moderne, Paris, purchase 1975
p. 141

Seated man, 1947
Oil on canvas
117 x 81.5 cm
Städtische Galerie im Lenbachhaus, Munich
p. 150

Big pumpkin event, 1948
Oil on canvas
114 x 162 cm
Private collection
p. 146

Still life with pumpkin, 1948
Oil on canvas
140 x 70 cm
Fonds national d'Art contemporain, Ministère de la Culture et de la Communication, Paris
On deposit with the Musée des Beaux-Arts, Nantes
p. 127

Still life with carnation, 1948
Oil on canvas
92 x 65 cm
Private collection
p. 134

Nude leaning on elbow, 1948–49
Oil on canvas
116 x 81 cm
Collection of David Hélion
p. 108

Star-nude with smoker and daily-reader, 1949
Oil on canvas
155 x 200 cm
Private collection
p. 111

Star-nude with trousers, 1949
Oil on canvas
89 x 116 cm
Private collection
p. 106

The big daily read, 1950
Oil on canvas
130 x 195 cm
Courtesy Robert Miller Gallery, New York
p. 153

Big mannequin event, 1951
Oil on canvas
129.5 x 161.5 cm
Musée d'Art moderne de la Ville de Paris
p. 147

Daily allegory, 1951–53
Charcoal, paint and mixed media on canvas
194.7 x 259.6 cm
Musée Zervos, Vézelay
p. 151

Back with breads, 1952
Oil on canvas
130.1 x 97 cm
Tate, London, purchase 1988
p. 113

Rabbit event, 1952
Oil on canvas
92 x 60 cm
Private collection, Paris
p. 128

The studio, 1953
Oil on canvas
81 x 100 cm
Private collection
p. 101

The snack, 1953
Oil on canvas
89 x 147 cm
Private collection, Paris
p. 131

Odalisque, 1953
Oil on canvas
60 x 92 cm
Private collection
p. 109

Autumn leaves, 1954
Oil on canvas
97 x 130 cm
Collection Paolo Zanasi, Modena
p. 126

Chamber music, 1960
Oil on canvas
130 x 89 cm
Collection Paolo Zanasi, Modena
p. 130

The Dragon Street triptych, 1967
Acrylic on canvas
275 x 875 cm (whole)
Central panel 275 x 425 cm,
side panels 275 x 225 cm
Fonds régional d'Art contemporain
de Bretagne
pp. 142–44

Métro exit, 1969
Acrylic on canvas
130 x 180 cm
Private collection
p. 155

Cabbage patch, 1972
Acrylic on canvas
161 x 114 cm
Private collection
p. 133

Leeks, 1973
Acrylic on canvas
60 x 73 cm
Private collection
p. 132

Lobster and its reflection, 1975
Acrylic on canvas
100 x 73 cm
Private collection, Mulhouse
p. 129

Coat-tree and echo, 1975
Acrylic on canvas
130 x 97 cm
Musée d'Art moderne, Saint-Étienne
p. 121

Leggery, 1977
Acrylic on canvas
132 x 163 cm
Collection of David Hélion
p. 120

Mannequin event – sale, 1978
Acrylic on canvas
195 x 130 cm
Private collection
Courtesy galerie Art Attitude Hervé Bize,
Nancy
p. 116

First flea-market collection in the studio,
1978
Acrylic on canvas
114 x 162.5 cm
Collection of the Grand-Ducal Court,
Luxembourg
p. 117

The Last Judgment of things,
1978–79
Triptych, acrylic on canvas
200 x 845 cm (whole)
Central panel 200 x 145 cm,
side panels 200 x 350 cm
Private collection
pp. 160–62

The accident, 1979
Acrylic on canvas
97 x 130 cm
Collection of Nicolas Hélion
p. 99

As beautiful as a …, 1979
Acrylic on canvas
116 x 89 cm
Collection of Raphaël and Emmanuel
Hélion
p. 122

Find the cyclist, 1979
(Arpeggios)
Acrylic on canvas
162 x 130 cm
Musée national d'Histoire et d'Art
du Grand-Duché de Luxembourg,
Luxembourg
p. 119

The exhibition of 1934, 1979–80
Acrylic on canvas
130 x 195 cm
Centre Pompidou, Musée national
d'art moderne, Paris, purchase 1981
p. 83

The real and the dream, 1979–81
Acrylic on canvas
114 x 162 cm
Private collection
p. 110

Ballet of chairs at Skyros, 1980
Acrylic on canvas
145 x 200 cm
Private collection, Paris
p. 135

Best wishes to Richard Lindner, 1981
Acrylic on canvas
129.5 x 194.5 cm
Centre Pompidou, Musée national
d'art moderne, Paris,
accepted in lieu of tax 1991
On deposit with the Musée des Beaux-
Arts, Orléans
p. 123

1 jumble for Émile, 1981
Acrylic on canvas
145 x 200 cm
Fonds régional d'Art contemporain
d'Auvergne
p. 118

The day's events, 1982
Acrylic on canvas
200 x 300 cm
Private collection, Geneva
p. 157

The moment after, 1982
Acrylic on canvas
200 x 145 cm
Collection of David Hélion
and Jean-Jacques Bichier
p. 104

Last tumble, 1983
Acrylic on canvas
145 x 200 cm
Collection of Jacqueline Hélion
p. 98

Fire with nude, 1983
Acrylic on canvas
97 x 146 cm
Centre Pompidou, Musée national
d'art moderne, Paris,
accepted in lieu of tax 1991
On deposit with Musée des Beaux-Arts,
Orléans
p. 112

Another daily scene, 1983
Acrylic on canvas
175 x 250 cm
Private collection
p. 156

The painter trampled by his model, 1983
Acrylic on canvas
200 x 145 cm
Fonds régional d'Art contemporain
de Picardie
p. 105

Upturns, 1983
Acrylic on canvas
114 x 162 cm
BNP/PARIBAS
p. 96

Bench scene, 1983
Acrylic on canvas
114 x 162 cm
Collection of Nicolas Hélion
p. 152

Trombone pour une citrouille, 1983
Acrylic on canvas
130 x 162 cm
Private collection
p. 154

Trumpet for a painter, 1983
Acrylic on canvas
175 x 250 cm
Collection of Louis Hélion Blair,
United States
p. 107

The city, 1983
Acrylic on canvas
200 x 350 cm
Galerie Piltzer
p. 158

II. Drawings

Hands of a lighter up, 1939
Ink and wash, white gouache,
charcoal on cream paper
60.4 x 45.3 cm
Centre Pompidou, Musée national d'art
moderne, Paris, accepted in lieu of tax
1991

Umbrella, 1939
Charcoal on Ingres paper
62 x 47.5 cm
Centre Pompidou, Musée national d'art
moderne, Paris, gift of the Société des
Amis du Musée national d'art moderne,
1980
p. 166

Girl with her hair undone, 1946
Brush and Chinese ink
79 x 100 cm
Private collection, Paris
p. 172

Woman with her hair undone, 1946
Brush and Chinese ink
72 x 56 cm
Private collection, Paris

Woman leaning on her elbows, 1946
Brush and Chinese ink
73 x 59 cm
Private collection, Paris
p. 173

Mother and daughter pumpkin, 1948
Charcoal on paper
44.2 x 56.1 cm
Centre Pompidou, Musée national d'art
moderne, Paris, accepted in lieu of tax
1991
p. 169

The bed, 1948
Charcoal, watercolour, heightened with
white gouache, on paper
50.5 x 65 cm
Centre Pompidou, Musée national d'art
moderne, Paris, accepted in lieu of tax
1991

Items 21, 1949
Charcoal with watercolour heightening
on paper
49.7 x 64.7 cm
Centre Pompidou, Musée national d'art
moderne, Paris, gift of the Société des
Amis du Musée national d'art moderne,
1980
p. 167

Barred nude, 1949
Charcoal, watercolour on laid paper
62.5 x 48.5 cm
Centre Pompidou, Musée national d'art
moderne, Paris, accepted in lieu of tax
1991

Duster, 1949
Charcoal, watercolour on cream paper
65.4 x 50.3 cm
Centre Pompidou, Musée national d'art
moderne, Paris, accepted in lieu of tax
1991

Crumpled newspaper, 1950
Charcoal with ink heightening on stuck-
down paper
50.5 x 65.3 cm
Centre Pompidou, Musée national d'art
moderne, Paris, gift of the Société des
Amis du Musée national d'art moderne,
1980
p. 168

Chrysanthemums, 1951
Charcoal with watercolour heightening on
watermarked laid paper
63 x 48 cm
Centre Pompidou, Musée national d'art
moderne, Paris, gift of the Société des
Amis du Musée national d'art moderne,
1980

Nu slumped, 1951
Charcoal on laid paper
48.2 x 63.1 cm
Centre Pompidou, Musée national d'art
moderne, Paris, accepted in lieu of tax
1991
p. 175

La Spring, 1951
(Inverted nude)
Chalks on paper
30.5 x 24 cm
Centre Pompidou, Musée national d'art
moderne, Paris, purchase 1976
p. 174

Nude leaning on elbows, 1952
Charcoal, gouache, watercolour on grey
laid paper
46.8 x 60.8 cm
Centre Pompidou, Musée national d'art
moderne, Paris, accepted in lieu of tax
1991

Roofs, 1953
(Study)
Charcoal on canvas
96 x 128.5 cm
Centre Pompidou, Musée national d'art
moderne, Paris, accepted in lieu of tax
1991
p. 177

Sacrificial victims, 1977
Pastel and wash on brown Canson paper
75 x 106 cm
Centre Pompidou, Musée national d'art
moderne, Paris, accepted in lieu of tax
1991
p. 170

Flea-market stuff, 1977
Charcoal, pastel and inks on green
Canson paper
75.4 x 110.5 cm
Centre Pompidou, Musée national d'art
moderne, Paris, accepted in lieu of tax
1991
p. 171

Last symbol, 1982
Pastel, charcoal and inks on green
Canson paper
44.2 x 31.8 cm
Centre Pompidou, Musée national d'art
moderne, Paris, accepted in lieu of tax
1991
p. 176

INDEX OF NAMES

**The Fonds Jean Hélion
at the Institut Mémoires de l'Édition Contemporaine (IMEC)**

The Jean Hélion archives cover nearly fifty years of the artist's
intellectual life and career in France and in the United States, where
he stayed on numerous occasions from 1932 onwards and made
important friendships. His correspondence with other artists and
writers extends from the end of the 1930s to the 1970s, and includes
letters from, among others, John Ashbery, Pierre-Georges Bruguière,
André Du Bouchet, Roger Caillois, Alexander Calder, Jean Cassou,
Jean Dubuffet, Marcel Duchamp, William Einstein, Peggy
Guggenheim, Wassily Kandinsky, Joan Miró, László Moholy-Nagy,
Ben Nicholson, Francis Ponge, Georges Simenon and Saul
Steinberg.

These archives were entrusted to IMEC in 1993 by Jacqueline Hélion,
the artist's wife, and illustrate the phases and development of Hélion's
career (post-cubist, abstract, figurative) and his indefatigable activity
as a writer and as a theoretician of art.

The *fonds* also contains a complete set of press cuttings (obtained
through an agency over thirty years), papers documenting the
preparations for exhibitions, original manuscripts of writers and critics
on the subject of the artist, exhibition catalogues, posters, unpublished
texts by the artist, periodicals and reviews, and further illustrative
material, which have been extensively exploited for this catalogue.

IMEC

9 rue Bleue
75009 Paris
Tél. : +33 1 53 34 23 23

Abbaye d'Ardenne
14280 Saint-Germain-la-Blanche-Herbe
Tél. : +33 2 31 29 37 37

Photographic Credits

Rachel Adler Fine Art, New York, p. 72
Albright Knox Art Gallery, Buffalo, p. 86
Herta et Paul Amir, Beverly Hills, p. 61
Galerie Art Attitude Hervé Bize, Nancy, p. 116
The Art Institute of Chicago, p. 90
AV-Studio De Boni, Schaan, pp. 67, 133
Bibliothèque nationale de France, département des Estampes et de la Photographie, Paris,
pp. 14–15, 35, 53, 184 centre right, 193 left and right, 196 left and right, 199 right, 203 left
BNP/PARIBAS, p. 96
Camara, p. 110
Galerie Louis Carré, p. 60
CNAC/MNAM/dist. RMN, pp. 27, 176, 187 right, 191 right, 192 centre, 202 right / Jacques Faujour,
pp. 58, 128, 192 left / Béatrice Hatala, p. 63 / Jacqueline Hyde, pp. 166–68, 174, 190 right /
Georges Meguerditchian, pp. 83, 97, 139 / Philippe Migeat, pp. 59, 106, 108, 112, 123, 169–71,
175, 177, 197 right, 203 right / Jean-Claude Planchet, pp. 22, 109, 134, 137 / Bertrand Prévost,
p. 89
Centre Pompidou, Bibliothèque Kandinsky, Paris, pp. 45, 46 left, 47 left, 49, 199 left
Collection Cour Grand-Ducale, Luxembourg / Jochen Herling, p. 117
Jean Dubout, p. 131
Fondation Torres-García, Montevideo, p. 17 left
Fonds Jean Hélion / IMEC, pp. 9, 180–183, 184 left and right, 185, 186, 187 left, 188, 189, 190
left, 191 left, 192 right, 193 centre, 194, 195, 196 centre left, 197 left, 198, 199 centre, 200, 201,
204 / A. Bonnesœur, Lers (Orne), p. 180 centre / Thomas Bouchard, p. 192 right, 193 centre right /
Pierre-Georges Bruguière, p. 185 right / Pierre Descargues, p. 188 below / Collection René Gaude,
p. 190 left, 191 left / Douglas Glass, p. 189 above / A.D. Litton, p. 201 right / A.D. Litton, Stanley
Geist, p. 202 right / Charles Marks, p. 194 right / André Morain, p. 201 left / Pascal Poucet, p. 198
left, 204 / Selon Édition, p. 195 / Studio Iris, p. 197 left / Clovis Vail, p. 189 below, 198 right
Fonds régional d'Art contemporain de Bretagne, Chateaugiron, pp. 142–44
Fonds régional d'Art contemporain de Picardie, Amiens, p. 105
The Solomon Guggenheim Foundation, New York / David Heald, pp. 75, 79
David Hélion, pp. 31, 108, 120
David Hélion and Jean-Jacques Bichier, p. 104
Jacqueline Hélion, p. 98
Louis Hélion Blair, Paris, pp. 21, 70, 107
Nicolas Hélion / Serge Veignant, pp. 99, 152
Raphaël and Emmanuel Hélion, Saint-Chéron, p. 122
Galerie Marwan Hoss, Paris, p. 154
Jacqueline Hyde, p. 120
Hamburger Kunsthalle, Hambourg / Elke Walford, p. 71
IVAM, Valencia / Juan Garcia Rosell, p. 74
Denis Luttenbacher, p. 129
Paul Lutz, p. 118
Collection Daniel Malingue, Paris, p. 93
The Metropolitan Museum of Art, New York, p. 87
The Robert Miller Gallery, New York, p. 153
Musée d'Art moderne de Saint-Étienne, p. 121
Musée de Grenoble, p. 62
Musée des Beaux-Arts de la Ville de Nantes / Patrick Jean, p. 127
Musée Malraux, Le Havre, p. 63
Musée national d'Histoire et d'Art, Luxembourg, p. 82 / Christof Weber, p. 119
Musée Zervos, Vézelay, pp. 30, 151
Museo nacional, Centro de Arte Reina Sofia, Madrid, p. 27
The Museum of Modern Art, New York, p. 24
Philadelphia Museum of Art, p. 46 / Lynn Rosenthal, p. 44 / Graydon Wood, pp. 47, 51
(Holtzman Trust)
Photothèque des Musées de la Ville de Paris / Jean-Yves Trocaz, pp. 69, 147
Galerie Piltzer, Saint-Martin-en-Bière / Thierry Jacob, p. 158
San Diego Museum of Art, Californie, p. 78
Southern Illinois University at Edwardsville, p. 25
Sprengel Museum Hannover, Hanover, p. 26 left
Städtische Galerie im Lenbachhaus, Munich, p. 150
Tate, London, pp. 39, 40, 42, 80, 113 / A.J. Hepworth p. 42 right
Galerie Patrice Trigano, p. 165
Sarah Wells, p. 26 right
The Whitney Museum of American Art, New York / Geoffrey Clements, p. 50
Yale University Art Gallery, New Haven, p. 18
Collection Paolo Zanasi, Modena / Pugnaghi, pp. 126, 130

Reproductions by Arciel Graphic, Paris
Printed by Artegrafica, Verona